Bus

Keith
Her Majest
Studies, He

Norm
Senior Lect

Kevin
Senior Lect
Liverpool J

8th Edition

Reprint inc
The Amen
    sexual a
    gender i
The Wolf
The Emplo
The Sale &
The Crimi
The Equal
The Treat
The Cons
The Comp
The Cons
The Employment Equality (Age) Regulations 2006

SOUTH-WESTERN
CENGAGE Learning™

Australia • Brazil • Japan • Korea • Mexico • Singapore • Spain • United Kingdom • United States

SOUTH-WESTERN
CENGAGE Learning™

Business Law, 8th Edition

Keith Abbott, Norman Pendlebury
and Kevin Wardman

Publishing Director: Linden Harris

Publisher: Patrick Bond

Editorial Assistant: Alice Rodgers

Production Editor: Lucy Mills

Marketing Manager: Leo Stanley

Production Controller: Paul Herbert

Cover design: Hannah Dale, HL Studios

Text design: Design Deluxe, Bath

© 2007, Cengage Learning EMEA

For product information and technology assistance,
contact **emea.info@cengage.com**.
For permission to use material from this text or product,
and for permission queries,
email **clsuk.permissions@cengage.com**.

British Library Cataloguing-in-Publication Data
A catalogue record for this book is available from the British Library.

ISBN: 978-1-84480-461-0

Cengage Learning EMEA
Cheriton House, North Way, Andover, Hampshire, SP10 5BE,
United Kingdom

Cengage Learning products are represented in Canada by Nelson Education Ltd.

For your lifelong learning solutions, visit **www.cengage.co.uk**

Purchase your next print book, e-book or e-chapter at
www.cengagebrain.com

Printed by TJ International, United Kingdom
5 6 7 8 9 10 – 12 11 10

PREFACE

The new edition is able to provide extensive coverage of the following examination syllabuses:

ACCA	Professional Qualification Diploma in Financial Management	F4 Corporate and Business Law Module A
CIMA	Certificate In Business Accounting 2000 2006	Business Law Fundamentals of Ethics, Corporate Governance & Business Law
ICSA	Diploma In Business Practice Self-Standing Awards: Certificate and Diploma in Company Secretarial Practice	Business Law in Practice Share Registration Practice Advanced Company Secretarial Practice
ICSA	Pre-Professional	Business Law and Corporate Law
IPD	Electives	Employment Law and Health and Safety

Since its first edition the main purpose of Business Law has been to fulfil the needs of students taking any introductory law course. It is therefore widely used on, for example, Association of Accounting Technicians (AAT), Institute of Legal Executives (ILEX) and Institute of Credit Management (ICM) courses. It is also very relevant for the GNVQ Business Law option.

The bulk of the text is devoted to the presentation of legal rules in a straightforward style and format which will help students understand the subject, assimilate the necessary facts and achieve success in examinations. In addition there are introductory chapters on Learning Methods and Examination Technique and 46 past examination questions with suggested answers. Further resources for lecturers and students can be found on the companion website at www.thomsonlearning.co.uk/abbott8.

The law is stated as at 30 July 2006.

K. R. Abbott
N. Pendlebury
K. Wardman
July 2006

ACCA, 29 Lincoln's Inn Fields, London WC2A 3EE

CIMA, 26 Chapter Street, London SW1P 4NP

ICSA, 16 Park Crescent, London W1N 4AH

IPD, Camp Road, London SW19 4UX

TABLE OF CASES

TABLE OF STATUTES

CHAPTER 1

Methods of Learning

INTRODUCTION

1. 'The skills of learning are themselves learned, but seldom taught!' In fact this chapter does not set out to teach a person how to learn. Learning is a very individual process and there is no set procedure which is best for everyone regardless of their personality. The contents of this chapter amount to a series of suggestions, some or all of which may be integrated into whatever method of learning a student has already developed. It therefore

    a.   Outlines the various *resources* available to a student;

    b.   Explains the essential *requirements* necessary to pass a law examination;

    c.   Gives some advice on the approach to learning; and

    d.   Suggests some methods of using the resources to achieve the requirements.

2. *Resources*

    a.   Lectures and the lecturer.

    b.   Lecture notes, both written and taped.

    c.   Textbooks.

    d.   Past questions.

    e.   Suggested answers to past questions.

    f.   Discussions with fellow students and arranged visits, for example, to the courts.

    g.   This book.

3. *Requirements*. Three qualities are necessary to pass law examinations

    a.   Understanding the principles of law,

    b.   Learning the relevant legal facts, and

    c.   Skill in applying the principles and facts to examination questions.

This chapter suggests the best available resources for attaining the requirements of understanding and learning. Chapter 2 deals with the third requirement of application.

4. *Approach*

a. *Mental approach*. It is vital to neither underestimate nor overestimate your own ability or the standard of the examination. Both undue pessimism and overconfidence can be the cause of failure. The methods described below should minimise the risk of failure because of an unrealistic assessment of either personal ability or of what is expected by the examiner. The best approach is summed up in a Chinese proverb:

'That the birds of worry and care fly above your head, this you cannot change, but that they build nests in your hair, this you can prevent.'

b. *Physical approach*

i. *Timetabling*. When the course is nearing its conclusion, ie six–eight weeks before the examination, it is generally advisable to prepare a revision timetable which allows roughly equal time for each paper that is to be taken. The timetable need not be complex, eg Mondays – Law; Tuesdays – Accounts; Wednesdays – Economics. A target number of hours should be set for each day, and if time is lost one day, it should be made good as soon as possible. Timetabling avoids time wasted deciding what to study each day, and it ensures that no subjects are neglected. The timetable may be changed occasionally if the revision time considered necessary for a particular subject changes as the examination draws near.

ii. *When to work*. This is mainly a matter for personal preference. It is, however, generally accepted that chances of success are not improved by working so late at night that you get less sleep than you need. A more contentious question is whether or not you should work up to the 'last minute' before an examination. The authors believe that you should do so. The evening before the examination is more usefully spent on revision rather than trying to relax watching television.

UNDERSTANDING

5. *Law is Easy to Understand!*

a. Such a statement by an author or lecturer may appear to reveal a lack of sympathy with the problems faced by students. This is not the case. It is merely that our experience has shown that most people who fail law examinations do not do so because they are unable to understand the subject. Law is after all a human creation. It is relevant to everyday life, and the medium of expression is words. Subjects, such as mathematics, with abstract concepts and more indirect relevance are arguably more difficult to understand. All students can therefore approach law with confidence that they will not encounter insurmountable difficulties in understanding the subject.

b. If, however, you do encounter a principle, rule, or case that you do not understand, you must never accept defeat. Read about it in several textbooks if necessary, ask your lecturer for a second explanation or

ii. Acts of Parliament and case law do not become inoperative merely due to old age. For example the TREASON ACT 1351 was considered in JOYCE v DPP (**1946**).

b. *Absence of codification*. In some countries most of the law has been reduced to written codes which contain the whole of the law on a particular subject. Generally this is not so in England.

c. *The system of precedent*. This means that a judge is bound to apply rules of law formulated in earlier cases provided the facts of the case before him are sufficiently similar, and the earlier case was heard in a court of superior, or (subject to exceptions) equal status.

d. *The judiciary*. English judges are independent of both Parliament and the Civil Service. This is evident from the fact that they often give judgement against the Crown or a Government Department. In addition, a judge will be immune from liability provided he acts honestly in the belief that he is within his jurisdiction. The judiciary is important because the judges of the superior courts have a great effect on development of the law. They do not merely apply statutory rules, they *make* law when interpreting statutes and by developing the doctrine of judicial precedent.

e. *Common law and equity*. English law is based on two complementary systems of law known as common law and equity. Common law was the first system to develop. Its rules were rigid and sometimes harsh. Equity evolved to supplement the common law with more flexible rules based on principles of good conscience and equality.

f. *The accusatorial procedure*. In both civil and criminal cases the court remains neutral and hears the arguments presented by each side. In countries where an inquisitorial procedure is used the court plays a more active part, itself questioning the witnesses.

CIVIL AND CRIMINAL LAW

6. There are many ways to classify law, the most fundamental distinction being that drawn between criminal and civil law.

7. *Criminal Law*

a. A crime is regarded as a wrong done to the State. Prosecutions are usually commenced by the State, although they may be brought by a private citizen. If the prosecution is successful the accused person (the defendant) is liable to punishment. Some crimes, for example rape, have specific victims. Others, for example treason or speeding, can be committed without causing loss to any particular person. If there is a victim he will not usually have a say in whether or not a prosecution is brought, nor will he benefit from a conviction, since fines are payable to the State.

b. Criminal and civil hearings take place in different courts with different rules of procedure. There is also a different standard of proof. In a criminal trial the prosecution must prove the accused's guilt *beyond reasonable doubt*. In a civil action the plaintiff must prove his case on the *balance of probabilities*.

8. *Civil Law*. Civil actions may be commenced by any person who seeks compensation for a loss which he has suffered. If the claimant is successful he will usually be awarded damages. The damages must be paid by the defendant. Their purpose is to compensate the claimant for his loss rather than to punish the defendant. There are many categories of civil law, for example:

a. *Contract*. This determines whether promises made by persons are enforceable.

b. *Tort*. A tort is defined as the breach of a general duty imposed by law, for example the duty not to be negligent, and the duty not to trespass on another person's property.

c. *Property law*. This includes the law relating to freehold and leasehold land, and the ownership and possession of goods.

d. *Company law*. There is a need to regulate the relationship that a company has with its directors, shareholders, creditors, and employees.

e. *Commercial law*. This term covers contractual matters relating to business transactions, for example the law relating to sale of goods, consumer credit and cheques.

f. *Employment law*. This also involves contractual relationships, in this case between employer and employee. The term also includes redundancy, unfair dismissal and health and safety at work.

g. *Family law*. Marriage, divorce, nullity, guardianship and legitimacy are within the scope of family law.

9. *Crime or Civil Wrong?*

a. The distinction between a crime and a civil wrong is not found in the nature of the act itself, but in the legal consequences that follow it. Thus if a taxi driver crashes he may commit:

   i. A breach of contract, ie failure to deliver the passenger to his destination.

   ii. A tort, ie negligence if he causes damage to any person or property.

   iii. A crime, for example dangerous driving.

b. In some situations the facts will therefore indicate both a criminal offence and a possible civil action. In such cases the victim will not be able to have both actions heard in the same court. He will have to start a civil action separate from any prosecution brought by the State. However, *S.11* CIVIL EVIDENCE ACT *1968* provides that in any civil proceedings the fact that a person has been convicted of an offence shall be admissible to prove that he committed that offence. The effect is to raise a presumption that he committed the offence, unless the contrary is proved.

THE TITLE OF CASES

10. *Criminal Cases*

    a. Where the offence is particularly serious or complex, for example murder or perjury, the Director of Public Prosecutions may investigate and prosecute. In addition some statutes require actions to be brought by the DPP, for example for election offences under the REPRESENTATION OF THE PEOPLE ACT *1949*.

    b. Prosecutions involving the more serious criminal offences, known as indictable offences, are brought in the name of The Queen. The case will then be known as, for example, 'R v Jones', R being short for either Regina or Rex.

    c. Prosecutions for less serious offences, known as summary offences, are usually commenced in the name of the actual prosecutor (normally a police officer), for example 'Evans v Jones'.

11. *Civil Cases*

    a. The parties' names are used, the claimant's name being placed first, for example 'Rylands v Fletcher'. This is, however, traditionally pronounced 'Rylands and Fletcher'.

    b. Sometimes there will not be a claimant and a defendant, for example if an application has been made to the court to interpret Brown's will the case would be known as 'Re Brown'.

12. *Appeal Cases*. When a party appeals he is called the appellant, and the other party is the respondent. Since the appellant's name is always placed first, when a defendant appeals the name of the case will be reversed, thus Peek v Derry in the High Court, and on appeal, became Derry v Peek in the House of Lords.

CHAPTER 4

The Main Sources of English Law

THE MEANING OF 'SOURCES OF LAW'

1. The previous chapter classified the law into civil and criminal by reference to the subject matter of the dispute and the legal consequences which result from the dispute. Law may also be classified by reference to its source, ie the means by which the law is brought into existence. There are four *legal sources* of law, namely custom, judicial precedent, legislation, and European law.

2. Sometimes other meanings are attributed to the term 'sources of law':

    a. The *literary source* describes where the law is physically found, ie in law reports and statutes.

    b. The *formal source* describes the authority which gives force to the rules of law, ie the State.

    c. The *historical sources* are generally regarded as common law and equity, although the term is sometimes used to refer to the reasons behind the creation of the law, for example a report by the Law Commission.

3. This chapter concentrates on the four legal sources, but since methods of classification of law are only matters of convenience, there is an inevitable overlap between these legal sources, civil and criminal law, and common law and equity.

CUSTOM

4. *Uses of the Word 'Custom'*. The word 'custom' may be used in several different senses. In one sense it is the main source of English law since it is the original source of common law. It would, however, be wrong to equate 'common law' and 'custom' today since most common law rules owe their origins to judicial decisions rather than ancient custom. In its second sense 'custom' describes a conventional trade usage. Custom in this sense is not a source of law, but a means by which terms are implied into contracts.

5. *Local Custom*. The third use of custom is to describe rules of law which apply only in a particular area, for example a county or parish. In this sense

custom is a distinct source of law. In addition to the characteristic of restriction to a particular locality, it must be an exception to the common law. For example, under the custom of 'Gavelkind', which operated in Kent, an intestate's property passed to his sons in equal shares, whereas over most of the country it would all pass to the eldest son. Gavelkind was abolished in 1925. A valid local custom may be limited to a class of persons within a locality such as fishermen, but it cannot apply to a class of persons throughout the country, since then it would not be an exception to common law, but a part of it.

6. *Proof of Existence of a Local Custom.* Local custom also differs from common law in that if an alleged custom is to be incorporated into the law it must be proved to exist in Court. It is then said to be 'judicially noticed' and will be enforced by other courts. Thus a person who alleges the existence of a custom must prove its existence by satisfying the following tests laid down by Blackstone in 1765:

a. *Antiquity.* Local custom must have existed since 'time immemorial'. This has been fixed by statute at 1189, the first year of the reign of Richard I. In practice proof back to 1189 is never possible, so the Court will accept proof of existence within living memory. If this is shown the person denying the existence of the custom must prove that it could not have existed in 1189.

In SIMPSON v WELLS (1872) Simpson, who had been charged with obstructing a public foot-way, by setting up a refreshment stall, alleged that he had a customary right to do so deriving from 'statute sessions' (ancient fairs held for the purpose of hiring servants). It was shown that statute sessions were first authorised in the 14th century, so the right could not have existed in 1189.

b. *Continuity.* The *right* to exercise the custom must not have been interrupted. This does not mean that the custom itself must have been continuously exercised.

In MERCER v DENNE (1905) D owned a section of beach and wished to build on it. P, a fisherman, claimed a customary right to dry his nets on the beach and asked for an injunction to prevent the building. D's defence was that the custom was only exercised occasionally, and that before 1799 the beach ground was below the high water mark, and until recent times was unsuitable for use for drying nets.

It was held that the custom was valid. Its existence throughout living memory was proved, and the fluctuations in use were due to variations in wind and tide. However, the fisherman had always claimed the right to use such ground as was available, and so the custom extended to the additional ground now available. (Throughout the text P = Plaintiff, D = Defendant.)

c. *Peaceable enjoyment.* A custom can only exist by common consent. It must not have been exercised by the use of force, secrecy, or permission. (Nec per vim, nec clam, nec precario.)

d. *Obligatory force*. Where a custom imposes a specific duty that duty must be compulsory, not voluntary. Blackstone said:

'A custom that all the inhabitants shall be rated towards the maintenance of a bridge will be good, but a custom that every man is to contribute thereto at his own pleasure is idle and absurd, and indeed no custom at all.'

e. *Certainty*. An alleged custom allowing tenants to take away turf 'in such quantity as occasion may require' was held void for uncertainty. (WILSON V WILLES (1806).)

f. *Consistency*. Customs are by their nature inconsistent with common law, but they cannot, in a defined locality, be inconsistent with one another.

g. *Reasonableness*. A custom must be reasonable.

In DAY V SAVADGE (1614) a custom which allowed an Officer of the City of London Corporation to certify what customs were valid in matters in which the Corporation was interested was held to be invalid because it was unreasonable.

A custom cannot be reasonable if it conflicts with a fundamental principle of common law.

In WOLSTANTON V NEWCASTLE-UNDER-LYME CORPORATION (1940) the alleged custom allowed the landlord to undermine and remove minerals from his tenant's land without paying compensation for buildings damaged as a result. This was held to be unreasonable.

7. In recent years the tendency has been to standardise law by statute. This has led to the decline of custom as a source of law so that it is now almost extinct. The types of customary rights that do still exist are, for example, rights of way and rights to indulge in sports or pastimes on a village green.

JUDICIAL PRECEDENT

8. *The History of Judicial Precedent*

a. The doctrine of binding precedent did not become firmly established until the second half of the 19th century. In the common law courts the former practice was to apply the declaratory theory of common law, ie the law was contained in the customs of the land, and judges merely declared what it was. Thus although judges regarded precedents as persuasive they did not consider them to be binding. In FISHER V PRINCE (1762), Lord Mansfield said:

'The reason and spirit of cases make law, not the letter of particular precedents.'

b. As time passed judges paid more and more attention to previous decisions and in MIREHOUSE V RENNELL (1833), Baron Parke said that notice must be taken of precedents. The court could not 'reject them and abandon all analogy to them'.

c. In the Court of Chancery there was no declaratory theory, the judges merely tried to do justice in each individual case. This system lacked certainty and criticism was strong. From about 1700 the court began to pay increasingly greater respect to its previous decisions.

d. The modern doctrine of binding precedent is about 125 years old. Its present form is due to two factors. Firstly in 1865 a Council was established by The Inns of Court and The Law Society to publish under professional control the decisions of the superior courts. Prior to this private reports were published, some were good, others were unreliable, and many cases were not reported at all. Secondly, the JUDICATURE ACTS 1873–1875 established a clear court hierarchy. The doctrine of precedent depends for its operation on the fact that all courts stand in a definite relationship to one another.

9. *An Outline of the Doctrine*. Despite the inevitable tendency of judges to create law, binding precedent is *based* on the view that it is not the function of a judge to make law, but to decide cases in accordance with existing rules. *Two* requirements must be met if a precedent is to be binding:

a. It must be a *ratio decidendi* statement, and

b. The court must have a superior, or in some cases equal status to the court considering the statement at a later date.

If these requirements are met, and the material facts as found are the same, the court is bound to apply the rule of law stated in the earlier judgement.

10. *The Ratio Decidendi*

a. Judgements contain:

   i. *Findings of fact*, both direct and inferential. An inferential finding of fact is the deduction drawn by the judge from the direct, or perceptible facts. For example from the direct facts of the speed of a vehicle, the road and weather conditions, and the length of skid-marks, the judge may infer negligence. Negligence is an inferential finding of fact. Findings of fact are not binding. Thus even where the direct facts appear to be the same as those of an earlier case the judge need not draw the same inference as that drawn in the earlier case.

   ii. *Statements of law*. The judge will state the principles of law applicable to the case. Statements of law applied to the legal problems raised by the facts as found upon which the decision is based are known as 'ratio decidendi' statements. Other statements, not based on the facts as found, or which do not provide the basis of the decision, are known as 'obiter dicta' statements. For the purpose of precedent the *ratio decidendi*, which literally means 'reason for deciding', is the vital element which binds future judges.

   iii. *The decision*. From the point of view of the parties this is the vital element since it determines their rights and liabilities in relation to the action, and prevents them from reopening the dispute.

b. Sometimes it is difficult to ascertain the *ratio decidendi* of a case. For example:

    i. A statement intended by the judge to be the *ratio* is not accepted by a subsequent court as the *ratio*, however, his other reasons are accepted.

    ii. In the Court of Appeal or House of Lords the different members of the court may reach the same decision, but for different reasons.

    iii. A judge may intend two rationes, one of which may be treated by a later judge as an *obiter dicta* statement because it was not essential to the decision.

11. *The Hierarchy of the Courts*. The doctrine of precedent depends for its operation on the fact that each court stands in a definite position in relation to every other court. Section 2 of the Human Rights Act 1998, requires all courts and tribunal to take account in any judgement, decision, decleration of advisory opinion, the provisions of the Act.

a. *The European Court*. Its decisions bind all British courts, but not its own future decisions.

b. *The House of Lords*. Its decisions are binding on all English courts, however, since 1966, following a statement by Lord Gardiner L.C., the House need not follow its own previous decisions.

c. *The Court of Appeal (Civil Division)*. In YOUNG v BRISTOL AEROPLANE CO. (**1944**) it was held that the court is bound by its own previous decisions unless

    i. There are two previous conflicting Court of Appeal decisions, in which case it may choose which to follow.

    ii. The previous decision conflicts with a later House of Lords judgement, or

    iii. The previous decision was given per incuriam. 'Per incuriam' means through lack of care because some relevant statute or precedent was not brought before the court.

d. *The Court of Appeal (Criminal Division)*. The rules are the same as the Civil Division, except that the court need not follow its own previous decisions where this would cause injustice to the appellant. The reason is that where human freedom is at stake the need for justice exceeds the desire for certainty. – R v GOULD (**1968**).

e. *The High Court (Divisional Courts)*. The High Court is bound by its own previous decisions subject to the rule in Young's Case and, in criminal cases, R v Gould.

f. *The High Court (Judges at First Instance)*. Their decisions are not binding on other High Court judges, but are of persuasive authority.

g. *Inferior courts*. Magistrates courts, county courts, and other inferior tribunals are not bound by their own previous decisions since they are less authoritative and are rarely reported.

12. *Persuasive Precedents*. These are statements which a later court will respect, but need not follow. There are several kinds of persuasive precedent:

    a. *Obiter dicta*. There are two types of *obiter dicta*:

        i. A statement based upon facts which were not found to exist.

        In RONDEL v WORSLEY (**1969**) the House of Lords stated an opinion that a barrister might be held liable in negligence when not acting as an advocate, and that a solicitor when acting as an advocate might be immune from action. Since the case actually concerned the liability of a barrister when acting as an advocate these opinions were *obiter dicta*.

        ii. A statement which although based on the facts as found, does not form the basis of the decision, for example a dissenting (minority) judgement.

    b. *Ratio decidendi* of inferior courts.

    c. *Ratio decidendi* of Scottish, Commonwealth, or foreign courts, and statements of the Judicial Committee of the Privy Council.

13. *Overruling and Reversing*

    a. Precedents can be overruled either by statute or by a superior court. Judges are usually reluctant to overrule precedents because this reduces the element of certainty in the law.

    b. Overruling must be distinguished from reversing a decision. A decision is reversed when it is altered on appeal. A decision is overruled when a judge in a different case states that the earlier case was wrongly decided.

14. *Distinguishing, Reconciling and Disapproving*

    a. A case is distinguished when the judge states that the material facts are sufficiently different to apply different rules of law.

    b. Cases are reconciled when the judge finds that the material facts of both cases are so similar that he can apply the same rules of law.

    c. A case is disapproved when a judge, without overruling an earlier case, gives his opinion that it was wrongly decided.

15. *Advantages and Disadvantages of Precedent*

    a. *Advantages*

        i. *Certainty*. It provides a degree of uniformity upon which individuals can rely. Uniformity is essential if justice is to be achieved. The advantage of certainty by itself outweighs the several disadvantages of precedent.

        ii. *Development*. New rules can be established or old ones adapted to meet new circumstances and the changing needs of society.

        iii. *Detail*. No code of law could provide the detail found in English case law.

      iv.   *Practicality*. The rules are laid down in the course of dealing with cases, and do not attempt to deal with future hypothetical circumstances.

      v.   *Flexibility*. A general *ratio decidendi* may be extended to a variety of factual situations. For example the 'neighbour test' formulated in DONOGHUE v STEVENSON (**1932**) determines whether a duty not to be negligent is owed to a particular person whatever the circumstances of the case.

  b. *Disadvantages*

      i.   *Rigidity*. Precedent is rigid in the sense that once a rule has been laid down it is binding even if it is thought to be wrong.

      ii.   *Danger of illogicality*. This arises from the rigidity of the system. Judges who do not wish to follow a particular decision may be tempted to draw very fine distinctions in order to avoid following the rule, thus introducing an element of artificiality into the law.

      iii.   *Bulk and complexity*. There is so much law that no-one can learn all of it. Even an experienced lawyer may overlook some important rule in any given case.

      iv.   *Slowness of growth*. The system depends on litigation for rules to emerge. As litigation tends to be slow and expensive the body of case law cannot grow quickly enough to meet modern demands.

      v.   *Isolating the ratio decidendi*. Where it is difficult to find the *ratio decidendi* of a case this detracts from the element of certainty.

16. *The Importance of Precedent Today*

  a. It may appear that since the volume of statute law is increasing rapidly as government intervention in such areas as employment and consumer affairs increases, then the relative importance of case law must be decreasing. In fact the reverse is true, since as more Acts are passed, judges will more often be called upon to create new precedents when interpreting this new law. In addition some Acts deliberately and unavoidably vest a wide discretion in the judiciary. For example, the *UNFAIR CONTRACT TERMS ACT 1977* (as amended) has the underlying theme that an exemption clause must be reasonable if it is to be valid, but it is, of course, left to the judge to decide what is reasonable in each particular case.

  b. In recent years the judges' jurisdiction over common law and equity has given rise to some notable developments. For example Lord Denning's judgement in CENTRAL LONDON PROPERTY TRUST v HIGH TREES HOUSE (**1947**) has now been generally accepted as having created a new principle of equity, ie equitable estoppel. More recently in SHAW v DPP (**1962**) the House of Lords found Shaw guilty of 'conspiracy to corrupt public morals', an offence previously unknown to the criminal law. Thirdly, in MILIANGOS v GEORGE FRANK TEXTILES (**1976**) the House of Lords effected a major reform by deciding that courts could, in future, express their judgements in foreign currency.

c. The traditional view that judges merely apply the law is useful to emphasise the fundamental feature of the constitution, namely the Sovereignty of Parliament, but it does not reflect reality, especially when a judge is faced with a 'first impression' case where there is no existing precedent and no provision in an Act of Parliament. In such cases the judge must of necessity create new law. Precedent is therefore a very important source of law, the other main source being legislation.

17. *Law Reporting*

It is vital for the operation of judicial precedent to have a comprehensive and accurate system of law reporting. Prior to 1865 the quality and accuracy of law reporting varied tremendously; since 1865 the Modern Reports are published by an independent body the Incorporated Council of Law Reporting for England and Wales. The Council's reports are know as the Law Reports and they are divided into four series. The Appeal Cases series reports on the decisions of the House of Lords and the Privy Council. The other series are known as, Queen's Bench, Family Division and Chancery Division. The facts of a case and decision are set out briefly, there then follows a detailed description of the facts and arguments of the case followed by the judgments of the various judges. The Council also publish a series called the Weekly Law Reports, which appear earlier than the Law Reports.

LEGISLATION

18. *Introduction*

a. The most important source of law at the present day is legislation. Statutes are passed by Parliament which is the supreme law making body in the United Kingdom. In theory, at least, there is nothing which Parliament cannot do by statute. In practice statutes often amend, and sometimes abolish, established rules of common law or equity, overrule the effects of decisions of the courts, or make entirely new law on matters which previously have not been the subject of legislation.

b. There are two types of legislation, parliamentary and delegated legislation. The functions of Acts of Parliament are as follows:

i. *Law reform*. Relatively few statutes are concerned with changing substantive rules of law. Where such a change does take place it often follows from an unpopular decision of the House of Lords, or is based on a recommendation of the Law Commission.

ii. *Consolidation*. Where existing legislation is gathered into one Act this is known as consolidation.

iii. *Codification*. This takes place when all the law on a topic (both case law and statute law) is included in one Act.

    iv.   *Revenue collection.* The annual Finance Acts which implement the Budget proposals are the main revenue collection statutes.

    v.   *Special legislation.* These Acts are concerned with the day-to-day running of society, for example the RENT ACT *1974*.

  c.   An Act will come into force on the day on which it receives the Royal Assent, unless some other date is specified in the Act itself. It will cease to have effect only when it is repealed by another Act. Whilst in force an Act is presumed to be operative throughout the United Kingdom and nowhere else, unless the Act states otherwise.

19. ***The Superiority of Legislation.*** The rationale for the supremacy of legislation is that the will of elected representatives should prevail over that of appointed judges. The evidence for its supremacy may be summarised in three statements.

  a.   No court may question the validity of an Act of Parliament.

     In CHENEY v CONN (**1968**) the plaintiff objected to his tax assessment under the FINANCE ACT *1964* because the government was spending part of the tax collected on making nuclear weapons. He alleged this was contrary to the GENERAL CONVENTIONS ACT *1957* and in conflict with international law. The court, however, held that the 1964 Act gave clear authority to collect the taxes and being more recent it prevailed over the 1957 Act. It was said that

     'It is not for the court to say that a parliamentary enactment, the highest law in this country, is illegal.'

  b.   An Act of Parliament may expressly or impliedly repeal an earlier statute.

     In VAUXHALL ESTATES v LIVERPOOL CORPORATION (**1932**) if compensation for compulsory purchase were assessed under an Act of 1919 the plaintiffs would receive £2,370, whereas if it were assessed under an Act of 1925 they would only receive £1,133. Furthermore the 1919 Act provided that any Act inconsistent with it would have no effect. It was held that this provision did not apply to subsequent Acts, ie Parliament cannot bind its successors. The 1925 Act impliedly repeals the 1919 Act so far as it was inconsistent with it, and the plaintiffs therefore received £1,133.

  c.   A statute may be passed to vary or revoke the common law or even to retrospectively reverse a judicial decision. The WAR DAMAGE ACT *1965* operated to remove vested rights to compensation from the Crown and was controversially expressed to apply to proceedings commenced before the Act came into force. It thus reversed the decision of the House of Lords in BURMAH OIL v LORD ADVOCATE (**1965**).

20. ***The Need for Statutory Interpretation.*** Where the words of a statute are absolutely clear the need for statutory interpretation will not arise, because the persons affected by the statute will have no difficulty in conducting their affairs according to the statute. However, where there is ambiguity or uncertainty interpretation is necessary.

  a.   *Ambiguity* is caused by an error in drafting whereby the words used are capable of two or more literal meanings.

b. *Uncertainty* arises when the words of a statute are intended to apply to various factual situations and the courts have to decide whether the case before them falls within the factual situations envisaged by the Act. Uncertainty is far more common than ambiguity.

21. *Judicial Approaches to Interpretation.* There are three recognised judicial approaches to statutory interpretation. The approach chosen will depend on the particular judge, so it is not possible to know in advance which will be used. They are known as 'rules' although they are not rules in the accepted sense of the word.

   a. *The literal rule.* This is the basic rule of interpretation. It states that the words used must be given their literal or usual meaning even if the result appears to be contrary to the intention of Parliament.

   In FISHER v BELL (**1961**) the RESTRICTION OF OFFENSIVE WEAPONS ACT 1959 made it an offence to '*offer for sale*' certain weapons including 'flick knives'. A shopkeeper who displayed these knives in his window was found not guilty of the offence, since although he had displayed the goods, accepted buyers' offers, and sold the goods he had not offered them for sale, because goods on display are not an offer to sell, they are an invitation to treat. (See Chapter 13.)

   b. *The golden rule.* This states that the literal must be followed unless to do so produces an absurd result. Where a statute permits two or more literal meanings application of the golden rule is not inconsistent with the literal rule since the literal rule cannot be applied in such cases. However, in rare cases a judge will apply the golden rule to a statute which has only one literal meaning:

   In RE SIGSWORTH (**1935**) the golden rule was applied to prevent a murderer from inheriting on the intestacy of his victim although he was, as her son, her only heir on a literal interpretation of the ADMINISTRATION OF ESTATES ACT 1925.

   The golden rule may be criticised as being subjective, since a judge who decides that a literal interpretation is absurd, and therefore contrary to the intention of Parliament, must be ascertaining the intention of Parliament from a source other than the statute itself. This is strictly speaking beyond his function.

   c. *The mischief rule.* Where an Act is passed to remedy a mischief the court must adopt the interpretation which will have the effect of remedying the mischief in question. For example the AFFILIATION PROCEEDINGS ACT 1957 refers to a 'single woman'. This has been interpreted to include not only unmarried women, but any woman with no husband to support her, because the mischief which the Act was passed to remedy was the possibility of a woman having an illegitimate child with no means of supporting it.

22. *Further Rules of Interpretation*

   a. The statute must be read as a whole, and each section must be read in the light of every other section, especially an interpretation section.

b. *The Eiusdem Generis Rule*. Where general words follow two or more particular words they must be confined to a meaning of the same kind (*eiusdem generis*) as the particular words. For example 'cats, dogs and other animals' means other domestic animals.

c. Where a criminal statute is uncertain or ambiguous it is generally interpreted in favour of the individual.

In R v HALLAM (**1957**) it was held that the offence of 'knowingly possessing an explosive' required the accused to know, not only that he possessed the substance, but also that it was explosive.

Contrast RE ATTORNEY-GENERAL'S REFERENCE (**No. 1 of 1988**) where the accused received unsolicited information from an employee of a firm of merchant bankers, to the effect that there was to be a merger between two companies. He knew that if this information were generally known it would affect the price of the shares. He also knew that it was confidential information, however, within 10 minutes he had instructed his stockbroker to purchase shares in one of the companies. The merger was announced the following day and a few weeks later the accused sold the 6,000 shares that he had purchased at a profit of £3,000. He was accused under *S.1 COMPANY SECURITIES (INSIDER DEALING) ACT 1985* which, among other things, required him to 'knowingly obtain' price sensitive information. He was originally acquitted on the basis that 'obtaining' meant actively obtaining the information, rather than passively obtaining it. This interpretation was rejected by both the Court of Appeal and the House of Lords on the grounds that the approach would water down the effect of the legislation and also require the courts to make almost imperceptible factual distinctions. The House of Lords recognised the importance of the general rule that in a penal statute the words would normally be given their narrower meaner, but felt that this was not appropriate in the present case.

d. Where a statute does not make an alteration of the law absolutely clear it will be presumed that Parliament did not intend to alter the law. For example prior to 1898 a wife was not permitted to give evidence against her husband. The *CRIMINAL EVIDENCE ACT 1898* made her competent to do so, but in the absence of express provision, it was held in LEACH v R (**1912**) that she could not be compelled to give evidence against her husband.

23. *Statutory Interpretation and Judicial Precedent*. Precedent and legislation are sometimes mistakenly regarded as separate sources of law. This is not the case because once a superior court in the hierarchy has interpreted the words of an Act, an inferior court is bound to adopt that interpretation if faced with the same words in the same Act. Thus statutory interpretation forms a link between the sources of precedent and legislation.

24. *Delegated Legislation*

a. Delegated legislation comes into being when Parliament confers on persons or bodies, particularly Ministers of the Crown in charge of government departments, power to make regulations for specified purposes. Such regulations have the same legal force as the Act under which they are made.

b. *Types of delegated legislation*

   i. *Orders in Council.* This is the highest form of delegated legislation, many Acts of Parliament being brought into operation in this way, the power to make the Order being contained in the Act. In theory an Order in Council is an order of the Privy Council, but in fact an Order in Council is usually made by the Government and merely approved by the Privy Council. This has the effect of conferring wide legislative power on government departments.

   ii. *Rules and regulations.* A statute may authorise a minister or a government department to make a wide variety of rules and regulations. These rules, and Orders in Council, are collectively known as statutory instruments.

   iii. *By-laws.* These are rules made by local authorities. Their operation is restricted to the locality to which they apply.

c. *Advantages of delegated legislation*

   i. It saves the time of Parliament, allowing Parliament to concentrate on discussing matters of general policy.

   ii. It can be brought into existence swiftly, enabling ministers to deal with urgent situations, such as a strike in an essential industry.

   iii. It enables experts to deal with local or technical matters.

   iv. It provides flexibility, in that regulations can be added to or modified from time to time without the necessity for a new Act of Parliament.

d. *Disadvantages of delegated legislation*

   i. Law making is taken out of the direct control of elected representatives and is placed in the hands of employees of government departments. This is in theory less democratic.

   ii. Parliament does not have enough time to effectively supervise delegated legislation or discuss the merits of the rules being created.

   iii. A vast amount of law is created, statutory instruments out-numbering by far the amount of Acts passed each year.

e. *Control of delegated legislation*

   i. *Judicial control.* If a minister, government department, or local authority exceeds its delegated power its action would be held by the court to be ultra vires (beyond the powers of) and therefore void.

   ii. *Parliamentary control.* There are several methods of parliamentary control. Some statutory instruments must be laid before Parliament and will cease to be operative if the House so resolves within 40 days. Others require a vote of approval from the House. In addition there is a Joint Committee of the Houses of Commons and Lords whose function is to scrutinise statutory instruments with a view to seeing whether the attention of Parliament should be drawn to the instrument on one of a number of specified grounds, for example because the instrument is obscurely drafted, or because it imposes a tax on the public.

LEGISLATION OF THE EUROPEAN UNION

25. *The European Union and the Single Market*

a. The European Economic Community was set up by the TREATY OF ROME *1957*. The six signatories were France, Germany, Italy, Belgium, Holland and Luxembourg. On 1st January 1973 Great Britain, Eire and Denmark joined as a result of the Brussels TREATY OF ACCESSION. Greece joined in 1981 and Spain and Portugal in 1986. The Community was renamed the European Union in 1993. The most recent new members are Austria, Sweden and Finland, who joined on 1st January 1995. The TREATY OF NICE *2003* allows for ten more countries to join the Union as from 1st May 2004, these are: Cyprus, the Czech Republic, Estonia, Hungary, Latvia, Lithuania, Malta, Poland, Slovakia and Slovenia; and Bulgaria and Romania will join in 2007. Negotiations for Turkey to join the Union are currently underway.

b. The object of creating a common market goes back to the TREATY OF ROME *1957*. However, in 1985 EU Heads of Government committed themselves to progressively establishing a single market over a period expiring on 31st December 1992. This commitment was included in a package of treaty reforms known as the SINGLE EUROPEAN ACT *1986* (SEA). The Act assisted the free movement of goods by breaking down technical barriers (for example differing national product standards) national restrictions, subsidy policies and so on. The SEA also sped up EU decision making by extending majority voting to most major areas of the single market programme. This replaces the unanimous voting requirements which applied before the Act came into force.

c. In November 1993 the TREATY OF EUROPEAN UNION, signed in Maastricht, came into force. It gave the EU more powers. In particular

   i. It provided for the introduction of a common currency by 1999.

   ii. It introduced European Citizenship. A number of consequences follow from this, including the right of any EU national to reside in any member state.

   iii. It increased the powers of the European Parliament, by introducing new rights, for example the right to reject proposed legislation in certain areas if no agreement can be reached with the Council of Ministers and the right to initiate legislation by requiring the Commission to submit a proposal.

   iv. It gave the EU a more active role in many areas, for example consumer protection, public health, industry policy, education and (with the exception of the UK) social policy.

   v. It introduced a common foreign and security policy.

26. *European Union Institutions*

a. *The Commission*

    i.   This is the executive body of the EU, and consists of 20 Commissioners appointed by mutual agreement of the member governments. There must not be more than two from any country, and the present practice is for the five larger countries – France, Germany, Italy, Spain and Britain to appoint two each, and the ten smaller countries one each.

    ii.   The Commission is responsible for the formulation of EU policy. It acts collectively, but individual commissioners specialise in particular areas such as agriculture, transport and social affairs.

    iii.   The Commission has wide legislative functions. It initiates and drafts most EU legislation, and puts its proposals before the Council for enactment. The Commission also has executive functions to ensure the enforcement of Council decisions.

    iv.   The Commission represents the EU in negotiations with non member states and administers certain budgets and funds. In general it acts as the day-to-day executive of the EU.

    v.   Each Commissioner is assisted by a small private staff whose members tend to be of the same nationality as the Commissioner they serve. In addition the Commission has a staff of about 17,000, divided between various departments and auxiliary services.

b. *The Council*

    i.   The Council is the EU's decision-making body. It agrees legislation on the basis of proposals put forward by the Commission.

    ii.   Each Council meeting will deal with a particular area of policy, for example agriculture, finance or industry and will be attended by the relevant Minister from each member state.

    iii.   There are three methods of decision making (a) unanimity (b) simple majority voting, ie at least nine member states in favour, and (c) qualified majority (weighted) voting based on the relative population of member states. Most proposals are subject to qualified majority voting.

c. *The European Parliament*

    i.   This directly elected body has 626 members, 87 from the UK. It has consultative and advisory functions which are exercised through 19 standing committees dealing with specialist topics, for example agriculture, transport, legal affairs and women's rights.

    ii.   Under the EU Treaties its formal opinion is required on many proposals before they can be adopted by the Council. Most proposals are subject to the co-operation procedure introduced by the SEA. This enables the Parliament to give an opinion when the Commission makes a proposal and again when the Council has reached agreement in principle (known as a 'Common Position'). Members of the European Parliament are elected for a period of five years.

d. *The Court of Justice*. The European Court of Justice (the ECJ) is a court of first instance from which there is no appeal. It consists of 15 judges, selected from persons whose independence can be relied on and who are either recognised legal experts or qualified for judicial office in their respective countries. The judges hold office for six years. They are assisted by nine Advocates General who present the cases in an unbiased manner. The decision of the Court is a single judgement, dissenting opinions are not expressed. Its decisions are binding on the national courts of member states. The jurisdiction of the Court includes:

i. Actions brought against member states either by other member states or by the Commission on the ground that Treaty obligations are not being fulfilled.

ii. Actions brought against EU institutions by member states, private individuals, or corporate bodies.

iii. Rulings on the interpretation of the Treaties or on the validity of any of the acts of the EU institutions.

27. *The Sources of EC Law*

a. *Treaties*. The primary sources of EC law are foundation treaties of Paris and Rome. The TREATY OF PARIS *1951* established the European Coal and Steel Community (ECSC). The TREATY OF ROME *1957* established the European Atomic Energy Community (EURATOM). A second TREATY OF ROME *1957* established the European Economic Community (EEC), now contained in the TREATY OF EUROPEAN UNION *1992*, consolidated into the TREATY OF AMSTERDAM.

b. *Direct effect and direct applicability* are key concepts of European Community Law. Direct applicability means that some provision of European Community Law is directly, ie automatically, part of the domestic (national) law of a member state of the European Union. It is not necessary for a member state to incorporate the provision in domestic legislation. Direct effect, on the other hand, means that some provision of European Community Law creates individual rights, which can be enforced in national (domestic) courts. In fact, direct effect takes two forms viz 'vertical direct effect', ie individual rights which can be enforced against a national (member) state and 'horizontal direct effect', ie individual rights, which can be enforced against other individuals.

The distinction between direct applicability and direct effect forms the background to European Community 'secondary' legislation, ie Regulations, Directives and Decisions. It is necessary, therefore, to examine each of these in turn.

c. *EC primary legislation*. Contained in the Treaties these are mainly concerned with economic matters such as free trade, agriculture, and transport. The Treaties set out in broad terms the objectives to be achieved and leave many of the details to the Council and the Commission. These bodies have law making powers *secondary legislation* – which they may exercise in accordance with the Treaties.

EC *secondary legislation* may be classified as:

i.   *Regulations*. These are of general application, binding in their entirety and directly applicable in all member states without the need for further legislation. They confer individual rights and duties which the national courts of the member states must protect. Their object is to obtain uniformity of law throughout the member states.

ii. *Directives*. Unlike regulations, directives do not have immediate binding force in all member states. They are addressed to member states, requiring the national Parliament to make whatever changes are necessary to implement the directive within a specified time.

iii. *Decisions*. These may be addressed either to a member state or to an individual or institution. They are a formal method of enunciating policy decisions and they are binding on those to whom they are addressed.

d.   *The legislative process*

i.   EU legislation is the result of lengthy and complex negotiations and consultations involving several Council and Commission working parties and other committees provided for by the Treaties.

ii. Briefly the procedure is for the Commission to discuss the proposal with officials from member states and other interested parties before adopting it as a formal proposal. It is then submitted to the Council and the European Parliament. Parliament may give an opinion and, depending on the Article of the Treaty on which the proposal is based, the Council can either adopt the proposal or agree a common position by qualified majority voting. In the latter case the European Parliament may give a second opinion before the proposal is returned to the Council to be finally adopted as Community Law.

e.   *Interpretation of EU legislation*. EU legislation is drafted in terms of broad principle, the courts being left to supply the detail by giving effect to the intention of the legislature. This can be ascertained because regulations, directives and decisions are required to state the reasons on which they are based. Thus in the interpretation of EU legislation the 'golden rule' and the 'mischief rule' are applied, rather than the 'literal rule'.

28. *Acceptance of EU Law by the UK*

a.   THE EUROPEAN COMMUNITIES ACT 1972 provides that any enactment of the UK Parliament shall have effect subject to the directly applicable legislation of the Communities. 'Directly applicable' means that a provision confers directly on individuals rights enforceable by them in the courts of a member state without the need for further legislation by that state. Thus UK legislation is repealed by subsequent directly applicable EU legislation to the extent that the two are inconsistent. Parliament has therefore been obliged to give up sovereignty so far as EU matters are concerned. It is, however, clear that the basic principle of Parliamentary Sovereignty has not been impaired.

EU law is only enforceable in the UK because the 1972 Act so stated and it was said in MACARTHYS V SMITH (1978) that 'Parliament's recognition of European Community Law...by one enactment can be withdrawn by another.'

b. The EU is concerned primarily with economic and commercial matters, and the effect of UK entry is being felt initially in those fields. Company law is experiencing wide changes as movement is made towards a uniform set of rules applicable to business organisations throughout the EU. Commercial law, particularly concerning monopolies and restrictive trade practices, is also being affected. However, criminal law, contract, tort, property law and family law will not be affected.

29. *The European Convention on Human Rights*

In the past human rights in the UK have not been contained in any written document or code; rights have been traditionally protected in two ways, one, by the courts adopting an approach which is that if the law does not prohibit an act then it is lawful and, two, through the ability to scrutinise any institutional excesses by way of judicial review. Although the UK is a signatory to the 1951 EUROPEAN CONVENTION ON HUMAN RIGHTS, it was never incorporated into UK law. In 1998 Parliament passed the HUMAN RIGHTS ACT 1998 which came into effect in 2000, and now incorporates the European Convention on Human Rights into UK law. The main provisions of the Act are: S.3 all existing legislation must, so far as is possible, be read as being compatible with the Convention, with any new legislation before Parliament requiring that a relevant Government minister make a written statement that the proposed legislation is compatible with the Convention. And S.7 creates the right of individuals to bring legal proceedings against public authorities for violations of the Convention. Key rights under the Convention are:

Article 1 contracting States shall ensure that all persons within their jurisdiction be given the rights and freedoms contained in the Convention.

Article 2 all persons shall have a right to the preservation of life as afforded by law.

Article 3 no person shall be subjected to any torture, inhumane or degrading treatment or punishment.

Article 4 no person shall be held in slavery or servitude or be required to perform compulsory labour (there are exceptions here where this is the consequence of an order of the court).

Article 5(1) no person shall be deprived of their liberty except where: it is consequent upon a lawful conviction of a court, is done to stop the spread of infectious diseases or is necessary to treat the mentally ill or prevent alcohol or drug abuse.

Article 5(2) any person arrested has the right to be informed promptly of the reason for that arrest and of any charges and Article 5(3) requires that such persons be brought promptly before a judge.

Article 6 provides for the right to a fair trial in public by an independent, impartial court or tribunal and Article 6(2) provides the right to a presumption of innocence until proven guilty. Article 6(3) gives minimum rights to those charged with criminal offences; these include:

prompt information as to the details of the charge

adequate time and facilities to prepare a defence

the right to choose a lawyer and receive free legal assistance

the same right to require witnesses to attend as given to the prosecution

the right to cross-examine witnesses

the right to have the assistance of an interpreter free where one is needed

Article 8 lays down that all persons have the right to respect for their private and family life, home and correspondence; Article 8(2) allows for exceptions in the interests of national security and the general public interest.

Article 9 gives the right to freedom of thought, conscience and religion.

Article 10 provides for freedom of expression.

Article 11 the right to peaceful assembly and freedom of association with others including the right to form and be a member of a trade union.

Article 12 members of the opposite sex who are of marriageable age have the right to marry and form a family.

Article 13 any individual whose rights or freedoms, as set out in the Convention, are violated has the right to an effective remedy.

Article 14 the rights stated in the Convention must be afforded without any discrimination on any ground whatsoever.

Article 15 derogations from the Convention are allowed in time of war.

It is generally felt that the impact of the Human Rights Act on UK law, both civil and criminal, will be significant. For business organisations in particular employee rights under existing employment law are likely to be affected.

CHAPTER 5

The Subsidiary Sources of Law

1. The following sources are subsidiary in the sense that they are not currently responsible for the direct creation of law. They are either records of the law (the Law Reports), historical explanations of the existence of laws (Law Merchant, Roman Law or Canon Law), or opinions of what the law is or should be (textbooks and the Law Commission).

THE LAW REPORTS

2. *The History of Law Reporting*

a. *1272–1535.* The earliest reports were 'Year Books', which were first compiled in the reign of Edward 1. They dealt mainly with matters of procedure rather than rules of substantive law.

b. *1535–1865.* The year books ceased in about 1535, and were replaced by private sets of reports published under the name of the law reporter. The standard varied greatly, the most reliable reports being produced by Coke (1572–1616) and Burrow (1751–1772). Many of the private reporters were also judges.

c. *1865–Present day.* In 1865 a Council was established by the four Inns of Court and the Law Society to publish under professional control the decisions of the superior courts. Since incorporation in 1870 it has been known as The Incorporated Council of Law Reporting. The Council publishes 'The Law Reports' and 'The Weekly Law Reports'. In addition to the Council's reports some private reports are published by Butterworths. There are also private reports on specialist areas for example *Simon's Taxes*.

3. *Law Reporting and Judicial Precedent*

a. The doctrine of precedent is closely linked to law reporting. It was only after the Council of Law Reporting was formed that the law reports became completely reliable, and consequently, only then was precedent able to function efficiently.

b. There is, however, no rule which states that a court may only rely on a precedent if it is reported. It is sufficient that the decision be vouched for by a member of the bar who was present when judgement was delivered. Nevertheless personal recollections by judges and barristers would be too haphazard to form the basis of a workable system, therefore precedents are almost always contained in law reports.

c. Although law reports are fundamental to the doctrine of precedent the courts themselves have never created a methodical system of producing law reports. This is left to private enterprise, so that even now there is an element of chance and individual preference in the choice of whether or not to report a case.

d. Law reporters are barristers, and they must be present when judgement is delivered if their report is to be valid.

LAW MERCHANT

4. The law of contract administered in the common law courts in the 13th and 14th centuries was very unsophisticated. In addition their jurisdiction was limited to claims involving less than 40 shillings. They were therefore badly equipped to deal with the increasing volume of disputes arising from England's growth as a trading centre. A new set of courts therefore evolved to deal with disputes between merchants. They were not common law courts since their rules originated partly in trade custom, and partly in international law.

5. *Courts Administering Law Merchant*

a. *Courts of Pie Poudre.* These were courts held at fairs and markets (where most trade was conducted). The power to hold the court would be granted by the King to officers of the borough in return for dues known as 'tolls'. The courts attracted the merchants because of their speed and simple procedure (in contrast with common law courts), and because they gave effect to the merchants' own customs. The 13th and 14th centuries were the heyday of these courts, thereafter various factors contributed to their decline. By the 18th century almost all of these courts had ceased to function. The name 'pie poudre' comes from the French 'pieds poudres', after the 'dusty feet' of the traders who used the courts.

b. *Staple Courts.* In order to facilitate the collection of taxes from foreign merchants, dealings in certain basic commodities such as wool and tin were confined to certain towns. In each of these 'staple' towns was a court which had exclusive criminal and civil jurisdiction over merchants. These courts applied a mixture of common law and merchants' customs.

c. *The High Court of Admiralty.* Mercantile law and maritime law have always been closely connected, both having their origins in mercantile custom. The High Court of Admiralty was created in the 14th century and originally had both civil and criminal jurisdiction over matters arising at sea. It later acquired jurisdiction over contracts made on land, but this was removed by Sir Edward Coke on his accession to the bench in 1606.

6. *The Content of the Law Merchant.* Law merchant is responsible for the concept of negotiability, and is the basis of many of the rules of partnership, insurance and agency. Over the years many of the rules of the law merchant were incorporated into the common law and later into statute, for example the BILLS OF EXCHANGE ACT *1882* and the SALE OF GOODS ACT *1893*.

CANON LAW

7. Canon Law (the law of the Catholic church) influenced the growth of English Law in two ways.

   a. *Influence on common law and equity.* For example the punishment of imprisonment, family rights, and the strong moral content of equity, are concepts which originated in Canon law.

   b. *Application in the Ecclesiastical Courts.* Like the Pie Poudre and Staple courts these courts were independent of the common law courts. They dealt mainly with offences against morality, eg adultery and slander. They also had jurisdiction over the law of succession. They kept this jurisdiction until 1857 when the Divorce Court and the Probate Court were established. Until about 1500 the ecclesiastical courts also tried all persons accused of felonies provided the accused person claimed 'the benefit of the clergy'. (See Chapter 6.12.)

ROMAN LAW

8. Although it is the basis of most continental systems of law, Roman law is of little importance as a source of English law. Its influence was mainly felt in the ecclesiastical courts and, since the Church used to play a part in the distribution of a deceased person's property, in the rules relating to the requirements of a valid will. A soldier's privileged will (ie a verbal will) is an example of a current law which has Roman origins.

TEXTBOOKS

9. *Early Textbooks.* Although they are not original sources of law early text books are sometimes regarded as authoritative statements of the law at that time. For example *Littleton's Tenures* (approximately 1480) and *Coke's Institutes* (1628). *Coke* was relied on in REID v POLICE COMMISSIONER OF THE METROPOLIS (1973).

10. *Modern Textbooks.* These are sometimes used by barristers in court, but are of little importance as a source of law since this function is fulfilled by the law

reports and statutes. However, some writers have had the distinction of court recognition of their work. For example *Pollock's* definition of consideration was accepted by the House of Lords in DUNLOP V SELFRIDGE (**1915**) and *Winfield's* definition of nuisance was accepted in READ V LYONS (**1947**).

THE LAW COMMISSION

11. The Law Commission was established in 1965. It consists of solicitors, barristers, and academic lawyers who are appointed on a full-time basis by the Lord Chancellor. The Commission's function is to review areas of law where there is a need for reform, simplification or modernisation. It produces a steady flow of reports, recommendations and draft Bills, most of which have been enacted by Parliament, for example the CRIMINAL LAW ACT *1967* and the THEFT ACT *1968*.

CHAPTER 6

English Legal History

THE ORIGINS OF THE COMMON LAW

1. Prior to 1066 there existed a primitive legal system based on local custom. The effect of the Norman Conquest was to set in motion the unification of these local customs into one system of law with the King at its head. The system was common to all men and for this reason was known as 'common law'.

2. The ascendancy of the King's courts over the local courts took about 300 years, during which the King gradually assumed control through his itinerant justices, and established a central system of courts. The growth of the King's courts was resisted by the local barons, landowners and sheriffs whose jurisdiction (and revenue) was being diminished.

3. Many factors accounted for the growth of the King's courts and the decline of the local courts including:

   a. *The evolution of the writ system*. The King, as the source of justice, would grant a writ where there was a denial of justice in the local courts. These writs became standardised and provided specific rights which could be enforced in the King's courts. This led to a decline in the civil jurisdiction of the local courts, since most early writs were concerned with protecting rights in land, and disputes over land were the main business of the local courts.

   b. The *STATUTE OF GLOUCESTER 1278*. This was passed in an attempt to limit the jurisdiction of the King's courts over personal actions. It actually provided that no action for less than 40 shillings could be commenced in the King's courts. It was, however, deliberately misinterpreted by the royal judges who took it to mean that no personal action for more than 40 shillings could be tried in the local courts.

THE COURTS OF THE COMMON LAW

4. *The Curia Regis (King's Court)*. Although called a 'court' it had legislative, administrative and judicial functions. It was therefore the predecessor of Parliament as well as the courts. It originally consisted of the King and his tenants-in-chief. These were men to whom land had been granted in return for

some service such as the provision of men or arms. The King would travel the country, and the Curia Regis would meet wherever the King was. In medieval times a pattern developed whereby courts separated from the Curia Regis and eventually acquired a jurisdiction separate from it. The King, however, retained a residual judicial power which later led to other courts deriving their jurisdiction from him, notably The Court of Chancery and The Star Chamber. The common law courts which split from the Curia Regis were the courts of Exchequer, Common Pleas and King's Bench.

5. ***The Court of Exchequer.*** This became a separate court in the reign of Henry I (approximately 1140) and originally dealt with the collection of royal revenue, and at a later date disputes over debts. The judges were known as Barons. It acquired jurisdiction over the writ of debt through the fiction of 'Quominus'. This depended on a fictitious allegation of a debt owed by the plaintiff to the Crown which he was unable to pay because of a debt owed to him by the defendant. The King's interest was thus involved and the royal court could try the substantive dispute between the parties.

6. ***The Court of Common Pleas.*** Since it was impractical for litigants to follow the King around the country the MAGNA CARTA *1215* provided that common pleas should be heard in a 'certain place' which was fixed as Westminster. The judges were full-time lawyers and the court's jurisdiction extended to all disputes which did not concern the King's interest, for example personal actions of debt. It also tried actions for trespass where the title to land was concerned. It was the most widely used court, since it exercised jurisdiction over land, and most disputes concerned land, since only landowners could afford to use the courts.

7. ***The Court of the King's Bench.*** This was the last of the three courts to break away from the Curia Regis, its first Chief Justice being appointed in 1268. Its original jurisdiction was exercised principally in civil matters, although its judges did have criminal jurisdiction in the assize courts. It also had, because of its association with the King, the jurisdiction to issue the prerogative writs of mandamus, prohibition, and certiorari, which restrain abuses of jurisdiction by inferior courts and public officials. In addition it had appellate jurisdiction over the Court of Common Pleas.

8. These three royal courts all basically exercised a civil jurisdiction, with some overlap of their functions. They were abolished by the JUDICATURE ACTS *1873–1875*. Most criminal matters were dealt with by the itinerant justices in the assizes.

9. ***Assizes and Itinerant Justices***

   a. It has always been impossible to administer justice on the basis of all trials taking place in London. The Normans therefore adopted the system of sending out royal justices to hold '*assizes*' or sittings of the Royal Courts. Their original main function was the supervision of local administration and tax collection. They also had some criminal jurisdiction. Later their powers were extended to civil proceedings. The system was so successful that in the 12th century the country was divided into circuits, and each was visited three or four times a year by the justices.

b. The early justices were either judges of the common law courts, members of the clergy, or prominent laymen. They held office by reason of commissions issued by the King. The commission of *Oyer and Terminer* and the commission of *Gaol Delivery* conferred criminal jurisdiction. Civil jurisdiction was granted by the commission of *Assize*. Civil jurisdiction was however, limited, most cases being heard at Westminster. This was inconvenient because of the difficulty of transporting local juries to Westminster. The STATUTE OF NISI PRIUS *1285*, therefore extended the civil jurisdiction of the justices by providing that in certain civil actions, eg trespass, a jury should be summoned to Westminster on a certain day unless before (*nisi prius*) that date the case had been heard at a local assize.

c. The itinerant justices were of considerable importance in the development of common law. At first they administered local customs ascertained with the help of a local jury. When not on circuit the justices would meet and discuss the merits of the various customs they had discovered. Some would be rejected, other gained general acceptance, and were gradually applied throughout the whole country. This formed the basis from which the common law was developed.

10. *Quarter Sessions and Justices of the Peace*

a. The original function of J.P.s (approximately 1200) was administrative rather than judicial. However, in the early 14th century their civil function declined and, since the assizes could not deal with the growing number of offenders, they were given a criminal jurisdiction.

b. The original of the modern J.P. is the STATUTE OF LABOURS *1361*. This provided for the appointment of lay justices and compelled them to hold sessions in each county four times a year (quarter sessions). In 1590 J.P.s were given jurisdiction over all criminal offences. It was not until 1842 that the jurisdiction of quarter sessions was limited to exclude treason, murder and some of the other more serious offences. Trial at quarter sessions was by jury.

c. In the 15th century J.P.s were given statutory power to try the less important criminal cases outside quarter sessions. These sittings became known as 'petty sessions'. The jurisdiction of the petty sessions was entirely statutory, and the court sat without a jury. Such courts are now termed 'magistrates' courts'.

d. The administrative function of J.P.s declined as their criminal jurisdiction grew. However, certain functions remain to the present day, for example the power to issue warrants for arrest, and the task of conducting preliminary investigations into indictable offences (committal proceedings).

11. *The General Eyre.* A wider commission than was issued to itinerant justices and J.P.s was issued to the justices of the General Eyre. They were concerned to safeguard royal interests of all kinds, for example the collection of revenue and fines, trying prisoners in gaol, and the questioning of local officials. The

Eyre was held once every seven years, and was very unpopular. It ceased in about 1340.

THE ORIGINS OF EQUITY

12. The early common law was rigid and often harsh. This was to some extent reduced through the use of legal fictions. Fictions were used for three purposes:

    a. To reduce the severity of the criminal law. For example stolen property in fact worth more than one shilling would be valued by the court at less than one shilling, thus classifying the offence as a misdemeanour rather than a felony and consequently reducing the severity of the sentence. Another example is the 'benefit of the clergy'. – If a person could show that he was a member of the clergy he could be tried in the ecclesiastical courts where the penalties were less severe. The test to determine whether a person was a clergyman was whether he could read. To show ability to read he had only to recite a verse of Latin commonly supposed to have been Psalm 51 Verse I which most people therefore learnt by heart – just in case!

    b. To extend the scope of writs beyond their literal scope.

    c. To acquire jurisdiction from other courts, for example the fiction of 'Quominus' (5. above). Such fictions cannot be explained by a desire to improve the common law, but by the fact that judicial salaries depended upon the number of cases heard.

13. Fictions were not, however, capable of remedying all the defects of the common law. For example

    a. The plaintiff either had to fit his action into the framework of an existing writ, or show that it was similar to such a writ. If he could do neither, he had no remedy.

    b. In civil actions the only remedy which the common law courts could give was an award of damages.

    c. There were elaborate rules governing the procedure which had to be followed in bringing a case, and any slight breach of the rules might leave a plaintiff who had a good case without a remedy.

14. In many of these cases dissatisfied persons would petition the King, since the Curia Regis was not subject to the limitations of the common law courts, and could exercise the royal prerogative as it thought fit. For a time the King determined these petitions himself, but he later delegated this function to his Chancellor. The Chancellor was one of the most important members of the Curia Regis. He was in charge of the Chancery which was responsible for the issue of writs. Since he was already concerned with the legal process it was logical that the Chancellor should preside at hearings of petitions. Initially the Chancellor issued decrees in the King's name. In 1474 a Chancellor first issued a decree in his own name. At this point in time the Court of Chancery was created. Like the common law courts it had now become independent of the King.

THE COURT OF CHANCERY

15. The early Chancellors were members of the clergy who were very concerned to order what was, as a matter of conscience, fair between the parties. The first lawyer to be appointed Chancellor was Sir Thomas More in 1529. At first there were no fixed rules on which the Court proceeded. Gradually the Court began to be guided by its previous decisions, and formulate general principles, known as the 'maxims of equity', upon which it would proceed. Finally the Court of Chancery evolved a body of law the principles of which were as firm as those of the common law.

16. *The Maxims of Equity.* These are principles which the Court of Chancery followed when deciding cases, and which are applied today when equitable relief is claimed. There are many maxims, the following being some of the more well known examples:

    a. *He who seeks equity must do equity.* A person who seeks equitable relief must be prepared to act fairly towards his opponent as a condition of obtaining such relief. For example a mortgagor who wishes to exercise his equitable right to redeem must give reasonable notice of his intention.

    b. *He who comes to equity must come with clean hands.* Not only must the plaintiff 'do equity' by making proper present concessions to the defendant, he must also have acted properly in his past dealing with the defendant. For example D.C. BUILDERS V REES (1966) (Chapter 13).

    c. *Equality is equity.* For example since equity does not allow the remedy of specific performance to be invoked against a minor (a concession to his youth), it will also not allow a minor to claim the benefit of this remedy.

    d. *Equity looks at the intent rather than the form.* For example if an agreed damages clause in a contract is not a genuine pre-estimate of the loss that would result from a breach, equity would regard the clause as a penalty clause and treat it merely as a device to induce performance of the contract. The court would therefore enforce the contract as written, but would award the innocent party his actual loss.

17. *The Achievements of the Court of Chancery.* These were considerable, in particular the court developed the law relating to trusts and mortgages, and discretionary remedies namely:

    a. *Injunction* – An order of the court compelling or restraining the performance of some act.

    b. *Specific performance* – An order of the court compelling a person to perform an obligation existing under either a contract or trust.

    c. *Rectification* – The alteration of a document so that it reflects the true intention of the parties.

    d.   *Rescission* – The restoration of the parties to a contract to their precontract state of affairs.

18. **The Defects of the Court of Chancery**

    a.   The court inevitably bore the characteristics of the Chancellor. This was a good feature in that excellent lawyers such as Sir Thomas More and Sir Frances Bacon were able to contribute greatly to the development of equity. It was a bad feature when the shortcomings of other Chancellors brought the court into disrepute, for example in the 17th century the sale of offices was widespread and in 1725 when Lord Macclesfield was Chancellor, a deficiency of about £100,000 was discovered in court funds. In addition it was clear that there was a variation in the standard of justice dispensed by different Chancellors.

    b.   The sale of offices resulted in an excessive number of court officials, who tended to try to extend the scope of their duties so as to increase their revenue. This meant that procedure became very slow and expensive.

    c.   In contrast to the excess of officials there was a scarcity of judges. At first the Chancellor was the only judge, but he was later assisted by his Chancery Masters. The chief of these was the Master of the Rolls, who was effectively a second judge. It was not until 1813 that the first Vice-Chancellor was appointed by Lord Eldon.

COMMON LAW AND EQUITY

19. **Similarities between Common Law and Equity**

    a.   Both common law and equity are law. In ordinary language 'equity' means natural justice, but although inspired by these ideas, equity no longer represents the flexible concept of natural justice. It is now a branch of the law.

    b.   Common law and equity have both developed in an English context. They are not imported systems, and have only been subject to minimal foreign influence.

    c.   Both have been partly embodied in statute, for example the *SALE OF GOODS ACT 1979* (common law) and the *TRUSTEE ACT 1925* (equity).

    d.   Since the *JUDICATURE ACTS 1873–1875* both have been administered in the same courts.

20. **Differences between Common Law and Equity**

    a.   The most important difference is that common law was constructed as a complete and independent system, whereas equity developed to remedy the defects of the common law, and would be meaningless if considered in isolation, since it pre-supposes the existence of common law. For example the doctrine of equitable estoppel in contract developed as an exception to the arguably harsh rule of PINNEL'S CASE (**1602**). (See Chapter 13.)

b. Historically each system had different procedural rules since, until 1875, they were administered in separate courts. In the common law courts an action was commenced by the issues of a writ, whereas in the Court of Chancery an action was commenced by a petition, which allowed a greater scope to the plaintiff.

c. Although the administration of common law and equity has now been fused, their content nevertheless remains separate. Thus to say that a rule or remedy is 'equitable' means that it must be interpreted in an equitable atmosphere, and that the principles of equity apply. Thus the equitable remedies, for example specific performance and rescission are discretionary, whereas the common law remedy of damages exists as a right if a wrong is proved. A recent example of the exercise of this discretion was MILLER v JACKSON (**1977**) where although the plaintiff 'won' the case the injunction he sought was refused. (See Chapter 26.5.)

d. By its nature the Court of Chancery was certain to come into conflict with the common law courts. For example the Chancellor would rescind a contract where the common law courts would enforce it as originally drawn. In such cases equity would have to prevail or it would be of no effect. This has been clear since 1615 when there was a dispute between Sir Edward Coke who was Chief Justice of the Common Pleas and Lord Ellesmere, the Lord Chancellor. This dispute was only resolved when King James I, after consulting the Attorney-General, (Sir Francis Bacon,) decided in favour of the Court of Chancery.

THE REFORMS OF 1873–1875

21. By the second half of the 19th century the court structure was coming under heavy criticism for several reasons:

a. Procedure was complex and out of date.

b. The separate existence of common law courts and the Court of Chancery was not satisfactory. It has been said that one court was set up to do injustice and another to stop it.

c. The appeals procedure was in need of reform.

22. The necessary reforms were implemented by the *JUDICATURE ACTS 1873–1875* which came into operation together in 1875. Their main effect was to create a new Supreme Court of Judicature to which was transferred the jurisdiction of all the superior courts of law and equity. The Supreme Court was divided into two parts, the High Court and the Court of Appeal. The Judicature Acts did not affect the other courts. Thus, for example, the House of Lords and County

Courts are not part of the Supreme Court. The Judicature Acts changed the court structure as follows:

Before 1875	Created in 1875 HIGH COURT	Today
Court of Queen's Bench Court of Common Pleas Court of Exchequer	Queen's Bench Division Common Pleas Division Exchequer Division	Queen's Bench Division (Merger in 1880)
Court of Chancery Court of Bankruptcy	Chancery Division	Chancery Division
Court of Probate Court of Admiralty Court of Divorce	Probate, Divorce and Admiralty Division	Family Division (Re-named by The Administration of Justice Act 1970)
Court of Appeal in Chancery Court of Exchequer Chamber	COURT OF Split APPEAL in 1966	The Court of Appeal (Civil Division) The Court of Appeal (Criminal Division)

23. The above changes had the effect of fusing the administration of common law and equity. It did not, however, fuse their content. It also enacted the established rule that in cases of conflict the rules of equity shall prevail.

24. Finally the Judicature Acts simplified procedure by creating a single set of rules to apply throughout the Supreme Court. This considerably reduced the chance of a case being lost due to an error in pleading.

CHAPTER 7

The Courts

THE COURT STRUCTURE

1. The English court structure is fairly complex. It has four basic levels – the House of Lords; the Court of Appeal; the High Court (including the Crown Court); and the Inferior Courts (including County Courts and Magistrates Courts). Within this structure there is neither a clear division into criminal and civil courts, nor a division into first instance and appeal courts. For example the Queen's Bench Division of the High Court hears both civil and criminal cases and operates as both a first instance and an appeal court.

2. *The Structure of the Civil Courts*

3. *The Structure of the Criminal Courts*

MAGISTRATES COURTS

4. *Composition*

a. Magistrates courts are composed of Justices of the Peace. The court consists of at least two, but not more than seven justices (usually three) or a stipendiary magistrate.

b. J.P.s (except stipendiary magistrates) are not legally qualified, but they must live within 15 miles of their commission area and they are required to undertake basic training in judicial science. Each court has a legally qualified Clerk to the Justices. He advises the justices on the law, but he does not assist them with their decision on the facts. There is no jury in magistrates courts.

c. Any person may apply, or be proposed, to be a magistrate. Selection is made by a Lord Chancellor's advisory committee, of which there is one per county. Membership of these committees is secret and the criteria which they use to make their choice is also secret. Selection criteria therefore vary from one county to another. Magistrates are unpaid, but they may claim expenses.

d. J.P.s keep their full-time jobs, hearing cases perhaps one day in every two weeks. They must retire at 70.

e. Stipendiary magistrates are full-time paid magistrates. They are appointed by the Crown on the advice of the Lord Chancellor, from barristers or solicitors with at least seven years general advocacy experience. They are only appointed in certain urban areas and they usually sit alone.

5. *Criminal Jurisdiction*

a. *Summary offences*. The court's criminal jurisdiction exists mainly over summary offences, all of which are statutory offences. The maximum penalty that can be imposed was increased by the CRIMINAL JUSTICE ACT 2003 to 12 months' imprisonment (65 weeks for two or more offences). Most summary offenders are convicted of motoring offences. Since convictions were so numerous, the MAGISTRATES COURTS ACT 1957 introduced a procedure enabling persons to plead guilty by post. There are over 1½ million persons a year found guilty of summary offences.

b. *Indictable offences*. The most serious indictable offences are triable only in the Crown Court, for example murder, manslaughter, rape, bigamy and conspiracy. Statute does, however, specify some offences which are both indictable and summary. In such cases, if the accused consents, the case may be tried summarily, although an accused of 17 or over may demand the right to a jury trial in the Crown Court. If tried in the Magistrates Court and found guilty, the accused may be sent to the Crown Court for sentence if the magistrates consider that he deserves a greater punishment than they have the power to impose. The CRIME AND DISORDER ACT 1998 gives magistrates the power to impose Anti Social Behaviour Orders on offenders aged 10 and above.

6. *Transfer Procedure*

a. The CRIMINAL JUSTICE AND PUBLIC ORDER ACT 1994 abolished committal proceedings and substituted a new procedure for transfer of cases from the Magistrates Court to the Crown Court for trial.

b. Cases which are triable on indictment will now automatically be transferred to the Crown Court without a hearing in the Magistrates Court. If a defendant considers that there is no case to answer, a written application for dismissal must be made to the Magistrates Court. The written representations of both prosecution and defence will be considered and a decision made to dismiss the charge, amend it, or transfer the charge or amended charge to the Crown Court for trial. A magistrates hearing will only take place if the defendant is not legally represented or if the case is particularly complex or difficult. Oral representations will then be made by both parties, but no witnesses can be called. The CRIMINAL JUSTICE ACT 2003 limits the circumstances in which a defendant may be sent to the Crown Court for sentencing.

7. *Family Proceedings Courts and Youth Courts*

a. *Care and supervision proceedings*

   i. If a person under the age of 18 is beyond parental control or in some other trouble, his situation may be considered by the Family Proceedings Court. Under *S.31 CHILDREN ACT 1989*, if the child is suffering or is likely to suffer significant harm because the care being given to the child is not what it would be reasonable to expect, or because the child is beyond parental control, a care order may be made. This transfers parental responsibility to the local authority and puts a duty on the authority to provide accommodation for and maintain the child. The local authority must, however, allow the child reasonable contact with parents or guardians. A care order cannot be made in respect of a married child aged 16 or 17.

ii. A supervision order provides for the supervision of the child by local authority social workers. Their duty is to advise, assist and befriend the child.

iii. If the child is not receiving full-time education suitable to his age, ability or aptitude the court may make an education supervision order on the application of the local education authority.

b. *Criminal proceedings*

i. Children (aged 10 to 13) and young persons (aged 14 to 17) will have their case heard by magistrates sitting as a Youth Court. This court will sit in private in a different building or room from that in which other courts are held. Alternatively it must sit on a different day. The court consists of three magistrates drawn from a special panel. At least one magistrate must be a woman. Children under the age of 10 are presumed to be incapable of committing a crime (CHILDREN AND YOUNG PERSONS ACT 1963).

ii. Under the CRIMINAL JUSTICE ACTS 1982 and 1988 persons under 21 years of age cannot be sent to prison for any offence. The court may impose a fine or a community order, ie a probation order, a curfew order, a supervision order or an attendance centre order. An attendance centre order requires a young offender to spend a specified number of hours (up to a maximum of 24) at an attendance centre. The court may also order detention in a young offenders institution. This is only available for persons aged 15 to 20. The court must not impose this custodial sentence unless it is satisfied that there is no other way of dealing with the offender. The maximum custodial sentence for an offender aged 15 to 17 is 12 months. If the person commits an offence for which the penalty is life imprisonment, the person must be sentenced to custody for life, although a person aged under 17 who is convicted of murder must be detained during Her Majesty's pleasure.

8. *Civil Jurisdiction.* Magistrates' civil jurisdiction is less important than their criminal jurisdiction, but it is varied and includes, for example:

a. The recovery of certain civil debts including income tax, electricity and gas bills and council tax.

b. Domestic proceedings under the DOMESTIC PROCEEDINGS AND MAGISTRATES COURTS ACT 1978 (see below).

c. The granting of gaming and liquor licences.

9. *Domestic Courts*

a. These courts are constituted under the 1978 Act (see 8.b. above) to hear domestic proceedings. 'Domestic proceedings' are defined to include, for example, affiliation, adoption, guardianship and matrimonial proceedings.

b. The only people allowed to be present at the hearing are the officers of the court, the parties and their legal representatives, witnesses and other persons directly concerned with the case, and other persons whom the court may permit to be present.

c. Under the 1978 Act either party to a marriage may apply for an order on the ground that the other:

   i. Has failed to provide reasonable maintenance for the applicant;

   ii. Has failed to provide, or make a proper contribution towards, reasonable maintenance for any child of the family;

   iii. Has behaved in such a way that the applicant cannot reasonably be expected to live with the respondent; or

   iv. Has deserted the applicant.

d. If one of the above grounds is proved the court has a variety of orders available, for example:

   i. Periodical payments and/or a lump sum (of up to £500) to or for the benefit of the applicant or any child of the family;

   ii. Orders for custody or access;

   iii. Orders committing children to the care of a local authority;

   iv. Orders excluding one spouse from the matrimonial home.

10. *Advantages and Disadvantages of Lay Magistrates*

a. *Advantages*

   i. Public participation in the legal process reduces the remoteness of the law from the public.

   ii. The system is cheap since magistrates are not paid, but it nevertheless appears to attract high quality personnel.

   iii. Lay magistrates reduce the pressure on professional lawyers, leaving them to hear the more serious offences and most civil cases.

   iv. Although not legally qualified, magistrates may be better qualified in other respects, for example to hear children's cases. In addition the use of lay magistrates reduces the risk of the child perceiving himself as a young criminal.

b. *Disadvantages*

   i. Magistrates tend to be drawn from a narrow background. The majority are male, middle-aged and middle class. For example less than 10% of magistrates are under 40.

    ii. It has been argued, although not proved, that magistrates are too willing to accept police evidence.

    iii. There is also evidence that sentencing policies differ widely from one area to another. A person convicted of an offence may have three or four times the chance of going to prison if he comes from an area where the magistrates prefer custodial sentences to alternative sentences such as community service, probation and fines.

THE CROWN COURT

11. **Creation.** The Crown Court was created by the COURTS ACT 1971. It replaced the Assizes and Quarter Sessions and was made part of The Supreme Court of Judicature. The Assizes and Quarter Sessions were local courts, but in contrast the Crown Court is a single court which has buildings throughout the country and may sit anywhere in England and Wales, its jurisdiction is in no sense local. When sitting in the City of London it is known as The Central Criminal Court (The Old Bailey).

12. *Judges*

    a. Crown court judges are either

        i. *High Court judges*, usually of the Queen's Bench Division; or

        ii. *Circuit judges*, ie full-time judges appointed from the ranks of barristers or solicitors of 10 years standing, or from recorders of at least three years standing.

        iii. *Recorders*, ie part-time judges who are either barristers or solicitors of 10 years standing.

    b. The judge will usually sit alone unless an appeal is being heard from a Magistrates Court, when the judge will be joined by two, three or four lay magistrates. The court, sitting in this form, also exercises a limited civil jurisdiction, mainly over appeals concerning liquor and gaming licences.

13. *Criminal Jurisdiction*

    a. The criminal jurisdiction of the Crown Court concerns all cases above the level of Magistrates Courts. The more serious offences are tried by the High Court judges and the less serious by the circuit judges and recorders.

    b. When hearing appeals from the Magistrates Courts, the court may allow the appeal, reduce the sentence, or increase the sentence up to the maximum that could have been imposed by the Magistrates Court.

14. *The Jury*

The court sits with a jury of 12, and a majority verdict of 10–2 will be sufficient to convict the accused.

COUNTY COURTS

15. *Introduction*

a. County courts were created by the COURTS ACT 1846 to try civil cases involving small sums of money. Originally the upper limit of their jurisdiction was fixed at £20. This limit has been extended on many occasions so that today they deal with the majority of the country's civil litigation.

b. Jurisdiction is, however, limited in three respects:

   i.   It is entirely statutory, so that if in any matter statute provides no jurisdiction then none exists;

   ii. They have no appellate jurisdiction;

   iii. Jurisdiction is local, so there must be a connecting factor between the action and the county court district in which it is tried.

c. There are about 400 county court districts grouped into circuits, each of which is presided over by one or more circuit judges. The term 'county court' is misleading since these circuits are not based on county boundaries.

16. *Jurisdiction*

a. The extent of county court jurisdiction was extended considerably from 1st July 1991 by the COUNTY COURT JURISDICTION ORDER 1991 under the provisions of the COURTS AND LEGAL SERVICES ACT 1990. The Order abolished many existing financial limits, resulting in many cases being triable in either the county court or the High Court.

In general terms the extent of county court jurisdiction is:

   i.   Contract and tort actions for less than £25,000 shall normally be tried in a county court and actions for £50,000 and over in the High Court. Actions which fall in the middle range or have no quantifiable value can be tried in either court, depending on the complexity of the facts.

   ii. Personal injury claims unless the claim is worth £50,000 or more.

   iii. Equity and probate when an estate has a value of not more than £30,000.

   iv. Mortgages – up to £30,000 amount owing.

   v.   Enforcement of payment of fines.

   vi. Action to recover solicitors' costs up to £5,000.

b. In addition some courts outside London have bankruptcy jurisdiction which is unlimited in amount. The courts with such jurisdiction also have the power to wind-up companies where the paid-up capital is less than £120,000. Some courts in coastal areas also have Admiralty jurisdiction limited to £5,000 (£15,000 in salvage cases).

c. Some county courts are designated as 'Divorce' County Courts. They have jurisdiction in undefended matrimonial matters. In addition matrimonial cases must be commenced in a divorce county court and decided there, unless they are transferred to the High Court on the application of one of the parties or on the direction of the court. Consequently most divorce proceedings take place in divorce county courts. If the case involves any dispute with regard to children, for example as to the parent with whom the child will live, the case will be heard by a nominated circuit judge who by virtue of experience and training is a specialist in family work.

17. *Composition*

a. A county court is presided over by a circuit judge.

b. The COUNTY COURTS ACT 1984 contains provisions enabling judges of the Court of Appeal and High Court and recorders to sit in the county court. The judge usually sits alone, without a jury, although in some cases, for example fraud, there is provision for trial by a jury of eight.

c. Each county court also has a district judge who acts as an assistant judge and clerk to the court. He must be person with at least seven years general advocacy experience. In his administrative capacity he maintains the court records, arranges for the issue and service of summonses, deals with money paid into court, and a large number of similar functions. In practice much of the work is delegated to clerks and bailiffs. The district judge's function is narrower than that of the judge. He may hear undefended cases, cases where the amount at stake does not exceed £5,000 and (if the judge and parties agree) any other action.

d. In most ordinary actions the district judge will conduct a pre-trial review. The purpose is to encourage the parties to settle the claim, thus avoiding the time and expense involved in going to trial. If no compromise can be reached, the district judge will fix a date for the trial.

18. **Small Claims.** If a claim does not exceed £5,000 (except for personal injury cases), is straightforward and does not require a substantial amount of preparation with legal costs unlikely to be large, then, under recent reforms (see below) a judge may allocate the procedure onto what is called 'the small claims track'. Legal costs are not generally recoverable under the small claims track and, from April 2000, legal aid is not available in personal injury claims; this being replaced by a scheme of 'no win no fee'.

19. *The Woolf Reforms*

In 1999 significant changes were introduced with regard to procedure in the civil courts. The changes were based on the findings that the civil justice system was expensive, slow, excessively complicated and not meeting the needs of clients. Changes were introduced by the CIVIL PROCEDURE ACT 1997. The key thrust of the changes is to move the management of cases from litigants to judges. Initially it will be for a judge to decide which of three possible tracks a case is to proceed upon: the small claims track, the fast track or the multi-track. In addition time periods will be set by judges for the completion of certain procedures by litigants and wherever possible the parties will be encouraged to agree key points outside of the court. In this way it is hoped that cases will proceed more quickly and efficiently. New rules amend legal terminology to be in accord with more modern language; key changes are:

Old Term	New Term
Plaintiff	Claimant
Writ	Claim form
Pleading (the reason for the claim)	Statement of case
Minor/ infant (person under the age of 18)	Child
Affidavit	Statement of truth
In chambers or in camera	In private
Ex parte	Without notice
Subpoena	Witness summons
Discovery (of documents)	Disclosure
Anton Pillar order (power to enter and search)	Search orders
Interlocutory injunction	Interim injunction
Mareva injunction (stopping a transfer of assets)	Freezing injunction
Next friend (an adult who acts on behalf of a child in litigation)	Litigation friend

20. *Importance.* The practical importance of the County Courts is that they deal with the majority of the country's civil litigation. Over 1½ million actions are commenced each year, although only about 5% result in trials since most actions are discontinued or settled out of court before the trial stage is reached. Several factors may, however, prevent county courts being as effective a means of resolving small disputes as was originally intended. These factors may be expressed as three questions:

a. Does X know that he has suffered a wrong which entitles him to a legal remedy? He may, for example, be unaware that an exemption clause is invalidated by the UNFAIR CONTRACT TERMS ACT 1977.

b. Does X wish to involve the law? He may see the law as a middle or upper class institution, which is 'not for me'.

c. Can X afford to risk losing his case, possibly incurring expenses in excess of his original claim?

    This may be a particularly difficult decision to take if the potential defendant is an institution or company with resources to employ the best lawyers to fight the case regardless of cost.

THE HIGH COURT

21. *Creation and Composition*

   a. The High Court was established by the *JUDICATURE ACTS 1873–1875*. Prior to 1971 it sat in the Royal Courts of Justice in London, although when the judges tried a case on assize they constituted a court of the High Court. The *COURTS ACT 1971* abolished all courts of assize, but provided that sittings of the High Court could take place anywhere in England or Wales. The centres where sittings are held are determined by the Lord Chancellor.

   b. The High Court is divided into three divisions, namely the Queen's Bench Division, the Chancery Division, and the Family Division. Each division has a head and a number of puisne judges.

   c. High Court judges are appointed by the Queen on the advice of the Lord Chancellor. They must be barristers of not less than 10 years standing. The division to which they are appointed depends on the practice followed prior to appointment. The maximum number of High Court judges is fixed by Order in Council at 85.

   d. The trial is usually before a judge sitting alone, or before two or three judges in appeal cases. A jury may sit in defamation, false imprisonment, and fraud cases.

22. *The Queen's Bench Division*

   a. The jurisdiction of the Queen's Bench Division is wider than that of the other two divisions. It is both civil and criminal, and original and appellate.

   b. The most important aspect of its business is its *original civil jurisdiction*, mainly over contract and tort actions. Jurisdiction over commercial matters is exercised by a Commercial Court which is part of the division. It sits in London, Liverpool and Manchester. The division also has an Admiralty Court which deals with claims for damage, loss of life or personal injury arising out of collisions at sea, claims for loss or damage to goods carried in a ship, and disputes concerning the ownership or possession of ships.

   c. The *appellate civil jurisdiction* of the division is relatively minor. A single judge has jurisdiction to hear appeals from some tribunals, for example the Pensions Appeal Tribunal. A divisional court, consisting of two or more judges may hear appeals by way of 'case stated' from magistrates courts, the Crown Court, and from the Solicitors' Disciplinary Tribunal. '*Case stated*' means that the magistrates write down the arguments put forward by the parties, their findings, and their decision, together with reasons. This will go to the divisional court who will consider whether the decision is correct in law. If the appellant disputes an issue of fact, they may not bring an appeal by way of case stated.

   d. The *criminal jurisdiction* of the High Court is exercised exclusively by the Queen's Bench Division. This is entirely appellate and is exercised by the divisional court, usually consisting of three judges, and often including the head of the division, the *Lord Chief Justice*. The jurisdiction is over appeals by way of 'case stated' from magistrates courts and the Crown Court.

e. The divisional court also exercises a *supervisory jurisdiction*. It may issue the prerogative writ of habeas corpus, and it may make orders of mandamus, prohibition, and certiorari by which inferior courts and tribunals are compelled to exercise their powers properly, and are restrained from exceeding their jurisdiction.

f. Finally the jurisdiction of Queen's Bench Division judges extends to hearing trials in the Crown Court. Judges of the division spend about half their time 'on circuit' and half their time in the Royal Courts.

g. About 55 judges are appointed to the Queen's Bench Division.

23. *The Chancery Division*

a. The nominal head of the division is the *Lord Chancellor*, although he never sits in first instance cases.

b. The jurisdiction includes trusts, mortgages, bankruptcy, company law and partnership, and contentious probate business. There is some overlap of jurisdiction with the Queen's Bench Division. For example ESSO PETROLEUM LTD V HARPER'S GARAGE (STOURPORT) LTD (1967) was tried in the Queen's Bench Division, whereas PETROFINA (GREAT BRITAIN) LTD V MARTIN (1965) was tried in the Chancery Division. (These cases are very similar, and will be discussed in Chapter 17.)

c. The Chancery Division currently has about 15 judges.

24. *The Family Division*

a. This division, set up in 1970, deals with defended divorces, wardship, adoption, guardianship, legitimacy, disputes concerning the matrimonial home, and non-contentious probate cases. It also hears appeals from magistrates and county courts on family matters.

b. The head of the division is the *President*, and he is assisted by about 20 puisne judges.

25. *The Restrictive Practices Court*

a. This court was originally set up in 1956 and now deals with enforcement of the *RESTRICTIVE TRADE PRACTICES ACT 1976* and the *RESALE PRICES ACT 1976*. These acts prevent manufacturers entering into agreement which restrict free competition and fix prices with regard to their goods. However, since 1973 the court has also had the power to consider restrictive agreements in respect of services.

b. If the court considers that such agreements are contrary to the public interest it may enforce its rulings by an injunction. In practice this rarely occurs since the *RESTRICTIVE TRADE PRACTICES ACT 1976* requires potential restrictive trading agreements to be registered with the Director General of Fair Trading (see Chapter 17.).

c.   The court consists of five High Court judges assisted by ten laymen appointed by the Lord Chancellor from persons with knowledge and experience of industry, commerce or public affairs. Each case is heard by one judge and two laymen, unless it is solely an issue of law, in which the court will consist of a judge sitting alone.

THE COURT OF APPEAL

26. The Court of Appeal was split into civil and criminal divisions in 1966. The head of the civil division is the *Master of the Rolls* and the head of the criminal division is the *Lord Chief Justice*.

27. There are 28 Lord Justices of Appeal, Appeals are normally heard by three judges, but certain cases may be heard by two judges and occasionally a 'full court' of five or more judges will sit for an important case. For example YOUNG V BRISTOL AEROPLANE CO (**1944**) (Chapter 4.11) was heard by a court of six judges. A majority decision is sufficient and a dissenting judgement is expressed.

28. The appeal takes the form of re-hearing the case by drawing on the judge's notes and the official shorthand writer's transcript and by listening to arguments from counsel. Witnesses are not heard again nor is fresh evidence usually admitted. The court may uphold or reverse the decision in whole or part, it may alter the amount of damages awarded and it may make a different order as to costs. If new evidence is discovered it may order a new trial.

29. The Civil Division hears appeals from the County Court, any Division of the High Court and from some tribunals, for example the Employment Appeal Tribunal. The Criminal Division hears appeals from the Crown Court, either against conviction or against sentence. The Home Secretary may also refer cases to the Court of Appeal. For example in R V MAGUIRE (**1991**) the court quashed the conviction of alleged IRA terrorists who had previously been convicted of a bomb attack on a Birmingham public house. The Attorney General may also

   a.   Refer to the court for an opinion on a point of law arising from a charge which has resulted in an acquittal or,

   b.   Refer a case for an increased sentence if he considers that the judge in the Crown Court has been too lenient.

THE HOUSE OF LORDS

30. The House of Lords is the final court of appeal for all internal cases. There are 13 Lords of Appeal in Ordinary. The minimum number to hear an appeal is

three, but five judges usually sit. As in the Court of Appeal, a majority decision is sufficient and dissenting judgements are expressed. The Law Lords are, of course, professional lawyers, not lay members of the House of Lords.

31. The leapfrog procedure was introduced in 1969 because it was thought that two appeals from the High Court the Court of Appeal and then to the House of Lords were unnecessary. Appeal direct from the High Court to the House of Lords is allowed if

    a. The trial judge grants a certificate on the ground that the case involves a point of law of general importance, for example a matter of statutory interpretation

    b. The parties consent

    c. The House of Lords grants leave for a direct appeal.

    Since its introduction in 1969 the leapfrog procedure has rarely been used.

32. ARTICLE 141 of the TREATY OF ROME affects the jurisdiction of the House of Lords. It provides that a court of a member state against whose decisions there is no judicial remedy under national law must refer certain questions to the European Court for a preliminary ruling, and having obtained the ruling is bound to follow it. The questions concern:

    a. The interpretation of a Treaty; or

    b. The validity and interpretation of acts of the institutions of the European Union; or

    c. The interpretation of the statutes of bodies established by an act of the Council of Ministers.

    In 2004 the Government introduced the CONSTITUTIONAL REFORM BILL which will create a Supreme Court to replace the House of Lords sitting as an appellate court.

CHAPTER 8

Tribunals and Arbitration

1. *Statutory Tribunals*

    a. Statutory tribunals (also called administrative tribunals) are specialised courts established by statute to deal with disputes between government agencies and individuals or between two individuals in a less formal manner than is normal in a court.

    b. Tribunals have developed because the growth of social legislation in the 20th century has resulted in many new types of dispute. These disputes are often well suited to a procedure which is comparatively cheap, quick and informal. They are also far too numerous to be dealt with by the ordinary courts. Important statutory tribunals include:

        i. *Employment Tribunals;*

        ii. *the Employment Appeal Tribunal;*

        iii. *the Social Security Appeals Tribunal;*

        iv. *the Rent Assessment Committee;*

        v. *the VAT and Duties Tribunals;*

        vi. *the Lands Tribunal.*

    c. The main difference from the ordinary courts is their composition, their members being lawyers, judges, or laymen with a specialised knowledge of the field in which the tribunal operates.

    d. In recent years the control of tribunals, in particular by the courts, has increased. The TRIBUNALS AND INQUIRIES ACT 1971 provides that in the case of certain specified tribunals the chairman is to be selected from a panel appointed by the Lord Chancellor. In addition there is a Council on Tribunals which keeps under review the working of tribunals and reports on them from time to time. Tribunals subject to the scrutiny of the council include, for example the Lands Tribunal, National Insurance Tribunals and Rent Tribunals.

2. Some private or professional associations have tribunals to resolve disputes between members or exercise control and discipline over them. The jurisdiction of these tribunals is based on contract in that by becoming a member of the association a person accepts the jurisdiction of the governing tribunal. In some

cases the powers of the tribunal are defined by statute, for example The *SOLICITORS ACT 1974* and The *MEDICAL ACT 1978* define the powers of the Solicitors Disciplinary Tribunal and the Professional Conduct Committee of the General Medical Council respectively. There is normally an appeal from such tribunals to the High Court. If the powers of the tribunal are based solely on contract, for example the tribunals of trade unions or private clubs, there is no appeal to the courts, although the High Court may declare that the tribunal has acted beyond its contractual powers and that its action is void.

3. *Tribunals of Inquiry.* Parliament may, on occasions, set up a tribunal to inquire into a matter of urgent public importance. The tribunal will usually be given many of the procedural powers of the High Court, such as summoning witnesses, requiring the production of documents and examining witnesses on oath. The tribunal will sit in public unless the public interest requires otherwise. Persons appearing before the tribunal may, at the discretion of the tribunal be represented by a barrister or solicitor.

4. *Local Statutory Inquiries.* Many statutes confer jurisdiction upon Ministers to hold local inquiries. Such inquiries often arise when an order made by a local or public authority is submitted to a Minister for confirmation, for example an order for the compulsory acquisition of land. The inquiries are conducted by local inspectors but ultimate responsibility lies with the Minister. Procedure is governed by the statute under which the inquiry is held. However, the *TRIBUNALS AND INQUIRIES ACT 1958* requires the Minister to give the reasons for his decision if requested to do so.

5. *The Criminal Injuries Compensation Board.* Sometimes tribunals are set up to determine an individual's right to compensation from public fund. Thus the Criminal Injuries Compensation Board was established in 1964 to provide compensation to victims of crimes of violence (or if the victim dies, his dependants). Compensation is assessed on the same basis as common law damages and is paid as a lump sum.

6. *Control by the Courts*

   a. The Donoughmore Committee in 1932 recommended four types of safeguard:

      i. Against excess of jurisdiction.

      ii. Against failure to observe natural justice, ie both sides must be heard, and no person may be the judge of his own case.

      iii. Through publication of reports of tribunals. (This was implemented by the *TRIBUNALS AND INQUIRIES ACT 1958.*)

      iv. Through the exercise of supervisory and appellate jurisdiction.

   b. The supervisory control of the courts over tribunals is exercised in two ways:

      i. By the issue of the prerogative orders of mandamus, certiorari and prohibition. *Mandamus* is an order compelling the performance of a duty by a person or body of persons. *Prohibition* is the opposite, it is an order to prevent something from being done. *Certiorari* is an order to bring before the High Court a case which has been adjudicated upon, or which is in progress so that the High Court can decide whether or not the inferior court has acted in excess of its jurisdiction, or contrary to natural justice.

ii. By allowing an individual to bring an action against the officers of the tribunal claiming an injunction or a declaration as to his rights.

c. *Appeals from tribunals.* The TRIBUNALS AND INQUIRIES ACT 1971 provides for any party to appeal or to require the tribunal to state a case on a point of law to the High Court. However, there is often no right to appeal from the decision of a local inquiry.

7. *Advantages and Disadvantages of Tribunals*

a. *Advantages*

i. Tribunals specialise in a particular field and use personnel with specialised knowledge and experience.

ii. They are as informal as is consistent with the proper conduct of their affairs.

iii. They are less expensive than the courts.

iv. They are able to meet by appointment, and therefore act more quickly than the courts.

b. *Disadvantages*

i. As a result of their flexibility decisions can be inconsistent and difficult to predict.

ii. Some tribunals do not give reasons for their decisions and others hear cases in private.

iii. In some cases there is no representation by professional lawyers.

In May 2000 a review of the tribunal system was undertaken. The report, *Tribunals for Users: One System, One Service*, was published in 2001. The object of the report was to recommend a system that is independent, coherent, professional, cost-effective and user-friendly. The government has accepted the need for reform and published a White Paper in 2003 setting out the proposed reforms.

ALTERNATIVE DISPUTE RESOLUTION

8. *Introduction*

a. In the field of commerce in particular many parties prefer to refer their disputes to alternative dispute resolution (ADR), rather than have them resolved in court though litigation. The main advantages of these alternatives to litigation are that the proceedings tend to be less costly, take place more quickly and are held in private; they are also much more conducive to the parties reaching a compromise agreement.

b. An agreement to refer disputes to a form of arbitration is a contract, and is therefore subject to the ordinary law of contract. If the provision attempts to oust the jurisdiction of the courts it is void as being contrary to public policy. The parties may, however, include a 'SCOTT v AVERY (1856) clause'. Such a clause makes reference to arbitration a condition precedent to a court action. The court may therefore stay proceedings until an arbitrator has first heard the case.

c. The CONSUMER ARBITRATION AGREEMENTS ACT 1988 provides that arbitration clauses in consumer contracts cannot be enforced against a non-consenting consumer if the amount involved is less than £1,000. Therefore the consumer may either choose the contractual arbitration procedure or the county court small claims procedure. If the consumer's claim exceeds £1,000, the court will allow the arbitration clause to be operative if to do so would not be detrimental to the consumer's interests.

9. *Procedure*

The ARBITRATION ACT 1996 allows the parties to contract out of its mandatory and non-mandatory sections. The Act lays down three principles which are to govern its application:

i. the object of arbitration is to obtain a fair resolution of disputes by an impartial tribunal without unnecessary delay or expense;

ii. the parties should be free to agree how their disputes are resolved, subject only to such safeguards as are necessary in the public interest and the court should not intervene except as provided by the Act;

iii. an arbitrator is required to act fairly and impartially as between the parties and, in an attempt to reduce formality, the arbitrator need not follow High Court procedures but should adopt procedures suitable to the particular circumstances.

The parties are required to do all that is necessary for the proper and expeditious conduct of proceedings.

10. *Other forms of ADR*

a. *Early neutral evaluation.* This is where a neutral person, perhaps a lawyer or an expert in a particular field, gives a non-binding opinion on the merits of the case. This can then be used by the parties to negotiate or reach agreement.

b. *Expert determination.* Here an expert is agreed upon by the parties to settle the dispute which is legally binding.

c. *Mediation.* This involves a mediator working with the parties to reach a settlement or agreed position. Mediation takes two forms: 'evaluative', where the mediator assesses the strengths and weaknesses of the case, or 'facilitative', where his/her role is to facilitate/broker an agreement. Mediation has significant advantages in that costs and conflict can be much reduced. If agreement is reached the parties may set out their agreement in a binding contract.

d. *Conciliation*. This is similar to mediation with the conciliator – an outside person – actively seeking and putting forward a suggested basis for agreement between the parties. For example ACAS (the Advisory Conciliation and Arbitration Service) has a role in relation to proceedings that may be brought before an Employment Tribunal. The procedure is that when a complaint is presented to an Industrial Tribunal, a copy is sent to the Conciliation Officer. He may try to settle the dispute if asked to do so by either party, or if in his opinion there is a good chance of a settlement. The parties should feel able to speak openly to the Conciliation Officer, since a person's statement is not admissible in evidence in an Industrial Tribunal without that person's agreement.

e. *Med-AB*. This is a procedure that combines mediation and arbitration. Mediation is first tried; if this fails, the dispute is referred to arbitration. It is not unusual for the same independent person to act as both mediator and arbitrator.

f. *Neutral fact finding*. This process is commonly used in cases where there are complex technical issues to be determined. An expert in the field reviews the merits of the case and makes an assessment; this may then be used as a basis for further negotiations.

11. *Appointment of Arbitrators*

a. Where an agreement refers a dispute to arbitration it will be presumed that this means reference to a single arbitrator, but where a specific provision is made for two arbitrators they must appoint an umpire who, if they cannot agree, will break the deadlock.

b. The parties may appoint any person they wish to act as arbitrator. Lawyers are often appointed, but in some cases a person with relevant technical knowledge is appointed. The High Court has the power to appoint arbitrators in default of appointment by the parties, and to revoke the authority of an arbitrator on the ground of delay, bias or improper conduct.

12. *Appeal and Enforcement*

Parties to the proceedings can apply to the court challenging an award on grounds of serious irregularity, for example, failure of an arbitrator to act fairly and impartially with a reasonable opportunity being given to both sides to put their case, avoiding unnecessary delay and expense. Further grounds for appeal are where the arbitrator is alleged to have exceeded his/her powers, and on a point of law.

13. *Ombudsmen*

Here a formally appointed commissioner or official, acts as a referee in disputes between government and the citizen. Their job is to investigate complaints of misadministration by government departments or public bodies. They have no power to impose a remedy, but only to make recommendations.

They deal with such issues as, unreasonable delay, bias, unfairness, mistakes, failure to follow correct procedures and discourtesy.

14. *Regulators*

These are individuals specially appointed to deal with issues relating to the way utilities industries – gas, water, electricity, telecommunications – have dealt with complaints. Different regulators are appointed for each utility.

CHAPTER 9

The Personnel of
the Law

1. This chapter deals with solicitors, barristers, judges and juries. Both lay and stipendiary magistrates are personnel of the law, but they are discussed in Chapter 7.

SOLICITORS

2. *The Provision of Legal Services.* The COURTS AND LEGAL SERVICES ACT 1990, has significantly affected the traditional work of solicitors and barristers, for example

   a. The Act sets up a Lord Chancellor's Advisory Committee on legal education and conduct. This Committee may consider applications by professional and other bodies to be granted rights of audience in court.

   b. The Act also provides a framework for persons other than solicitors to conduct pre-trial work, for example the issue of writs. Such persons would have to demonstrate to the Advisory Committee that they have the necessary education and training and will be bound by an appropriate code of conduct.

   c. The Act also widens rights to engage in conveyancing, by setting up the Authorised Conveyancing Practitioners Board, which can authorise, supervise and discipline persons authorised to do conveyancing work. Such persons are an addition to the licensed conveyancers that have been working since 1985.

   d. In connection with probate services the Act establishes machinery for bodies to apply for their members to become probate practitioners. Prior to the Act it was an offence for anyone other than a solicitor or a barrister to prepare for payment papers leading to a grant of probate.

3. *Functions of Solicitors*

   a. There are about 100,000 solicitors practising in the UK. They perform a wide variety of work including conveyancing, probate, divorce, company and commercial matters, and general litigation. Some solicitors, particularly in the city centres, are specialists, concentrating for example on company law or maritime law. Many others are general practitioners, deriving most of their income from conveyancing and general litigation, but prepared to undertake most work requested by their clients.

b. If a person wishes to seek a legal remedy or use the facilities of the law, for example to sell his house or make a will, he will usually consult a solicitor. If a barrister's services are needed, either to present a case in court or to give an expert opinion, the solicitor will instruct the barrister. A layman cannot, in general, instruct a barrister direct.

c. Solicitors have had a right of audience in magistrates and county courts for many years. In 1993 solicitors in private practice (but not employed solicitors) were also given the right to appear in higher courts. The decision was taken by Lord Mackay, the Lord Chancellor, under machinery set up by the *COURTS AND LEGAL SERVICES ACT 1990*. The main advantage of the change is that it widens choice for consumers and has the potential to reduce costs. The decision was welcomed by the Law Society who had been arguing for increased rights of audience for solicitors for several years.

d. There is no legal obligation to employ a solicitor when seeking a legal remedy. A person may conduct his own case in any court in the land. He can do his own conveyancing, draw up his own will, and conduct his own divorce provided he has the time and common sense to understand and apply the basic procedures involved. Furthermore, since 1985 practising solicitors have lost their monopoly on conveyancing, since this may now be done by licensed conveyancers who are not qualified solicitors.

4. *The Law Society*

a. The solicitors' governing body is the Law Society. Its main functions are

    i. To control entry requirements to the profession.

    ii. To make rules governing the handling of clients' money by solicitors.

    iii. To issue practising certificates and protect the public against work by unqualified persons.

    iv. To administer the legal aid scheme.

    v. To run a compensation fund for persons who have suffered as a result of wrongful acts by solicitors.

    vi. To supervise solicitors' charges and provide a complaints system.

b. Solicitors are liable to the general criminal law, and to a solicitors disciplinary tribunal consisting of the Master of the Rolls, solicitor members and lay members. Solicitors, however, cannot be sued for negligence in their conduct of a case in court.

5. *Legal Executives.* Solicitors usually employ legal executives. They work under the control and authority of the solicitor, and usually specialise in a particular field, for example conveyancing. The governing body of legal executives is the Institute of Legal Executives. It sets its own examinations, however, qualification as a legal executive does not entitle a person to practise on his own account.

BARRISTERS

6. *Functions of Barristers*

a. Only a minority of qualified barristers practise at the bar, currently about 11,000. His/her work will then be in industry or education. Barristers' work includes advocacy in all courts, and giving written opinions on their specialist areas.

b. Prior to the COURTS AND LEGAL SERVICES ACT *1990* a barrister could only take instructions from a solicitor. However, S.61 now allows a barrister to enter into a contract with a client for the provision of services and payment of fees. Barristers may also make contracts with other professionals, for example accountants who are not involved in litigation, but who wish to obtain an expert opinion.

c. A successful barrister will usually 'take silk', ie become a Queen's Counsel. His work will then be exclusively advocacy. Barristers have a right to be heard in any court, but they may not form partnerships, nor may they sue for their fees.

7. *Liability of Barristers*

a. Barristers may not be sued for negligence as a result of their conduct of a case in court. In RONDEL v WORSLEY (**1969**) P contended that D, a barrister, had been negligent in the conduct of his case. The claim was struck out as disclosing no cause of action. The main reason given was that if a barrister could be sued for negligence it would mean a re-trial of the original case. This would open the door to every dissatisfied litigant and lead to dozens of pointless actions. (See Chapter 24:2 dii HALL v SIMONS (**2000**).)

b. Barristers are not immune from action as a result of pre-trial acts or omissions. The immunity is confined to work which 'is intimately connected with the conduct of the case in court' (SAIF ALI v SYDNEY MITCHELL (**1978**)).

8. *The Bar Council.* This is the barristers' governing body. It was formed in 1894. Its purpose is to maintain the standards and independence of the bar. It also deals with questions of professional etiquette, but it has no disciplinary powers.

9. *Fusion of the Legal Profession*

a. The division of the legal profession into two branches has been a topic of much discussion in recent years. In July 2003 a Consultation Paper was published asking whether the distinction between the two be abolished. In May 2004 the Government invited the Bar Council and Law Society to develop a new scheme for accrediting advocates. It seems likely that in the near future the two professions will become one.

The main arguments for and against fusion are as follows:

b. *Arguments against fusion*

i. *The service provided to the public.* It is argued that if fusion took place the specialist barristers would join the large firms and the clients of small firms would accordingly to be denied access to such specialists. This would result in the decline of small firms of solicitors.

    ii. *The service provided to judges.* In a judicial system that relies heavily on oral trials judges need clear argument and guidance to lead them to the correct decision. Such a service can only be provided by a select group of professional advocates.

c. *Arguments in favour of fusion*

    i. Functions overlap in the present system, both in advocacy and in specialisation in subject matter. Many solicitors are advocates and spend much of their working life in magistrates and county courts and, particularly in the larger firms, many solicitors are highly specialised.

    ii. The present system is inefficient since it involves duplication of effort, and the quality of work is affected because responsibility is divided. Also the custom whereby a barrister only receives his brief one or two days before the trial, is seriously prejudicial to the client.

    iii. *Cost.* The client will usually have to pay two experts to bring his case to court, and if a Queen's Counsel is employed three lawyers would have to be paid.

d. A number of reforms have been suggested, for example solicitors could be given a full right of audience in all courts and all barristers could be permitted to form partnerships with solicitors. Alternatively all lawyers could qualify in the same way and then practise as they please, in partnership or alone, taking instructions from lay clients or other lawyers. One class of lawyers would exist, some would be specialists and others general practitioners. Each lawyer could adjust his own practice to the needs of his clients, and his own preferences. The decisions as to which lawyers to use, and in what combinations, could then be taken by the client in his own best interests. Since the passing of the COURTS AND LEGAL SERVICES ACT 1990 it is clear that no unification of the profession is likely to take place in the foreseeable future.

10. Other legal personnel include:

a. *Public notaries*; who are authorised to draw up deeds, prepare wills and to administer oaths and take statements of truth – an *affidavit*. Most notaries are solicitors.

b. *Legal executives*; these are employed by solicitors to carry out routine work, such as conveyancing.

MINISTERS OF THE CROWN

11. The United Kingdom does not have a Minister of Justice. The link between Parliament and the Judiciary is provided by four ministers:

a. *The Lord Chancellor* is the Speaker of the House of Lords, appointed by the Crown on the advice of the Prime Minister. He is chosen from eminent lawyers or judges who support the party in office and he has a seat in the Cabinet. The Lord Chancellor:

i.   Is Head of the Judiciary;

ii. Presides over the House of Lords in both its legislative and judicial capacities;

iii. Is responsible for advising the Crown on the appointment of High Court (puisne) judges;

iv. Is Head of the Chancery Division of the High Court;

v.   Is responsible for the work of the Law Commission, the Land Registry, the Public Trustee and the Public Record Office;

vi. Acts as general legal advisor to the Government and as its spokesman in the House of Lords.

The office of Lord Chancellor is soon to be abolished and to be replaced by a Secretary of State for Constitutional Affairs. The purpose behind the reform is to strengthen the separation of the 'powers of state' – between the executive, legislature and judiciary.

b. *The Home Secretary* is a member of the House of Commons and of the Cabinet. His responsibilities include:

i.   The Prison, Borstal and Probation services. (Borstals were replaced in 1953 by detention centres and youth custody centres);

ii. The Police;

iii. The administration of the Metropolitan Courts; and

iv. Advice to the Government on the treatment of offenders and on the prerogative of pardon.

c. *The Attorney-General* is a barrister and a member of the House of Commons. As senior law officer of the Crown he represents the Crown in important civil and criminal matters. He appoints and supervises the Director of Public Prosecutions.

d. *The Solicitor-General* is also a barrister and member of the House of Commons. He assists and deputises for the Attorney-General both in the Commons and in Court.

NB. The *Director of Public Prosecutions (DPP)* is a barrister or solicitor with at least 10 years experience. He is appointed by the Home Secretary and assisted by a staff of professional lawyers and civil service administrators. His role concerns the administration of criminal justice and his duty is to institute proceedings:

i.   When the offence is punishable by death;

ii. When a case is referred to him by a government department; and

iii. In other cases where he considers that his intervention is needed.

JUDGES

12. *Appointment*

    a.   Judges above puisne judges are appointed by the Crown on the advice of the Prime Minister. Two posts deserve special mention:

        i.   *The Lord Chief Justice.* He is the head of the Criminal Division of the Court of Appeal and the Queen's Bench Division.

        ii.   *The Master of the Rolls.* He is the head of the Civil Division of the Court of Appeal. He also has duties in connection with the admission of solicitors.

    b.   High Court (puisne) judges, circuit judges, and recorders are appointed by the Crown on the advice of the Lord Chancellor.

        i.   *Puisne judges* must be barristers of at least 10 years standing or circuit judges who have held office for at least two years. They are usually appointed to the division of the High Court in which they practised, but they may sit in any division. There are 85 puisne judges. Appointment is by invitation. On retirement a knighthood is automatic.

        ii.   *Circuit judges* number about 622. Any barrister of at least seven years standing may apply to become a circuit judge, but in practice these judges are appointed from the middle ranks of barristers. Top barristers often do not apply because they are unwilling to take a drop in salary.

        iii.   *Recorders* must be barristers or solicitors of at least three years standing. They are part-time judges who sit in the county court for about 20 days each year. At present there are about 1,342 recorders.

    Judges can only be removed on an address by both Houses of Parliament. No judge has been removed from office since before 1700. Judges must now retire at 70, and circuit judges at 72.

13. *Constitutional Position*

    a.   Judges are not under the control of Parliament, or the Civil Service. The independence of the judiciary is a fundamental principle of constitutional law. Closely related to judicial independence is the doctrine of judicial immunity. In SIRROS v MOORE (**1975**) it was held that any judge will be immune from action provided he acts honestly and in the belief that he is within his jurisdiction.

    b.   Judicial immunity extends to the parties, witnesses, advocates, the verdict of the jury and fair, accurate and contemporaneous newspaper reports.

14. *The Function of Judges*

    a.   The traditional function of judges is to apply existing rules of law to the case before them. It is, however, being increasingly accepted that judges are capable of 'making law' both through the interpretation of statutes and the doctrine of precedent. Furthermore it is clear that when an Act of Parliament makes no provision for the case in question and there is no existing precedent, the judge must, of necessity, create new law.

b. In the following notable cases the judiciary went beyond the application of existing legal rules:

   i. In CENTRAL LONDON PROPERTY TRUST v HIGH TREES HOUSE (**1947**) Denning J. (as he then was), in the view of many writers, created a new rule of equity, namely equitable estoppel.

   ii. In SHAW v DPP (**1962**) Shaw published a directory of prostitutes. He was found guilty of 'conspiracy to corrupt public morals', an offence previously unknown to the criminal law.

   iii. In MILIANGOS v GEORGE FRANK TEXTILES (1975) the House of Lords effected an important reform by holding that English courts have power to give judgements expressed in foreign currency.

c. Judges also exercise certain administrative functions, for example:

   i. The Court of Protection (Chancery Division) supervises the affairs and administers the property of persons of unsound mind.

   ii. A rule committee chaired by the Lord Chancellor makes rules to govern procedure in the Supreme Court.

Circuit judges, district judges (who assist in the county court) and recorders do not create precedents.

JURIES

15. *The History of the Jury*

a. The trial of criminals by jury evolved in the 13th century to replace trial by ordeal which the church condemned in 1215. Most civil cases were also tried by jury until 1854.

b. Juries were originally summoned for their local knowledge, but by the 15th century their function had changed from witnesses to judges of fact. Nevertheless it was not until BUSHELL'S CASE (**1670**) that it was established that jurors could not be punished for returning a verdict contrary to the direction of the trial judge.

c. Until the present century the jury was widely regarded as one of the chief safeguards of the individual against the abuse of prerogative and judicial power. However, particularly in civil cases, juries were unpredictable and liable to make errors. In 1854 the COMMON LAW PROCEDURE ACT therefore provided that in civil cases the trial could be heard by a judge sitting alone if both parties consented.

In 1933 the ADMINISTRATION OF JUSTICE (MISCELLANEOUS PROVISIONS) ACT abolished civil juries in most cases, the main exceptions being fraud and defamation. The jury has also declined in criminal cases, but the loss of faith in the criminal jury has been far less marked.

16. *The Present Day Jury*

   a. Jurors are summoned by the Lord Chancellor and selection is by random ballot. An incomplete jury may be completed by summoning any person in or near the court to serve. A juror is in contempt of court if he refuses to serve or if he is drunk. MPs, lawyers, doctors, the clergy, some ex-prisoners and the mentally unsound do not qualify for jury service. Before a juror is sworn the defence may make a challenge. Since 1988 such a challenge must be supported by reasons. The reasons must not be stated in the presence of the jurors (and the juror who has been challenged) but must be argued in private before the judge. Jurors may also be successfully challenged if they know the defendant.

   b. Juries used to be criticised because the property-ownership qualification produced a jury that was not representative of the population. However, the property qualification was abolished in 1972, and now any registered elector resident for five years or over, between 18 and 70, may be summoned for jury service.

   c. The jury sits in private and in general a majority verdict of 10–2 is necessary for a conviction.

17. *Criticisms of the Jury*

   a. To some people the whole idea of a jury seems absurd. 12 individuals usually with no prior contact with courts are chosen at random to listen to evidence, often of a highly technical nature. They are given no training, they deliberate in secret, they do not give reasons for their verdict, and they are responsible to no one but themselves. After making a decision affecting the liberty of another individual they merge back into the community.

   b. More specific criticisms are

      i.   The random method of selection may produce a jury which is not intellectually capable of weighing the evidence and following the arguments presented.

      ii. Jurors are thought to be biased towards the motorist in motoring offences, and against newspapers in libel cases.

      iii. Jurors can be taken in by skilled speakers, and are not experienced in weighing evidence.

      iv. The system is not popular with jurors since attendance is compulsory and unpaid.

      v.   In a comprehensive study published in 1979, John Baldwin and Michael McConville found that the jury was representative of the population in terms of age and social class, but unrepresentative in terms of sex and race. Their research did not, however, find a consistent relationship between the composition of the jury and its verdict. A more important aspect of their study was to look at 'questionable' convictions and acquittals. They found that the incidence of such decisions was sufficiently high to 'shake the dogmatic and complacent attitudes that tend to characterise opinions about the jury system'.

18. *Defence of the Jury*

a. There are many passionate defenders of the jury. They argue that it is a check upon unpopular laws, that it is the best means for establishing the truth, that it serves an important political function by involving laymen in the administration of justice, and most important that it is a safeguard of liberty. Lord Devlin wrote:

    'No tyrant could afford to leave a subject's freedom in the hands of 12 of his countrymen. So that trial by jury is more than an instrument of justice and more than one wheel of the constitution: it is the lamp that shows that freedom lives.'

b. It is also clear that in general the jury enjoys the confidence of the public, the judiciary, lawyers, and the police, and although Baldwin and McConville show that its verdicts are questionable more often than was previously thought, it may well be that it reaches the right decision as often as can reasonably be expected of any tribunal.

CHAPTER 10

Procedure and Evidence

'Procedure' and 'Evidence' are both topics of considerable substance and complexity. This chapter does not attempt to explain these topics in detail. It merely explains some of the basic rules, procedures and terminology. It is primarily intended to indicate that particular rules exist rather than describe their detailed content.

CIVIL PROCEDURE

1. **Introduction**. The term 'procedure' covers all the steps necessary to turn a legal right into a satisfied judgement, it does not merely refer to the trial itself. The proceedings prior to trial, particularly in larger civil cases usually take many months and often result in a settlement being reached before any trial takes place. Proceedings after trial may also take many months, for example appeals procedure and the enforcement of the judgement. This section will be concerned with bringing an action in the Queen's Bench Division of the High Court, which may be regarded as the standard procedure. There are, however, many variations from this where an action is brought, for example, in bankruptcy. Procedure in the Queen's Bench Division is governed by the Rules of the Supreme Court. These rules are delegated legislation and are made by a Rule Committee under powers conferred by the *JUDICATURE ACT 1925*. It is important to note that these rules are purely procedural and will be declared ultra vires if they attempt to deal with substantive rules of law. In 1994 Lord Woolf was asked to undertake a review of the rules of procedures in the civil courts. His proposals for reform radically changed procedure in the civil courts. The *CIVIL PROCEDURE ACT 1997* brought in new Civil Procedure Rules in April 1999. The main changes are as follows.

   a. New terminology. For example, 'plaintiff' is now known as claimant and 'writs' are called 'claim forms'. A summary of the key changes in legal terminology are:-

Old Term	New Term
Plaintiff	Claimant
Writ	Claim Form
Pleading	Statement of case
Minor	Child
Affidavit	Statement of truth

Old Term	New Term
In chambers	In private
Ex parte	Without notice
Subpoena	Witness summons
Discovery	Disclosure
Anton Piller Orders	Search orders
Interlocutory injunction	Interim injunction
Mareva injunction	Freezing of assets injunction
Next friend	Litigation friend

b. *Encouragement of settlement*

Alternative Dispute Resolution is to be actively encouraged at various stages.

Pre-action protocols. These lay down a code for the parties to follow in pre-trial procedures; they include such things as timetables for the exchange of documents and use of expert witnesses.

Costs and payments into court. This gives greater discretion to the judge for the award of costs and allows for the taking into account of the conduct of the parties and the manner in which they have conducted themselves in court procedures. There is also the ability of a defendant to make an offer to settle, prior to the judge's summing up, with the effect that if the claimant's case does not exceed that amount there will be no costs awarded to the claimant with the added penalty that he will have to pay part of the defendant's costs also.

c. *A single jurisdiction.* The High Court and County Courts become a single jurisdiction operating to common procedural rules.

d. There are three tracks which cases may be allocated to:

　i. A small claims track – for cases up to £5,000; excluding personal injury and housing cases where the limit is £1,000.

　ii. A fast track – for claims between £5,000 and £15,000. These cases are heard by the county court within 30 weeks.

　iii. A multi-track for claims over £15,000. These are dealt with by the High Court where timetables are monitored and estimated costs agreed.

2. Summary Procedure

The basic steps involved are as follows:

a. The action is begun by issuing and serving a claim form.

b. The defendant acknowledges service.

c. An exchange of statement of case takes place.

d. Preparation is made for the trial, including discovery and inspection of documents.

e. The trial.

f. If there is no appeal the matter is concluded by enforcement of the judgement.

3. **Commencement of Proceedings**

   a. *Statement of claim.* The usual method of commencing an action is to issue a claim form. This places the matter on official record. A copy of the claim form must be served on each defendant either personally or by some other means such as service on his solicitor.

   b. *Petitions.* Some actions are commenced by a petition rather than a statement of claim, for example a divorce or a company liquidation.

   c. *Acknowledgement of service.* If a person on whom a statement of case is served proposes to enter a defence he must, within 14 days of service of the claim form, deliver an acknowledgement. The form of acknowledgement is served by the claimant with the claim form. After acknowledging service the defendant has a further 14 days in which to file a defence.

4. **Statement of Case**

   a. The object of the statement of case is to define the area of contention between the parties. A statement of case must contain a brief statement of the facts relied on, but not the evidence by which they will be proved. If a matter is not included in the pleadings it cannot usually be raised at the trial.

   b. The statements are:

      i. The *statement of claim*. This is the first statement and it is made by the claimant.

      ii. The *defence*, ie the defendant's answer. If the defendant has a complaint against the claimant he may include a *counterclaim* with his defence.

      iii. The *reply*. This is the claimant's answer to the defence.

   c. A typical series of statement of case may appear as follows:

In the Queen's Bench Division of the High Court.
Between

ACME BUILDERS LTD	*Claimant*
and	
JOHN BROWN	*Defendant*

Particulars of Claim

The Claimant's claim is for the balance of the agreed price for materials supplied and work done at the Defendant's factory at 30 Newton Street, Luton, between November 2004 and June 2005.

Particulars

Agreed price of work	£20,000
Received on account	£16,000
Balance	£4,000
And the Claimant claims:	£4,000

Defence and Counterclaim

1. The Defendant admits that the Claimant agreed to build an extension to the Defendant's factory for the sum of £20,000 to a specification prepared by the Claimant and agreed by the Defendant in a letter dated 30th September 2004.

2. It is admitted that the Claimant purported to carry out the work contracted for and that the sum of £4,000 is outstanding therefore. The Defendant will seek to set off his counterclaim in extinction of the sum due to the Claimant.

Counterclaim

3. It was a term of the contract that Claimant would carry out the work in a workmanlike manner.

4. In breach of contract certain work has been carried out in a defective manner and not in accordance with the agreed specification.

5. Particulars of the defects are shown on the attached schedule. The total estimated cost of rectification shown therein is £5,000.

And the Defendant Counterclaims: £5,000

Reply and Defence to Counterclaim

1. The Claimant admits the facts and matters set out in the Defence.

2. Paragraph 3 of the counterclaim is admitted. Paragraph 4 is denied. It is denied that any of the work is defective or fails to comply with the specification.

---

   d. If either party needs more information he may ask for 'further and better particulars' of specific matters.

5. ***Default Judgements.*** If the defendant fails to acknowledge service or if he fails to serve a defence the claimant may obtain a default judgement without the necessity of resorting to a trial.

6. ***Summary Judgements.*** If the claimant feels that there is no defence to the action he may apply for a summary judgement. The application will be dealt with by a Master of the Court. He is an official who has most of the powers of a judge. His decision can be set aside on appeal to the judge.

7. ***Procedure from Close of Pleadings to Trial***

   a. Between close of pleadings and trial much preparatory work must be done by the parties' solicitors.

   b. *Disclosure and inspection of documents.* Disclosure refers to the requirements of each side to disclose to the other all documents which are relevant to the dispute. Certain privileged documents need not be disclosed, for example letters between the party and his solicitor and experts' reports.

   c. *Summons for directions.* The interlocutory proceedings (proceedings until trial) are concluded by the taking out by the claimant of a summons for directions. A Master will hear the summons for directions. He will fix such matters as the date and venue of the trial and the numbers of expert witnesses that may be called by each side.

This would then be allocated to the *small claims track*.

8. *Payments into Court*

A payment into court is a sum of money paid by the defendant (or the claimant in respect of a counterclaim) into the court office. It is allowed at any time prior to commencement of the judge's summing up in all actions for debt and damages. The purpose is to put pressure on the claimant to settle for an amount less than that originally claimed, ie for the amount paid in. If the claimant does not settle and goes on to be awarded less than the amount paid in the plaintiff will have to pay both his own costs and the defendant's costs incurred after the payment in. In the absence of a payment in a winning plaintiff would usually have his costs paid by the defendant. The judge is not told of the payment in until after he has decided the amount of damages to award. It is now also possible for the claimant to make an offer to settle which has a similar effect on costs.

9. *Trial*

   a. In the High Court the parties are usually represented by barristers although they may appear in person. Solicitors have a right of audience in the County Court and in magistrates courts but not in the High Court.

   b. The trial starts with the claimant's barrister outlining the issues involved and calling witnesses. The defendant's barrister then outlines his case and calls the evidence for the defence. Next the defendant's barrister and then the claimant's barrister will make a closing speech. Finally the judge gives the decision in the form of a reasoned judgement which may be delivered as soon as the case is concluded, or reserved to a later date if the judge wishes to consider the case further.

10. *Enforcement of the Judgement.*
The final stage is enforcement of the judgement. If the defendant does not pay a judgement debt there are several ways by which the judgement creditor can obtain payment. The most important of these is the writ of *fieri facias* (fi fa) which orders the bailiff to seize the debtor's goods and, if necessary, sell them to pay the claimant out of the proceeds. The creditor may also be able to obtain a *charging order* on the defendant's land. If the debt is not paid the creditor will eventually be able to have the land sold and recover the judgement debt from the proceeds. A *freezing injunction* may be sought preventing the defendant from transferring assets out of reach of the court – for example, transferring money abroad.

11.
Proceedings in County Courts are broadly similar to High Court actions, although rather less formal and complex.

CHAPTER 11

The Law of Persons

INTRODUCTION

1. A legal person is a being that is regarded by the law as having rights and duties. There are two basic types of legal person – natural persons and corporations. A corporation is an artificial person which is recognised in law as a separate legal entity once the formalities for its creation have been complied with. A corporation must be distinguished from an unincorporated association, which does not have a legal identity separate from that of its members. The most significant types of corporation and unincorporated association are limited companies and partnerships respectively. These are discussed in detail in Part V.

NATURAL PERSONS

2. Human beings generally have full legal capacity, and consequently are potentially subject to any rule of law. The actual rules to which a person is subject depends on the factual situation in which he finds himself. These factual situations which affect a person's rights and capacities are called statuses. One person may have many statuses, for example husband, father, employer. Other examples include minor, guardian, wife, and mentally disordered person.

3. *Husband and Wife*

   a. *Formation.* In HYDE v HYDE (**1866**) marriage was defined as the 'voluntary union for life of one man and one woman to the exclusion of all others'. The union is based on contract, but since the contract alters the legal status of the parties there are special rules for its formation and dissolution, together with a number of legal consequences.

   In order to make a valid marriage:

   i.   Both parties must be at least 16 years old

   ii. The parties must not be within the prohibited degrees of relationship, for example a person cannot marry his sister or mother

   iii. The parties must be respectively male and female

     iv.   Neither party may be already married

     v.   Certain formal requirements must be complied with.

If any of the above requirements are not complied with the marriage will be void. In certain other situations a marriage will be voidable, for example if at the time of the marriage the man did not know that the woman was pregnant by another man.

b.   *Consequences of marriage.* The main consequences are

     i.   Both spouses are under a duty to cohabit unless separated by agreement, or by a court order

     ii.   The husband normally has a duty to maintain his wife

     iii.   Both have a right to occupy the matrimonial home

     iv.   Both have rights regarding succession on the death of the other

     v.   Either may apply to the court for the determination of any dispute arising between them as to the title or possession of property. Since 1968 one spouse may be prosecuted for stealing from the other, although the prosecution will normally require the consent of the Director of Public Prosecutions.

     vi.   Each can sue the other in contract and tort

     vii.   A wife takes her husband's domicile.

c.   *Dissolution of marriage.* The sole ground for divorce is that the marriage has broken down irretrievably. To establish this the petitioner must satisfy the court on one of the following facts:

     i.   That the respondent has committed adultery and the petitioner finds it intolerable to live with the respondent

     ii.   That the respondent has behaved in such a way that the petitioner cannot reasonably be expected to live with the respondent

     iii.   That the respondent has deserted the petitioner for a continuous period of at least two years immediately preceding the presentation of the petition

     iv.   That the parties have lived apart for the continuous period of at least two years immediately preceding the presentation of the petition and the respondent consents to a divorce

     v.   That the parties have lived apart for a continuous period of at least five years immediately preceding the presentation of the petition.

A petition cannot normally be presented within the first three years of the marriage. However, a judge may give leave to present a petition on the grounds of exceptional hardship to the petitioner or exceptional depravity of the respondent.

4. *Minors.* A minor is any person who has not reached the age of 18. In addition to the contract and tort rules applicable to minors which are dealt

with in Chapters 14 and 23, there are a number of general points that should be noted.

a. A minor cannot marry under 16, and requires his parents' consent to marry under 18.

b. A minor cannot vote and cannot become a member of parliament, or an elected councillor, until the age of 21.

c. A minor cannot make a will, nor can he hold a legal estate in land, but he can hold an equitable interest.

d. A minor cannot take part directly in civil litigation, but must sue through his 'next friend' and defend through his 'guardian ad litem'. This will usually be the mother or father. A minor may, however, defend himself if charged with a crime.

e. There are many other rules concerning for example driving, drinking, smoking, school attendance and work that affect minors.

f. In addition to the supervision proceedings and criminal proceedings described in Chapter 7, minors may be the subject of orders introduced in the *CHILDREN ACT 1989*, to ensure their protection.

    i. An *emergency protection order*, removing the child from its parents can be made if the court is satisfied that (a) there is reasonable cause to believe that the child is likely to suffer significant harm or (b) local authority enquiries have been frustrated by denial of access to the child or (c) the applicant (who must be an authorised person) has reasonable cause to suspect that the child is suffering, or is likely to suffer, significant harm and their enquiries are being frustrated by lack of access.

    ii. A *child assessment order* may be made if the court is satisfied that the child is suffering, or is likely to suffer, significant harm and that an assessment is needed which requires the child to be taken away from home. Unlike the emergency protection order this is not necessarily designed for emergencies, it may follow from professional observation of one or more suspicious or unsatisfactory circumstances.

NATIONALITY

5. Nationality is the relationship between a person and a particular state or political unit. It is a person's political status and is important in determining the applicability of immigration law and certain other rights and duties such as the right to vote and the duty to serve on a jury.

6. The *BRITISH NATIONALITY ACT 1981*. This Act created three new categories of citizenship to replace Citizenship of the United Kingdom and Colonies. The new categories are:

a. *British Citizenship*, ie persons born, registered, adopted or naturalised in the UK. This category has the right of abode in the UK and freedom from immigration control.

b. *Citizenship of the British Dependent Territories*, ie persons who held a UK passport before 1981 and who were born, registered or naturalised in a British dependency, for example Bermuda, Gibraltar and The Falklands. Such persons have no automatic right of entry to the UK.

c. *British Overseas Citizenship*, ie granted to pre-1981 passport holders in East Africa, India and Malaysia.

7. A person may acquire British Citizenship by naturalisation. The conditions are

a. Residence in the UK for the preceding 12 months plus four of the seven years preceding that year.

b. Full age, ie 18.

c. Good character.

d. Ability to speak English.

e. Intention to remain resident in the UK.

8. British citizenship may be lost:

a. By *renunciation*. A declaration of renunciation must be made. This will be registered by the Secretary of State provided he is satisfied that the person will acquire some other citizenship or nationality.

b. By *deprivation*. The main ground is that the Secretary of State is satisfied that registration or naturalisation was obtained by fraud or misrepresentation.

DOMICILE

9. A person is domiciled in a country if he is resident in the country and has the intention of remaining there. Domicile implies a link with a particular system of law, in contrast to nationality which involves allegiance to a particular sovereign.

10. No person can be without a domicile, and no person can have more than one domicile at one time. The types of domicile are:

a. *Domicile of origin*. This attaches to a person at birth.

 i. If he is legitimate he will take the domicile of his father.

 ii. If illegitimate, or if the father died before the child was born, it will be that of his mother.

b. *Domicile of choice*. A person over 16 may adopt a domicile of choice. This has two elements:

 i. The fact of living in a territory, and

 ii. The intention to stay there. All relevant factors will be taken into account in determining this intention, for example whether or not a house has been purchased.

    c.   *Domicile of dependence*. This type of domicile applies to children under 16. The dependent domicile of a legitimate child under 16 is that of his father, ie if the father's domicile of origin changes then the child's domicile also changes. Similarly if the mother of an illegitimate child takes a new domicile that domicile will become the dependent domicile of the child. If the father of a legitimate child dies the dependent domicile of the child will usually be the domicile of the mother.

The main importance of domicile is that it governs jurisdiction in many family matters, for example marriage and divorce.

RESIDENCE

11. Residence is a question of fact to be determined by the courts. The word implies a degree of permanence. The residence of a wife is prima facie that of her husband.

12. Residence is relevant in determining domicile, liability to taxation, and the jurisdiction of the courts, but it is not the only factor in each case.

CHAPTER 12

Property Law

CLASSIFICATION

1. Property is anything that can be owned. It is divided into real property (realty) and personal property (personalty or chattels). Property is classified into real and personal according to the historical action necessary to recover it:

   a. If dispossessed of real property the plaintiff had a right to get back the very thing he had lost. This was known as a right *in rem* (a right in the thing) and was enforced by a real action.

   b. If dispossessed of anything else (including leasehold land) a person's only right was to monetary compensation from the person who had dispossessed him. This was known as a right *in personam* and was enforced by a personal action.

2. *Real property* consists of all freehold (as opposed to leasehold) interests in land.

3. *Personal property* is sub-divided into:

   a. Chattels real, ie leasehold interests in land, and

   b. Chattels personal (pure personalty). These are further sub-divided between:

      i. Choses in possession, ie tangible, moveable objects such as a car, wristwatch, or the family pet. It is possible to enjoy a right over such objects by physical possession.

      ii. Choses in action, ie rights such as debts, patents and copyrights which may only be enforced or protected by bringing a legal action. Other examples are trade marks, stocks and shares, business goodwill and cheques.

LEGAL ESTATES AND LEGAL INTERESTS

4. Since the Norman Conquest in 1066 it has been accepted that only the Crown may 'own' land in the absolute way that other property may be owned. Other persons hold an estate or interest in land which gives them certain rights over that land for a definite or indefinite period of time. These rights may be

broadly classified as legal estates, legal interests, and equitable interests. Since the LAW OF PROPERTY ACT 1925 only two legal estates can now exist:

a. Fee simple absolute in possession (or freehold estate) and

b. Term of years absolute (or leasehold estate).

5. Fee Simple Absolute in Possession

a. The meaning of this term may be clarified as follows:

i. *Fee*. This means that the estate is capable of being inherited. It may devolve to any person under the deceased's will, or if he died without leaving a will it would devolve to his relatives. A fee estate would end if a person died leaving no will and no relatives. In such a case the land would revert to the Crown. A fee estate must be distinguished from a life estate. For example land bequeathed 'to A for life remainder to B' is not a fee estate because A cannot bequeath the land in his will.

ii. *Simple*. This means without a provision as to tail. Thus a fee simple may pass to any relative or anyone else under a will, whereas a fee tail can only pass to lineal descendants. It cannot pass, for example to a brother or parent, or as a gift in a will.

iii. *Absolute*. This means not subject to any conditions.

iv. *In possession*. The person is entitled to immediate physical possession, although he will still hold the freehold (ie be regarded as in possession) where he grants a lease of the land in return for a rental.

b. The distinctive characteristic of a freehold estate is that it is of uncertain duration since it cannot be known when the estate will revert to the Crown.

6. A Term of Years Absolute

a. This is an estate which, in contrast to a freehold estate, is of a certain duration, for example 99 years, 5 years or one month. It does not matter if the period is for less than a year provided the lease has a certain duration, nor does it matter if the estate does not take effect immediately, since there is no requirement that it must be 'in possession'.

b. A tenancy agreement made on a weekly or monthly basis is not a legal estate since there is no certainty as to duration. It is an equitable interest.

7. The LAW OF PROPERTY ACT 1925 also provided for the creation of legal *interests*. The most important of these are easements and mortgages.

a. An *easement* is a right to use or restrict the use of another person's land in some way. For example a right of way or a right of light.

b. A *mortgage* is a form of security for a loan. It involves the transfer of an interest in land from the borrower (or mortgagor) to the lender (or mortgagee) with a provision for redemption on repayment of the loan.

EQUITABLE INTERESTS

8. The two legal estates referred to above must be distinguished from equitable interests. There are several different equitable interests. Their common factor is that they can only exist as the result of an express or implied trust.

For example A conveys his property 'to B for the use of an in trust for C'. The common law took no notice of A's intention that B (the trustee) should hold the land for C (the beneficiary). C's only protection was in equity. Equity acknowledged that at common law the legal estate was vested in B, but as a matter of conscience compelled B to act in accordance with A's intentions.

9. The distinction between legal estates (and interests) and equitable interests is important because:

   a. If a person purchases land which is subject to a legal estate or legal interest of which he is not aware he is nevertheless bound by the legal estate or interest, but

   b. If he is a bona fide purchaser for value of a legal estate, which is subject to an equitable interest, he will take the estate free from the equitable interest if he had no notice (actual or constructive) of it.

   For example – A, the owner of the fee simple of 'Courtlands' grants by deed a lease to B over part of the land. (This creates a legal estate.) A also grants by means of a written contract a lease to C over another part of the land. (Since this lease is not by deed it only creates an equitable interest.) While A retains the fee simple both B and C have remedies against him, although C's remedies being equitable are discretionary. If, however, A sells his fee simple to D, who is a bona fide purchaser for value without notice of C's equitable interest, or B's legal estate, then D will take the land free from C's interest, but subject to B's estate. C's interest in the land is said to be 'overreached', ie converted to an interest in the sale proceeds, and A must account to him with an amount of the sale proceeds equal to the value of his interest.

   c. Note the meaning of 'constructive notice'. This refers to the ability to fix the whole world with notice of an equitable interest by registering it at HM Land Charges Registry. All persons are then deemed to have notice (ie have constructive notice) of the interest regardless of whether or not they have actual notice of it.

OWNERSHIP AND POSSESSION

10. The law has not developed concise definitions of these terms. Both however, are relationships between persons and property.

11. *Possession* has two elements:

   a. The means to exercise control over the thing by direct or indirect means, for example through an employee, and

b. The intention to exclude others.

If a person has a. above, but not b. he has custody of the property.

12. A problem arises when considering whether or not a person can possess something which he does not know is on his person or on his land. The answer depends on the context:

   a. If unknown to an occupier something is buried on his land, he will possess it for the purposes of the civil law of trespass and he will be able to sue any person who wrongfully disturbs it.

   b. If, however, the thing buried is a dangerous drug, an occupier without knowledge of its presence will not be criminally liable as possessor of the drug.

   c. It was held in R v HALLAM (1957) that the offence of 'knowingly possessing an explosive' requires knowledge on the part of the accused that the substance possessed is explosive, not merely that he possessed the substance.

13. *Ownership* has been defined by Pollock in his book 'Jurisprudence' as

   'The entirety of the powers of use and disposal allowed by law.'

   This definition illustrates that a person's rights over the property he owns are limited by law. For example:

   a. Planning permission is necessary to build on land, or to change the use of land.

   b. Gold and silver found under land belong to the Crown.

   c. Adjoining land has a natural right to support.

   d. Buildings or trees may be subject to preservation orders.

   e. A person cannot use his land in such a way that it constitutes a nuisance.

   f. Land may be subject to a compulsory purchase order.

14. Ownership may be acquired in the following ways:

   a. Originally by

      i. Creating something, for example a painting.

      ii. Receiving the benefit of a transaction that creates something, for example an inventor is granted a patent.

      iii. Occupation, ie taking possession of something that has no owner, such as a wild animal.

      iv. Accession, ie something new is added to something already owned, for example a cat has a kitten.

   b. Derivatively, ie acquired from a previous owner who intends ownership to pass, for example a gift or a sale.

   c. Succession, ie by reason of the death of the previous owner.

THE ASSIGNMENT OF CHOSES IN ACTION

15. A chose in action is a personal property right which can only be protected or enforced by bringing a legal action. A chose may be legal, for example a simple debt, or equitable, for example a beneficiary's interest in a trust fund. Assignments of choses in action are possible both at law, and in equity.

16. *Easements and Profits.* We noted earlier that one estate in land is the Term of Years Absolute – a leasehold estate. This gives a right to use land belonging to another for a certain fixed period in return for a payment of rent. It is also possible to own other rights in another's property.

   a. *Easements.* These come in various forms:

      i. *right of way.* For example, a right to cross another's land for access.

      ii. *a right to light.* This stops the occupier of adjoining land from building so close to another's land that light is denied to such an extent that the land affected can only gain sufficient light by artificial means.

      iii. *a right of support.* This easement gives a right to support from another adjoining building; for example, a common support wall.

   b. *Profits.* This is a right to take from the land of another, for example, fishing or mining rights. Unlike an easement these rights are not restricted to adjoining land. The LAND REGISTRY ACT 2002 provides for profits to be registered on the Land Registry.

17. *Assignments at Law*

   a. A legal assignment of a legal chose must comply with *S.136 LAW OF PROPERTY ACT 1925* if it is to be valid. This section requires:

      i. That the assignment is in writing and signed by the assignor, and

      ii. That it is absolute, ie the whole of the interest is transferred to the assignee, and

      iii. That written notice is given to the debtor.

   b. The effect of such an assignment is that the assignee becomes the legal owner of the chose, and can sue the debtor without making the assignor a party to the action. Consideration for the assignment is not required by *S.136*.

18. *Assignments in Equity*

   a. Equitable assignments of both legal and equitable choses are possible. For example, an attempted legal assignment will take effect as an equitable assignment if it does not comply with *S.136* because, for example, only part of a debt is assigned. In general equity looks at the intent rather than at the form and will therefore enforce an assignment provided there is:

      i. Intention to assign,

      ii. Identification of the chose, and

      iii. Communication to the assignee.

b. Writing is not necessary for the equitable assignment of a legal chose, but by *S.53* LPA 1925 an equitable assignment of an equitable chose must be in writing and signed by the assignor.

c. Notice to the debtor is not necessary to complete an equitable assignment, although it is advisable to prevent the debtor paying the assignor. The effect of the assignment is to enable the assignee to sue the debtor in his own name, except where the assignment is non-absolute, in which case equity requires the assignor to join in the action.

Coursework Questions 1–7 (for answers see pages 641–50)

Typical Exam Questions

1. Explain the doctrine of binding precedent in English law paying particular regard to:
   (a) the hierarchy of the courts;   (5 marks)
   (b) the relative advantages and disadvantages of the doctrine.   (5 marks)
   (10 marks)
   ACCA June 2004

2. 'In English law, parliament is sovereign.' Discuss.

   (20 marks)
   ICSA November 2004

3. Within the context of EU law, explain 'direct applicability' and 'direct effect' and their significance for European 'secondary' legislation.

   (20 marks)
   ICSA November 2004

4. 'The English legal profession is divided into two branches. This division operates for the benefit of the profession's clients.' Explain and discuss.

   (20 marks)
   ICSA November 2004

5. What is the basis of the legal distinction between real and personal property and what are the main differences between them as regards their creation and transfer?

6. Courtrooms are not the only places where legal disputes are resolved. Frequently administrative rather than legal action is needed to resolve a problem, and thus there is a system of administrative tribunals to which appeals may lie on a variety of matters. Similarly, the process of arbitration may provide a speedy and cost-effective alternative dispute resolution to the courts.

   Explain how arbitration, administrative tribunals and other alternative dispute resolution can be a useful and effective alternative to the resolution of disputes by the courts. What are the advantages and disadvantages of these alternative forms of dispute resolution?

7. *Objective test questions are awarded 2 marks each.*

Question 1.1

Which of the following statements is *correct*?

(i) In the event of a conflict between equity and the common law, the common law prevails.
(ii) An Act of Parliament can overrule any common law or equitable rule.

A (i) only. **B** (ii) only. **C** Neither (i) nor (ii). **D** Both (i) and (ii).

Question 1.2

All criminal cases commence in
A the County Court.
B the Crown Court.
C the Court of Appeal.
D the Magistrates Court.

CIMA November 2001

PART II

THE LAW OF CONTRACT

THE CONCEPT OF A CONTRACT

1. A contract is an agreement which legally binds the parties. Sometimes contracts are referred to as 'enforceable agreements'. This is rather misleading since one party cannot usually force the other to fulfil his part of the bargain. The usual remedy is damages.

2. The underlying theory is that a contract is the outcome of 'consenting minds', each party being free to accept or reject the terms of the other. However, to speak of consenting minds is no longer accurate because, for example:

   a. Parties are judged by what they have said, written, or done, not by what is in their minds, ie an objective standard is applied.

   b. Mass production and nationalisation have led to the standard form contract. The individual must usually 'take it or leave it', he does not really agree to it. For example, the customer has to accept his supply of electricity on the electricity board's terms – he is not likely to succeed in negotiating special terms.

   c. Public policy sometimes requires that the freedom of contract should be modified. For example, the RENT ACT 1968, and the UNFAIR CONTRACT TERMS ACT 1977.

   d. The law will sometimes imply terms into contracts because the parties are expected to observe certain standard of behaviour. A person is bound by these terms even though he has never agreed to them, or never even thought of them. For example S. 12–15 SALE OF GOODS ACT 1979.

   e. The law of agency enables the agent to bind his principal provided the agent acts within the scope of his apparent authority, even if he goes beyond his actual authority. As a result a principal may find himself bound by a contract that he did not intend to make.

3. The essential elements of a contract are:

   a. That an agreement is made as a result of an offer and acceptance.

b.   The agreement contains an element of value known as consideration, although a gratuitous promise is binding if it is made by deed.

c.   The parties intend to create legal relations.

4. The validity of a contract may also be affected by the following factors:

a.   *Capacity.* Some persons, eg children have limited capacity to make contracts.

b.   *Form.* Most contracts can be made verbally, but others must be in writing or by deed. Some verbal contracts must be supported by written evidence.

c.   *Content.* The parties may generally agree any terms, although they must be reasonably precise and complete. In addition, some terms will be implied by the courts, custom or statute and some express terms may be overridden by statute.

d.   *Genuine consent.* Misrepresentation, mistake, duress and undue influence may invalidate a contract.

e.   *Illegality.* A contract will be void if it is illegal or contrary to public policy.

5. A contract that does not satisfy the relevant requirements may be void, voidable or unenforceable.

a.   A *void* contract has no legal effect. The expression 'void contract' is a contradiction in terms since if an agreement is void it cannot be a contract. However, the term usefully describes a situation where the parties have attempted to contract, but the law will not give effect to their agreement because, for example there is a common mistake on some major term (such as the existence of the subject matter). When a contract is void, ownership of any property 'sold' will not pass to the buyer, so he will not be able to sell it to any one else. The original seller (ie the owner) will therefore be able to recover the property from the person in possession.

b.   When a contract is *voidable* the law will allow one of the parties to withdraw from it if he wishes, thus rendering it void. Voidable contracts include some agreements made by minors and contracts induced by misrepresentation, duress or undue influence. A voidable contract remains valid unless and until the innocent party chooses to terminate it. Therefore if the buyer resells the goods before the contract is avoided, the sub-buyer will become the owner and will be able to keep the property, provided he took it in good faith.

c.   An *unenforceable* contract is a valid contract and any goods or money transferred cannot be recovered, even from the other party to the contract. However, if either party refuses to perform his part of the contract the other party cannot compel him to do so. A contract will be unenforceable when the required written evidence of its terms is not available, eg the written evidence for a contract for the sale of land.

CHAPTER 13

The Formation of a Contract

INTRODUCTION

1. The method by which the courts determine whether an agreement has been reached is to enquire whether one party has made an offer which the other party has accepted. For most types of contract the offer and acceptance may be made orally or in writing, or they may be implied from the conduct of the parties. The person who makes the offer is known as the *offeror* and the person to whom the offer is made is the *offeree*.

2. In addition to offer and acceptance the law imposes the requirements of consideration (value) and intention to create legal relations. These are elements in the formation of a contract and are dealt with in this chapter. The other requirements are contractual capacity and legality of object which are considered later.

OFFER

3. *Definition*

   a. An offer is a definite promise to be bound on certain specific terms. It cannot be vague as in GUNTHING V LYNN (**1831**), where the offeror promised to pay a further sum for a horse if it was 'lucky'. However, if an apparently vague offer is capable of being made certain, either by implying terms or by reference to previous dealings between the parties, or within the trade, then it will be regarded as certain. Thus in HILLAS V ARCOS (**1932**), a contract for the sale of timber 'of fair specification' between persons well acquainted with the timber trade was upheld.

   b. An offer may be made to a particular person, or class of persons, or to the public at large as in CARLILL V CARBOLIC SMOKEBALL CO (**1893**) (Paragraph 4. below.)

   c. An offer must not be confused with the answer to a question or the supplying of information.

In HARVEY v FACEY (**1893**) P telegraphed D

'Will you sell us Bumper Hall Pen? Telegraph lowest cash price.' D telegraphed the reply

'Lowest price for Bumper Hall Pen £900.' P then telegraphed

'We agree to buy Bumper Hall Pen for £900 asked by you.'

D then decided that he did not wish to sell Bumper Hall Pen to P for £900, and P claimed that a contract had been made, the second telegraph being an offer. The court held that there was no contract, the second telegram being merely an indication of what D would sell for, if and when, he decided to sell. It was supplying of information in response to a question.

4. *Invitations to Treat*. An offer must be carefully distinguished from an invitation to treat, which is an invitation to another person to make an offer. The main distinction between the two is that an offer can be converted into a contract by acceptance, provided the other requirements of a valid contract are present, whereas an invitation to treat cannot be 'accepted'. There are several types of invitations to treat:

a. *The exhibition of goods for sale in a shop*. For example FISHER v BELL (**1961**) (Chapter 4.21).

Also PHARMACEUTICAL SOCIETY OF GREAT BRITAIN v BOOTS CHEMISTS (**1953**) where by statute certain drugs had to be sold in the presence of a qualified pharmacist. Boots operated a self-service shop, with a qualified pharmacist present at the check-out, but not at the shelves on which the drugs were displayed. The precise location of the place of sale was therefore relevant to determine whether or not an offence had been committed. It was held that the display was an invitation to treat, the customer's tender of the drugs was the offer, and the taking of the money by the pharmacist was the acceptance. The sale therefore took place at the check-out, and Boots therefore did not commit an offence.

b. *General advertising of goods*. Thus a newspaper advertisement that goods are for sale is not an offer. Also in GRAINGER v GOUGH (**1896**) it was held that the circulation of a price-list by a wine merchant was only an invitation to treat.

However, advertisements of rewards for the return of lost or stolen property are offers since they clearly show an intention to be bound without the need for further negotiation. Similarly the promise to pay money in return for an act has been held to be an offer.

In CARLILL v CARBOLIC SMOKEBALL CO (**1893**) the defendant company manufactured a patent medicine, called a 'smokeball'. In various advertisements they offered to pay £100 to any person who caught influenza after having sniffed the smokeball three times a day for two weeks. They also stated that they had deposited £1,000 at The Alliance Bank in Regent Street to show their 'sincerity'. Mrs C used the smokeball as advertised, and contracted influenza after more than two weeks' treatment, and while still using the smokeball. She claimed her £100.

The company raised several defences:

i. The advertisement was too vague since it did not state a time limit in which the user had to contract influenza.

  – The court said that it must at least protect the user during the period of use.

ii. It was not possible to make an offer to the whole world, or to the public at large.

  – The court made a comparison with reward cases, and stated that such an offer was possible.

iii. Acceptance was not communicated.

  – Not necessary in such cases. A comparison was made with reward cases where no communication is necessary.

iv. The advertisement was a mere gimmick or 'puff' and there was no intention to create legal relations.

  – The deposit of £1,000 would indicate to a reasonable man that there was an intention to create legal relations.

v. C provided no consideration.

  – It was held that the actual act of sniffing the smokeball was consideration. (The purchase price was not consideration for a contract with the manufacturer, it was consideration for the contract with the retailer.)

c. *An invitation for tenders*

i. A tender is an estimate submitted in response to a prior request. An invitation for tenders does not generally amount to an offer to employ the person quoting the lowest price.

ii. An exception may occur where tenders have been solicited from selected persons and the invitation to tender sets out a prescribed clear procedure.

   In BLACKPOOL AND FYLDE AERO CLUB v BLACKPOOL COUNCIL (**1990**) the Council, who manage Blackpool Airport, intended to grant a concession to operate pleasure flights from the Airport. It sent invitations to tender to P and six other parties, all of whom were known to the Council. The invitation stated that tenders received after the last date would not be considered. P posted their tender in good time in the town hall letter-box, but this was not opened when it was supposed to be, consequently P's tender arrived late and was excluded from consideration. P sued in contract and negligence. The contract claim was that when inviting tenders the Council promised that it would consider tenders that were received in time. P succeeded, the Court of Appeal holding that it was possible to have exceptions to the rule that invitations to tender were not contractual offers. This would apply where tenders are invited from known and selected persons under a clear prescribed procedure.

   iii. If tenders are invited for an indefinite amount of goods eg 'sugar as requested during 1994', 'acceptance' of such a tender amounts to a standing offer by the supplier to supply goods set out in the tender as and when required by the person accepting it. When the buyer places an order a contract is made for that quantity, but if the buyer does not place any orders there will be no breach. Similarly the persons submitting the tender may withdraw the standing offer at any time, except with regard to goods already ordered by the buyer under the tender.

d. *An auctioneer's request for bids.* An advertisement stating that an auction is to be held, or a request for bids is an invitation to treat, and not an offer to sell to the highest bidder. The bid is the offer, and the fall of the auctioneer's hammer is the acceptance. Until this happens the bidder may retract his bid. *(S.57(2) SALE OF GOODS ACT 1979.)* However, where advertising that an auction will be held 'without reserve' means that the auctioneer must sell to the highest bidder, BARRY v HEATHCOTE BALL & CO (**2000**).

e. *A company prospectus.* A prospectus or advertisement inviting the public to subscribe for shares or debentures is an invitation to treat, even if (as is the custom) it is described as 'an offer for sale'. The member of the public makes the offer by completing and sending in an application form. The company may then accept this offer in whole or in part. Partial acceptance is an exception to the rule that acceptance must precisely correspond to the offer, however, the prospectus will make it clear that the company has the right to accept in respect of a proportion of the shares applied for.

f. In some cases it is not absolutely clear what amounts to an offer and what is an invitation to treat. For example:

   i. *Buses.* It is probable that the bus itself is the offer (WILKIE v LONDON TRANSPORT (**1947**)) since if the bus were an invitation to treat, and the passenger's tender of the fare an offer, then a passenger could board a bus and, not having seen the conductor, get off again without being in breach of contract.

   ii. *'Pay on exit' carparks.*

In THORNTON v SHOE LANE PARKING (**1972**) a ticket to a carpark was dispensed by an unattended machine. The court held that the offer was the sign 'Parking' outside the garage, and the acceptance was the customer placing his car on the spot which caused the automatic machine to operate. In this case the precise time at which the contract was made was important, since it determined whether or not conditions printed on the ticket dispensed by the machine were a part of the contract. In this case there had been an offer and acceptance before the ticket was issued. The conditions printed on the ticket therefore come too late to be incorporated into the contract.

5. *Termination of Offer*. An offer may be terminated in the following ways.

   a. *Revocation*, ie withdrawal of the offer. Note that

      i. A promise to keep an offer open for a fixed period does not prevent its revocation within that period. However, a person may buy a promise to keep an offer open for a fixed period, ie he may buy an option to purchase. The offer cannot then be revoked without breach of this 'option contract'.

      ii. Revocation is ineffective until communicated to the offeree. Thus revocation by post is ineffective until it reaches the offeree. However, if the offeree must know that the offer has been revoked he cannot accept it, even if he obtained his information through a third party.

        In DICKENSON V DODDS (**1876**) D offered to sell a house to P for £800, and the offer was to be left open until 9 am Friday. On Thursday D sold the house to a Mr Allan, and a Mr Berry told P of this sale. P nevertheless wrote a letter of acceptance which he handed to D before Friday 9 am. It was held that there was no contract, the offer having been withdrawn before acceptance and communication by a third party being valid. An offer to sell a particular item is withdrawn by implication if that item is sold to another person.

      iii. Where the offer consists of a promise to pay money for the performance of an act the offer cannot be revoked once performance has commenced. For example if a promise is made to pay £100 to the first person to swim the English Channel four times non-stop, the offer cannot be revoked once the swim has commenced.

   b. *A refusal or a counter-offer.*

      i. In HYDE V WRENCH (**1840**) D offered his farm to P for £1,000. P wrote saying he would give £950 for it. D refused this, and P then said he would pay £1,000 after all. D had by now decided that he did not wish to sell to P for £1,000. P sued for breach. His action failed because his offer of £950 was a counter offer which terminated D's offer of £1,000, thus when P purported to accept at £1,000 there was no offer in existence, and therefore no contract was formed.

      ii. A counter-offer must be distinguished from a request as to whether or not other terms would be acceptable, since such a request does not, by itself, terminate an offer.

        In STEVENSON V MCLEAN (**1880**) D offered to sell iron to P for cash. P wrote and asked for four months credit. This inquiry was not held to be a counter-offer, but a request for information. It did not therefore terminate D's offer.

   c. *Lapse of time.* The offer will terminate at the end of the period stated in the offer, or if no period is fixed, it will terminate after a reasonable time.

      In RAMSGATE VICTORIA HOTEL V MONTEFIORE (**1866**), in June 1864 D offered to take shares in P's hotel. P did not reply to this offer, but in

101

November he allotted shares to D, which D refused to take. It was held that the refusal was justified, since P's delay had caused D's offer to lapse.

d. *Failure of a condition subject to which the offer was made.*

In FINANCINGS LTD v STIMSON (1962) D who wished to purchase a car signed a hire-purchase form on the 16th of March. This was the offer. The form stated that the agreement would only become binding when the finance company signed the form. On the 24th of March the car was stolen from the dealer's premises, and it was recovered badly damaged. On the 25th March the finance company signed the form. It was held that D was not bound to take the car. There was an implied condition in D's offer that the car would be in substantially the same condition when the offer was accepted as when it was made.

e. *Death.* The position depends on who dies.

   i.   If the offeree dies the offer lapses.
   ii. If the offeror dies the offer lapses if the offeree knows of the death at the time of his purported acceptance, or if the contract requires personal performance by the offeror, for example playing in an orchestra.

ACCEPTANCE

6. *What Amounts to Acceptance*

   a. The acceptance may be in writing, or oral, or it may be inferred from conduct, for example by dispatching goods in response to an offer to buy.

   b. The acceptance must be unqualified and must correspond to the terms of the offer. Accordingly:

      i.   A counter-offer is insufficient and, as stated above, causes the original offer to lapse.
      ii. A conditional assent is not enough, for example when an offer is accepted 'subject to contract'.

   c. Where it is intended to make a contract by means of sealed competitive bids, a submission by one bidder of a bid dependant for its definition on the bids of others is invalid.

   In HARVELA INVESTMENTS v ROYAL TRUST COMPANY OF CANADA (1985) a seller of shares (Royal Trust (RT)) had by a telex dated 15th September agreed to accept the highest bid made by Harvela (H) or Outerbridge (O). H bid 2,175,000 Canadian dollars. O's bid was as follows '2,100,000 Canadian dollars or 101,000 Canadian dollars in excess of any other offer which you may receive...which ever is higher'. On 29th September RT telexed O stating that in the circumstances they were bound to accept O's offer. H objected and commenced this action. The House of Lords had to decide two issues:

i. Was the status of the telex of 15th September such that a contract had been formed between RT and H?

ii. Was there a second contract (as claimed by O) as a result of the telex of 29th September?

It was held that the telex of 15th September was not an invitation to treat, but a unilateral offer, conditional upon the happening of a specified event. Such an event could only be done by one of the promisees, not both. Since the intention was to create a fixed bidding sale, the court rejected the referential bid (O's bid) and held (reversing the Court of Appeal) that a binding contract existed between RT and H. Any other decision would recognise a means by which sealed competitive bidding could be wholly frustrated. Concerning the second contract it was held that no such contract had been formed because there was no intention on the part of the parties. RT's only intention, manifested in the telex of 28th September was to perform the legal obligation that it mistakenly thought it had incurred.

d. In complex commercial contracts which are the result of lengthy negotiations, it can be difficult to say when an offer has been made and accepted, since any draft agreement may go through several changes as new demands are made or concessions granted. In the event of a dispute the court will need to look at all the correspondence and take oral evidence to decide, on an objective basis, what was agreed by the parties.

In TRENTHAM V ARCHITEL LUXFER (1993) P, the main contractors on a building contract, entered into negotiations with D, who were subcontractors, to supply and install doors and windows. After D had completed the work and been paid, P tried to claim a contribution from D towards a penalty they had incurred under the main contract. D argued that no contract existed because although there had been various telephone calls and letters there was no matching offer and acceptance, nor any agreement as to whose standard terms would govern the contract. The Court of Appeal held that there was a contract, that the approach to the issue of formation should be objective (ie does not take account of subjective expectations and unexpressed reservations of the parties) and a precise match of offer and acceptance is not necessarily required where a contract is alleged to have come into existence, as a result of performance. It was also held that where a contract comes into existence, during and as a result of, performance it will often be possible to hold that the contract impliedly and retrospectively covers pre-contractual performance.

This case is important for two main reasons:

i. It weakens the dominance of the 'offer and acceptance' approach to contract formation, reviving to some extent an approach advocated by Lord Denning, ie that you should look at the correspondence as a whole and the conduct of the parties.

ii. It recognises that where work is done before any formal agreement is reached, that work will generally be regarded as covered by the agreement, ie it will have a retrospective effect.

7. *The Communication of Acceptance – General Rules*

a. Acceptance is not effective until communicated to and received by the offeror. Thus if an acceptance is not received because of interference on a telephone line, or because the offeree's words are too indistinct to the heard by the offeror, there is no contract.

b. Acceptance must be communicated by the offeree or by someone with his authority.

In POWELL v LEE (1908) P applied for the post of headmaster of a school. He was called for interview and the managers (D being one) passed a resolution appointing him, but they did not make any arrangements for notifying him. However, one of the managers, without authority, informed P that he had been appointed. The managers subsequently re-opened the matter and appointed another candidate. It was held that P failed in his action for breach of contract since acceptance had not been properly communicated to him.

c. The offeror may expressly or impliedly prescribe the method of communicating acceptance, although there will be valid acceptance if the offeree adopts an equally expeditious method, unless the offeror has made it clear that no method other than the prescribed method will be adequate.

d. A condition that silence shall constitute acceptance cannot be imposed by the offeror without the offeree's consent.

In FELTHOUSE v BINDLEY (1863) P was engaged in negotiations to purchase his nephew's horse. There was some confusion as to the price so P wrote to his nephew saying:

'If I hear no more about him I consider the horse is mine at £30 15s.' The horse was at the time in the possession of D, an auctioneer. The nephew, wishing to sell at £30 15s therefore told D not to sell the horse, but D sold the horse by mistake. P therefore sued D in conversion (a tort alleging wrongful disposal of the plaintiff's property by the defendant). D's defence was that the horse did not belong to P, since there was no valid contract between P and his nephew, because the condition that silence constituted acceptance was ineffective. This defence succeeded.

e. Acceptance is not effective if communicated in ignorance of the offer. However, if a person knows of the offer, the fact that he has a motive for his acceptance, other than that contemplated by the offeror, does not prevent the formation of a contract.

f. There is no contract if two offers, identical in terms, cross in the post. For example, A offers to sell his car to B for £500 and B offers to buy A's car for £500. There is no contract because although there are 'consenting minds' there is no acceptance.

8. *The Communication of Acceptance – Exceptions*

a. *Unilateral contracts.* These are contracts where the offer consists of a promise to pay money in return for the performance of an act. In such cases performance of the act is sufficient acceptance, however, consideration is not complete until performance has finished.

b. *Postal rules*. Where the parties contemplate acceptance by post, acceptance is complete when the letter is posted, even if the letter is lost in the post.

In HOUSEHOLD FIRE INSURANCE CO v GRANT (1879) D applied for shares in the company. A letter of allotment (the acceptance) was posted to him, but it never arrived. The company later went into liquidation and D was called upon to pay the amount outstanding on his shares. It was held that he had to do so. There was a contract between the company and himself which was completed when the letter of allotment was posted, regardless of the fact that it was lost in the post.

Note that:

i. If the letter is lost or delayed in the post because the offeree has addressed it incorrectly the 'post rule' will not apply.

ii. 'Posted' means put into the control of the post office in the usual manner, and not for example, by handing it to a postman.

iii. The post rule applies to telegrams, but where communication is instantaneous, ie telephone, fax, telex and email the general rule applies.

iv. The parties may decide to exclude the operation of the post rule by contrary agreement. This may be wise in international sales, where the possibility of delayed communication is much greater. The post rule will also be excluded if it is clearly inconsistent with the nature of the transaction and/or the words used by the parties.

In HOLWELL SECURITIES v HUGHES (1974) D granted P an option to purchase land to be exercised 'by notice in writing'. A letter exercising the option was lost in the post. It was held that the words 'notice in writing' meant that the notice must actually be received by the vendor.

CONSIDERATION

9. *Definition*. A promise is only legally binding if it is made in return for another promise or an act (either a positive act or something given up), ie if it is part of a bargain. The requirement of 'something for something' is called consideration. It may be defined as some benefit accruing to one party, or some detriment suffered the other. There have been several case law definitions, for example from CURRIE v MISA (1875):

'Some right interest profit or benefit accruing to one party, or some forbearance, detriment, loss or responsibility given suffered or undertaken by the other'.

10. *Executory, Executed and Past Consideration*. Consideration may be executory or executed, but it may not be past.

a. *Executory consideration*. Here the bargain consists of mutual promises. The consideration in support of each promise is the other promise and not a performed (executed) act.

For example A orders a greenhouse from B to be paid for when it is delivered next week. There are two promises for the law to enforce, B's promise to deliver the greenhouse and A's promise to pay for it.

b. *Executed consideration.* Here the consideration for the promise is a performed, or executed act. For example, fertiliser is ordered and paid for, and it is agreed that delivery will take place within 10 days. If delivery is late the buyer may sue, putting forward his executed act (ie payment) as consideration. Similarly a person who returns a lost dog, having seen an offer of reward may claim the reward. His act of returning the dog is executed consideration. The sequence of events in both examples is first the promise, and subsequently the act.

c. *Past consideration.* If the act put forward as consideration was performed before any promise of reward was made it is not valid consideration.

For example X promises to give Y £10 because Y dug X's garden last week. Y cannot sue because when X's promise was made Y's act was in the past.

In ROSCORLA v THOMAS (1842) P purchased a horse from D. After the sale was complete D gave an undertaking that the horse was not vicious. This proved to be wrong. P sued on this undertaking He failed since his consideration was in the past. The act put forward as consideration, ie the payment of the price, was complete before the undertaking was given. P therefore gave nothing new in return for the undertaking. It is not possible to sue in a 'something for nothing' situation.

In deciding whether consideration is past the courts do not always take a strictly chronological view. If the consideration and the promise are substantially the same transaction it does not matter in which order they are given. Thus manufacturers may give guarantees to persons who buy their products from retailers. The buyer then sends a card to the manufacturer to claim the benefit of the guarantee, and he usually does this after he has bought the goods.

d. *Exceptions to the past consideration rule*

i. Past consideration will support a bill of exchange (*S.27 BILLS OF EXCHANGE ACT 1882*).

ii. Where a subsequent promise is made to pay for services rendered at the defendant's request. The explanation is that when the request was made there was an implied understanding that there would be some payment, and the subsequent promise merely fixed the amount.

In LAMPLEIGH v BRAITHWAIT (1615) D killed a man and asked P to obtain for him a royal pardon. P did so and D then promised to pay him £100. D broke this promise and P sued him. P succeeded in this action because D's request was regarded as containing an implied promise to pay, and the subsequent promise to pay £100 was merely fixing the amount.

11. *'Consideration Must Move from the Promisee'.* This maxim represents an alternative way of stating the basic rule of privity of contract. It means that the

only person who can sue on a contract is the person who paid the price. For example if John orders flowers to be sent to Mary, who is in hospital, and those flowers are not sent, then it is John who is entitled to a remedy against the shop. Although Mary was to have had the benefit of the flowers, she cannot sue because she did not pay the price.

12. *Consideration Must be of Some Value*

    a.   As long as some value is given the court will not ask whether it is proportionate in value to the thing given in return. In other words there is no remedy for someone who makes a bad bargain.

        In THOMAS v THOMAS (**1842**) executors agreed to convey the matrimonial home to a widow provided she paid £1 per year rent and kept the house in repair. In an action on the promise to convey it was held that the promise of payment and doing the repairs were valuable consideration.

    b.   Some acts, although arguably of some value, have been held to be no consideration:

        i.   Payment on the day that a debt is due of less than the full amount of the debt is not consideration for a promise to release the balance (PINNEL'S CASE (**1602**)). However, if the creditor agrees to take something different from what he is entitled to, or if payment is made at his request at an earlier date there is sufficient consideration.

           In D.C. BUILDERS v REES (**1965**) D owed P £482 and knowing that they were in financial trouble offered them £300 in full settlement of the debt. P accepted this cheque, but later sued for the balance of £182. P succeeded because:

           (a) D paid P a cheque, and the court did not consider this as different from the cash to which P was entitled.

           (b) The payment was made at D's suggestion and not at P's request.

           (c) Equitable estoppel was not an available defence for D, because she had attempted to take advantage of P's financial difficulties and had not therefore come to equity with 'clean hands'.

        ii. A promise to do what the promisee can already legally demand.

           In STILK v MYRICK (**1809**) P was a seaman who had agreed to work throughout a voyage for £5 per month. During the voyage two of the crew of eleven deserted, and the captain promised to divide their wages between the rest of the crew if they would complete the voyage. On completion of the voyage P requested his share, and was refused. His legal action failed on the grounds that he was already contractually bound to complete the voyage and did not therefore provide any consideration for the promise of the deserters' wages.

           Contrast HARTLEY v PONSONBY (**1857**) where 17 out of a crew of 36 deserted. The remainder were promised an extra £40 each to work the ship to Bombay. P, a seaman, had to sue to recover his £40. He succeeded, mainly because the large number of desertions made the voyage more dangerous, and this had the effect of discharging the original contract. (It was now fundamentally different from the voyage bargained for.) This left P free to enter into a new contract under which his promise to complete the voyage constituted consideration for the promise to pay £40.

Contrast also WILLIAMS v ROFFEY (**1990**) where D engaged P to carry out carpentry work in a block of flats at an agreed price of £20,000. P soon realised that the price was too low for him to operate satisfactorily and make a profit. D was concerned that P would not complete the work on time and therefore made an oral agreement to pay P a further sum of £10,300. Seven weeks later, after D had paid P only a further £1,500 P ceased work and later sued D for the additional sum promised. The Court of Appeal held that where D promised to pay P a sum of money additional to that already agreed as the contract price, in return for P's promise to perform his existing obligations on time, the resultant benefit to D was capable of being consideration for D's promise to make the additional payment (provided there was no economic duress or fraud). The court considered that this did not contravene the principle in STILK v MYRICK (**1809**), but merely limited its application. P was therefore successful in obtaining the additional amount promised.

iii. A promise to discharge a duty imposed by law.

In COLLINS v GODEFROY (**1831**) P was called by subpoena to give evidence in a case involving D. He afterwards alleged that D had promised to pay him six guineas for his loss of time. P failed in his action since he was bound by law to attend the trial (this is the effect of the subpoena) and he did not therefore do anything for D that he was not already bound to do. P therefore had not provided any consideration.

13. *Equitable Estoppel*

a. Strict application of the rule in PINNEL'S CASE (**1602**) could cause hardship to a person who relies on a promise that a debt will not be enforced in full. Equitable promissory estoppel mitigates this harshness.

It may be expressed as follows:

Where a person promises that he will not insist upon his strict legal rights, and the other party acts upon that promise, then the law will require that such a promise be honoured and that he be *estopped* from going back on that promise even though it is not supported by consideration.

In CENTRAL LONDON PROPERTY TRUST v HIGH TREES HOUSE (**1947**) P leased a block of flats to D. Due to the war D was unable to sub-let the flats, and so P agreed to accept half rent. Six months after the war P claimed the full rent for the post-war period. This claim succeeded. However, the court also considered whether P would have succeeded if he had claimed the full rent back to the start of the war. Denning, J. (as he then was), said that he would not have been successful because he would have been estopped in equity from going back on his promise.

b. Note that

    i. The effect of equitable estoppel is suspensory, ie when circumstances change, so as to remove the reasons for the promise, the original rights of the promisor become enforceable again as in the High Trees case.

    ii. The principle acts as 'a shield and not a sword' – Birkett L.J. Thus it only prevents the promisor from insisting on his strict legal rights when it would be unjust to allow him to do so, it does not enable the promisee to sue on an action unless he has given consideration.

In COMBE v COMBE (1951) A husband during divorce proceedings promised to pay his wife an annual allowance. The wife, relying on this promise, agreed not to apply to the court for a maintenance order, and later sued to enforce the husband's promise. At first instance her claim succeeded on the authority of the High Trees case. The Court of Appeal reversed this decision because:

    a) Equitable estoppel may only be used when a person who promises not to enforce his strict legal rights goes back on this promise. It does not give effect to a new contract. Any new contract must be supported by consideration in the usual way. (It is said to operate as a *shield not a sword*.)

    b) The wife had not supplied consideration since her forbearance to apply for a maintenance order was not at the husband's request.

14. *Consideration and Existing Duties, the Modern Approach*

a. Although consideration has always been a popular topic with examiners, problems rarely occur in practice. When they do arise it is usually because the parties to a binding contract have suffered a change in circumstances and agree to vary the original terms in a manner which confers a benefit on only one party. Then, at a later stage, the other party seeks to enforce the original terms.

b. The modern approach to such situations, expressed by the Court of Appeal in the important case of WILLIAMS v ROFFEY, is that a promise to pay an additional sum to secure performance of an existing and unchanged obligation is enforceable unless it was obtained by duress (ie economic duress) or the promisor received no benefit. The court will, however, regard a promise that ensures the timely performance of an obligation as conferring a benefit. In ROFFEY the defendants had contracted to refurbish some flats for the plaintiff. Due to underestimating the costs involved Williams communicated to the defendants that he could not complete the work. The defendants then agreed to pay an extra amount per flat as they were worried that they would be subject to a heavy penalty clause for late completion with the owner of the flats. The court held that Williams was entitled to the extra money. The carrying on of the work, though an existing obligation, brought a significant additional benefit to the plaintiff through their avoiding the penalty clause; it amounted to fresh consideration.

c. Although the Court of Appeal claimed to distinguish STILK v MYRICK, most commentators believe that the court went far beyond refinement or limitation, arguably abolishing the doctrine of consideration and removing the need to resort to the complexities of equitable estoppel to enforce a change to promise.

d. Instead the courts will consider, to a much greater extent than before, whether unfair economic pressure has been brought to bear on the defendant by a plaintiff seeking to enforce an altered agreement.

e. Commentators have generally welcomed this more flexible approach, which allows re-negotiation of contract terms in the light of changed circumstances. There is, however, some danger that it will open the door to commercial blackmail falling short of provable duress.

INTENTION TO CREATE LEGAL RELATIONS

15. Where the parties have not expressly denied an intention to create legal relations, what matters is not what the parties had in their minds, but the inferences that reasonable people would draw from their words or conduct, ie it is an objective test. See CARLILL v CARBOLIC SMOKEBALL CO (1893) (Chapter 13.4 above). The decision in this case might have been different if there had been no deposit of money to show sincerity.

16. *Commercial Agreements*

a. *Agreements 'subject to contract'*. Where there is a commercial agreement it is presumed the parties intend to create legal relations. However, if the parties expressly deny intention by stating that negotiations are 'subject to contract' or that any agreement is to be 'binding in honour only' then there is no contract.

In JONES v VERNONS POOLS (1938) P claimed that he had sent D a football coupon on which the draws he had predicted entitled him to a dividend. D denied having received the coupon. They relied on a clause printed on the coupon which stated that the transaction should not 'give rise to any legal relationship...but...be binding in honour only'. It was held that this clause was a bar to an action in court.

b. *Comfort letters*. If a person has an interest in credit being allowed to another person they may write a 'comfort letter' to the lender encouraging an offer of credit. Depending on its wording the comfort letter may amount to

i.   A binding guarantee of the loan,

ii. A legally binding agreement short of a guarantee, or

iii. No agreement at all.

In KLEINWORT BENSON v MALAYSIA MINING CORPORATION BERHAD (1989) a holding company (D) refused to guarantee a new loan by P to one of its subsidiarie(S). D however, wrote to P stating it is our policy to ensure that the business (ie its subsidiary) is at all times in a position to meet its liabilities. S later became insolvent and was unable to repay the bank. It was held that, since D had refused to give a guarantee, the comfort letter did not amount to a contract, but was only a statement of D's policy.

17. *Domestic agreements*

a. Where there is a domestic agreement the presumption is that legal relations are not intended for example an agreement by a man to pay his wife £50 per week 'housekeeping' money. However, it is possible for a man to make a binding contract with his wife, for example as part of a separation agreement.

    In MERRITT V MERRITT (**1970**) a husband left his wife and when pressed by her to make arrangements for the future, agreed that if she would pay the outstanding mortgage instalments he would, when all the payments had been made, transfer the house into her name. It was held that there was a binding contract since the presumption that legal relations are not intended does not apply if husband and wife are separated or about to separate.

b. Where adult members of a family (other than husband and wife) share a household, the financial arrangements which they make may well be intended to have contractual effect.

    In PARKER V CLARK (**1960**) a young couple were induced to sell their house and move in with elderly relations by the latter's promise to leave them a share of the home. It was held that legal effect was intended, otherwise the young couple would not have taken the important step of selling their own home.

c. An agreement between persons who share a household, but which has nothing to do with the management of the household will probably be intended to be legally binding.

    In SIMPKINS V PAYS (**1953**) three ladies who lived in the same house took part in a fashion competition run by a newspaper. They agreed to send their entries on one coupon and to share any prize money. The court rejected the contention that the agreement to share was not intended to be legally binding since the contract had nothing to do with the routine management of the household.

CHAPTER 14

Capacity to Contract

In order for an agreement to be a valid contract both parties must have capacity to contract. In general all persons have full power to enter into any contract they wish. Different rules apply to minors, corporations, mental patients and drunks. For more detail on corporations please refer to Chapter 37.

MINORS

1. *Introduction*

   a. A minor is a person who has not yet reached his 18th birthday. When the age of majority was reduced from 21 to 18 in 1969 the practical importance of the rules governing minors' contracts was reduced since most of the decided cases concerned persons aged between 18 and 21. Problems today are most likely to arise with contracts of employment and hire purchase agreements.

   b. The law governing minors' contracts shows how the law must compromise between two principles. The first, and more important is that the minor must be protected against his own inexperience. The second is that in pursuing this object the law should not cause unnecessary hardship to those who deal with minors. The compromise between these principles results in certain contracts with minors being valid (contracts for necessaries and contracts of service), others are void or voidable, and in some cases the minor may be liable in tort, or in equity. These categories are considered below:

2. *Contracts for Necessaries*

   a. *S.3 SALE OF GOODS ACT 1979* provides that a minor must pay a reasonable price for necessaries sold and delivered. The section also defines necessaries as 'goods suitable to the condition in life of such minor and to his actual requirements at the time of sale or delivery'.

   b. Note that:

      i. The term 'necessaries' is not confined to goods but also includes necessary services and, if the minor is married, necessaries for his family.

      ii. The minor is only bound to pay a reasonable price, and not the contract price.

      iii. If the necessaries are sold but not delivered (ie if the contract is executory, the adult not having performed his part) the minor is not bound.

    iv.   If the goods are delivered, but not paid for the minor is bound because the goods are 'sold and delivered'. The time of payment is not relevant in deciding whether or not a sale has been made.

  c. The burden of proving that the goods are necessaries lies on the seller.

    i.   Firstly, he must show that they are capable of being necessaries. Items of mere luxury, eg a racehorse can never be necessaries, but in PETERS v FLEMING (**1840**), it was shown that a luxurious item of utility such as a gold watch may be a necessary. This broad definition of necessaries was clearly not adopted for the benefit of the minor, but to give protection to suppliers who gave credit to young men from wealthy families.

    ii. Secondly, the seller must show that the goods are in fact necessary for the particular minor in question.

In NASH v INMAN (**1908**), a tailor sued a minor for the price of clothes, including 11 waistcoats. His action failed because he could not show that the minor was not already adequately supplied. A minor is not liable if he has an adequate supply, even if the supplier did not know this.

3. *Contracts of Service*

  a. A contract of service or apprenticeship is binding on a minor if, looked at as a whole, in the light of the circumstances when it was made, it is for his benefit. He may be bound even if some of the clauses of the contract do not turn out to be to his advantage.

In CLEMENTS v LAND NW RAILWAY (**1894**) a young porter agreed to join an insurance scheme to which his employers contributed, and to give up any claim for personal injury he might have under the *EMPLOYERS' LIABILITY ACT 1880*. The scheme covered a wider range of injuries than the Act but the scale of compensation was lower. The minor was injured in such a way that would have entitled him to compensation under the Act, but it was held that the contract was binding on him since, looked at a whole, in the light of the circumstances when it was made, the insurance scheme was more beneficial to him than the Act.

  b. A minor will therefore not be bound if the contract is on the whole harsh or oppressive.

In DE FRANCESCO v BARNUM (**1890**) a girl was apprenticed for stage dancing by a contract which provided that she should be entirely at the disposal of her master; that she would only be paid if he actually employed her (which he was not bound to do); that she could not marry during the apprenticeship; that he could end the contract if he found her unsuitable; and that she could not accept any professional engagement without his consent. She accepted a professional engagement with D without the master's (P's) consent. It was held that P could not sue D in the tort of inducing a breach of contract since, as the contract was unreasonably harsh, it was invalid.

4. *Voidable Contracts*

a. 'Voidable' means that the contract will bind both parties, unless it is avoided by the minor before, or within a reasonable time after, reaching 18. In EDWARDS v CARTER (1893) 4½ years after reaching the age of majority (at that time 21) was held to be an unreasonable delay. The other party cannot avoid the contract.

b. Voidable contracts include those by which the minor acquires an interest in subject matter of a permanent or continuing nature, such as land, shares in a company, or contracts of partnership.

c. When a minor avoids a contract he escapes liabilities such as rent which are not yet due, but he can be sued for liabilities (again rent is a possible example) which have accrued.

d. Avoidance will not entitle the minor to recover money paid by him under the contract unless there has been a total failure of consideration, ie unless he has received absolutely nothing for his money.

In STEINBERG v SCALA (1925) a minor purchased some shares in a company. When she was required to pay the balance of the purchase price she attempted to avoid the contract, and recover the money that she had already paid. It was held that she did not have to pay the balance, but she could not recover what she had already paid, because she had received some benefits, such as the right to vote at company meetings, and the right to receive dividends. There had not been a failure of consideration since she had received something for her money.

Contrast CORPE v OVERTON (1833) where a minor agreed to enter into a partnership to be formed in the future. He paid £100 in advance. He later changed his mind, and attempted to recover the £100. His action succeeded because, since the partnership had not yet been formed, he had received absolutely nothing for his money, ie there was a total failure of consideration.

e. Similarly, if a minor delivers goods under a contract which is not binding on him, he cannot get them back unless there has been a total failure of consideration.

5. *Purchase of Non-necessary Goods*

a. A minor will not be bound on a trading contract or on a contract for the purchase of non-necessary goods.

In MERCANTILE UNION GUARANTEE CORPORATION v BALL (1937) a minor purchased on hire-purchase a lorry for use in his haulage contractor business. It was held that this was a trading contract rather than a contract for necessaries and so the minor was not bound.

b. A minor will, however, be bound if he ratifies the contract after reaching 18. No new consideration is required for the ratification.

c. The minor who purchased the goods can give a good title to a third party who takes them bona fide and for value (STOCKS v WILSON (1913)). The person who sold to the minor cannot recover from the third party. However, if the minor still has the property, or any property representing it, the court has the power, if it considers it just and equitable, to require the minor to return the property to the vendor (S.3 MINORS CONTRACTS ACT 1987). Clearly it would not be equitable to order restitution if the minor has paid for the property, although it is no longer a condition of restitution that the minor obtained the goods by fraudulently misrepresenting his age. If the minor has sold the goods it is unlikely that restitution will apply to the sale proceeds, since they will not be identifiable as 'property representing the goods'. If the goods are returned in a damaged state the vendor will not be able to obtain compensation from the minor.

6. *Loans and Guarantees*

   a. Loan to minors are not binding unless ratified by the minor after reaching the age of 18. No new consideration is required for ratification.

   b. By *S.2 MINORS CONTRACTS ACT* 1987 a guarantee by an adult of a minor's loan or transaction will be enforceable against the guarantor despite the fact that the main transaction cannot be enforced against the minor.

7. *Liability in Tort*. A minor cannot be made indirectly liable on a void contract through being sued in tort, but he can be sued in tort if his act is of a kind not contemplated by the contract.

   In BURNARD v HAGGIS (**1863**) a minor hired a horse subject to a condition that he was not to use it for jumping. He broke this provision, and the horse died in a jumping accident. In this case the owner's tort action succeeded because the minor had done an act not contemplated by the contract, and had thus taken himself out of the scope of the law of contract, and the protection it affords to minors.

   Contrast JENNINGS v RUNDALL (**1799**) when a minor hired a horse for 'riding' and rode it so hard that it was injured. He was held not liable in tort because all he did was an act contemplated by the contract, ie riding, although in an excessive manner. Since he was not liable in contract, he could not be made indirectly liable on the contract by bringing a tort action.

8. *The Effect of Equity on Minors' Contracts*

   a. *Subrogation.* If a minor borrows money to buy necessaries and he actually spends money for this purpose, the lender may 'step into the shoes' of the seller and recover from the minor the reasonable price which the seller could have recovered. The lender is said to be subrogated to the rights of the seller.

   b. *Specific performance.* This will not be granted to a minor, since equity will not grant it against a minor. The equitable maxim 'equality is equity' applies.

MENTAL DISORDER AND DRUNKENNESS

9. a. If a person's property is placed under the management of the court under the *MENTAL HEALTH ACT 1983* the person will have no capacity to contract with regard to that property. However, the patient's representatives may hold the other party to the contract.

b. If a person is temporarily incapable of understanding what he is doing because of mental illness, drunkenness or drugs the contract will be valid unless he can prove:

    i. That he did not understand the nature of the contract and,

    ii. The other party knew or ought to have known of this disability.

        Such a contract will be binding if it is later ratified at a time when the person is able to understand what he is doing.

c. Where necessaries are sold and delivered to a person who by reason of mental incapacity or drunkenness is incompetent to contract, he is bound to pay a reasonable price. *S.3 SALE OF GOODS ACTS 1979.*

CORPORATIONS

10. There are three types of Corporation, classified according to their mode of creation:

a. *Chartered corporations.* A corporation created by Royal Charter has power to do whatever an individual can do. If it makes a contract which offends the spirit of the Charter the contract is valid, although the Charter may be withdrawn.

b. *Statutory corporations.* They have only the powers expressly or impliedly conferred on them by the creating statute.

c. *Companies registered under the COMPANIES ACT 1985.*

    i. When a company is registered it must file various documents with the Registrar of Companies. One of these documents is its Memorandum of Association. This contains the company's 'objects clause' which lays down the permitted range of activities which the company can follow.

    ii. Prior to the COMPANIES ACT 1989 the basic rule was that an act outside the objects clause was *ultra vires* and void and therefore could not be enforced by the company or by an outsider. This was unpopular with companies (for whom it could be inconvenient to have restricted powers) and outsiders (who might find that their contract could not be enforced). This was generally the case even if the outsider did not actually know of the restriction on the company's power, because of the doctrine of *constructive notice*, by which everyone was deemed to know of the contents of the company's registered documents.

    iii. Companies therefore sought to avoid the ultra vires rule by drafting lengthy objects clauses allowing them to do almost anything they could ever wish to do. They also usually included general powers allowing anything incidental to any of their other objects and powers.

iv. The 1989 Act reduces the importance of the objects clause in two ways:

    a) It provided that it is sufficient for the memorandum to state that the object of the company is to carry on business as a general commercial company. This allows the company (a) to carry on any trade or business whatsoever and (b) to do all such things as are incidental or conducive to the carrying on of any trade or business by it.

    b) It also provided that the validity of an act done by a company shall not be called into question on the ground of lack of capacity by reason of anything in the company's memorandum. Consequently a completed act will have total protection from the ultra vires rule and will be enforceable by both the company and an outsider.

v. The Act does retain the power of members to bring proceedings to restrain ultra vires acts. However, it is most unlikely that a company taking advantage of the provision described above will ever make an ultra vires contract.

CHAPTER 15

Form of Contracts

1. The general rule is that a contract may be in writing, or oral, or inferred from conduct, or a combination of any of these. It is a common mistake to think that a binding contract must be in writing. Writing makes it easier to prove the contents of the contract, but it is not usually necessary. There are, however, three categories of exceptions.

2. ***Contracts which Must be by Deed***

    a. A conveyance or transfer of a legal estate in land (including a mortgage) or the grant of a lease for three or more years must be by deed. A conveyance is the document which transfers the title of unregistered land. A transfer is the document which transfers title to registered land.

    b. Consideration is not necessary for a deed. Therefore a binding gratuitous promise can be made by deed. The essentials of a deed are:

        i. *Writing*.

        ii. *Signature*.

        iii. *Witness and Attestation*. The LAW OF PROPERTY (MISCELLANEOUS PROVISIONS) ACT 1989 removed the requirement that a deed must be sealed. However, it provided that the signature of the individual making the deed must be witnessed and attested. Attestation consists of a statement that the deed has been signed in the presence of a witness.

        iv. *Delivery*. This means conduct indicating that the person executing the deed intends to be bound by it. No physical transfer of possession is necessary.

        v. *Intention to create a deed*. The 1989 Act also provided that it must be clear on the face of the document that it is intended to be a deed. This requirement can be satisfied together with the requirement of attestation by using the words 'signed as a deed by AB in the presence of YZ'.

    c. By *S.36A COMPANIES ACT 1985* there is now no requirement for a company to have a seal. Any document (including a deed) will be executed if signed by two directors or a director and the secretary, provided it is expressed to be executed by the company.

    d. The effect of non-compliance with the above is that the contract is void. Therefore any money paid or property transferred can be recovered. However, an unsealed lease operates in equity as an agreement to enter into a lease. It will therefore bind the parties. However, if it has not been registered at the Land Registry, it will not bind a third party who purchases the landlord's interest without notice of the tenant's interest. If it has been registered the purchaser of the freehold will be regarded as having notice of the lease, whatever his actual knowledge.

3. *Contracts which Must be in Writing*

   a.   The main types are:

      i.   The sale of disposition of land or an interest in land (other than contracts for leases of three years or less). By *S.2 LAW OF PROPERTY (MISCELLANEOUS PROVISIONS) ACT 1989* the contract must be in writing and must incorporate all the terms that have been expressly agreed in one document, or where contracts are to be exchanged in each contract. Both parties must sign the contract.

      ii.   Consumer credit agreements (including hire purchase agreements) which are regulated by the *CONSUMER CREDIT ACT 1974*, ie the credit does not exceed £15,000 and the customer is not a company. These must be in writing and must contain all the terms of the agreement other than implied terms. The agreement must be signed by the customer in person and by or on behalf of the creditor or owner.

      iii.   Bills of exchange and cheques.

      iv.   The transfer of shares in limited companies.

      v.   Policies of marine insurance.

      vi.   Legal assignments of choses in action.

   b.   The effect of non-compliance varies, depending on the type of agreement. Usually the contract will be void, but in the case of consumer credit transactions the effect of non-compliance by the seller is to make the agreement unenforceable against the debtor unless the creditor (seller) obtains a court order – *S.127 CONSUMER CREDIT ACT 1974*. The debtor may therefore keep the goods if they are already in his possession.

4. *Contracts which Must be Evidenced in Writing.* A contract of guarantee must be evidenced in writing to be legally enforceable.

   a.   *Nature of the contract.* For example if A contracts to buy goods from B, and C promises to pay B if A does not, a contract of guarantee is formed. This should be distinguished from a contract of indemnity in which the person giving the indemnity makes himself primarily liable by saying, for example, 'I will see that you are paid'. A guarantor, however, does not expect to be approached for payment. He may say, 'If he does not pay you then I will'.

   b.   *Written Evidence.* Any signed note of the material terms of the contract is sufficient. Besides the signature of the guarantor other evidence must include the names or identification of the parties, a description of the subject matter and any other material terms. Any consideration need not be stated. The evidence may be contained in several separate documents.

      In ACTIONSTRENGTH LTD v INTERNATIONAL GLASS ENGINEERING & SAINT-GOBAIN GLESS UK LTD (2003) a main contractor (IGE) fell behind with payments to a sub-contractor AS whereupon the customer, SGG, allegedly promised orally to pay any unpaid invoices owed by IGE to AS. The House of Lords held that SGG's oral guarantee was unenforceable because it had not been evidenced in writing as required by *S.4* of the STATUTE OF FRAUDS ACT *1677*.

5. *Electronic Communications*

Ecommerce is expected to play an increasing role in transactions between organisations in the UK. With this in mind the ELECTRONIC COMMUNICATIONS ACT *2000* has been passed to help facilitate the development of electronic commerce, it provides for:

i. a voluntary system of registration to provide cryptography support services, such as electronic signature and confidentiality services;

ii. the legal recognition of electronic signatures;

iii. the removal of the need for paper in other legislative provisions and the ability to modify legislation by ministerial order to facilitate the use of electronic communications and storage.

CHAPTER 16

The Contents of Contracts

1. A contract may contain three types of clause, namely express terms (other than exemption clauses), implied terms, and exemption clauses (which are always expressly agreed).

EXPRESS TERMS

2. *Contract Terms and Representations*

A statement may be an express term of the contract or a representation inducing its formation. The importance of the distinction is that different remedies are available if a term is broken or a representation is untrue. Which it is depends on the intention of the parties (objectively assessed). It may be helpful to consider:

a.   The stage of negotiations at which the statement was made. The later it was made the more likely it is to be a term.

b.   Whether the statement was reduced to writing after it was made. If it was it is clearly regarded as more important, and is therefore probably a term of the contract.

c.   Whether the maker suggests that the other party should check the statement. If so it is likely to be a representation.

d.   Whether the maker of the statement possessed special skill or knowledge as compared with the other party.

In OSCAR CHESS v WILLIAMS (1975) D, a private individual, sold to P, car dealers, for £280 a car honestly described as a 1948 Morris 10. It was in fact a 1939 model worth £175. The statement that it was a 1948 model was held not to be a term of the contract, since D had himself been sold the car as a 1948 model, being given a forged log book. D thus had no special knowledge as to the age of the car, whereas P, being a dealer was in at least as good a position as D to know whether the statement was true.

Contrast DICK BENTLEY PRODUCTIONS v HAROLD SMITH MOTORS (1965). A dealer sold a Bentley car stating that it had only done 20,000 miles since a replacement engine, whereas it had in fact done 100,000 miles since then.

This statement was held to be a warranty since the dealer was in a better position to know the mileage than the purchaser.

3. *Conditions and Warranties*

   a. There are two basic types of express term:

      i. A *condition* is a vital term, going to the root of the contract, breach of which normally entitles the innocent party to treat the contract as at an end (ie to repudiate the contract) and to claim damages.

      ii. A *warranty* is a term which is subsidiary to the main purpose of the contract, breach of which only entitles the innocent party to damages.

   b. Classification as a condition or warranty depends on the intention of the parties, but in many cases their intention is not expressed and the clause will not obviously be a condition or a warranty. Such terms are called *intermediate or innominate terms*. They remain unclassified until the seriousness of a breach can be judged. If the breach goes to the root of the contract, depriving the plaintiff of the major benefits of the contract, the relevant term will be classified as a condition.

      In HONG KONG FIR SHIPPING CO v KAWASAKI KISEN KAISHA (**1962**) a ship delivered under a 24 month charterparty was unseaworthy, and took seven months to repair. The court said that many contractual undertakings could not be categorised simply as 'conditions' or 'warranties', and the innocent party should be entitled to rescind only if the effect of the breach is to substantially deprive him of the benefit of the contract. Since the ship was available for 17 out of 24 months rescission was not granted.

   c. The use by the parties of 'condition' or 'warranty' is not conclusive. If breach of a term expressed to be a condition can only produce a very small loss it may be held that the breach will not justify rescission.

      In WICKMAN v SCHULER (**1974**) it was a 'condition of a four year agreement that a representative of the plaintiff should visit six named customers once a week to solicit orders'. The plaintiff failed to make some of the required visits and the defendant terminated the contract. The court held that the plaintiff could recover damages for wrongful termination. It was not likely that the parties intended that failure to make a few visits out of a total of over 1,400 visits should justify rescission.

   d. On occasions the parties will classify terms as conditions, which in the absence of agreement would be treated as warranties. For example in a commercial contract a delivery date for goods is normally regarded as very important and will be assumed to be a condition. On the other hand a deadline for payment is not regarded as so important and would normally be classified as a warranty. However, if the parties make time of payment 'of the essence' it will be a condition.

      In LOMBARD NORTH CENTRAL v BUTTERWORTH (**1987**) an agreement for the hire of computers stated that prompt payment was 'of the essence'. The hirer was late paying one instalment. This was held to be a breach of condition entitling the owner to treat the contract as at an end, repossess the computers and claim damages for breach.

4. *Incomplete Contracts*

    a.   A legally binding agreement must be complete in its terms.

        In SCAMMELL v OUSTON (**1941**) an agreement for the purchase of a van provided for the balance of the price to be paid over two years 'on hire purchase terms'. It was held that there was no agreement since it was uncertain what terms of payment were intended. Hire purchase terms may vary over intervals between payments, rate of interest, etc.

        However, the parties may leave an essential term to be settled by specified means outside the contract. For example it may be agreed to sell at the ruling open market price (if there is a market) on the day of delivery, or to invite an arbitrator to determine a fair price. It is also possible for the price to be determined by the course of dealing between the parties.

    b.   In HILLAS v ARCOS (**1932**) a contract for the supply of timber in 1930 contained an option for the purchaser to buy a quantity of timber in 1931, but made no reference to the price. It was held that the missing terms of the 1931 purchase could be deduced from the conduct of the parties in their 1930 transaction when the price was determined by reference to an official price list.

    c.   If the parties used non-essential words, for example standard printed conditions some of which are inappropriate, such words may be disregarded.

        In NICOLENE v SIMMONDS (**1953**) a contract provided that the 'usual conditions of acceptance apply'. However, there were no usual conditions of acceptance. It was held that this phrase was non-essential and meaningless. It could therefore be ignored.

5. *Standard Form Contracts*

Many agreements are not individually negotiated, indeed it would be impossible for business to cope if every agreement had to be negotiated by the parties. Standard form contracts are usually used by large organisations in their contracts with consumers, for example British Telecom. They are also often used in commercial transactions. There are two main ways in which a problem with the agreed terms can arise.

    a.   There will be a problem of consistency when blank parts of a standard term contract are completed in a way that is inconsistent with the printed words. However, the basic rule of construction is that the particular overrides the general, thus the written words inserted in the contract override inconsistent printed words.

    b.   The second problem occurs when both parties have their own standard terms. A buyer will order on his standard terms but the seller will purport to accept on his standard terms which of course will be inconsistent with those of the buyer.

        In BUTLER MACHINE TOOL COMPANY v EX-CELL-O CORPORATION (**1979**) the seller offered machine tools subject to certain terms and conditions which 'shall prevail over any terms and conditions in the buyer's order'. The conditions included a price variation clause. The buyer replied by placing an order for the machine on terms and conditions which were materially different from those put forward by the seller and which, in particular, made no provision for a variation of price. At the foot of the buyer's order there was a tear-off acknowledgement of receipt of the order stating that 'we accept your order on the terms and conditions stated thereon'. The seller completed the acknowledgement and returned it to the buyer. When the seller came to deliver the machine they claimed that the price had increased by about £2,900. The buyer refused to pay the increased price and contended that the contract had been concluded on his rather than the seller's terms and therefore constituted a fixed price contract. The judge found for the seller and the buyer appealed. The Court of Appeal found for the buyer because:

i.   Applying the rules of offer and acceptance, the buyer's order was a counter-offer which destroyed the offer made in the seller's quotation. The seller by completing and returning the acknowledgement form, accepted the counter-offer on the buyer's terms.

ii. The documents comprising a 'battle of forms' were to be considered as a whole. If the conflicting terms and conditions of both parties were irreconcilable, then the acknowledgement of the order was the decisive document since it made it clear that the contract was on the buyer's and not the seller's terms.

IMPLIED TERMS

6. Terms may be implied by custom, the courts, or by statute.

7. *Custom*. The parties are presumed to have contracted by reference to the customs prevailing in the trade or locality in question, unless they have shown a contrary intention.

In BRITISH CRANE HIRE v IPSWICH PLANT HIRE (1974) both firms were in the business of hiring out cranes and heavy plant. D urgently needed a crane for work on marshy ground and agreed to hire such a crane from P. The method of payment was agreed but the hire conditions were not. P then sent D a copy of their standard conditions (which were similar to those used throughout the trade) which provided that the hirer would be liable for all expenses arising out of the crane's use. Before these conditions were signed the crane sank into the marshy ground, and P incurred expenses in recovering it. P claimed these expenses from D. Their action succeeded since both parties were in the same trade, and had equal bargaining power, and the evidence was that they both understood that P's standard conditions of hire would apply.

8. *The Courts*

a.   The courts will imply two types of terms into contracts. Firstly, terms which are so obvious that the parties must have intended them to be included. These are called terms implied in fact. Secondly, terms which are implied to maintain a standard of behaviour, even though the parties may not have intended them to be included. These are called terms implied in law.

b. *Terms implied in fact.* The implied term must be both obvious and necessary to give 'business efficacy' to the contract. The courts will not imply a term merely because it is reasonable to do so. The test used is known as the 'officious bystander' test, ie if when the parties were making the contract and officious bystander had asked 'Is X a term of the contract?' and if he would have received the reply 'Yes, obviously' then the term will be implied.

In THE MOORCOOK (1889) D were wharf owners contracted to allow P to unload their ship at the wharf. The ship grounded at low water, and was damaged by settling on a ridge of hard ground. D were held to be in breach of an implied term that the wharf was safe.

In EYRE V MEASDAY (1986) P underwent a sterilisation operation. The surgeon had advised her that the operation was irreversible and consequently P believed that she would be sterile. The fact that there was a slight risk of pregnancy after the operation was not pointed out. Later the plaintiff became pregnant and gave birth to a son. It was held that the word 'irreversible' did not amount to a guarantee of success, it merely indicated that the procedure could not be reversed, which is quite different. Applying the 'officious bystander' test the courts said that although it would be reasonable for P to assume that she was sterile, it would not be reasonable for her to think that she had been given a guarantee that she was sterile. If she had wanted such a guarantee she should have asked for it. P was therefore unsuccessful.

c. *Terms implied in law.* Terms implied in law cover many classes of contract. Thus in a contract of employment the employee impliedly undertakes, for example, to faithfully serve his employer, and that he is reasonably skilled. The employer impliedly undertakes that he will not require the employee to do an unlawful act, and that he will provide safe premises. Similarly in a tenancy agreement the landlord impliedly covenants that his tenant shall have quiet possession, and the tenant impliedly agrees not to commit waste.

In LIVERPOOL CITY COUNCIL V IRWIN (1977) it was held that where parts of a building have been let to different tenants, and where rights of access over the parts of the building retained by the landlord eg the stairs, have been granted to these tenants, then a term could be implied that the landlord would keep these parts reasonably safe.

9. *Statute*

a. The most well known examples are the terms implied by *S.12–15 SALE OF GOODS ACT 1979*:

i. That the seller has the right to sell.

ii. That in a sale by description the goods shall correspond with the description.

iii. That the goods supplied are of satisfactory quality, and fit for the purpose for which they are required. 'Satisfactory quality' was substituted for 'merchantable quality' by the SALE AND SUPPLY OF GOODS ACT 1994.

    iv. That where the goods are sold by sample the bulk will correspond with the sample.

b. The SUPPLY OF GOODS AND SERVICES ACT 1982 has given similar protection to persons who are supplied with (as opposed to sold) goods, and to persons who are supplied with services.

These three Acts are considered in more detail in Chapter 31.

EXEMPTION CLAUSES

10. An exemption clause is a term in a contract which seeks to exempt one of the parties from liability, or which seeks to limit his liability to a specific sum if certain events occur, such as a breach of warranty, negligence, or theft of goods.

11. An exemption clause may become a term of the contract by signature or by notice.

a. If a person signs a document he is bound by it even if he does not read it.

In L'ESTRANGE v GRAUCOB (1934) P, who was the proprietor of a cafe, purchased a cigarette vending machine. She signed, without reading, a sales agreement which contained a large amount of 'small print'. The machine was defective but the vendors were held to be protected by an exemption clause contained in that small print.

b. A person may not be bound by a signed document if the other party misrepresented its terms.

In CURTIS v CHEMICAL CLEANING CO (1951) P took a white satin wedding dress, trimmed with beads and sequins to the cleaners. The assistant gave her a form to sign, and when asked about its contents said that it excluded the company's liability for damage to the beads and sequins. P then signed the form, which in fact contained a clause excluding the company from all liability. When the dress was returned it was badly stained. The company attempted to rely on their exemption clause but it was held that they could not do so since the assistant had misrepresented (albeit innocently) the effect of the form.

c. Where a document is not signed the exemption clause will only apply if

    i. The party knows of the clause, or if

    ii. Reasonable steps are taken to bring it to his notice before the contract is made.

In OLLEY v MARLBOROUGH COURT (1949) P booked in at the D's hotel. When she went to her room she saw a notice on the wall stating that the hotel would not be liable for articles lost or stolen unless they were handed in for safe keeping. P left some furs in the bedroom, closed the self-locking door, and hung the key on a board in reception. The furs were stolen. It was held that the exemption clause was not effective. The contract was completed at the reception desk, and accordingly a notice in the bedroom came too late to be incorporated into the contract.

d. The more outlandish the clause (whether it is an exemption clause, a limitation clause or an agreed damages clause) the greater the effort that must be made to bring it to the other party's attention.

In INTERFOTO PICTURE LIBRARY v STILETTO VISUAL PROGRAMMES (1988) D, an advertising agency, hired 47 transparencies from P. They arrived with a delivery note requiring them to be returned by a specified date. The delivery note included nine 'small print' conditions which D never read. One of the conditions stated that if the transparencies were returned late there would be a charge of £5 per transparency per day. D returned the transparencies 14 days late and was billed for over £3,500. P's claim failed since the clause imposed an unusual and exorbitant charge and they had not taken sufficient steps to bring it to the attention of a person with whom they had never previously dealt.

e. The court will not enforce an exemption clause unless the party affected by it was adequately informed of it when he accepted it. Thus the exemption clause must be put forward in a document which gives reasonable notice of the liability conditions proposed by it.

In CHAPELTON v BARRY UDC (1940) there was a pile of deckchairs and a notice saying 'hire of chairs 2d per session of 3 hours.' P took two chairs, paid for them and received two tickets. One of the chairs collapsed and he was injured. The Council relied on a notice on the back of the tickets by which it disclaimed liability for injury. It was held that the notice advertising chairs for hire gave no warning of limiting conditions and it was not reasonable to communicate them on a receipt. The disclaimer of liability was not effective.

Contrast THOMPSON v LMS RAILWAY (1930) where an elderly lady who could not read asked her niece to buy her a railway excursion ticket on which was printed 'Excursion. For conditions see back.' On the back it was stated that the ticket was issued subject to conditions contained in the company's timetables. These conditions excluded liability for injury. It was held that the conditions had been adequately communicated and therefore accepted.

A further distinction between the two cases is that in Chapelton's case the ticket was a mere receipt, it did not purport to set out the conditions for the hire of the chair, it only showed the time for which it was hired and that a fee had been paid. However, in Thompson's case it would have been obvious to a reasonable person that the ticket had contractual effect since tickets of that kind generally contain contract terms.

f. If the parties have had long and consistent dealings on terms incorporating an exemption clause, then the clause may apply to a particular transaction, even if the usual steps to incorporate it were not taken. If there are only a few transactions spread over a long period it would not be reasonable to assume that the person has agreed to the term.

In HOLLIER v RAMBLER MOTORS (1972) on three or four occasions over a period of five years H had had repairs done at the garage. On each occasion he had signed a form by which the garage disclaimed liability for damage caused by fire to customers' cars. On the latest occasion he did not sign the form. The car was damaged by fire caused by negligence of garage employees. The garage contended that the disclaimer had by course of dealing, become an established term of any contract made between them and H. It was held that the garage was liable. There was insufficient evidence to show that H knew of and agreed to the condition as a continuing term of his contracts with the garage.

12. *Limitations on the Use of Exemption Clauses*

a. In considering the validity of exemption clauses the courts have had to strike a balance between:

    i. The principle that parties should have complete freedom to contract on whatever terms they wish, and

    ii. The need to protect the public from unfair exemption clauses in standard form contracts used by large business enterprises.

b. The use of exemption clauses by large organisations to abuse their bargaining power is clearly indefensible. Nevertheless exemption clauses do have a proper place in business. They can be used to allocate contractual risk, and thus determine in advance who is to insure against that risk.

They also make it possible for a contracting party to quote different rates according to the risk borne by him. Thus between businessmen of similar bargaining power exemption clauses are a legitimate device, but limitations on their use have been necessary in contracts involving the public. The main limitations are now contained in the *UNFAIR CONTRACT TERMS ACT 1977*, and in the past were exercised through the doctrine of fundamental breach.

13. *The Unfair Contract Terms Act 1977*

a. The Act uses two techniques for controlling exemption clauses – some types of clause are stated to be ineffective, whereas others are subject to a test of reasonableness.

b. The contract and tort provisions of the Act (with the exception of S.6)

    i. Are limited to liability which arises *in the course of a business*, and

    ii. Do not apply to contracts made before 1st February 1978. The main provisions of the Act are:

c. *S.2 Exclusion of negligence liability.*

    i. A person cannot by reference to any contract term restrict his liability for death or personal injury resulting from negligence.

    ii. In the case of other loss or damage a person cannot restrict his liability for negligence unless the term is reasonable.

d.   *S.3 Standard term contracts and consumer contracts.* The party who imposes the standard term contract or who deals with the consumer cannot, unless the term is reasonable

   i.   Restrict his liability for his own breach, or

   ii. Claim to be entitled to render substantially different performance, or no performance at all.

e.   *S.5 'Guarantee' of consumer goods.* Where goods are of a type ordinarily supplied for private use or consumption and loss or damage arises because the goods are defective in consumer use and the manufacturer or distributer was negligent, liability for loss or damage cannot be excluded or restricted by reference to a term contained in a 'guarantee' of the goods.

f.   *S.6 Sale of goods.*

   i.   *S.12 SALE OF GOODS ACT 1979* cannot be excluded.

   ii. *S.13–15 SALE OF GOODS ACT 1979* cannot be excluded in a consumer sale, but can be excluded in a non-consumer sale if the exemption clause is reasonable.

g.   *S.11 The requirement of reasonableness.* The term must be a fair and reasonable one having regard to all the circumstances which were, or ought reasonably to have been known to or in the contemplation of the parties when the contract was made. The burden of proving reasonableness lies on the person seeking to rely on the clause. In contracts for the sale of goods Schedule 2 UCTA 1977 lays down guidelines for determining reasonableness.

   i.   The strength of the bargaining positions of the parties relative to each other.

   ii. Whether the customer received an inducement (such as a lower price) to agree to the term. – If he did, the term is more likely to be reasonable.

   iii. Whether the customer knew or ought reasonably to have known of the existence and extent of the clause (having regard to any trade customs and any previous dealing between the parties).

   iv. Where the term excludes or restricts any relevant liability if some condition is not complied with, whether it was reasonable at the time of the contract to expect that compliance with that condition would be practicable.

      In GRANVILLE OIL AND CHEMICALS LTD v DAVIS TURNER & CO LTD (2003) a contract was entered into for the delivery of paint. The contract was subject to standard terms and conditions which required any legal action be brought within nine months. The claimant brought a claim for damaged goods more than a year after the nine-month period arguing that the term was void under the *UNFAIR CONTRACT TERMS ACT 1977*. The Court of Appeal held that the nine month clause was not void under the Act. The parties were both in business, they were of equal bargaining strength and the claimant might have been able to contract on different terms. Moreover, the clause had been brought to the claimant's attention. It was reasonably practicable for the claimant to comply with the clause as goods could have been checked on delivery. The clause would be effective in barring the claim.

v. Whether the goods were manufactured to the special order of the customer. – If they were, the term is again more likely to be reasonable.

A common situation was considered by the House of Lords.

In SMITH V ERIC BUSH (1989) P wished to purchase a house. She approached the Abbey National for a mortgage and paid for a survey including a valuation report by the surveyor hired by the Building Society (Eric Bush). In view of her limited resources P did not hire her own surveyor, but relied on the building society's valuation. However, the surveyor had negligently failed to notice that the removal of the chimney breasts had left the chimneys in a dangerous state. A few months after P moved in they collapsed, causing considerable damage. Although P was allowed to see the valuation report, the mortgage application form stated that neither the Abbey National nor the surveyor gave any warranty that the report was accurate, and that it was supplied without responsibility on their part. The House of Lords held that this disclaimer of responsibility was unreasonable in circumstances where the surveyor knows that the borrower will be supplied with a copy of the report and would be likely to rely on it despite the disclaimer. P was successful in her action. When considering all of the relevant circumstances the question for the court is limited to whether the clause satisfied the requirement of reasonableness *in relation to the particular contract*, not every contract in which it might be used.

In PHILLIPS PRODUCTS V HYLAND (1984) Phillips hired a JCB, plus driver (Hyland) from a plant hire company. An exclusion clause in the contract stated 'when a driver or operator is supplied by the owner to work the plant, he shall be under the direction and control of the hirer. Such drivers or operators shall for all purposes in connection with their employment in the working of the plant be regarded as their servants.' Hyland nevertheless made it clear to Phillips that he would not tolerate interference in the way he operated his machine. He then drove it negligently causing over £3,000 of damage to Phillips' buildings. It was held that the exclusion clause was not reasonable the plaintiff hire company were therefore liable for Hyland's negligence.

h. *S.12 The definition of consumer.* A person deals as a consumer if

i. He neither makes the contract in the course of a business, nor holds himself out as doing so, and

ii. The other party does make the contract in the course of a business, and

iii. The goods are of a type ordinarily supplied for private use or consumption.

The person who claims that the other party does not deal as a consumer must show that he does not. Where a business engages in an activity (for example buying a car) that is merely incidental to their business (for example as shipping brokers) that activity will not be 'in the course of the business unless it is an integral part of it, and it will not be an integral part unless it is carried on with a degree of regularity' (R & B CUSTOMERS BROKERS V UNITED DOMINIONS TRUST (1988)).

14. *THE UNFAIR TERMS IN CONSUMER CONTRACTS REGULATIONS 1999.*

   a. These regulations implement an EC directive on unfair contract terms.

   b. They apply to terms which have not been individually negotiated in contracts for the sale or supply of goods or services to consumers. The regulations therefore cover the vast majority of consumer contracts.

   c. An unfair term is defined as

   'Any term which contrary to the requirement of good faith causes a significant imbalance in the parties rights and obligations under the contract to the detriment of the consumer.'

   d. When deciding on 'good faith' the court will consider all relevant factors, examples of which may include:

   i. The strength of the bargaining positions of the parties.

   ii. Whether the consumer had an inducement to agree to the term.

   iii. Whether it was a special order of the consumer.

   iv. The extent to which the seller or supplier dealt fairly with the consumer.

   e. The regulations give 18 examples of terms which may be regarded as unfair, including

   i. Excluding or limiting liability of the seller when the consumer dies or is injured, where this results from an act or omission of the seller (the *UNFAIR CONTRACT TERMS ACT 1977* only covers negligent acts or omissions).

   ii. Excluding or limiting liability where there is incomplete performance by the seller.

   iii. Making a contract binding on a consumer where the seller can still avoid performing the contract.

   f. Two remedies are available

   i. The unfair term can be declared void, leaving the remainder of the contract in operation.

   ii. An individual, consumer group or Trading Standards Department can complain to the Director General of Fair Trading or other qualifying body to seek an injunction to prohibit use of the term. Other qualifying bodies are listed as: Director Generals of Gas, Electricity, Water and Telecommunications, the Consumers' Association, and all weights and measures authorities.

g. The regulations overlap with the UNFAIR CONTRACT TERMS ACT 1977. Businesses dealing with consumers will have to have regard to both laws until consolidation takes place. There are a number of similarities between the 1977 Act and the Regulations, most notable of which is the test of *reasonableness* under the Act and *fairness* under the Regulations.

15. *The Requirement of Reasonableness and the End of Fundamental Breach*

a. It has now become clear that the statutory requirement of reasonableness has replaced the common law rules on fundamental breach. The problem was that some breaches were so serious that they amounted to totally different performance or no performance at all. There used to be a rule that an exemption clause could not apply to such a fundamental breach. In 1967 this was changed by the House of Lords and it was said that if a clause was sufficiently well constructed it was possible to exclude liability for a fundamental breach. For example:

In PHOTO PRODUCTIONS v SECURICOR TRANSPORT (1980) P engaged D to provide a visiting patrol service to their factory at a charge of £8.75p per week. One night an employee of D intentionally started a fire at the factory causing damage of £615,000. D sought to avoid liability by relying on a clause which stated:

'Under no circumstances shall the company (Securicor) be responsible for any injurious act or default by any employee of the company unless such act or default could have been foreseen and avoided by the exercise of due diligence on the part of the company as his employer.'

It was not suggested that D could have foreseen and avoided the act of their employee. However, the Court of Appeal held that there was a fundamental breach to which the exemption clause did not apply. The House of Lords unanimously reversed the decision, holding that as a matter of construction, the words of the exemption clause clearly relieved D from the liability which they would have otherwise incurred.

b. The case that finally laid to rest the doctrine of fundamental breach was decided by the House of Lords in 1983. It was the first time that the House had had to consider a statutory provision giving power to override an exemption clause.

In GEORGE MITCHELL v FINNEY LOCK SEEDS (1983) P, who was a farmer, ordered 30 Ib of cabbage seed from D, who were seed merchants. The purchase price was about £200. D's standard term contract limited their liability for the supply of defective goods to replacement or refund of the amount paid by P. P planted the seed over a wide acreage but when the crop came up it was not fit for human consumption but consisted of unusable weeds. P claimed about £61,500 damages and about £30,500 interest. P's arguments were based both on the common law ground of fundamental breach and on the statutory ground of reasonableness. It was held that at common law the exemption clause would have protected D, but the court decided in favour of P, relying exclusively on the statutory ground. Lord Bridge said that fundamental breach had been 'forcibly evicted' from our system. Thus it will no longer be necessary to use this artificial method of analysing contract terms now that it is possible for the court to set aside the term if it does not satisfy the requirement of reasonableness. It is hoped that the application of this test will lead to less uncertainty.

Note: Since the contract in the above case was made before 1st February 1978 (when the UNFAIR CONTRACT TERMS ACT came into force) the provision which applied was *s.55 of SCHEDULE 1* of the *SALE OF GOODS ACT 1979*. This applies to contracts made between 18th May 1973 and 1st February 1978 and it adopts a requirement of reasonableness very similar to the *UNFAIR CONTRACT TERMS ACT*.

The UK government has indicated an intention to consolidate the provisions of the *UNFAIR CONTRACT TERMS ACT 1977* and the *UNFAIR TERMS IN CONSUMER CONTRACTS REGULATIONS 1999*.

CHAPTER 17

Vitiating Factors

These are factors which affect the validity of an otherwise effective contract.

MISTAKE

1. *Introduction*

a. It is in the interest of business generally that apparent contracts be enforced. Thus most mistakes, for example as to the quality of a product, will not affect the validity of the contract.

In BELL v LEVER BROS LTD (1932) two directors were removed by the majority shareholder LB Ltd. As there was a period of time left still to run on both directors' five year contracts, LB Ltd agreed to pay compensation to the directors for loss of office. It subsequently emerged that past misconduct by the directors could have rendered them liable to dismissal without compensation. LB Ltd sought to recover the money paid by arguing that the agreement to pay them compensation was void for mistake. The House of Lords ruled that both parties believed there was an entitlement to be paid and an obligation to pay (the directors' successfully arguing that they had forgotten about their previous wrongdoings). This was a mistake by LB Ltd as to the *qualities* of the directors and as such was not the kind of mistake that would invalidate a contract.

This was further illustrated in LEAF v INTERNATIONAL GALLERIES (1950) where both the buyer and seller were mistaken as to the true identity of the artiste of a particular painting. When it was later discovered the court ruled that this was a common mistake as to quality and value of the painting and that this did not affect the validity of the contract.

In a more recent case, GREAT BRITAIN PEACE SHIPPING LTD v TSAVLIRIS SALVAGE LTD (2002) a contract was entered into to charter a vessel on the understanding, subsequently shown to be incorrect, that the vessel chartered was the nearest one to a particular location. It transpired that other vessels were nearer. The Court of Appeal held that the mistake as to distance was not such as to confound the common assumption of both parties that the vessel hired was sufficiently close to the location to carry out the service for which it had been chartered. The contract was valid and the defendants were liable to pay the hire charges.

The common law rules on mistake, if applicable, render the contract *void*, but these rules are exercised within narrow limits. In equity the rules have a wider scope, but their effect is less drastic. If a document is signed by mistake special rules apply.

b. It is very important to distinguish a contract which is *void for mistake* from one which is merely *voidable for misrepresentation*. The distinction is of little importance to the parties themselves, since the goods or money can be recovered from the other party to the contract if they are still in his possession. The distinction is, however, very significant if the goods have been sold to a third party. For example if A 'sells' his car to B and then B re-sells the car to C, if the contract between A and B was void for mistake, then A can recover the car from C because no title passes under a void contract. C will be able to sue B for breach of the implied condition that he had a right to sell and pass title. However, in a similar situation if the contract between A and B is only voidable for misrepresentation, then provided the sale to C took place before A avoided the contract, C will obtain good title, since 'voidable' means valid until avoided. A would then have to seek a remedy for misrepresentation (innocent, negligent or fraudulent) against B.

2. *Common Law.* The following types of mistake render a contract void, provided the mistake actually induces the contract.

a. Mistake as to the existence of the subject matter.

In GALLOWAY V GALLOWAY (**1914**) a man and a woman made a separation agreement, believing that they were married. In fact they were not married because, unknown to them, at the time of their marriage ceremony the man's wife was still alive. The separation agreement was held to be void for mistake because the 'marriage' which was the basis for the agreement was void.

b. Mistake as to the possibility of performing the contract.

In SHEIK BROS V OCHSNER (**1957**) a contract was made for the exploitation of sisal grown on a specific plot of land. The contract provided for an average delivery of 50 tons of sisal per month. The contract was held to be void because the land was not capable of producing 50 tons per month.

c. Mistake as to the identity of the subject matter.

i. For example A intended to buy product X, but B intended to sell product Y.

In RAFFLES V WICHELHAUS (**1864**) P agreed to sell to D a consignment of cotton which was to arrive 'ex Peerless from Bombay'. There happened to be two ships called Peerless sailing from Bombay, one in October and one in December. P was thinking of one ship and D of the other. It was held that there was no contract.

In SHOGUN FINANCE V HUDSON (**2004**) a rogue purchased a vehicle from a garage pretending that he was another person, a Mr Patel. He produced Mr Patel's driving licence and was checked for credit-worthiness based upon the assumed identity. When the vehicle was subsequently sold by the rogue to an innocent purchaser, the garage sought to have the vehicle returned claiming the contract was void due to mistake as to identity. The House of Lords ruled that this was an agreement concluded in writing and that the particulars in the agreement were only capable of applying to Mr Patel, it was the intention of the rogue that the garage should identify Mr Patel as the purchaser. Before entering the agreement the garage checked that Mr Patel existed and that he was worthy of credit. On that basis they decided to contract with him and no-one else. As the agreement was concluded without his authority it was a nullity and the vehicle must, therefore, be returned.

ii. It is important to be able to distinguish a mistake as to identity from a mistake as to quality.

In SMITH v HUGHES (1871) P was shown a sample of oats by D, and thinking that they were old oats he bought them. They were in fact new oats, and he refused to accept them. It was held that his mistake did not invalidate the contract. The parties were at cross-purposes, but not to such an extent that there was no agreement at all. The mistake was only one of quality, and as such does not operate to render the contract void.

iii. A mistake as to quality will only invalidate the contract if it is a mistake as to the fundamental quality by which the thing is identified not if it is a mistake as to one of the various other qualities of the product.

d. Mistake as to the identity of the other party. It is clear that such a mistake cannot be made when parties deal face to face, unless there is clear evidence to the contrary.

In INGRAM v LITTLE (1973) X entered into a contract to purchase jewellery from Y. X wanted to pay by cheque and was informed by Y that the goods could not be delivered until the cheque cleared. X then made representations that he was a well known respectable person whereupon Y agreed to let some of the jewellery be taken by X. The cheque proved worthless. The court held that the contract had been concluded before the indentity of X became important, there was a valid contract which was not void because of mistake. It would almost certainly have been void however on the grounds of misrepresentation (see PHILLIPS v BROOKS (1919)).

In such a situation a person can only make a mistake as to the attributes (ie the quality) of the other party, and not his identity. An agreement apparently made between X and Y will be void if X can prove:

i. That at the time of the agreement he regarded the identity of the other party as of importance.

ii. That he did not intend to contract with Y, but with a different existing person – Z, and

iii. That this fact was known to Y.

In CUNDY v LINDSAY (1878) Blenkarn, a rogue trader, wrote to the claimant ordering linen from an address where a highly respected business also resided in the same street. He sought to further disguise his identity through a signature that looked like that of the reputable firm. Goods were duly delivered which were then sold on to a good faith purchaser. The Court held that the contract between the claimant and Blenkarn was void for mistake and therefore title could not pass and the goods must be returned to the claimant.

Contrast LEWIS v AVERAY (**1971**). P advertised his car for sale, and was induced to accept a cheque from a crook who said he was the famous actor Richard Greene. The cheque was dishonoured. P then claimed the car from D. who had bought it in good faith from the crook. The claim failed because his contract with the crook was not void for mistake, since the presumption that he intended to contract with the person physically before him had not been overcome. P's mistake was as to the credit-worthiness of the other party, and not as to his identity. The contract between P and the crook was voidable for fraud. Voidable, however, means valid until avoided, and P had not avoided by the time the crook sold the car to D. The contract was therefore valid, and the crook was able to pass title to D.

In KINGS NORTON METAL v EDRIDGE MERRETT (**1897**) P received an order for wire from 'Hallam and Co'. The letterhead depicted a large factory and described Hallam and Co as a substantial firm. In fact Hallam and Co did not exist, being merely an alias for a crook named Wallis. P sent the goods to 'Hallam and Co' on credit. Wallis took possession of them and re-sold them to D. It was held that as Wallis and 'Hallam and Co' were the same person, P had not made a mistake as to identity, but had intended to contract with the writer of the letters. Thus the contract was only voidable for fraud, and since Wallis sold to D before P avoided the contract D obtained title to the goods.

e. Mistake as to the terms of the contract of which the other party is aware.

In HARTOG v COLIN AND SHIELDS (**1939**) a seller of hare skins mistakenly offered them at a price 'per pound' instead of 'per piece', there being about three pieces to the pound. The buyer, knowing of the mistake, accepted the offer, and later sued the seller for non-delivery. His action failed since he knew that the seller did not intend to contract on the terms stated.

f. *Terminology*. Different terminology is often used to describe the various types of mistake.

   i. *Unilateral mistake*. This occurs when one of the parties is mistaken about some fundamental fact and the other party knows or should know this, for example CUNDY v LINDSAY (**1878**).

   ii. *Bilateral (or common) mistake*. This occurs when both parties make the same mistake. Usually this will be a mistake as to the existence of the subject matter, for example GALLOWAY v GALLOWAY (**1914**).

   iii. *Mutual mistake*. This occurs when the two parties mean different things. It will normally be a mistake as to the identity of the subject matter of the contract, for example RAFFLES v WICHELHAUS (**1864**).

3. *Equity*. Equity will in limited situations relieve a party from the effects of his mistake where the common law would hold him to the contract. There are two equitable remedies:

   a. *Rescission*. The circumstances when this remedy will be granted have never been precisely defined. In general it will only be granted if the party seeking to rescind was not at fault, and provided justice can be done to the other party by imposing conditions.

In GRIST v BAILEY (**1966**) the contract concerned the sale of a house which was occupied by a tenant. Both parties believed that the house was subject to rent control, and they agreed a price of £850. In fact the house was not subject to rent control, and so was worth £2,250. The contract for sale at £850 was rescinded in equity, with the condition imposed that the vendor should give the purchaser first option to buy the house at the correct market price.

b.   *Rectification.* Where there has been a mistake, not in the actual agreement, but in its reduction into writing, equity will rectify the written document so that it coincides with the true agreement of the parties provided:

    i   The terms were clearly agreed between the parties

    ii.   The agreement continued unchanged up to the time it was put into writing, and

    iii. The writing fails to express the agreement of the parties.

In WEEDS v BLANEY (**1976**) P orally agreed with D to sell him a farmhouse and some land. P's solicitor in error prepared a contract which included further land owned by P. The error was not noticed and the land was transferred to D who became the registered owner. It was held that P was entitled to rectification of the contract and the transfer.

4.   *Non Est Factum* (It is not my act). The general rule concerning signed documents is that a person is bound even if he does not read or understand the document (L'ESTRANGE v GRAUCOB (**1934**), Chapter 16.11). However, an apparent signed contract will be regarded as void if a party can successfully plead the defence of *non est factum*. Three conditions must be satisfied:

a.   The signature must have been induced by fraud.

b.   The document must be fundamentally different from that thought to be signed. A mistake as to the contents is not sufficient to allow *non est factum* to be raised.

c.   The party seeking to avoid liability must prove that he acted with reasonable care.

In LEWIS v CLAY (**1897**) D was induced to sign two promissory notes by the fraudulent misrepresentation that his signature was required as a witness. The rest of the document apart from the space for the signature was covered by blotting paper, D being told that the documents were of a private nature. It was held that the defence of non est factum applied even though D could not say precisely what type of document he thought he had signed.

Contrast SAUNDERS v ANGLIA BUILDING SOCIETY (**1970**). The original plaintiff (a Mrs Gallie who died before 1970) wanted to help her nephew, Parkin, to raise money on the security of her leasehold house, provided she could continue to live there rent free for the rest of her life. Parkin did not want to raise the loan or become owner of the house himself as he feared this would enable his wife (from whom he was separated) to enforce a claim for maintenance against him. He therefore arranged that his friend, Lee, should raise the money on a mortgage of Gallie's house, and then given the money to him. Before Lee could mortgage the house it had to be transferred to him. An assignment was prepared under which the lease of the house was transferred to Lee for £3,000 (a reasonable price was included in the assignment so as not to subsequently arouse the Building Society's suspicions). When Gallie was asked to sign the assignment she did not read it because her glasses were broken, but Lee told her it was a deed of gift to Parkin (who witnessed the document). Lee then raised money by mortgaging the property to The Anglia Building Society, but he did not pay any money to Parkin, nor did he pay the £3,000 to Gallie.

It was held that *non est factum* did not apply to Gallie's signature of the assignment, since her mistake was not sufficiently serious. She believed the document would enable Parkin to raise money on the security of the house, and the document was designed to achieve this aim, though by a different method than that contemplated by Gallie. It was also stated that Mrs Gallie's carelessness prevented her from relying on *non est factum*.

MISREPRESENTATION

5. *General Definition.* A misrepresentation is an untrue statement of fact which is one of the causes which induces the contract. Note that

    a. It must be a statement of fact. Such a statement may be written, spoken or made by conduct.

        i. A *statement of opinion*, for example that the goods represent good value, cannot amount to a misrepresentation unless the maker of the statement is an expert or has special knowledge.

        In BISSETT v WILKINSON (**1927**) the vendor of land stated that it would support 2,000 sheep. It turned out that this was not the case, but the vendor was not liable because the land had not previously been used for sheep and the purchaser knew this. The statement was therefore held to be one of opinion not fact.

        A statement of opinion may by implication involve a statement of fact.

        In SMITH v LAND AND HOUSE PROPERTY CORPORATION (**1884**) the vendor of a hotel described it as 'let to Mr Frederick Fleck (a most desirable tenant)'. The tenant was in fact in arrears with his rent. It was held to be statement of fact since the vendor was impliedly stating that he knew the fact that supported his opinion that the tenant was 'desirable'.

        ii. A *statement of intention* is not a misrepresentation unless it can be proved that the alleged intention never existed.

        In EDGINGTON v FITZMAURICE (**1885**) P was induced to lend money to a company because the directors said they intended to use the money to finance expansion. In fact this intention never existed since the directors needed the money to pay off company debts. It was held that there had been a fraudulent misrepresentation.

        iii. A false statement as to the law cannot be a misrepresentation, since everyone is presumed to know the law.

    b. Silence is not usually misrepresentation except

        i. When a statement made in the course of negotiations subsequently becomes false and is not corrected, or

        ii. When silence distorts a literally true statement.

          In R v KYLSANT (**1931**) a company when inviting the public to subscribe for its shares, stated that it had paid a regular dividend throughout the years of the depression. This clearly implied that the company had made a profit during those years. This was not the case since the dividends had been paid out of the accumulated profits of the pre-depression years. The company's silence as to the source of the dividends was held to be a misrepresentation since it distorted the true statement that dividends had been paid.

        iii. Where the contract is of utmost good faith (*uberrimae fidei*).

    c. The misrepresentation must induce the contract. The plaintiff therefore cannot avoid the contract if

        i. He knew the statement was false, or

        ii. He would have made the contract despite the misrepresentation, or

        iii. He did not know that there had been a misrepresentation.

        In HORSFALL v THOMAS (**1862**) the vendor of a gun concealed a defect in the gun (a misrepresentation by conduct). The buyer purchased the gun without examining it. Therefore the concealing of the defect could not have affected his decision as to whether or not to purchase it. His action therefore failed.

6. *Fraudulent Misrepresentation*

    a. *Definition*. A statement which is known to be false, or made without belief in its truth, or recklessly, not caring whether it is true or false.

        In DERRY v PEEK (**1889**) a company had a power conferred by a special Act of Parliament to run trams by animal power and with Board of Trade consent by steam or mechanical power. The company invited applications for shares from the public and stated in the prospectus that they had power to run trams by steam power. They had assumed that Board of Trade permission would be granted, but in the event it was not. As a result the directors were sued for fraud. The court formulated the definition of fraud stated above and held that the directors were not liable since they honestly believed their statement to be true.

    b. *Remedies*. If the innocent party has suffered loss he may claim damages, based on the tort of deceit. In addition he may:

        i. Refuse to perform the contract and

        ii. Claim rescission of the contract.

Since fraud makes a contract voidable, the innocent party may chose to affirm the contract.

c.   When a contract is voidable, it will generally be valid until the other party is informed of the avoidance. However, where the seller has a right to avoid for fraud he does so if, on discovering the fraud, he takes all reasonable steps to recover the goods.

In CAR AND UNIVERSAL FINANCE v CALDWELL (1964) a person was induced by fraud to sell his car to a crook. The crook's cheque was dishonoured, and the crook could not be found. Immediately the cheque was dishonoured the former owner informed the police and the Automobile Association, and asked them to find his car. It was held that since he had done all he could in the circumstances he had successfully avoided the contract. It is clearly vital to avoid a contract induced by fraud as soon as possible. Since fraud makes a contract voidable, (and not void,) if the crook sells the goods to a third party before avoidance he passes a good title and the original owner bears the loss. If the crook 'sells' after avoidance he cannot pass title, thus the third party to whom he has 'sold' must bear the loss.

The House of Lords stated in STANDARD CHARTERED BANK v PARKINSON NATIONAL SHIPPING CORPORATION (2003) that the maker of a fraudulent misrepresentation cannot raise a defence of contributory negligence.

7. *Innocent Misrepresentation*

a.   An innocent misrepresentation is a statement which the maker honestly and reasonably believes to be true. The law on this topic represents an attempt to strike a balance between two innocent parties, the maker of the statement and the person who has been induced to make a contract in reliance on that statement. In such situations the law often becomes very complex. This is true of innocent misrepresentation where the rules originate from three sources, common law, equity and statute.

b.   *Remedies.* The innocent party has no right to damages, but may ask the court to grant the equitable remedy of rescission, ie restoration, to the pre-contract state of affairs.

   i.   Under *S.1 MISREPRESENTATION ACT 1967* the remedy of rescission is not lost if the representation is later incorporated into the contract.

   ii. Under *S.2(2)* the court has a discretion to award damages in lieu of rescission if it thinks it equitable to do so, for example if the misrepresentation is trivial it may be too drastic to rescind the contract. *S.2(2)* damages may be awarded even if the *S.2(1)* defence of reasonable belief is available (see below) but they may not be awarded in addition to rescission since the section specified 'in lieu of rescission', ie instead of rescission.

   iii. As with a fraudulent misrepresentation the innocent party may choose to affirm contract.

8. *Negligent Misrepresentation*

a. A negligent misrepresentation is a false statement made by a person who had no reasonable grounds for believing it to be true.

b. The innocent party has a right to damages for misrepresentation if he has suffered loss. However, if the maker of the statement proves that he had reasonable grounds for believing, and in fact did believe, up to the time the contract was made that the facts represented were true, then he has a defence. *S.2(1) MISREPRESENTATION ACT 1967.*

c. The measure of damages is the same as in a claim for the tort of deceit, ie the plaintiff is entitled to be put in the position which he would have been in if the representation had not been made, rather than the position in which he would have been in if the representation had been true. The deceit measure also entitles the plaintiff to recover all losses, whether foreseeable or not, provided they are not otherwise too remote.

In NAUGHTON v O'CALLAGHAN (1990) P purchased a racehorse (Fondu) for 26,000 guineas on the basis of a negligent misrepresentation by D as to its pedigree. At the time, if the pedigree had not been misrepresented, it would have been worth about 23,500 guineas. The misrepresentation was discovered two years later, during which time Fondu had been raced very unsuccessfully and was worth about £1,500. P claimed the difference between the purchase price of 26,000 guineas and £1,500, plus training fees and expenses. D claimed the damages were limited to the difference in value at the time of sale ie 2,500 guineas. Normally the courts would award the difference between the value of the goods as represented and the actual value at the time of sale. However, P succeeded since there were reasons for departing from the usual position, ie

i. P had purchased a completely different animal from that described in the catalogue.

ii. The fall in value was due to Fondu's lack of success not a general fall in the value of racehorses. It probably would not have occurred if Fondu had had the pedigree described in the catalogue.

iii. The training fees and expenses were losses directly and naturally resulting from the misrepresentation.

iv. If the misrepresentation had been discovered immediately, Fondu could have been sold for 23,500 guineas in which case damages would have been 2,500 guineas.

In F AND H ENTERTAINMENTS v LEISURE ENTERPRISES (1976) P purchased the lease of a club premises from D for £23,100 having been told that the rent was £2,400 per year, and that no rent review notices had been served. P went into occupation and spent £4,000 on re-equipping and preparing the premises for use. The landlords then requested the revised rent of £6,500 (valid rent review notices had in fact been served). P vacated the premises and sought rescission and damages. It was held that damages under *S.2(1)* would be awarded and that they would include compensation for expenditure properly and not prematurely incurred, ie the £4,000. Rescission was also granted.

d. A negligent misrepresentation may also give rise to the possibility of a negligence action under the principle in HEDLEY BYRNE v HELLER (1964) (Chapter 24.4). The rules for measure of damages suggest that, given the choice, a plaintiff would benefit from an action under *S.2(1)* rather than a claim for negligence. If the misrepresentation has been incorporated into the contract, and not the remoteness is an issue, it may also benefit the plaintiff to bring an action under *S.2(1)*, since the remoteness rule in the contract limits losses to what may reasonably be supposed to have been in the contemplation of the parties. This is narrower than the negligence test of reasonable foreseeability, which in turn is narrower than the deceit measure described above.

9. *Bars to Rescission.* The remedy of rescission will not be available in the following situations:

   a. If the innocent party, with knowledge of his rights, affirms the contract.

      In LONG v LLOYD (1958) P was induced to buy a lorry from D after hearing representations as to its condition, and a statement that it would do eleven miles to the gallon. P then drove the lorry home from Hampton Court to Sevenoaks. The next Wednesday P drove to Rochester, and during the journey the dynamo ceased to function, an oil leak developed, a crack appeared in one of the wheels, and petrol consumption was five miles per gallon. He complained to D who offered to pay half the cost of a new dynamo, and this offer was accepted. The next day the lorry broke down on a journey to Middlesbrough, and P asked for his money back. A subsequent examination by an expert showed that the lorry was unroadworthy. It was held:

      i. That the representations as to the condition of the lorry were innocent.

      ii. The journey to Rochester was not affirmation because P had to have an opportunity to test the vehicle in a working capacity.

      iii. The acceptance of the offer to pay half of the cost of the dynamo, and the subsequent journey to Middlesbrough, did amount to affirmation and therefore rescission could not be granted.

      If this case had been heard after 1967 P may have succeeded under *S.2(1)* MISREPRESENTATION ACT *1967*. It is unlikely that D could have proved that he had reasonable grounds for believing that the lorry was in good condition.

   b. Lapse of time.

      i. Where the misrepresentation is fraudulent lapse of time does not itself bar rescission because time only begins to run from discovery of the truth.

      ii. Where the misrepresentation is innocent lapse of time may bar rescission.

      In LEAF v INTERNATIONAL GALLERIES (1950) P was induced to buy a painting by an innocent misrepresentation that it was by John Constable.

Five years later he discovered the truth and immediately claimed rescission. He could not therefore have affirmed the contract but his claim was held to be barred by lapse of time.

Two further points of interest were made in Leaf's case. Firstly, the contract was not void for mistake, the mistake being merely as to quality. Secondly, Lord Denning said that a claim to rescind for innocent misrepresentation must be barred when the right to repudiate for breach of condition is barred, ie when there is 'acceptance' within the meaning of S.35 SALE OF GOODS ACT 1893. (*Now S.35 SGA 1979.*)

c. If restitutio in integrum is impossible, ie if restoration to the pre-contract state of affairs is impossible, because for example a partnership's capital has been converted into shares in a limited company as in CLARKE v DICKSON (**1858**). A more obvious example of impossibility of restoration is where the subject matter is food which has been eaten. A modern tendency is for the courts to award rescission if the substantial identity of the property remains even though the parties cannot be precisely restored to their pre-contract position, financial adjustments being made if necessary.

d. The intervention of third party rights. Thus a person cannot rescind an allotment of shares in a company after the company has gone into liquidation, since at this point third party rights intervene because the assets of the company have to be collected to distribute among the company's creditors.

10. *Exempting Liability for Misrepresentation.* If a contract purports to take away any liability or remedy for misrepresentation that provision is of no effect unless it satisfies the requirement of reasonableness as defined by *S.11 UNFAIR CONTRACT TERMS ACT 1977.*

11. *Trade Descriptions.* Note that the TRADE DESCRIPTIONS ACT 1968 which prohibits mis-descriptions of goods relates to criminal law, not the law of contract.

DURESS AND UNDUE INFLUENCE

12. *Duress*

a. This is a common law doctrine, and its effect if proved is that the contract is voidable. It is limited in scope to illegal violence or threats of violence to the person of the contracting party. To threaten a person's property is not duress, but to threaten unlawful imprisonment is duress.

In CUMMING, v INCE (**1847**) an old lady was threatened with unlawful confinement in a mental home if she did not transfer certain property rights to one of her relatives. The subsequent transfer was set aside since the threat of unlawful imprisonment amounted to duress.

b. Duress does not need to be the only factor inducing the contract, as long as it is one of the reasons.

In BARTON v ARMSTRONG (**1976**) there was a dispute between two shareholders in the same company (A and B), including a threat by A to kill B.

Later B purchased A's shares on terms that were very favourable to A. The contract was set aside on the grounds of duress, even though there may have been other factors inducing B to sell his shares.

13. *Undue Influence*

a.   In developing this doctrine equity recognised that consent may be affected by influences other than physical ones. Its effect is to make the contract voidable. The burden of proof of undue influence will depend on the relationship between the parties.

b.   If there is no special relationship the party seeking to avoid must prove that he was subjected to influence which excluded free consent.

In WILLIAMS v BAYLEY (**1866**) a father agreed to mortgage his property to a bank if the bank would return to him promissory notes on which his son had forged his signature. The bank had hinted at prosecution and 'transportation' of the son if the father did not agree to execute the mortgage. The agreement to execute the mortgage was set aside because undue influence had been proved.

c.   Where a confidential relationship exists between the parties it is for the party in whom confidence is placed to show that undue influence was not used. Examples of such relationships are trustee/beneficiary, solicitor/client, parent/child, however, the presumption applies whenever the relationship is such that one of them is by reason of the confidence placed in him able to take unfair advantage of the other.

In TATE v WILLIAMSON (**1866**) D became financial adviser to an extravagant Oxford undergraduate. The undergraduate sold his estate to D for about half its value, and died of alcoholism at the age of 24. His executors were successful in having the sale of the estate set aside.

d.   A transaction will not be set aside on the ground of undue influence unless it can be shown that the transaction is to the manifest disadvantage of the person subjected to undue influence. Also a presumption of undue influence will not arise merely because a confidential relationship exists, provided the person in whom confidence is placed keeps within the boundaries of a normal business relationship.

In NATIONAL WESTMINSTER BANK v MORGAN (**1985**) a wife (W) signed a re-mortgage of the family home (owned jointly with her husband H) in favour of the bank to prevent the original mortgagee from continuing with proceedings to re-possess the home. The bank manager told her in good faith but incorrectly, that the mortgage only secured liability in respect of the home. In fact it covered all H's debts to the bank. W signed the mortgage at home in the presence of the manager, and without taking independent advice. H and W fell into arrears with the payments and soon afterwards H died. At the time of his death nothing was owed to the bank in respect of H's business liabilities. The bank sought possession but W contended that she had only signed the mortgage because of undue influence from the bank and therefore it should be set aside. The House of Lords held, reversing the Court of Appeal, that the manager had not crossed the line between explaining an ordinary business transaction and entering into a relationship in which he had a dominant influence, furthermore the transaction was not unfair to W, therefore the bank was not under a duty to ensure that W took independent advice. The order for possession was granted.

e. Where there is a commercial relationship the courts will recognise the existence of economic duress as part of the concept of undue influence.

In THE ATLANTIC BARON (1979) the parties reached agreement on the purchase price to be paid for a ship. There was then a currency devaluation and as a result the vendor claimed a 10% increase in price. The purchaser refused to pay. The vendor then stated that if the extra was not paid he would terminate the contract and amicable business relations would not continue. Due to this threat the purchaser agreed to the increase in price. It was later held that the threat to terminate the contract and discontinue amicable business relations amounted to undue influence. The contract was therefore voidable.

In ATLAS EXPRESS V KAFCO (IMPORTERS AND EXPORTERS) (1989) D made a contract with Woolworths for the delivery of its goods to about 800 Woolworths stores. D then made a contract with P, a well known company of forwarders, for carriage of the goods. P later decided that the carriage charge was too low and presented D with a revised invoice showing higher carriage charges. They also refused to accept any goods for delivery unless invoice showing the higher charges was signed. D protested the increase, but since they were committed to Woolworths (who would probably withdraw their business if the goods were not delivered) they signed the invoice. They subsequently refused to pay the increased rate of charges. When sued by P they pleaded economic duress.

This defence was accepted by the court. It was also held that P had provided no consideration for the second agreement. Contrast WILLIAMS V ROFFEY (1990) Chapter 13.12.

ILLEGALITY

14. *Introduction.* The law will clearly refuse to give effect to a contract if it involves the commission of a legal wrong, or if it is invalidated by statute. Also classed as illegal contracts are contracts which do not involve the commission of a crime or tort, but which are not enforced by the courts because they are contrary to public policy. The most important of these are contracts in unreasonable restraint of trade.

15. *Classification.* There are many different ways to approach the classification of illegal contracts. For convenience the following categories will be used:

a. Contracts involving the commission of a legal wrong.

b. Contracts illegal by statute.

c. Contracts contrary to public policy.

16. *Contracts Involving the Commission of a Legal Wrong.* The following are examples only and not a complete list:

    a.   Where the object is to commit a crime or a civil wrong as in NAPIER V NATIONAL BUSINESS AGENCY (**1951**), where the contract was drawn up so as to deceive the Inland Revenue.

    b.   A contract to pay money on the commission of an unlawful act.

17. *Contracts Illegal by Statute.* For example:

    a.   *Wagering contracts.*

        i.   *S.18* GAMING ACT *1845* makes all contracts of wagering void and provides that no action can be brought to recover any money or valuable thing alleged to be won on a wager.

        ii.   A wagering contract is a contract by which two persons professing to hold opposite views as to the outcome of a future uncertain event agree that, dependent on the determination of such event, one shall win and the other shall lose, a sum of money or other stake; neither of the parties having any interest in the contract other than such sum or stake, there being no other consideration by either. It is essential that each party may either win or lose.

    b.   *Restrictive trade agreements.* These are agreements where producers or suppliers restrict the manufacture, supply or distribution of goods by, for example, fixing a minimum selling price for goods or regulating the supply of goods. The RESTRICTIVE TRADE PRACTICES ACT *1976* does not make such agreements automatically void, but provides machinery whereby their validity is tested. (19.c below.)

    c.   *Statutes in general.* If one party in performing a contract does an act, prohibited by statute, the act only may be illegal, or the whole contract may be illegal. It depends on whether or not the statute was intended to prohibit the whole contract.

        In ARCHBOLDS V SPANGLETT (**1961**) D contracted to carry whisky belonging to P in a van which was not licensed to carry goods which did not belong to him. In carrying the whisky D therefore committed a statutory offence. The whisky was stolen on the journey and P sued for damages. D pleaded the illegality for his defence. The Court of Appeal rejected this defence because:

        i.   The Act in question did not prohibit the contract expressly or by implication, and

        ii.   P did not know that D did not have the correct licence.

18. *Contracts in Contravention of Public Policy.* For example:

    a.   Contracts promoting sexual immorality.

        In PEARCE V BROOKS (**1866**) a contract to hire out a carriage to a prostitute for the purposes of her profession was held to be illegal.

    b.   Contracts which detract from the institution of marriage. For example:

        i.   Marriage brokage contracts.

       ii.   Contracts in restraint of marriage.

      iii.   Contracts for the future separation of husband and wife.

    c.   Sales of offices and honours.

       In PARKINSON v COLLEGE OF AMBULANCE (1925) a contract to obtain a knighthood was held to be illegal since it could lead to corruption and was 'derogatory to the dignity of the Sovereign'. It has since been made a criminal offence to make such a contract.

    d.   Contracts made with an enemy in wartime.

    e.   Contracts which involve doing an illegal act in a friendly foreign country.

       In FOSTER v DRISCOLL (1929) a contract was made to smuggle whisky into the USA during the period when the sale of liquor in the USA was forbidden. This contract was held to be illegal.

    f.   Contracts in unreasonable restraint of trade (see below).

19. ***Restraint of Trade.*** A contract in restraint of trade is one which restricts a person from freely exercising his trade or profession. Such contracts are prima facie illegal. However, some types of restraint can be justified if they are reasonable so far as the parties are concerned, and provided they are not contrary to public interest. When assessing the validity of contracts in restraint of trade the courts have had to balance the desire to allow complete freedom to contract with the fact that most restraints (especially restrictive trade practices) are contrary to public interest because they restrict the choice or bargaining power of the public. There are four types of contract in restraint of trade which may be held to be valid depending on the circumstances:

    a.   Restraints imposed on ex-employees.

        i.   If the restraint is to be reasonable between the parties it must be no wider than is necessary to protect the promisee's trade secrets or business connections. Therefore a restraint imposed on an employee who has no knowledge of his employer's secrets or influence over his customers will be illegal, as it would be an attempt to prevent competition. However, if trade secrets and business connections are legitimately protected, the fact that the restraint incidentally reduces the ex-employee's power to compete does not invalidate it.

       ii.   The court will also consider any time limits imposed by the restraint and/or the area it covers.

          In MASON v PROVIDENT CLOTHING (1913) a canvasser employed to sell clothes in Islington covenanted not to enter into similar business within 25 miles of London for three years. The restraint was held to be void because the area of the restraint was about 1,000 times as large as the area in which he had been employed.

In FITCH v DEWES (1921) a lifelong restraint on a solicitor's managing clerk not to practise within seven miles was upheld. In contrast to the previous case, the main objection concerned the duration of the restraint rather than the area covered. However, a solicitor's business is one to which clients are likely to resort for a long time, thus the lifetime restraint was not unreasonable. If the business to be protected is of a more fluctuating nature, long restraints will not be upheld.

iii. The court may grant judgement for a person against an association of employers who do not have a contractual relationship with the person concerned, but whose rules place an unjustified restraint on his liberty of employment.

In GREIG v INSOLE (1978) the Test and County Cricket Board sought to ban World Series cricketers from Test and County cricket by means of a change of their rules. The change of rules was held to be ultra vires since it was an unreasonable restraint of trade.

b. *Restraints imposed on the vendor of a business.* The restraint will only be effective if:

   i. There is a genuine sale of the goodwill of the business.

   In VANCOUVER MALT AND SAKE BREWING CO v VANCOUVER BREWERIES (1934) a company which was licensed to brew beer, but which did not in fact brew any, agreed to sell its business, and to refrain from manufacturing beer for 15 years. Since the company was not actually brewing beer the purchaser could only have paid for the tangible assets, because there were no intangible assets (ie goodwill) to sell. The purchaser had not therefore bought the promise not to brew beer, and so he could not enforce it.

   ii The restraint must be no more than is necessary to protect the particular business bought by the purchaser. In assessing the reasonableness of the restraint the area covered, the duration of the restraint, and the type of business are again important. However, it is possible even for a worldwide restraint to be upheld.

   In NORDENFELT v MAXIM NORDENFELT (1894) the owner of an armaments business sold it to a company and covenanted not to carry on a similar business for 25 years except on behalf of the company. The covenant was held to be valid although it prevented competition anywhere in the world.

c. *Agreements between traders by which prices or output are regulated*

   i. Such agreements were usually valid at common law, since they were generally made between persons of equal bargaining power, and were of benefit to both parties. They were, however, often contrary to the public interest. Parliament has therefore passed several Acts to protect the consumer.

   ii. The *RESTRICTIVE TRADE PRACTICES ACT 1976* requires certain types of restrictive trading agreements to be registered with the Director

General of Fair Trading. After registration the agreement is placed on a register open to public inspection and brought before the Restrictive Practices Court to determine whether the restriction is contrary to the public interest. If it is then the offending provisions are void. Failure to register a registrable agreement also renders the restrictions in it void. Any restriction is presumed to be contrary to the public interest unless it falls within one or more of eight 'gateways' referred to in the Act, for example the agreement benefits the public because it reduces the risk of injury, or the agreement maintains export trade.

iii. The RESALE PRICES ACT 1976 provides that if an agreement between a supplier and a dealer seeks to establish a minimum price to be charged by the dealer such a provision will be void. However, there is a power for the Restrictive Practices Court to grant exemption in certain cases.

d. *Solus agreements*. This is the name given to a contract by which a trader agrees to restrict his orders to one supplier. A solus agreement may be part of a mortgage or lease. The duration of the restraint is the most important factor in assessing the reasonableness, and thus the legality of these agreements.

In ESSO PETROLEUM v HARPER'S GARAGE (1967) D, who owned two garages, entered into solus agreements with P in respect of each garage. He agreed only to sell petrol supplied by P, to keep the garage open at all reasonable times, and not to sell the garage without ensuring that the purchaser entered into a similar agreement with P. One solus agreement was for a period of 4½ years, and the other (which was contained in a mortgage of his land to P) was for 21 years. The House of Lords held that the 4½ year agreement was valid, but that the 21 year agreement was invalid since it was of unreasonable duration, and was contrary to the public interest. In addition the obligation to sell only to a purchaser who was willing to enter into a similar solus agreement made the garage unsaleable.

In PETROFINA v MARTIN (1965) Martin's agreement with Petrofina was almost identical to Harper's agreement with Esso. In this case, however, the duration of the restraint was 12 years. D broke the agreement by selling other makes of petrol, and P sought to enforce it by means of an injunction preventing D from doing this. It was held that the restraint was invalid because it was of unreasonable duration.

20. *Consequences of Illegality*

a. *Contracts illegal as formed*. ie The contract is incapable of lawful performance, or is intended to be performed illegally as in PEARCE v BROOKS (1866). Such contracts are void and unenforceable. Therefore money paid or property handed over usually cannot be recovered.

b. *Contracts illegal as performed*. ie Legal at the outset, but later used for an illegal purpose.

i. The guilty party has no remedies.

In COWAN v MILBOURN (1867) D agreed to let rooms to P. He later discovered that P was going to use the rooms to give blasphemous lectures, which was an illegal purpose. D therefore refused to carry out the contract. P failed in his claim for possession since he was the guilty party.

ii. The innocent party has his normal contractual remedies, except in respect of anything done by him after he learns of the illegal purpose.

c. *Contracts in contravention of public policy.* Many such contracts, for example contracts in restraint of trade may not fall simply into the categories specified above, but will contain many different promises. These contracts will not be wholly void, but void in so far as public policy is contravened. The court may therefore sever the illegal part of the contract, leaving the remainder valid provided:

i. The void promise is not substantially the whole consideration given by the party making it.

ii. The contract can be construed as severable without destroying the main substance of what was agreed.

In LOUND v GRIMWADE (**1888**) D, who had committed a fraud making him both criminally and civilly liable, promised to pay P £3,000 if P promised not to take 'any legal proceedings' in respect of the fraud. P's claim for the £3,000 failed as a substantial part of the consideration for the promise to pay it was his own illegal promise to stifle a criminal prosecution.

In GOLDSOLL v GOLDMAN (**1915**) D sold his business in imitation jewellery to P, and agreed that he would not for two years deal in real or imitation jewellery in the UK or specified foreign countries. The restriction was held to be too wide in area, since D had never traded abroad, and in respect of subject matter since he had hardly ever dealt in real jewellery. It was, however, held that the references to foreign countries and real jewellery could be severed, so that D could be restrained from dealing in imitation jewellery in the UK for two years.

CHAPTER 18

Discharge of Contracts

1. There are four ways by which the rights and obligations of the parties may come to an end, namely performance, agreement, frustration and breach.

PERFORMANCE

2. *General Rule*

    a. A person who performs a contract in accordance with its terms is discharged from any further obligations.

    b. If a person's obligation is to pay money, exactly the right amount of cash must be tendered. For example a contract will not be discharged by offering a £20 note in settlement of a £10 debt, because it is not reasonable to compel the other party to provide change. Of course if the creditor provides change without any objection the contract will be discharged. If a debtor pays by cheque, he will not be discharged until the cheque is honoured by his bank.

    c. If a person's obligation is to deliver goods the goods must be tendered at a reasonable hour, not, for example in the middle of the night. The goods must also comply exactly with the contract terms. If the seller tenders too few goods, too many goods, or the right amount of goods mixed with other goods, the buyer may reject all of them because performance is not exact. The same applies if the goods are not packed in accordance with the contract.

    In RE MOORE AND LANDAUER (**1921**) A supplier of tinned fruit agreed to supply the goods in cases containing 30 tins each. When he delivered the goods about one half were packed in cases of 24 tins each. The correct total amount of tins were delivered, and the market value of the goods supplied was unaffected, however, there was a breach of contract (*S.13(1) SALE OF GOODS ACT 1893*) and this entitled the buyer to reject the whole consignment.

    d. Many contracts state the order in which parties must perform their obligations. For example if Fred agrees to work for Abdul for £300 per week, payable in arrears, clearly Abdul need not pay Fred until Fred has done the week's work.

3. *Exceptions.* There are six exceptions to this rule:

    a. *Severable contracts.* Where a contract may be divided into several parts, payments for parts that have been completed can be claimed. Whether a contract is severable or not depends on the intention of the parties. In the absence of evidence as to intention the courts are reluctant to construe the contract so as to require complete performance before any payment becomes due.

In ROBERTS v HAVELOCK (1832) P agreed to repair a ship. The contract did not state when payment was to be made. It was held that P was not bound to complete the repairs before claiming some payment.

b. *Acceptance of part performance.* Where A has accepted the partial performance of B, having an option to reject, a promise to pay is implied and a quantum meruit may be claimed by B. A quantum meruit action is a claim for a percentage of the contract price in direct proportion to the percentage of work done.

In SUMPTER v HEDGES (1898) P agreed to build a house for D for £565. He partially erected the building, doing work to the value of £333. He then stopped the job because he ran out of funds. D, using P's materials that had been left on the site, finished the job himself. P claimed £333 for work done plus the value of his materials used by D. He failed in his claim for the £333 because although D had 'accepted' P's part performance D had no option to reject. It is impossible to reject a half-built house since the status quo cannot be restored. P, however, obtained judgement in respect of his materials that D had used to complete the house.

c. *Prevention of performance.* Where one party is prevented by the other from completely performing the contract he may bring a quantum meruit action to claim for the work done. (See Chapter 19.9.)

In PLANCHE v COLBURN (1831) P agreed to write a book on costume and armour which was to appear in serial form in D's periodical. P was to be paid £100 on completion. After P had done some research, and written some of the book, but before he had completed it, D stopped publishing the periodical. It was held that P had been wrongfully prevented from performing the contract, and he was entitled to a quantum meruit.

d. *Substantial performance.* Where a contract has been substantially performed an action lies for the contract price less a reduction for the deficiencies. This exception only applies when the defect relates to the quality of performance. If the defect concerns quantity, for example of goods supplied, the general rule applies.

In HOENIG v ISAACS (1952) P agreed to decorate and furnish D's flat for £750. The furniture had several defects which could have been made good for £55. D argued that P was only entitled to reasonable remuneration for work done under the contract. The court, however, held that P was entitled to the full contract rate, less the cost of making the defects good, since he had substantially performed the contract.

Contrast BOLTON v MAHADEVA (1972) A plumber agreed to install a central heating system for £560. His work was defective in that the system did not heat adequately and it gave off fumes. The defects cost £174 to repair. The plumber failed in his action to recover the price less a reduction of £174, since he could not be said to have substantially performed the contract. He therefore recovered nothing and the defendant got a £560 heating system for £174. The decision may seem unfair. However, the court must draw the line so as not to encourage bad workmanship. It would also be unfair to allow every workman who did not complete a job to be paid pro rata for work done.

e. Where the *LAW REFORM (FRUSTRATED CONTRACTS) ACT 1943* applies (see below).

f. *Time of performance.* At common law a party who failed to perform his obligations within a given time was in breach of contract. The equitable rule, which now prevails, is that time is only of the essence of the contract if

    i. The parties expressly state, or if

    ii. A party who has been guilty of undue delay is notified by the other party that unless he performs within a reasonable time, the contract will be regarded as broken.

In RICKARDS v OPPENHEIM (1950) a contract for the sale of a car provided for delivery on 20th March. The car was not delivered on that date but the buyer continued to press for delivery. On 29th June he told the seller he must have the car by 25th July at the latest. It was held that the buyer could not have refused delivery merely because the original date had not been met, but he could do so on giving the seller a reasonable time to deliver. Here the notice did give a reasonable time, so the buyer was justified in refusing delivery after 25th July.

4. *Tender of Performance*

a. Where an obligation under a contract is to deliver goods or render services, tender of the goods or services, which is refused, discharges the party tendering from further obligation and entitles him to damages for breach.

b. Where money is tendered it must be 'legal tender' and it must be the exact sum. If such a tender is refused it does not release the debtor from his obligation to pay, but if he is sued he may pay the money into court, and the creditor will have to pay the costs of the action.

c. If the debtor sends money in the post and it is lost he will have to pay again unless

    i. The mode of delivery was requested by the creditor, and

    ii. The debtor took reasonable care.

d. *Appropriation of payments.* When a debtor makes a payment to his creditor which is insufficient to discharge all amounts outstanding, the payment is appropriated as follows:

    i. The debtor may tell the creditor which debt or debts should be discharged by the payment.

    ii. If the debtor does not do this then the creditor may appropriate the payments to debts as he chooses, including statute-barred debts.

iii. If the debtor pays the exact amount of a particular debt, it is presumed that the payment is in discharge of the debt of that amount.

iv. If there is a current account it is presumed that the payments are appropriated to the oldest debts first.

AGREEMENT

5. The basic rule is that an agreement to discharge a contract is binding only if it is by deed, or if it is supported by consideration. It is not necessary for this type of agreement to be reached by means of an offer from one party which is accepted by the other. The legal position depends on whether the discharge is bilateral or unilateral.

6. *Bilateral Discharge.* ie The contract is executory or partly executory on both sides (both parties have obligations outstanding).

   a. The consideration requirement is automatically present since both parties will surrender something of value – ie the right to insist on the other party's performance.

   b. Cases of waiver, ie forbearance, for example of the right to insist on performance at the agreed time, fall within the principle of equitable estoppel established in CENTRAL LONDON PROPERTY TRUST v HIGH TREES HOUSE (1947). Therefore a voluntary concession granted by one party, upon which the other has acted, remains effective (ie binding on the promisor) until it is made clear by reasonable notice that the strict obligations of the contract are to be restored. Note also WILLIAMS v ROFFEY (1990) (Chapter 13.12).

7. *Unilateral Discharge.* ie Only one party has rights to surrender.

   a. Where one party has completely performed his side of the contract, ie it is wholly executed on one side, any release by him of the other party must be by deed, or supported by fresh consideration.

   b. Where there is a release supported by fresh consideration there is said to be 'accord' and 'satisfaction'.

      i. The accord is the agreement by which the obligation is discharged.

      ii. The satisfaction is the consideration which makes the agreement effective.

      iii. The satisfaction may be executory.

8. There are two further ways in which a contract may be discharged by agreement.

   a. *Novation.* For example A owes B £100 and B owes C £100. A agrees to pay C, if C will release B from his obligation to pay him. All three parties must agree to the arrangement.

   b. *Condition subsequent.* Sometimes a clause in a contract will provide for its discharge if a particular event occurs in the future, ie subsequent to the formation of the contract.

FRUSTRATION

9. *The Basis of the Doctrine*

a. The general rule is that if a person contracts to do something he is not discharged if performance proves to be impossible.

In PARADINE v JANE (**1647**) A tenant who was sued for rent pleaded that he had been dispossessed of the land for the last three years by the King's enemies. His plea failed. It was said:

'When a party by his own contract creates a duty or charge upon himself, he is bound to make it good, notwithstanding any accident by inevitable necessity, because he might have provided against it by his contract.'

b. This severe rule is mitigated by the doctrine of frustration, which, if it applies, automatically discharges the contract.

c. In general if an event is to frustrate a contract it must be:

   i.   Not contemplated by the parties when the contract was formed.

   ii. One which makes the contract fundamentally different from the original contract.

   iii. One for which neither party was responsible.

   iv. One which results in a situation to which the parties did not wish originally to be bound.

10. *The Application of the Doctrine.* Frustration occurs:

a. If the whole basis of the contract is the continued existence of a specific thing which is destroyed.

In TAYLOR v CALDWELL (**1863**) D contracted to let a music hall to P for four days. Before the first day the music hall was accidentally burnt down. P claimed damages, but it was held that D was discharged from his obligation when the music hall burned down. The contract was frustrated.

b. If either party to a contract of personal service dies, becomes seriously ill, or is called up for military service.

In CONDOR v BARRON KNIGHTS (**1966**) P was the drummer in a pop group. Owing to illness he was forbidden by his doctor from performing more than a few nights per week. Since the nature of the work required him to be present seven nights a week the contract was held to be frustrated.

c. If the whole basis of the contract is the occurrence of an event which does not occur.

In KRELL v HENRY (**1903**) D hired a flat in Pall Mall for the purpose of viewing the coronation procession of Edward VII, although this was not expressly stated in the contract. He paid £25 at the time of the agreement and was to pay a further £50 two days before the procession was to take place. Before the £50 had been paid the procession was cancelled due to the illness of the King. The contract was held to be frustrated. Performance was not physically impossible, but the court said that frustration was not limited to such cases but included 'the cessation or non-existence of an express condition or state of things going to the root of the contract, and essential to its performance'. P's claim for the balance of £50 therefore failed, as did D's counter-claim for return of the £25 already paid. D's claim would now be subject to the LAW REFORM (FRUSTRATED CONTRACTS) ACT 1943.

Contrast HERNE BAY STEAMBOAT CO v HUTTON (1903). A boat was hired 'for the purpose of viewing the naval review and for a day's cruise round the fleet'. The review was to form part of Edward VII's coronation celebrations, but it was cancelled due to his illness. The fleet was, however, still assembled. The contract was not frustrated, since it was construed merely as a contract for the hire of a boat, which could still be performed even when one of the motives of the hirer was defeated.

The above two cases are very difficult to reconcile. A clue may be found in a passage in one of the judgements from KRELL v HENRY. It was stated that a contract for the hire of a cab to go to Epsom on Derby day would not be frustrated if the Derby was cancelled. The contract would be construed as one to get the passenger to Epsom and not the Derby. In KRELL v HENRY the contract was not construed as one merely to provide a flat since it was extremely unusual for flats to be let by the day for very high rents. Contracts to carry passengers to Epsom are, however, often made on days other than Derby days.

d. If the government prohibits performance of the contract for so long that to maintain it would impose on the parties fundamentally different obligations from those bargained for. All the circumstances are relevant, for example both the duration of the contract and the duration of the interruption.

In TAMPLIN STEAMSHIP CO v ANGLO-MEXICAN PETROL (1916) a ship was requisitioned by the government for use as a troopship. The charterparty under which the ship was hired was for five years, and there were 19 months left to run. The owners claimed that the contract was frustrated so that they, and not the hirers, would obtain the government compensation (which exceeded what they would receive under the charterparty). It was held that the contract was not frustrated since there may have been months during the remaining period during which the ship would be available, and because the charterers were still prepared to pay the agreed price.

e. If the performance of the main object of the contract subsequently becomes illegal.

In BAILY v DE CRESPIGNY (1869) a landlord covenanted that neither he nor his successors in title would permit building on a paddock which adjoined the land let. The paddock was then compulsorily acquired for a railway, and a station was built. It was held that the landlord was not liable for breach of the covenant because it was impossible for him to secure performance of it.

11. *The Limits to the Doctrine*

a.   A contract is not frustrated if it becomes unexpectedly more expensive or burdensome to one of the parties. If the contract is to be discharged performance must become 'radically different'.

In DAVIS CONTRACTORS V FAREHAM UDC (1956) P agreed to build 78 houses at a price of £94,000 in 8 months. Labour shortages caused the work to take 22 months at a cost to P of £115,000. P wished to claim that the contract was frustrated so that they could then claim for their work on a quantum meruit. Lord Radcliffe, however, said that hardship, material loss, or inconvenience did not amount to frustration, the obligation must change such that the thing undertaken would, if performed, be a different thing from that contracted for.

b.   A party cannot rely on a self-induced frustration, ie frustration due to his own conduct.

   i.   The doctrine of frustration clearly does not protect a person whose own breach is actually the frustrating event.

   In THE EUGENIA (1964) a charterer in breach of contract ordered a ship into a war zone. The ship was detained. It was held that the charterer could not rely on the detention as a ground for frustration.

   ii.   Deliberate failure to perform a condition precedent may not amount to a self-induced frustration. In each case the position must be determined in accordance with the proper construction of the contract.

   In GYLLEHAMMER V SOURBRODOGRADEVNA INDUSTRILA (1989) the parties had an outline agreement for the construction of a bulk carrier. The contract was subject to several conditions precedent (ie conditions that had to be complied with before the contract could be regarded as valid). One of these provided that the contract would be void if the shipbuilders did not obtain bank performance guarantees. When it appeared that a change in economic climate would render the building uneconomic, the shipbuilders did not seek the relevant guarantees. They then argued that their absence rendered the contract void. The purchasers claimed that it was not open to the other party to frustrate the inception of a contract by failing to take steps to allow conditions precedent to be fulfilled. The court held that this was not the case. It was clear that there would be no contract in the absence of bank guarantees and that their absence could be pleaded by the shipbuilders, whatever the reason for that absence.

   iii.   It is probable that negligence prevents a party claiming frustration. Thus if the fire in TAYLOR V CALDWELL had been started due to the defendant's negligence their plea of frustration would have failed.

c.   Frustration will not apply where the parties have expressly provided for a contingency which has occurred. It is a means by which risk is allocated, and loss apportioned in circumstances which neither party has foreseen.

12. *The Effect of Frustration*

    a.   The contract is discharged automatically as to the future, but it is not made void from the beginning.

    b.   At common law the loss lay where it fell, ie money paid before the frustration could not be recovered (KRELL v HENRY (1903)) and money payable before the frustration remained payable, unless there was a total failure of consideration.

        In FIBROSA v FAIRBAIRN (1942) a purchaser of machinery for £4,800 paid £1,000 on placing the order. The machinery was to be delivered in Poland. Shortly after the contract was made war broke out and Poland was occupied by Germany. It was therefore impossible to deliver the machinery. The plaintiff succeeded in his action to recover the £1,000 since he had received absolutely nothing in return for his £1,000, ie there was a total failure of consideration.

    c.   The position is now governed by *THE LAW REFORM (FRUSTRATED CONTRACTS) ACT 1943* whereby

        i.   Money paid before the frustrating event is recoverable and money payable before the frustrating event ceases to be payable, but if one party has incurred expenses the court may allow him to retain or be paid an amount not exceeding the amount of the expenses.

        ii.   If one party has obtained a valuable benefit (other than money) because of something done by the other party in performance of the contract, he can be ordered to pay a just sum for it, not exceeding the amount of the benefit.

BREACH

13. *Definition.* Breach occurs:

    a.   If a party fails to perform one of his obligations under a contract, for example he does not perform on the agreed date, or he delivers goods of inferior quality, or

    b.   If a party, before the date fixed for performance, indicates that he will not perform on the agreed date. This is an anticipatory breach.

14. *Effect of Breach.* Breach does not automatically discharge the contract

    a.   Breach of warranty only entitles the innocent party to damages.

    b.   Breach of condition entitles the innocent party to damages, and gives him an option to treat the contract as subsisting or discharged.

15. *Affirmation of the Breach*

    a.   If the innocent party elects to treat the contract as still subsisting, and can complete his side without the co-operation of the other, he is entitled to do so, and claim the whole sum due under the contract.

In WHITE AND CARTER (COUNCILS) v MCGREGOR (1961) P agreed to advertise D's business for three years on plates attached to litterbins. D repudiated the contract on the same day that it was made. P nevertheless manufactured and displayed the plates as originally agreed, and claimed the full amount due under the contract. A majority of the House of Lords upheld the claim, their reason being that a repudiation does not, of itself, bring the contract to an end. Its effect is to give the innocent party a choice of whether or not to determine the contract. If he chooses to affirm the contract it remains in full effect.

b. Affirmation does not of itself exclude a finding of reasonableness in relation to any exemption clause S.9(2) UNFAIR CONTRACT TERMS ACT 1977. This prevents the court being forced into a situation where it would feel compelled to find an exemption clause unreasonable, so as not to exclude an innocent party's remedies when he had affirmed a contract that he could have terminated.

16. *Termination*

a. If the innocent party elects to end the contract he is not bound to accept further performance, and he may sue for damages at once.

b. Where if it is to be valid, an exemption clause has to satisfy the requirement of reasonableness, it may be found to do so, and be given effect, even though the contract has been terminated by the innocent party. S.9(1) UNFAIR CONTRACT TERMS ACT 1977, ie a valid termination of a contract does not terminate an exemption clause. Clearly if it did exemption clauses would be useless in every case of a breach which entitled the innocent party to end the contract.

17. *Anticipatory Breach*

a. Where there is an anticipatory breach, and the innocent party elects to treat the contract as discharged, he can sue for damages at once.

In HOCHSTER v DE LA TOUR (1853) D agreed to employ P as a courier for three months commencing on 1st June. Before this date D told P that his services would not be required. This was to be an anticipatory breach of contract, and it entitled P to sue for damages immediately.

This decision could lead to difficulties, especially if the trial takes place before the date fixed for performance. For example if X contracts to deliver goods to Y in two years time, and then indicates that he does not intend to perform, Y's damages are in general quantified by reference to the market price at the time fixed for performance. Clearly if the trial takes place before this date the market price cannot be known.

b. If the innocent party elects to treat the contract as still subsisting, he keeps it alive for the benefit of both parties, so that frustration may intervene to release the party at fault from further liability.

In AVERY v BOWDEN (1855) D chartered a ship from P to carry goods from Odessa. The charter allowed 45 days for loading. During this period D's agent told the captain (P's agent) that he had no cargo and that he would be wise to leave. The captain, however, remained in Odessa and pressed for performance. Before the 45 days had expired the Crimean War broke out and frustrated the contract. If P had accepted D's anticipatory breach immediately he could have sued for damages. Since he did not do so, he kept the contract alive for the benefit of both parties, so the frustration operated to relieve D from liability. P's claim for damages therefore failed.

 c. The doctrine of anticipatory breach is important because

  i. It helps to minimise the total loss, because if the plaintiff could not sue immediately he would be more likely to keep himself available for performance. Whereas, since he may sue at once he has an incentive to abandon the contract and avoid the extra loss that he might have suffered had he waited.

  ii. It protects a person who has paid in advance for future performance. It would be unfair if such a person could not sue until the time fixed for performance, since his advance payment may have reduced his ability to make an alternative contract.

18. *Instalment Contracts.* If in an instalment contract there is a breach with regard to one or some instalments the main tests as to whether the breach entitles the innocent party to treat the contract as at an end are

 a. The ratio that the breach bears to the contract as a whole, and

 b. The degree of probability that the breach will be repeated.

In MAPLE FLOCK CO V UNIVERSAL FURNITURE PRODUCTS (**1934**) the contract provided for 100 tons of rag flock to be delivered in instalments of $1\frac{1}{2}$ tons at the rate of three instalments a week. The sixteenth instalment was defective and the buyers claimed to be entitled to rescind. Their claim failed mainly because the single instalment was a small quantity when compared with the contract as a whole.

CHAPTER 19

Remedies for Breach of Contract

1. There are both common law and equitable remedies for breach of contract. The common law remedies are damages, an action for an agreed sum, and a quantum meruit claim. The equitable remedies are specific performance and injunction. By far the most commonly sought remedy is damages.

DAMAGES

2. A claim for damages raises two questions

   a. For what kind of damage should the plaintiff be compensated? ie Remoteness of damage.

   b. What monetary compensation should the plaintiff receive in respect of damage which is not too remote? ie Measure of damages.

3. Note carefully the distinction between damage and damages. Damage is the loss suffered by the plaintiff. Damages are the financial compensation awarded to him. It is very important to use the correct word. For example 'Remoteness of damages' is a meaningless phrase.

4. *Remoteness of Damage*

   a. Damage is not too remote if it is

   'such as may fairly and reasonably be considered either as arising naturally, ie according to the usual course of things from the breach itself, or such as may reasonably be supposed to have been in the contemplation of both parties at the time they made the contract, as the probable result of the breach'.

   In HADLEY v BAXENDALE (1854) P's mill shaft broke and had to be sent to the makers at Greenwich to serve as a pattern for a replacement. D agreed to transport the shaft to Greenwich, but in breach of contract delayed delivery causing several days loss of production at the mill. P claimed £300 in respect of lost profit. Alderson B stated the rule quoted and applied it as follows:

   i. The loss did not arise naturally since D could not foresee that his delay would stop the mill. It was quite possible that P might have had a spare shaft or been able to get one.

    ii.   The loss could not have been contemplated by both parties at the time of the contract as the probable result of the breach. If D had been told that delay would stop the mill such loss would have been in his contemplation and he may then have sought to limit his liability, however, he did not have this information.

b.   The above rule can be analysed into two parts, briefly summarised as loss 'naturally arising' and loss 'in the contemplation of both parties…as the probable result of the breach'. An example of the application of the first part is PINNOCK v LEWIS (1923). The distinction between the two parts is illustrated by PILKINGTON v WOOD (1953).

In PINNOCK v LEWIS (1923) the seller of poisonous cattle food was held liable for the loss of the cattle to which it was fed. This loss arose naturally from his breach.

In PILKINGTON v WOOD (1953) P bought a house in Hampshire, his solicitor, D, failing to notice that the title was defective. D was held liable for the difference between the value of the house with good title and with defective title – this was loss 'naturally arising'. However, P's job shortly moved to Lancashire and he wished to sell his house. The defective title made the sale difficult and meant that P was delayed in paying off his bank overdraft out of the sale proceeds. D was held not liable for this additional loss as he could not have anticipated that P would shortly want to move, nor did he know that P had an overdraft, ie the loss was not, and could not reasonably be supposed to have been in his contemplation.

c.   HADLEY v BAXENDALE, broadly speaking, represents the law today. It was considered by the House of Lords in KOUFOS v CZARNIKOW (1969) when all five law lords approved the rule, although saying that the loss must be contemplated as 'a real danger' or 'a serious possibility' rather than as 'the probable result of the breach'.

In KOUFOS v CZARNIKOW (1969) a ship was chartered to carry sugar from Constanza to Basrah. The charterer intended to sell the sugar immediately on its arrival. The ship owner did not know this, but he did know that there was a market for sugar at Basrah. In breach of contract the ship owner deviated and arrived nine days late during which time the market value of the sugar had fallen by about £4,000. The House of Lords unanimously upheld P's claim for this amount, approving the rule in HADLEY v BAXENDALE subject to the qualifications mentioned above. The case is interesting in that although there was a roughly equal chance of the price of sugar rising or falling, the fact that it fell was nevertheless foreseeable as 'a serious possibility'.

d.   When the breach of contract consists of failure to pay a sum of money the general rule is that only the sum of money, not interest or damages can be recovered (LONDON, CHATHAM AND DOVER RAILWAY v SOUTH EASTERN RAILWAY (1893)). This rule is considered to be unsatisfactory and there are a number of exceptions. In particular it does not apply to claims for special damages under the second limb of the rule in HADLEY v BAXENDALE. For example:

In INTERNATIONAL MINERALS AND CHEMICALS CORPORATION v HELM (1986) a debt was due to be paid to an American plaintiff in Belgian francs.

Between the due date and the judgement date the value of Belgian francs as against US dollars had fallen by 40%. It was held that the loss was recoverable since D knew that such a loss was not an improbable consequence of their default.

e. Note that the contract and tort tests for remoteness differ. In tort the loss must be the 'reasonably foreseeable' result of the tort. The tort test is therefore more generous to the plaintiff.

5. Measure of Damages

a. The general rule is that the plaintiff recovers his actual loss (in respect of damage which is not too remote). ie He is placed in the same position as if the contract had been performed. Therefore in assessing damages for breach of contract to pay a pension, or up to £10,000 damages for wrongful dismissal (INCOME AND CORPORATION TAXES ACT 1970, as amended), regard must be had to the plaintiff's liability to taxation.

b. SECTIONS 50 AND 51 SALE OF GOODS ACT 1979 provide respectively that in an action for damages for non-acceptance or non-delivery, where there is an available market, the measure of damages is the difference between the contract price and the market price on the date fixed for acceptance or delivery or, if no date was fixed, at the time of refusal to accept or deliver. The provisions of these two sections are only prima facie rules and may not be applied if they would not indemnify the plaintiff for his loss.

In THOMPSON V ROBINSON GUNMAKERS (1955) D purchased a 'Standard Vanguard' car from P and later refused to accept delivery of it. P's profit on the sale would have been £61, but D argued that they were not liable for this amount, since the profit would still be made when the car was sold to another customer. The court rejected this argument since the supply of this model exceeded the demand. Therefore if P had found another customer he could have sold a car to him in addition to selling a car to D.

Contrast CHARTER V SULLIVAN (1957) D refused to accept delivery of a 'Hillman Minx' car that he had bought from P. P claimed £97 15s loss of profits. In contrast with the above case his claim failed, because the demand for Hillman Minx cars exceeded the supply. He could therefore sell every car that he could obtain from the makers and had accordingly not lost a sale.

c. In assessing the award of damages the court may take into account inconvenience and annoyance.

In JARVIS V SWAN TOURS (1973) P paid £63 for a two week winter sports holiday. It differed vastly from what was advertised. There was very little holiday atmosphere, the hotel staff did not speak English, and in the second week he was the only guest at the hotel. P recovered £125 damages for his upset and annoyance due to having his holiday spoilt.

d. The defence of contributory negligence under the LAW REFORM (CONTRIBUTORY NEGLIGENCE) ACT 1945 (Chapter 24.9) cannot be used to justify a proportionate reduction in damages for breach of contract (BASILDON

DISTRICT COUNCIL v LESSER (1984)). However, the plaintiff's negligence may result in his claim being defeated.

In LAMBERT v LEWIS (1982) P used a trailer coupling after realising that it was clearly defective. This negligent action relieved the supplier from contractual liability for the loss that occurred as a result of the ensuing accident.

6. *Mitigation*

a. The above rules are subject to the limitation that the plaintiff must do what is reasonable to mitigate his loss, and cannot recover any part of it which the defendant can prove has resulted from failure to mitigate, ie the plaintiff cannot recover for a loss that he ought to have avoided.

In DARBISHIRE v WARREN (1963) P owned a car of which he was particularly proud. Although it was old he maintained it in excellent condition. It had a market value of about £85. The car was damaged by D's negligence and P was advised it would cost him £192 to get it repaired. P went ahead with the repairs and claimed £192 from D (less the money he had received from his insurance company, and plus the cost of hiring a car while the repairs were carried out). His claim failed. The court held that the expenditure on repairs was not justified. P should have mitigated his loss by buying a replacement vehicle on the open market.

b. WHITE AND CARTER (COUNCILS) v MCGREGOR (1961) (Chapter 18.15) illustrates that mitigation is only relevant to a claim for damages and not to a claim for an agreed sum.

7. *Liquidated Damages and Penalties*

a. Where no provision for damages is made in the contract then the court will assess the damages payable. These are unliquidated damages. However, the courts recognise that within the basic right of freedom to contract there is a right to specify the damages to be paid in the event of a breach. Equity, however, gives relief in circumstances where this right is abused by a party who has attempted to take an unfair advantage of his stronger bargaining position.

b. Where the parties have agreed in a contract how much is to be payable on a breach, this sum is recoverable if it is liquidated damages, ie a genuine pre-estimate of the loss, but not if it is a penalty, ie an amount fixed as a threat to prevent a breach.

c. Where it is a penalty the plaintiff can only recover his actual loss in respect of damage which is not too remote.

In LAMDON TRUST v HURRELL (1955) D purchased a car from P on hire-purchase. The hire-purchase price was £558. After he had paid £302 D defaulted and P re-possessed the car, and resold it for £270. A provision in the hire-purchase agreement provided that if it was terminated due to a hirer's default, the hirer must pay as compensation the difference between the sums paid (in this case £302) and £425, ie £123. Since P had already received £572 for the car (£302 plus £270), D objected to their claim for

£123. The court held that the compensation clause was a penalty and since P had already received more than the original price of the car D was not liable to pay him any more compensation. The effect of P's clause could be more vividly seen if D had defaulted after payment of £10. D could have claimed £415 under their compensation clause and resold the car probably for at least £500, giving them a total compensation of £915. Clearly this is not a genuine estimate of loss.

d. Whether a particular sum is liquidated damages or a penalty depends on the parties' intentions. The words used by the parties are not conclusive evidence of intention, the courts will look at the following tests

   i. Is the sum stipulated extravagant in comparison with the greatest loss which could have followed from the breach? If so it is a penalty.

   In KEMBLE v FARREN (**1829**), an actor's contract provided that if either he or the theatre management broke their contract then the party in breach must pay the other £1,000 as 'liquidated damages'. This was held to be a penalty clause because it was disproportionate both to the actor's daily fee of £3 6s 8d, and to the greatest possible loss that would result from the breach.

   ii. Where a lump sum is payable on the occurrence of certain events, some of which are serious and some of which are not, the lump sum is presumed to be a penalty, but where a precise estimate of the consequences of the breach is impossible the court may regard the lump sum as a genuine pre-estimate.

   In DUNLOP PNEUMATIC TYRE CO v NEW GARAGE AND MOTOR CO (**1915**) P offered a trade discount to dealers who promised:

   a) not to sell below certain list prices;

   b) not to supply certain named persons;

   c) not to exhibit any of the goods; and

   d) to pay £5 'by way of liquidated damages and not as a penalty' for each breach of the agreement. This clause was held to be enforceable since £5 was not an excessive figure to place on a breach the actual loss from which would be impossible to forecast.

In ARISTON v CHARLY (**1990**) P agreed to manufacture records and print sleeves for D. D entrusted P with certain metal parts, artwork, label information, negatives and lacquer necessary for the work. Since this equipment was valuable the contract provided that if P did not return the items within 10 days of D's request they would pay a penalty of £600 per day for late delivery. Following a request P returned most of the equipment within the required time. The action was commenced by P claiming amounts outstanding on their invoices, D counter-claimed £600 per day for failure to return the equipment. It was held that the clause was unenforcable because it was a penalty. £600 per day may have been a reasonable estimate of loss resulting from the failure to return all of the equipment, but under the clause the same amount was payable even if only one item were retained. It was not therefore a reasonable pre-estimate of the loss.

OTHER COMMON LAW REMEDIES

8. *Action for an Agreed Sum.* A contract will often provide for the payment by one party of an agreed sum in exchange for performance by the other, for example goods sold for a fixed price. Provided the duty to pay the price has arisen the innocent party may sue the contract breaker for the agreed sum. Such action is different from an action for damages, since the plaintiff recovers the agreed sum, neither more nor less. Therefore questions of remoteness and measure cannot arise.

9. *Quantum Meruit*

Where either work has been done or accepted under a void contract or where one party abandons a contract (as in PLANCHE v COLBURN (1831), Chapter 18.3) the injured party, instead of claiming damages, may claim payment for what has been done under the contract. This is known as a *quantum meruit* claim. Quantum meruit means 'how much it is worth'. The claim is not based on the original contract, but on an implied promise by the other party arising from the acceptance of executed consideration.

EQUITABLE REMEDIES

10. *Specific Performance.* Specific performance is a decree issued by the court which orders the defendant to carry out his obligations. It is a remedy which

   a. Is discretionary, although the discretion must be exercised within well established principles.

   b. Is not normally awarded if damages would be an adequate remedy. It is most likely to be awarded in contracts for the sale of land.

   c. Must be available to either party. Thus it is not available to an infant in respect of a contract not enforceable against him.

   d. Is not available in respect of certain types of contract, such as those requiring personal services, for example as a butler, or contracts which require extensive supervision, for example building contracts.

11. *Injunction*

   a. A *mandatory injunction* orders a person to take action to undo a breach of contract. For example he may be ordered to take down an advertising sign erected in breach of contract.

b. A *prohibitory injunction* is an order of the court which prohibits a person from doing something. Such an injunction could be granted to prevent the breach of a reasonable restraint of trade clause.

In WARNER BROTHERS v NELSON (**1937**) D, an actress, agreed to act for P and undertook that she would not act for anyone else during the period of the agreement without P's written consent. It was held that she could be restrained by an injunction from breaking this undertaking. This did not of course force her to act for P, nor did it prevent her from obtaining different types of work.

c. A *Mareva injunction* orders a defendant not to remove specified assets from the jurisdiction of the English courts. It is a temporary injunction granted when a case is pending in court, its purpose being to prevent the defendant from nullifying the effect of a judgement which the plaintiff is likely to obtain. It is therefore ancilliary to other proceedings which must have been commenced by the time the injunction is granted. The name 'Mareva injunction' derives from the case of MAREVA COMPANIA NAVIERA v INTERNATIONAL BULK CARRIERS (**1975**), but it is now granted by virtue of *S.37 SUPREME COURT ACT 1981*.

d. An *Anton Pillar injunction* authorises the inspection, photographing, custody or removal of documents or property.

In ANTON PILLER v MANUFACTURING PROCESSES (**1976**) such an injunction was granted when a manufacturer of computer components feared that his agent would pass on confidential information to a competitor.

The injunctions are now granted by virtue of *S.33 SUPREME COURT ACT 1981*. They will only be granted in exceptional circumstances, the inspection or removal normally being carried out by the applicant's solicitor, accompanied by police officers.

12. Rescission and rectification are also equitable remedies. They were discussed in Chapter 17.

LIMITATION OF ACTIONS

13. The *LIMITATION ACT 1980* lays down periods of six years for a simple contract, and 12 years for a deed. Time runs from the date when the breach occurred and failure to discover the breach does not usually stop time running. There are two exceptions to this rule:

a. Where the action is based on the fraud of the defendant, or the breach is concealed by the fraud of the defendant.

In LYNN v BAMBER (**1930**) P bought plum trees from D that were warranted to be 'purple pershores'. Seven years later he discovered they were not purple pershores and sued for damages. D pleaded that the action was statute barred. P succeeded because D's fraudulent misrepresentation and concealment of the breach of warranty were a good defence to the plea that the action was statute barred.

b.   Where the action is for relief from the consequences of a mistake.

In PECO ARTS v HAZLITT GALLERY (1983) P purchased a drawing from D in 1970 for $18,000. In 1976 it was revalued by an expert for insurance purposes. In 1981 it was discovered that the drawing was a fake. P alleged that the contract was a void for mistake and claimed rescission and recovery of the purchase price plus interest. D's only defence was the LIMITATION ACT. It was held that they could succeed since there was no lack of diligence on their part, ie they could not have been expected to obtain independent authentication at the time of purchase and they were entitled to conclude that it was original, since no doubts had been cast upon it at the time of the 1976 valuation.

This case does not contradict LEAF v INTERNATIONAL GALLERIES (1950) (Chapter 17.9b) since Peco's case concerned the time limit for claiming relief from the consequences of an operative mistake, whereas Leaf's case was concerned with lapse of time following an innocent misrepresentation.

c.   When there is fraud or mistake time runs from when the fraud or mistake was, or ought to have been, discovered, whichever is the earlier.

14. If at the time the cause of action accrued the plaintiff was a minor or a mentally disordered person, the action must be commenced within six years of the cessation of the disability. Provided there is no interval between two disabilities, for example the minor becomes mentally ill, then the two disabilities can be added together. However, if the disabilities are separated by an interval time will not be stopped from running by the second disability.

15. Where a claim is made for a contract debt time starts running afresh if before, or after, the limitation period has expired:

a.   A written acknowledgement of the debt is given by the debtor to the creditor, or

b.   A payment of part of the debt is made.

The LIMITATION ACT does not apply to equitable remedies, but the maxim 'delay defeats equity' may apply.

In POLLARD v CLAYTON (1855) D agreed to sell P all the coal that he raised from a particular mine. In breach of the agreement he sold the coal elsewhere and 11 months later P sought specific performance of the contract. It was held that the right to this equitable remedy was barred by the unreasonable length of time that had elapsed since the breach.

CHAPTER 20

Privity of Contract

1. ***The Basic Rule.*** The common law doctrine of privity of contract states that no one can sue or be sued on a contract to which he is not a party. This was clearly illustrated in the following two House of Lords' decisions.

In SCRUTTONS v MIDLAND SILICONES (**1962**) A shipping company agreed to carry drums of chemicals belonging to P from America to England, the contract limiting their liability to $500 per drum. The shipping company hired a firm of stevedores (D) to unload the ship, and due to D's negligence the chemicals were damaged to the value of $1,800 per drum. P were successful in their tort action against D, recovering their full loss. The court held that D could not rely on the exemption clause in the contract between P and the shipping company because they were not a party to this contract, nor were they protected by a similar exemption clause in their contract with the shipping company because P were not a party to this contract.

In BESWICK v BESWICK (**1967**) A Mr Beswick (B) entered into an agreement with his nephew (also Mr Beswick), the defendant in this case (D), whereby D was to take over B's business in return for a payment of £6.50 per week to B during his life, and after his death £5 per week to his widow. When B died D stopped the payments. B's widow sued D both in her personal capacity and in her capacity as administratix of his estate. She failed in her personal capacity, but succeeded as administratix and was awarded a decree of specific performance against D.

If a person dies leaving a will he will name an executor in the will. If a person leaves no will his affairs will be handled by an administrator who is usually his nearest relative. A female administrator is called an administratix.

2. *Exceptions*

   a. *Statutory exceptions*

      i. The MARRIED WOMAN'S PROPERTY ACT 1882 provides that a man (or woman) may insure his (or her) life for the benefit of his wife (or husband) and children. On his death the insurance company becomes a trustee of the money due to his wife, and she as a beneficiary may sue to recover it, although she was not a party to the insurance contract.

      ii. The ROAD TRAFFIC ACT 1972 provides that in certain cases an injured third party may proceed directly against the insurance company.

      iii. The BILLS OF EXCHANGE ACT 1882 provides that certain persons who come into possession of a cheque may sue the drawer of the cheque, even though they have no contract with him.

b. *Equitable exceptions.* Occasionally equity may confer a benefit on a third party by using the device of an implied trust.

In GREGORY AND PARKER v WILLIAMS (**1817**) P, who owed money to both G and W, agreed with W to transfer his property to him if W would pay his (P's) debt due to G. The property was duly transferred but W refused to pay G. The common law doctrine of privity prevented G from suing on the contract between P and W. Equity, however, held that P could be regarded as a trustee for G, and that G could therefore bring an action, jointly with P against W.

c. *Covenants*

i.   At common law the assignee of a lease takes it with the benefits of, and subject to the burdens of, the assignor. Although there is no contract between the lessor and the assignee there is 'privity of estate' and the assignee may therefore sue and be sued by the lessor.

ii. In equity the case of TULK v MOXHAY (**1848**) established that restrictive covenants run with the land, ie a purchaser is bound by a covenant entered into by a previous owner if he has notice of the covenant.

iii. Distinguish covenants in leases, which may be positive, eg to pay rent, or negative, for example not to keep a dog, from restrictive covenants which may apply to freehold land, for example not to build within fifteen feet of the road.

d. *Assignment*

i.   A party can assign or transfer to another person the rights contained in the contract, but cannot, without the consent of the other person, assign the burden of his contractual obligations.

ii. By *S.136 LAW OF PROPERTY ACT 1925* a legal assignment must be in writing and signed by the assignor. The whole of the interest must be transferred to the assignee and written notice must be given to the other party.

iii. Rights that are highly personal to the original parties, for example those arising from a contract of service, cannot be assigned without the consent of the other party to the contract.

e. *Resale price agreements.* Where a resale price agreement has been approved under provisions in the *RESALE PRICES ACT 1976* a supplier of goods may bring an action to enforce a minimum resale price against a person who was not a party to a contract with the supplier. Such resale price agreements are comparatively rare.

f. *Collateral contracts*

i.   A collateral contract arises when a promise that is not part of the main contract is nevertheless part of another contract related to the same subject matter.

ii. The usual situation is that a person (A) is persuaded by the statement of another (B) to enter into a contract with a third party (C). The main contract will be between A and C. The collateral contract will be between A and B based upon B's statements.

In SHANKLIN PIER v DETEL PRODUCTS (1951) P hired contractors (X) to paint Shanklin Pier. They specified that X use paint to be purchased from D, because D had assured P that the paint would last seven to 10 years. X purchased and used the paint but it only lasted three months. P successfully sued D on the basis of their assurance that the paint would last seven years even though the contract for the sale of the paint was from D to X. It was held that there was a collateral contract between P and D. The consideration given by P was that they caused X to make the contract with D.

The same principle applies when a person buys goods and is given a manufacturer's guarantee. The basic contract is between the customer and the retailer but the guarantee amounts to a collateral contract between the customer and the manufacturer.

3. *Conclusion*

a. The case of BESWICK v BESWICK is important because in the Court of Appeal the doctrine of privity was challenged by Lord Denning. He had said that the widow could also sue in her own right because the doctrine of privity was 'at bottom...only a rule of procedure' and could be overcome if the intended beneficiary joined the promisee in the action. The House of Lords did not consider it necessary to comment on this view since they already had sufficient reason to find the widow's favour. However, the speeches all assume the correctness of the generally accepted view that a contract can only be enforced by the parties to it. Thus in BESWICK v BESWICK the House of Lords affirmed the continued existence of the doctrine of privity in the face of critics who have suggested that a remedy should be provided for a party who has been given specific rights under a contract, and despite Lord Denning's attempt to give effect to this suggestion.

b. Privity has also been criticised by the Law Commission. In 1991 the Commission proposed that the general rule that a third party cannot acquire rights under a contract to which he is not a party should be substantially amended by Parliament. One possible reform would be to allow a third party to sue whenever a contract happens to benefit them. However, the Commission rejects this as too wide. Its basic recommendation is that a third party should be allowed to bring an action where the parties to the contract intend to confer an *enforceable legal obligation* (not merely a benefit). This could be expressly stated or implied from the circumstances. It would not be necessary for the beneficiary to be named, although doing so would reduce doubts both over the identity of beneficiaries and the desire to create an enforceable benefit.

Pressure for reform has resulted in the *CONTRACTS (RIGHTS OF THIRD PARTIES) ACT 1999* being enacted. The Act, whilst retaining the principle of privity, gives, in certain circumstances, the right to third parties (outsiders to the agreement) to enforce the contract. *S.1* lays down two circumstances where this will occur:

i.   where the contract expressly so provides;

ii. where a term of the contract purports to give a benefit to the third party and, upon a proper construction of the contract, the parties did not intend that it be not enforceable by the third party. This means that a presumption of third party enforceability will arise where, under the contract, a clear benefit is to be bestowed upon a person, unless evidence can be produced to rebut the presumption.

The Section goes on to require that the third party must be expressly identified in the contract. Where the Act is found to apply, the third party has the same remedies as would be available if she/he had entered the contract personally; this will include the ability to seek benefits from any exclusion clauses.

The proposals if enacted would meet many of the criticisms of the present situation and would have been likely to have led to a different outcome in most of the leading cases, including BESWICK v BESWICK.

Coursework Questions 8–16 (for answers see pages 651–62)

(for answers see pages 651–62)

THE LAW OF CONTRACT

Typical Exam Questions

8. In relation to contract law distinguish between offers and invitations to treat and explain why it is important to make such a distinction.

(10 marks)

ACCA June 2004

9. In the law of contract describe the rules relating to:

   (a) remoteness of damage;   (5 marks)

   (b) the measure of damages.   (5 marks)

(10 marks)

ACCA June 2004

10. Explain how the law determines whether negotiating parties have reached agreement.

(15 marks)

CIMA 2002

11. In what circumstances will frustration discharge a contract?

(20 marks)

ICSA November 2004

Multiple choice questions:

12. a. The vast majority of contracts are 'simple'. What is the meaning of the word 'simple' in this context?

   A   The terms of the contract are set out in writing.

   B   The contract does not need to be in any particular form to be binding.

   C   The contract contains fewer than ten provisions.

   D   The contract is not supported by consideration.

b. A Ltd placed the following advertisement in a local newspaper:

'*We are able to offer for sale a number of portable colour television sets at the specially reduced price of £5.90. Order now while stocks last.*'

The advertisement contained a mistake in that the television sets should have been priced at £59.00. B Ltd immediately placed an order for 100 television sets.

Which ONE of the following statements is *correct*?

A B Ltd has accepted an offer and is contractually entitled to the 100 television sets.

B A Ltd can refuse to supply B Ltd as the advertisement is not an offer, but an invitation to treat.

C A Ltd can only refuse to sell the television sets to B Ltd if it has sold all its stock.

D As B Ltd has not yet paid for the television sets, the company has no contractual right to them.

c. Which ONE of the following statements is *correct*?

A If a person signs a contract, he/she is bound by all its terms.

B A contract which has not been signed is not binding on any of the parties.

C A person who signs a contract is deemed to have read it.

D A person who has not read a contract cannot be bound by it.

d. Which ONE of the following statements is *correct*?

A If the creditor agrees to accept less than the full amount due, the debt is discharged at common law.

B At common law, a creditor who has agreed to accept less than the full amount due, may go back on his word and recover the balance.

C Payment of less than the full amount due by a third party cannot discharge the whole debt.

D Payment of less than the amount due cannot discharge the whole debt, even if made early at the request of the creditor.

e. Which ONE of the following is *not* an equitable remedy?

A Damages.

B Specific performance.

C Rescission.

D Injunction.

f. Which of the following statements is *correct*?

i. As a general rule, a contract will only be discharged if all its terms have been precisely performed.

ii. If a contract becomes impossible to perform through no fault of either contracting party, the contract is frustrated and unenforceable, unless its terms provide for the frustrating event.

A (i) only. **B** (ii) only. **C** Neither (i) nor (ii). **D** Both (i) and (ii).

g. In breach of contract, C Ltd refused to sell a motor car to D Ltd at the agreed price of £10,000. If the type of motor car is readily available on the market at a price of £9,000, which ONE of the following is *correct*?

A D Ltd is entitled to an order of specific performance, forcing C Ltd to carry out its contract.

B D Ltd is entitled to damages of £1,000.

C D Ltd is entitled to nominal damages only.

D D Ltd is not entitled to damages.

CIMA November 2001

Other sample questions:

13. a. What must a plaintiff prove in order to satisfy a court that he has been induced to enter into a contract as a result of a misrepresentation? If he succeeds, what remedies will then be available to him?

(14 marks)

b. Whilst negotiating to sell his business to Ivan, Henry made a true statement which gave total figures for turnover and profits for the previous five years. This created an impression that the business was in a healthy state. Henry did not disclose, nor did Ivan request, a breakdown of figures which would have revealed a steady decline in profitability over this period. Ivan, having purchased the business, discovered the true state of affairs.

What remedies, if any, does Ivan have?

(6 marks)

(**20 marks**)

14. a. In what circumstances will mistake prevent the formation of a valid contract?

(12 marks)

b. Victoria offers two expensive cars for sale and John and Mary call in response to the advertisement. John says that he is a well-known businessman, agrees to buy the first car and gives Victoria a cheque for the purchase price. Mary says that she merely wishes to hire the second car for a forthcoming event. Victoria agrees, accepts a cheque for the hire price and signs, without reading, what she believes to be a contract of hire; it is, in fact, a contract of sale. Both John and Mary are then allowed to drive away the cars.

The cheques have now been dishonoured and Victoria seeks your advice. Advise her as to whether she may claim ownership of the cars.

(8 marks)

(20 marks)

15. a. When, if ever, does payment of a smaller sum discharge a debt owed to a creditor?

(10 marks)

   b. D owned a fleet of lorries.

   i. He agreed with E to deliver E's grain to his warehouse. E then asked D to deliver the grain to a different destination 50 miles away, and offered him extra remuneration. E did not pay the extra remuneration.

   ii. He agreed with F to deliver F's steel to G. G agreed to assist D with unloading the steel. When the steel was delivered G refused this assistance.

   Advise D.

(10 marks)

(20 marks)

16. Explain how the courts and Parliament have sought to limit the effect of exclusion clauses in the law of contract

(20 marks)

PART III

THE LAW OF TORTS

CHAPTER 21

The Nature of a Tort

1. A tort cannot be defined by reference to a particular act or omission. It is only possible to define it by reference to the origin of the rule and the legal consequences of its breach. Professor Winfield stated that 'Tortious liability arises from the breach of a duty primarily fixed by law: such duty is towards persons generally and its breach is redressible by an action for unliquidated damages.' (Unliquidated damages are damages determined by the court, and not previously agreed by the parties.)

2. The law of tort deals with a wide variety of wrongs, for example

   a. Intentionally or negligently causing physical injury to another (trespass to the person and negligence).

   b. Interfering with the enjoyment of another's land (nuisance, trespass to land and the tort known as 'Rylands v Fletcher').

   c. Defamation (libel and slander).

3. A tort must be distinguished from:

   a. A *breach of contract*, where the obligation of which a breach is alleged arose from the agreement of the parties.

   b. A *breach of trust*, where the duty broken is known only to equity and not to common law and where the remedy is equitable or discretionary and not the common law right to damages.

   c. A *crime*, where the object of proceedings is to punish the offender rather than compensate his victim.

4. Each individual tort has its own particular rules governing liability, but in general the plaintiff must prove the following:

   a. That the defendant's conduct has been intentional or negligent, ie liability is usually based on fault. There are, however, some instances of 'strict liability', ie liability irrespective of fault.

   b. That the tortious act or omission caused some damage to the plaintiff. However, some torts are actionable 'per se' (without proof of loss), for example trespass and libel.

5. *Malice in Tort*

   a. Malice means acting from a bad motive. The general rule is that the defendant's motives are irrelevant. Therefore a good motive will not excuse a tortious act, and a bad motive will not turn an otherwise innocent act into a tortious one.

In BRADFORD CORPORATION v PICKLES (1895) in an effort to induce the Corporation to buy his land, D sank a well on his land and abstracted water which would have otherwise reached the Corporation's reservoir. It was held that an injunction would not be granted to the Corporation. The right to abstract water is not (like the right to make noise on one's land) limited by the requirement of reasonableness. It is an absolute right and an element of malice could not make it a nuisance.

b.   There are several exceptions to the general rule stated above:

    i.   The plaintiff must prove malice in the torts of malicious prosecution and injurious falsehood.

    ii.   In the tort of defamation if the plaintiff can prove malice this will prevent the defences of qualified privilege and fair comment.

    iii.   In nuisance the plaintiff will sometimes succeed if he shows that the defendant's malice turned an otherwise reasonable act into an unreasonable one.

In HOLLYWOOD SILVER FOX FARM v EMMETT (1936) D, a developer, felt that a notice board inscribed 'Hollywood Silver Fox Farm' was detrimental to his neighbouring development. When P refused to remove the notice D caused his son to discharge guns on his land to interfere with the breeding of the foxes. It was held that his action constituted a nuisance.

CHAPTER 22

General Defences

INTRODUCTION

1. A defence need only be argued by the defendant once the basic requirements of the tort have been established by the plaintiff. The general defences described in this chapter are not usually the 'first line of defence' for a defendant. Initially he will probably try to refute the allegation that he has committed the tort. For example:

'I did not commit the tort of negligence because the plaintiff has failed to prove that I did not act as a reasonable man. I was reasonable because...'

If the plaintiff does establish that the tort has been committed then, and only then, need the defendant argue a defence. For example:

'I accept that I was negligent, but the loss the plaintiff has suffered is not sufficiently closely related to my negligent act.'

This is the defence of remoteness. The distinction is illustrated by the following case.

In WOOLDRIDGE V SUMNER (1963) P was a professional photographer. He was standing inside a show jumping arena when a horse ridden by D galloped off the course and into him. The judge found that there was an error of judgement by D. P's negligence action against D failed because this error of judgement did not amount to a breach of D's duty of care to P. The tort of negligence had not therefore been committed. The rider did not therefore have to argue that P consented to run the risk of injury by standing inside the arena.

VOLENTI NON FIT INJURIA (CONSENT)

2. The general rule is that a person has no remedy for harm done to him if he has expressly or impliedly consented to suffer the actual harm inflicted, or if he has consented to run the risk of it. Thus, for example, a boxer could not sue as a result of a broken jaw suffered in the ring.

3. *The Meaning of 'Consent'*

   a. Mere knowledge does not necessarily imply consent. The plaintiff must both appreciate the nature of the risk of injury and consent to run that risk.

In SMITH v BAKER (1891) P, who worked in a quarry, was injured when a stone fell from a crane which his employers negligently used to swing stones above his head. When sued his employers pleaded the defence of volenti. They were able to show that P knew of the risk of injury, but they could not show that he freely consented to run that risk. – He may have continued to work under the crane through fear of losing his job. P's action succeeded.

b. Consent need not be expressly given. It is sufficient that the plaintiff voluntarily agrees to the risk of injury.

In ICI v SHATWELL (1965) P and his brother, who were experienced in handling explosives, disregarded their employer's instructions and tested some detonators without taking adequate precautions. P was injured due to his brother's negligence, and sued ICI (the employers) claiming that they were vicariously liable for his brother's negligence. ICI's defence of volenti succeeded.

P knew the risk he was taking, but he took the risk voluntarily. Note that P could have chosen to sue his brother. If he had done so the brother could have successfully pleaded volenti.

c. A consent given under protest is no consent, as where an employee has the choice between incurring a risk, or giving up a job which is not normally dangerous.

In BOWATER v ROWLEY REGIS CORPORATION (1944) D ordered one of their employees (P) to take out a horse which they knew was unsafe. P was injured. D's defence of volenti failed because P took out the horse because he was in fear of losing his job. His consent was not therefore freely given.

d. An apparent consent may be negated by statute. For example:

   i. The *ROAD TRAFFIC ACT 1972* makes void any agreement between a driver and passenger whereby the passenger travels at his own risk since the Act makes passenger insurance compulsory.

   ii. The *UNFAIR CONTRACT TERMS ACT 1977* provides that a person cannot by reference to any contract term exclude or restrict his liability for death or personal injury resulting from negligence.

4. *Rescue Cases*

a. If a defendant who has placed a third party, or himself, in a position of danger is sued by the plaintiff in respect of injuries suffered while taking steps to effect a rescue, he cannot plead volenti as a defence. The plaintiff's moral duty to effect a rescue excludes any real consent by him.

In HAYNES v HARWOOD (1935) a boy threw a stone at a horse which had been left unattended, causing the horse to bolt into a crowded street. P, a policeman, was injured when he tried to stop the horse. P's action against the owners of the horse succeeded. They could not claim the defence of volenti since he was acting under a duty to effect a rescue, and had not therefore freely consented to run the risk of injury.

b. The general principle is similar where injuries are suffered in an attempt to rescue property, although the risks to which a plaintiff may reasonably expose himself are less than when life is endangered.

c. If there is no immediate danger, only inconvenience, the defence of volenti is likely to succeed.

In CUTLER v UNITED DAIRIES (1933) P attempted to catch a horse which had bolted into an empty field. In this case the owner's defence of volenti succeeded since, as no person was in danger, P was not effecting a rescue but was acting voluntarily.

REMOTENESS OF DAMAGE

5. Causation and Remoteness

a. Before the question of remoteness arises, the plaintiff must show that the defendant's conduct was a substantial factor in bringing about his injury. Thus if the plaintiff would have suffered the same injury despite the defendant's conduct he will not receive compensation.

In BARNETT v CHELSEA HOSPITAL MANAGEMENT COMMITTEE (1969) P went to the hospital complaining of vomiting and was sent away to see his own doctor without being given a proper examination. Shortly afterwards P died of arsenic poisoning. P's widow's negligence action failed because P would have died whatever action the hospital doctor had taken. The careless examination was not the *cause* of the death.

b. Causation and remoteness are different parts of the same series of events. For example the causes and consequences of a car accident can be represented as follows:

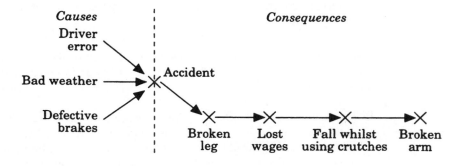

Causation is concerned with factors to the left of the dotted line, and remoteness with the consequences shown to the right of the line.

6. *The Test for Remoteness*

a. When causation has been established and the basic elements to the tort have been proved, the defendant may be able to escape payment of some or all of the damages claimed by showing that there is not a sufficiently close connection between his behaviour and the damage suffered by the plaintiff, ie that the loss is too remote.

b. The test for remoteness is '*Reasonable foreseeability*', ie the defendant is only liable for the consequences of his act that a reasonable man would have foreseen. This test was established in OVERSEAS TANKSHIP (UK) v MORTS DOCKS (THE WAGON MOUND) (**1961**), which overruled RE POLEMIS (**1921**), a case which stated that the defendant was liable for all loss which was the 'direct result' of his tort.

In THE WAGON MOUND (**1961**) an action was brought by the owners of a wharf against the owners of *The Wagon Mound* (a ship). The ship had discharged oil into Sydney harbour which ignited when hot metal from welding operations being carried on in the harbour fell onto a piece of cotton waste floating in the oil. The court held that damage to the wharf by fouling was foreseeable, but not damage by fire, since oil on water does not usually ignite. The ignition of the oil only occurred because the hot metal fell on to highly combustible cotton waste. Such an event was not reasonably foreseeable.

c. Note that

   i. The test is objective, ie what matters is not what the defendant actually foresaw (ie his subjective foresight), but what a reasonable man would have foreseen as the consequences of the tort, had he applied his mind to it.

   ii. The tort test is wider (more generous to the plaintiff) than the contract test. In contract the loss must be foreseeable as the probable result of the breach.

d. The following case shows that policy considerations play a part in deciding remoteness issues, ie even if the loss is regarded as foreseeable the plaintiff may not be awarded damages.

In MEAH v McCREAMER NO 2 (**1986**) a negligent car driver (McCreamer) crashed, causing head injuries to his passenger (Meah). Meah underwent a personality change and three years later sexually assaulted and wounded two women and raped a third. He was sent to prison. In the first action resulting from these events (MEAH v McCREAMER (**1985**)) Meah received damages that compensated him for the personality change and prison sentence. The second action was a claim against Meah for damages by his victims. Liability was admitted and £17,000 was awarded. In the final action (MEAH v McCREAMER NO 2 (**1986**)) Meah sought to recover this £17,000 from McCreamer. The judge regarded this as a problem of remoteness. He pointed out that:

i.   The defendant must take his victim as he finds him even if he has an 'eggshell personality', ie he was the worst possible person to receive an injury of this type.

ii. The remoteness rules did not require the precise nature of the damage to be foreseeable, only the general type of damage.

iii. Policy considerations would have to be taken into account when deciding whether a particular loss should be recoverable.

Meah's barrister argued that as the claim for imprisonment was successful then it followed that he must be able to recover the damages that he had to pay to his victims. The judge, however, said that there was a distinction between imprisonment of and injuries to Meah himself, and indirect loss suffered as a result of having to compensate someone else. Furthermore it was necessary to draw the line somewhere. It would not for example be reasonable to impose on the driver (McCreamer) liability to support any child born to the victim of the rape. It was held that the damage was too remote and the case was dismissed.

7. *Novus Actus Interveniens*

a.   When a chain of events results from a tort, sometimes the loss suffered is not within the scope of compensation merely because it is not reasonably foreseeable. For example:

| Accident | Broken back | Lost wages | Lost chance of promotion |

Unless there was a very good chance of promotion the third consequence would probably be too remote.

b.   In other cases the chain of events is said to be 'broken' by an intervening event known as a *novus actus interveniens*. This may be an act of the plaintiff himself or the act of a third party over whom the defendant had no control.

In LAMB v CAMDEN BOROUGH COUNCIL (1981) council workers broke a water main, causing serious damage to L's house. In fact the house became unsafe and the tenant to whom it was let moved out pending repairs. Squatters then moved into the empty house and caused £30,000 damages. The Court of Appeal awarded P damages in respect of damage due to flooding (liability was admitted by the Council) but rejected the claim for damage caused by squatters because this was not a reasonably foreseeable result of the Council's negligence.

In KNIGHTLY v JOHNS (1982) D, a motorist negligently crashed his car, blocking a one-way traffic tunnel. A police inspector then told P, a police constable, to ride the wrong way down the tunnel to stop more motorists from entering.

P was injured when he struck a vehicle that was entering the tunnel. It was held that D was not liable for P's injuries since P's accident was not a reasonably foreseeable result of D's negligence.

c. To refer to a novus actus interveniens is in fact merely another way of saying that the loss is not reasonably foreseeable. In the example given in 5.b. above it could be said that the broken arm is too remote because it is not reasonably foreseeable or because the fall from crutches is a novus actus interveniens.

d. Some intervening acts (even if not foreseeable) will not break the chain of events which links the defendant's tort with the plaintiff's loss. For example:

   i. An act done 'in the agony of the moment' created by the defendant's tort.

   In SCOTT v SHEPHERD (1773) D threw a lighted firework into a crowded market place. Several people threw the firework away from their vicinity until it exploded in P's face. D claimed that the onward throwing of the firework was a novus actus interveniens. The court however, held that the onward throwing was an instinctive act, done in the 'agony of the moment'. It did not therefore break the link between P and D. P was awarded damages.

   ii. Where the intervening act is a rescue.

8. *'Thin Skull' Cases.* The Wagon Mound decision does not alter the common law rule applicable in 'thin skull' cases. Thus the defendant must still take his victim as he finds him, he cannot plead the medical condition of his victim as a defence, even if this condition means that the loss suffered is not reasonably foreseeable.

In SMITH v LEECH BRAIN (1962) P was injured at work when due to the negligence of one of D's employees a piece of molten zinc hit him on the lip. Most people would have been burned and nothing more, but P was susceptible to cancer and the accident brought it on – P died. The court applied the rule that the defendant must take his victim as he finds him, and his estate was awarded full compensation for the loss. The loss was clearly outside the scope of 'reasonable foreseeability', but the judge made it clear that he did not think the Wagon Mound decision was intended to alter the common law rule applicable in 'thin skull cases'.

9. *Strict Liability Torts.* In torts of strict liability, ie breach of statutory duty and 'Rylands v Fletcher' the reasonable foreseeability test does not apply. The defendant will have to compensate the plaintiff for all the damage which is the direct result of his tort.

OTHER GENERAL DEFENCES

10. *Mistake.* The general rule is that mistake is no defence to a tort action. There are three exceptions. In each case the success of the defence depends on whether or not the defendant acted reasonably in making the mistake.

   a. False imprisonment. – If a policeman without a warrant arrests somebody who has not committed a crime when he reasonably believes that they have.

   b. Malicious prosecution. – If the person who commenced the prosecution (the defendant in the present tort action) was under the mistaken belief that the plaintiff was guilty of a crime.

   c. Defamation. – See Chapter 28.7 (unintentional defamation).

11. *Inevitable Accident*

   a. It has been said that a defendant is not liable if he can prove that damage is due to an 'inevitable accident', ie that he is 'utterly without fault'.

   In STANLEY V POWELL (1891) D fired his gun at a pheasant but the bullet hit a tree, and ricocheted into P. D was held to be completely blameless and not therefore liable in negligence.

   b. Professor Winfield has suggested that the defence has very little relevance since the decision in FOWLER V LANNING (1959) which pointed out that since the burden of proving fault lies with the plaintiff, a defence which involves the defendant proving that he is without fault is superfluous.

   c. In any event the plea of inevitable accident cannot be raised in cases of strict liability.

12. *Act of God.* This means circumstances which no human foresight can guard against. Act of God differs from inevitable accident since

   a. It is available as a defence in strict liability cases; and

   b. The 'act' must be caused by the forces of nature without human intervention.

13. *Self-Defence.* A person may use reasonable force to defend himself, or his property, or another person against unlawful force. What is reasonable depends on the facts of each case, however, retaliation will never be reasonable.

14. *Necessity*

   a. This defence may be used where the defendant has inflicted loss on an innocent plaintiff while attempting to prevent a greater loss to himself.

   In COPE V SHARPE (1912) a fire broke out on P's land. D, a gamekeeper on adjoining land, entered P's land and burnt some of the heather to form a firebreak to prevent the fire spreading to his employer's land. When sued for trespass his defence of necessity succeeded (even though the firebreak had proved to be unnecessary), since there was a real threat of fire, and D had acted reasonably.

   b. The difference between self-defence and necessity is that self-defence is used against a plaintiff who is a wrongdoer, and necessity is used against an innocent plaintiff.

15. *Statutory Authority*

   a. Absolute statutory authority (ie where the statute has expressly authorised the thing done, or the thing done is a necessary consequence of what is authorised) is a complete defence, provided the defendant can prove he used all proper care.

In ALLEN v GULF OIL (1981) a 450-acre oil refinery dominated the small village of Waterston near Milford Haven, causing both noise and smell. P's nuisance action was one of 53 brought by local residents. D's defence was that their activities were authorised by the *GULF OIL REFINING ACT (1965)*. After some disagreement between the Court of Appeal and the House of Lords on the extent of authority granted by the statute the House of Lords held that it authorised both the construction and use of a refinery together with its vast complex of jetties and railway lines. Furthermore it operated as a complete defence to an action for private nuisance. It is perhaps unfortunate that the House did not take the view of the majority of the Court of Appeal and Lord Keith in the House of Lords. They were of the opinion that although the statute enabled Gulf to make the installation and operate it (ie an injunction could not be granted), it did not excuse them from paying compensation for injury done to those living in the neighbourhood.

b. Conditional statutory authority (ie where the injury is not a necessary consequence of what is authorised), is no defence.

CHAPTER 23

Capacity

PARTIES TO WHOM SPECIAL RULES APPLY

1. Generally any person can sue or be sued, but there are exceptions.

2. *The Crown*

   a. The CROWN PROCEEDINGS ACT 1947 preserves the immunity of Her Majesty in her private capacity from any legal process, but provides machinery whereby (with some exceptions) the Crown can be sued in respect of the torts of subordinates.

   b. Actions under the Act are brought against the appropriate government department.

3. *The Post Office*

   a. No proceedings in tort lie against the Post Office for any act or omission of its servants in relation to a postal packet or telephonic communication (*POST OFFICE ACT 1969*).

   b. However, the Post Office is liable for loss or damage to a registered inland letter if caused by a wrongful act or omission of an employee or agent of the Post Office.

4. *Minors*

   a. A minor can sue in tort, although proceedings must be brought through his 'next friend', ie his nearest adult relative.

   b. Minority is generally no defence, however,

      i. Extreme youth may be relevant in cases where some special mental element is needed, such as malice, or in considering the standard of care to be expected.

      ii. A minor cannot be sued in tort where this would be an indirect way of enforcing a contract on which he is not liable. Contrast BURNARD V HAGGIS (1863) with JENNINGS V RUNDALL (Chapter 14.7).

   c. A parent is not liable as such for his child's tort, but he may be liable on other grounds. For example:

      i. If he employs the child he may be vicariously liable as employer;

      ii. If he expressly authorises the tort; or

iii. If he negligently allowed his child the opportunity of causing harm, for example by allowing a young child to possess a dangerous weapon.

5. *Husband and Wife*

   a. A husband is not affected if his wife is sued and vice versa.

   b. Each may sue the other as if they were not married.

6. *Corporations*

   a. They can sue for such torts as can be committed against them and not, for example, for trespass to the person.

   b. They can be sued for the torts of an employee committed whilst he was acting in the course of his employment.

7. *Unincorporated Organisations*

   a. Such bodies have no legal existence separate from that of their members and cannot therefore sue or be sued, although members who committed or authorised the tort are liable.

   b. Where the tort arises from the use of the organisation's property a representative action may be brought against one member of the organisation, representing himself and the other members.

   c. There are provisions for partnerships to sue and be sued in the firm's name.

8. *Judicial Immunity*. Judges, magistrates and magistrates' clerks have immunity for acts in their judicial capacity. Barristers and witnesses have immunity in respect of all matters relating to the cases with which they are concerned. This is mainly relevant to prevent actions against them for slander.

9. *Executors*

   a. At common law a personal action died with the injured person. Now under the *LAW REFORM (MISCELLANEOUS PROVISIONS) ACT 1934* (as amended) on the death of any person, all causes of action (except defamation) whether as defendant or plaintiff survive against the estate or for the benefit of the estate. However, the damages recoverable

      i. Cannot be exemplary and

      ii. Where the tort caused the death, must be calculated without reference to any loss or gain to the estate resulting from the death (for example the proceeds of life assurance) except that funeral expenses may be included.

      The estate may therefore claim damages for the period between injury and death, for example for pain and suffering, loss of earnings and medical expenses. However, there is no claim for loss of expectation of life or for loss of income after death.

   b. If the person is killed as a result of, for example negligence, a second separate action may be brought by dependents under the *FATAL ACCIDENTS ACT 1976*. Under this Act a person whose negligence caused the death of another will be liable to certain relatives if they have suffered financial loss because of the death. No action may be brought if more than three years have elapsed between injury and death. Also if the deceased was guilty of contributory negligence the damages will be reduced according to the extent to which he was at fault. In assessing damages under the *FATAL ACCIDENTS ACT* any benefits arising from the death, for example insurance policies, pensions or gratuities are to be disregarded.

10. *Joint Tortfeasors*

   a. If two or more people are jointly liable in tort, either or both may be sued.

   b. If only one is sued and is required to pay damages he may usually recover a contribution from the other under the *CIVIL LIABILITY (CONTRIBUTION) ACT 1978*. The amount of contribution will be decided by the court on the basis of what is just and equitable given the responsibility of each party for the injury.

VICARIOUS LIABILITY

11. 'Vicarious liability' means liability for the torts of others, and arises because of a relationship between the parties. The relationship may be either

   a. Employer/independent contractor, or

   b. Employer/employee (master/servant)

12. *Liability for the Torts of Independent Contractors*

   a. An independent contractor is a person who undertakes to produce a given result, and who in the actual execution of the work is not under the control of the person for whom he does it.

   b. The general rule is that an employer is not liable for the tort of his independent contractor.

   In PADBURY v HOLLIDAY AND GREENWOOD (**1912**) an employee of a contractor engaged to fit windows, negligently left a hammer lying on a window sill. A gust of wind caught the window which, as it moved, knocked the hammer onto P, a passer-by. D were not held liable since the tort was committed by an employee of their independent contractor.

   c. Exceptions:

   i. Strict liability under the rule in Rylands v Fletcher;

   ii. Where the employer was negligent in the hiring of the independent contractor;

   iii. Where the duty is personal, for example an employer has a duty to provide employees with a reasonably safe plant and a reasonably safe system of work. If he employs a contractor in the discharge of this duty he remains liable for any negligence by the contractor.

iv. Where the work is 'extra hazardous'. For example

In HONEYWELL AND STEIN v LARKIN BROTHERS (1934) an independent contractor used magnesium flares to take pictures of the inside of a cinema. The negligence of the contractor caused a fire to start. In this case the employer of the contractor was held liable since he had ordered the performance of what was regarded as a hazardous activity.

13. *Liability for the Torts of Servants*

a. A person is a servant if his employer retains a right to control not only the work he does, but also the way in which he does it. The test is the right of control, not how much control was in fact exercised. This is the traditional test, but difficulties arise when applying it to professional persons such as doctors. In such cases it may be necessary to consider such criteria as payment of salaries and the power of dismissal.

b. The rule is that a master is vicariously liable for the torts of his servant that are committed within the *course of his employment*. The tortious act must be a wrongful way of doing what the employee is employed to do.

In LIMPUS v LONDON GENERAL OMNIBUS CO (1862) a bus driver whilst racing a bus caused an accident. His employers were held liable because he was doing what he was employed to do, ie driving a bus, although in an improper way.

Contrast BEARD v LONDON GENERAL OMNIBUS CO (1900). A bus conductor attempted to turn a bus around at the end of its route and in doing so he caused an accident. His employers were not liable since he was employed only to collect fares and not to drive buses.

c. An act of violence will usually take the employee outside the scope of employment and the employer will not be liable.

In WARREN v HENLYS (1948) a petrol pump attendant assaulted a customer during an argument over payment for petrol. It was held that the employer was not liable.

d. The employer may be liable even if the employee acts contrary to clear instructions.

In ROSE v PLENTY (1976) D was a milkman. His employer did everything possible to stop the common practice of taking young children on the van and paying them to help deliver the milk. A notice at the depot said

'Children must not in any circumstances be employed by you in the performance of your duties.'

Contrary to this instruction D employed P. While moving from one delivery point to another the boy had one leg dangling from the van so that he could jump off quickly. D drove negligently and P's foot was crushed between the van and the kerb.

It was held that D's employer was liable because D had been acting within the scope of his employment, ie delivering milk and collecting empty bottles, although in an improper way.

e. Sometimes a prohibition imposed by an employer on an employee will limit the scope of employment. Thus in TWINE v BEAN'S EXPRESS (1944) a prohibition against drivers giving lifts to hitchhikers was held to limit the scope of employment. However, this was not considered relevant to Rose v Plenty since Rose was not a mere passenger being given a lift, but he was the method by which Plenty did his job.

f. An employee may be within the course of his employment even though he has acted fraudulently.

In LLOYD v GRACE, SMITH (1912) the defendants were solicitors who employed a managing clerk to do conveyancing. The managing clerk fraudulently induced P to convey two cottages to him by representing that this was necessary in order to sell the cottages. The clerk then resold the cottages and absconded with the sale proceeds. The solicitors were held liable on the grounds that by allowing him to perform conveyancing transactions they had given him apparent authority to act as he did. He was acting within the scope of his employment even though his act was fraudulent.

g. An employee who wrongfully uses his own property to carry on his job may still be within the course of his employment.

In MCKEAN v RAYNOR BROTHERS (1942) an employee was told to deliver a message using the firm's lorry. Although he took his own car he was still held to be in the course of his employment.

If an employer allows an employee to use the employer's vehicle for the employee's own use, the employer will not be liable for any accident that may occur.

If an employer provides a vehicle for the employee's use, the employee may be regarded as the employer's agent if he gives another employee a lift, even though it is not within the scope of his employment to do this.

In VANDYKE v FENDER (1970) an employee who was provided with a company car gave other employees a lift to work. There was an accident and one of the other employees was injured. He was successful in his claim for damages against the company since Mr Fender, although not a paid driver, was driving the car as the company's agent and they were therefore liable for his negligence.

h. When an employee who is on a journey deviates from the authorised route, it is a question of degree whether he has started on a fresh journey ('a frolic of his own') which relieves the employer from liability.

i. Where the employer is held liable for his employee's tort, the employee is also generally liable, but if a blameless employer is held liable for his employee's tort, a term is implied in their contract that the employee will indemnify the employer (LISTER v ROMFORD ICE (1957)).

CHAPTER 24

Negligence

1. *Basic Requirements*. If he is to succeed in a negligence action the plaintiff must prove:

   a. That the defendant owed to him a legal duty of care, and

   b. That the defendant has been guilty of a breach of that duty, and

   c. That damage has been caused to the plaintiff by that breach.

Note in particular that the burden of proof is placed on the plaintiff. Each of these requirements is now considered in turn.

THE DUTY OF CARE

2. *The Neighbour Test*

   a. The courts have always taken the view that a careless person should not have to compensate all the people who suffer as a result of his conduct. For example when a van driver is injured due to the negligence of another driver several people may also be affected. There may be a witness to the accident who suffers nightmares as a result of his experience and a trader to whom the driver was delivering goods may lose profits because of inadequate stock. In such cases the task of the court is to consider the interests of the victims whilst being fair to the careless person.

      This is achieved by asking two questions:

      i. Is there a sufficient relationship of *proximity* between the plaintiff and the defendant?

      ii. If so are there any *policy* reasons for negating or reducing the class of persons to whom a duty is owed?

      If these questions are applied to the above example the result will be compensation for the van driver, but for policy reasons the witness and trader are unlikely to be compensated.

   b. 'Proximity' does not mean physical proximity, it is based on reasonable foreseeability and is generally known as the '*neighbour test*'. The first case to establish this principle of proximity was in 1932.

      In DONOGHUE v STEVENSON (1932) P's friend purchased a bottle of ginger beer manufactured by D and gave it to P. P drank most of the bottle, but then noticed the decomposed remains of a snail in the bottom of the bottle. P subsequently became ill and sued D in negligence. D's defence was that he did not owe a duty of care to P because there was no contract between D and P (the purchaser having been P's friend).

The court, however, held that a contractual link should no longer be the test for determining whether or not a duty of care was owed. The House of Lords stated that a duty of care is owed to any person who we can reasonably foresee will be injured by our acts or omissions. The court described such persons as 'neighbours'. It was held that D could reasonably foresee that somebody apart from the original purchaser may consume his product and he was therefore held liable to P.

c. The neighbour test has been applied in numerous cases since 1932, for example:

In KING v PHILLIPS (1952) D carelessly drove his taxi over a boy's cycle. The boy, who was not on the bicycle, screamed. His mother (P) heard the scream and on looking out of the window saw the crushed bicycle, but not her son. As a result she suffered shock which made her ill. She failed in her action against D because it was held that a driver could only reasonably foresee that his carelessness would affect other road users and not persons in houses. He did not therefore owe a duty of care to P.

In TUTTON v WALTER (1985) P kept bees on land near to D's farm. D had a crop of oil seed rape which, when in flower, is particularly attractive to bees. Despite clear written instructions to the contrary D sprayed his crop while it was in flower, with a pesticide that was fatal to bees. His defence to P's action was that no duty was owed because he was doing on his own land something that he was entitled to do, and that the bees came on to the land without permission and were basically trespassers. The judge did not accept these arguments. It was held that the duty was owed under the neighbour principle and it had been broken. P therefore received compensation for the loss of his bee colony.

In HOME OFFICE v DORSET YACHT CO (1970) it was held that the Home Office owed a duty of care to the Yacht Club in respect of the detention of Borstal trainees who had escaped from an institution and caused damage to P's yachts. The duty to people whose property might be damaged in an escape was based on the control which the Home Office has over Borstal trainees.

d. In certain situations the courts will not apply the neighbour test without qualification. The main areas concern economic loss, negligent statements, and nervous shock, each of which are considered below (paragraphs 3–5). In addition a plaintiff who is within the neighbour test may not receive compensation:

   i.   Where the defendant is guilty of an *omission* which results in foreseeable harm, for example by failing to save a small child drowning in shallow water. This exception will only apply if there is a 'pure omission', ie if the defendant's prior conduct gives rise to a duty, the fact that an omission is the direct cause of the harm will not save the defendant from liability – clearly a car driver cannot avoid liability by claiming that the accident was caused by his omission to apply the brake.

ii. Where a barrister is sued for professional negligence as a result of his conduct of a case in court (RONDEL v WORSLEY (1969) Chapter 9.7). In HALL v SIMONS (2000), the House of Lords ruled that immunity of barristers for negligence in their work in court was no longer sustainable. This was unanimously agreed in respect of civil litigation and by a majority in respect of criminal cases.

iii. If a person is the occupier of land and the injured person is a trespasser. (The extent of the duty is defined by the OCCUPIERS LIABILITY ACT 1984.)

iv. If the injured person is an accomplice in crime.

In ASHTON v TURNER (1981) D, a burglar driving a get-away car caused an accident in which P, his accomplice, was injured. Both P and D were drunk. It was held for public policy reasons that D was not liable.

3. Economic Loss

a. Where negligent conduct causes economic loss (ie financial loss that it not consequential upon physical injury to person or property) the courts have been generally unwilling to hold that a duty of care exists.

In MUIRHEAD v INDUSTRIAL TANK SPECIALISTS (1986) P established a lobster farm. He intended to purchase lobsters cheaply in the summer, keep them alive until Christmas, and then sell them at a higher price. A constant supply of circulating sea water was needed to keep the lobsters alive. He installed the necessary tanks and pumps. Unfortunately the pump motor (supplied by a French firm) could not cope with the fluctuations in English voltage and a large number of lobsters were lost as a result of a pump failure. P claimed compensation for the loss of lobsters and loss of potential profit. It was held that he could recover for the loss of the lobsters and any financial loss suffered in direct consequence, but could not recover for any loss of profit.

b. Numerous economic loss cases have concerned the liability of persons involved in the design, approval and construction of buildings. The position was reviewed by the House of Lords.

In MURPHY v BRENTWOOD DISTRICT COUNCIL (1990) P claimed £35,000 from D as compensation for the reduction in the value of his house which suffered as a result of defects in the design. The defective design had been approved by the Council. P relied on a 1977 case (ANNS v MERTON LBC) where, in a similar situation, the plaintiff had been successful. However, a seven member House of Lords unanimously overruled the Anns decision on the grounds that it did not proceed on the basis of established principles, but introduced a potentially indeterminate liability covering a wide range of situations. In Murphy's case the court held that such loss was purely economic (not physical) and was not therefore within the scope of the duty of care owed by D to P. They made it clear that the right to recover for pure economic loss, not flowing from physical injury, must be determined by the principle in HEDLEY BYRNE V HELLER (see 4. below).

In DEPARTMENT OF THE ENVIRONMENT V THOMAS BATES (1990) P had a 42 year lease of part of an office block constructed by D. Eleven years after the offices had been constructed it was discovered that low strength concrete had been used in various supporting pillars. The building was still safe for its existing load, but the pillars were not strong enough to support the design load of the building. P carried out remedial work and then sued D for negligence. The court applied the decision in Murphy's case, holding that the loss was purely economic and was not recoverable in tort, because when the remedial work was carried out the building was not unsafe, but merely subject to a defect in quality which made P's lease less valuable.

c.   Hedley Byrne has been applied on many occasions. Examples include SMITH V ERIC BUSH (1989) (Chapter 16.13) and HARRIS V WYRE FOREST DISTRICT COUNCIL (1989).

In HARRIS V WYRE FOREST DISTRICT COUNCIL (1989) P paid a valuation fee to the Council in connection with a loan application. On the basis of the valuation report the Council lent P £8,500 out of a purchase price of £9,000. P did not personally see the valuation report. Serious settlement was later discovered which required extensive repair. The House of Lords held that D was liable since although P had not seen the valuation report, it was reasonable for him to assume that the surveyor conducting the valuation had not found any serious defects.

Unfortunately the SMITH and HARRIS decisions are arguably inconsistent with MURPHY V BRENTWOOD DC, in that a surveyor who carries out a negligent valuation is liable to a purchaser who suffers economic loss (the SMITH and HARRIS cases) but a surveyor who negligently approves defective plans or foundations will not be liable to a purchaser (MURPHY'S case).

d.   The cautious approach exemplified in Murphy's case has recently been applied to accountants in the leading case of CAPARO INDUSTRIES V DICKMAN (1990) and the James McNaughton case described below.

In CAPARO INDUSTRIES V DICKMAN (1990) the plaintiff company sued two directors of Fidelity plc and the accountants Touche Ross & Co, the auditors of Fidelity. The plaintiff had taken over Fidelity and alleged that the profits were much lower than shown in the audited accounts, consequently they had suffered financial loss. The House of Lords considered whether a duty of care is owed to persons who rely on the accounts to deal with the company or to buy and sell its shares. The House stated that the criteria for the imposition of a duty were:

(a) Foreseeability of damage,

(b) Proximity of the relationship, and

(c) The reasonableness or otherwise of imposing a duty.

To establish proximity all of the following factors will typically need to be present:

i.   The advice was required for a purpose made known to the adviser when the advice was given

ii. The adviser knew his advice would be communicated to the recipient in order that it should be used for this purpose

iii. It was known that the advice was likely to be acted upon without independent inquiry

iv. It was acted on to the recipient's detriment.

The House was prepared to acknowledge that liability for negligent audit can exist, but the above factors were not present in Caparo's case. The plaintiff's action therefore failed.

In JAMES MCNAUGHTON PAPER GROUP v HICKS ANDERSON (1990) P was known to be interested in taking over the MK Paper Group. D, who were MK's accountants had recently produced a draft profit and loss account showing a loss of £48,000. However, they told P that following a rationalisation MK was now breaking even. The take-over proceeded, but it was later discovered that there were a number of errors in the accounts. P's negligence action against D failed because the Court of Appeal adopted the restrictive approach of CAPARO v DICKMAN and held that no duty of care was owed by the accountants to P. Unlike Caparo, it was known that P was considering a take-over, however, the court was not prepared to attribute to D the knowledge that P would rely on the accounts, without further enquiry or advice, for the purpose of finalising an agreement. The court clearly felt that P should have realised that the company was in a poor state and should have consulted its own advisers.

4. *Negligent Statements*

a.   The usual rules of liability apply when the negligent statement results in physical injury. For example

In CLAY v CRUMP (1963) D, an architect, stated that a wall on a demolition site was safe and could be left standing. It later collapsed injuring P. P succeeded in his action against D for his negligent statement.

b.   Where the negligent statement results in financial loss different rules of liability apply. The difference concerns the persons to whom a duty of care is owed. Instead of the 'neighbour test' laid down in DONOGHUE v STEVENSON (1932) the courts initially formulated in HEDLEY BYRNE v HELLER (1964), a much narrower test based on a 'special relationship' between the parties.

In HEDLEY BYRNE v HELLER (1964) D were bankers and P were advertising agents. They had a mutual client E Ltd who wished to place advertisements on television. E requested credit from P, so P asked D for references. D stated that E was a respectably constituted firm and was considered good, although the statement was made without responsibility on their part. P therefore incurred personal liability on several advertising contracts.

E then went into liquidation and P were unable to recover over £17,000 owed to them. P therefore sued D on his negligent statement. It was held that he did have a possible action, and he would have succeeded, but for the disclaimer of responsibility. In order to succeed in such a case the plaintiff must show a special relationship by proving that:

i. He relied on the special skill and judgement of the defendant, and

ii. The defendant knew or ought to have known of this reliance and thus accepted responsibility for making the statement carefully.

c. In some exceptional situations a plaintiff may succeed even if he does not rely on any statement by the defendant, although in such cases there must be close proximity between the plaintiff and the defendant.

In ROSS v CAUNTERS (1979) D was a solicitor. One of his clients bequeathed some property to the plaintiff. At the time the will was executed D had failed:

i. To tell the testator that the will must not be witnessed by the spouse of any beneficiary;

ii. To check that the will had been properly executed;

iii. To notice that P's husband had witnessed the will; and

iv. To draw the testator's attention to this fact. (It was admitted that if the testator had been told of the error he would have put it right.)

As a result of iii. above P was prevented from inheriting under the will. She was however, successful in her negligence action against D, despite the fact that she clearly had not relied on any statement by D. The judge did not adopt the 'reasonable foreseeability' test or the 'special relationship' test. He chose a point between the two, in effect there must be a *close proximity* between P and D – P *individually (or as a member of a specific and limited class) must be in the defendant's direct contemplation as someone likely to be closely and directly affected by his acts.*

This requirement was satisfied in ROSS v CAUNTERS because

i. P was named in the will;

ii. The proximity was in no way accidental or unforeseen, but arose out of D's duty to his client. In fact the aim of the transaction between D and his client was to confer a benefit on P.

d. If there is a subsequent contract between the plaintiff and the defendant, based wholly on a negligent statement made by the defendant, the plaintiff will not be confined to contractual remedies, but may also have a remedy in tort.

In ESSO PETROLEUM v MARDON (1976) Esso found a site for a filling station on a busy main road. A company executive with 40 years experience of the petrol trade estimated that sales would be 200,000 gallons per year by the third year (assuming access to the main road), so Esso bought the site. However, planning permission was then refused for direct access to the main road, thus reducing potential sales. Despite this the executive later represented to M that sales would be 200,000 gallons per year. Even though M's own estimate was 100,000–150,000 gallons per year he accepted a tenancy relying on the accuracy of the executive's statement. His rent was based on expected sales of 200,000 gallons per year. In the first 15 months sales were only 78,000 gallons and M could not therefore pay the rent. He was sued by Esso. In return he brought a counter-claim against Esso, claiming damages in contract for breach of warranty and damages in tort for a negligent statement. It was held by the Court of Appeal

i. On the contract point: That since the party making the statement had expertise it could be interpreted as a warranty (ie a term of the contract rather than a mere representation inducing the contract) breach of which entitled the innocent party to damages.

ii. On the tort point: That if a person professing to have special knowledge or skill makes a representation which induces the other to contract with him he is under a duty to take reasonable care to see that the representation is correct. Esso were therefore liable in damages. Esso's defence to the tort claim was that HEDLEY BYRNE v HELLER could not apply since it was concerned solely with liability in tort, and not where a pre-contract statement made in negotiations later resulted in a contract – in which case the law of contract provides the plaintiff's only remedies. This defence clearly failed.

e. A disclaimer of responsibility by the defendant (as in HEDLEY BYRNE v HELLER) will be sufficient to exclude the duty of care. However, since the *UNFAIR CONTRACT TERMS ACT 1977*, the exemption clause must satisfy the requirement of reasonableness. See SMITH v ERIC BUSH (**1989**) (Chapter 16.13).

5. Nervous Shock

a. Nervous shock occurs when a person is so affected by a horrifying event that they suffer an identifiable psychiatric illness. Ordinary grief and sorrow, which is reasonably foreseeable, does not amount to nervous shock. The courts have been very reluctant to regard a duty as owed to persons who suffer nervous rather than physical injuries. There are several reasons for this:

i. Fear of fraudulent claims;

ii. The difficulty of fixing a monetary value to such loss;

iii. Unfairness to defendants if damages become out of proportion to the negligent conduct complained of.

b. It used to be thought that to claim for nervous shock the plaintiff must fear injury to himself or a near relative and that the shock must result from actually seeing the accident itself rather than the aftermath. However, decided cases have extended the basis for a claim.

In CHADWICK v BRITISH RAILWAYS BOARD (**1967**) the Board were held liable in negligence for a serious railway accident in which 90 people died. P was a voluntary rescue worker who worked all night in the wreck. As a result he later suffered from neurosis which necessitated hospital treatment. P succeeded in his action against BRB. It was held that in the circumstances injury by shock to volunteer rescue workers was foreseeable. Accordingly a duty was owed to such persons and damages could be awarded even though the shock did not arise from fear of injury to himself or his family.

In McLOUGHLIN v O'BRIEN (1982) P's husband and three children were injured in a car accident caused by D's negligence. One of the children died almost immediately. At the time of the accident P was at home about two miles away. About an hour later the accident was reported to her by a neighbour who said that he thought her son was dying. The neighbour then drove her to hospital where her fourth child (who was not in the accident) told her that her youngest daughter aged three, was dead. At the hospital she saw through a corridor window her other daughter (aged seven) crying, with her face cut and covered in dirt and oil, she could also hear her son (aged seventeen) shouting and screaming. As a result of seeing these injuries and the distressing way in which she learned of them P suffered a severe shock, depression and a change of personality. The House of Lords awarded damages since the loss was reasonably foreseeable and the injury was an illness rather than 'normal' grief and sorrow. The House was not impressed by the public policy argument that such a decision 'would open the flood gates'.

c. More recently the House of Lords has laid down more restrictive principles for nervous shock cases.

In ALCOCK v CHIEF CONSTABLE OF WEST YORKSHIRE (1991) the case resulted from the disaster at Hillsborough Football Ground in Sheffield when too many people were allowed into the ground. Nearly 100 people were killed and many more injured as they were crushed against railings and barricades. The scenes were witnessed on nationwide television. The House of Lords established the principle that the person at fault owes a duty of care to a person who is not actively involved in the accident only if

i. There is a close tie of love and affection with the primary victim such that it is reasonably forseeable he will suffer nervous shock and,

ii. There is proximity in time and space, ie the claimant must see or hear the accident or its immediate aftermath with his own unaided senses.

It was therefore held that only the parents or spouses of the victims could recover damages for nervous shock, provided they had actually seen the accident by being at the ground or as a result of identifying bodies afterwards. Parents or spouses who had only seen the disaster by viewing live television could not get damages.

d. It has been held that damages for nervous shock can be recovered as a result of witnessing damage to property.

In ATTIA v BRITISH GAS (1987) P suffered a nervous shock when, on returning home, she saw that the whole of her house was on fire as a result of D's negligence.

THE STANDARD OF CARE

6. The defendant will discharge his duty if he takes reasonable care. This is an objective test, ie the test is 'Did the defendant exercise the care that a reasonable man would have exercised?' It is not 'Did he do his best?'

The care which a reasonable man would show varies with the circumstances. Some relevant factors may be:

a.   The magnitude of the foreseeable risk.

In LATIMER v A.E.C. (1953) a thunderstorm flooded D's factory, making the floor slippery. D did all they could to clear the water and make the factory safe. P nevertheless slipped and was injured. P alleged negligence, claiming that the factory should have been closed. It was held that the risk of injury did not justify such a drastic measure. P's claim failed.

b.   The known characteristics of the party exposed to the risk.

In PARIS v STEPNEY BOROUGH COUNCIL (1951) P, who only had one eye, worked for the council as a vehicle welder. He was blinded completely when a spark flew into his one good eye. He sued his employers for negligence claiming that he should have been supplied with goggles. The evidence was the goggles were not thought necessary for two-eyed welders. However, since the loss of a person's only good eye is far more serious than the loss of one of two good eyes, goggles should have been supplied to P. The council had broken their duty of care.

c.   Whether the defendant was faced with an emergency.

In WATT v HERTFORDSHIRE C.C. (1954) P, a fireman, was injured when a jack slipped in a lorry while going to an accident. The lorry was not equipped to carry the jack, but it had been used because the fire brigade were faced with an emergency. P's action failed, the council had not broken its duty of care.

d.   Whether a special relationship exists, such as that of competitor to spectator as in WOOLDRIDGE v SUMNER (1963) (Chapter 22.1).

e.   The state of health of the defendant. If the defendant causes a road accident he will only escape liability if his actions at the relevant time were wholly beyond his control, as in a case of sudden unconsciousness.

In ROBERTS v RAMSBOTTOM (1980) D collided head on with a parked vehicle, causing injury to its occupants. D claimed that he was not liable because 20 minutes earlier he had unknowingly suffered a stroke.

This affected his mind so that he could not drive properly. It also meant that he could not appreciate that he was unfit to drive. He did, however, have sufficient awareness of his surroundings and traffic conditions to continue to control the car, although in an inadequate way. It was held that where a driver retains some control, even if imperfect, he must be judged by the objective standard of a reasonable driver. In this case, even though D was not morally to blame because of the nature of the disabling symptoms, D had fallen below this objective standard and was liable.

f. In addition to any statutory and contractual duties owed by an employer to his employee an employer has a common law duty to act with reasonable care towards his employees. To assess whether he has discharged this duty it will be necessary to consider, among other things, whether he has provided:

   i.   A competent staff,

   ii. Proper tools, machinery and premises, and

   iii. A safe system of work and supervision.

   Where work is done on another person's premises the employer's duty is less onerous, although he must still show reasonable care.

   In WILSON v TYNESIDE WINDOW CLEANING CO (1958) the employer discharged his duty of care by telling window cleaners employed by him to take reasonable care, and not to clean windows if it was dangerous to do so.

7. *Res Ipsa Loquitur*

a. In some situations the plaintiff will not need to prove a breach of the duty of care. This is where the maxim *res ipsa loquitur* (the thing speaks for itself) applies.

b. The maxim applies when:

   i.   The 'thing' is under the control of the defendant;

   ii. The defendant has knowledge denied to the plaintiff; and

   iii. The damage is such that it would not normally have happened if proper care had been shown by the defendant.

c. If these requirements are fulfilled there is prima facie evidence of a breach of duty. The burden of proof is then shifted to the defendant, who must prove that he did show reasonable care.

d. The maxim does not apply when the facts are sufficiently known because it depends on an absence of explanation.

e. 'Res Ipsa Loquitur' was considered in the following four cases. In the first two it was held to apply; in the latter two it did not apply. However, even when it does apply (ie b.i–iii are present), it does not guarantee success for the plaintiff. It merely shifts the burden of proof to the defendant, who may be able to show that despite the facts he acted as a reasonable man at all times.

   In BYRNE v BOADLE (1863) A barrel of flour fell from D's warehouse injuring P, a passer-by. No explanation could be given by D for the incident and P was in no position to prove a breach of duty by D. The court therefore placed the burden of proof on D, who had to show that he had not broken his duty of care. He was unable to do this and P therefore succeeded in his action.

In MAHON v OSBORNE (1939) a swab was left in a patient's body after an operation. Clearly the patient could not prove a breach of duty, since he was under an anaesthetic. However, the presence of the swab raised the inference of a breach of duty (*res ipsa loquitur*). The surgeon was unable to show that he had used reasonable care and was accordingly held liable.

In FISH v KAPUR (1948) P's jaw was found to be broken after D, a dentist, had extracted a tooth. It was held that this was not a *res ipsa loquitur* situation since there were reasons other than the dentist's breach of duty which could have accounted for the broken jaw. For example P may have had a weak jaw. P was therefore compelled to prove the three requirements of negligence in the usual way.

In TURNER v MANSFIELD CORPORATION (1975) P was a driver of a corporation dustcart. For some reason, which was never explained, the movable body of the cart rose and hit a bridge, causing the cab section to rise from the ground and jamming the dustcart under the bridge. P jumped from the cab and was injured in his fall to the ground. The Court of Appeal held that this was not a case to which *res ipsa loquitur* applied. It was for P who was in control of the dustcart to give an explanation of the accident. Since he could not do this, his action failed.

DAMAGE

8. The plaintiff must show that as a result of the breach of duty he has suffered some damage. If a person's unreasonable conduct fortunately injures no one then that person cannot be liable in negligence (although he may be guilty of a criminal offence, eg careless driving). The rules on damage have already been covered, but are summarised below.

   a. The damage must be *caused* to a substantial extent by the defendant's conduct.

   b. The damage must be sufficiently closely related to the negligent act, ie it must not be too *remote*.

   c. In most cases the damage must be either physical injury to the plaintiff's person or property or economic loss consequential upon physical injury, eg lost wages as a result of a broken leg.

   d. In cases of identifiable psychiatric illness the courts may award damages if such illness is reasonably foreseeable, but considerations of public policy limit the scope of such damages.

   e. If the damage is economic loss unaccompanied by any injury to person or property a 'special relationship', based on reliance, must exist between the plaintiff and the defendant (HEDLEY BYRNE v HELLER (1964)).

CONTRIBUTORY NEGLIGENCE

9. a. At common law if the plaintiff was guilty of any negligence which contributed to the cause of the accident, he recovered nothing.

   b. Since 1945 by virtue of the *LAW REFORM (CONTRIBUTORY NEGLIGENCE) ACT 1945* where a person suffers damage partly as a result of his own fault, and partly due to the fault of another, the damages recoverable will be reduced according to his share of responsibility.

   c. A person can be guilty of contributory negligence if his conduct while in no way contributing to the accident itself, contributed to the nature and extent of his injuries.

   In O'CONNELL v JACKSON (**1971**) D, a car driver, knocked P off his moped, the accident being entirely D's fault. P suffered severe head injuries which the evidence showed would have been less serious if he had been wearing a crash helmet. It was held that the plaintiff's damages would be reduced by 15%. And in BADGER v MINISTRY OF DEFENCE (2005) the claimant had his award of compensation for injuries sustained through asbestos poisoning whilst employed by the MOD, reduced by 20% because of the contributory nature of his unwillingness to give up smoking which contributed to his subsequent death.

   d. The court does not approach the problem by saying 'What injuries would he have suffered if he had been wearing a crash helmet – we shall compensate him for such injuries.' The court says – 'Given that he has suffered injuries X, Y and Z what was his percentage of fault either in causing the accident or contributing to such injuries – his damages shall be reduced by this percentage.'

   e. To prove contributory negligence it is not necessary for the defendant to show that the plaintiff owed him a duty of care, only that he failed to take reasonable care for his own safety. For example:

   In FROOM v BUTCHER (**1976**) it was held that failure to wear a seat belt amounted to contributory negligence.

   In OWENS v BRIMMELL (**1977**) P's damages were reduced by 20% because he accepted a lift in D's car knowing that D was drunk.

OCCUPIERS' LIABILITY TO LAWFUL VISITORS

10. The duty of occupiers of premises towards lawful visitors is governed by the *OCCUPIERS' LIABILITY ACT 1957*.

    a. An '*occupier*' is a person who has some degree of control over the premises. He need not necessarily be the owner. It is also possible for there to be more than one occupier.

b. 'Premises' includes land, buildings, fixed or movable structures such as pylons and scaffoldings; and vehicles, including ships and aeroplanes.

c. 'Visitors' are persons lawfully on the premises, such as customers in shops and factory inspectors. A trespasser will be deemed to be a lawful visitor for the purposes of the Act if the occupier has granted him implied permission by habitual acquiescence in his known trespass.

11. The extent of the duty is laid down in S.2(2) of the Act:

'A duty to take such care as in all the circumstances of the case is reasonable to see that the visitor will be reasonably safe in using the premises for the purpose for which he is permitted by the occupier to be there.'

This duty is merely an enactment of the common law duty to act as a reasonable man (see 6. above). The Act states that all the circumstances of the case are relevant in determining the duty owed. Therefore the occupier:

a. Must be prepared for children to be less careful than adults. In the case of very young children the occupier is entitled to assume that they will be accompanied by an adult.

b. May expect a person who is doing his job to guard against the ordinary risks of his job.

In ROLES v NATHAN (1963) the plaintiffs, who were chimney sweeps, were employed by D to block up holes in the flues of a coke-fired heating system. Despite a warning from D they attempted to do this while the coke fire was lit, and they were both killed by carbon monoxide gas. Their executor's action failed since it was a risk incidental to their job which they should have foreseen and guarded against.

Contrast SALMON v SEAFARERS RESTAURANTS (1983) when a fire broke out at D's fish and chip shop due to the negligence of one of the employees. The fire melted a seal of a gas meter, gas escaped and there was an explosion. P, a fireman, was injured. D contended that they were only liable if a fireman was injured as a result of some foreseeable but nevertheless exceptional risk, not risks ordinarily incidental to the job of a fireman. It was held that the duty was not limited in this way, the duty owed was the same as that owed to any other visitor. In this case it was foreseeable that firemen would be needed and that such an explosion might result from the fire. D was therefore liable.

c. Will not be liable if the injury results from the faulty work of an independent contractor, provided the occupier took reasonable steps to ensure that the contractor was competent, and that the work was properly done.

d. May be able to escape liability by giving an adequate warning of any danger. However, it must be remembered that under the UNFAIR CONTRACT TERMS ACT 1977 an occupier of business premises cannot exclude liability for causing death or personal injury through negligence and cannot exclude liability for other loss or damage unless the exclusion clause satisfies the Act's requirement of reasonableness (Chapter 16.13).

12. The Act preserves the right of the occupier to plead the defence of volenti non fit injuria in respect of risks 'willingly accepted' by the visitor.

13. The *DEFECTIVE PREMISES ACT 1972* provides that any person who undertakes work for, or in connection with the provision of a dwelling owes a duty of care to:

    a.   The person who orders the work; and

    b.   Any person who subsequently acquires an interest in the dwelling.

OCCUPIERS' LIABILITY TO TRESPASSERS

14. The *OCCUPIERS' LIABILITY ACT 1984* has replaced the common law rules governing the duty of occupiers of premises to persons other than visitors. The Act covers not only trespassers but also persons using rights of way who fall outside the meaning of 'visitor' under the *OCCUPIERS' LIABILITY ACT 1957*.

15. For several years prior to 1984 the occupier's duty to trespassers was to act with common sense and humanity. This required all the surrounding circumstances to be considered, for example the seriousness of the danger, the type of trespasser likely to enter, and in some cases the resources of the occupier.

   In BRITISH RAILWAYS BOARD v HERRINGTON (1972) BRB's electrified railway ran near a park used by children. The fences on each side of the railway were in poor condition and BRB knew that people used to climb through the broken fence to take 'short-cuts' across the railway. H, aged six, got through the fence and was seriously injured when he touched the live rail. The House of Lords held that the old rules relating to liability towards trespassers no longer applied, and although an occupier does not owe the same duty of care to a trespasser as he owes to a visitor, he must act by standards of common sense and humanity and warn or exclude, within reasonable limits, those likely to be injured by a known danger. BRB were therefore held liable.

16. The main provisions of the 1984 Act are:

    a.   *Duty owed.* The occupier owes a duty if:

         i.   He is aware of the danger or has reasonable grounds to believe that it exists; and

         ii.   He knows, or has reasonable grounds to believe, that someone is in (or may come into) the vicinity of the danger; and

         iii. The risk is one against which in all the circumstances of the case he may reasonably be expected to offer that person some protection.

    b.   *Duty broken.* The duty is to take such care as is reasonable in all the circumstances to see that the person to whom the duty is owed does not suffer injury on the premises by reason of the danger concerned.

    c.   *Damage.* The occupier can only be liable for injury to the person. The Act expressly provides that the occupier incurs no liability in respect of any loss of or damage to property.

    d.   *Warnings*. The duty may be discharged (in appropriate cases) by taking reasonable steps to give warning of the danger. The Act also preserves the right of the occupier to plead the defence of volenti.

17. The Act does not significantly change the law, all the circumstances remain relevant, including what the occupier does know and ought to know both about the existence of the danger and the likelihood of trespassers. It is therefore very unlikely that Herrington's case or the other cases described below would be decided differently under the Act, and it will still be rather difficult to predict the outcome of many cases, contrast for example the cases of Penny and Harris.

In HARRIS v BIRKENHEAD CORPORATION (1975) P, aged four, fell from the upper window of a derelict vandalised house. The house had been acquired for demolition by the council. Due to an administrative oversight the doors and windows had not been boarded up in the usual way. It was held that the council were liable because the house was a dangerous and tempting place for young children, therefore a humane and commonsense person should take precautions.

In PENNY v NORTHAMPTON BOROUGH COUNCIL (1974) a trespasser threw an aerosol can into a fire started by boys on a council tip. The can burst and injured an eight-year old trespasser. It was held that the council were not liable.

In PANNETT v McGUINNESS (1972) D, who were demolition contractors, were burning rubbish on a demolition site. They appointed three workmen to supervise the fire and keep a lookout for children. P, aged five, fell into the fire while the men were away and was badly burned. Although P was a trespasser, and the men had on many occasions in the past chased children away, D was held liable since he had failed to keep a proper lookout.

Contrast WESTWOOD v THE POST OFFICE (1974). P, an adult employee of the post office, was injured when he entered an unlocked room which had warning of danger on the door. Although the room should have been locked P's claim failed since a notice of danger is regarded as adequate warning to an adult.

CHAPTER 25

Strict Liability

1. Strict liability is liability which arises without fault. There are two torts dealt with in this chapter. The first is known as the tort of 'Rylands v Fletcher' the second is 'Breach of Statutory Duty'. The chapter also deals with the strict liability and criminal liability imposed by the CONSUMER PROTECTION ACT 1987.

RYLANDS V FLETCHER

2. The rule stated by Blackburn J. is

'The person who for his own purposes brings on his lands and collects and keeps there anything likely to do mischief if it escapes, must keep it at his peril, and if he does not do so is prima facie answerable for all the damage which is the natural consequence of its escape.'

In RYLANDS V FLETCHER (1868) the defendant, a mill owner, employed independent contractors to build a reservoir on his land for the purpose of supplying water for his mill. During the work the contractors found some disused mine shafts which unknown to them connected with the plaintiff's mines under adjoining land. The contractors failed to seal these shafts and when the reservoir was filled with water, the water escaped through these shafts and flooded the plaintiff's mine. Blackburn J. held that the defendant was liable. Note that:

a. Since the defendant employed competent workmen and did not know of or suspect the existence of the disused mine shafts, it follows that liability is absolute (strict) and does not depend on negligence.

b. The words of the rule make it clear that the defendant's liability was personal, not merely vicarious liability for the negligence of his independent contractor.

3. The rule applies to water, animals, chemicals, filth, industrial use of gas or electricity, and exceptionally humans.

In ATTORNEY-GENERAL V CORKE (1933) D allowed gypsies to occupy his land, living in caravans and tents. The gypsies fouled and caused damage to adjoining land. It was held that Rylands v Fletcher applied since although it was lawful to allow gypsies onto land, it was not a natural use of land, and therefore the owner had to bear the risk of damage due to this non-natural use.

Following PAGE MOTORS v EPSOM BOROUGH COUNCIL (**1980**) it is clear that where gypsies are concerned an action in nuisance is more appropriate (Chapter 26.4).

4. There must be a non-natural use of land, ie some special use bringing with it increased danger to others. The rule does not therefore apply to:

   a. Damage due to things naturally on the land, although in such cases an action may lie in nuisance. (See LEAKEY v NATIONAL TRUST (**1980**) (Chapter 26.2).)

   b. Damage due to a natural use of the land, for example domestic gas, electricity or water.

      In RICKARDS v LOTHIAN (**1913**) D was the occupier of business premises and P was the lessee of the second floor. One evening an unknown person deliberately blocked a sink on the fourth floor and turned on the tap. Consequently P's stock was found next morning badly damaged. P's Rylands v Fletcher action against D failed because

      i. domestic water was not a non-natural use of the land, and

      ii. because the escape was caused by the deliberate act of an unknown person.

   c. Recently it has been held that the storage of chemicals by a firm based in an 'industrial village' was a natural use of the land.

      In CAMBRIDGE WATER COMPANY v EASTERN COUNTIES LEATHER (**1991**) the judge rejected P's claim with regard to pollution of a nearby public water supply borehole because the storage of chemicals by firms involved in the local tanning industry was a natural use of the land for the purposes of the rule in RYLANDS v FLETCHER. This decision represents a significant relaxation of the rule.

5. There must be an escape beyond the boundaries of the defendant's land.

   In READ v J. LYONS (**1947**) P was employed as an inspector of munitions factories. She was injured by a shell which exploded while being manufactured. She claimed under the rule in Rylands v Fletcher, but failed because there had been no escape of the dangerous thing over the boundaries of the defendant's land.

6. *Defences*

   a. The escape was caused by:

      i. The plaintiff.

      ii. Act of God.

      iii. The deliberate act of a third party over whom the defendant had no control as in RICKARDS v LOTHIAN (**1913**).

   b. The accumulation was made:

      i. With the plaintiff's express or implied consent (volenti).

         In PETERS v PRINCE OF WALES THEATRE (BIRMINGHAM) (**1943**) D leased to P a shop in the same building that contained the theatre. The theatre had installed (and P knew this) a sprinkler system as a fire precaution.

During a frost the water in the sprinkler system's pipes froze, cracking the pipes. In the following thaw P's shop was flooded and his stock damaged. There was no liability under Rylands v Fletcher because the sprinkler system was for the common benefit of both the theatre and P's shop, and because P had impliedly consented to run the risk of accidents involving the system.

ii. With absolute statutory authority.

BREACH OF STATUTORY DUTY

7. Whether or not a tort action is possible by a person injured due to a breach of statutory duty depends on the construction of the particular statute.

Generally an action will lie, unless it is clear from the statute, or the pre-existing law that this was not intended. However, no action will lie if:

a. It is clear that the penalty provided by the Act was intended to be the only remedy.

In ATKINSON v NEWCASTLE WATERWORKS (1877) P's timber yard was destroyed by fire because there was insufficient water pressure in the mains to put it out. The WATERWORKS CLAUSES ACT 1874 provided a £10 penalty if a waterworks company allowed the pressure to fall below a specified minimum. The pressure was below this minimum. However, P's action to recover his full loss did not succeed, since the statute did not disclose a cause of action by individuals for damage of this kind, because this would amount to the waterworks company providing a gratuitous fire insurance service. It was clear that the £10 penalty was the only penalty intended to be imposed by the Act.

b. The Act was passed for the benefit of the public generally rather than particular individuals, for example the TRADE DESCRIPTIONS ACT 1968.

c. The Act was passed for the benefit of a section of the public of which the plaintiff is not a member.

In HARTLEY v MAYOH AND CO (1954) P, a fireman, was electrocuted while fighting a fire at D's premises. His electrocution was due to D's breach of statutory regulations. P, however, failed to recover compensation because the regulations were expressed to be for the benefit of 'employees' and he was not a member of this class of persons.

d. The plaintiff suffered damage different from that which the statute was intended to prevent.

In GORRIS v SCOTT (1874), in a storm sheep were swept from the deck of a ship because they were not in pens. However, the purpose of the statutory requirement of 'penning' sheep was to prevent the spread of infection and not to stop them being washed overboard. The plaintiff therefore recovered nothing.

e. If the plaintiff suffers *economic loss* caused by a highway authority's breach of its statutory duty to repair a highway.

In WENTWORTH v WILTSHIRE COUNTY COUNCIL (1992) P's dairy farm was served by a road which fell into disrepair. As a result, from January 1980, Milk Marketing Board tankers could not use the road to collect milk. Initially the Council denied that the road was maintainable at public expense, but at a Crown Court hearing in November 1981 it was established that it was a public highway and that the Council had the statutory duty to maintain it. Nine months later it was repaired, but this was too late to save the farm. P claimed approximately £77,500 damages for economic loss due to breach of statutory duty. The Court of Appeal (reversing the High Court) held that Parliament's intention, based on the construction of the *HIGHWAYS ACT 1959*, was that compensation for economic loss was not payable. The remedy for breach of the Act is to obtain a court order that the highway be put into proper repair. No other means of enforcement was indicated by the Act. P's claim was unsuccessful.

8. The statutory duty may be absolute, or to take reasonable care, depending on the construction of the statute. If it is absolute (ie liability is strict), then contributory negligence is an available defence, but it will be no defence to plead

   a. Volenti non fit injuria.

   b. That the duty has been delegated to a competent person, or

   c. That reasonable care was taken.

9. The fact that the statutory penalty is applied for the benefit of the injured party does not exclude a remedy in tort.

   In GROVES v LORD WIMBORNE (1898) P, a factory employee, was injured when he caught his hand in machinery which by statute should have been fenced. The statute provided that an employer must pay a fine for breach of this statutory duty, and also provided that the fine may be applied for the benefit of the injured party. P therefore received 'double compensation' he was awarded damages in tort for breach of statutory duty (he did not, of course, have to prove fault only that the statute had been broken and that he had been injured) and he had the fine imposed by the criminal law given to him.

PRODUCT LIABILITY

THE CONSUMER PROTECTION ACT 1987

10. *Introduction*

   a. Consumer groups have argued for some time that the law governing civil liability for damage due to defective goods is unfair. For a consumer to sue a manufacturer he must either proceed via a chain of contractual actions (possibly being defeated by an exemption clause) or he must sue for negligence and prove fault. This means that the law often fails to regulate the conduct of those responsible for the damage.

b. Industrial groups have opposed strict product liability on the ground that insurance would be prohibitively expensive and some smaller businesses could be forced to close.

c. After many years of deliberation the EC issued a directive on product liability in July 1985. This has been implemented in the CONSUMER PROTECTION ACT 1987. The Act has three main parts dealing with product liability, consumer safety and misleading price indications.

11. *Part I. Product Liability. Basic Rule. S.2.*

a. To succeed in a product liability claim against a manufacturer the plaintiff must show four things:

  i. That the product contained a defect

  ii. That the plaintiff suffered damage

  iii. That the damage was caused by the product and,

  iv. That the defendant was a producer, 'own brander' or importer of the product.

b. A supplier will also be liable if he fails to identify the producer or importer when requested to do so.

c. The effect of this section is that in future liability will no longer be decided by reference to the fault of the manufacturer or some other person, but by reference to the state of the product in question, ie strict liability is introduced. Even so the plaintiff may experience some difficulty proving that the defect in the product caused the injury.

d. A 'product' must be moveable and industrially produced, eg cars are products, buildings are not. Products of the soil, stock farming and fishing are not products unless subjected to industrial process, eg potatoes are not, but potato crisps are products.

12. *The Meaning of 'Defect'*

a. There are three types of product defect:

  i. A *manufacturing defect* occurs when a product fails to comply with the manufacturer's product specifications and consequently deviates from the norm. The frequency of such defects can be calculated fairly accurately and the producer will be able to spread the risk via insurance and pricing.

  ii. A *design defect* occurs when the product specifications are themselves at fault and present a hazard. This type of defect is far more serious and has led to major claims for compensation, particularly in defective drug cases, for example the Thalidomide case.

  iii. A *duty to warn defect* refers to the producer's responsibility to provide appropriate warnings and instructions to enable the consumer to use the product safely.

b. *S.3* lays down the criteria for judging defectiveness. There is a defect in a product if the safety of the product is not such as persons generally are entitled to expect, taking all circumstances into account, including:

    i. The presentation of the product, including instructions and warnings.

    ii. The use to which it could reasonably be expected to be put.

    iii. The time when the product was supplied.

c. The above test is satisfactory in respect of manufacturing and duty to warn defects, but it is less appropriate for design defects. This is because it is based on consumer expectations and consumers will not know what to expect because they will not usually know how safe it is possible to make the product.

d. The omission of 'reasonably' from the phrase 'entitled to expect' suggests a stricter standard than that normally applied in tort. However, reasonableness is retained in the factors that the court must take into account.

In A & OTHERS V NATIONAL BLOOD AUTHORITY & OTHERS (2001) the NBA were held liable for damage done to recipients of blood infected by Hepatitis C following blood transfusions. The Court found that the danger was known in 1988 but the NBA did not introduce screening tests until 1991. Blood and blood products contaminated with the virus were 'defective products' under *S.3* of the CONSUMER PROTECTION ACT 1987.

13. *Defences (S.4)*

a. Any person has a defence if he can show:

    i. That the defect is attributable to compliance with any enactment.

    ii. That he did not at any time supply the product.

    iii. That the supply was otherwise than in the course of a business.

    iv. That the defect did not exist in the product at the time of supply.

    v. That the state of scientific and technical knowledge at the relevant time was not such that the producer might be expected to have discovered the defect.

    vi. That the defect constituted a defect in a product in which the product in question had been comprised and was wholly attributable to the design of the subsequent product.

    vii. More than 10 years has elapsed since the product was first supplied.

b. The most important defence is v. above, since it directly challenges the basic concept of strict liability for product defects. It is known as the '*state of the art*' defence. It is particularly significant in the area of drugs where new products are constantly being developed on the boundaries of medical and scientific knowledge. A defect in a new drug could affect thousands of users but they would not be compensated if the defect was unknowable at the time of the product's circulation.

   c.   The impact of the 'state of the art' defence will depend on the attitude of the courts. There are two possible approaches:

       i.   The stricter approach is based on the assumption that the producer will be aware of all the available information and technology relating to his product at any given time. There will be two issues for the court. Firstly, was the knowledge available? Secondly, whether the producer applied the knowledge.

      ii.   The second approach pays more regard to the practicalities of the situation and would allow the producer to escape liability if the product was as safe as possible bearing in mind cost, utility, consumer expectations, the availability of safe alternatives and so on. Thus a producer would not be expected to make a product safe if to do so would be prohibitively expensive or if it would reduce the product's utility.

14. *Part II. Consumer Safety*

Part II is intended to provide the public with better protection from unsafe consumer goods. It primarily imposes criminal sanctions, but will also assist the plaintiff in a civil action for negligence since, if a manufacturer has been found guilty under the Act, the plaintiff will be able to rely on the breach of statutory duty, rather than have to prove a breach of the duty of care. The main provisions are:

   a.   A person is guilty of an offence if he supplied consumer goods which are not reasonably safe (*S.10*).

   b.   The Secretary of State may make safety regulations (for example with regard to flammability or toxicity) governing the making and supplying of goods. Such regulations cover for example children's nightdresses and electric blankets.

   c.   The Secretary of State may serve a 'prohibition notice' upon a supplier, prohibiting him from supplying goods which are unsafe. A 'notice to warn' may also be served requiring the supplier to publish, at his own expense, a warning to customers about unsafe goods.

15. *Part III. Misleading Price Indications*

   a.   *S.20* provides that a person commits an offence if, in the course of a business, he gives consumers an indication which is misleading as to the price at which any goods, services, accommodation or facilities are available.

   b.   Examples of misleading price indications include

       i.   An understatement of the price

      ii.   Failing to make it clear that some other additional charge will be made

     iii.   Falsely indicating that the price is expected to be increased, reduced or maintained

     iv.   Making a false price comparison, for example by falsely stating that the price has been reduced.

c. The Office of Fair Trading has issued a code of practice on misleading price indications. Compliance or non-compliance with the code may be taken into account by the court when determining whether or not an offence has been committed (*S.25*).

d. The Act provides various defences, for example

   i. That the defendant took all reasonable precautions and exercised all due diligence to avoid the commission of an offence (*S.39*).

   ii. That the defendant was an innocent publisher or advertising agency who was unaware, and who had no ground for suspecting, that the advertisement contained a misleading price indication (*S.24*).

e. The courts have tended to interpret the 'due diligence' defence fairly strictly, although less rigorous precautions are expected of small firms.

In RILEY v WEBB (**1987**) the defendants supplied pencils containing poisonous substances contrary to the *PENCILS AND GRAPHIC INSTRUMENTS (SAFETY) REGULATIONS 1974*. The defendants' order to their suppliers included a general condition requiring conformity with statutory safety requirements. It was held that this was insufficient, since the defendants should have brought the particular regulations to the attention of their suppliers and obtained a positive assurance that they would comply with them.

CHAPTER 26

Nuisance

PRIVATE NUISANCE

1. A private nuisance is an unlawful interference with the use or enjoyment of another person's land. It will not usually be an unlawful activity. The interference may consist of:

   a. Actual injury to property, for example fumes killing shrubs, or roots undermining a wall.

   b. Interference with health or comfort, for example noise, smoke, or smell.

   c. Interference with easements or natural rights.

2. Whatever the type of harm it does not follow that any harm constitutes a nuisance. Regard must be had to the rule of 'give and take' between neighbours. It may therefore be relevant to consider:

   a. *How far the act complained of is unusual or excessive.*

      In FARRAR v NELSON (**1885**) D bred and kept pheasants on his land. Had he kept only a reasonable number the inconvenience caused to his neighbour would not have constituted a nuisance. D, however, kept an excessive amount of pheasants and this was held to amount to a nuisance.

   b. *Duration.* – The longer the duration of an interference the more likely it is to be a nuisance. An isolated act cannot be a private nuisance.

      In BOLTON v STONE (**1951**) D hit a cricket ball out of the ground hitting P. The evidence was that on only about eight occasions had balls been struck out of the ground in 35 years. P sued in negligence and nuisance.

      P's negligence action failed because she was not owed a duty of care. Injury to passers-by was only foreseeable as a remote possibility, it was not reasonably foreseeable.

      It was held not to be a nuisance because it was an isolated act. A private nuisance must be a continuing state of affairs.

   c. *The defendant's intention.* – An act that would not otherwise be actionable may become a tort if it is done with intention to injure or annoy as in HOLLYWOOD SILVER FOX FARM v EMMETT (**1936**) (Chapter 21.5).

   d. *The character of the neighbourhood.* – A person in a town cannot expect silence and clean air. Thus the standard of comfort protected by the law varies from place to place. However, the character of the neighbourhood is only relevant where the interference is to health and comfort and not where actual damage to property is caused. If actual damage is caused it is a nuisance regardless of the neighbourhood.

e. *Sensitivity.* – The law gives no special protection to abnormally sensitive persons or property. Thus no remedy lies if sensitivity is the sole reason for the damage.

In ROBINSON V KILVERT (**1889**) heat which rose from D's flat damaged exceptionally sensitive paper stored by P in the above flat. There was no suggestion that the heat was excessive. P did not receive compensation because the paper was only damaged because it was very sensitive.

f. *The defendant's lack of care.*

i. If lack of care allows an annoyance to become excessive the defendant may be liable.

In ANDRAE V SELFRIDGE (1938) P, a hotel owner, recovered damages from D, who was demolishing the adjoining premises. Although building and demolition do not usually constitute a nuisance, since they are socially desirable, if the amount of noise and dust created is unnecessarily great, as in this case, a nuisance will be committed.

ii. If a landowner's lack of care allows his land to encroach upon his neighbour's land he may be liable in either nuisance or negligence.

In LEAKEY V NATIONAL TRUST (**1980**) soil and tree stumps had fallen onto P's land from a natural mound on D's land, the movement being caused by natural subsidence due to weather and soil conditions. It was held that an occupier of land owes a general duty of care to neighbouring occupiers to take reasonable steps to prevent the natural or non-natural state of the land from causing damage to neighbours. In such cases it does not matter whether the action is brought in negligence or nuisance. It was suggested by D that the rule in Rylands v Fletcher indicated that there was no liability for the natural state of the land. It was, however, held that although liability under Rylands v Fletcher is restricted to non-natural use of the land it does not exclude or deny liability for natural hazards.

3. *Persons Who Can Sue*

a. Since the interference must be with the enjoyment or use of land it follows that the only person who can usually sue is the occupier of the land, not his lodger, guest or wife.

In MALONE V LASKEY (1907) M occupied a house which was leased by D to his (M's) employers. M's wife (the plaintiff) was injured when a lavatory cistern fell on her due to being loosened by vibrations from D's electric generator which was in adjoining premises. P's nuisance claim failed since she was not D's tenant, and in nuisance it is the tenant who must sue and no other persons on the premises.

b. A reversioner can also sue if there is a permanent injury to his interest in the property. (A reversioner is an owner of freehold property who has granted a lease. His interest is called the freehold reversion. He may also be called a lessor or landlord.)

4. *Persons Who Can be Sued*

a. The person who created the nuisance may be sued even if he has vacated the land.

b. The person in possession may be sued unless:

   i. The nuisance was caused by an independent contractor, *except* where the work necessitated special precautions by the occupier.

   In BOWER v PEATE (1876) P and D owned adjoining houses, each having a right of support from the other. D hired an independent contractor to pull down and rebuild his house, and the contractor undertook to support P's house while the work was in progress. The contractor was however, negligent, and P's house was damaged. D was held liable because the duty to support his neighbour's house could not be delegated by D. – If D wished to work on his house then he must himself accept the risk of damage to P's house. (The nuisance in this case was the interference with an easement, ie the right of support that each could expect from his neighbour.)

   ii. The nuisance was caused by a trespasser, or

   iii. The nuisance existed before the occupier acquired the property, except where the occupier failed to take reasonable steps to abate it.

c. An occupier will be liable for a nuisance committed by a trespasser if he adopts the nuisance:

   In SEDLEIGH-DENFIELD v O'CALLAGHAN (1940) a trespasser (the county council) entered D's land and laid a drainage pipe in a ditch. The council protected the end of the pipe with grating so that it would not get blocked with leaves. The grating was unsatisfactory and every few months one of D's employees used to unblock the grating. On one occasion a blockage caused the flooding of P's land (which adjoined D's land). Usually proof that a nuisance was caused by a trespasser is a defence. However, in this case D had, on finding out about the nuisance, acquiesced in its presence and continued it himself. He was therefore held liable.

   In PAGE MOTORS v EPSOM BOROUGH COUNCIL (1980) D leased P land for use as a car showroom and garage. At the start of the lease there were a few gypsies on D's adjoining land, but the number rapidly increased. D had a statutory duty to provide adequate sites for gypsies in the area, but they did not do so. P alleged that the gypsies were a nuisance – there was smell from bonfires, uncontrolled dogs, obstruction of access and customers and suppliers had become reluctant to visit the garage. Eventually, over three years after the lease was granted, sites were established and the gypsies left the area. It was held that although D had not caused the nuisance they had allowed it to continue for far too long and were liable for any loss suffered by P. The judge appreciated that the council had difficulties because of the lack of alternative sites and pressure from the Department of the Environment not to move gypsies needlessly. However, he pointed out that his decision was just in that it had the effect of sharing the burden of a local problem among the whole community on whose behalf the council was acting rather than allowing it to fall on one individual.

d. A landlord out of possession is not liable, unless he permits his tenant to commit the nuisance.

5. *Defences*

a. Volenti non fit injuria.

b. Absolute statutory authority.

c. The nuisance was caused by a stranger and the defendant could not possibly have known of it.

d. Long use, ie 20 years, provided the nuisance is capable of forming the subject matter of an easement. An *easement* is a right to use or restrict the use of another person's land in some way, for example a right of way or a right of light.

e. It may be a defence to establish that commission of a nuisance is in the public interest. There are, however, two conflicting Court of Appeal cases on this point.

In MILLER v JACKSON (1977) a majority of the Court of Appeal (Geoffrey–Lane and Cumming–Bruce L.J.) held that a cricket club were guilty of negligence and nuisance in allowing cricket balls to be struck out of the ground into P's adjoining premises, but a different majority (Lord Denning M.R. and Cumming–Bruce L.J.) refused an injunction and awarded damages on the basis that the greater interest of the public in being able to play cricket on a ground where it had been played for over 70 years should prevail over the hardship of a few individual householders, who had recently purchased their houses, and were deprived of the use of their gardens while the game was in progress.

Contrast KENNAWAY v THOMPSON (1980) where the nuisance complained of was noise from motor boat racing and water-skiing. The Court of Appeal held that a nuisance existed and they granted an injunction which limited the number of days on which large-scale activities could take place and limited the noise level on other occasions. They refused to follow Miller v Jackson, feeling that it was wrong to allow a nuisance to continue merely because the wrongdoer is willing and able to pay for any injury he may inflict. The court felt that the two reasons for refusing to grant an injunction in Miller v Jackson (i. the public interest and ii. that the plaintiff 'came to the nuisance') were contrary to earlier authority and were not binding on the court.

6. *Ineffective Defences*

   a. That the plaintiff came to the nuisance.

   In STURGES v BRIDGEMAN (**1879**) D had for many years been manufacturing sweets in premises adjoining P's garden. P, a doctor, then built a consulting room that adjoined the manufacturing premises. He then sued D in nuisance, due to the noise and vibrations caused by D's machinery. D's defence was in effect 'I was here first'. However, this defence is ineffective, and particularly in view of the area (Wimpole Street) the noise and vibrations were held to constitute a nuisance. D also claimed that he had acquired a right to commit the nuisance through long use. It was held that this was not possible – any right acquired through long use (20 years) must be capable of forming the subject matter of an easement.

   b. That reasonable care has been taken.

   In RAPIER v LONDON TRAMWAYS (1893) D kept about 200 horses in stables adjoining the P's land. Although D took reasonable measures to minimise any nuisance a certain amount of noise and smell was caused by the horses. D were held liable in nuisance – it was no defence to say that they had done everything possible to prevent it.

   c. That the defendant's conduct would not have amounted to a nuisance had it not been for the contributory acts of others.

7. *Abatement of Nuisances*. In addition to the usual remedies of damages and/or an injunction the law will sometimes allow the remedy of abatement, ie removal of the nuisance.

   a. If there are two ways of abating a nuisance the less mischievous must be selected.

   b. Entry onto the land of a third party is not permissible.

   c. Notice should be given to the occupier of the land in which the nuisance arises except:

   i.   Where abatement is possible without entry, or

   ii. In cases of emergency, such as a fire.

   d. Abatement allows a person to cut off the branches of his neighbour's trees which overhang his land.

   e. Abatement is also applicable to public nuisance.

PUBLIC NUISANCE

8. A public nuisance is an unlawful act or omission which endangers the health, safety, or comfort of the public (or some section of it) or obstructs the exercise of a common right, for example selling contaminated food, or obstructing a highway. For example AB AND OTHERS v SOUTH WEST WATER SERVICES (**1992**) (Chapter 29.4).

9. It differs from private nuisance in that:

    a. It is a crime as well as a tort.

    b. An isolated act may be a public nuisance.

    c. It need not involve an interference with the use of enjoyment of land.

    d. Several people at least must be affected.

        In R v MADDON (1975) **D** dialled 999 and informed the telephonist that there was a 200 lb bomb at the local steelworks. The call was a hoax and D was charged with the offence of committing a public nuisance. The only people who knew of the call and its contents were the telephonist, eight security guards, and the police – who conducted an hour-long search until the hoax was discovered. It was held that the offence of public nuisance had not been committed since not enough people were affected.

    e. A right to commit a public nuisance cannot be acquired by long use.

10. Potentially the same people may sue and be sued as in private nuisance, except that a private individual may only sue if he has suffered some special damage different from that suffered by the class of persons affected.

In CAMPBELL v PADDINGTON CORPORATION (**1911**) the Council erected a stand in Burwood Place, London so that Council members could view King Edward VII's funeral procession. P owned a flat in Burwood Place which she often let for the purpose of viewing public processions. The Council's stand obstructed this view, so that she could not let her flat. Since the stand was a public nuisance, and since she had suffered special damage in excess of that suffered by the public at large, she was successful in her action against the Council.

11. If the same act is both a public and private nuisance the right of a private individual to sue for private nuisance is not affected.

12. *Highway Nuisances*. Common examples of public nuisances are obstructions on highways or dangerous premises adjoining the highway. Principles of 'give and take' also apply to public nuisance. Thus a temporary obstruction, if reasonable in its size and duration, may be permissible. However:

    a. Liability is strict for the collapse of an artificial projection over the highway, for example a lamp. If the projection is natural the occupier will be liable only if he knew or ought to have known of the danger.

        In NOBLE v HARRISON (**1926**) the branch of a tree on D's land that overhung the highway suddenly fell and damaged a passing coach. The owner of the land was not held liable, because a reasonable examination would not have revealed the tree's defect.

    b. If something projects above the highway this will not constitute a public nuisance if no obstruction is caused.

    c. If a local authority allows a highway to become dangerous it may be liable unless it can be shown that reasonable care has been taken having regard to various matters such as the expected volume of traffic, and the standard of maintenance appropriate to such a highway.

13. *Remedies*

a. Criminal aspect. – A prosecution, or an application for an injunction by the Attorney General.

b. Civil aspect. – An application for an injunction and/or damages by the person suffering loss.

CHAPTER 27

Trespass and Conversion

TRESPASS TO THE PERSON

1. *Definition* A trespass to the person is an intentional interference with the person or liberty of another. It was formerly thought that an action for trespass to the person could be brought where personal injuries were caused negligently though directly. However, since LETANG v COOPER (**1965**) it has been clear that the phrase 'trespass to the person' is restricted to intentional acts. Where an unintentional act causes physical injury the correct action is negligence. Trespass to the person is actionable per se (without proof of loss) unless the defendant establishes that his act was justified. It may take three forms – assault, battery and false imprisonment.

2. *Assault*

   a. An assault is an act of the defendant which causes the plaintiff reasonable fear of an immediate battery on him by the defendant.

   b. Words are no assault, but they may prevent the act that they accompany from being an assault.

       In TUBERVELL v SAVAGE (**1669**) during an argument D brandished his sword saying, 'If it were not assize time I would not take such language from you.'

       However, since it was assize time (ie the local criminal courts were in session), these words prevented the brandishing of the sword from being an assault.

   c. It has been suggested that if a person rounds a corner and is confronted by a motionless gunman, the gunman may commit an assault if he does not move the gun barrel away from the other person. However, it is generally accepted that some movement is necessary to commit an assault.

       In INNES v WYLIE (**1844**) a policeman stood motionless in order to block a doorway. This was held not to be an assault.

3. *Battery*

   a. Battery is the intentional application of force to another person. The amount of harm inflicted is relevant to the amount of damages awarded, but not to the determination of liability.

   b. It is a battery to throw something, eg water, at the plaintiff so that it hits him; or to remove a chair from under him; or to set a dog on him; or to drag him away from something for his own good.

c. Consent is a defence to battery, but the defence will not apply if the defendant does some act which was not contemplated by the plaintiff.

In NASH v SHEEN (1953) P went to the hairdresser for a permanent wave, but was instead given a tone-rinse which changed the colour of her hair and caused a rash over the rest of her body. The hairdresser was held to have committed a battery.

d. It is not a battery to touch a person to attract his attention.

4. *False Imprisonment*

a. This is the infliction of bodily restraint not authorised by law.

b. The restraint must be total.

In BIRD v JONES (1845) D closed off the public footpath over one side of Hammersmith Bridge, and charged people admission to his enclosure to watch the Boat Race. P climbed into the enclosure from one side, and was prevented from leaving from the other side. He was, however, told that he could go out the same way that he came in. It was held that there was no false imprisonment since the restraint was not total.

c. The plaintiff need not know that he is being detained.

In MEERING v GRAHAME – WHITE AVIATION CO (1919) P was suspected of thefts from his employers, although he did not know that he was a suspect. When he was asked to answer some questions concerning the thefts he voluntarily agreed – he still did not realise that he was a suspect. He later found out that while he was being questioned there were two of the works security guards outside the door who would have prevented him leaving if he had attempted to do so. He succeeded in his false imprisonment action, not on the grounds of his discomfort, but because of the injury to his reputation caused by his employer's action.

d. It is no tort to refuse to allow a person to leave premises when he does not fulfil a reasonable condition subject to which he entered them.

In ROBINSON v BALMAIN NEW FERRY CO (1910) the terms of a contract to travel on a ferry provided that the passenger must pay one penny on entering the wharf and a further penny on leaving. P paid his penny to enter, but just missed the ferry. He attempted to leave without paying another penny, but was restrained from doing so until he had paid. He failed in his false imprisonment action. The court said there was no duty on a person to make exit from his premises gratuitous, where a person had entered on the basis of a definite contract which involved their leaving in another way.

e. In addition to the usual remedy of damages the remedies of self-help (ie breaking out) and an application for a writ of habeas corpus are available. *Habeas corpus* is a prerogative writ designed to provide a person, who is kept in confinement without legal justification, with a means of obtaining release. An application may be made, for example, by the parents of a child who is being kept in an institution against their wishes.

5. *Justification of Trespass to the Person*

a. Defence of person or property. Reasonable force may also be used to remove a trespasser.

b. Parental authority. Reasonable and moderate punishment may be administered.

c. Lawful arrest. A person arrested without warrant must be told of the reason for the arrest, and taken to a magistrate or police station as soon as possible.

d. Judicial authority.

e. Necessity.

In LEIGH v GLADSTONE (1909) P, who was on hunger strike in prison was forcibly fed by warders in order to save her life. The defence of necessity was successfully raised against her action for battery.

f. Inevitable accident. (See STANLEY v POWELL (1891) Chapter 22.11.)

TRESPASS TO LAND

6. Trespass to land is the *direct interference* with the *possession* of another person's land without lawful authority. It is a tort actionable per se, ie without proof of loss.

7. *Possession.* – Since trespass is a wrong done to the possessor only he rather than the owner can sue. Possession includes not only physical occupation, but occupation through servants and agents. Mere use, for example as a lodger, is not possession.

8. *Interference*

a. This must be direct, either by

   i. Entering on land, or

   ii. Remaining on land after permission to stay has ended. An exception is a lessee, who if he remains at the end of his lease retains possession and therefore does not become a trespasser.

   iii. Placing objects on land.

b. If a right to enter is abused this may be a trespass.

In HARRISON v THE DUKE OF RUTLAND (1893) the Duke owned a grouse moor. A road led across this moor which he allowed the public to use. P however, abused this right of entry by deliberately frightening the grouse just as the Duke and his party were about to shoot. P was physically restrained by members of the shooting party and he brought an action for false imprisonment. His action failed because proportionate and reasonable force may be used to restrain or eject a trespasser and P, because he had abused his right of entry, was a trespasser.

c. Entry below the surface is a trespass, as is entry into airspace, if it takes place within the area of ordinary use.

In KELSEN V IMPERIAL TOBACCO CO (1957) P and D occupied adjoining premises, D, however, occupied a taller building than P. D attached an advertising sign to their wall which projected a few inches into the airspace about P's premises. P was successful in obtaining a court order compelling D to remove the sign since it was a trespass.

d. *S.76 CIVIL AVIATION ACT 1982* exempts civil aircraft flying at a reasonable height from liability for trespass, but it imposes strict liability on the owner of the aircraft for all damage caused by things falling from it.

e. If a person enters in exercise of a common law or statutory right and abuses the right by a positive act he is deemed to be a trespasser from the moment he entered the premises, ie a trespass ab initio (from the beginning).

In *THE SIX CARPENTERS CASE* (*1610*) six carpenters entered a public house and consumed a quantity of wine and bread. They then refused to pay the price. They were not held to be trespassers ab initio since their act was a non-feasance (an omission) and not a misfeasance.

9. *Defences*

a. The general defences of volenti, necessity, inevitable accident, self-defence and statutory authority all apply, but mistake is no defence.

b. Entry to exercise a common law right. For example A enters B's land to re-possess his goods that B has wrongfully taken onto his land.

c. Entry by licence. For example theatre guests. When the licence expires the person becomes a trespasser when he does not leave, in contrast to a lessee who remains in possession.

d. *Jus tertii.* – There is a rule which states that a person claiming land from another who is in possession of it can succeed only by showing a stronger title than the person in possession. If the land rightfully belongs to neither of them, but to a third party, the person in possession will have the defence of *jus tertii*.

In DOE D. CARTER V BARNARD (1849) P was wrongfully turned off certain land by D. In her action to recover possession it became evident that neither P nor D were entitled to the land. P's action to recover the land therefore failed since she could not show a better title than D. D could therefore claim the defence of *jus tertii*.

10. *Remedies*. The remedies available to the plaintiff depend on whether or not he is in possession of the land. If an owner has been wrongfully dispossessed he cannot sue for trespass since he is not in possession.

a. Remedies available to the person in possession:

i. Damages, nominal or compensatory.

ii. Injunction.

iii. Ejection of the trespasser. Reasonable and proportionate force may be used (ie proportionate to the amount of force that the trespasser is using to prevent ejection).

b. Remedies available to an owner who has been wrongfully dispossessed:

    i. Re-entry, however, the re-entry must be peaceful.

In HEMMINGS v STOKE POGES GOLF CLUB (**1920**) P refused to leave his cottage when his tenancy had been lawfully ended by notice to quit. The landlords, using reasonable force, removed P and his furniture and re-entered the premises. It was held that they were entitled to do this. (The law regarding tenants has now been changed so that it is illegal to remove a tenant without first obtaining a court order. Reasonable force may, however, be used to remove a licensee remaining on premises after the termination of his licence.)

    ii. An action for the recovery of land. The limitation period for this remedy is 12 years.

    iii. Having recovered possession as above, such person is deemed by the doctrine of Possession by Relation to have been in possession since the moment his right to possession accrued. He can therefore maintain an action for mesne profits, ie profits lost to the plaintiff while the defendant was wrongfully in possession.

11. *Criminal Liability*

a. *Squatters*. The fact that trespass is not usually a crime has led to problems with persons who trespass and take up residence on other people's property.

    i. S.6 CRIMINAL LAW ACT 1977 created the offence of using or threatening violence to secure entry to premises on which there is another person who opposes entry. This offence, however, cannot be committed by a displaced residential occupier, or someone acting for him.

    ii. By S.7 CRIMINAL LAW ACT 1977, it is an offence for a trespasser to fail to leave premises when required to do so by a displaced residential occupier.

b. *Travellers*. S.39 PUBLIC ORDER ACT 1986 gives senior police officers the power to direct trespassers to leave land. The officer must reasonably believe that two or more trespassers intend to reside there, that reasonable steps have been taken by the occupier to ask them to leave, and that either

    i. Damage has been caused to property;

    ii. The trespassers have used threatening, abusive or insulting words or behaviour towards the occupier; or

    iii. That the trespassers have brought at least 12 vehicles onto the land.

Failure to comply with the police officer's direction is a criminal offence.

TRESPASS TO GOODS

12. A trespass to goods is the direct interference with the possession of goods. The interference must be direct and not consequential, although in some cases

physical contact is not necessary, for example to chase cattle is a trespass to goods. Generally the interference will take one of three forms:

a. Taking the goods,

b. Damaging goods, or altering their physical condition,

c. Interfering with goods, for example moving them about.

13. Only persons in possession (ie having immediate physical control) can sue. Some persons not in actual possession are deemed to have possession for this purpose. For example a master who has given custody of his goods to his servant, or the personal representative of a deceased person, is deemed to be in possession.

14. Defences include

a. Inevitable accident

In NATIONAL COAL BOARD v EVANS (1951) in the course of excavating the foundations of a building D damaged a cable belonging to the NCB. It was held that since the presence of the cable was unforeseeable D was not liable, having the defence of inevitable accident.

b. Reasonable defence of person or property. For example injuring a dog which is attacking somebody.

c. Pursuance of a legal right or legal process. For example levying distress for rent.

d. In addition trespass to goods or land will not be unlawful if it is by police following procedures laid down in the *POLICE AND CRIMINAL EVIDENCE ACT 1984*, for example if the police enter premises without a warrent to make an arrest, or if the police enter premises with a search warrant the police may take articles found on premises if they reasonably believe that they are evidence in relation to an offence.

CONVERSION

15. *Definition*

Conversion is some dealing by the defendant in relation to the plaintiff's goods which is a denial of the plaintiff's right to possess and use those goods. It is the main method by which rights in personal property are protected.

16. *The Wrongful Act*

a. The defendant may be liable in conversion even if he never possessed the goods provided his dealing constituted an unjustifiable denial of title.

In VAN OPPEN v TREDEGARS (1921) P delivered goods by mistake to a firm. D purported to sell the goods to the firm. The firm disposed of the goods in the course of their business. D was held liable.

b. The defendant will not be liable if he merely moves goods without any denial of title.

In FOULDES v WILLOUGHBY (**1841**) D moved P's horses from D's ferry, hoping that this would also induce P to leave. P remained and was ferried across the river. It was held that there is no conversion since there had been no denial of P's title to the horses.

c. The usual form of conversion is an abuse of existing possession by for example:

    i.   Destroying goods;

    ii.   Altering their nature;

    iii. Wrongfully refusing to return them;

    iv. Selling and delivering them to the third party, even if the defendant dealt innocently with the goods. (Note the exceptions in *S.22, 24 and 25 SALE OF GOODS ACT 1979* (Chapter 31).)

       In HOLLINS v FOWLER (**1875**) D, a broker, sold and delivered cotton belonging to P. He was acting on behalf of a crook although he did not know this at the time. He was held liable in conversion because he had sold and delivered goods in denial of P's title.

d. Involuntary receipt of goods is not conversion, although the recipient must not wilfully damage or destroy them unless they become a nuisance. However, a person who receives unsolicited goods will be entitled to deal with them as if they were a gift if the sender fails to take them back within six months, or at some earlier date if the recipient gives notice to the sender (*UNSOLICITED GOODS AND SERVICES ACT 1971*).

e. Conversion may arise in situations where a seller of goods includes a term in his contract reserving title until payment.

In CLOUGH MILL v MARTIN (**1985**) a contract for the sale of yarn had a reservation of title clause stating that the ownership of the yarn remained with the seller until the seller had received payment in full, or the yarn was sold by the buyer in a bona fide sale at full market value. When a receiver was appointed, the seller claimed a quantity of the yarn. The receiver refused to return it. The seller's claim was upheld and the receiver was held personally liable in conversion.

17. *The Plaintiff's Rights*

a. At the time of the conversion the plaintiff must have been in possession of the goods, or have had a right to immediate possession.

b. Where the plaintiff has been deprived permanently of the goods the measure of damages is their market value at the time of the conversion unless:

    i.   The defendant has the goods and refuses to deliver them, in which case it is their value at the time of refusal;

    ii. The value has increased since the date of the conversion, in which case the measure may be the value at the date of judgement (provided the plaintiff sues promptly).

CHAPTER 28

Defamation

1. A defamatory statement is a false statement that tends to injure the plaintiff's reputation, or causes him to be shunned by ordinary members of society. There are two forms of defamation, namely libel and slander.

2. *Distinctions Between Libel and Slander*

   a. A defamatory statement is libel if it is in permanent form, or if it is for general reception. For example writing, pictures, films, radio, television, the theatre, records, or waxworks. If the statement lacks permanence it will be slander. For example spoken words or gestures.

   b. Libel is a crime as well as a tort, whereas slander is only a tort.

   c. Libel is actionable per se, slander is not unless:

      i. It imputes a crime punishable by imprisonment.

      ii. It imputes certain existing diseases, such as venereal disease or Aids.

      iii. It imputes unchastity, adultery, or lesbianism in a woman.

      iv. It is calculated to damage the plaintiff in any office, trade, or profession held or carried on by him.

3. If the plaintiff is to succeed in a defamation action he must show three things

   a. That the statement is defamatory;

   b. That it refers to the plaintiff;

   c. That it has been published by the defendant.

   In addition to the above requirements in most cases of slander (ie where it is not actionable per se) the plaintiff must prove damage, ie material loss capable of monetary evaluation, such as loss of employment, and not mere loss of friends or reputation.

   Each of the three main requirements is now considered in turn.

4. *The Meaning of 'Defamatory'*

   a. A useful guide was laid down by Lord Atkin in SIM v STRETCH (**1936**). He said.

   'Would the words tend to lower the plaintiff in the estimation of right thinking members of society generally?'

   In SIM v STRETCH (**1936**) a housemaid left P's employment, and went to work for D, for whom she had worked in the past. D then sent P the following telegram.

'Edith has resumed her services with us today. Please send her possessions and the money you borrowed, also her wages.'

P alleged this telegram was defamatory in that it implied he was in financial trouble, having to borrow off a housemaid, and not having paid her wages. The House of Lords held that the telegram was not defamatory, since if a statement has a number of good interpretations, it is unreasonable to seize upon a bad one to give a defamatory sense to the statement.

b. A statement would satisfy Lord Atkin's test if it

    i.   Reflects on a person's trading or professional ability.

    ii.   Imputes dishonesty, criminality or immorality.

    iii. Imputes insanity, certain diseases, or that the plaintiff has been raped.

In YOUSSOUPOFF v M.G.M. PICTURES LTD (1934) M.G.M. made a film about the life of Rasputin. In the film Rasputin was represented as having raped a Princess Natasha. In the film Princess Natasha was also represented as being in love with the man who was eventually to murder Rasputin.

In real life the plaintiff, a Russian Princess (whose name was not Natasha) was married to a man who was undoubtedly concerned with the murder of the real-life Rasputin. P alleged that because of her marriage reasonable people would think it was she who had been raped. P succeeded in her libel action.

It appears rather illogical that it is defamatory to accuse a person of something, which if it had happened, would have been actively resisted by that person, for example rape, or the catching of certain diseases. It does, however, probably reflect the reality of life in that so-called 'reasonable people' may in fact shun a person who has been raped or who is ill.

c. A statement is not defamatory if the plaintiff's reputation suffers in the eyes of only a section of the community in circumstances where the majority of the community would approve of his action.

In BYRNE v DEANE (1937) D was the proprietor of a golf club and P was a member. There were some illegal gaming machines in the clubhouse, P informed the police of this and the machines had to be removed. A few days later a poem appeared on the wall near where the machines had been. The poem referred to the machines and ended as follows:

'But he who gave the game away, May he Byrne in hell and rue the day.'

P alleged that this was defamatory, in that it showed that he was disloyal to his fellow members. It was held that the words were not defamatory because 'right-thinking members of society' would not think less of a person who upheld the law. It was not sufficient that he was shunned by the members of the golf club.

d. A problem may arise if the words used are not prima facie defamatory. In this case an innuendo is required if the plaintiff is to succeed. An innuendo is a statement by the plaintiff of the meaning that he attributes to the words.

In TOLLEY v J.S. FRY AND SONS LTD (**1931**) D, a chocolate manufacturer, published an advertisement showing a picture of P, and a poem including P's name and D's name. P was a well known amateur golfer and he had not given his consent for his name and picture to be used in this way. The picture and poem were not by themselves defamatory. However, P brought a libel action alleging an innuendo. He alleged that reasonable people would think that he had been paid for the use of his name and that he therefore was not a genuine amateur golfer. It was held that this was a reasonable inference. He succeeded in his libel action.

In CASSIDY v DAILY MIRROR (**1929**) D published a picture of Cassidy and a young woman with a statement that their engagement had been announced. This information was given to the paper by Cassidy himself. Cassidy was, however, already married and his wife brought a libel action claiming that the photograph and statement contained an innuendo to those who knew her that she was not married to her husband, and was accordingly 'living in sin' with him. The evidence was that some people who knew her were given this impression. She therefore succeeded in her action. Note that:

    i.   The young woman would probably have succeeded if she had brought an action. The innuendo would have been that she was the type of person who went out with married men. This would have been the thoughts of people who knew Cassidy was already married.

    ii.   If the case had occurred after 1952 the paper may have been able to succeed in the defence of unintentional defamation. (See below.)

e.   The statement must also be false. The legal presumption is that it is false. Thus the defendant has to prove its truth, rather than the plaintiff its falseness.

5. *Reference to the Plaintiff*

a.   The plaintiff need not necessarily be named.

In J'ANSON v STUART (**1789**) a newspaper, speaking of a swindler (without naming him) described him as follows: 'He has but one eye, and is well known to all persons acquainted with the name of a certain noble circumnavigator.'

The plaintiff was able to succeed in his defamation action because he only had one eye and a name similar to that of a famous admiral.

b.   Except where a plea of unintentional defamation succeeds, it is no defence to say:

    i.   That the defendant did not intend to refer to the plaintiff.

    In HULTON v JONES (**1910**) a humorous newspaper article described the immoral life of a fictitious churchwarden from Peckham called Artemus Jones. There existed, however, a real Artemus Jones, who was a barrister. The evidence was that the people who knew him thought the article referred to him. Artemus Jones was awarded damages of £1,750.

    ii.   That the words were intended to refer to a third person of whom they were true.

In NEWSTEAD v LONDON EXPRESS (1939) the newspaper published a statement that Harold Newstead a thirty-year old Camberwell man had been convicted of bigamy. Unfortunately there were two thirty-year-old Harold Newsteads in Camberwell, and whilst the statement was true in respect of one of them it was untrue of the other. The Harold Newstead who had not been convicted of bigamy therefore recovered damages.

6. *Publication by the Defendant.* The plaintiff must prove that the statement was published, ie communicated to at least one person other than himself. However:

    a.   A person is not liable if publication occurs only as a result of an act which is not reasonably foreseeable by him, for example, a letter being opened by the plaintiff's butler. (It is, however, reasonably foreseeable that a letter will be opened by the plaintiff's wife.)

    b.   Two or more persons may be responsible for the same publication, for example, the author, printer, publisher, and bookseller. The bookseller will have a defence if he did not know of the libel and could not be expected to know of it.

7. *Defences*

    a.   *Justification.* The defence of justification is available if the statement is true in substance. Small inaccuracies do not defeat this defence.

In ALEXANDER v N.E. RAILWAY CO (1865) P had been convicted of failing to pay his rail fare. The railway published a poster stating that his sentence was a fine or three weeks imprisonment. In fact the alternative was two weeks imprisonment. It was held that this small inaccuracy did not defeat the defence of justification. Note that:

    i.   A defendant can plead inconsistent defences. For example if an innuendo is alleged, the defendant could plead firstly that there is no possible innuendo, and secondly that if there is then it represents the truth.

    ii.   If, for example, A says, 'B said C is a thief.' Then to succeed in the defence of justification he must prove that C is a thief, and not just that B said C is a thief.

    iii.   An honest belief that the statement is true is no justification.

    iv.   By *S.5 DEFAMATION ACT* 1952 where the words complained of contain two or more distinct charges against the plaintiff the defence does not fail merely because the truth of each charge is not proved if the charge not proved to be true does not materially injure the plaintiff's reputation having regard to the true charges. For example if A calls B 'a thief and a murderer' and B is a murderer, but not a thief, B would be unlikely to succeed in a defamation action against A since a murderer's reputation can hardly be lowered by being called a thief, albeit incorrectly.

b. *Fair comment.* This defence will apply where the statement is a fair comment made in good faith on a matter of public interest. Note that:

   i. The subject matter must be of public interest, for example the conduct of politicians, or crime reporting.

   ii. The statement must be opinion not fact.

   iii. The comment must be based on facts which, if stated with the comment, must be true.

   iv. The comment must be fair, ie an honest expression of the defendant's opinion. It cannot therefore be motivated by malice.

   v. An example of fair comment would be 'Mr X raped Miss C; he is a disgrace to the community'. The second part of the quotation is a comment on the first, it is also opinion. Since crime is a public interest, if Mr X did rape Miss C the defence would be available to the maker of the statement.

c. *Absolute privilege.* No action lies for defamation, however, false or malicious the statement, if it is made:

   i. In Parliament;

   ii. In parliamentary papers;

   iii. In the course of state communications;

   iv. In judicial proceedings;

   v. In newspaper reports of judicial proceedings, provided they are fair, accurate and contemporaneous. 'Newspaper' in this context includes weekly but not monthly publications.

d. *Qualified privilege.* The defence will be available in the following situations, provided the statement was not published more widely than necessary, and provided it was not motivated by malice:

   i. Where A makes a statement to B about C and A is under a legal, social or moral duty to make the statement to B, and B has an interest in receiving it.

   In WATT v LONGSDON (**1930**) D, a company director, received allegations of drunkenness, dishonesty, and immorality by P, who was an employee of the company. He showed these allegations to the chairman of the company and to P's wife. The communication to the chairman was held to be subject to qualified privilege since both the duty to make the statement, and an interest in receiving it were present.

   It was held, however, that he had no legal, social or moral duty to communicate the allegations to P's wife. Thus in respect of the communication to her the defence of qualified privilege failed.

237

ii. Where A makes a statement to B about C and A has an interest to protect and B has a duty to protect it.

In SOMERVILLE v HAWKINS (1851) D told two servants that he had dismissed P for robbing him. D could plead the defence of qualified privilege because he had an interest to protect, ie his own property.

iii. For fair and accurate reports of judicial or parliamentary proceedings, whether or not they are in a newspaper, and whether or not they are contemporaneous.

iv. For fair and accurate reports in a newspaper or broadcast on various matters, such as public meetings (*S.7 DEFAMATION ACT 1952*). The *S.7* definition of 'newspaper' includes monthly publications.

v. For professional statements between solicitor and client.

e. *Unintentional defamation (S.4 DEFAMATION ACT 1952).* This defence only applies to words published innocently, ie where:

i. The publisher did not intend to refer to the plaintiff, and

ii. The words were not prima facie defamatory, and the publisher did not know of any possible innuendo, and

iii. The publisher was not negligent.

Where the above conditions are satisfied the publisher may make an 'offer of amends', ie an offer of a suitable correction and apology, and an offer to take reasonable steps to notify persons who have received copies of the alleged defamatory words. If the offer is accepted, the matter is closed. If the offer is refused, the publisher has a defence if he can prove:

i. That the words were published innocently

ii. That the offer was made as soon as possible, and

iii. That the author wrote them without malice.

8. *Mitigation.* The defendant may mitigate his payment of damages by:

a. Apology.

b. Proof of provocation.

c. Evidence of the plaintiff's bad reputation prior to the publication of the defamation.

CHAPTER 29

Remedies and Limitation Periods

REMEDIES

1. *Damages*. It will be clear from the previous chapters that the main remedy for the victim of a tort is an award of damages. Damages are a sum of money payable by the defendant. The defendant may, however, choose, or be required by law, to insure against the payment of damages. Tort damages are always unliquidated, ie they clearly cannot be fixed by prior agreement between the parties. There are three main types of damages.

2. *Compensatory Damages*

   a. Their purpose is to put the plaintiff so far as money can do, in the position that he would have been in if the tort had not been committed. This sum must take into account future loss, since usually only one action may be brought. The damages awarded will be itemised under several 'heads', for example,

      i.   Loss of amenity;

      ii. Pain and suffering;

      iii. Loss of expectation of life;

      iv. Loss of income, both actual and prospective.

   b. The relationship between iii. and iv. has been reviewed by the House of Lords.

      In PICKETT V BRITISH RAIL ENGINEERING (1980) the court held that a plaintiff, (provided he survived the tort), could recover damages for loss of income on the basis of his pre-accident life expectancy. This overrules the Court of Appeal decision in OLIVER V ASHMAN (1962) which decided that damages for future loss of income should be awarded only for the period during which the plaintiff is expected to remain alive.

   c. Where damages are awarded for loss of earnings, the fact that the plaintiff would have paid tax on his earnings must be taken into account, thus reducing the award of damages (BRITISH TRANSPORT COMMISSION V GOURLEY (1955)). The notional tax reduced is not paid to the Inland Revenue, it could therefore be argued that this represents a benefit to the defendant or to his insurance company.

    d.   Social security benefits, for example for sickness or disablement, are also deducted, although if the plaintiff failed to make a national insurance claim, and had not acted unreasonably in failing to claim, the sum will not be deducted. Insurance benefits receivable because of the plaintiff's private payment of premiums are not deductable, nor is a disability pension received as of right.

    e.   Compensatory damages may be ordinary or special

        i.   Ordinary damages are assessed by the court as compensation for losses which cannot be positively ascertained, and will depend on the court's view of the nature of the plaintiff's injury. Such damages, for example for pain and suffering, need not be quantified in the statement of claim.

        ii.   Special damages can be positively ascertained, for example damage to clothing or costs of repairs to cars. Special damages must be specifically claimed.

3. *Nominal Damages.* If a tort is actionable per se, and the plaintiff proves the elements of the tort without showing actual loss, he will be awarded a small sum of money, for example £1 in recognition of the fact that he has suffered a wrong.

4. *Exemplary Damages.* These are granted in rare cases, their purpose being to punish the defendant in addition to compensating the plaintiff. They may be awarded for:

    a.   Oppressive, arbitrary or unconstitutional acts of public officials.

    In AB AND OTHERS v SOUTH WEST WATER SERVICES (1992) the plaintiffs suffered ill effects as a result of drinking contaminated water from D's water system which had been polluted in July 1988 when 20 tons of aluminium sulphate was accidentally introduced into the system at a water treatment works. D was subsequently prosecuted and convicted for contamination of the water supply, for which they as the water authority were responsible. The plaintiffs brought a number of actions against D, ie under the CONSUMER PROTECTION ACT 1987, under the rule in RYLANDS v FLETCHER, for breach of contract, in nuisance and in negligence. They also claimed exemplary damages because D acted in an arrogant and high-handed manner in ignoring complaints and deliberately misled the plaintiffs by sending a circular letter to all customers asserting that the water was safe to drink, when it was known to be unfounded as no adequate tests had been carried out. They further failed to give any proper information to public health authorities, hospitals, doctors and customers as to any precautions that should be taken to minimise the effects of consumption of contaminated water. Finally they failed to close down the treatment works or provide clean water from an alternative source, but continued to supply contaminated water for a longer period than they would have done had they been properly informed.

    The Court of Appeal held that exemplary damages are not limited by the cause of action sued on but by the status of the defendant and the quality of his conduct. Exemplary damages may therefore be awarded in a claim of public nuisance against a water authority which has deliberately interfered with a person's rights as a member of the public.

b.   When the defendant's conduct has been calculated to make a profit for himself.

In CASSELL V BROOME (1972) D published a book, knowing that it was defamatory of P, because they thought that any damages awarded to P would be less than the profits of the book. The court, however, awarded exemplary damages against D, awarding P more than his actual loss to ensure that D did not profit from his tort.

5. *Injunction*

a.   An injunction is an equitable remedy. It may be an order of the court commanding something to be done (a *mandatory injunction*) or it may forbid the defendant from doing something (a *prohibitory injunction*). Like other equitable remedies, the award of an injunction is at the court's discretion. An example of the exercise of this discretion is MILLER V JACKSON (1977) (Chapter 26.5) when although the plaintiff 'won' the case he was not granted the injunction that he wanted.

b.   A valuable feature of this remedy is the power of the court to grant an *interlocutory* (until trial) *injunction*. Thus a temporary remedy may be obtained within days or even hours of the complaint arising. The matter must, however, be serious, and the judge must consider that there would be a high chance of success for the plaintiff at a full hearing of the case.

6. *Other Remedies*. Other remedies may be appropriate for particular torts, for example

a.   Abatement of nuisance;

b.   Escape from false imprisonment;

c.   Ejection of trespassers;

d.   Application for a writ of habeas corpus.

LIMITATION OF ACTIONS

7. Time limits for action in tort are governed by the *LIMITATION ACT 1980* and the *LATENT DAMAGE ACT 1986*.

a.   An action for the recovery of land must be brought within 12 years. (*S.15 LA 1980*).

b.   An action for damages in respect of personal injury caused by negligence, nuisance, or breach of duty must be brought within three years (*S.11 LA 1980*).

c.   An action under the *FATAL ACCIDENTS ACT 1976* must be brought within three years (*S.12 LA 1980*).

d. An action for a claim not involving personal injury may not be brought later than six years from the date on which the cause of action accrued or three years from when the plaintiff knew or ought to have known about the damage. There is an overriding time limit of 15 years from the date of the defendant's breach of duty.

e. There is a special three-year time limit in cases of libel and slander (subject to an extension of one year by the High Court (*ADMINISTRATION OF JUSTICE ACT 1985*)).

8. *The Point When Time Starts to Run*

a. Where a tort is actionable per se, time runs from the moment of the wrongful act.

b. Where a tort is actionable only on proof of damage, time runs from the moment damage was first suffered. Problems have occurred in cases of 'latent damage', ie damage which does not manifest itself until some time after the act or omission which causes it. In such cases time does not begin to run until such time as the plaintiff discovers the damage, or ought, with reasonable diligence, to have discovered it.

In HAWARD v FAWCETTS (**2006**) the House of Lords ruled that time runs when the claimant knew enough, ie had knowledge. for it to be reasonable for him to embark upon an investigation as to potential negligence.

c. Where a cause of action is based on or concealed by fraud, time does not begin to run until the plaintiff discovers the fraud, or could with reasonable diligence have done so.

d. Where a tort is of a continuing nature, for example nuisance or false imprisonment, a fresh cause of action arises daily, and an action lies for such instances of the tort as lie within the statutory period.

9. *Discretion to Exclude Time Limits*

a. By *S.33 LA 1980* the court is given a discretion to 'disapply' the time limits specified in *S.11* and *12* of the Act. In the words of Ormrod L.J. 'Parliament has now decided that uncertain justice is preferable to certain injustice, in other words certainty can be bought at too high a price.' When deciding whether or not to override the time limits in *S.11* and *S.12* the court must consider all the circumstances, for example:

i. The period of, and reasons for, the delay.

ii. The difficulties that will be suffered by witnesses when they are asked to recall facts.

iii. The conduct of the defendant after the cause of action arose, including the extent to which he responded to reasonable requests for information from the plaintiff.

b. There have been several cases on *S.33*.

In BUCK v ENGLISH ELECTRIC (**1978**) P contracted pneumoconiosis from work in 1959. By 1963 he was sufficiently disabled to realise that he had a cause of action. By 1973 he was so disabled that he had to give up work. He died in 1975 shortly after issuing a writ. It was held that although the action was statute barred by the delay (from 1963–1975) that discretion to override what is now *S.11* would be exercised in favour of P. The main reason was that D would not be prejudiced because there were other similar claims against them and it was unlikely that their evidence would be less cogent.

In WALKLEY V PRECISION FORGINGS (**1979**) by virtue of a solicitor's negligence P failed to prosecute a claim under a writ issued in 1971. In 1976 a fresh writ was issued bringing the same cause of action. It was held that *S.2* (now *S.33*) had no application in such a case. The prejudice to P was not to the time limits imposed by the Act but was due to the negligence of the solicitors.

Coursework Questions 17–29
(for answers see pages 662–76)

(for answers see pages 662–76)

	THE LAW OF TORTS

Typical Exam Questions

17. 'The rule in 'The Wagon Mound (1961)' governs remoteness of damage in the tort of negligence. Discuss.

(20 marks)

ICSA November 2004

18. Distinguish briefly between liability in tort arising under the following.

   a. The Occupiers' Liability Act 1957

(10 marks)

   b. The Occupiers' Liability Act 1984

(10 marks)
ICSA November 2004

19. Which of the following is a correct statement of the law? In the tort of negligence, if a claimant is partly responsible for his/her own injuries, then

   A no compensation can be recovered from the defendant;

   B the defendant is fully liable if he/she was mainly responsible for the injuries;

   C if the defendant was negligent, he/she remains fully liable for all the injuries caused;

   D the compensation will be reduced to take account of the claimant's share of the responsibility.

CIMA November 2001

20. a. What is meant by *res ipsa loquitur* in the law of tort?

   b. Harry is driving his car when suddenly the brakes fail. He is unable to stop and crashes into a motorcycle ridden by Susan, damaging the motorcycle and injuring Susan. Advise Harry as to his civil liability.

21. a. Define public nuisance and distinguish it from private nuisance.

   b. The noise and vibrations from the Acme Plastics Ltd's factory annoy all the residents of Park Road. One of the residents, Mr Evans, is particularly annoyed because on one occasion a piece of hot plastic waste material from one of the factory chimneys fell on to his house causing damage to the roof. Advise the residents and Mr Evans.

22. Advise Thomas whether an action for negligence is likely to succeed against each of the parties in the following cases, explaining the relevant principles of law involved.

    a. Albert, a practising accountant, upon whose advice Thomas made an investment which proved to be worthless.

    b. Bernard, a barrister, who represented Thomas in a recent case and who conducted the case badly.

    c. Charles, a car driver, whose car skidded and crossed on to the wrong side of the road where it collided with Thomas's car.

    d. David, a demolition worker, who carelessly injured a fellow worker thereby causing Thomas, who was passing at the time to suffer nervous shock.

23. a. What is the distinction between libel and slander, and why is it important?

    b. Mike, a radio journalist, recorded a private interview on his tape recorder with one Quip, a prominent politician, in which Quip accused Red, a political opponent, of being a traitor to his country and that he had 'sold out to the Russians'. Is this statement defamatory, and if so, is it libel or slander? Would your answer be the same if Mike broadcast the interview from the radio station for which he works?

24. a. In what circumstances is an employer liable for the wrongful acts of his employees?

(14 marks)

    b. Eric, an accountant, is sent by his employer to audit the accounts of a client. Eric's instructions prohibit him from giving any advice on the investment of surplus funds. However, he does give such advice carelessly and, in acting upon it, the client suffers loss. To what extent is the employer liable for this loss?

(6 marks)
(20 marks)

25. Mr Adams and Mrs Barker are neighbours. Mr Adams has, in the last two years, done the following things on Mrs Barker's land without her permission:

    a. He has allowed the roots of his tree to extend into Mrs Barker's garden, where they have undermined the foundations of Mrs Barker's house;

    b. He has moved the boundary fence which he shares with Mrs Barker one metre into Mrs Barker's land;

    c. He has dug a hole in Mrs Barker's garden, and taken soil from it for his own garden. What torts, if any, has Mr Adams committed?

26. a. What is meant in the law of torts by a *novus actus interveniens*?

    b. Arthur is employed by A B Ltd. Because of his employer's negligence Arthur sustains a broken leg. Consider A B Ltd's liability if

     i.   Arthur is left with a severe limp because of an error made by the surgeon who set his leg in plaster.

    ii.   Arthur's workmates, believing that he has merely dislocated a joint attempt to manipulate his leg back into place. This makes Arthur's injury much worse and it becomes necessary to amputate his leg.

27. To what extent is a supplier of goods liable in civil law (both for negligence and under the CONSUMER PROTECTION ACT (1987) for injuries caused by those goods to people with whom he has no contractual relationship?

(20 marks)

28. a. Explain the meaning and effect of the following defences which may be put forward to an action in tort

    i.   consent   (4 marks)

    ii.   contributory negligence   (4 marks)

    iii. statutory authority   (4 marks)

    b. What remedies may follow a successful tort action?

(8 marks)

(20 marks)

29. a. An occupier owes a common duty of care to lawful visitors who enter his premises. Explain this statement.

(12 marks)

    b. Walter, the owner of a warehouse, spreads rat poison on slices of bread with the intention of putting it down to attract and destroy vermin.

Simon, an employee with learning difficulties, who has forgotten his lunch, finds the bread and eats a slice, as does Young, a small boy who has wandered into the warehouse.

Both Simon and Young become seriously ill.

Discuss the possible liabilities of Walter.

(8 marks)

(20 marks)

PART IV

COMMERCIAL LAW

CHAPTER 30

Agency

INTRODUCTION

1. An agent is a person who is used to effect a contract between his principal and a third party. The agent may be an employee of the principal, for example a salesman in a shop, or he may be an independent contractor, for example an estate agent. Whatever the type of agent the distinctive characteristic of the relationship is that the agent has the power to make a binding contract between a principal and a third party without himself becoming a party to the contract.

2. There are several different types of agent, the more important being considered later. However, all agents will fall into one of three general categories:

   a. A *special agent's* authority is limited to the performance of a specific act, such as buying a particular car.

   b. A *general agent* has authority to perform any of the duties which are normally within the scope of the business entrusted to him, for example a solicitor.

   c. A *universal agent* is appointed by a deed known as a 'power of attorney'. He has unlimited authority and may perform any acts that his principal could have performed including the execution of a deed on his behalf.

3. Since an agent does not contract on his own behalf he need not possess full contractual capacity – he may, for example, be a minor. The principal, however, must have full capacity to make the contract in question.

4. In everyday language the word 'agent' is often used to describe anybody who buys and sells goods. For example a car dealer may be described as the 'sole agent' for a particular make of car. This does not mean that the dealer acts as the legal agent of the manufacturer when he sells the car to a customer. In practice the dealer acts on his own account when he buys from the manufacturer and sells to the customer. This wider use of the word 'agent' must be distinguished from the narrow legal usage. In law an agent is someone whose purpose is to make a contract between his principal and a third party.

APPOINTMENT OF THE AGENT

5. Agency may be created in the following four ways.

6. *Express Agreement*. The agent may be appointed verbally or in writing, unless he is authorised to execute a deed, in which case the appointment must be by deed.

7. *Implication*

   a. Agency will arise when, although there is no specific agreement, a contract can be implied from the conduct or relationship of the parties.

   b. The test is objective and agency may therefore be implied even if the principal and agent did not recognise the relationship themselves (GARNAC GRAIN CO. v H.M. FAURE (**1967**)).

   c. If an alleged agent is a partner in a firm, he will be held to be acting as the agent of his co-partners if the contract that he made is within the usual scope of the partnership business.

   d. Cohabitation (rather than marriage) raises a presumption that the woman has authority to pledge the man's credit for necessaries. In defining necessaries regard is had to the man's style of living rather than to his actual means. The presumption can be rebutted by evidence that, for example, the trader had been told not to supply goods to the woman on credit, or that the woman had sufficient funds to purchase necessaries.

   e. An implied agency may arise by estoppel. Thus if a person by his words or conduct represents another as having authority to make contracts on his behalf, he will be bound by such contracts as if he had expressly authorised them. ie He is *estopped* by his conduct from denying the existence of an agency.

   In PICKERING v BUSK (**1812**) a broker was employed by a merchant to buy hemp. After he had completed the purchase the broker retained the hemp at his wharf, at the request of the merchant. He then sold the goods. The purchaser was held to have obtained a good title to the goods because the broker was apparently an agent to sell, and the merchant was estopped by his conduct from denying the agency.

8. *Necessity*. Agency of necessity is formed by operation of law (ie automatically). Thus the principal may be bound to a contract made on his behalf without authority and which he refuses to ratify. Three conditions must be satisfied:

   a. There must be an emergency, making it necessary for the agent to act as he did.

   In PRAGER v BLATSPIEL (**1924**) A bought skins as agent for P but was unable to send them to P because of prevailing war conditions. Since A was also unable to communicate with P he sold the skins before the end of the war. It was held that A was not an agent of necessity, because he could have stored the skins until the end of the war. There was no real emergency.

   b. It must be impossible to get instructions from the principal.

   In SPRINGER v GREAT WESTERN RAILWAY (**1921**) a consignment of fruit was found by the carrier to be going bad. The carrier sold the consignment locally instead of delivering it to its destination. It was held that the carrier was not an agent of necessity because he could have obtained new instructions from the owner of the fruit. He was therefore liable in damages to the owner.

c. The agent must have acted in good faith, and in the interests of all the parties.

In GREAT NORTHERN RAILWAY v SWAFFIELD (1874) a horse was sent by rail and on its arrival at its destination there was no one to collect it. GNR incurred the expense of stabling the horse for the night. It was held that GNR was an agent of necessity who had implied authority to incur the expense in question.

9. *Ratification*

a. If a duly appointed agent exceeds his authority, or a person having no authority purports to act as agent, the principal is not bound.

b. The principal may, however, adopt the contract at a later date, provided:

   i. The agent named his principal and specifically informed the third party that he was contracting as agent.

   ii. The principal had contractual capacity at the date of both the contract and the ratification, and if the principal is a company, it must have been incorporated at the time of the contract.

   In KELNER v BAXTER (1866) P sold wine to D who purported to act as agent for a company which was about to be formed. When it was formed the company attempted to ratify the contract made by D. It was held that it could not do so, since it was not in existence when the contract was made. D was therefore personally liable to pay for the wine.

   iii. The principal had full knowledge of all material facts, or was prepared to ratify in any event.

c. A void contract cannot be ratified. Similarly a forged signature cannot be ratified because forgery is an illegal act, and because a forger does not purport to act as an agent.

In BROOK v HOOK (1871) a man forged his uncle's signature on a promissory note. When a third party came into possession of the note and discovered the forgery, he intended to bring proceedings against the forger. The uncle then purported to ratify his nephew's act by signing the note, but later refused to honour it. It was held that the ratification was ineffective and the promissory note was therefore void.

d. If A, who has no authority to do so, contracts with X, on behalf of P, any ratification by P relates back to the making of the contract by A.

In BOLTON PARTNERS v LAMBERT (1888) the managing director of a company acting as an agent of the company, but without authority to do so, accepted an offer by the defendant for the purchase of company property. The defendant later withdrew his offer, but the company then ratified the manager's acceptance. It was held that D was bound by the contract as the ratification was retrospective to the time of the manager's acceptance.

THE RELATIONSHIP BETWEEN PRINCIPAL AND AGENT

10. *The Duties of an Agent*

a. He must carry out his principal's lawful instructions, unless he is acting gratuitously.

In TURPIN v BILTON (**1843**) an insurance broker, in return for a fee, agreed to effect insurance on P's ship. He failed to do so and the ship was lost. The broker was held liable to P.

b. He must exercise reasonable care and skill in the performance of his duties. The degree of skill expected of him depends on the circumstances. More skill is expected of a professional person than of a layman who merely advises a friend. If a payment is made this will also be taken into account in assessing the care and skill expected but even an unpaid agent may be liable in tort for negligence if he gives bad advice. (HEDLEY BYRNE v HELLER (**1964**) (Chapter 24).)

c. He must act in good faith and for the benefit of his principal.

   i. He must not let his own interests conflict with his duty to his principal. It does not matter that the contract is made without intent to defraud, for example if an agent appointed to buy sells his own property to the principal at a proper market price. The reason for the rule is to prevent the agent from being tempted not to do the best for his principal.

   In ARMSTRONG v JACKSON (**1917**) P employed D, a stockbroker, to buy some shares for him. In fact D sold his own shares to P. It was held that P could rescind the contract. The agent's interest as seller was to sell at the highest possible price, whereas his duty as agent was to buy at the lowest possible price – clearly a conflict of interest and duty.

   ii. He must not make a secret profit, ie he must not use his position to secure a benefit for himself.

   In LUCIFERO v CASTEL (**1887**) an agent appointed to purchase a yacht for his principal bought the yacht himself and then sold it to his principal at a profit, the principal being unaware that he was buying the agent's own property. The agent had to pay his profit to the principal. (This case also illustrates i. above.)

   The agent must pay the profit to the principal even if the principal could not have earned the profit himself.

   In READING v ATTORNEY GENERAL (**1951**) a sergeant in the British Army in Egypt agreed to accompany lorries carrying illicit spirits. He was paid £20,000 so that his presence in uniform would ensure that the vehicles were not searched. It was held that as he made his profit through the use of his position, he had to account to the Crown as his employer. (The sergeant was not strictly an agent, but he was held to have a fiduciary relationship with his employer similar to a principal/agent relationship.)

iii. He must not misuse confidential information regarding his principal's affairs. If the principal fears that the agent will destroy or dispose of confidential information the principal may apply for an *Anton Piller injunction*, authorising the principal's representative to enter the agent's premises to remove the confidential material. An Anton Piller injunction is an ex parte injunction, ie it is granted on the application of the principal without the agent being represented. The name derives from the case ANTON PILLER KG v MANUFACTURING PROCESSES (1976) where it was first granted.

iv. Certain employees owe fiduciary duties to their employer, for example the managing director of a company. Sometimes senior managers are also regarded as having an agency type of relationship with their employer. Such persons generally have a duty to disclose their own breaches of duty and any breaches by other employees.

In CYBRON CORPORATION v ROCHEM (1983) a 'European Zone Controller' received on retirement a generous package of benefits. It was then discovered that he had, with other employees, set up a rival business and participated in large scale commercial fraud. The company sued to recover the money paid to him on his retirement. The court held that even if the person concerned had no duty to disclose his own breach (this was not made clear) he was under a duty to disclose breaches by other employees. Such a duty does not apply to all employees in all situations, it depends on the particular employee and the circumstances in general, however, it clearly applies to a zone controller who is responsible for a large section of his employer's business. The company was therefore successful and the agreement concerning payments on retirement was voidable for non-disclosure.

v. A breach of duty by the agent may result in the agent losing his right to remuneration, but this will not be the case if the right to remuneration accrued before the principal exercised his right to terminate the contract for breach.

In ROBINSON SCAMMELL v ANSELL (1985) an estate agent had been engaged to sell P's house. The agent found purchasers, but when P's own house purchase fell through A informed the purchasers that the sale might not proceed and suggested alternative properties for them to look at. On discovering this P informed A that the agency was terminated. They then contacted the original purchasers and successfully completed the sale to them. The agents claimed their fee and their client refused to pay. It was held that the right to remuneration accrued before the breach. The estate agents were therefore awarded their commission. The Court of Appeal based their decision on KEPPEL v WHEELER (1927) where although the plaintiff was awarded damages for breach, the agent received his commission because the breach was not sufficiently serious to justify termination of the agency agreement.

d. He must not delegate the performance of his duties, unless the principal expressly or impliedly authorises the agent to appoint a sub-agent. An agent does not, however, 'delegate' by instructing his own employees to do necessary acts in connection with the performance of his duty.

e. He must not mix his own financial affairs with those of his principal, for example by paying money received on behalf of his principal into his own account. In addition he must render accounts to the principal when required.

11. *Duties of the Principal*

a. He must pay the agent the commission or other remuneration that has been agreed. If nothing has been agreed the agent is entitled to what is customary in the particular business, or in the absence of custom, to reasonable remuneration. The exact point in time at which the right to commission arises depends on the terms of the contract between the principal and the agent. This has given rise to difficulty, particularly in cases concerning estate agents.

In LUXOR (EASTBOURNE) v COOPER (1941) the contract provided that the vendor of land should pay the estate agent his commission 'on completion of sale'. A prospective purchaser was introduced by the agent. He was ready, willing and able to buy, but the sale did not take place because the owner refused to deal with him. It was held that the agent was not entitled to commission.

Contrast SCHEGGIA v GRADWELL (1963). A similar contract provided that the vendor should pay commission as soon as 'any person introduced by us enters into a legally binding contract to purchase'. It was held that an agent was entitled to his commission when the purchaser signed a binding contract, although the vendor later rescinded the contract because of the purchaser's breach.

b. He must indemnify the agent for losses and liabilities incurred by him in the course of the agency.

In ADAMSON v JARVIS (1827) an auctioneer sold goods on behalf of his principal, being unaware that the principal had no right to sell. The auctioneer was held liable to the true owner in conversion, but was entitled to an indemnity from the principal.

It has been held that an agent may be indemnified when he makes a payment on behalf of his principal which is not legally enforceable by the third party, but which is made as a result of some moral or social pressure.

In READ v ANDERSON (1884) an agent was employed to bet on a horse. The horse lost and the agent paid the bet. It was held that he was entitled to an indemnity from the principal since if he had not paid he would have been recorded as a defaulter.

12. *Commercial Agents*

   a.   The COMMERCIAL AGENTS (COUNCIL DIRECTIVE) REGULATIONS 1993 were
        passed to clarify the relationship between commercial agents and their
        principals.

   b.   A *commercial agent* is a self-employed intermediary who has the authority
        to negotiate the sale or purchase of goods on behalf of another person. In
        relation to these agents the regulations state that the duty of good faith
        specifically includes

        i.   a duty of the *agent* to make proper efforts to negotiate and conclude
             transactions and to communicate all necessary information to the
             principal;

        ii. a duty of the *principal* to provide the agent with necessary
             documentation and information, and to notify the agent if he expects
             the volume of transactions to be significantly lower than anticipated.

THE AUTHORITY OF THE AGENT

13. *Express, Implied and Apparent Authority*

   a.   Where the agent is given *express authority* an act performed within the
        scope of this authority will be binding on the principal and the third party.

   b.   Where an agent is employed to conduct a particular trade or business he
        has *implied authority* to do whatever is incidental to such trade or busi-
        ness. This is the case even if the principal told the agent that he did not
        have such authority, unless the third party knew of the lack of authority.

        In WATTEAU v FENWICK (1893) the manager of a public house was instructed
        by D, the owner, not to purchase tobacco on credit. P, who was not aware
        of this restriction sold tobacco to the manager, and the manager was unable
        to pay for it. P then successfully sued D. It was held that the purchase of
        tobacco was within the usual authority of a manager of a public house, and
        it was this authority upon which the seller was entitled to rely.

   c.   If a person's words or conduct lead another to believe that an agent has
        been appointed and has authority, he will usually be estopped from denying
        the authority of the agent, even though no agency was agreed between the
        principal and agent. The agent is said to have *apparent authority*.

14. *Breach of Warranty of Authority*

   a.   A person who professes to act as agent, and who either has no authority
        from the alleged principal, or has exceeded his authority, is liable in an
        action for breach of warranty of authority at the suit of the party *with
        whom he professed to make the contract*.

   b.   The agent is not liable if the third party knew of his lack of authority at
        the time the contract was made.

c. The agent is liable whether he acted fraudulently or innocently. For example where his authority is terminated without his knowledge by the death or insanity of his principal.

In YONGE v TOYNBEE (**1910**) a solicitor was conducting litigation on behalf of a client who went insane. After this happened, but before the solicitor heard of it, he took further steps in the action. As a result the other party to the litigation incurred further costs. It was held that he could recover these costs from the solicitor since the solicitor had continued the action after the agency had been ended by the client's insanity. It made no difference that the solicitor had acted in good faith and with reasonable care.

WHO CAN SUE AND BE SUED

15. The question of whether or not the agent can sue or be sued by the third party depends on the parties' intention. If their intention is not clear, the following rules apply:

16. *If the Agent Names the Principal.* The agent generally incurs neither rights nor liabilities, and drops out as soon as the contract is made. Only the principal can sue and be sued.

17. *If the Agent Discloses the Existence but not the Name of the Principal.* Again the general rule is that the agent can neither sue nor be sued, but a contrary intention is more easily inferred than when the principal is named. Regardless of whether or not the principal is named, in the following exceptional cases the agent may be personally liable:

   a. If he signs his own name to a deed in which his principal is not named.

   b. If he signs a negotiable instrument in his own name without adding words indicating that he is signing as agent.

   c. If the custom of the particular trade makes him liable.

   d. If he agrees to be liable.

18. *If the Agent Does Not Disclose the Existence of the Principal*

   a. The agent may sue and be sued on the contract.

   b. The undisclosed principal may also sue on the contract provided:

      i. The agent's authority to act for him existed at the date of the contract, and

      ii. The terms of the contract are compatible with agency.

      In HUMBLE v HUNTER (**1842**) An agent entered into a charterparty and signed it as 'owner'. It was held that the word 'owner' was incompatible with an agency relationship. Evidence was not admissible to show that another was principal. The principal could not therefore sue on the contract.

c. On discovering the principal, the third party may choose to sue him instead of the agent. The commencement of proceedings against either the principal or agent does not necessarily amount to a conclusive election so as to bar proceedings against the other. (CLARKSON, BOOKER V ANDJEL (**1964**)). A judgement against one is, however, a bar to an action against the other.

19. *Torts of the agent.* The principal is liable together with the agent, for a tort committed within the scope of the agent's actual or apparent authority.

In UNITED BANK OF KUWAIT V HAMMOND (**1988**) a solicitor signed guarantees and undertakings, without actual authority. The result was that the bank lent money to a fraudulent third party. It was held that the bank was reasonable in its belief that the solicitor was acting with the firm's authority. The firm was therefore held liable.

TYPES OF AGENT

The following are examples of the more important types of agent.

20. *Auctioneers*

a. An auctioneer is an agent to sell goods at a public auction.

b. He has authority to receive the purchase price and can sue for it in his own name.

c. He has a lien on the goods for his charges.

d. He has implied authority to sell without a reserve price and even if he sells below a reserve price specified by the owner the contract will be binding. If, however, he declares that the sale is 'subject to a reserve' then a sale below the reserve price is not binding on the owner.

21. *Factors*

a. A factor is an agent 'employed to sell goods or merchandise consigned or delivered to him by or for his principal for a compensation' (Story, *Agency*). Factors are also known as mercantile agents.

b. His powers are:

i. To sell in his own name;

ii. To give a warranty, if it is usual in the course of the business;

iii. To receive payment for goods sold, give valid receipts, and grant reasonable credit;

iv. To pledge the goods under the Factors Acts. (To pledge means to deposit as security.)

c. In addition a factor has a lien on the goods for his charges, and he has an insurable interest in the goods.

22. *Brokers*. A broker has been defined by Story as 'An agent employed to make bargains and contracts in matters of trade, commerce or navigation between other parties for a compensation commonly called brokerage'. In contrast with a factor:

    a.   He rarely has possession of goods and therefore has no lien on them.

    b.   He does not buy and sell in his own name, unless there exists a trade custom enabling him to do so.

    c.   He has no power to pledge the goods.

23. *Stockbrokers*. A member of the Stock Exchange has an implied authority to make contracts for his principal in accordance with the rules of the Exchange. These rules bind the principal even if he is not aware of them, provided they are neither illegal nor unreasonable.

24. *Del Credere Agents*. An agent who guarantees to his principal that the purchasers he finds will pay for the goods sold to them is called a *del credere* agent. Therefore if the buyer does not pay the principal the agent will have to do so. A *del credere* agent does not guarantee that a buyer will accept delivery, so if the buyer does not accept delivery, the agent is not liable.

TERMINATION OF AGENCY

25. *By the Act of the Parties*

    a.   The parties may at any time mutually agree to terminate the agency.

    b.   The principal may revoke the agent's authority at any time, subject to the following restrictions:

        i.   If the agent is also an employee then proper notice must be given to terminate his contract of employment.

        ii.   The principal should give notice of the revocation to third parties with whom the agent has dealt, otherwise he will be estopped from denying the capacity of the agent, should the agent make subsequent contracts with these third parties.

        iii.   A termination in breach of contract will entitle the agent to damages.

           In TURNER v GOLDSMITH (1891) G, a shirt manufacturer, employed T as an agent to sell such goods as should be forwarded to him. The agency was for 5 years, determinable by either party at the end of that time by notice. After two years G's factory was burned down and he ceased business. T's action for loss of commission succeeded since there was a definite agency agreement for 5 years and this contract was not frustrated merely because the factory in which G manufactured shirts was burnt down.

        iv.   Where the principal has given the agent an authority coupled with an interest he cannot revoke. For example if the agent is authorised to collect debts on behalf of his principal and retain a part of the sum collected.

c.   If an agent commits a serious breach of an express or implied duty for example making a secret profit by failure to disclose the correct selling price of the principal's goods, the principal may terminate the agency agreement without notice and sue for damages. If the agent has made a secret profit the principal is entitled to it even if he could not have made the profit himself.

26. *By Operation of Law*

a.   On the death or insanity of either the principal or the agent.

b.   On the bankruptcy of the principal.

c.   If the subject-matter or the operation of the agency agreement is frustrated or becomes illegal, for example if the principal becomes an alien enemy.

27. *By Completion of the Agency Agreement*

a.   Either the period fixed for the agreement comes to an end, or

b.   The purpose for which the agreement was created is accomplished.

CHAPTER 31

Sale of Goods

INTRODUCTION AND DEFINITIONS

1. A sale of goods is the most common type of commercial transaction. Most of the common law relating to the sale of goods was first codified by the *SALE OF GOODS ACT 1893*. This was amended by the *SUPPLY OF GOODS (IMPLIED TERMS) ACT 1973* and the law has now been consolidated by the *SALE OF GOODS ACT 1979* the most recent amendment to the Act being the *SALE AND SUPPLY OF GOODS TO CONSUMERS REGULATIONS 2002*. References in this chapter to sections are to sections of the 1979 Act, unless otherwise stated.

The *SALE AND SUPPLY OF GOODS TO CONSUMERS REGULATIONS 2002* implemented a 1999 EC Directive on the Sale of Goods and Associated Guarantees. The Regulations, which came into force in March 2003, introduce some significant changes to the legal framework for the sale and supply of consumer goods. These are:

a. Where a seller, in the course of a business, delivers consumer goods which do not conform with the contract of sale, for example, they do not meet satisfactory levels of quality or performance, it is presumed that any lack of conformity existed at the time of delivery if discovered within the first six months. This in effect reverses the burden of proof onto the seller for a period of six months from the date of delivery, that is, *he* must show to the satisfaction of the court that at the time of delivery the goods did comply with the contract.

b. A hierarchy of remedies is set where there is a lack of conformity.

   i. The consumer is entitled to a repair or replacement free of charge within a reasonable period and without major inconvenience to the consumer. If this is impossible or disproportionate, or the seller has not remedied the defect within a reasonable time, or without major inconvenience to the consumer;

   ii. The consumer will be entitled to either, a reduction in price, or rescission of the contract (unless the shortcoming is minor).

c. The Regulations introduce an automatic legally binding consumer guarantee.

2. The *UNFAIR CONTRACT TERMS ACT 1977* is also very important to contracts for the sale of goods. In addition to the statutory rules the ordinary principles of

contract law are also applicable, for example the rules relating to mistake, misrepresentation, offer, acceptance and agency.

3. *Contract of Sale Distinguished From Other Transactions*

    a.   'A *contract of sale of goods* is a contract whereby the seller transfers or agrees to transfer the property in goods to the buyer for a money consideration called the price' *(S.2(1))*.

    b.   A *mortgage* is the transfer of the general property in the goods from the mortgagor to the mortgagee to secure a debt.

    c.   A *pledge* is the delivery of goods by one person to another to secure payment of a debt. It differs from a mortgage because a mortgagee obtains the general property in the goods whereas a pledgee only obtains a special property necessary to secure his rights, ie only possession passes, coupled with a power to sell. By *S.62(4)* the Act does not apply to a transaction in the form of a contract of sale which is intended to operate by way of mortgage, pledge, or other security.

    d.   A contract for *work and labour* is sometimes difficult to distinguish from a sale of goods. The test is whether the substance of the contract is the skill and labour exercised for the production of the item. Contracts for work and labour are governed by THE SUPPLY OF GOODS AND SERVICES ACT *1982*.

       In ROBINSON v GRAVES (**1935**) it was held that a contract with an artist to paint a picture was not a sale of goods because the substance of the contract was the skill and experience of the artist and it was immaterial that some paint and canvas would also pass to the purchaser. Similarly a contact for the repair of a car is not a sale of goods even if the repairs involve fitting some new parts.

    e.   A sale presupposes a 'price'. Therefore if the consideration is goods alone the contract is one of *exchange* and the Act will not apply. A part exchange, for example where a second-hand car plus cash is given in return for a new car, is a sale of goods.

4. *Sale and Agreement to Sell Distinguished*

    a.   The term 'contract of sale' in the Act includes both actual sales and agreements to sell *(S.61(1))*.

       i.   Where under a contract of sale, the property in goods is passed from the seller to the buyer, the contract is called a '*sale*' *(S.2(4))*.

       ii.   Where the transfer of the property in the goods is to take place at a future time or subject to some condition later to be fulfilled the contract is called an '*agreement to sell*' *(S.2(5))*.

       iii.   An agreement to sell becomes a sale when the time elapses or the conditions are fulfilled subject to which the property in the goods is to be transferred *(S.2(6))*.

b. The distinction is important because several consequences follow from the passing of property:

    i. Unless otherwise agreed the risk passes with the property. (See paragraph 25, below.)

    ii. If the property has passed to the buyer the seller can sue for the price.

    iii. If the seller re-sells the goods after the property has passed to the buyer, the second buyer acquires no title unless he is protected by one of the exceptions to the '*nemo dat*' rule. (See 27. below.) Similar principles apply if the buyer re-sells goods before the property has passed to him.

c. '*Property*' means the right of ownership. It is of course possible to transfer possession of goods without transferring the ownership of them, for example hire purchase contracts and contracts whereby the seller has reserved his title as in ALUMINIUM INDUSTRIE B.V. v ROMALPA (**1976**). (See 22. below.)

5. *Goods*

a. '*Goods*' means 'All chattels personal other than things in action and money'. The definition includes industrial growing crops, and has been held to include a ship and a coin sold as a collector's item.

b. The Act also distinguishes between:

    i. '*Specific goods*', ie 'goods identified and agreed upon at the time a contract of sale is made', eg 'My Ford Escort M123 ABC'.

    ii. '*Future goods*', ie 'goods to be manufactured or acquired by the seller after the making of the contract of sale', eg a wedding cake.

    iii. '*Unascertained goods*', ie goods defined only by a description applicable to all goods of the same class or goods forming part of a larger consignment, eg six bottles of Chateau Laffite 1961 or eg half of that lorry load of sand.

c. The distinction between specific and unascertained goods is important because, for example S.6 and 7 only apply to specific goods (see 26. below) and because the rules governing the passing of property are different.

CAPACITY, FORM, SUBJECT MATTER AND PRICE

6. *Capacity*

a. Capacity is regulated by the general law concerning capacity to contract, but where necessaries are sold and delivered to a minor, or a person who by reason of mental incapacity or drunkenness is incompetent to contract, he must pay a reasonable price for them (*S.3*).

b. 'Necessaries' are goods suitable to the condition of life of the minor or other incompetent person, and to his actual requirements at the time of sale and delivery. (See Chapter 14.2.)

7. *Form*. Subject to various statutory provisions a contract of sale may be in writing, by word of mouth, or implied from conduct (*S.4*).

8. *Subject matter*. The goods may be existing goods, owned or possessed by the seller, or future goods (*S.5*).

9. *The price*

   a. The price must be in money. It may be:

      i.   Fixed by the contract;

      ii. Left to be fixed in the manner agreed in the contract; or

      iii. Determined by the course of dealing of the parties.

   b. If it is not determined as above the buyer must pay a reasonable price (*S.8*), however, the absence of agreement as to price may render the contract void for uncertainty.

   c. Where the contract specifies that the price shall be fixed by the valuation of a third party and the third party does not make the valuation the contract is avoided. If, however, the goods or part of them have been delivered to and appropriated by the buyer he must pay a reasonable price for them. If the failure to value is the fault of the buyer or seller that party is liable to pay damages (*S.9*).

THE TERMS OF THE CONTRACT

10. The following questions, which were considered in Chapter 16, are also relevant to sales of goods:

    a. Is a statement made in negotiations a mere representation inducing the contract, or a term which is part of the contract?

    b. If it is a term, is it a condition or a warranty?

    c. If a term has not been expressly agreed, can it be included in the contract by implication?

    d. Are any exemption or limitation clauses valid?

11. *Conditions and Warranties*

    a. Of the four questions stated above, that relating to conditions and warranties merits revision and further discussion.

    b. A *condition is* a vital term, going to the root of the contract, breach of which normally entitles the innocent party to repudiate the contract and claim damages.

c.   A *warranty* is a subsidiary term, breach of which only entitles the innocent party to damages.

d.   The intention of the parties determines whether a clause is a condition or warranty, but in the absence of evidence of intention the courts will consider the commercial importance of the term, or less usually, the effects of the breach as in HONG KONG FIR SHIPPING v KAWASAKI KISEN KAISHA (**1962**).

e.   In the above case it was stated that many contracted undertakings could not be categorised simply as 'conditions' or 'warranties'. It has since been held that the division into conditions and warranties is not exhaustive. A term may be an 'intermediate term' in which case the remedy would depend upon the nature of the breach rather than the status of the term. If the breach goes to the root of the contract repudiation is justified, in other cases repudiation is not justified.

In CEHAVE NV v BREMER (**1975**) B agreed to purchase for £100,000 a shipment of animal feed. The contract between S and B provided that the goods should be 'shipped in good condition'. When the shipment arrived at its destination it was unloaded into containers. It was then discovered that some of the goods had been damaged in transit and B refused to accept delivery. The container owners applied to court and it was ordered that the goods be sold. In 'somewhat strange circumstances' they were sold to an importer for £30,000 who then re-sold them to B the same day for £30,000. The Court of Appeal held that there was a breach of the term that the goods be 'shipped in good condition' but this term was neither a condition nor a warranty, but an 'intermediate term'. Since breach of this term did not go to the root of the contract B was not entitled to reject the goods. The Court also decided that B could not reject for breach of the implied condition as to merchantable quality, it being concluded that the goods were merchantable.

12. *The Treatment of Conditions as Warranties*

a.   By *S.11(2)* a buyer may waive a breach of condition by the seller, or elect to treat it as a breach of warranty.

b.   By *S.11(4)* a 'buyer *must* treat a breach of condition as a breach of warranty where the contract is *non-severable* and he has *accepted* the goods or some of them. Note that:

   i.   *S.11(4)* does not apply to a breach of *S.12(1)* (see below).

   ii.   The meaning of non-severable contracts and acceptance is discussed below – *S.31* and *S.35*.

   iii.   *S.11(4)* must be read subject to the amended *S.35*.

13. *Stipulations as to Time*

a.   By *S.10* unless a different intention appears from the terms of the contract, stipulations as to *time of payment* are not deemed to be of the essence of the contract. Whether any other stipulation as to time is of the essence of the contract depends on the terms of the contract.

b. Where a party has waived a stipulation, for example as to the time for delivery, which was of the essence of the contract, he may again make that stipulation of the essence by giving the other party reasonable notice of his intention to do so. (RICKARDS v OPPENHEIM (**1950**) (Chapter 28.3).)

14. The implied terms of the Act were outlined in Chapter 16. They will now be considered in more detail.

15. *Title*

a. By *S.12(1)* there is an implied *condition* that the seller has the right to pass good title to the goods.

In NIBLETT v CONFECTIONERS' MATERIALS CO (**1921**) cans of condensed milk were labelled in a way that infringed the trade mark of a third party. The third party could therefore have restrained the sale by S to B by obtaining an injunction. It was held that S were in breach of the implied condition that they had the right to sell the cans. This case shows that *S.12* will be broken not only where the seller lacks the right to pass the property in the goods to the buyer, but also where he can be stopped by process of law from selling the goods.

b. By *S.12(2)* there is an implied *warranty* that the goods are free of any encumbrance not made known to the buyer, and the buyer will enjoy quiet possession of the goods except so far as it may be disturbed by the owner or other person entitled to the encumbrance disclosed.

In MICROBEADS v VINHURST ROAD MARKINGS (**1975**) S sold to B road marking equipment. At the time of the sale, unknown to S, a third party had applied for a patent in respect of the equipment. At the time of the sale the third party could not have objected to B's use of the equipment. Two years after the sale, the third party, who had now been granted patent rights informed B that he was infringing a patent. B then sued S for breach of *S.12(1)* and *S.12(2)*. It was held that there was no breach of *S.12(1)* since at the time of sale S could not have been prevented by injunction from selling the goods. However, there was a breach of *S.12(2)*. The activities of the third party amounted to an infringement of B's quiet possession of the goods. S was therefore liable even though he did not know of the patent application.

c. Since the essence of a contract is the transfer of property, if the seller breaks *S.12(1)* there will be a total failure of consideration and the buyer will be entitled to recover the whole price with no deduction for his use.

In ROWLAND v DIVALL (**1923**) B purchased a car from S for £334. Both B and S dealt in good faith. Four months later it was discovered that the car was stolen and B had to return it to the true owner. B sued to recover the price paid to S. S argued that since B had accepted the car he was limited by *S.11(4)* to a claim for damages for breach of warranty, and that in assessing these damages an allowance should be made for his use. Both these arguments failed. Atkin L.J. said that there could not be acceptance if there was nothing (ie no title) to accept, and that since B had paid for the property in the car and not merely the right to use it, there had been a total failure of consideration, entitling him to recover the whole purchase price without any set off for the use of the car. This has been criticised in that it is unrealistic to say that consideration has failed totally when B had four months use of the car before he had to return it.

16. *Description*

a. Where goods are sold by description there is an implied *condition* that:

   i. The goods will correspond with the description (*S.13(1)*), and

   ii. If the sale is by sample, as well as by description, the bulk of the goods will also correspond with the sample (*S.13(2)*).

   In GRANT v AUSTRALIAN KNITTING MILLS (**1936**) a buyer of underpants contracted dermatitis because of an excess of sulphite in the garment he purchased. It was held:

   a) A sale may be 'by description' even if the buyer has seen the goods before buying them provided he relied essentially on the description, and any discrepancy between the description and the goods is not apparent. There was therefore a breach of *S.13*.

   b) Reliance on the seller's judgement is readily inferred in retail sales because a buyer will go into a shop with confidence that the seller has selected his stock with skill.

   c) The buyer did not need to specify his purpose because it is obvious and therefore may be implied. *S.14* was therefore also broken.

b. A sale of goods is not prevented from being a sale by description solely because goods being exposed for sale are selected by the buyer (*S.13(3)*).

   The Section does not therefore require written or verbal descriptions to be given by the seller, for example goods selected by the buyer from a supermarket shelf may be sold by description. On the other hand even if the seller does describe the goods, it will not be a sale by description if there is no reliance whatsoever by the buyer on that description.

   In LIENSTER ENTERPRISES v CHRISTOPHER HULL FINE ART (**1990**) S informed B that he had two paintings by Gabriele Munter of the German impressionist school. However, S had no expertise in German impressionist paintings and B knew this. B later visited S, inspected the paintings and bought them. It was later found out that the paintings were not by Munter. It was held that B had not relied on S's statement as to the artist, but had relied entirely on his own skill and judgement. It was not therefore a sale by description. The court also rejected B's claim that the painting was not of merchantable quality.

c. A sale by description may include such matters as measurements and methods of packing, for example RE MOORE AND LANDAUER (**1921**) (Chapter 18.2).

d. It is possible to be in breach of *S.13*, without being in breach of *S.14*, since goods that are of merchantable quality and/or fit for their purpose may nevertheless not comply with the seller's description.

17. *Satisfactory Quality and Fitness for Purpose*

   a. By *S.14(1)* there is no implied condition or warranty as to quality or fitness for a particular purpose of the goods sold, except as provided by the following sub-sections, or by *S.15*. This sub-section preserves the basic rule of *caveat emptor* (let the buyer beware).

   b. *Satisfactory quality*

   i. Until 1994 the Act implied a condition of 'merchantable quality'. This terminology was both old fashioned and confusing, since it was defined by reference to fitness for purpose, which is the subject of *S.14(3)*. Merchantable quality has now been replaced by satisfactory quality. This terminology is more in line with current trading conditions and the Act gives improved guidance on its meaning.

   ii. *S.1* SALE AND SUPPLY OF GOODS ACT *1994* inserts a new *S.14(2)* in the 1979 Act. It states that where goods are sold in the *course of a business* there is an implied *term* that the goods *supplied* under the contract are of *satisfactory quality*.

   The new section uses the word '*term*' to include both conditions and warranties and it refers to goods *supplied* under the contract, not just goods sold. It would therefore cover the quality of a 'free gift' offered as an inducement to purchase goods.

   iii. Goods are of a satisfactory quality if they meet the standard that a reasonable person would regard as satisfactory, taking into account any description, the price (if relevant) and all other relevant circumstances. This definition makes it clear that defects which would render new goods unsatisfactory will not necessarily be unacceptable if they occur in second-hand goods, it is a matter of degree. In this respect it is similar to the old *S.14(2)*. For example in SHINE v GENERAL GUARANTEE FINANCE (**1988**) it was held that a 20-month-old second-hand car was not of merchantable quality at the time of sale when the buyer later discovered that eight months earlier it had been written off by insurers, since it had been totally submerged in water for over 24 hours.

   iv. The new section differs from the old in that examples are given of aspects of quality of goods. The list is not exhaustive and the court may, of course, consider any relevant aspect of quality when deciding whether quality is satisfactory. The Act's guidelines include

   – state and condition

   – fitness for all the purposes for which goods of the kind in question are commonly supplied

   – appearance and finish

   – freedom from minor defects

   – safety, and

   – durability

v. The implied term does not extend to any matter making the goods unsatisfactory

- which is specifically drawn to the buyer's attention before the contract is made

- where the buyer examines the goods and the examination ought to reveal the matter

- which, in a sale by sample, would have been apparent on a reasonable examination of the sample

c. *Fitness for purpose*

i. By *S.14(3)* where goods are sold in the *course of a business* and the buyer makes known to the seller the purpose for which the goods are being bought there is an implied *condition* that the goods are reasonably fit for that purpose, except where the circumstances show that the buyer does not rely, or that it is unreasonable for him to rely, on the skill or judgement of the seller.

In ASHINGTON PIGGERIES v CHRISTOPHER HILL (1972) B asked S to compound food for minks in accordance with a recipe supplied by B. The recipe included herring meal, which is toxic to minks. S compounded the food, which was later fed to the minks with the result that many died. S argued that they were not liable because B had supplied the recipe, and B and themselves were in the same line of business. S were, however, held liable. The court said that reliance on the seller's skill and judgement need not be total but it must be substantial and effective.

ii. Where the purpose for which the goods are required is obvious, it need not be made known expressly because it is clearly implied.

In GODLEY v PERRY (1960) a six-year-old boy purchased a toy plastic catapult. The catapult broke whilst being used and the boy lost an eye. His action against the shopkeeper who sold it to him was successful. There was no need for the boy to make known the purpose of his purchase since it was known by implication.

iii. This section also applies to second-hand goods, but the standard of fitness expected is lower. Like *S.14(2)* it does not apply to a private seller who does not sell in the course of a business.

The relationship between *S.14(2)* and *S.14(3)* was well illustrated in, JEWSON LTD v KELLY (2003). Here the buyer purchased a number of boilers from Jewson for installation into some newly converted flats. When he failed to pay for the goods and the Jewson brought proceedings, the buyer counterclaimed for damages for breach of *S.14(2) and (3)*. The buyer claimed that the boilers were not of satisfactory quality in that they did not meet the particular energy efficiency ratings required for the flats and that this was causing problems in finding buyers. The Court of Appeal held that it was the function of *S.14(3)* to impose any special obligation on the seller based upon the particular circumstances of the buyer, not *S.14(2)*. There had been no argument by the buyer that the boilers were unsatisfactory in themselves,

S.14(2), the issue was whether the particular circumstances of the buyer in needing them to help meet certain energy efficiency targets, rendered them unsatisfactory. The buyer did not provide Jewson with any special information about the particular nature of the purchase – the need to achieve key energy saving ratings – as such he could not show that he relied upon their skill and judgement with regard to the boiler's particular suitability for the particular purpose required. The buyer could only show reliance on the seller as to the intrinsic qualities of the boilers under *S.14(2)* and here they were reasonably fit for their purpose. The seller was not liable.

18. *Sale by Sample*

    a.   *S.15* provides that where there is a sale by sample, *conditions* are implied that

        i.   The bulk will correspond with the sample;

        ii.   The buyer will have a reasonable opportunity of comparing the bulk with the sample; and

        iii.   The goods shall be free from any defect making their quality unsatisfactory, which would not be apparent on reasonable examination of the sample.

    b.   If a sale is by sample and description the goods supplied must correspond with both the sample and the description.

        In NICHOL v GODTS (**1854**) the seller sold 'foreign refined rape oil warranted only equal to sample'. When it was delivered the bulk did correspond with the sample but the sample was not 'foreign refined rape oil'. It was held that both *S.13* and *S.15* were broken because if the sale is by sample and description there is an implied condition that the goods correspond with both sample and description.

19. *Exemption Clauses*. The acceptability of exemption clauses is governed by the UNFAIR CONTRACT TERMS ACT 1977. This was considered in more detail in Chapter 16. *S.6* of the Act (as amended) refers to contracts for the sale of goods and states that:

    a.   *S.12 SGA 1979* cannot be excluded.

    b.   *S.13–15 SGA 1979* cannot be excluded in a consumer sale, but can be excluded in a non-consumer sale if the exemption clause is reasonable.

    c.   The regulations made under *S.22* FAIR TRADING ACT 1973 make it a criminal offence for someone in the course of a business to display at a place where consumer transactions take place a notice of an exemption clause which is void under *S.6* UNFAIR CONTRACT TERMS ACT 1977.

THE TRANSFER OF THE PROPERTY IN THE GOODS TO THE BUYER

20. Property (ownership) and possession must be distinguished since the property in goods sold may pass to the buyer although the seller retains possession of

the goods. The moment property passes is important for several reasons. (See paragraph 4.b. above.)

21. By *S.16* where there is a contract for the sale of *unascertained goods* (ie goods defined by description only, and not identified until after the contract is made), no property passes to the buyer unless and until they are ascertained. Thus if a large consignment of goods are handed to a carrier who is directed to set aside the contractual goods, no property passes until the carrier has done so because until then the goods are unascertained.

In HEALY v HOWLETT AND SONS (1917) B ordered 20 boxes of fish from S. S consigned 190 boxes by rail and directed railway officials to set aside 20 boxes for B's contract. The train was delayed and the fish had deteriorated before 20 boxes had been appropriated for B. It was held that since property did not pass until appropriation the fish were at S's risk at the time of deterioration and B was not therefore liable to pay the price.

22. By *S.17* if the contract is for the sale of *specific or ascertained* goods the property passes when the parties intend it to pass. Intention is ascertained from the terms of the contract, the conduct of the parties, and the circumstances of the case. This section enables the parties to agree to 'reserve title' to the goods until the buyer's outstanding debts are paid.

In ALUMINIUM INDUSTRIE BV v ROMALPA (1976) the plaintiffs, who were sellers of aluminium provided in their conditions of sale that 'The ownership of the material to be delivered by AIV will only be transferred to the purchaser when he has met all that is owing to AIV no matter on what grounds.'

After having taken delivery of a consignment of aluminium the purchaser went into liquidation. S who had not received the purchase price sought to enforce the above provision so as to secure payment prior to the distribution of B's assets to the general creditors. It was held that S could recover the consignment.

This decision created a remedy for an unpaid seller in addition to those provided by *S.39 SGA*. This remedy of possession is wider than the remedy of lien since a lien is for the price only, whereas the Romalpa remedy may be exercised until 'all that is owing' has been paid. It is also wider than stoppage in transit since the right to stop in transit ends when transit ends, whereas the Romalpa remedy may be exercised after delivery of the goods. However, a Romalpa clause will not apply where the material is subjected to a manufacturing process. For example:

In RE PEACHDART (1983) leather was sold on reservation of title terms. The intention was that it be used in the manufacture of handbags. It was held that the supplier's title ceased to exist when the leather had been made into handbags.

To increase the protection afforded by a reservation of title clause it is advisable for the supplier

a. To require that the material in question be kept separate from the buyer's other stock; and

b. To reserve a right of access to the buyer's premises.

23. Where the parties have not shown a definite intention at the time of contracting *S.18* states that the following 'rules' shall be applied to decide the time at which property shall pass.

   a. *Rule 1*. Where there is an unconditional contract for the sale of specific goods in a deliverable state the property passes when the contract is made, and it is immaterial whether the time of payment or delivery or both are postponed.

   In TARLING v BAXTER (**1827**) B purchased a haystack. Before he took it away it was destroyed by fire. B was held liable to pay for the haystack because the property passed when the contract was made.

   Note that:

   i.   If, after the contract has been made, the parties agree that the property will pass at a certain time, the agreement will be ineffective if the property has already passed under Rule 1.

   In DENNANT v SKINNER & COLLOM (**1948**) a crook purchased a car at an auction. He was allowed to take the car away on payment of a cheque on condition that he signed a document whereby it was agreed that the property would not pass until the cheque had cleared. The crook then re-sold the car to the defendant. The cheque was later dishonoured. It was held that the defendant got good title to the car because property had passed to the crook under Rule 1 before the agreement was signed. The agreement was therefore of no effect.

   ii. 'Deliverable state' means such a state that the buyer would under the contract be bound to take delivery of them (*S.61(5)*).

   b. *Rule 2*. Where the contract is for specific goods and the seller is bound to do something to the goods to put them into a deliverable state, the property does not pass until this has been done and the buyer has notice thereof.

   In UNDERWOOD v BURGH CASTLE BRICK AND CEMENT SYNDICATE (**1922**) the contract was for the sale of an engine, weighing 30 tons. At the time of sale it was imbedded in a concrete floor. Whilst being detached from its base and loaded into a railway truck the engine was damaged. The seller nevertheless sued for the price. It was held that the goods were not in a deliverable state when the contract was made so that the property did not pass under Rule 1. Also property would not pass under Rule 2 until the engine had been safely loaded into the truck.

   c. *Rule 3*. Where the specific goods are in a deliverable state but the seller has still to do something, such as weighing, measuring or testing the goods, the property does not pass until such act has been done and the buyer has notice thereof.

   i.   For example B purchases a sack of potatoes from S. The price of potatoes is 25 pence per pound, but the total weight of the sack is not known. If it is agreed that the seller will weigh the potatoes to ascertain the total price payable property does not pass until this is done and the buyer has notice of it.

  ii. Both Rule 2 and Rule 3 are confined to acts done by the seller. If the buyer is to do the act, the property would pass on making the contract.

d. *Rule 4.* Where goods are delivered on approval or on sale or return the property passes

  i. When the buyer signifies his approval or acceptance to the seller, or

  ii. When he does any other act adopting the transaction, such as pawning the goods, or

  iii. If he does not signify approval or acceptance, property passes when he retains the goods beyond the agreed time or, if no time was agreed, beyond a reasonable time.

In POOLE v SMITH'S CAR SALES (BALHAM) LTD (1962) P left his car with D on 'sale or return' terms in August 1960. After several requests D returned the car in November 1960 in a badly damaged state due to use by D's employees. It was held that since the car had not been returned within a reasonable time the property in the car had passed to D and he was accordingly liable to pay the price agreed.

e. *Rule 5(1).* Where there is a contract for the sale of unascertained or future goods by description the property passes when the goods of that description and in a deliverable state are unconditionally appropriated to the contract by one party with the express or implied assent of the other.

In PIGNATARO v GILROY (1919) S sold 140 bags of rice to B. Fifteen bags were appropriated by S for the contract and B was told where he could collect them. The bags were then stolen through no fault of S before B was able to collect them. B failed in his action to recover the price paid for the 15 bags. It was held that S's appropriation of the bags for the contract, without any objection by B, constituted transfer of title to those bags. They therefore belonged to B when they were stolen.

f. *Rule 5(2).* A seller who delivers goods to the buyer or to a carrier for transmission, without reserving a right of disposal, is deemed to have unconditionally appropriated the goods to the contract.

In EDWARDS v DDIN (1976) S filled B's petrol tank and B drove off without paying. It was held that B was not guilty of theft because the property had passed to him. It was impossible for the seller to reserve a right of disposal to petrol which at the point of delivery is mixed with the petrol already in B's tank. At that point the petrol is unconditionally appropriated to the contract with the consent of both parties. (B would now be guilty of the offence of making off without payment (*S.3 THEFT ACT 1978*).

Note that:

  i. Rule 5 must be considered in conjunction with *S.16.* Under *S.16.* no property passes until the goods are ascertained. Rule 5 shows when goods are ascertained.

  ii. An example of an implied assent to appropriation would be where B orders goods to be sent by post. When S dispatches the goods this amounts to appropriation by S with B's consent.

24. By *S.19* the seller may reserve the right of disposal of the goods until certain conditions are fulfilled and the property will not then pass until the conditions imposed by the seller are fulfilled.

25. *Risk (S.20)*

   a.   The general rule has already been stated, ie that the risk 'follows' the property. Thus the owner must bear any accidental loss.

   b.   This rule may be varied by trade usage or by agreement.

   In STERNS v VICKERS (**1923**) S agreed to sell 120,000 gallons of spirit out of a tank containing 200,000 gallons which was on the premises of a third party. A delivery warrant was issued to B, but he did not act on it for some months, during which time the spirit deteriorated. It was held that although no property had passed (because there had been no appropriation) the parties must have intended the risk to pass when the delivery warrant (ie the authority requiring the third party to release the spirit to B) was issued to B. B therefore remained liable to pay the price.

   c.   If delivery is delayed through the fault of either party the goods remain at the risk of that party as regards any loss which might not have occurred but for the delay.

   In DEMBY HAMILTON v BARDEN (**1949**) S agreed to send 30 tons of apple juice by weekly consignments to B. B delayed in taking delivery of some of the juice which as a result went bad. B was held liable to pay the price since the loss was his fault.

26. *Perishing of Goods*

   a.   Where there is a contract for the sale of *specific* goods, and the goods without the knowledge of the *seller* have perished at the time the contract is made, the contract is void *(S.6)*. The section is limited to specific goods, but also applies where part of a specific consignment of goods has perished before the contract is made.

   In BARROW LANE AND BALLARD v PHILLIPS (**1929**) S sold 700 bags of nuts. Unknown to the sellers 109 bags had already been stolen at the time of sale. It was held that the specific consignment of 700 bags had perished because a substantial part of it was missing.

   b.   Where there is an agreement to sell *specific* goods and subsequently the goods, without any fault on the part of the seller or buyer, perish before the risk passes to the buyer, the agreement is thereby avoided (*S.7*).

   c.   Note that:

   i.   *S.6* is a partial enactment of the common law rules relating to mistake in the formation of a contract.

   ii.   *S.7* is an enactment of the common law rule relating to frustration when there is a sale of specific goods. *S.7* cannot apply if the risk passes to the buyer at the time of sale, ie if *S.18* Rule 1 applies.

   iii   *S.6* and 7 do not apply to sales of unascertained goods.

SALE BY A PERSON WHO IS NOT THE OWNER

27. The basic common law rule is *nemo dat quod non habet*. Literally translated this means 'no man gives that which is not his own'. If there is a 'sale' by a person who is not the owner, the buyer will generally acquire no title and will have to return the goods to the true owner. The buyer may of course sue the seller for breach of *S.12(1)*, but is not entitled to any compensation from the true owner unless money was spent improving the goods before the buyer discovered they were not his.

The basic *nemo dat* rule is enacted in *S.21* which provides that where goods are sold by a person who is not the owner, the buyer acquires no better title than the seller unless:

a. The seller had the authority or consent of the owner, or

b. The owner is precluded by his conduct from denying the seller's authority to sell. For example

In EASTERN DISTRIBUTORS v GOLDRING (1957) M owned a van and he wanted to buy a car from C. However, he did not even have enough money for a hire-purchase deposit. M and C therefore devised a scheme whereby C would pretend to a finance company (ED) that he owned both the car and the van – he would sell them both to ED, and then buy both back on hire-purchase. In order to convince ED that C owned both the car and the van M signed a form to this effect. C then sold the van to ED, but ED did not accept the car. However, C told M that the *whole deal* had fallen through. Neither C nor M paid any of the hire purchase instalments for the van. M, who had been in possession of the van all the time, then sold it to G. (M believed he was the owner since C had told him that the deal had fallen through.) ED then sued to recover the van from G. It was held that since M had acted as if C was the true owner of the van (by signing a form to this effect so as to trick ED) he was estopped from denying C's right to sell. ED therefore acquired a good title to the van from C. M therefore had no title to pass to G. ED therefore succeeded in their action to recover the van from G.

Note that:

i. Where there is an estoppel the effect is to pass title to the buyer.

ii. The mere fact that the owner gives possession of the goods to a third party does not estop him from denying that person's authority to sell.

In CENTRAL NEWBURY CAR AUCTIONS v UNITY FINANCE (1957) A agreed with B that A would sell a car to a finance company, which would then let it to B on hire-purchase. A then handed the vehicle and registration book to B before the arrangements with the finance company had been completed. The finance company then refused B's application for hire purchase. B, however, was a crook and he had in the meantime sold the car to C. It was held that C did not get title to the car because B had no title to pass to him, and A's conduct in handing over the car and its registration book did not estop him from disputing B's authority to sell.

28. Apart from the two general exceptions contained in *S.21* there are several other exceptions (29–33 below).

29. *Sale Under a Voidable Title*

   a. Under *S.23* where a seller of goods has a *voidable title*, but this title has not been avoided at the time of sale, the buyer acquires a good title provided he buys in good faith without notice of the seller's defect in title.

   b. This provision only applies to contracts which are voidable, for example for fraud, and not those which are void for mistake. Contrast LEWIS v AVERAY with CUNDY v LINDSAY. Note also CAR AND UNIVERSAL FINANCE v CALDWELL (Chapter 17.2 and 17.6).

30. *Mercantile Agents*

   a. Under *S.2* FACTORS ACT *1889* any sale, pledge, or other disposition by a mercantile agent in possession of goods or documents of title with the consent of the owner, and in the mercantile agent's ordinary course of business, to a bona fide purchaser for value without notice of any defect in his authority is as valid as if expressly authorised by the owner.

   b. A mercantile agent is an agent having in the customary course of his business authority to sell goods, or raise money on the security of goods. This definition includes an auctioneer or broker, but not a clerk or warehouseman.

   c. It has been held that in the case of second-hand vehicles to be within 'the ordinary course of business' the sale must be accompanied by delivery of the registration book (PEARSON v ROSE AND YOUNG (**1951**)).

31. *Dispositions by a Seller who Remains in Possession After a Sale*

   a. By *S.24* where a person having sold goods continues in possession of them or documents of title to them the delivery or transfer by him, or by a mercantile agent acting for him, of the goods or documents under any sale, pledge or other disposition, is as valid as if authorised by the owner, provided the second buyer takes in good faith without notice of the previous sale.

   b. The usual sequence of events would be:

      i. A sale by X to Y under which the property passes, but X remains in possession.

      ii. A second sale by X to Z and delivery to Z.

   c. For the section to apply the seller must continue in actual physical possession of the goods after the first sale, but not necessarily as seller. He may retain possession as, for example, a hirer or a trespasser.

   In WORCESTER WORKS FINANCE v COODEN ENGINEERING (**1971**) A sold a car to B, B paying by cheque. B re-sold the car to C but remained in possession of it. When B's cheque was dishonoured A went to B to re-possess the car and B allowed A to take it away. When C discovered this he sued A in conversion. It was held that although B was not a seller (since he never had title to the car) but a trespasser, the section nevertheless applied to him since continuity of physical possession was the vital factor, not the character of that possession. Note also that 'other disposition' was widely construed so as to include a retaking of the goods with the seller's consent. This case clearly does not follow the usual sequence referred to above.

d.   Consider the following example:

X, who wishes to raise some money, sells his car to a finance company for £1,000, and then takes it back on hire purchase, paying a deposit and the balance by instalments. Throughout the transaction X keeps possession of the car. X then sells the car to Y for £900. Advise Y. *S.24* is the correct advice and Y may keep the car. The finance company could have avoided this result by requiring the car to be delivered to them, and then immediately delivering it back to X. X would not then have 'continued in possession'.

e.   *S.24* gives no protection to the seller, he remains liable to the first buyer.

32. *Dispositions by a Buyer Who Obtains Possession After an Agreement to Sell*

a.   By *S.25* where a person having bought or agreed to buy goods obtains possession of the goods or documents of title with the seller's consent the delivery or transfer by that person or by a mercantile agent acting for him of the goods or documents under any sale, pledge or other disposition to a person receiving them in good faith and without notice of any lien or other right of the original seller has the same effect as if the person making the delivery or transfer were a mercantile agent in possession of the goods or documents with the owner's consent.

b.   The usual sequence is:

i.   X agrees to sell to Y and Y is given possession of the goods although the property in the goods has not yet passed.

ii.   Y 'sells' and delivers the goods to Z who takes them in good faith.

c.   The person making the disposition must have bought or agreed to buy the goods, the section does not apply to someone who only has an option to purchase as in a hire purchase agreement (HELBY v MATTHEWS (**1895**)), nor does it apply to someone who has taken the goods on approval or on sale or return.

d.   The disposition must have been one which could have been made by a mercantile agent acting in the ordinary course of business (NEWTONS OF WEMBLEY v WILLIAMS (**1964**)).

e.   The section is not intended to take title away from an owner from whom goods have been stolen.

In NATIONAL MUTUAL AND GENERAL INSURANCE ASSOCIATION v JONES (**1988**) thieves stole a car. They sold it to A, who sold it to B, who sold it to C, who sold it to D, who sold it to Jones. All the parties (A, B, C, D and Jones) were innocent and unaware of the defect in title. C and D were car dealers. It was held that Jones did not obtain title to the car because A did not make a contract of sale with B, and A and B could not properly be described as 'seller' and 'buyer'. Thus A did not deliver the goods to B 'under a sale' as required by the section, because a contract of sale supposed that the seller had, or was going to have, a general property in the goods.

f. In 1985, there was an interesting case involving both *S.25* and reservation of title clauses.

In FOUR POINT GARAGE v CARTER (1985) Carter purchased a new car from X Limited. X Limited did not have the car in stock so it arranged to buy the car from Four Point who delivered it direct to Carter (who was unaware of Four Point's involvement). The contract between Four Point and X Limited reserved title to the car until the price had been paid. A few days after Carter had taken delivery X Limited went into liquidation without having paid Four Point. Four Point claimed that they were entitled to recover the car under their reservation of title clause. Carter claimed the protection of *S.25*. As regards *S.25* it was held that there was no difference between a delivery direct to a sub-purchaser and a delivery to a buyer who then delivered to a sub-purchaser. X Limited would be regarded as having taken constructive delivery, therefore Four Point delivered to Carter as X Limited's agent. Concerning the reservation of title clause it was held that the basic form of clause used did not preclude implication of a term authorising the garage to sell the car in the ordinary course of business. Carter was therefore successful on both arguments.

33. The final exception is where there is a disposition under a common law or statutory power of sale, or under a court order.

34. *Market Overt*

The exception relating to market overt (*S.22*) was repealed by the SALE OF GOODS (AMENDMENT) ACT 1994.

35. *Conclusion*. The reasons for the general rule and its exceptions were summed up by Lord Denning in BISHOPSGATE MOTOR FINANCE v TRANSPORT BRAKES. He said:

'In the development of our law two principles have striven for mastery. The first is the protection of property. No one can give a better title than he himself possesses. The second is the protection of commercial transactions. The person who takes in good faith for value without notice should get a good title. The first principle has held sway for a long time, but it has been modified by common law itself and by statute so as to meet the needs of our times.'

PERFORMANCE OF THE CONTRACT

36. *Delivery*

a. Delivery is the physical transfer of possession from one person to another. It does not necessarily mean transportation. Delivery may be actual or constructive, for example when the keys to a warehouse in which the goods are stored are handed to the buyer.

b. It is the duty of the seller to deliver the goods and the buyer to accept and pay for them (*S.27*).

c. Payment and delivery are concurrent conditions unless otherwise agreed, for example if the sale is on credit (*S.28*).

37. *Place of Delivery (S.29)*

   a. Except where there is a provision in the contract the place of delivery is the seller's place of business, unless the contract is for specific goods, which to the knowledge of the parties are in some other place, in which case that other place is the place of delivery.

   b. If the goods are in the possession of a third party there is no delivery until the third party acknowledges to the buyer that he holds the goods on his behalf.

   c. If goods are to be sent, the seller must send them within a reasonable time, and demand or tender of delivery must be made at a reasonable hour to be effective.

38. *Incorrect Delivery (S.30)*

   a. If the seller delivers a larger or smaller quantity of goods than ordered the buyer may

      i. Reject the whole, or

      ii. Accept the whole, or

      iii. Accept the quantity ordered and reject the rest.

   b. If he chooses ii. or iii. above he must pay for the goods at the contract rate. He cannot accept the incorrect goods. He will only be able to accept them if the seller first offers to sell them to him.

39. *Instalment Deliveries (S.31)*

   a. The buyer is not bound to accept delivery by instalments unless so agreed.

   b. Where a contract provides for delivery in stated instalments which are to be separately paid for, and the seller makes defective deliveries, or the buyer fails to take delivery of, or pay for one or more instalments, it is a question of construction whether this amounts to a repudiation of the whole contract or to a severable breach giving a right to compensation, but not a right to treat the whole contract as at an end. The tests to be used in applying this section were laid down in MAPLE FLOCK CO V UNIVERSAL FURNITURE PRODUCTS (**1934**) (Chapter 18.18) as follows:

      i. The ratio quantitatively which the breach bears to the contract as a whole, and

      ii. The degree of probability that the breach will be repeated.

   c. If instalments are to be separately paid for the contract is more likely to be construed as severable. *S.11(4)* is relevant to severable and non-severable contracts. As a result of this section if an instalment contract is non-severable and the buyer accepts the first instalment this will prevent his rejection of later defective deliveries, and will limit his remedy to damages for breach of warranty.

40. *Acceptance*

a. By *S.35* (as amended by the SALE AND SUPPLY OF GOODS ACT *1994*) the buyer accepts the goods when he:

   i. Intimates to the seller that he has accepted them; or

   ii. Does any act to the goods which is inconsistent with the ownership of the seller, such as subselling and delivering the goods; or

   iii. Retains the goods, after the lapse of a reasonable time without intimating to the seller that he has rejected them.

In BERNSTEIN v PAMSONS MOTORS (**1986**) P bought a new car from D. A defect caused the engine to seize up three weeks after purchase, the car having only covered 140 miles. P sought rescission. It was held that the car was neither of merchantable quality, nor reasonably fit for its purpose. However, P's claim was rejected because he was deemed to have accepted the car under *S.35*. He was therefore limited to damages for breach of warranty. The judge clearly took the view that 'lapse of reasonable time' meant reasonable time to try out the goods generally, it did not mean reasonable time to discover the defect. Thus presumably the result would have been the same even if the plaintiff had not used the car at all. It is suggested that it is unsatisfactory and that the judge's decision was borderline.

b. Where goods are delivered to a buyer which he has not previously examined, he is not deemed to have accepted them until he has had a reasonable opportunity of examining them to ascertain conformity with the contract. The seller is bound to afford this opportunity if so requested. In the case of a contract for sale by sample the buyer must have a reasonable opportunity of comparing the bulk with the sample.

c. The buyer is not deemed to have accepted goods merely because

   i. He asks for, or agrees to, their repair by or under an arrangement with the seller, or

   ii. The goods are delivered to another under a sub-sale or other disposition

d. *Right of partial rejection.* If a seller supplies some goods which are in breach of contract together with others which are unaffected by the breach, a new section *(35A)* inserted by the 1994 Act gives the buyer a right to accept the goods which were unaffected by the breach without losing his right to reject the rest. This effectively replaces *S.30(4)* which is repealed.

THE RIGHTS OF THE UNPAID SELLER

41. *Lien (S.41–43)*

a. A lien is the right to retain possession of goods (but not to resell them) until the contract price has been paid.

b. The unpaid seller's lien is for the price only. When the price is tendered it does not enable him to retain possession for any other purpose, for example to recover the cost of storing the goods during the exercise of the lien.

42. *Stoppage in Transit (S.44–46)*

a. After the seller has parted with the possession of the goods to a carrier for transmission to the buyer he can stop the goods and retake possession on the buyer becoming insolvent (ie if the buyer is unable to pay his debts as they fall due).

b. The period of transit operates from the time when the goods are handed to the carrier until the time when the buyer takes delivery of them. Transit is also terminated if:

i. The buyer obtains delivery before the arrival of the goods at the agreed destination, for example because the carrier hands them to the buyer's agent during transit; or

ii. If, on reaching the agreed destination, the carrier acknowledges to the buyer that he is holding the goods to the buyer's order; or

iii. If the carrier wrongfully refuses to deliver the goods to the buyer.

43. *Resale of Goods.* The general rule is that lien and stoppage in transit do not give the unpaid seller any right to re-sell the goods. By *S.48* the exceptions are:

a. Where they are of a perishable nature; or

b. Where the buyer, after being given notice by the seller that he intends to resell, does not pay for them within a reasonable time; or

c. Where the seller has expressly reserved the right to resell if the buyer defaults in payment.

44. *Repossession of Goods*

a. If the seller has reserved title to the goods until the contract price, or any other debt owing to him by the buyer is paid, then he may re-possess the goods if the buyer, being a company, goes into liquidation or receivership. (ALUMINIUM INDUSTRIE BV v ROMALPA (**1976**) paragraph 22. above.)

b. The right to re-possess from a buyer who is a private individual would arise:

i. If he were adjudged bankrupt, or

ii. If it were intimated in some other way that the goods would not be paid for.

45. *Remedies Against the Buyer.* The above remedies are all enforced against the goods. The remedies against the buyer are:

a. An action for the contract price, provided the property in the goods has passed to the buyer.

b. An action for non-acceptance. *S.50* provides that in an action for damages for non-acceptance, where there is an available market the measure of damages is, prima facie, the difference between the contract price and the market price on the date fixed for acceptance, or if no date was fixed, at the time of refusal to accept. Note THOMPSON V ROBINSON GUNMAKERS (1955) and CHARTER V SULLIVAN (1957) (Chapter 21.5).

THE REMEDIES OF THE BUYER

46. The buyer may:

a. Sue for non-delivery. *S.51* provides that in an action for damages for non-delivery, where there is an available market the measure of damages is, prima facie, the difference between the contract price and the market price on the date fixed for delivery, or if no date was fixed, at the time of refusal to deliver.

b. Sue to recover any money paid to the seller.

c. Repudiate the contract for breach of a condition by the seller, unless:

   i. He has waived the breach, and elected to treat it as a breach of warranty; or

   ii. The contract is non-severable and he has accepted the goods or part of them (*S.11(4)*).

d. In respect of a breach of warranty:

   i. Set up the loss in diminution of the price, or

   ii. Sue for damages.

e. Sue for specific performance. This equitable remedy is at the discretion of the court and will not normally be granted when damages are an adequate remedy. The goods will need to be specific or ascertained and not readily available elsewhere in the market. The remedy is appropriate for goods which have a special value or which are unique, for example a classic car or a painting.

f. Seek a compensation order for 'any personal injury, loss or damage', where a trader is convicted of a criminal offence under the provisions of the *POWERS OF CRIMINAL COURTS (SENTENCING) ACT 2000*. Magistrates can award up to £5,000, there is no limit in the Crown Court. This can be a useful remedy where the consumer has, for example, suffered minor harm with a stand alone civil action not worth bringing or where the consumer has no civil remedy.

AUCTION SALES

47. By *S.57* the following rules apply to auction sales.

a. Each lot is deemed to be the subject of a separate contract of sale.

b. The sale is complete when the auctioneer announces its completion by the fall of the hammer or in other customary manner. Until this happens the bidder may retract his bid or the seller may withdraw the goods. Generally an auction sale will be an unconditional contract for the sale of specific goods within the meaning of *S.18 Rule 1*. Property will therefore pass when the contract is made, ie on the fall of the hammer.

In DENNANT v SKINNER (**1948**) P sold a car by auction to X. Later X gave P a cheque for the price and signed an agreement that ownership would not pass until the cheque had cleared. Before the cheque cleared X sold to D. It later became apparent that the cheque would not be honoured. It was held that P could not recover the car from D since X had acquired title when it was knocked-down to him. The subsequent agreement that ownership would not pass until the cheque was cleared did not transfer title back to P.

  c. A sale may be subject to a reserve price, ie a minimum price below which the goods cannot be sold.

  d. A seller may expressly reserve the right to bid, provided this is notified at the sale.

  e. Where a sale is not notified to be subject to a right to bid on behalf of the seller, it is not lawful for the seller to bid (or employ any person to bid) nor is it lawful for the auctioneer to knowingly take any such bid. Any sale contravening this rule may be treated as fraudulent by the buyer.

THE SUPPLY OF GOODS AND SERVICES ACT 1982

48. The Act has two main parts. Part I amends the law with respect to terms implied in certain contracts for the supply of goods. Part II codifies the common law rules applicable when a person agrees to carry out a service.

49. *Part I*

  a. Many modern commercial transactions where property is transferred do not fall within the definition of a sale of goods. For example:

    i. Contracts for work and materials, for example building, car repair, and contracts to install central heating or double glazing.

    ii. Contracts of exchange or barter. Provided there is no money consideration these are not sales of goods. A contract of part-exchange is a sale of goods. (See paragraph 3.e. above.)

    iii. 'Free Gifts'. If a buyer is given a gift of 'product x' if he buys 10 units of 'product y', he will own product x although it was not sold to him.

    iv. Contracts for the hire of goods.

  b. The problem was that Sale of Goods Act protection did not apply to goods supplied under such contracts. This could be unfair. For example when someone supplied work and materials his obligations in respect of the materials were those implied at common law, but if he only supplied the materials he would be subject to the more stringent requirements of the SALE OF GOODS ACT.

c. This anomaly has been remedied by the 1982 Act. The Act applies to 'contracts for the transfer of property in goods' and 'contracts for the hire of goods'. *Sections 2–5* provide for statutory implied terms on the part of the seller similar to those in *S.12–15* SALE OF GOODS ACT 1979. Thus:

 i. By *S.2* there is an implied condition that the transferor has the right to transfer the property in the goods.

 ii. By *S.3* there is an implied condition that the goods will correspond with their description.

 iii. By *S.4* there are implied conditions relating to quality and fitness for purpose.

 iv. By *S.5* there is an implied condition that where the transfer is by reference to sample the bulk will correspond with the sample.

d. Contracts for the hire of goods are defined in *S.6* and *S.7–10* provide for statutory implied conditions similar to *S.12–15* SALE OF GOODS ACT 1979.

50. *Part II*

a. In October 1981 the National Consumer Council published a report entitled *Service Please*. This reported widespread dissatisfaction with regard to consumer services, the main areas of complaint concerned poor quality workmanship, delays in carrying out work and complaints about the price charged. These problems are clearly very important because of the vast number of service contracts made each day, involving for example storage, repairs, cleaning, transport, holidays, banking, dentistry, law, accounting and advertising. The purpose of the Act is to codify the common law relating to the three areas mentioned above, namely skill, time and price.

b. The Act applies to contracts 'under which a person agrees to carry out a service'. However, it does not apply to contracts of employment, apprenticeships, services rendered to a company by a director and the services of an advocate before a court or tribunal.

c. By *S.13* there is an implied term that where the supplier is acting in the course of a business he will carry out the service with reasonable care and skill.

d. By *S.14* there is an implied term that where the supplier is acting in the course of a business and the time for the service to be carried out is not fixed by the contract or determined by the course of dealings between the parties, the supplier will carry out the service within a reasonable time.

e. By *S.15* there is an implied term that where the consideration is not determined by a contract or in a manner agreed in the contract or by the course of dealing between the parties, the party contracting with the supplier will pay a reasonable price.

51. *Exclusion of Liability.* *S.7* UNFAIR CONTRACT TERMS ACT 1977 (as amended by the SUPPLY OF GOODS AND SERVICES ACT 1982) deals with contracts for the supply of goods other than contracts of sale or hire purchase. *S.2* of the 1977 Act is relevant to Part II of the 1982 Act.

a. If the exclusion clause relates to title it will be void (*S.7(3A) UCTA 1977*).

b. If the exclusion clause relates to description, quality, fitness or sample

   i. If the buyer deals as a consumer the clause is void (*S.7(2)*).

   ii. If the buyer does not deal as a consumer the exclusion clause must satisfy the requirement of reasonableness (*S.7(3)*).

c. If the exclusion clause relates to poor quality work, ie a breach of *S.13* the clause must satisfy the requirement of reasonableness (unless the negligent work causes personal injury or death, in which case it is void) (*S.2 UCTA 1977*).

d. If there is a complaint in a consumer contract for work and materials it will be necessary to discover the exact nature of the complaint. If it concerns defective materials the exclusion clause will be void. On the other hand if the materials are acceptable but the workmanship is negligent the exclusion clause will have to satisfy the reasonableness test. *S.2* of the 1977 Act does not distinguish between consumer and non-consumer contracts, however, recent cases have shown that it is becoming more difficult for a trader to exclude liability for negligence when he deals with a consumer. For example:

In WOODMAN V PHOTO TRADE PROCESSING (**1981**) (a test case supported by the Consumers Association), P took some film of a friend's wedding to a shop for developing. The shop displayed a notice limiting their liability to the cost of the film. Due to the processor's negligence the film was ruined. It was held that the exemption clause in the shop was unreasonable and P was awarded £75 to compensate him for his disappointment.

CHAPTER 32

Competition Policy

Open and fair competition is seen as being vital to a fair and efficient market with the best possible prices amongst producers and suppliers. However, unfettered competition leads to unfair practices with monopolies and unfair agreements being reached between manufacturers and service providers; such as price fixing or practices which deter other competitors from entering the market. It can lead to relationships between producers and suppliers being co-operative rather than competitive. It is thus necessary to regulate the market. The key legislative provisions in this area are, the *COMPETITION ACT 1998*, which came into force in 2000, and the *ENTERPRISE ACT 2002*, which came into force in 2003.

1. As a member of the European Union the UK is subject to EC law on regulating competition between member states; these are principally, *Articles 81* and *82* of the *TREATY OF ROME*. *ARTICLE 81* prohibits agreements between organisations that restrict or distort competition: these include price fixing, market sharing, restricting competition. The European Commission will grant certain exemptions and gives block exemptions for certain categories of agreement. In CREHAN V INNTREPRENEUR PUB COMPANY (IPC) AND BREWMAN GROUP LIMITED (B) (2003) C was a tenant of two public houses. As a part of the tenancy agreement he was required to buy all of his beer from B. This led to C going out of business because other untied public houses could buy their beer from whomever they chose which had the effect of them being able to gain much lower prices for their beer. C complained that the tied agreement was a breach of *Article 81*. The High Court held that two conditions had to be satisfied for a successful claim under *Article 81*; firstly, having regard to the legal and economic context of the leases, whether it was difficult for other businesses to enter the market or increase their market share, and secondly, whether there existed a network of similar leases that had the effect of sealing off the market. The court found that a significant number of estates had been sold recently following UK legislation (the *SUPPLY OF BEER (TIED ESTATES) ORDER 1989*), and it was not difficult for newcomers to enter the market or existing participants to increase their market share, there was no infringement of *Article 81*.

   Article 82 prohibits abuse of a dominant position; this is where a small number of suppliers or producers have in effect a monopoly in the market, this might include imposing unfair buying or selling prices. In PUBLISHERS' ASSOCIATION V COMMISSION OF THE EC (1992) UK publishers were seeking to continue enforcing a minimum resale price on books sold in the UK and other EC member states (the Net Book Agreement). The European Commission found the agreement contrary to *Article 81* and required its abolition. This was subsequently confirmed by the European Court of Justice.

The European Commission also has power to control mergers and takeovers with a view to ensuring that they do not impede effective competition.

2. UK competition law is contained in the COMPETITION ACT 1998. The Act mirrors the two *Articles 81* and *82*. Organisations may apply to the Office of Fair Trading for individual or block exemptions. Individual exemptions are granted where it can be shown that any agreement leads to improving production or distribution or promotes developments which will ultimately benefit the consumer. Any restrictions in such agreements must be indispensable to achieving these aims and the agreement must not lead to the elimination of competition. Block exemptions are based on the same criteria as individual agreements but apply automatically to certain sections of the market.

The Competition Commission was established under the COMPETITION ACT its role is to:

i.   hear appeals against decisions of the Office of Fair Trading

ii. investigate specific markets or the conduct of companies or mergers, here it reports to the Secretary of State with recommendations for any course of action.

The ENTERPRISE ACT 2002 introduced a number of changes to UK competition law setting up new statutory bodies such as the Competition Appeal Tribunal and a new system for market investigations. Also, individuals who dishonestly engage in cartel agreements may be prosecuted and lastly, there is a new power to allow the Office of Fair Trading to apply for a disqualification order for directors who have committed breaches of competition law.

CHAPTER 33

Consumer Credit

INTRODUCTION: *THE CONSUMER CREDIT ACT 1974* (as amended)

1. The consumer credit industry is regulated by the CONSUMER CREDIT ACT 1974.

2. The purposes of the Act are:

   a. To introduce a uniform system of statutory control over the provision of credit. (The CONSUMER CREDIT ACT 2006 amends the CONSUMER CREDIT ACT 1974.)

   b. To protect the interests of consumers by introducing a new system of licensing those who offer credit, and by increasing the protection of purchasers of credit by redressing bargaining inequality, controlling trading malpractices and regulating the remedies for default.

3. Previous credit legislation has imposed different rules according to the status of the creditor and the type of lending. The Act treats all lenders alike and regulates in the same way, so far as possible, all forms of credit, for example a cash loan, a sale of goods on credit, a credit card transaction, or a hire purchase deal. It provides hirers of goods with similar protection to credit purchasers of goods, recognising that hire is often an alternative to credit. It also recognises that:

   a. Prior to entering into an agreement the consumer needs an adequate supply of information to make an informed choice;

   b. The imposition of trading standards and the provision of consumer protection is needed at every stage of the transaction; and

   c. The credit industry is not made up of creditors only but also a wide range of ancillary businesses for example debt collectors, debt counsellors, credit reference agencies and brokers – either a 'broker' in the traditional sense, or a retailer offering the financial services of a creditor in order to sell his goods.

4. The responsibility for the operation of the Act rests with the Director General of Fair Trading, whose duties include:

   a. Supervision of the working and enforcement of the Act, and

   b. Administration of the licensing system.

5. The Act reforms the consumer credit industry within a framework of new and different terminology. The Act applies to '*regulated agreements*'. A regulated agreement may be either a *consumer credit agreement* or a *consumer hire agreement*.

6. *Regulated Consumer Credit Agreements*

a. A consumer credit agreement is a credit agreement by which the creditor (who may be an individual or a corporation) provides the debtor (who must be an individual) with credit not exceeding £25,000. The term 'individual' is defined to include partnerships and other unincorporated bodies even though they are not usually thought of as 'consumers'. Companies cannot be debtor 'individuals'.

b. *S.10* provides that credit may be either

    i. *'Running Account'* credit, ie credit up to an agreed limit, for example a bank overdraft or a credit card; or

    ii. *'Fixed Sum'* credit, ie credit of a definite amount, for example a bank loan or a hire purchase agreement.

c. *S.11* provides for the classification of credit agreements according to the purpose for which the credit is given. It refers to

    i. *Restricted-use credit.* – The credit facility may be used for a stipulated purpose only, for example a hire purchase agreement or a shop budget account.

    ii. *Unrestricted-use credit.* – The debtor may use the loan as he pleases, for example an overdraft facility or an 'Access' card if it is used to obtain cash.

d. *S.12* and *S.13* provide a further type of classification based on the relationship between the creditor and the supplier:

    i. *Debtor-Creditor-Supplier* agreements, ie where credit is provided to finance a transaction between a debtor and a supplier. If the supplier of the goods also supplied the credit it is still a debtor-creditor-supplier agreement. The usual type of hire purchase transaction involving a consumer, a dealer and a finance company is a debtor-creditor-supplier agreement (see below).

    ii. *Debtor-Creditor* agreements. – In effect any agreement to supply credit which is not a debtor-creditor-supplier agreement, for example a personal bank loan.

    iii. The categorisation between debtor-creditor-supplier and debtor-creditor agreements is necessary because under the Act the creditor under a debtor-creditor agreement does not incur any liability for the quality of goods supplied, whereas the creditor who finances sales of goods directly, or in the course of an agreement with the supplier, does have such liability.

e. The Act also regulates *credit-token* agreements. A credit-token is, for example a Visa, MasterCard, or 'Barclaycard', a Cash Dispenser Card, or a credit card issued by a retailer. The extent of the credit card holder's liability is defined in the Act (*SS.66* and *84*). The card holder is not liable for another person's use of the card unless he has previously accepted the card or the use by another person amounted to acceptance. A card holder accepts the card when he (i) signs it; (ii) he signs a receipt for it: or (iii) it is first used, either by the card holder himself or a person he authorises to use it.

7. ***Regulated Consumer Hire Agreements.*** A consumer hire agreement is a bailment of goods to an individual for a period of more than three months, for not more than £25,000, and which is not a hire purchase agreement. (A hire purchase agreement is a consumer credit agreement.)

A recent House of Lords judgement provides a good illustration of how the framework of regulation applies in practice. In DIAMOND V LOVELL (2000) a Mrs Diamond hired a replacement car following an accident for which she was not responsible. Mr Lovell's insurance company paid for the repairs to Mrs Diamond's car but refused to pay the hire fee. The insurance company put forward two lines of defence. Firstly, the agreement between Mrs Diamond and the hire company was a regulated consumer credit agreement and was unenforceable because it did not comply with the *CONSUMER CREDIT ACT*. Secondly, Mrs Diamond had not mitigated her loss; she could have hired a car at a much lower rate, the particular hire company specialised in accident repair hire vehicles requiring no payment from the hirer simply a claim on the final settlement. The House of Lords held that the agreement was a consumer credit agreement and unenforceable because it did not contain all the terms 'prescribed' in regulations made under the *CONSUMER CREDIT ACT*. As to mitigation of loss, Mrs Diamond acted reasonably in engaging the services the hire company but this did not mean she was entitled to recover the full amount. She had obtained additional services – not having to pay or pursue a claim for car hire, benefits which she would not be entitled to claim for under English law; any claim would have been limited to a general market hire rate.

HIRE PURCHASE – PRELIMINARY MATTERS

8. Probably the most common method of obtaining the possession and use of goods before making full payment is to enter into a hire purchase agreement. A hire purchase is a bailment of goods (ie a delivery of possession of goods) plus the grant of an option to purchase the goods. The consumer does not 'agree to buy' the goods at the time of the contract. Therefore if he sells the goods before he has exercised his option to purchase he does not pass title to them.

In HELBY V MATTHEWS (1895) the owner of a piano hired it to a bailee. The agreement provided that the bailee should pay monthly instalments, he could terminate by delivering the piano to the owner, and if he paid all the instalments punctually he would become the owner of the piano, but until such time the piano would be the property of the owner. Before paying all the instalments the bailee pledged the piano with a pawnbroker as security for an advance. It was held that the owner could recover the piano from the pawnbroker because the bailee had not 'agreed to buy' the piano, he merely had an option either to purchase the piano by paying all the instalments, or to return the piano. Consequently he could not pass title to the pawnbroker.

9. *The Role of the Finance Company*. Usually when a consumer wishes to purchase goods on hire purchase the dealer himself does not provide the credit. The dealer sells the goods to a finance company for cash. The finance company (now the owner) then hires the goods to the consumer, the rights and obligations being between the finance company and the consumer, rather than between the dealer and the consumer.

10. *The prescribed form for credit or hire agreements*

There are certain requirements which must be met. These include:

Prior to the agreement a debtor or hirer must be given details of the agreement he is about to sign, and the agreement must be:

i.   readily legible,

ii   contain all the terms,

iii   comply with regulations as to its form and content, eg correctly stating the amount of the loan or hire,

iv   where appropriate, give details of any right to cancel,

vi   be signed personally by the debtor or hirer.

In WILSON V SECRETARY OF STATE FOR TRADE AND INDUSTRY (2003) W, a borrower, was charged a 'document fee' of £250 which, because she did not pay it immediately, was added to the loan. W claimed under *S.127* of the CONSUMER CREDIT ACT that the agreement was unenforceable as it did not correctly state the amount of the loan. The House of Lords confirmed the Court of Appeal's view that the 'document fee' was not credit and as a result one of the prescribed terms was incorrect rendering the agreement unenforceable.

11. *Obligations in Relation to Hire Purchase Contracts*

   a. *Obligations of the creditor (owner)*

      i.   The SUPPLY OF GOODS (IMPLIED TERMS) ACT 1973 imposes obligations relating to title, description, quality and fitness for purpose, and sample very similar to those imposed by the SALE OF GOODS ACT 1979. The creditor also has an obligation to deliver the goods at the agreed time, or if no time is agreed, within a reasonable time.

      ii. The restrictions on the use of exemption clauses imposed by the UNFAIR CONTRACT TERMS ACT 1977 apply to hire purchase in the same way as they apply to sale of goods.

      iii. If the creditor breaks an express or implied *condition of* the contract the bailee can treat the contract as at an end and claim damages. He is entitled to repayment of all the instalments that he has paid, but he must allow the creditor to re-possess the goods. If the creditor breaks a *warranty* the bailee may claim damages.

      iv. By *S.56* if a dealer arranges with a consumer for goods to be sold to a finance company the dealer is deemed to have conducted the negotiations as agent for the creditor. Thus the creditor will be liable for any representations or contractual promises made by the dealer.

b. *Obligations of the dealer (credit-broker)*

i. Although the usual type of hire purchase contract will create a contractual relationship between the finance company (the owner) and the consumer, the dealer may be liable on an implied collateral contract.

In ANDREWS v HOPKINSON (1956) a car dealer said of a second-hand car 'It's a good little bus; I would stake my life on it; you will have no trouble with it.' A hire purchase agreement was entered into. A week later P was injured in a collision caused by a serious defect in the car. P could not sue the finance company because of an effective exemption clause, but he was successful in his action against the dealer, the court holding that there was an implied contract between P and D and express term of which was 'you will have no trouble with it'. Since this term was broken P received damages. This case is not affected by S.56 (above) since that section also preserves the personal liability of the dealer.

ii. The dealer is deemed to be the agent of the creditor for the purposes of receiving any notice of revocation, cancellation or rescission, and where such notice or payment is received he is deemed to be under a contractual duty to transmit the notice or payment to the creditor.

c. *Obligations of the debtor*

i. To take delivery of the goods.

ii. To take reasonable care of the goods. The debtor is not liable for fair wear and tear, but he will be liable for damage caused by his own negligence, or if he deals with the goods in a manner which is clearly unauthorised by the creditor. If the goods are stolen the agreement will be discharged by frustration and both parties will therefore be free from further liability.

iii. To pay the instalments, unless the debtor has exercised his option to terminate (see below).

12. *Hire Purchase, Conditional Sale, and Credit Sale Agreements.* In addition to the more common hire purchase agreements the Act also regulates conditional sale and credit sale agreements.

a. A *conditional sale* is an agreement for the sale of goods whereby the price is payable by instalments and ownership remains with the seller until fulfilment of all conditions governing payment of instalments and other matters specified in the agreement. The 'buyer' under a conditional sale agreement is not regarded as a person who has bought or agreed to buy the goods. Thus he will be treated the same way as a debtor under a hire purchase agreement and will not be able to pass good title to the goods.

b. A *credit sale* is an agreement for the sale of goods, the purchase price being payable by five or more instalments, not being a conditional sale agreement. Under such agreements the ownership of the goods passes to the buyer at once, and he may therefore pass on good title to another person.

FORMATION OF THE AGREEMENT

13. *Licensing*

    a. Any person who wishes to carry on a consumer credit or consumer hire business must first obtain a licence from the Director General of Fair Trading, who must be satisfied that the applicant is a fit person to engage in such business.

    b. A person who engages in activities for which a licence is required when he does not have a licence, commits a criminal offence and in general the agreement will be unenforceable against the debtor or hirer.

14. *Seeking Business*

    a. *Advertising of credit.* An advertisement must give a fair and reasonably comprehensive picture of the credit offered, for example the 'true' rate of interest. An offence is committed if the advertisement:

        i.   Gives information which is false or misleading in a material respect.

             In METSOJA v NORMAN PITT (1989) a car dealer advertised a new car with a 0% credit facility. The dealer also operated a part exchange facility, however, the part exchange allowance was lower if a new car was bought on credit than it would be if the car were purchased for cash. It was held that the lower allowance on part exchange for persons purchasing on credit was a hidden charge for credit contrary to the Act.

        ii. Fails to comply with the regulations that are from time to time in force.

        iii. Advertises restricted-use credit where the person offering the credit does not hold himself out as prepared to sell the goods or services for cash.

    b. *Canvassing.* It is an offence:

        i.   To solicit entry by an individual into a regulated debtor-creditor agreement *off trade premises*, unless in response to a written request.

        ii. To send an unsolicited credit-token.

        iii. To send a circular to a minor soliciting the use of credit or hire facilities.

15. *Formal Requirements*

    a. Prior to making the agreement certain information must be disclosed to ensure that the debtor is aware of his rights and duties and the protection and remedies available to him under the Act. In particular the lender must disclose the annual percentage rate of interest (APR). All lenders must work this out in the same way so that consumers can make a fair comparison. To calculate the APR a lender will add all interest and other charges together and take into account how and when payments are made.

    b. The agreement itself must:

        i.   Be in writing;

    ii.   Contain all express terms in a clearly legible form;

    iii. Be signed by the debtor personally and by or on behalf of the creditor or owner;

    iv. Comply with the current regulations as to form and content; and

    v.   In the case of a cancellable agreement, contain a notice in the prescribed form indicating the right of the debtor to cancel the agreement, including how and when the right is exercisable and the name and address of a person to whom notice of cancellation may be given.

  c. *Copies of the agreement.* The debtor must receive:

    i.   Immediately upon signing – a copy of the form that the debtor signs.

    ii. Within seven days – a second copy of the completed agreement. This second copy is only necessary if the agreement was not completed by the debtor's signature (ie if the creditor has not previously signed it). In the case of a cancellable agreement this copy must be sent by post and must contain details of the debtor's right to cancel.

    iii. Within seven days (if no second copy is required) – a notice sent by post giving details of rights concerning cancellation of cancellable agreements.

  d. Non-compliance with the required formalities renders the agreement unenforceable against the debtor except on a court order. In some situations, for example if the creditor fails to give notice of the right to cancel, the court must refuse to enforce the agreement.

16. *The Debtor's Right to Cancel*

  a. A regulated agreement is cancellable:

    i.   If its prior negotiations included oral representations made in the presence of the consumer by the owner, or creditor, or by a person acting on their behalf, and

    ii. Provided the consumer signed the agreement at a place *other than the place of business* of the owner, creditor, or person acting on their behalf.

  b. Notice of cancellation must be given before the end of the 5th day following the day on which the consumer received the second copy (where necessary) or, if there was no second copy, notice of his cancellation rights. Thus if the consumer signs an unexecuted agreement (ie not yet signed by the creditor) on 1st May, and receives his second copy on 7th May, the cancellation or 'cooling off' period will expire at midnight on 12th May.

  c. Notice of cancellation must be in writing and may be served on either

    i.   The creditor;

    ii. The credit-broker (for example a garage in a tripartite hire purchase agreement for the sale of a car) or supplier who negotiated the agreement; or

    iii. Any person specified in the notice of cancellation rights.

d.   Notice of cancellation is effective when posted, even if it is lost in the post.

e.   The effect of cancellation is that the agreement is treated as if it had never been entered into. Therefore any deposit paid, or goods handed over in part exchange by the consumer must be returned to him, and he has a lien on the goods in his possession until this is done. The consumer need not send the goods back himself, but he must retain them and permit their collection in response to a written request. He has a duty to take reasonable care of the goods for 21 days, but thereafter owes no duty of care unless he has unreasonably refused to comply with a request to permit collection, in which case the duty continues until such request is complied with.

f.   Non-cancellable agreements include non-commercial restricted-use credit arranged to finance the purchase of land, or arranged in connection with a bridging loan (ie a loan to enable the purchase of a house prior to the sale of the purchaser's previous house) and all agreements signed *on business premises*.

g.   The debtor's rights to cancel was extended by the CONSUMER PROTECTION (CANCELLATION OF CONTRACTS CONCLUDED AWAY FROM BUSINESS PREMISES) REGULATIONS 1987. These give the consumer the right of cancellation not only if the contract is made during the trader's visit, but also if during the visit, the consumer makes an offer which is subsequently accepted by the trader. Even where the trader's visit was requested by the consumer, the agreement will still be cancellable if the consumer requested a visit in connection with a possible supply of a particular type of goods or service and the resulting agreement is for a different type of goods or service which the consumer, when requesting the visit, could not reasonably have known was part of the trader's business.

The Regulations exempt certain types of agreement, for example agreements for the sale of land, to finance the purchase of land, agreements for building work, agreements for the supply of food and drink, and insurance

MATTERS ARISING DURING THE AGREEMENT

and investment agreements. Also excepted are agreements where the total payments to be made by the consumer do not exceed £35.

17. The main obligations of the creditor, dealer and debtor have already been considered. However, there are a number of other matters which may arise during the period of a consumer credit agreement.

18. *Additional Information.* The debtor is entitled to receive, in return for a request in writing and a payment of 15 pence, another copy of his agreement and a statement of the current financial position of his account.

19. *Appropriation of Payments.* A consumer might have two or more agreements with the same creditor and tender a payment insufficient to discharge the total amount due under all the agreements. In such a case

a. The consumer may allocate his payment between the various agreements as he thinks fit.

b. In the absence of allocation by the consumer the creditor must appropriate the payment towards the various sums in due proportion that they bear to one another. He cannot appropriate them to the agreements that would best serve his interests.

20. *Early Payment by the Debtor.* The debtor is entitled, at any time, by notice to the creditor and payment of all amounts outstanding, to discharge his indebtedness.

21. *Variation of Agreements.* Where, under a power conferred by the agreement, the creditor varies the agreement, for example by increasing the rate of interest payable, the variation does not take effect until notice of it is given to the debtor in the prescribed manner.

22. *Death of the Debtor*

a. If the agreement is fully secured the creditor may not take action.

b. If it is unsecured or partly secured the creditor may take action on an *order of the court* provided he can prove that he has been unable to satisfy himself that the present and future obligations of the consumer are likely to be discharged.

23. *Liability of Creditor for Supplier's Default*

a. In the usual triangular hire purchase agreement where a customer requires goods or services from a supplier and is provided with credit from a creditor, the creditor will be liable for the supplier's default if the creditor has himself contracted with the customer to supply the goods or services. The creditor will be personally liable for breach of implied conditions as to title, quality, fitness for purpose and so on. He will also usually be liable for misrepresentations made by the dealer to the customer, since under *S.56* the dealer is deemed to have conducted negotiations as agent for the creditor.

b. In a debtor-creditor-supplier agreement where the creditor has not personally contracted to supply goods or services to the customer, *S.75* provides that if the debtor (customer) has a claim against the supplier for misrepresentation or breach of contract, the debtor has a similar claim against the creditor. For example if the debtor uses a credit card to pay for goods then he may choose to bring a claim against the creditor (the credit card company) rather than the supplier, provided the cash price for the goods is more than £100, but less than £30,000. *S.75* providing connected lender liability will cover transactions entered into abroad (OFFICE OF FAIRTRADING v LLOYDS TSB BANK PLC (2006)).

In UNITED DOMINIONS TRUST v TAYLOR (**1980**) a car dealer introduced the customer to UDT. UDT lent the customer the money to enable him to purchase the car from the dealer. Taylor did not make loan repayments and was sued by UDT. His defence was that he had purchased the car because of misrepresentations by the dealer as to its condition and that the dealer was in breach of contract, ie the contract by which he bought the car. Taylor therefore claimed he had a right to rescind the contract with the dealer and, by virtue of *S.75*, a similar right to rescind the loan agreement. It was held that this was the effect of *S.75* and judgement was given in Taylor's favour.

DEFAULT AND TERMINATION

24. **Default Notices.** Whenever a consumer defaults a creditor is stopped from taking any action to enforce the agreement unless he has first served on the consumer a 'default notice' which must specify

   a. The alleged breach;

   b. The action required to put it right if it is capable of remedy; and if not –

   c. What sum, if any, is required to be paid as compensation; and

   d. The date by which such action must be taken, which must be not less than seven days after the service of the default notice.

25. *Further Restriction on Remedies for Default*

   a. Where goods are bought on hire purchase *S.90* provides that once one-third or more of the total price of the goods has been paid the creditor cannot recover possession of them except on an order of the court. Such goods are known as 'protected goods'.

   b. The section does not apply if the debtor voluntarily surrenders the goods.

   c. If goods are recovered by the creditor in contravention of *S.90* the agreement will terminate and the debtor is released from all liability. In addition he is entitled to recover from the creditor all sums paid under the agreement.

   d. Entry on to any premises by the creditor to take possession of goods subject to hire purchase, conditional sale, or consumer hire agreements is prohibited except by court order. Clearly this is of importance if the goods are not protected under *S.90*.

   e. The charging of default interest at a higher rate than the basic rate of interest is prohibited.

26. *Termination*

   a. The debtor may, at any time before the final payment falls due, terminate a *hire purchase* or *conditional sale agreement* by giving notice in writing to any person authorised to receive the sums payable under the agreement.

   b. The debtor's liability is to pay the sums which have accrued, plus the amount, if any, by which one half of the total price exceeds the total of the sums paid, or such lesser amount as may be specified in the agreement. He is also liable to compensate the creditor for any damage to the goods if he has failed to take reasonable care of them.

   c. If any contract term is inconsistent with these provisions, for example a term which imposes additional liability on the debtor, such term is void. The contract may, however, grant the debtor more favourable terms for termination than those provided by the Act.

d. Different rules apply to the termination of a *consumer hire agreement.* Termination does not affect any liability which has already accrued. The right to terminate does not arise until the agreement has been in existence for 18 months, unless the agreement itself provides for a shorter period. The period of notice which must be given is one instalment period or three months, whichever is less. The right to terminate a consumer hire agreement does not apply:

    i. Where the total hire payments exceed £,1500 per year; or

    ii. Where the goods are hired for a business, and are freely chosen by the hirer from a supplier, and the hiring arrangement is not made until the goods have been chosen; or

    iii. Where the hirer obtained the goods so that he could in turn hire them out in the course of his business.

JUDICIAL CONTROL

Judicial control over the provisions of the Act is exercised by the County Court.

27. *Enforcement Orders*

a. In several situations, for example if the agreement is 'improperly executed' the Act provides that, before he can enforce the agreement, the creditor must obtain a court order, ie an *'enforcement order'*.

b. As a general rule the court must dismiss the application if in all the circumstances justice appears to require this. In some cases the court has no choice but to dismiss the application, for example where the agreement was a cancellable one, but the consumer was not given proper notice of his right to cancel it.

28. *Time Orders*. On an application for an 'enforcement order', or on an application to recover possession of goods after service of a default notice, the court may grant a *'time order'*. This gives the consumer more time to pay, or to do something else he should have done, such as maintaining any security in good repair. While a time order is in force the consumer is protected against the consequences of his default, thus a security cannot be enforced, and the goods cannot be recovered by the creditor.

29. *Return and Transfer Orders*

a. Where a creditor seeks to recover, because of a breach by the consumer, goods which he has let on hire purchase, the court may order the consumer to return the goods under a *'return order'*. Where it thinks fit, the court may suspend the return order so long as the consumer keeps up revised payments under a 'time order'.

b. As an alternative (in cases where goods may be divided up) the court may make a *'transfer order'* giving ownership of part of the goods to the consumer and returning the rest to the creditor, depending on how much the consumer has already paid in respect of the total price of all the goods.

30. *Unfair Credit Relationship Test*

Sections 19–22 of the CONSUMER CREDIT ACT *2006*, amends the 1974 Act in allowing the court to examine alleged unfair credit agreements by taking account of all relevant factors over the entire duration of the agreement and not simply those relevant at the time the agreement was made (as was the case under the previous CONSUMER CREDIT ACT *1974*). *S140A(1)* gives power to the court to make an order if it finds that an agreement between creditor and debtor unfair. In taking account of all relevant circumstances this may include one or more of the following:

i.   any terms of the agreement or of any related agreement;

ii. the way in which the creditor has exercised or enforced any of his rights under the agreement;

iii. any other thing done (or not done) by, or on behalf of, the creditor.

The Act also allows consumers to access an alternative dispute resolution scheme rather than having recourse to the courts. It provides consumers with free access to a quick and efficient resolution of consumer credit disputes. Creditors will have a duty to refer complaints to the Financial Ombudsman Service.

Another factor in assessing fairness might be European legislation; the UNFAIR COMMERCIAL PRACTICES DIRECTIVE *2005/29/EC*. This will apply to consumer credit and has a non-exhaustive list of commercial circumstances that may be considered unfair.

31. *Interest on Trade Debts*

Small businesses have traditionally suffered from late payment for goods and services supplied to larger companies; their weak bargaining position making it difficult for them to include in their contracts to supply late payment interest charge clauses. The LATE PAYMENT OF COMMERCIAL DEBTS (INTEREST) ACT *1998* now gives to small businesses a statutory right to claim interest on late payment of commercial debts for the supply of goods and services to other businesses and public bodies. A small business is defined as one with fewer than 50 full-time employees, a large business is one where there are over 50 full-time employees. Interest becomes payable the day after the 'relevant date', this is either the date agreed by the parties or 30 days after the supplier has performed his obligations. Any attempt to exclude the Act will be subject to there existing some other substantial remedy within the contract, otherwise such terms will be of no effect.

CHAPTER 34

Insurance

PRINCIPLES OF INSURANCE LAW

1. *The Contract of Insurance*

   a. Insurance is a contract whereby the insurer, in return for a sum of money called the premium, contracts with the insured to pay a specified sum on the happening of a specific event, for example death or accident, or to indemnify the insured against any loss caused by the risk insured against, for example fire.

   b. It differs from a wager in that, although risk is the essence of the contract, the insured takes out insurance to guard against the risk of loss, whereas in a wager the contract itself creates the risk. In insurance the insured must therefore have some interest apart from the contract, ie an insurable interest.

   c. Many insurance contracts provide that the answers submitted by the insured in his proposal form are 'the basis of the contract'. This has the effect that all the terms of the contract are treated as conditions and the insurers will be able to avoid liability if the proposal form is incorrect, even if the wrong answer was given innocently and does not relate to a material fact. For example:

   In DAWSONS v BONNIN (1922) In response to a question on a proposal form as to where a lorry would be garaged, the proposer inadvertently inserted the wrong address. The lorry was later lost due to fire and a claim was made under the policy. It was held that since the proposal form was expressed to be 'the basis of the contract', all answers were conditions, the inaccuracy of which entitled the insurer to avoid the policy, even if, as in this case, the answer to the question did not affect the premium charged.

2. *The Principle of Good Faith*

   a. All contracts of insurance are *uberrimae fidei*. They are therefore voidable at the option of the insurer for non-disclosure of any material fact which was known, or ought to have been known, to the insured at the time of making the contract.

   b. A fact is material if it would influence the judgement of a prudent insurer in deciding whether to accept the risk, and if so at what premium and on what conditions.

   In LONDON ASSURANCE v MANSEL (1879) D failed to disclose that several insurance companies had declined proposals to insure his life. This was held to be a material factor which should have been disclosed. Rescission of the contract was therefore granted.

c. A policy of insurance, like any other contract is voidable for misrepresentation, whether innocent or fraudulent. The insurer however, can only avoid if the misrepresentation is materially and substantially false. Where an insurer avoids a voidable contract, they need not return any premiums paid.

3. *Insurable Interest*

a. Insurable interest means that the insured must be so circumstanced in relation to the subject matter of the insurance as to benefit by its existence or be prejudiced by its destruction (LUCENA V CRAUFURD (1806)). Thus for example, a person has an insurable interest in his property and in his own life or in that of his wife.

b. The common law does not require the insured to have an insurable interest. However:

   i. If the contract is one of indemnity (see below) an insured who has no interest at the time of the loss will have no claim – he loses nothing, therefore no indemnity is necessary.

   ii. Any policy in which the insured at the time of the policy has no insurable interest and no expectation of acquiring one is a wager, and void under the GAMING ACT 1845.

   iii. The LIFE ASSURANCE ACT 1774 provides that any insurance on the life of a person is void unless the person taking out the policy has an insurable interest in the life insured. Despite its name this Act also applies to personal accident and fire insurance policies.

   The effect of i.–iii. above is that an insurable interest must be present in all contracts of insurance. What 'insurable interest' means in relation to specific types of insurance contract is considered below under the appropriate heading.

4. *Indemnity*

a. An indemnity policy is one under which the insured will be compensated (ie indemnified) for his actual loss so far as it does not exceed the sum insured. For example if X insures his house for £20,000 and it is burnt down, if £5,000 will restore it, then he may claim £5,000 and no more. If it will cost £40,000 to restore it, then he may claim £20,000.

b. A 'valued policy' may, however, agree the measure of indemnity at the time when the policy is issued instead of waiting until the time of the loss. Such a contract is valid unless the overvaluation is so gross as to amount to a wager. The insured can recover the agreed value if the loss is total. If the loss is partial he can recover such proportion of the agreed value as is represented by the depreciation in the actual value. For example:

In ELCOCK V THOMSON (1949) a house was insured against fire. In the policy its value was agreed at £106,850. The house was damaged in a fire.

In fact its actual value before the fire was £18,000 and after the fire was £12,600, ie the depreciation in actual value was £5,400. The court therefore held that the insured was entitled to recover:

$$\frac{5,400}{18,000} \times 106,850 = £32,055$$

c.   The insured can never recover more than the sum for which the property is insured. For example:

In DARRELL v TIBBITTS (1880) a house was damaged by a gas explosion. The landlord recovered £750 from insurers. The tenant was, however, obliged under the terms of his lease to repair the damage. He did this with money received from the local authority (whose negligence caused the explosion). It was held that the insurers could recover the £750 paid to the landlord because clearly he had suffered no loss. To allow him to keep the money would be to award him double compensation.

d.   Provided the policy is not a 'valued policy' the measure of indemnity

   i.   In the event of total loss, is not the cost price, but the market value of the property at the time and place of the loss. For example:

   In LEPPARD v EXCESS INSURANCE CO (1979) a cottage was insured for £10,000, this sum being stated to be the amount necessary to replace the property in its existing form if it was completely destroyed. When the cottage was destroyed the insured claimed £10,000. The Court of Appeal, however, only awarded him the market value of the cottage at the time of its destruction, namely £3,000.

   ii.   In the event of partial loss, is the cost of repairs.

e.   If the property is under-insured (ie insured for less than its market value), the insurer is still liable for a partial loss up to the full limit of the sum insured. Some policies guard against this by including a 'subject to average' clause, whereby if the amount insured is less than the value the insurers are only liable for that proportion of the actual loss which the sum insured bears to the value of the property. For example the market value of X's house is £20,000, but it is only insured for £10,000. If X suffers fire damage to the extent of £5,000, he can only recover £2,500 from the insurer.

f.   All contracts of insurance are contracts of indemnity except:

   i.   Life assurance.

   ii.   Insurance against accident to, or illness of, the insured himself.

5. *Subrogation*

a.   If the contract is one of indemnity the insurers have a right of subrogation, ie having paid the insured his compensation, they are permitted to take over any rights that the insured has against the person who caused the loss. The insurers bring the action in the name of the insured, who must lend his name in return for a promise that he will not be liable for costs. The insurers are said to 'step into the shoes' of the insured, ie they are subrogated to his rights. For example A has insured his property against damage by fire with X Ltd. A fire is caused by B's negligence. X Ltd must pay A under the policy, but they are then entitled to sue B in negligence. If they recover the damages from B which exceed the amount they have had to pay to A, the excess received belongs to A.

b. If the insured renounces or compromises any right of action he has against a third party, he must repay to the insurers the benefit of which he has thereby deprived them.

In PHOENIX ASSURANCE v SPOONER (1905) D's premises were insured against fire with P. The local authority then issued a compulsory purchase notice, but before the purchase had been completed the premises were destroyed by fire. The local authority then completed the purchase having agreed with D to pay a sum which reflected the fact that D had received some money from P. In addition it was agreed that the local authority would indemnify D against any claim brought by P. When P did claim it was held that, since fire insurance is a contract of indemnity, P was entitled to all the rights that D had against the local authority, and this included a right to the full market value of the property. Since D had accepted less than the market value (because she had received some insurance money) she had deprived P of their opportunity to obtain the market value from the local authority. D therefore had to pay compensation to P, but could re-claim the amount paid from the local authority under her agreement with them.

6. *Contribution*

a. Where there is more than one policy enforceable at the time of loss covering the same subject matter, risk and interest, the insured may recover the total loss from either insurer.

b. Any insurer who pays more than his share may claim a contribution from the others in proportion to the sum insured with each.

7. *Risk*

a. Loss resulting from negligence is covered.

In HARRIS v POLAND (1942) the insured deliberately hid her jewellery in the grate of her fireplace. Later, having forgotten this, she lit the fire, and damaged her jewellery. Her claim succeeded even though she had been negligent and despite the fact that the fire had not escaped from its usual boundaries.

b. Clearly loss resulting from negligence is precisely what motor vehicle insurance is designed to cover. A claim will in fact lie even if the driving is so negligent that it amounts to a criminal offence.

c. A loss will not be covered if it is a loss of profits or if it is caused by:

i. The insured's own wilful misconduct. (The burden of proving this lies on the insurer.)

ii. Ordinary wear and tear.

TYPES OF INSURANCE CONTRACT

8. *Life Assurance*

    a.   A life assurance contract is one by which the insurer in return for either a lump sum or annual payments over a specified period, undertakes to pay the person for whose benefit the insurance is made, a sum of money on the death of the person whose life is insured. The term '*assurance*' is used where the event concerned must occur, in this case death. The term '*insurance*' is used when the event may occur, for example an accident or theft.

    b.   *Insurable interest*:

        i.   The interest must be a pecuniary interest, and must exist at the date of the contract but need not continue until the date of the death. Thus a man may take out a policy on the life of his wife, and even if they divorce he may claim under the policy when his former wife dies.

        ii.   A person may insure his own life for his own benefit for any sum he wishes, even though he intends when insuring to assign the policy to another person.

        iii.   Spouses have an unlimited insurable interest in each other's lives, but other relatives, such as father and son, have no insurable interest in the lives of each other.

        iv.   A creditor has an insurable interest in the life of the debtor up to the amount of the debt at the date of insurance.

        v.   An employee has an insurable interest in his employer's life to the extent of his wages, and an employer may insure against the loss of his employee's services through death.

    c.   *Suicide*:

        i.   If the insured is insane when he commits suicide the insurance money is recoverable unless the policy otherwise provides.

        ii.   If the insured is sane the position is unclear. Prior to 1961 suicide was a crime, and since it is contrary to public policy to allow a person to profit from his crime the insurance money could not be recovered by his personal representatives. Suicide is no longer a crime, however, it is probable that the money is irrecoverable, because money is not generally payable under a policy when the insured deliberately brings about the event insured against.

    d.   *Assignment*:

        i.   Assignment means that the right to receive the policy money is transferred from the person originally entitled to the asignee.

        ii.   The assignee need not have an insurable interest in the policy.

iii. The assignee must protect his interest in the policy by notifying the insurers.

iv. The assignee has a right to sue the insurers, if necessary, for the policy money.

9. *Fire Insurance*

a. A fire insurance contract gives the insured an indemnity covering loss caused by fire during a specified period.

    i. 'Fire' means ignition and not merely overheating.

    ii. 'Loss caused by fire' does not merely include items burned, it could include damage caused by the water used to fight the fire.

b. Clearly the insured cannot recover if he deliberately starts the fire, but if the loss is merely caused by his negligence this does not defeat his claim. – HARRIS V POLAND (**1942**) (see 7. above).

c. In contrast to life assurance, since the contract is one of indemnity, the insurable interest must exist not only when the contract is made, but also when the loss occurs. Any legal or equitable interest in the subject matter suffices as an insurable interest. For example an interest as an owner, tenant, mortgage, trustee, beneficiary, or personal representative. However, a shareholder has no interest in and cannot insure the property of a company, even if it is a 'one-man' company. – MACAURA V NORTHERN ASSURANCE CO (**1925**) (Chapter 39.4).

d. Restoration of the building.

    i. At common law the insured was not bound to use money received from the insurance company to reinstate the property. He was entitled to be indemnified in cash which he could use as he wished.

    ii. However, the FIRES PREVENTION (METROPOLIS) ACT *1774*, which despite its name applies throughout the country, provides that any person (for example a tenant) interested in a building destroyed by fire can require the insurer to spend the insurance money on the reinstatement of the building.

10. *Motor Vehicle Insurance*

a. Under the ROAD TRAFFIC ACT *1988* a motorist must insure against any liability he may incur as a result of causing the death or injury of a third party. The third party has a right to sue the insurers direct despite the general privity of contract rule.

b. If the user of a motor vehicle is not insured against liability for causing injury to third parties both the owner and the user have committed a criminal offence. In addition to their criminal liability any person who does not have the required compulsory insurance is liable to pay damages for breach of statutory duty if there is no other remedy available to the injured party.

In MONK v WARBEY (**1935**) D lent his car to a friend. The friend's driver drove negligently causing injury to P. The friend was not covered by insurance and D's policy only applied when the owner was driving it. D was therefore liable to pay damages to P for breach of statutory duty.

c. A provision in the policy which purports to exclude the insurer's liability to indemnify the insured because of his age, physical or mental condition, the condition of his vehicle, or the number of passengers carried is void. However, a limitation as to user, for example for 'private' purposes only, will prevent a third party from recovering damages from the insurer if he is injured while the car is being used in another way, for example as a taxi.

d. *Unsatisfied judgements*. In 1946 motor vehicle insurers agreed to set up the Motor Insurers Bureau (M.I.B.). The M.I.B. will satisfy a judgement where the driver does not have the compulsory cover, because for example he had not taken out a policy, or the insurers have gone into liquidation. The conditions are:

   i. Notice of proceedings is given to the M.I.B. before, or within 7 days after their commencement, and

   ii. The liability is one that is required to be covered by the Road Traffic Act.

e. The M.I.B. has also agreed to compensate 'hit and run' victims if

   i. Neither the owner nor driver can be traced.

   ii. On the balance of probabilities the owner or driver would be liable to compensate the victim.

   iii. The victim was a compulsory risk within the meaning of the ROAD TRAFFIC ACT.

   iv. The accident was not a deliberate attempt to run down the victim, and

   v. The claim is made in writing within three years of the accident.

11. *Insurance Against Theft*

   a. The principles applicable to life and fire insurance also apply to theft. For example:

   In ROSELODGE v CASTLE (**1966**) when insuring their stock against theft diamond merchants failed to disclose that the sales manager had a previous conviction for smuggling diamonds. It was held that this amounted to nondisclosure of a material fact, and the insurers could avoid the claim, even though the sales manager was not the thief.

   b. The insurer may avoid the contract if, for example

   i. The property has been deliberately overvalued; or

   ii. The stolen property was illegally imported, with the intention of evading customs duty. The rationale here is that if the insured was indemnified for the theft, he would profit from his illegal act of importing the goods.

12. *Accident Insurance*

    a. Life assurance policies usually also cover personal injury to the policy holder.

    b. A person who does not have life assurance may either insure himself against personal injury or insure against liability arising from injuries to third parties. He will not, however, be able to claim under a liability policy in respect of a deliberate unlawful act by himself.

        In GRAY V BARR (**1971**) D shot and killed Gray in a fight. He was acquitted of both murder and manslaughter but Gray's personal representatives made a claim against him under the *FATAL ACCIDENTS ACT*. D sought an indemnity under his accident liability policy in respect of any damages he might have to pay. It was held that even if the death was an 'accident' within the terms of the policy, the policy would not cover accidents which occurred as a result of threatening unlawful violence with a loaded gun.

    c. An injured third party may sue the insurer direct if the insured is bankrupt, or if the insured is a company which has gone into liquidation.

13. *Employers' Compulsory Insurance.* The *EMPLOYERS' LIABILITY (COMPULSORY INSURANCE) ACT 1969* makes it compulsory for every employer (except nationalised industries and local authorities) to insure himself against liability for injury or disease sustained by his employees and arising in the course of their employment.

CHAPTER 35

Patents, Copyright, Trade Marks and Passing-off

INTRODUCTION

1. In order to encourage new inventions and original works and to protect the goodwill of those who have built up a business the law gives statutory protection to patents, designs, copyright and trade marks. These rights are governed by the *COPYRIGHT, DESIGNS AND PATENTS ACT 1988* and the *PATENTS ACT 1977* (as amended). In addition the economic tort of 'passing-off' prevents a person from conducting himself so that customers will mistake his goods, services or business for that of someone else. This branch of law is known as intellectual property law.

DESIGNS

2. *Design Right*

   a. A *design right* is a new property right created under the 1988 Act. Hardware is automatically protected and does not need to be registered. The right subsists in an original design. It does not apply to the following:

      i.   Method of construction.

      ii. Interface (enabling the article to be placed in or against another article in order that either article may perform its function).

      iii. Surface decoration.

   b. *Duration.* The design right expires 15 years from the end of the calendar year in which first recorded in a design document, or an article was made to the design. If the design was made available for sale or hire within five years from first being recorded or an article being made, expiry is 10 years from the end of the year in which this occurred. Designs registered with the Registered Designs Act 1949 expire 10 years from the 12th January 1988 (commencement date of the 1988 Act).

    c.   *Remedies for infringement*. The following remedies are available:

        i.   Damages.

        ii.   Order for delivery-up. The articles delivered up would be disposed of by forfeiture to the design right owner or by destruction.

PATENTS

3. *Definition*

A patent is the name given to a bundle of monopoly rights which give the patentee the exclusive right to exploit the invention for a given period of time. It is a right to stop others, an inventor does not need a positive right to exploit his own invention.

4. *Applying for a Patent*

    a.   An application is made to the Patent Office. If the invention has been made by an employee in the course of his employment, the employer owns the invention and may apply for a patent with the inventor's consent. Alternatively a joint application may be made, or the employee may apply, in which case the grant will be subject to the employer's interest.

    b.   At the Patent Office a document called a '*Complete Specification*' is filed. This contains a description of the article, process or machine, including working instructions and a statement of 'claims' which define the scope of the invention for which the inventor seeks his monopoly. It is against these claims that any infringement is judged.

    c.   The Patent Office carries out '*research*' to test for novelty. According to the result of this search the applicant may decide to abandon or modify his application or request an *examination* by a qualified Patent Office examiner. The main task of the examiner is to see that the claims of the specification describe things that are not only new, but also inventive. Once the examiner is satisfied the specification is published and for three months afterwards any interested party can object by notice to the Patent Office.

        A bagless cyclonic vacuum cleaner invented and patented by Dyson was held to have been infringed subsequently by Hoover (DYSON APPLIANCES LTD V HOOVER LTD (2000)).

    d.   In the event of no opposition or failure of objections the '*Letters Patent*' will be sealed and the patentee can sue in the High Court (or in some cases the County Court) for any infringement.

    e.   Once granted the patent covers the UK and is in force for four years, and it can be renewed annually for a further 16 years, after which it can be extended by an application to the High Court for a further five or 10 years.

5. *International Application Procedure*

An application at the British Patent Office will only result in the grant of a British Patent. Until recently an applicant who wanted protection in other countries had to file applications in each country for which a patent was required. This was costly and resulted in the application being examined with varying degrees of thoroughness in each country. Two systems now exist to minimise the need for separate national applications.

a. The *PATENT CO-OPERATION TREATY* (in operation since 1978) provides for the filing of a single application designating the countries for which the applicant seeks protection. A single search is carried out and the application is then sent to each of the designated countries for separate examination as a national application according to their local laws.

b. The *EUROPEAN PATENT CONVENTION* (in operation since 1978) to which EEC member states (except Greece) and some other European countries belong, provides for an application to be filed at the European Patent Office in Munich. The application is searched and examined at the European Patent Office and if the invention satisfies the requirements of the Convention separate national patents are granted for the specified countries.

6. *Patentability*

Patents must fulfil the following requirements specified in the *PATENTS ACT 1977*:

a. It must be a patentable invention which is capable of industrial application. The Act does not define what is patentable, instead it lists a number of things that are not patentable inventions, for example:

    i. Discoveries, scientific theories or mathematical methods;

    ii. Literary, dramatic, musical or artistic works;

    iii. Schemes, rules or methods for performing a mental act, playing a game, doing business or programming a computer;

    iv. The presentation of information.

b. *Novelty.* The invention must be new, ie it must not have been made available to the public anywhere in the world by written or oral description, by use or in any other way.

c. *Inventive steps.* An invention involves an inventive step if it is not obvious to a person skilled in the art, having regard to state of the art knowledge.

7. *Employee Inventions*

Since most inventions are made by company employees, the question of rights to the invention are important. The Act provides that an invention made in the course of employment shall belong to the employer, but it also establishes a statutory award scheme to compensate employees for inventions made on behalf of their employers. The award will ensure a fair share to the employee having regard to the benefit derived by the employer. Any contract term which diminishes the employee's rights under the Act is void.

8. *Ownership, Assignment and Licensing*

    a.   A patent, or an application for a patent, is personal property, but it is not a chose in action.

    b.   An assignment must be in writing and signed by both parties, otherwise it is void.

    c.   Licensing is a method of developing a patent whereby the patentee gives permission for the sale or manufacture of the patented article, subject to express conditions.

9. *Licences of Right for Drugs*

The 1988 Act brings in legislation in respect of 'licences of right' for drugs. The intention is to bring the law in Great Britain into agreement with the laws of nearly all other countries. It was considered in the public interest that there should be the right of free use of inventions for the manufacture of food and medicine. Patents may be taken out for these purposes but the patents would not be used to restrain manufacture of them.

In the case of a patent for drugs, without waiting for the three-year period applicable to other patents, a licence could be had by any person interested on such terms as the comptroller thought fit to secure that drugs should be available to the public at the lowest prices consistent with the patentees deriving a reasonable advantage from their patent rights. The applicant for a licence of right of this nature may make his application in the 16th year of the patent.

10. *Infringement*

    a.   There are two questions in relation to infringement:

        i.   Does the scope of the invention as defined in the claims cover the product or process concerned?

        ii.   Is the defendant's conduct prohibited by the Act?

    b.   The Act provides that a person infringes a patent if he does any of the following:

        i.   If the invention is a product, he makes, disposes of, uses or imports the product, or keeps it for disposal or otherwise;

        ii.   If the invention is a process, he uses it or offers it for use, when he knows or should know that there would be an infringement, or if he disposes of, uses, imports or keeps any product obtained by means of that process;

        iii.   Supplies means essential for putting an invention into effect to a person not entitled to work the patent, when he knows, or should know, that the means are suitable and that they are intended to be used to put the invention into effect.

    c.   An inventor whose patent is infringed is entitled to an injunction, delivery of the infringing articles and damages, which may be assessed on a loss of profits or royalty basis. He will also be given a 'certificate of contested validity' which entitles him to larger costs in any future infringement action. If the patentee loses the grant of the patent may be revoked or the specifications may be found not wide enough to cover the defendant's product or process.

The *PATENTS ACT 2004* has been passed to assist, particularly small businesses, to enforce patent rights. It enables the Patent Office to provide an independent non-binding opinion on patent validity or alleged infringement thus limiting recourse to litigation. The legislation encourages the out of court settlements of disputes and deters patent owners from making unreasonable allegations of infringement. There is also provision for a European Community patent to be granted with a centralised Community Patent Court with jurisdiction over invalidity and infringement proceedings.

COPYRIGHT

11. *Definition*

Copyright protects the independent skill, labour and effort which has been expended in producing work and prevents others from helping themselves to too large a portion of that skill, labour and effort. Unlike a patent, a copyright is not a monopoly, it is a right of protection against copying. Copyright is acquired by bringing a work into existence. There is no requirement of, nor provision for, registration.

12. *Statutory Protection*

   a. *Subsistence of copyright*. Works eligible for copyright protection are put into three groups:-

      i. Literary, dramatic, musical or artistic works.

      ii. Sound recordings, films, broadcasts or cable programmes.

      iii. Typographical arrangement of published editions.

      A computer program is treated as literary work.

   b. *Artistic works*. The following are protected:

      i. Paintings, drawings, sculptures, engravings and photographs, *irrespective of artistic quality*.

      ii. Works of architecture, being either buildings or models of buildings.

      iii. Works of artistic craftsmanship, not included in the above categories.

      The phrase 'irrespective of artistic quality' has enabled the courts to hold that engineering production drawings are entitled to copyright.

   c. *Ownership*. The 1988 Act simplifies the provisions regarding ownership of copyright, the only case where the case in a literary, dramatic or musical work does not initially rest in the author is where the work is made by an employee in the course of his employment in which case the employer is the first owner of the copyright unless there is some agreement to the contrary. The Act also introduces a concept of literary, dramatic, musical or artistic work which is computer generated in circumstances in which there is no human author. The author is taken to be the person by whom arrangements necessary for creation of the work are undertaken.

d. *Duration*. The present term of copyright protection is the life of the creator plus 70 years.

e. *Right of the copyright owner*. The copyright in a work is the exclusive right to do the following acts in the UK.

    i. Copy the work. (Copying includes storing in any medium by electronic means.)

    ii. Issue copies to the public.

    iii. Perform, show or play the work in public.

    iv. Broadcast or include in a cable programme service.

    v. Make an adaptation of the work.

Copyright in the typographical arrangement of a published edition includes not only the right to copy the work but also the right to issue copies to the public.

The 1988 Act introduces the moral rights of an author as follows:

    i. *Paternity right*. An author of a literary, dramatic, musical or artistic work, or the director of a film has a right to be identified as author or director in certain circumstances.

    ii. *Right of integrity*. An author has the right not to have his work subjected to derogatory treatment amounting to distortion or mutilation of the work or which is otherwise prejudicial to the honour or reputation of the author or director.

These two rights subsist throughout the duration of the copyright.

    iii. *Privacy*. A person who commissions a photograph or film for private or domestic purposes has a right not to have:

      1) copies issued to the public

      2) the work exhibited in public

      3) the work broadcast or included in a cable programme. An entitled person may waive the above rights.

13. *Indirect Copying*

Copying a product which has been manufactured from drawings amounts to indirectly copying the drawings and is an infringement of copyright.

In BERSTEIN v SIDNEY MURRAY (1981) a dress designer saw P's design at an exhibition and later marketed dresses which were a copy of P's both in materials and design. It was held that although the dresses themselves were not protected by copyright D had indirectly copied the sketches made by P.

Contrast BRITISH LEYLAND v ARMSTRONG PATENTS (1986) where D declined to obtain a licence from P to produce spare parts for BL cars, but nevertheless produced replacement exhaust pipes by copying the shape and dimensions of the original. P alleged that D had by indirect copying infringed the copyright in P's original drawings of the exhaust system. The High Court and Court of Appeal granted an injunction in favour of P, but the House of Lords reversed this decision. It was held that although exhaust pipes were purely functional articles which were neither patentable nor a registerable design, the replacements produced by D were clearly recognisable as copies of P's drawings in which artistic copyright subsisted. Therefore D had infringed P's copyright but car owners had an inherent right to repair their cars in the most economical way possible and must have access to a free market for spares. P was not entitled to derogate or interfere with that right by asserting their copyright against a person manufacturing parts solely for repair.

Manufacturers have protested that this decision amounts to a 'pirates charter' in that it allows a producer of spares to copy the original design of an article and sell it at a cheaper price than the manufacturer. The spare parts industry has welcomed the decision as a liberalisation of the market of considerable benefit to the consumer.

14. *Restricted Acts*

   a. The acts restricted by copyright in artistic work are:

      i. Reproducing the work in any material form, including converting a two-dimensional work into a three-dimensional work and vice versa.

      ii. Publishing the work, including television broadcasts.

      There will be no infringement with regard to drawings if the article is not regarded by non-experts as a reproduction.

   b. There is no copyright in a name because of the improbability that a name could amount to an original work.

15. *Infringement*

   a. Infringement occurs when a person, without the consent of the copyright owner, contravenes the rights of the copyright owner. Secondary infringement will occur if:

      i. A person, without permission, transmits a work by means of a telecommunication system if he knows that infringing copies will be made on reception.

      ii. A person supplies a copy of a sound recording or film, knowing or believing that the recipient will make infringing copies.

313

b. *Electronic infringement of copyright.* The 1988 Act introduces measures for copyright protection in respect of the latest forms of technology which have an impact on the copyright system.

Where copies of a protected work are issued to the public in an electronic form which is 'copy protected' any person who makes or trades in, or advertises any device specifically designed to circumvent the copy protection or who publishes information intended to help persons to circumvent it commits an infringement of copyright.

Copyright is also infringed by a person who dishonestly receives a programme either broadcast or distributed by cable transmitted from the UK with the intention of avoiding payment.

c. *Remedies for infringement.* The following remedies are available:

i. Injunction.

ii. Damages.

iii. Order for delivery-up.

iv. Account for profit.

The 1988 Act makes it a criminal offence if a person knew or had reason to believe that copyright would be infringed in the event of making or dealing with infringing articles.

The TRADE MARKS (OFFENCES AND ENFORCEMENT) ACT 2002 should aid enforcement in that the Act gives police the power to obtain warrants to search and seize property from any business that they believe is using unlicensed software and to subsequently prosecute.

The COPYRIGHT AND RELATED RIGHTS REGULATIONS 2003 have been introduced to help the music and film industries from unauthorised downloading of their works on the Internet. It makes it a criminal offence for those making infringing copies or illicit recordings who communicate them to the public.

16. *Licensing*

a. The 1988 Act renames the Performing Rights Tribunal – the Copyright Tribunal and gives the Secretary of State additional powers of supervision over and regulation of the licensing of right.

b. The new regime of control will operate where rights are either licensed pursuant to a licensing scheme or licensed by a licensing body. A licensing scheme is defined as a scheme setting out:

i. The classes of case in which the operator of the scheme is willing to grant copyright licences, and,

ii. The terms on which licences would be granted in those classes.

c. A licensing body is a society or other organisation which has as a main object the negotiation or granting of copyright licences and whose objects include the granting of licences covering works of more than one author.

d.   A copyright licence means a licence to do or authorise the doing of any of the acts restricted by copyright.

The following disputes may be referred to the tribunal:

i.   Over the terms of a scheme proposed to be operated by a licensing body.

ii.   Over the terms of a scheme already in operation.

iii.   In respect of a scheme already subject to an order by the tribunal.

iv.   Between a person who claims to be covered by a scheme but complains that the operator of the scheme has either refused a licence or offered one on unreasonable terms.

The tribunal's jurisdiction over licences from licensing bodies is with respect to disputes concerning licences proposed, granted or withheld by a licensing body but not pursuant to a licensing scheme, eg a dispute between the Performing Rights Society and the BBC would be appropriate in this case.

17. *Performances* The 1988 Act repealed the PERFORMERS' PROTECTION ACTS *1958–1972*.

a.   *Persons Protected*. The following persons are protected:

i.   Those who act, sing, deliver, declaim, play in or otherwise perform literary, dramatic, musical or artistic works.

ii.   Those having recording rights in relation to a performance.

b.   *Rights of action*. Performers and persons having recording rights have civil rights of action for damages, an injunction, that illicit recordings be delivered up or the seizure of illicit recordings exposed for sale or hire. The seizure remedy is subject to the safeguards that the police must be given advance notice, only premises with public access may be entered and force may not be used. In addition to civil remedies performers are also protected by penal provisions.

c.   *The Copyright Tribunal*. The tribunal is given a limited jurisdiction with respect to performances, ie a person wishing to make a recording from an existing recording may apply to the tribunal where:

i.   The identity of the performer cannot be ascertained or

ii.   The performer unreasonably withholds consent.

d.   *Extent of rights*. The rights last for 50 years from the day when the performance took place.

TRADE MARKS

18. *Definition*

a.   A trade mark is a mark used in relation to goods or services so as to indicate a connection in the course of trade between the goods and some person having a right to use the mark.

b. The commercial purpose of a trade mark is to distinguish the goods or services of a company from those of its competitors. Many trade marks indicate quality and induce customers to buy the goods.

c. The legal purpose of a trade mark is to prevent others from using the mark and thus benefiting from the goodwill attached to the mark.

d. Like patents, trade marks constitute 'industrial property'. However, trade marks are concerned with commercial features and sales, rather than the technical features which are crucial to patents. While the life of a patent is limited to 20 years a trade mark can be renewed indefinitely. Another difference is that the cost of registering, renewing and enforcing trade mark rights is much less expensive than for patents.

e. Trade marks are defined in the TRADE MARKS ACT 1994, which was passed to implement the EU directive on trade marks. A trade mark is defined as 'any sign capable of being represented graphically which is capable of distinguishing goods or services of one undertaking from those of another'. Trade marks can consist of words (including personal names), designs, letters, numerals or the shape of goods or their packaging.

NESTLE SA'S TRADE MARK APPLICATION (HAVE A BREAK) (2003) The High Court rules that registration of these words would not be granted because the phrase was not distinctive.

BECKHAM v PETERBOROUGH FOOTBALL CLUB (2003). Victoria Beckham failed to get an injunction to restrain the football club from using the word 'Posh' a registered trade mark. The term had been used by the club for a number of years. The Court found that the use of the term in the particular context would not lead to any public confusion.

f. The fact that the shape of goods can be a trade mark overrules the House of Lords decision in COCA COLA TRADE MARKS (1986), however, there is no protection if the shape

   i. Results from the shape of the goods

   ii. Is necessary to obtain a technical result, or

   iii. Adds substantial value to the goods.

g. Smells, colours and sounds can be protected if they can be represented graphically. Geographic names can be protected where the mark acquires a distinctive character.

SHIELD MARK BV v KIST (2004) here a mark consisting of the first five notes of a Beethoven composition were held to be capable of being the subject of a trade mark.

h. The 1994 Act also introduces *collective marks* which are marks which can be used by anyone who is a member of a certain association owning a mark.

19. *Registration*

Registration at the Patent Office confers a statutory monopoly on the use of the mark and a registered owner may sue for infringement.

20. *Infringement*

a.   Infringement occurs when any person, without permission, uses in the course of a trade, a mark identical to the registered mark or so similar as to be likely to deceive or cause confusion. Infringement also occurs if a person compares his goods with those of a trade mark owner and refers to the latter's goods by the trade mark, for example a comparative price list setting out the trader's brand and comparing it with a famous name product.

ARSENAL FOOTBALL CLUB PLC v REED (2003). The case arose out of two registered trade marks, the words, 'Arsenal' and Arsenal Gunners' along with its cannon and shield emblems. The marks were used on a wide variety of goods. Mr Reed sold unofficial Arsenal souvenirs outside the club's ground. Mr Reed had a notice by his stall indicating that his products were not official club merchandise. Upon referral to the ECJ the court ruled that the function of a trade mark is to avoid confusion as to the origin of goods and that the disclaimer did not remove the confusion. The Court of Appeal ruled that on the facts, Mr Reed was infringing the Arsenal trade mark in spite of his disclaimer.

b.   When considering whether marks are similar the idea conveyed by the mark must be looked at as well as any physical similarity.

In TAW v NOTEK (1951) P used a drawing of a car in the shape of a cat's body with the eyes as headlamps as their trade mark. D used the head of a cat with the eyes as car headlamps. It was held that although the drawings were visually dissimilar the idea was the same, so P's trade mark had been infringed.

c.   When infringement occurs the plaintiff is entitled to an injunction and damages on an account of profits and to an order for destruction or modification of the offending goods.

d.   Where goods are sold that infringe a trade mark title to those goods will not pass and the seller will be in breach of the implied condition in *S.12 SALE OF GOODS ACT 1979*.

21. *The Community Trade Mark*

This is a single trade mark right which extends throughout the EU. It is available to any member of the EU or person domiciled in a EU country. It may consist of any distinctive sign capable of being represented graphically. Applications can be made to the UK Registry in London or directly to the CTM office in Spain, known as the Office for Harmonisation in the Internal Market.

PASSING-OFF

22. *Definition*

Passing-off is a tort. X will commit a tort against Y if he passes off his goods or business as those of Y. Y need not prove that X acted intentionally, or with intent to deceive. Nor does he have to prove that anyone was actually deceived, if deception was likely. There is also no requirement for Y to prove damage.

In ASPREY & GARRARD LTD v WRA (GUNS) LTD (2002) the defendant, an ex-employee of the claimant, set up a rival company using his own name – William R. Asprey Esq. The High Court granted an injunction restraining the use of his own name for passing off and infringement of trade mark. The use of one's own name is an exception to the passing off rules and must not, as it did here, cause confusion.

23. *Types of Passing-off*

    a.   Passing-off is usually committed by imitating the appearance of the plaintiff's goods, or by selling them under the same or a similar name. If the name used by the plaintiff merely describes his goods then generally no action will lie. However, it is possible for a name that was originally only descriptive to come to signify goods produced by the plaintiff. It is also possible for a word to lose its trade meaning and become merely descriptive.

    b.   The tort may be committed by applying the name of the locality in which the plaintiff produces goods to the defendant's goods.

        In BOLLINGER v COSTA BRAVA WINE CO (1961) P, who manufactured champagne brought an action against D who were describing their product as 'Spanish champagne'. It was held that the word 'champagne' was generally regarded as referring exclusively to wine produced in the Champagne region of France and even with the prefix 'Spanish' purchasers could be misled. An injunction was granted to prevent D using the name.

    c.   A person may usually carry on business under his own name, unless he does so fraudulently. But he must not mark his goods with a name (even his own name) if this will have the effect of passing-off those goods as goods of another.

    d.   Passing-off may be committed by using another person's name or trade name.

        In HINES v WINNICK (1947) P broadcast with a band called 'Dr Crock and the Crackpots'. After he left the programme D gave the same name to a replacement band. It was held that the public were likely to be misled and an injunction was granted.

    e.   It is not necessary for the defendant's trade to be identical to that of the plaintiff if there is sufficient similarity to mislead the public.

        In HARRODS LTD v R. HARRODS LTD (1923) the famous Knightsbridge store successfully prevented a money-lending company from trading under the Harrods name. Although the nature of their business was different there was sufficient likelihood that the public would assume that they were connected.

        In contrast there have been many cases where a plaintiff has failed to prevent the use of a similar name because the likelihood of confusion or loss of business did not exist. For example the owners of 'Wombles' books and television programmes could not prevent a company from leasing 'Wombles' rubbish skips and a Mr Albert Edward Hall was allowed to continue to use the name the 'Albert Hall Orchestra' despite an objection from the proprietor of the Royal Albert Hall.

f. False advertising is not generally passing off, but it may be in exceptional circumstances.

In MASSON SEELEY v EMBOSSOTYPE MANUFACTURING (1924) D copied P's catalogue in such a way that the public would believe that the goods offered were P's goods. D's goods were, however, inferior to P's goods. It was held that this was passing-off.

'Switch selling' does not amount to passing-off.

In RIMA ELECTRIC v ROLLS RAZOR (1965) D advertised so as to lead the public to believe that they could buy 'Magicair' hairdryers for 5 guineas. However, they had no Magicair hairdryers so they offered other makes to enquirers. It was held that this was not passing off.

g. *Reverse passing-off.* Usually passing-off occurs when the defendant holds out his goods as being those of the plaintiff. However, passing-off may also occur when the defendant holds out the plaintiff's goods as being his own, hence the 'reverse' passing-off.

In BRISTOL CONSERVATORIES v CONSERVATORIES CUSTOM BUILT (1989) D showed prospective customers photographs of P's ornamental conservatories, which they held out as being examples of their own goods and workmanship. If the customer placed an order, he would then be supplied with a conservatory manufactured by D. In this case the Court of Appeal was concerned only with D's motion to strike out P's statement of claim as disclosing no reasonable cause of action. However, on the facts as alleged the Court held that there was a triable issue.

24. *Remedies*

The plaintiff may obtain an injunction and/or damages. Damages will reflect lost profit (if any) plus loss of goodwill and reputation.

CHAPTER 36

The Data Protection Act 1998

1. *Purpose of the Act*

The *DATA PROTECTION ACT 1998* builds upon previous legislation to give rights to individuals whose 'personal data' is stored on computers and certain manual files.

2. *Data Covered*

The Act defines 'data' as information which is:

i. Being processed by means of equipment operating automatically in response to instructions given for that purpose

ii. Is recorded with the intention that it should be processed by means of such equipment

iii. Is recorded as part of a relevant filing system or with the intention that it should form part of a relevant filing system, or

iv. Though not falling within i, ii, or iii, forms part of an accessible health, educational or publicly accessible record.

3. *Persons*

The Act defines specific persons associated with regulated data; these are:

a. *data controller* who is a person who determines the manner and purpose for which personal data is to be processed; a *data processor* who is any person (other than an employee of the data controller) who processes the data on behalf of the data controller; a *data subject* is an individual who is the subject of personal data.

Personal data has to relate to a living individual identifiable from the data already in the possession of the data controller or from data likely to come into his possession.

The Data Protection Registrar is renamed the Data Protection Commissioner and the process of 'registration' with the Commissioner is renamed 'notification'.

4. *Rights Conferred*

Under *S.*7 of the Act individuals have the right of access to their personal data. A data subject has the right to be told whether personal data is being processed by or on behalf of a data controller and of the nature of such data, the purpose for which it is being processed, and those to whom it will be disclosed. In addition an individual is entitled to a copy of any personal data and information the data controller has as to the source of that data. The obligation of a data controller to supply the above is conditional upon a request being made in writing by the data subject with payment of a fee. An individual has the right to instruct a data controller, upon giving reasonable notice, to cease processing his personal data for purposes of direct marketing.

Where a decision, which will significantly affect an individual, is to be made by a data controller based solely upon personal data being processed automatically, an individual has the right to prevent such a decision being taken by the giving of notice in writing; further, even where the data subject serves no such notice, a data controller, in such circumstances, must as soon as is reasonably practicable, inform the data subject that a decision was made on that basis. The individual then has 21 days to require the data controller to reconsider the decision and the data controller has 21 days in which to notify the individual of the steps taken to comply with the request.

5. *Rights*

A data subject may apply to a court to have inaccurate personal data rectified, blocked, erased or destroyed. A data controller who wishes to process personal data must first make a notification to the Commissioner to be included on the register.

6. *Data Protection Principles*

The Act lays down a number of principles which will govern personal data processing, these are that such data be:

a. Processed fairly and lawfully;

b. Obtained only for lawful purposes;

c. Adequate, relevant and not excessive in relation to the purpose for which it is to be processed;

d. Accurate and kept up to date;

e. Not kept for longer than is necessary for the stated purpose;

f. Processed in accordance with the rights given under the Act to data subjects;

g. Subject to measures of security to prevent unauthorised or unlawful processing, accidental loss, destruction or damage; not transferred to a country or territory outside of the European Economic Area unless that country or territory ensures an adequate level of protection for the rights and freedoms of data subjects.

7. *Sensitive Data*

Certain data is termed 'sensitive personal data'; this is defined as information relating to a person's racial or ethnic origin; political or religious beliefs; membership of a trade union; physical or mental health or condition; sexual life; alleged commission or commission of any offence or proceedings relating to such an offence. Here, when assessing compliance with principle a. above, ie that data be processed fairly and lawfully, certain specific conditions are stated as being relevant, these are whether:

a. the data subject has given explicit consent to the processing of his personal data;

b. the processing was necessary in order for the data controller to perform a right or obligation imposed on him in connection with employment;

c. the processing is necessary to protect the vital interest of the data subject;

d. the processing is carried out in the legitimate course of a non-profit-making body's activities; the information has been made public as a result of a deliberate act of the data subject;

e. processing was necessary for the purposes of legal proceedings or the administration of justice; processing is necessary for medical purposes and is undertaken by a health professional or some other person who owes a duty of confidentiality equivalent to that of a health professional; in the field of racial or ethnic origin processing is necessary to ensure that unequal treatment in these areas does not occur; processing is necessary for purposes set out by the Secretary of State.

There are exemptions from the data protection principles, data protection rights and the need to register in relation to: national security; crime and taxation; health education and social work; journalism, literature or art; and domestic purposes.

8. *Monitoring of Employee Communications*

Article 8 of the HUMAN RIGHTS ACT 1998 (see Chapter 4.29), giving the right to privacy, has raised particular concerns for employers. In HALFORD V UNITED KINGDOM (1997) complaints by an Assistant Chief Constable that her telephone calls made from the office were monitored in contravention of Article 8 were upheld. The Government argued that telephone conversations at work fell outside of the Convention and that employers should in principle be able to monitor calls made by employees on telephones owned by the employer. The European Court of Human Rights did not accept this argument and stated that an employee had a reasonable expectation of privacy. This raises the question of the extent to which employers can monitor employees' emails and Internet access. Is there any reason why emails should be treated differently from telephone calls giving employees the right to a reasonable expectation of privacy? S.1. of the REGULATION OF INVESTIGATORY POWERS ACT 2000 makes it unlawful for any person, without lawful authority, to intentionally intercept a communication in the course of its transmission by way of a public or private telecommunications system. However, it will be lawful where the interceptor believes that both parties have agreed to such monitoring. Also the Act gives powers to the Secretary of State to introduce regulations where it is felt to be a reasonable and legitimate practice for the purpose of carrying on any business. Obvious instances of this will be where the employer is required to monitor communications for purposes of national security or ensuring compliance with regulatory or self-regulatory practices or to detect or prevent crime.

9. *Enforcement*

Where the Commissioner can show reasonable grounds for believing that a data controller has or is about to contravene any data protection principles or commit or has committed an offence under the Act, he may apply to a circuit judge for a search warrant. Main offences created under the Act are:

a. Failure to specify changes in contravention of a notice to do so by the Commissioner;

b. Deliberately or recklessly making a false statement while purporting to comply with an enforcement notice;

c. Unlawfully obtaining, selling or offering to sell personal data.

10. *FREEDOM OF INFORMATION ACT 2000*

The Act requires that public authorities have in place an approved publication scheme. The scheme identifies information available from the authority and how it can be obtained. Individuals can request this and other information which must be made available within 20 days, subject to certain exemptions such as information relating to national security and information given in confidence. There is an approved fee payable. Public authorities is a wide term which covers central and local government, police and prosecution services, the health service and education which includes colleges and universities. There is an appointed Commissioner to deal with complaints. He has the power to issue notices:

i   A *decision notice*; requiring that a public authority responds as to whether a request has been dealt with;

ii An *information notice*; requiring a public authority to provide specified information;

iii An *enforcement notice*; requiring a public authority to provide the information requested.

CHAPTER 37

Regulatory Bodies

THE FINANCIAL SERVICES ACT 1986

1. *Historical Context*

   a. Prior to the FSA the regulation of financial services was on a piecemeal basis, combining government measures with a large element of self-regulation. The legislation included the COMPANIES ACT, the BANKING ACT 1979, the PREVENTION OF FRAUD (INVESTMENTS) ACT 1958 and several Acts concerned with the insurance industry. Self-regulation was provided by the Stock Exchange, and various accountancy, legal and other professional bodies which regulated the conduct of their own members.

   b. The rapidly changing markets of the 70s and 80s opened up loopholes in the regulatory system. In particular there was no regulation of investment management or of advice in areas other than securities. Also an increasing number of private investors were becoming involved in high risk investments such as commodities and futures, that were previously the preserve of professional investors.

   c. A special investigation by Professor Gower in 1982 and a subsequent White Paper in 1984 led to the FINANCIAL SERVICES ACT 1986. The main provisions of the Act came into force on 29th April 1988. The Act has wide effect, bringing sole practitioners and substantial investment firms within one framework. The guiding principle is basically one of self-regulation within a statutory framework. The Act is largely concerned with protecting the private investor by trying to ensure that he is not cheated or misled. It cannot, of course, provide a remedy if he simply makes a poor investment decision.

2. *Coverage*

   a. One of the main provisions allowed for the establishment of an agency to which most of the powers under the Act could be delegated *(S.114)*. This is called the Securities and Investments Board (SIB). However, not all of the regulatory powers in the Act have been transferred to the SIB. Excluded from its responsibilities are provisions concerning.

      i.   Listing requirements for public issues

      ii. Takeovers and mergers

      iii. Insider dealing investigation and prosecution.

b. The regulatory structure for investment business is headed by the SIB, which is assisted by several self-regulating organisations (SROs) and recognised professional bodies (RPBs). These must be recognised by the SIB, on the basis that their methods of regulating their members provide a sufficient level of investor protection.

c. In some cases the FSA confers authority on firms to carry out investment business, although those firms are responsible to another regulator for their mainstream business. For example:

   i. Banks continue to be supervised by the Bank of England so far as their banking business is concerned.

   ii. Insurance companies are regulated by the DTI, except for the marketing of life assurance and unit trusts.

   iii. Building societies are regulated under the FSA for investment business, but their traditional lending and borrowing activities are regulated by the Building Societies Commission.

3. *Investments*

a. The basic principle underlying the regulatory framework is that no-one may carry on an investment business unless they are either authorised or exempt *(S.3)*. Any person in contravention will have committed a criminal offence and any investment agreement entered into will be unenforceable *(S.4,5)*. The Act provides detailed definitions of 'investments' and 'investment business' which are briefly summarised below.

b. *Investments*. This is defined very widely to cover any right, asset or interest in the following categories

   i. Company shares, including shares of foreign companies.

   ii. Debentures, and any other instrument creating or acknowledging indebtedness, including cheques, bills of exchange, bankers drafts and bank notes.

   iii. Government, local authority or other public authority securities.

   iv. Warrants or other instruments entitling the holder to subscribe for investments in the above categories. Warrants give the holder the right to purchase or subscribe for a security at a pre-determined price on one or more of a number of future dates.

   v. Certificates or other instruments conferring rights to acquire, dispose of, underwrite or convert investments. For example, a depository receipt permitting trading in a security, where the security does not fulfil the requirements for listing on the Stock Exchange.

   vi. Units in collective investments schemes, for example units in unit trusts.

   vii. Options to acquire or dispose of certain investments, for example options on currencies, gold or silver. Options give the holder a right to buy (a call option) or sell (a put option) the investment at a fixed price. The option may normally be exercised at any time before the maturity date.

viii. Futures for investment purposes. These are defined as rights under a contract for the sale of a commodity, or of property, under which delivery is to be made at a future date and at a price agreed when the contract is made. Futures are excluded from regulation if the contract is made for commercial rather than investment purposes.

ix. Contract for differences. These are contracts designed to secure a profit, or avoid a loss, by reference to fluctuations in the value of property, any description in an index, or any other factor.

c. *Investment Business*. This includes

i. Dealing in investments, ie buying, selling, subscribing for or underwriting investments either as principal or as agent

ii. Arranging deals in investments

iii. Managing investments

iv. Advising on investments. Giving advice about the tax or legal consequences of an investment is excluded

v. Establishing, operating or winding up a collective investment scheme, including acting as a trustee of a unit trust scheme.

Certain activities which would otherwise constitute investment business are specifically excluded, for example:

i. Dealing as principal

ii. Arranging an employee's share scheme

iii. Supplying a financial package in connection with a sale of goods or a supply of services

iv. The sale of a private company. This exemption is not restricted to the sale of the whole of the company. The shares sold may carry as little as 75% of the voting rights

v. Trustees and personal representatives are not carrying on an investment business in respect of investments which they manage as a trustee or personal representative unless they hold themselves out as offering investment management services or receive additional remuneration for such services in addition to remuneration as a trustee

vi. Advice given in the course of a profession which is not investment business, provided the advice is a necessary part of other advice or services given in the course of that profession

vii. Newspapers. Advice in financial columns of newspapers and other periodicals is excluded.

THE SECURITIES AND INVESTMENTS BOARD

4. *Introduction*

a. One of the main provisions of the FINANCIAL SERVICES ACT *1986* was to require the Secretary of State for Trade and Industry to regulate the investment industry. It empowered him to delegate his tasks to a designated agency, which in the first instance must be the Securities and Investments Board. The SIB came into existence on 29th April 1988, when the main provisions of the FSA came into force.

b. The SIB occupies an unusual constitutional position. It is a private company limited by guarantee, financed entirely by the investment industry. Although it is not a government body it has delegated power to make rules which have legislative effect.

c. The SIB reports annually to the Chancellor of the Exchequer, who in turn lays its report before Parliament. The SIB's authority can be removed by Parliament on a proposal from the Chancellor. Individual members may be dismissed by the Secretary of State.

d. The SIB consists of practitioners from a wide variety of investment activities, together with independent lay members representing the users of financial services and public at large. It has a full-time executive chairman. Board members are appointed jointly by the Treasury and the Governor of the Bank of England.

5. *Authorised Investment Businesses*

a. The main aim of the SIB is to achieve a high level of investor protection by ensuring that anyone providing any form of investment service, including those who deal in or advise on investments, meet standards of honesty, competence and solvency. Thus investment businesses, unless they fall within very limited exempt categories, must gain authorisation from the SIB or from one of the other regulatory bodies set up under the Act. In order to be granted the necessary authorisation a firm must satisfy its regulatory body that it is 'fit and proper' to carry on investment business. The test of this includes consideration of its financial resources, the previous record of its officers, and their level of experience and competence. The SIB maintains a list of authorised firms. This is called the central register.

b. It is a criminal offence to carry on investment business without authorisation, and the SIB can prosecute anyone who has broken this rule. The maximum penalty is two years' imprisonment and/or an unlimited fine. It can also seek an injunction to stop such firms trading and/or a court order to restore clients' money. The SIB also has formal powers in investigation, with criminal sanctions in the event of obstruction. It can disqualify individuals from employment in the investment industry.

c. If a person, such as a solicitor or accountant is '*knowingly concerned*' with another person's (the contravener's) breaches of the FSA then, in default of payment by the contravener, the person concerned may be liable to repay the investor the purchase price of the shares comprised in the investment transaction *(S.6 FSA 1986)*.

In SECURITIES AND INVESTMENTS BOARD v PANTELL S.A. (**1992**) D carried on unauthorised investment business in the UK, selling unmarketable and worthless shares in a Utah Corporation. Their solicitors were joined in the action because it was alleged that they had knowledge of their client's contravention of the Act because they operated the company's bank account, assisted in the distribution of advertisements and paid cheques for UK investors into the company's account. The Court of Appeal held that the solicitors were '*knowingly concerned*' in the contravener's breaches of the Act and were liable to repay investors the price of their shares.

6. *The Central Register*

a. Before parting with money on the basis of investment advice it is prudent to check that the adviser is legitimately carrying on investment business and is subject to the rules of one of the regulatory bodies.

b. The central register is a computerised database of more than 40,000 investment firms. It also has an introductory section describing the regulatory system. A person consulting the register will be able to find out

    i. The name or trading name, address and telephone number of the firm's main place of business.

    ii. The firm's authorisation status. This is important since only investors who do business with authorised firms are eligible to make a claim on the investors' compensation fund. Also, as previously stated, any firm carrying on investment business without authorisation is committing a criminal offence.

    iii. Whether the firm is regulated by a Self-Regulating Organisation, or a Recognised Professional Body, or the SIB itself. The regulatory body is responsible for monitoring the firm's continuing financial soundness and the way in which it handles its customers' business. It is the organisation that should be contacted if any investor has a problem that cannot be resolved with the firm itself.

    iv. Whether the firm can handle clients' money. Some firms are only authorised to give advice, in which case any investment cheques would need to be made out to the firm running the investment scheme, not the financial adviser.

    v. The type of investment business which the firm is permitted to engage in. Firms must be authorised specifically for each type of investment business, for example business enterprise scheme management, discretionary portfolio management or options and warrants activities.

    vi. Any warning messages, for example that the firm is in liquidation or suspended as a result of disciplinary action.

c. The public may access the central register

    i. By writing to the SIB, whose staff will then send the relevant information, or by telephoning the SIB, who will then pursue the individual inquiry free of charge. A member of the public may also visit the SIB and access the register personally, without charge and without the need for an appointment.

    ii. By asking a financial adviser who has direct on-line access to the register for a printout of his entry in the register.

    iii. By accessing the public on-line service available to subscribers to Prestel or Telecom Gold. In some areas this will be available via libraries or the citizens advice bureau.

7. *Rules for Regulation of Investment Business*

a. In order to have a regulatory regime which encourages healthy competitive markets and enjoys the confidence of both users and practitioners, it is necessary to have rules to raise standards, maintain proper financial management and punish malpractice

b. These rules need to be sufficiently flexible to react to changes in the various markets. The SIB therefore has a three-tier rule structure consisting of

    i. Core rules which have to be incorporated into the rule books of each self-regulating organisation,

    ii. Rules written by each SRO for their particular members, and

    iii. Guidance notes for the interpretation of the rules.

c. The most important rules are as follows:

    i. Investment businesses must act in the best interests of the client and must therefore do their best to make sure that they are aware of that client's circumstances. Firms must subordinate their own interests to those of the client.

    ii. Firms must comply with advertising requirements, including requirements to warn investors about the volatility or the marketability of the advertised investment.

    iii. Firms must disclose information about fees, commissions or other remuneration. If the firm manages a portfolio on behalf of the client, it must periodically send details of investment performance.

    iv. There must be separation of the status of the salesman and adviser, so that the client knows whether he is dealing with a representative tied to one company's range of products, or an independent intermediary acting as an agent of the client and advising on the full range of available investments.

    v. Investment firms must keep their money separate from the client's money.

    vi. Firms must set out the basis of their relationship with a private client in a customer agreement letter, setting out the functions or services the firm is to provide, its responsibilities and its charges.

    vii. Unsolicited visits and telephone calls to sell investments are generally prohibited. The main exceptions are calls relating to life assurance and unit trusts. However, where such a call results in a sale, the customer will have a 14-day 'cooling off period' during which the investment can be cancelled.

    viii. Firms must adhere to a proper complaints procedure, fully investigating and dealing with all client complaints and keeping records of the investigation.

    ix. All published recommendations, must be fair and not misleading, must provide appropriate information about foreseeable risks, and any predictions or forecasts must be reasonably justified.

8. *Self-Regulating Organisations.* There are four SROs. Each will make rules for their members and issue guidance notes as to their interpretation. If their rules are broken they can issue warnings and reprimands or they can fine, suspend or withdraw authorisation from their members. The four SROs are

    a. *The Securities and Futures Authority Limited.* SFA member firms carry on business in connection with dealing and arranging deals in for example shares, debentures, government securities, futures, options, foreign currency and commodities. They may also advise corporate finance customers and arrange deals and manage portfolios for them.

    b. *Investment Management Regulatory Organisation.* IMRO member firms are engaged in

        i. The management and operation of collective investment schemes, for example authorised unit trusts

        ii. Selling and advising on transactions in unit trusts

        iii. Acting as a trustee of collective investment schemes

        iv. Arranging deals in investments related to business expansion scheme legislation

        v. In-house pension fund management and acting as pension fund trustees

        vi. Investment advice (other than corporate finance advice) to institutional or other corporate customers.

    c. *Financial Intermediaries, Managers and Brokers Regulatory Association.* FIMBRA member firms mainly advise on and arrange deals in life assurance, pensions and unit trusts. They give advice on a wide range of investments, for example life assurance shares, debentures and gilts and act as private portfolio managers.

    d. *Life Assurance and Unit Trust Regulatory Organisation.* LAUTRO member firms are normally insurance companies and friendly societies engaged in the retail marketing of life assurance. They may operate collective investment schemes and engage in the retail marketing of units in such schemes.

e.   A review of retail regulation in March 1992 recommended that a new SRO be created to regulate investment business done with the private investor. This will be known as the *Personal Investment Authority (PIA)*. Its scope will include activities currently regulated by FIMBRA and LAUTRO.

9. *Recognised Professional Bodies*

a.   Professional advisers such as accountants and solicitors provide an important source of investment advice and other investment services such as insurance broking, although this is not the main part of their activities. The system of regulation is built on the existing structure of monitoring and disciplinary arrangements that the main professional bodies already have, subject to a provision that this must provide adequate investor protection. A professional body which is recognised by the SIB will be able to issue a certificate to its members which will enable them to carry on investment business of the kind regulated by the body, without having to seek further authorisation. In keeping with the idea of limited involvement of professional firms in investment business, the Act requires the professional body to have rules imposing acceptable limits on the *kind* of investment business carried on by certified persons and the circumstances in which they may carry on such business. The *scale* of such business remains a matter of judgement for the RPB, but it is intended that it is limited to business incidental to the practice of the profession. The rules of the RPB will prohibit a certified person from carrying on investment business outside those limits, unless he has separate authorisation through registration with the SIB, or separate membership of an SRO. Members of professional bodies which are not RPBs must belong to an SRO, or be regulated directly by the SIB, if they carry on investment business.

b.   There are nine RPBs

   i.   Chartered Association of Certified Accountants (ACCA)

   ii.   Institute of Actuaries

   iii. Institute of Chartered Accountants in England and Wales (ICAEW)

   iv.   Institute of Chartered Accountants in Ireland

   v.   Institute of Chartered Accountants in Scotland

   vi.   Insurance Brokers' Registration Council (IBRC)

   vii. Law Society

   viii. Law Society of Northern Ireland

   ix.   Law Society of Scotland

10. *Recognised Investment Exchanges*

a.   Persons running a market or exchange will fall within the definition of carrying on an investment business and will therefore need to be authorised. An RIE will provide facilities for effecting transactions in investments, although it will not be authorised for any other type of investment business. Recognition means that the exchange (but not its members) is exempt from the requirement of authorisation as an investment business. Membership of an RIE is not therefore an alternative method of obtaining authorisation.

b. To obtain recognition an RIE must satisfy the SIB that it meets certain basic requirements including

    i. Sufficient financial resources to perform its functions

    ii. Rules and practices to ensure the orderly conduct of business and afford proper protection to investors

    iii. Dealings limited to investments in which there is a proper and reasonably liquid market

    iv. Satisfactory arrangements for recording transactions

    v. Effective monitoring and enforcement of rules

    vi. Arrangements for the investigation of complaints

    vii. Proper arrangements for the clearing and performance of contracts

c. RIEs include

    i. The Stock Exchange

    ii. The London Commodities Exchange

    iii. London International Financial Futures Exchange (LIFFE)

    iv. The London Metal Exchange

11. *Investors Compensation Scheme*

a. The investor protection framework cannot take the risk out of capital investment. No compensation is payable if, for example, the investment falls in value because of a fall in the market, or because an individual company collapses, or because inflation erodes the real value of the return or an investment. Compensation is only potentially available in the event of fraud or failure of the investment firm to which the investor has entrusted money.

b. The compensation scheme may be able to help if the following conditions are satisfied:

    i. The claimant is a private investor

    ii. The investment firm is fully authorised

    iii. The firm cannot pay out investors' claims

    iv. The firm owes the claimant money, or is holding shares or other investments on behalf of the claimant

    v. The claim arises out of business regulated by the FSA.

c. The compensation scheme is not available if

    i. The investment firm has gone into liquidation, but was not in breach of its rules, or the law, or

    ii. The investment firm is still in business. In this case if money has been lost through mismanagement or negligent advice, the claimant will have to take up the case with the firm's regulatory body.

d. The maximum compensation payable to any one individual is £48,000.

e. The scheme is the responsibility of the SIB and is run on a day-to-day basis by a separate management company. The directors include representatives of the investing public and of the regulatory organisations. The scheme is funded entirely by the investment industry up to a maximum of £100,000,000 per year, although from 1989 until 1991 the annual average compensation paid has been approximately £15,000,000.

FINANCIAL SELF-REGULATION

12. *The Financial Reporting Council*

a. *Introduction*

The Financial Reporting Council was established in 1990, following the Dearing Report ie the report of the Review Committee on Accounting Standards. Although the FRC has the support of government it is not government controlled, but is part of the private sector process of self-regulation. This is reflected in its constitution, membership and financing. Funds are provided approximately one third by the Department of Trade and Industry, one third from the Consultative Committee of Accountancy Bodies and one third from the London Stock Exchange and the banking and investment communities. The FRC is a company limited by guarantee. It has a chair and three deputy chairs appointed by the Secretary of State for Trade and Industry and the Governor of the Bank of England acting jointly. Council members are appointed by the chair and deputies and include representatives from the accountancy profession, city institutions (including the Stock Exchange) and commerce generally. The Council will normally meet three times a year.

b. The main purposes of the FRC are

    i. To provide support to its operational subsidiary bodies, the Accounting Standards Board and the Financial Reporting Review Panel.

    ii. To promote good financial reporting, from time to time making public reports on reporting standards.

    iii. To make representations to government on the current working of legislation and on any desirable developments.

    iv. To provide guidance to the Accounting Standards Board on work programmes and broad policy issues.

    v. To ensure that new arrangements are conducted with efficiency and economy and that they are adequately funded.

The Council's constitution provides for it to publish an annual report reviewing the state of financial reporting and making known the views of the Council on accounting standards and practice. The first report was published in autumn 1991.

13. *The Accounting Standards Board*

a. Like the FRC, the Accounting Standards Board is a company limited by guarantee. It is a subsidiary of the FRC which acts as its sole director.

b. Its role is to make, amend and withdraw accounting standards. In doing this it will focus, so far as possible, on general principles rather than the prescription of highly detailed rules. The ASB is an autonomous body, that does not need outside approval for its actions. However, in practice it consults widely on all its proposals. Thus for all new proposals there is a formal exposure draft stage, and any comments received are normally placed on public record.

c. The ASB has a sub-committee called 'the Urgent Issues Task Force'. This assists the board where an accounting standard or Companies Act provision exists, but where unsatisfactory or conflicting interpretations have developed. It also advises on significant developments in accounting and financial reporting where no legal provision or accounting standard exists at present. The Urgent Issues Task Force also consults widely, for example by regularly circulating information sheets to approximately 3,000 people, including the finance directors of all listed companies.

d. Membership of the ASB is limited to a maximum of 10. In December 1992 there were nine members, two full-time and seven part-time. They are appointed by an appointments committee consisting of the FRC chairman and deputy chairmen, plus three council members. A majority of six out of nine (or seven out of ten) is required for any decision to adopt, revise or withdraw an accounting standard.

e. At its first meeting the ASB agreed to adopt the 22 statements of standard accounting practice (SSAPs) issued by the former accounting standards committee. The ASB will review these SSAPs individually as opportunities arise during the course of its work.

14. *The Financial Reporting Review Panel*

a. Like the ASB, the FRRP is a company limited by guarantee and a subsidiary of the FRC which acts as its sole director. It is autonomous in carrying out its functions, needing neither outside approval nor approval from the FRC.

b. The role of the Panel is to examine departures for the accounting requirements of the COMPANIES ACT 1985 (as amended by the COMPANIES ACT 1989) and if necessary to seek a court order to remedy them. Its authority stems from a statutory instrument made by the Secretary of State for Trade and Industry in 1991.

c. By agreement with the DTI the work of the FFRP is limited to public and large private companies, the DTI dealing with all other cases.

d. The FRRP does not scrutinise all company accounts falling within its brief. Instead it acts on matters drawn to its attention, either directly or indirectly. Its main concern is to examine material departures from accounting standards with a view to assessing whether the accounts nevertheless meet the statutory requirement to give a true and fair view. A material departure from an accounting standard does not necessarily mean that the accounts will fail the true and fair test. However, the COMPANIES ACT requires large companies to disclose in their accounts any such departures, together with reasons, thus enabling them to be readily identified and considered.

e. When a case comes to the FRRP's attention it will be considered by a group of five or more members drawn from the overall Panel membership. The group will be responsible for carrying out the functions of the FRRP for that case, without any collective involvement by the other Panel members. The group will try to discharge its function by seeking voluntary agreement from the directors on any necessary revisions to the accounts. (This has been possible since amendments made by the COMPANIES ACT 1989.) If this approach fails, the Panel may seek a declaration from the court that the accounts do not comply with the requirements of the COMPANIES ACT and seek an order requiring the directors to prepare revised accounts. If the court grants such an order it may also require the directors to meet the costs of the proceedings and the cost of revising the accounts. If accounts are revised, either voluntarily or by order of the court, but the company's auditor had not qualified his audit report on the defective accounts, the FRRP will draw this fact to the attention of the auditor's professional body.

f. Appointments to FRRP are made by an appointments committee consisting of the FRC chairman and deputy chairmen plus three Council members. There is no upper limit to membership.

THE STOCK EXCHANGE

15. *Recent History*. Throughout the 1970s and 80s the Stock Exchange came under increasing pressure to change. There were three main reasons for this.

a. The Exchange's trading and settlement system was finding it increasingly difficult to deal with the volume of transactions. When a person buys shares their stockbroker telephones a market maker, establishes the price, and then purchases the shares on the client's behalf. He then passes information to the 'back office' for settlement. The clerk confirms the transaction with the market maker, the client and with the registrar of those shares. The registrar then processes the information and sends the share certificate to the client. Although the process was supported by a computerised clearing system known as *Talisman*, it came under heavy pressure in the mid to late 1980s because

    i. De-regulation (the big bang) resulted in a vast increase in the volume of trading; and

ii. Numerous privatisation issues significantly increased the number of shares in existence and saw the number of private investors rise from 2,000,000 to 7,000,000 in three years.

This caused huge backlogs, with many private investors being told by their brokers that they would not receive share certificates for between three and nine months. The problem eased significantly after the stock market crash in October 1987, since trading volumes dramatically reduced and have never recovered to their pre-1987 levels.

b. In 1978 the Government decided to take the Exchange to the Restrictive Practices Court, because it considered that its rules imposed restrictions in three main areas.

i. The operation of a scale of minimum commissions

ii. The separation of capacity between broker and jobber

iii. Restrictions on membership.

The situation continued until 1983, when the chair of the Exchange and the Secretary of State for Trade and Industry reached an out of court agreement, under which the Exchange undertook to abolish its system of minimum commissions and introduce other changes that came to be known as the 'big bang'.

c. In 1979 exchange control was abolished. This made it easier for UK institutions to invest overseas. The Exchange's member firms were for the first time exposed to competition from much larger overseas brokers. Major UK companies were also able to trade their shares on overseas markets. Fund managers increasingly chose to invest through foreign brokers.

16. *Deregulation.* There were several deregulatory changes in 1986, culminating in the big bang of 27th October 1986.

a. From 1st March 1986 member firms could be owned by a single outside corporation. Previously control had to be in the hands of individual members. Many firms were therefore bought by UK and overseas banks.

b. In November 1986 voting rights in the exchange were transferred to member firms, instead of residing with individual members.

c. Minimum scales of commission were abolished on 27th October 1986. Members became free to negotiate a commission with their clients, competing with each other on the basis of charges as well as services.

d. The rules and constitution of the Exchange were changed to end the separation of member firms into brokers and jobbers. Now all firms are brokers/dealers able to act as agency brokers representing clients in the market, or as principals buying and selling shares on their own account. Firms were also permitted to register as market makers, committed to making firm buying and selling prices at all times.

e. Possibly the most important change on 27th October 1986 was the introduction of a computer-based quotation system, known as Stock

Exchange Automated Quotations (SEAQ). SEAQ carries prices for over 2,000 securities. Market makers enter competing buying and selling prices into SEAQ and this information is then transmitted electronically into offices of brokers and investors. Up to the minute share price information can therefore be viewed directly by market participants around the world and is no longer limited to those who have physical access to a market floor. The SEAQ service shows the competing bid and offer prices from all registered market makers. It automatically selects and displays the best bid and offer price to enable brokers to see instantly who is offering the best price for any given security. Dealing then takes place on the telephone or through computer systems.

17. *Buying and Selling Shares*

a. There are two basic ways of buying shares in public companies.

   i. *Buying new issues*. Details of new issues must be disclosed in a prospectus and advertised in at least one daily newspaper. The applicant fills in an application form included in the prospectus and sends it, with a cheque, to the address given. This will usually be a merchant bank acting as an issuing house. Depending on the success of the issue and the method chosen for scaling down over-subscribed issues, the applicant may receive all, some, or none of the shares applied for.

   ii. *Buying existing shares*. The main function of the Stock Exchange is to allow existing shares to be bought and sold at any time. As members of the Exchange, stockbrokers buy and sell on behalf of private individuals and institutional clients.

b. *Stockbrokers*. In addition to specialist stockbroking firms, banks and building societies also provide stockbroking functions. There are various services that stockbrokers can provide

   i. *Dealing only* ie simply carrying out the client's instructions to buy and sell the shares and arrange settlement of the deal.

   ii. *Advisory*. The stockbroker will consider the merits of a particular company, advising whether to buy, sell or hold its shares. The broker may also suggest changes to the client's portfolio of shares.

   iii. *Discretionary*. In this case the broker will manage the portfolio totally, informing the client on a regular basis of shares bought or sold, the value of the portfolio, and the value of dividends credited to the client's account. If a broker is appointed in this way the client will be given a 'client agreement letter'. This is a requirement of the FINANCIAL SERVICES ACT and will set out the services offered and the terms under which the broker deals for the client.

Brokers advise on a wide range of investments, not just shares. These include unit trusts, investment trusts, warrants, options, personal equity plans and so on. When the client gives the stockbroker the order to buy shares, the broker contacts a market maker and purchases the shares at the best price at the time of the deal. From this time the client becomes the owner of the shares. The broker then draws up a contract note which is sent to the client within a few days. The share certificate will be sent later.

c. *Payment*. The year is divided into account periods of two weeks each. All deals made during a particular period are bundled together and must be paid for on account day. This is the second Monday following the end of the account period. If a client purchases UK equity shares this date will appear on the contract note as the settlement date. This is all the buyer has to do. The seller will have to sign a transfer form and return it with the share certificate to the stockbroker in order to be paid for the shares being sold.

d. *Taxation*

   i. *Income tax*. When a shareholder receives dividends, advance corporation tax equivalent to income tax at the basic rate will have been paid by the company. A basic rate tax payer will therefore have no further tax to pay, but a higher rate tax payer will have to pay additional tax at the end of the year.

   ii. *Capital gains tax*. The difference between the purchase price and selling price of shares (after expenses) is a capital gain, or loss. Liability for capital gains tax only arises when shares are sold or otherwise disposed of. It does not apply if the shareholder continues to hold the shares. Tax will be payable if the shareholder's total capital gains (less losses) in any one year exceeds the capital gains tax threshold set by the government for that year.

Coursework Questions 30–35 (for answers see pages 676–82)

(for answers see pages 676–82)

	COMMON LAW

Typical Exam Questions

30. Graham, a dealer, collects and sells rare books. Whilst visiting a local town he notices that Peter has three rare editions for sale in his second-hand bookshop. He negotiates and agrees a price of £500 for each of the rare editions.

On the assumption that he will have the books in his possession, he negotiates to sell the first book to Eric for £800. The second book is to be sold to Helen for £600, together with another rare book that Helen is to sell to Graham for £400 (as Graham has a buyer for this book in the sum of £600). The third book, which is the only surviving copy, is to be sold to Richard for the sum of £1,000. Graham has now returned to collect and pay for the three books from Peter as agreed. He is shocked when Peter informs him that the sale is off because he has received an offer from Bertram in the sum of £2,000 for the set of three books and has agreed to sell them to him.

Explain what remedies, if any, Graham has against Peter.

(20 marks)

ICSA November 2004

31. (a) Explain what consumers must determine before deciding whether they have a statutory claim for breach of the implied terms under *SALE OF GOODS ACT 1979*, as amended, or the *SUPPLY OF GOODS AND SERVICES ACT 1982*.

(12 marks)

(b) Explain what terms are implied into a contract regulated by the *SUPPLY OF GOODS AND SERVICES ACT* 1982, and where services only are involved and there is no formal agreement between the supplier and consumer.

(8 marks)

(**20 marks**)

ICSA November 2004

32. (a) Where the buyer is in breach of contract to the seller, the seller may exercise statutory rights against the goods, subject to certain conditions. Explain what those rights are.

(12 marks)

(b) The '*nemo dat quod non habet*' rule provides that if a person does not have the title to the goods they cannot pass good title. There are, however, a number of exceptions to this rule.

Explain how the following statutory exceptions apply in practice:

(i) Estoppel.

(ii) Common law or statutory power of sale.

(iii) Sale of a motor vehicle subject to hire purchase.

(8 marks)
(**Total: 20 marks**)
ICSA November 2004

33. (a) Explain the ways in which an agency agreement can be formed, using illustrative examples to support your answer. (10 marks)

(b) Explain in detail the ways in which an agency agreement not governed by the Commercial Agents Regulations 1993 can be terminated.

(10 marks)

(**20 marks**)
ICSA November 2004

34. (a) There has been considerable concern expressed by the music industry about the downloading from the internet of recording artists' copyrighted material.

Explain what is meant by 'copyright' in the context of intellectual property, with particular reference to how long copyright exists depending upon the 'property' involved. (10 marks)

(b) (i) What remedies are available for the owner of copyrighted material if his rights are infringed?

(4 marks)

(ii) What defences, if any, are available to a defendant in such an action?
(6 marks)
(**20 marks**)
ICSA November 2004

35. (a) Explain what is meant by the expression 'extortionate (unfair) credit bargain' and what action, if any, can be taken by the courts in respect of such a bargain. (10 marks)

(b) Explain the term 'protected goods', as defined in the CONSUMER CREDIT ACT 1974. What action must a creditor follow if they wish to repossess such goods? What are the consequences of unlawful repossession?

(10 marks)

(**20 marks**)
ICSA November 2004

PART V

SOLE TRADER, PARTNERSHIP AND COMPANY

CHAPTER 38

Non-corporate Bodies

THE SOLE TRADER

1. The *sole trader* can be described as an individual who carries on a business on his own account. Though he is likely to be a small business this may not be so, a sole trader could employ any number of employees. The key features of the sole trader are:

   i. If he chooses not to trade under his own name he must register the name under the BUSINESS NAMES ACT 1985.

   ii. He has sole responsibility for the debts of the business and is liable personally to the full extent of all he possesses in both business and private assets – he has *unlimited liability*. Where a sole trader business becomes insolvent – the assets no longer matching liabilities – he is said to be bankrupt brought about by the procedure known as bankruptcy laid down in the INSOLVENCY ACT 1986 as amended by the ENTERPRISE ACT 2002.

   iii. He usually makes all the decisions and takes all the profits or stands all losses.

   iv. There are no formalities for ending the business; he may cease trading at any time.

   v. Upon the death of the sole trader the business ceases.

THE PARTNERSHIP

2. *Introduction*

   Unincorporated associations consist of a number of persons who have come together for a matter of common interest, for example a sports club, a trade union, or a *partnership*. The associations do not have a separate legal entity from their members. Thus the property of an association is regarded as belonging to the members jointly, and if a wrong is committed by a member the general rule is that he alone is liable for what he has done. There are exceptions to this rule, in particular in connection with partnerships.

   When people wish to associate for business purposes they will usually form a company or a partnership. The law of partnership is based on agency, each partner becoming an agent of the others, and is only appropriate for a relatively small number of persons who have trust in each other and who are able to provide the funds for the business from their own resources.

3. *Definition of the partnership*

A partnership is defined by the PARTNERSHIP ACT 1890 as 'the *relation* which subsists between persons carrying on a *business in common* with a *view to profit*'.

a. A partnership is described as a '*relation*' because, unlike a company, it is not a legal entity separate from the partners.

b. The partners must carry on a '*business*', ie a trade, profession or vocation over a period of time. If they merely co-own property this does not create a partnership.

c. '*In common*' means the business must be carried on for the joint benefit of the persons who are partners.

d. '*View to profit*' means the partners must intend to make a profit. It does not mean that if the actual result is a loss there is no partnership.

4. *Creation*

a. No formalities are necessary, although for practical reasons writing is usually used.

b. The maximum number of partners is 20, except for certain professional partnerships, for example solicitors and accountants, where there is no maximum.

c. The partners may trade under any name they please, except that the word 'limited' must not be the last word of the name.

d. Any partnership agreement will usually deal with the following matters:

    i. The firm's name;

    ii. The place and nature of the business;

    iii. The date on which the partnership is to commence and its duration. If there is no fixed period then it is a partnership at will;

    iv. The proportions in which capital is to be provided, and whether interest is to be paid on capital before profits are divided;

    v. Details of the firm's bank account, including who is allowed to sign cheques;

    vi. Whether all or only some of the partners shall manage the business and whether all partners shall give their whole time to the business;

    vii. How profits are to be shared, and provisions for drawings;

    viii. Provisions for keeping regular accounts and the preparation of an annual profit and loss account and balance sheet;

    ix. What shall happen on the death or retirement of a partner. In the absence of an agreement to the contrary the death of a partner automatically dissolves the partnership;

x. Whether a retired partner is allowed (within limits) to compete with the firm;

xi. A list or description of what is agreed to be partnership property;

xii. Insurance against death or sickness of a partner and for the business generally;

xiii. Any limits on the business interests of the partners outside the firm;

xiv. An arbitration clause.

5. *Authority of Partners*

a. Every partner is an agent of the firm and therefore has *implied authority* to bind the firm by transactions entered into by him in the *ordinary course of business*. Thus an outsider who contracts with a partner within the scope of that implied authority may treat the firm as bound, despite any restriction on the authority of that partner to which the partners have agreed, unless the outsider knew of the restriction.

In MERCHANTILE CREDIT v GARROD (1962) A and B were partners in a firm which let garages and repaired cars. The partnership agreement expressly excluded buying and selling cars. Without B's knowledge, A, acting without the owner's consent, sold a car to a finance company for £700, paying the proceeds into the partnership account. It was held that B was liable to repay the £700 to the finance company. The prohibition on buying and selling in the partnership agreement did not entitle B (or the firm) to avoid liability since A's conduct was of a kind normally undertaken by persons trading as a garage, ie A apparently had authority to sell cars.

b. In a trading partnership the following acts are within the implied authority of a partner:

i. Borrowing money in the name of the firm and giving security by pledging its goods or by depositing title deeds to create an equitable mortgage;

ii. Signing cheques, and drawing, accepting or indorsing bills of exchange;

iii. Employing a solicitor to defend an action against the firm. However, it is doubtful if a partner would have authority to commence any proceedings other than routine actions to recover trade debts;

iv. Receiving payment of debts and giving valid receipts;

v. Buying and selling goods on account of the firm;

vi. Engaging employees to work for the firm. A partner probably does not have implied authority to dismiss employees.

c. The following acts are outside a partner's implied authority:

i. Consenting to a judgement against the firm;

ii. Executing a deed;

iii. Giving a guarantee in the absence of a trade custom to do so;

iv. Referring a dispute to arbitration;

v. Accepting property other than money in payment of a debt.

6. *Liability of Partners*

a. *Liability for torts.* On the usual principle of vicarious liability (since each partner is an agent of the others) all the partners are liable for a tort committed by a partner in the ordinary course of the firm's business, or with the authority of his co-partners.

In HAMLYN v HOUSTON (1903) a partner bribed a competitor's clerk to disclose confidential information relating to it. The partner used the information and the rival firm consequently suffered loss. It was held that the partner's firm was liable for his wrongful act since he was acting in the ordinary course of business when he obtained information about the rival.

Partners' liability in tort is joint and several. This means that a partner is liable jointly with the other partners and also individually liable. Thus a plaintiff may issue separate writs against each partner either at the same time or successively and judgement against one partner does not prevent an action being brought against the others.

b. *Liability for misapplication of money or property.* Where either:

i. One *partner*, acting within the scope of his apparent authority, receives money or property of a third person and misapplies it, *or*

ii. A *firm*, in the course of its business, receives money or property of a third person and the money or property is misapplied by one or more of the partners while in the custody of the firm, then the firm is liable to make good the loss.

c. *Liability in contract*

i. Every partner is liable jointly with his co-partners for all debts and obligations of the firm incurred whilst he was a partner.

ii. Where liability is joint it used to be the case that once a third party had sued one of the partners he could not sue the others. However, the CIVIL LIABILITY (CONTRIBUTION) ACT 1978 removed this limit on the number of actions. It also provides that a partner who has paid a debt of the firm can claim a contribution from his partners.

d. *Liability of a retired partner*

i. A partner who retires does not cease to be liable for partnership debts incurred before his retirement. These may include debts arising after his retirement from transactions during the period when he was a partner.

ii. A retired partner may be discharged from liability for debts incurred while he was a partner if the debts are later discharged by the new firm, or if the creditors agree to release him by novation (see below).

iii. A retired partner may be liable on contracts made after his retirement if he continues to be an 'apparent partner', by for example allowing his name to remain on the firm's notepaper.

e. *Liability of a new partner*

i. A person admitted as a partner does not thereby incur liability for debts incurred before he became a partner.

ii. There may be a contract of *novation* between a retired partner, the firm as reconstituted by the entry of a new partner, and the creditors. Under such a three party agreement, the creditors and the firm agree that the reconstituted firm will be liable for unpaid debts of the old firm and that the retired partner be discharged from liability.

7. *The Relationship of Partners to Each Other*

a. *Good faith.* There is duty of utmost good faith once the partnership is established, although the contract of partnership is not itself *uberrimae fidei*. Thus:

i. Partners are bound to render true accounts and full information on all matters affecting the partnership.

ii. A partner must account for any profit made by him without the consent of the others from using the firm's property, name, or trade connections.

iii. A partner may have a separate account unless he had agreed to the contrary, but a partner must account for any profit made in a business of the same kind as, and competing with, the firm.

b. *Management*

i. Subject to contrary agreement every partner is entitled to access to partnership books and may take part in the management of the business.

ii. Decisions on ordinary matters connected with the partnership business are by majority of the general partners. If there is a deadlock the views of those opposing any change will prevail, but unanimity is required for matters relating to the constitution of the firm, for example to change the nature of the partnership business or to admit a new partner.

c. *Capital, profits and losses*

i. Profits and losses are shared equally in the absence of contrary agreement. However, if the partnership agreement states that profits are to be shared in certain proportions then, prima facie losses are to be shared in the same proportions.

ii. No interest is paid on capital except by agreement. However, a partner is entitled to 5% interest on advances beyond his original capital.

d. *Indemnity.* The firm must indemnify any partner against liabilities incurred in the ordinary and proper conduct of the partnership business, or in doing anything necessarily done for the preservation of the partnership property or business.

e. *Partnership property*

i. The *initial* property of the partnership is that which the partners, expressly or impliedly agree shall be partnership property. It is quite possible that property used in the business should not be partnership property, but should, for example, be the sole property of one of the partners, it depends entirely on the intention of the partners.

ii. Property *afterwards* acquired is governed by the same principle, but clearly it will be partnership property if it is bought with partnership money.

8. *Dissolution*

a. Dissolution occurs:

i. By effluxion of time, if the partnership was entered into for a fixed term.

ii. By termination of the adventure, if entered into for a single adventure.

iii. By the death or bankruptcy of a partner, unless the partnership agreement otherwise provides.

iv. By subsequent illegality, ie an event which makes it unlawful to continue the business.

v. By notice of a partner.

vi. By order of the court, for one of several reasons, for example the permanent incapacity of a partner, or because it is just and equitable to order dissolution.

b. *Misrepresentation.* When a partner is induced to enter into a partnership by misrepresentation he remains liable to creditors for obligations incurred while a partner, but he has several remedies against the maker of the statement including, for example, rescission and/or damages.

c. After dissolution the authority of the partners continues so far as is necessary to wind-up the partnership affairs and complete transactions already begun.

d. On dissolution any partner can insist on realisation of the firm's assets, (including goodwill), payment of the firm's debts, and distribution of the surplus, subject to any contrary agreement.

9. *Limited Partnerships*

a. Limited partnership was established by the LIMITED PARTNERSHIP ACT *1907.* The use of this form of partnership has not been extensive due to the ease of incorporating a private company.

b. Under such a partnership there must be at least one general and one limited partner. The limitation on the number of partners applicable to ordinary partnerships also applies to limited partnerships.

c. The general partner is liable for all the firm's debts and liabilities but a limited partner is only liable to the extent of his capital contribution which may be in cash or in the form of property. Particulars of this contribution must be disclosed in the particulars registered with the Registrar of Companies and if this capital is later withdrawn, the limited partner will be liable for the firm's debts to the extent of the amount so withdrawn.

d. A limited partnership must be registered with the Registrar of Companies. Until this is done all the partners are deemed to be general partners. The registered particulars include, for example, the firm's name, the place and nature of business, and the full name of each partner.

10. *The Limited Liability Partnership (LLP)*

A partnership formed under the LIMITED LIABILITY PARTNERSHIP ACT 2000, will enjoy limited liability similar to that of the private limited company. Partners will not incur personal liability for the debts of the partnership. It is registered with the Registrar of Companies and once formed owns the assets of the business separate from the members and directors. The LLP was brought about largely through pressure from large firms of accountants and solicitors worried at the size of personal liability of individual partners for negligence for example auditors negligently approving accounts that are not accurate and which mislead investors. The LLP provides limited liability to the non-negligent partner(s) with the negligent partner/member incurring unlimited liability. The LIMITED LIABILITY PARTNERSHIPS REGULATIONS 2001 (S1 2001/1090) provide more details on the regulation of the LLP, broadly they apply, with appropriate amendments, company law provisions to the LLP. It is in this respect, with the consequent public disclosure requirements of an LLP, that the advantage of secrecy and privacy, an often important feature of the partnership, is lost.

CHAPTER 39

Corporate Bodies – The Company

1. *Companies and Partnerships*

   Partnerships historically were not adequate for the development of modern capitalism since (among other things) they originally did not provide any means for business people to limit their liability, and just as importantly, they did not enable access to sufficient capital. These aims could only be achieved through a framework which enabled business organisations to have a separate legal personality from their members. Such a structure could be used by a small family business, but more significantly it could accommodate large and complex organisations with fluctuating membership. The framework that developed was company law. At its heart is the ability of a group of people to register a company under the Companies Acts. From the date of registration a corporate person comes into being, having a legal personality distinct from that of its creators or members and subject to a wide range of legal rights and duties.

2. *Types of Company*

   There are three basic types of company classified according to their means of formation:

   a. *Chartered companies*. A chartered company is formed by the grant of a charter by the Crown under the Royal Prerogative or under special statutory powers. This method of incorporation is no longer used by trading companies since it is far quicker and cheaper to obtain incorporation by registration. It is only used by, for example, charitable organisations, learned and artistic societies and some schools and colleges. Chartered companies include the Institute of Chartered Accountants in England and Wales, the British Broadcasting Corporation and Oxford and Cambridge Universities.

   b. *Statutory companies*

      i. In the past companies were incorporated by special Act of Parliament when it was necessary for them to have special powers and monopolistic rights. This was the case when the supply of public services such as gas, water, electricity and railways was left to private enterprise. After the Second World War most of these statutory companies were nationalised and their functions taken over by public corporations. Some public services have been 'privatised', ie returned to public company status.

    ii.   There are also other types of organisation which owe their existence to statute. They include building societies, friendly societies and co-operative societies.

  c. *Registered companies.* The COMPANIES ACT 1985 provides for the registration of

    i.   Companies limited by shares;

    ii.   Companies limited by guarantee (Chapter 40.22);

    iii.   Unlimited companies (Chapter 40.23); and

    iv.   Partnership companies (paragraph 3.e. below).

The vast majority of companies are registered companies limited by shares. These companies may be public or private limited companies.

3. *Companies and Partnerships Compared*

  a. *Unincorporated associations and partnerships*

    i.   Unincorporated associations consist of a number of persons who have come together for a matter of common interest, for example a sports club, a trade union or a partnership.

    ii.   A partnership is defined by the PARTNERSHIP ACT 1890 as 'the relation which subsists between persons carrying on a business in common with a view to profit'. 'Business' includes any trade, occupation or profession.

  b. *The main differences between companies and partnerships*

    i.   A company is created by registration under the COMPANIES ACT 1985. A partnership is created by the express or implied agreement of the partners, no special form being required, although writing is usually used.

    ii.   A company incurs greater expenses at formation, throughout its life, and on dissolution, although the fees are not excessive.

    iii.   A company is an artificial legal person with a legal personality distinct from its members. In contrast a partnership is not a separate legal person, although it may sue and be sued in the firm's name. The partners own the property of the firm and are liable on its contracts.

    iv.   Shares in a public company are freely transferable, whereas a partner cannot transfer his share without the consent of all of his partners. He may assign the right to his share of the profits, but the assignee does not become a partner.

    v.   A company need only have one member and there is no upper limit on membership. A partnership must have at least two partners but must not consist of more than 20 persons, although there are some exceptions, for example solicitors, accountants, auctioneers and estate agents.

    vi.   Members of a company may not take part in its management unless they become directors, whereas all partners are entitled to share in management, unless the partnership agreement provides otherwise.

vii. A member of a company is not an agent of the company, and he therefore cannot bind the company by his acts. A partner is an agent of the firm, therefore it will be bound by his acts.

viii. The liability of a member of a company may be limited by shares or by guarantee. The liability of a general partner is unlimited, although it is possible for one or more partners to limit their liability provided there remains at least one general partner. In addition, as seen, the LIM-ITED LIABILITY PARTNERSHIP ACT 2000, does now provide a degree of limited liability for partnerships. The advantage of limited liability is unlikely to be real for many small companies and partnerships since lenders will usually require a personal guarantee of their loan from the directors and/or majority shareholders and partners.

ix. The powers and duties of a company are closely regulated by the Companies Acts, its constitution is specified in its Memorandum of Association, and its internal regulations are contained in its Articles of Association (although both can be freely altered by special resolution). In contrast, partners have more freedom to carry on any business they wish and to make their own arrangements with regard to the running of the firm.

x. A company must comply with more formalities, for example certain registers must be maintained and the accounts must be audited annually.

xi. Greater publicity must be given to the affairs of a company, for example to its directorate, its financial position and to charges on its assets.

xii. Company law requires maintenance of issued capital through the rule that dividends may only be declared out of profits. Partners' drawings of profit and capital are a matter of agreement.

c. *The similarity between companies and partnerships*. The main similarity is that both companies and partnerships are methods of carrying on business. Many companies are of course large and impersonal, having many institutional shareholders. Such companies bear little resemblance to partnerships. Small private companies are, however, often founded on the same basis as partnerships, ie a relationship of mutual trust and confidence.

d. *Conclusion*. Despite the greater degree of legal regulation affecting the registered company, the advantages of incorporation (for example separate legal personality, limited liability, transferability of shares, and possible tax advantages) have induced many partners and sole traders to convert their businesses into corporate form. However, partnership remains important, and in many cases mutual trust and confidence are more highly regarded than the benefits of incorporation. Thus, subject to a few exceptions, partnership is the compulsory form of association for many professional persons, for example solicitors. This preserves the principle of individual professional accountability towards the client, a policy central to professional ethics.

e. *Partnership companies*. As part of the Government's policy to encourage wider individual share ownership, it has introduced legislation making it easier to set up partnership companies. A partnership company is 'a company limited by shares whose shares are intended to be held to a substantial extent by or on behalf of its employees'. The Act allows the Secretary of State to prescribe, by regulations, a model set of articles appropriate for partnership companies, known as Table G.

THE CONSEQUENCES OF INCORPORATION

4. *A Separate Legal Entity*

a. The most important consequence of incorporation is that a company becomes a legal person distinct from its members.

In SALOMON v SALOMON & CO (**1897**) S formed a limited company with the other members of his family, and sold his business to the company for £39,000. He held 20,001 of the 20,007 shares which had been issued by the company, and £10,000 of debentures (documents acknowledging that S was a secured lender entitled to priority of repayment in a liquidation). The balance was payable in cash. About a year after its formation the company was wound-up. The assets at that time were just sufficient to discharge the debentures, but nothing was left for unsecured creditors with debts of about £7,500. The creditors claimed that they should have priority because S and the company were in effect the same person. The House of Lords, however, held that S and the company were separate legal entities, the company had been validly formed, and there was no fraud on the members or creditors. S was therefore entitled to the remaining assets.

b. Salomon's case was very important because it finally established the legality of family companies where one person holds the vast majority of the shares. It also showed that incorporation was available to small businesses as well as to large enterprises. However, it caused concern because it showed that it was possible to limit liability not merely to the money put into the company, but to avoid serious risk to some of that money by subscribing for debentures rather than shares. The decision has been criticised for this reason, but it can be justified on the grounds that persons who deal with a limited company know the risks, although it is not usually practical to take all the available precautions, such as a search of the company's file at the Companies Registry.

c. The fact that a company is a separate legal entity from its members is not necessarily beneficial to those members. For example if a trader sells his business to a company he will cease to have an insurable interest in its assets though he owns most of the shares.

In MACAURA v NORTHERN ASSURANCE (**1925**) M owned a timber estate. He formed a limited company and sold the timber estate to it. Like Salomon he was basically a 'one-man company'. Before he sold the estate to the company it had been insured in his own name. After the sale to the company he neglected to transfer the insurance policy to the company. The estate was destroyed by fire. It was held that M could not claim under the policy because the assets that were damaged belonged to a different person, namely the company, and M, as a shareholder, had no insurable interest in the assets of the company.

d. The effects of separate corporate personality are further illustrated by the following case.

In RE ATTORNEY-GENERAL'S REFERENCE (**No. 2 of 1982**) the respondents were accused of theft. They had appropriated for their own private purposes funds of various companies of which they were the sole shareholders and directors. Each acted with the consent of the other. Their defence was that they had appropriated their own property. The Court of Appeal held that even persons in total control of a company were capable of stealing its property. Furthermore it was not rational to treat the accused as having transmitted their knowledge to the company, so as to regard the company as having consented to the appropriation, in fact the company should be regarded as the victim of the crime.

e. *Corporate manslaughter*. The ability to prosecute a company for the death of a person or persons caused by its negligent operations, has recently been the subject of new legal proposals. The *CORPORATE MANSLAUGHTER BILL* will update existing laws on corporate killing. The proposed new criminal offence of corporate manslaughter will apply when someone has been killed because the senior management of a corporation has grossly failed to take reasonable care for the safety of employees or others. This tackles the key problem with current law: the need to show that a single individual at the very top of a company is personally guilty of manslaughter before the company can be prosecuted, a problem favouring the large public corporation with a large and diverse board and senior management. The new offence will mean that courts can look at a wider range of management conduct than at present. It focuses responsibility on the working practices of the organisation, as set by senior managers, rather than limiting investigations to questions of individual gross negligence by company bosses. The new offence will be clearly linked to the standards required under existing health and safety laws. The criminal liability of individual directors will not be affected by the proposals. Corporate manslaughter is an offence committed by organisations rather than individuals and will therefore carry a penalty of an unlimited fine rather than a custodial sentence.

5. *Other Consequences of Incorporation*

The following consequences of incorporation all flow from the fundamental consequence of separate legal personality:

a. *Limited liability*. All companies are liable without limit for their own debts. However, companies obtain their share capital from their members. Provided a company is formed on the basis of limited liability, its members are not liable for the company's debts. Complete absence of liability is not however, permitted. Each member is liable to contribute, if called upon to do so, the full nominal value of his shares so far as this has not already been paid. If he has agreed to pay more than the nominal value then his liability is limited to the amount he has agreed to pay.

b. *Property*. An important advantage of incorporation is that the property of the company is distinguished from that of its members. In contrast the property of a partnership is jointly owned by the partners. This can cause problems when defining the true nature of the interests of the partners, which will be necessary when a partner retires. There is no similar problem when the membership of a company changes since the members do not have any direct rights to the property of the company, they only have a right to their shares. Thus when shares are transferred, the company's property remains unaffected.

c. *Contractual capacity*. The question of contractual capacity is closely related to that of property ownership. Companies have contractual capacity and can sue and be sued on their contracts.

d. *Perpetual succession*. The continuity of the company is not affected by the death or incapacity of some or all of its members.

e. *Transferable membership*. Incorporation greatly facilitates the transfer of members' interests. Shares are items of property which are freely transferable provided the constitution of the company does not contain an express provision to the contrary.

f. *Increased borrowing powers*. It is logical to assume that unincorporated traders or partnerships would find it easier to borrow money because of their personal liability. This is not the case since a company can give as security a floating charge. This is not available to an unincorporated trader or partnership. A floating charge is a mortgage over the constantly fluctuating assets of a company. It does not prevent the company dealing with these assets in the ordinary course of business. Such a charge is very useful when a company has no fixed assets such as land which can be included in a normal mortgage, but nevertheless has a large and valuable stock-in-trade.

6. *The Veil of Incorporation*

The fact that the separate corporate personality of a company prevents outsiders from taking action against its members (even though the outsider can find out who they are and how many shares they hold) has led to comparison with a veil. The corporate personality is the veil, and the members are shielded behind this 'veil of incorporation'. However, the internal affairs of the company are never completely concealed from view since publicity has always accompanied incorporation. In addition there are several situations when the law is prepared to lift the veil of incorporation either to go behind the corporate personality to the individual members, or to ignore the separate personality of several companies in a group in favour of the economic entity constituted by the group as a whole.

7. *Examples of 'Lifting the Veil'*

a. *If the company is being used to enable a person to evade his legal obligations*

In GILFORD MOTOR CO v HORNE (1933) an employee covenanted that after the termination of his employment he would not solicit his former employer's customers. Soon after the termination of his employment he formed a company, which then sent out circulars to the customers of his former employer. The court lifted the veil of incorporation, granting an injunction which prevented both the former employee and his company from distributing the circulars even though the company was not a party to the covenant. However, in a more recent case the courts' strong support for the Salomon principle, even where there might be some evidence of apparent wrongdoing, was shown in a Court of Appeal decision; ORD & ANOR V BELHAVEN PUBS (1998). Here a defendant company pending legal action transferred its assets to another associated company. The plaintiff, concerned that insufficient assets remained to meet any future award of compensation, applied to have the associate company substituted as the new defendant. The Court refused stating that in the absence of evidence indicating some fraud or sham, the principle of separate legal existence as laid down in SALOMON V SALOMON must be upheld.

b. *Fraudulent or wrongful trading*

   i. By *S.213* of the INSOLVENCY ACT *1986*, if in the course of winding-up it appears that business has been carried on with intent to defraud creditors, the persons responsible may be made personally liable to make such contribution to the company's assets as the court thinks proper.

   ii. A more useful provision is *S.214* INSOLVENCY ACT *1986*, which enables the liquidator of an insolvent company to apply to the court to declare that a director be personally liable to contribute to the company's assets. Before making the order the court will have to be satisfied that the director knew or ought to have concluded that there was no reasonable prospect of avoiding insolvent liquidation and that he failed to take every step to minimise the creditors' loss.

c. *Groups and holding and subsidiary companies*

   Significant inroads to the concept of separate corporate personality have concerned holding and subsidiary companies. For certain purposes, in particular the presentation of financial statements, the companies in a group must be treated as one.

d. The UK courts have shown a marked reluctance to lift the veil within groups of companies where one company holds shares and controls another. In ADAMS V CAPE INDUSTRIES PLC (1991) the Court of Appeal refused to lift the veil of incorporation and hold a UK parent company liable for the acts of its subsidiaries abroad even though it could be shown that the UK parent had deliberately distanced itself from its subsidiaries in light of ongoing litigation; the Court finding that the fact that one company controls the actions of another does not make it 'at one' with that other, the *Salomon* principle must be upheld. However, within the European Union, the European Court of Justice has shown itself to be far more willing to lift the veil within groups of companies for purposes of applying Community rules on competition between member states.

   These instances of veil lifting will apply equally to the new Limited Liability Partnership (see paragraph 4 above).

PUBLIC AND PRIVATE COMPANIES

8. *Definitions*

   a. Public companies must

       i.   Be registered as public companies;

       ii. Have at least two members; and

       iii. State in their memorandum that they are public companies.

   b. *Private companies* are limited companies which are not registered as public companies, ie a company will be private unless it is specifically registered as public.

       Until July 1992 it was necessary for all companies to have at least two members. However, in response to an EC directive the COMPANIES (SINGLE MEMBER PRIVATE LIMITED COMPANIES) REGULATIONS 1992 now specify that a private company limited by shares or guarantee may be formed by one person and have one member.

9. *The Main Differences between Public and Private Companies*

   a. *Purpose*. Public and private companies fulfil different economic purposes. The purpose of a public company is to raise capital from the public to run the enterprise. This ability to offer shares to the public is now the only advantage of a public company. The purpose of a private company is to confer separate legal personality on the business of a sole trader or partnership.

   b. *Issue of capital*. A private company may not raise capital by issuing its securities to the public. There is no restriction on the offer of securities by a public company. A public company must, however, issue a prospectus (a document which gives minimum essential information to potential members) and comply with Stock Exchange rules to obtain a listing of the securities.

   c. *Transferability of shares*. The shares of a public company are freely transferable on the Stock Exchange. A private company will, in contrast, wish to remain under the control of the 'family' or 'partners' concerned. Its articles will therefore contain a clause restricting the right to transfer shares. The restriction may be:

       i.   An absolute power vested in the directors to refuse to register a transfer; and/or

       ii. A right of pre-emption (first refusal) granted to existing members when another member wishes to transfer shares.

   d. *Minimum share capital*. A public company must have a minimum allotted share capital of £50,000. A private company has no minimum share capital.

   e. *Company name*. The name of a public company must end with the words 'Public Limited Company', which may be abbreviated to 'PLC'. A private company's name must end with 'Limited'. This may be abbreviated to 'Ltd'.

f. *The memorandum.* A public company's memorandum must state that 'The company is to be a public company'.

g. *Payment for shares.* There are a number of differences in the rules relating to the consideration given in return for shares. For example if a public company issues shares in return for the transfer of a non-cash asset, that asset must be independently valued to ensure that the company is receiving an asset of a value at least as great as the value of shares issued in return. In a private company there is no requirement to obtain a report on the value of non-cash consideration received as payment for shares.

h. *Dividends.* There are detailed rules which differentiate between the ability of public and private companies to distribute their profits as dividends.

i. *Company administration.* The COMPANIES ACT 1989 made a number of changes designed to help small businesses by cutting the burden of regulation. Thus a private company may pass an *elective resolution* (this must be agreed by all members entitled to attend and vote at the meeting) if it wishes, for example (a) to dispense with the requirement to lay accounts and reports before the company in general meeting (b) to dispense with the requirement to hold an AGM or (c) to dispense with the requirement to appoint auditors annually.

j. *Written resolutions.* The 1989 Act also introduced a written resolution procedure for private companies. Anything which may be done by resolution of a private company in general meeting may now be done by a written resolution signed by or on behalf of all members.

k. *Other differences.* There are numerous other differences concerning, for example, directors, the secretary, commencement of business, the accounts and the minimum number of members.

REGISTRATION PROCEDURE

10. *The Functions of the Registrar of Companies.* The registrar is an official of the Department of Trade. His basic functions are:

a. To issue certificates of incorporation and change of name;

b. To be responsible for the registration and safe custody of documents required by statute to be filed with him and to pursue companies which fail to comply with such requirements;

c. To issue certificates of registration of mortgages and charges;

d. To provide facilities for the examination of filed documents by members of the public (the current search fee is £1) and to give copies of documents or certificates on payment of a fee;

e. At the conclusion of the winding-up of a company the registrar will complete final dissolution by striking the company off the register.

11. *Registration of New Companies*

    a. By *S.10* COMPANIES ACT *1985*, to obtain registration the promoters must deliver to the registrar:

        i. Memorandum of Association;

        ii. Articles of Association;

        iii. A statement containing the name, address, nationality, business occupation, other directorships and age of each person who is to be a first director or the secretary of the company. The statement must contain the signed consent of each person named to act.

        iv. Address of the registered office;

        v. A Declaration of Compliance, made by the solicitor engaged in the formation, or a person named as director or secretary, stating that the requirements of the Act have been complied with.

        vi. Registration fee of £20.

    b. The registrar could rely on the declaration of compliance, but in practice his staff check that the documents are formally in order and that the name and objects are legal. If satisfied the registrar will issue a *Certificate of Incorporation*. By *S.13* the certificate of incorporation is *conclusive evidence* that the formalities of registration have been complied with. This means that even if it is subsequently discovered that the formalities of registration were not in fact complied with, the registration will not be invalidated. The reason for this is that once a company has commenced business and entered into contracts it would be unreasonable for either side to be able to avoid the contract because of a procedural defect in registration.

12. *Re-registration of a Private Company as Public*

    a. By *S.43* the company must pass a *special resolution* that it should be re-registered as public. The special resolution must:

        i. Alter the company's memorandum so that it states that the company is to be a public company;

        ii. Make any other necessary changes to the memorandum, for example changing the name of the company so that it ends with 'Public Limited Company'; and

        iii. Make the necessary changes to the articles, for example by removing any restriction on the right to transfer shares.

    b. An application to re-register must then be sent to the registrar. This must be signed by a director or the secretary and must be accompanied by a printed copy of the new memorandum and articles and a number of specific documents primarily concerned with assuring that the company meets the capital requirements of public companies.

13. *Public Company to Re-register as Private*

    a.   By *S.53* the company must pass a *special resolution* that it should be re-registered as private. The special resolution must:

        i.   Alter the company's memorandum, in particular it must no longer state that the company is to be a public company. The name clause must also be changed;

        ii.   Alter the company's articles, probably to include a restriction on the right to transfer shares.

    b.   The application must be signed by a director or the secretary and sent to the registrar with a printed copy of the new memorandum and articles.

    c.   Within 28 days of the resolution holders of not less that 5% of the issued shares of any class *or* not less than 50 members, may apply to the court to cancel the resolution. The court may confirm or cancel the resolution, imposing such conditions as it thinks fit, for example that the dissenting members' shares be purchased, if necessary by the company itself.

Under proposals for *Company Law Reform 2005*, in future a memorandum of association will just be a statement that the subscribers intend to form a company. Other requirements of the memorandum will be transferred to the articles of association with the statement of authorised share capital being abolished and a statement of objects being optional. A procedure will be introduced for re-registration of a public company as an unlimited company.

PROMOTERS

14. A promoter is any person involved in the planning, incorporation, or initial running of a company, other than persons involved in a purely professional capacity. A promoter need not necessarily be the main person behind the incorporation, but he must have some executive function. The stereotype of a promoter may well be a city businessman, but any small trader who forms a company and sells his business to it is also a promoter.

15. *Duties of Promoters*. The law has to protect shareholders from the situation where a promoter forms a company, sell shares in the company for cash, and then sell his own property to the company in return for that cash, thus making a personal profit. The courts have established the principle that a promoter stands in a *fiduciary relationship* with the company which he is forming. This does not mean that he is barred from making a profit out of the promotion. It means that any profit made must be *disclosed* to the company. In this context 'the company' means existing and potential members. Thus a promoter cannot form a company and sell his own land to it at a vast profit, disclosing this only to a few of his associates who constitute the initial members, and then float off the company to the public. If the company is to be sold to the public the promoter's profit must be disclosed to potential members in the prospectus. Then, knowing what proportion of the price of their shares will go to the promoters,

the public are adequately informed when making the decision of whether or not to purchase the shares.

16. *Remedies for Breach of Duty*

In the event of non-disclosure of profits the company may commence proceedings for rescission or for recovery of the undisclosed profits.

a. The right to rescind is exercised on the usual contractual principles. Therefore:

   i. The company must have done nothing to ratify the agreement after finding out about the non-disclosure or misrepresentation; and

   ii. Restitution must be possible although the court can order financial adjustments to be made when ordering rescission, so the restitution rule rarely operates as any real restraint.

b. If the contract is rescinded the promoter's secret profit will normally disappear as a result. If, however, he has made a profit on some ancillary transaction this may also be claimed by the company. A secret profit may be recovered even if the company elects not to rescind.

c. The company may sue the promoter for damages under the *MISREPRESENTATION ACT 1967*, or for negligence, or for fraud. This will be useful if rescission is barred.

17. *Payment for Promotion*

a. Promoters are not entitled to payment because

   i. Before incorporation the company cannot contract to pay them since it does not exist; and

   ii. After incorporation any such contract would be void since the consideration would be past.

b. However, the articles will provide that 'the business of the company shall be managed by the directors who may exercise all the powers of the company'. The directors may therefore pay the promoters their expenses. In practice there will be few problems since the promoters will normally be the first directors.

c. Another method of payment would be for the promoter to sell property to the company at an over-valuation (the difference being the 'payment'). This would be acceptable provided all the disclosure requirements are satisfied.

PRE-INCORPORATION CONTRACTS

18. *The Effect on the Company*

a. A contract made on behalf of a company before its incorporation does not bind the company, nor can it be enforced or ratified by the company after incorporation.

In KELNER v BAXTER (1866) a company was about to be formed to buy an hotel. Before the company was formed the promoters signed a contract 'on behalf of' the proposed company for the purchase of a quantity of wine. The company was formed, the hotel purchased, and the wine was delivered and consumed, but before payment was made the company went into liquidation. It was held that the promoters were personally liable to pay for the wine, any purported ratification by the company being ineffective.

b.   Therefore any pre-incorporation agreements will either have to be binding in honour only, or the promoter will have to undertake personal liability.

19. *The Effect on the Person who Purports to Contract on Behalf of the Company*

a.   By *S.36C* where a contract purports to be made by a company, or by a person as agent for a company, at a time when the company has not been formed, then subject to any agreement to the contrary, the contract has effect as one entered into by the person purporting to act for the company or as agent for it, and he is personally liable on the contract.

b.   Although *S.36C* provides for an express agreement to the contrary, it does not envisage an agreement whereby the promoter incurs no liability and cannot enforce the contract since such an agreement would be invalid for lack of consideration. The Act envisages that the promoter protects himself by:

i.   Agreeing that the promoters' liability shall cease when the company, after incorporation, enters into a similar agreement; or

ii.   Agreeing that if the company does not enter into such an agreement within a fixed period either party may rescind.

20. *Contracts Made by a Public Company Before the Issue of a Certificate Under S.117*

a.   By *S.117* a public company may not commence business until it has obtained a certificate of compliance with the capital requirements of public companies (sometimes known as a 'trading certificate'). In contrast a private company may commence trading from the date of incorporation.

b.   If a public company does business in contravention of this section the transaction will be valid, but if the company fails to comply with its obligations within 21 days of being called upon to do so, the directors are liable to indemnify the other party if he suffers loss due to the company's failure to comply. This is an example of 'lifting the veil' of incorporation. In addition the company and its officers may be fined.

21. *Execution of Documents by Companies*

a.   Prior to 1989 a document was executed by affixing the company seal and adding the signature of two directors or one director and the secretary.

b.   By *S.36A* there is now no requirement for a company to have a seal. A document will be executed if signed by two directors or a director and the secretary, provided it is expressed to be executed by the company. This new provision relieves companies of the obligation to use seals, it does not prohibit them from continuing as before.

CHAPTER 40

The Memorandum and Articles of Association

INTRODUCTION

1. *Memorandum and Articles*

   The regulations of every company will be contained in two separate documents:

   a. The *memorandum* sets out its basic constitution and presents the company to the outside world.

   b. The *articles* deal with matters of internal administration, for example, the issue and transfer of shares, directors' powers, procedure at meetings, the payment of dividends and the secretary. 'Table A' is the model form for a company limited by shares. Table A is now contained in THE COMPANIES (TABLES A TO F) REGULATIONS 1985. By S.8 if a company does not register articles Table A will apply to that company. In practice companies will modify Table A to suit their own requirements.

   Current proposals contained in the White Paper, *Company Law Reform 2005*, will replace Table A with two sets of model articles: one for private limited companies and one for public companies. The proposed new model set of articles for the private limited company is much shorter and simpler than the present Table A.

2. *Contents of the Memorandum*

   a. Every *company* memorandum must contain the following six clauses:

      i.   Name;

      ii. Registered Office;

      iii. Objects;

      iv. Limitation of Liability;

      v.   Capital; and

      vi. Association.

b. In addition the memorandum of every *public company* must state that 'The company is to be a public company'.

THE NAME CLAUSE

3. *Basic Rules*

a. By *S.25(2)* the last word of a private company's name must be 'Limited'. This warns persons who deal with companies that they will not have access to the private funds of the members to satisfy their debts. 'Limited' may be abbreviated to 'Ltd'. A partnership name must not end with the word 'Limited'. Private companies limited by guarantee may apply to dispense with the word 'Limited' if their objects are to promote, for example, art, science or education and their articles prohibit the payment of dividends.

b. By *S.25(1)* a public company's name must end with the words 'Public Limited Company' or the abbreviation 'PLC'.

4. *Prohibition on Registration of Certain Names (S.26)*

A company may not be registered with a name:

a. Which includes any of the following (or abbreviations thereof) *other than* at the end of the name: 'limited', 'unlimited' or 'public limited company';

b. Which is the same as a name already appearing in the index kept by the registrar;

c. The use of which would, in the opinion of the Secretary of State, constitute a criminal offence;

d. Which in the opinion of the Secretary of State is offensive; or

e. Which would be likely to give the impression that the company is in any way connected with the Government or with a local authority.

5. *Change of Name (S.28)*

a. A company may change its name by *special resolution*. A new certificate of incorporation will be issued and the change is effective from the date of that certificate.

b. In certain circumstances the Secretary of State may order a company to change its name, for example

   i. If the name is too similar to a name already in the index.

   ii. If the name is so misleading as to be likely to cause harm to the public.

c. The court may also order a change of name following a successful 'passing off' action.

In EWING v BUTTERCUP MARGARINE CO (**1917**) E, whose business was called 'The Buttercup Dairy Company' was successful in his attempt to prevent a newly registered company from using the name 'Buttercup Margarine

Company' because it was considered that the public might think that the two businesses were connected.

6. *Publication of Name and Address*

a. Every company must publish its name:

    i. Outside all its places of business;

    ii. On all letters, orders, invoices, notices, cheques and receipts; and

    iii. On its seal, if it has a seal.

b. If a company does not comply with the above requirements, the company and every officer in default are liable to a fine. In addition if an officer or other person issues or signs any company letters, orders, cheques, etc which do not bear the full name of the company he may be fined and he will be liable to any creditor who has relied on the document if the company fails to pay him.

c. The place of registration (ie England or Scotland), the address of the registered office and its number in the index at the registry, must also appear on all business letters and order forms.

7. *Business Names*

a. Most companies, partnerships and sole traders trade under their own names, but sometimes they prefer to use another name. This is known as a business name.

b. The BUSINESS NAMES ACT 1985 requires any person (company, partnership or sole trader) who carries on business under a different name from his own

    i. To state its name and address on all business letters, invoices, receipts, orders and demands for payment;

    ii. To display its name and address in a prominent position in any business premises to which suppliers or customers have access; and

    iii. At the request of any person with whom it does business to supply a written notice of its name and address.

THE REGISTERED OFFICE

8. *The Registered Office Clause*

This clause does not state the address of the registered office, it merely states that the registered office will be situated in England and Wales (or Wales alone if it is to be a Welsh company) or Scotland, thus fixing the nationality and domicile of the company.

9. *The Purpose of the Registered Office*

The registered office is the official address of the company. It is also the place where writs, notices and other communications can be served, and where certain registers and documents are usually kept. It need not be a place of business of the company, in fact many companies arrange for the premises of their solicitors or accountants to be their registered office.

10. *Documents and Registers Kept at the Registered Office*

The following documents and registers are usually kept at the registered office, and must be kept there unless otherwise stated:

a.   The register of members, unless it is made up elsewhere in which case it can be kept where it is made up.

b.   The register of directors and secretaries.

c.   The register of directors' interests in shares and debentures. If the register of members is not kept at the registered office, the register of directors' interests may be kept with the register of members.

d.   The register of debenture holders. If the register is made up elsewhere it may be kept where it is made up.

e.   The register of charges.

f.   Copies of instruments creating the charges.

g.   The minute book of general meetings.

h.   Directors' service contracts. These may instead be kept at the principal place of business.

i.   The minute book of directors' meetings. This may be kept at any convenient place.

j.   The accounting records. These may also be kept at any convenient place.

k.   A copy of any contract for an off-market purchase, market purchase or contingent purchase by a company of its own shares (or if the contract is not in writing, a written memorandum of its terms) must be kept for 10 years from the date of completion of the purchase.

l.   A *public company* must keep a register of interests in shares. The level at which a holding becomes notifiable is 3%. This register must be kept with the register of directors' interests.

11. *Rights of Inspection of Documents and Registers*

The above registers and documents with the exception of d. and f. are the statutory books, ie the registers and documents which every company is required to keep by law. They are subject to the following rights of inspection:

a.   Members may inspect all except i. and j. free of charge.

b.   Creditors may inspect e. and f. free of charge.

c.   Debenture holders may inspect d. free of charge.

d.   Directors may inspect all of the documents and registers.

e.   The public may inspect a., b., c., d., e., and l. on payment of a small fee. They may inspect k. only if the company is a public company.

12. *Change of Address (S.287)*

    a.   The company cannot change the clause in the memorandum which states the country in which the registered office will be situated. It may, however, move the registered office within that country. This change of address is effected by *ordinary resolution*, or if there is authority in the articles, by a resolution of the board of directors.

    b.   The company is allowed 14 days from the date of the change (ie the date of registration of the change) to move its registers to the new registered office. Similarly if it is necessary to move registers quickly and it has not been practicable to give prior notice, no offence will be committed as long as notice of the change is given to the registrar within 14 days. Also, for 14 days following the change, a person may validly serve any document on the company at its previous registered office.

THE OBJECTS CLAUSE

13. *The Purposes of the Objects Clause*

S.2 requires every company to state its objects. This defines and limits its permissible activities. Originally the objects clause served two purposes:

    a.   Prospective members were told what kind of business they were investing in; and

    b.   Creditors were able to ensure that the funds from which they could expect payment were not used for unauthorised activities.

14. *Brief History*

    a.   Prior to 1989 the basic rule was that an act outside the objects clause was ultra vires and void and therefore could not be enforced by the company or by an outsider. This was unpopular with companies (for whom it could be inconvenient to have restricted powers) and outsiders (who might find that their contract could not be enforced). This was generally the case even if the outsider did not actually know of the restriction on the company's power, because of the doctrine of *constructive notice*, by which everyone was deemed to know of the contents of the company's registered documents.

    b.   Companies therefore sought to avoid the ultra vires rule by drafting lengthy objects clauses (30–40 paragraphs) allowing them to do almost anything they could ever wish to do. They also usually included general powers allowing anything incidental to any of their other objects and powers. The effect of the ultra vires rule was further restricted by *S.35 CA 85* (now repealed) which stated that if an outsider dealt with the company in good faith, any transaction decided on by the directors would be deemed to be within the company's capacity, regardless of any limitations in the memorandum or articles.

c. In 1985 the DTI commissioned a report from Dr Dan Prentice of Oxford University to advise on the implications of abolishing the ultra vires rule. His report recommended complete abolition. The Government, however, took the view that total abolition would be undesirable. The 1989 Act therefore abolished the application of ultra vires in respect of outsiders, but retained the power of members to bring proceedings to restrain ultra vires acts. This ensures that commercial transactions cannot be set aside once they have been entered into, but retains some members' rights.

d. The 1989 Act basically deals with four issues.

  i. Drafting the company's memorandum so as to widen its capacity

  ii. The protection of outsiders entering into contracts with the company

  iii. The ability of members to restrain ultra vires acts

  iv. The powers of directors to bind the company and restrictions on their powers (see Chapter 44).

15. *Statement of Objects in Memorandum*

a. By *S.3A* it is sufficient for the memorandum to state that the object of the company is to carry on business as a general commercial company. This is defined in the Act to allow the company

  i. To carry on any trade or business whatsoever and

  ii. To do all such things as are incidental or conducive to the carrying on of any trade or business by it.

b. This provision relieves companies of the need to draft long objects clauses. However, it is not clear that such a short statement will be sufficient for all purposes, for example it is not clear whether it will cover all types of gifts by companies, or the disposal of a business by general commercial company.

c. Where a company does adopt such a clause the effect will be to virtually abolish the ultra vires rule for internal purposes (see 17 below), the Act having already abolished it so far as outsiders are concerned.

16. *Validity of Acts Done by Companies*

a. By *S.35(1)* the validity of an act done by a company shall not be called into question on the ground of lack of capacity by reason of anything in the company's memorandum.

b. Consequently a *completed act* will have *total protection* from the ultra vires rule and will be *enforceable* by both the company and an outsider.

17. *Members' Right to Restrain Ultra Vires Acts*

By *S.35(2)* any member may bring proceedings to restrain an intended act which would be beyond the capacity of the company. However, this right is restricted by *S.35(3)* which allows the company to ratify an ultra vires act by *special resolution*.

18. *Constructive Notice*

    a.   *S.35B* makes it clear that an outsider is not bound to inquire as to whether an act is permitted by the memorandum or subject to any limitations on the authority of the directors. Furthermore *S.117A* provides that a person shall not be taken to have notice of any matter merely because it is disclosed in registered documents or made available by the company for inspection.

    b.   These sections abolish the doctrine of constructive notice subject to an exception preserved by *S.416* under which a person taking a charge over a company's property is deemed to have notice of any matter requiring registration and disclosed on the register of charges at the time the charge was created.

    c.   *S.142 CA 89* also provides that a person cannot rely on the fact that he did not have notice of certain matters if he failed to make such inquiries as should reasonably have been made in the circumstances.

19. *Alteration of Objects*

    a.   *Basic rule*

        By *S.4* a company may freely amend its objects clause by special resolution.

    b.   *Minority protection*

        i.   By *S.5* holders of 15% of the issued capital may apply to the court within 21 days of the resolution to have it set aside. The court may confirm or refuse the resolution, or it may arrange for the purchase of the dissentient members' interests, if necessary by the company itself.

        ii.   If no application is made the company must, within 15 days after the end of the 21 day period, deliver to the registrar a printed copy of the memorandum as altered.

LIMITATION OF LIABILITY

20. *Contents of the Clause*

Where a company is limited by shares or by guarantee this clause will merely state: 'The liability of the members is limited'.

21. *Companies Limited by Shares*

The vast majority of companies, both public and private are companies limited by shares. In such a company the capital is divided into shares, for example capital of £5,000 divided into 10,000 shares of 50 pence each. The members of the company are liable to pay for their shares, either in money or money's worth (ie non-cash assets, goodwill or know-how). Once they have paid for their shares they are under no further liability. The company is therefore said to be 'limited by shares'. It is, however, important to note that it is not the company's liability which is limited, it must discharge its debts as long as it has assets to do so. It is the members' liability to the company which is limited.

22. *Companies Limited by Guarantee*

    a.   Such companies are usually formed for educational or charitable purposes. They usually raise their funds by subscription. Limitation of liability by guarantee is not appropriate for trading companies.

    b.   The liability of each member is limited to the amount he has agreed to contribute in the event of winding-up. The amount (usually £1 or £5) will be specified in the memorandum. Moreover a member's liability is contingent, his money is only called-up in the event of liquidation.

23. *Unlimited Companies*

    a.   There is no limit to the liability of the members of such companies. Thus although the company is a separate legal entity, the members' liability resembles that of partners, except that technically their liability is to the company itself and not to the creditors.

    b.   Unlimited companies are not popular because of this personal liability. However, unlimited companies do have the advantage of greater privacy since they are not required to deliver copies of their accounts to the registrar.

OTHER CLAUSES

24. *The Capital Clause*

    a.   This states amount of capital and its division into shares of a fixed amount. For example Table B of The Companies (Table A to F) Regulations 1985 (the specimen form of memorandum for a company limited by shares), states that 'The share capital of the company is £50,000 divided into 50,000 shares of £1 each'.

    b.   The capital of a public company must be not less than the authorised minimum, at present £50,000.

    c.   When shares are first issued they may be issued at a premium (ie more than the nominal value), at par (ie at the nominal value), but not at a discount (ie less than the nominal value).

    d.   Once the shares have been allotted they will change hands at market value which may be above or below the nominal value. The two figures are not related. The nominal value is fixed by the promoters or directors of the company. The market value reflects the prosperity of the company and the extent of speculative dealing in the shares.

25. *The Association Clause*

In this clause the subscribers to the memorandum declare that they desire to be formed into a company, and agree to take the number of shares set opposite their names. Each subscriber signs the memorandum.

26. *Alteration of the Memorandum Generally*

Every clause of the memorandum may be altered except the registered office clause, ie the country of incorporation cannot be altered. In addition to the methods of alteration of the clauses required by statute, *S.17* allows the company to alter clauses that it has chosen to include in the memorandum instead of the articles. Such clauses can be altered by *special resolution* unless the memorandum provides for another method. Holders of 15% of the issued shares have 21 days to apply to court to challenge that alteration.

THE ARTICLES OF ASSOCIATION

27. *The Nature of the Articles*

The articles are the internal regulations of the company. They deal with, for example, the issue and transfer of shares, directors' powers, procedure at meetings, the payment of dividends and the secretary. Every company must have articles. 'Table A' is the model form for a company limited by shares. Table A is contained in THE COMPANIES (TABLES A TO F) REGULATIONS 1985.

28. *Alteration of Articles*

a. By *S.9* the articles may be altered by *special resolution*. Any provision which attempts to deprive the company of this power is void, for example a power given to a particular member to veto an alteration.

b. The articles of a *private company* may also be altered by *written resolution*. *S.113–114 CA 89* have introduced new rules allowing private companies to substitute the unanimous written agreement of all shareholders for any resolution passed at a general meeting. Clearly such a procedure can also be used, for example to change the company name or to alter the objects clause in the memorandum.

c. No alteration of the articles can constitute a fraud on the minority (see below), nor overrule the general law, the memorandum, or the provisions of the Acts. For example

   i. By *S.16* no increase of a member's liability is possible without his written consent, ie a member cannot be compelled to purchase more shares.

   ii. Minority protection provisions, for example the right of a dissenting 15% to object to a change of objects, cannot be excluded.

d. *Fraud on the minority.* The change must be for the benefit of the company, ie members in general. It would be improper if its purpose is primarily to injure other members.

In BROWN v BRITISH ABRASIVE WHEEL CO (1919) a resolution was passed adding to the articles a clause compelling a member to transfer his shares upon a request in writing by the holders of 90% of the issued shares. The change could not be for the benefit of the company as a whole, but solely for the benefit of the majority.

In future the case law concept of 'fraud on the minority' will become much less significant. *S.459–461* enable the court to restrain any actual or proposed act which is *unfairly prejudicial* to the interests of the members. These sections improve the position of the minority and would certainly be available if the alleged unfairly prejudicial act was an alteration of the articles.

e. *The effect of an alteration on outsiders.* An alteration of the articles which causes a breach of contract with an outsider is valid, and cannot be restrained by an injunction. The outsider's remedy is to claim damages for breach of contract.

In SOUTHERN FOUNDRIES v SHIRLAW (**1940**), Shirlaw had been appointed the managing director of Southern Foundries for 10 years. The articles stated that the managing director's appointment shall automatically cease if he should cease to be a director. Southern Foundries was then merged into a group called Federated Industries. All group members agreed to make certain alterations to their articles, one such change being that FI would have power to remove any director of a member company. FI then used this power to remove Shirlaw. As a result he automatically ceased to be managing director of SF, even though his contract had several years left to run. Shirlaw's claim for damages for wrongful dismissal succeeded because his contract as managing director was held to contain an implied term that the company would not do anything to make it impossible for him to continue as managing director.

29. *The Effect of the Memorandum and Articles*

By *S.14* the memorandum and articles when registered bind the company and the members as if they had been signed and sealed by each member and contained covenants on the part of each member to observe their provisions. The effects of this are that

a. *The company is bound to each individual member in his capacity as member.* Thus for example it must record a properly given vote. However, it is not bound by a right given by the articles to a member acting in another capacity, for example as company solicitor.

In ELEY v POSITIVE LIFE ASSURANCE CO (**1876**) the articles contained a clause appointing the plaintiff as company solicitor, and he acted as such for some time. The company then ceased to employ him and he brought an action for breach of contract. It was held that the articles did not constitute a contract between the company and Eley because even though he was a member they could not confer rights on him in any other capacity, including that of company solicitor.

b. *Each member is bound to the company.* Therefore a provision in the articles referring disputes between a member and the company to arbitration will be enforceable against the member provided the dispute concerns membership rights.

In HICKMAN v KENT SHEEP BREEDERS ASSOCIATION (1915) the articles provided for disputes between members and the company to be referred to arbitration. The Association wished to expel the plaintiff from membership of the Association and the plaintiff applied for an injunction to prevent this. It was held that the Association was entitled to have the action stayed since the dispute concerned membership rights and the articles provided for such disputes to initially be settled by arbitration rather than legal action.

c.   *The members are contractually bound to each other*. The main occasions when this question is likely to arise are when the articles give members pre-emption rights when another member wishes to sell his shares, or more rarely, when the articles place on members a duty to buy the shares of a retiring member. In such cases a direct action between the shareholders concerned is theoretically possible. However, a situation where members are able to sue other members may well give rise to practical difficulties. To avoid this modern articles will make the transaction a two stage process, each stage being a dealing with the company to which *S.14* clearly applies. The articles first require any member who intends to transfer his shares to inform the company. They then require the company to give notice to other members that they have an option to purchase the shares. If the first stage is not complied with, the company can sue the transferor. If the second stage is broken a shareholder may sue the company.

d.   *Differences between the contract in S.14 and other contracts*

   i.   The normal remedy of damages for breach of contract is not available because of the court's desire to maintain the capital of the company. A member may, however, obtain an injunction to prevent a breach by the company of any provision in the memorandum or articles and he may sue for a liquidated sum due to him as a member, for example unpaid dividends.

   ii. The contract does not guarantee the future rights and duties of members, since both the memorandum and articles may be altered. Thus when becoming a member a person agrees to a contract which is alterable by the other party (the company) at a future date.

CHAPTER 41

Share Capital

PUBLIC OFFERS FOR SHARES

1. *Raising Funds*

Private companies will usually raise their funds from their own membership or from a bank. Public companies are formed when it is necessary to obtain funds from an issue of shares or debentures to the public. This has led to many provisions to protect the investing public. These are now contained in *PARTS IV* and *V FINANCIAL SERVICES ACT 1986*.

2. *Listed and Unlisted Securities*

a. *Listed securities. PART IV* FSA *1986* deals with the official listing of securities, ie the Official List of the Stock Exchange. It provides for an application to be made to the '*competent authority*' (the Council of the Stock Exchange) by the method specified in the '*listing rules*'. These rules contain details of the information to be included in '*listing particulars*'.

b. *Unlisted securities. PART V* FSA *1986* deals with offers of unlisted securities which are to be admitted for dealing on an '*approved exchange*' for example the Unlisted Securities Market. In such cases no advertisement offering securities may be issued unless a '*prospectus*' has been approved by the exchange and delivered to the registrar of companies.

3. *Private Companies*

Two provisions in the Act make it clear that the Act does not apply to private companies:

a. By *S.143(3)* FSA a private company must not apply for its shares to be listed on the Stock Exchange.

b. By *S.170* FSA a private company must not issue any advertisement offering its shares for sale.

4. *Public Issue by 'Offer for Sale'*

a. This method may be employed when a public company wishes to raise money by issuing new shares. It involves the transfer of all the new shares to an issuing house (usually a merchant bank). The issuing house will then publish listing particulars inviting the public to purchase from it at a slightly higher price. This method is much more common than a '*direct offer*' by the company and it does not involve any risk for the company, although the issuing house will underwrite. The issuing house will not be registered as holder except in respect of shares which the public do not take. The practice is to issue renounceable letters of allotment to the issuing house. This enables it to assign its right to membership by signing forms of renunciation in favour of purchasers.

b. The term 'offer for sale' is rather misleading, since the listing particulars are in fact an invitation to treat, not an offer capable of acceptance by the public. The offer occurs when the applicant sends in the application form, it is then up to the company to accept.

5. *Rights Issues*

a. The modern practice when a public company wants to raise capital is to make a rights issue, ie new shares are created and offered to existing shareholders in proportion to their existing shareholding. Since 1980 it has been a legal requirement that existing shareholders be given a right of first refusal when new shares are issued *(S.89)*.

b. To make a rights issue attractive the shares will usually be offered at 10%–20% less than the current market value. This can give added worth to the existing shares until they go 'ex rights' when buying them will no longer entitle the holder to participate in the rights issue. After the issue the market may mark down the price of the shares since they will have lost some scarcity value.

6. *Application and Admission to the Official List*

a. No securities may be admitted to listing, ie quoted, unless an application has been made to the *competent authority* in the way required by the *listing rules*. The competent authority is the Council of the Stock Exchange. The listing rules are made by the Council. They specify the content of the listing particulars.

The information required is very detailed, but will include basic essential information, for example:

i. The names, addresses and descriptions of the directors.

ii. The capital to be subscribed, the amount to be paid in cash, and the nature of the consideration for the remainder.

iii. Voting and dividend rights for each class of share.

b. In addition to any matters required by the listing rules, the Act imposes a general duty to disclose information that investors and their advisers would reasonably require to make an informed decision on whether to buy the securities. It must enable them to ascertain the assets and liabilities, financial position, results and prospects of the issuer, and the rights attaching to those securities.

c. An application may be refused if

i. The Council considers that because of any matter relating to the issuer, the admission would be detrimental to investors.

ii. In the case of shares already officially listed in another EC state, the issuer has failed to comply with his obligations in connection with that listing.

d. The Council may discontinue the listing of any securities if it is satisfied that there are special circumstances which prevent normal regular dealings. It may also temporarily suspend listing. This sometimes occurs at the issuer's request, for example when rumours of a takeover bid distort the normal market for the securities.

7. *Remedies for Misrepresentation and Omission*

a. *Compensation.* Under *S.150–152* FSA a 'person responsible' for listing particulars (which includes the company, its directors or any other person who authorised any part of the particulars) shall be liable to compensate any person who acquires the securities in question and suffers loss as a result of any untrue or misleading statement or the omission of any of the required particulars. A number of defences are possible, for example:

i. Reasonable belief that the statement was true and not misleading, or that the matter was properly omitted.

ii. Reliance on a statement made by an expert, provided the expert consented to the inclusion of the statement and the person responsible can show reasonable belief in the expert's competence.

iii. That the loss resulted from the fair and accurate reproduction of a statement by an official person or contained in an official document.

iv. The plaintiff acquired the securities with the knowledge that the listing particulars were false or misleading.

b. *Damages.* There are three avenues leading to an award of damages. The action chosen will depend on several factors, including the type of misrepresentation.

i. By *S.2(1)* MISREPRESENTATION ACT *1967* the innocent party has a right to damages for misrepresentation if he has suffered loss. However, if the maker of the statement proves that he had reasonable grounds for believing, and in fact did believe, up to the time the contract was made, that the facts represented were true, then he has a defence.

The problem with *S.2(1)* is that the range of persons who can be sued is rather narrow. Only the other party to the contract can be sued. Thus directors and experts are excluded, as is the company, unless the securities were acquired directly from it.

ii. If the misrepresentation is fraudulent, damages may be recovered in tort for deceit. A fraudulent misrepresentation is a statement which is known to be false, or made without belief in its truth, or made recklessly, not caring whether it is true or false (DERRY v PEEK (1889)). The action will lie against all those who made the false statement, including the company.

iii. The third possibility is that damages for negligent misrepresentation may be claimed under the rule in HEDLEY BYRNE v HELLER (1964). The duty not to make negligent statements will be owed if the plaintiff can show that he relied on the special skill and judgement of the defendant, and the defendant knew, or ought to have known, of the reliance, thus accepting responsibility for making the statement carefully.

The persons liable will be those who both owed and broke the duty of care. This would include directors and experts, but it probably does not include the company.

c. *Rescission.* Since rescission is an equitable remedy its award is at the discretion of the court. In general the plaintiff will not be granted rescission in the following circumstances:

    i.   If he delays in seeking his remedy;

    ii.   If he affirms the contract, ie with knowledge of his right to rescind he acts in a way which is consistent with ownership of the shares, for example by voting at meetings or attempting to sell the shares; or

    iii. If the company goes into liquidation, since the rights of third parties, such as creditors and debenture holders, will then intervene.

The remedy of rescission is affected by *S.2(2)* MISREPRESENTATION ACT *1967* which gives the court a discretion to award damages in lieu of rescission if it thinks it equitable to do so.

TYPES OF CAPITAL AND ALTERATION OF CAPITAL

8. *Capital, Share Capital, and Loan Capital*

a. The word capital is generally used to describe the amount by which the assets of a business exceed its liabilities. This implies a fluctuating measure of the net worth of the business.

b. The share capital of a limited company is not a constantly fluctuating figure. It is the minimum value of net assets which must be raised initially, and so far as possible retained in the business, ie it is the amount that purchasers of shares have agreed to contribute to the company in return for their shares.

c. Share capital, which is subject to many rules of preservation and disclosure, must be distinguished from loan capital. When money is lent to a company the lender does not become a member of the company and the money raised is not subject to the same rules of preservation.

9. *Different Meanings of 'Share Capital'*

a. *Nominal or authorised capital.* Every company must state in its memorandum the amount of its nominal capital. This figure shows the maximum number of shares the company is authorised to issue and the nominal value of each share. It does not indicate that any shares have been issued and paid for.

b. *Issued capital.* Some or all of the nominal capital must be issued in return for cash or the transfer of non-cash assets. Issued capital is of far more importance than nominal capital since each shareholder is liable to pay the price of shares issued to him. It is the issued capital which, in theory, comprises a guarantee fund from which creditors can expect to be paid. It is therefore important that it is not wrongfully reduced, for example by using it to pay dividends to shareholders. However, it may of course, be quite legitimately lost in the normal course of business trading. Unless it is clear that some other meaning applies, all subsequent references to 'capital' are references to issued capital.

c. *Called-up capital*

   i.   *S.1 CA 85* provides that the liability of shareholders shall be limited to the amount, if any, unpaid on their shares. The Act therefore allows the issued shares to be partly called-up.

   ii. Called-up capital equals the aggregate of the calls made on shares, whether or not the calls have been paid, together with any share capital paid-up without being called and any share capital to be paid on a specified future date under the articles.

   iii. In practice companies usually require fairly prompt payment of the full amount of issued capital by instalments, so that issued capital and called-up capital are generally the same.

d. *Paid-up capital.* This is the sum of the payments received by the company. Unless some shareholders refuse to pay calls the paid-up capital will equal the called-up capital. Paid-up capital is important because if a company makes a reference on its stationery to the amount of its capital, the reference must be paid-up capital.

e. *Uncalled capital.* This is the difference between the amount already paid-up and the total nominal value of the issued shares. Uncalled capital is rare because it is unpopular with both companies and investors, companies because of the possibility that calls will not be met, and investors because of uncertainty as to when calls will be made. Where it exists, uncalled capital is a further guarantee fund for creditors. It is an asset equivalent to debtors, the debtors in this case being the members. The creditors can, however, only gain access to this fund in the event of a liquidation since they cannot compel the directors to make calls, nor can they levy execution on uncalled capital.

f. *Reserve capital.* In order that the guarantee fund referred to above can be removed from the directors' control and made more permanent, *S.120* provides that a company may, by *special resolution*, determine that it shall only be called up in the event of winding-up. The special resolution creating reserve capital is irrevocable. Reserve capital, which is also known as 'reserve liability' must not be confused with 'General Reserve' or 'Reserve Fund'. These terms refer to undistributed profits.

10. *Alteration of Capital*

By *S.121 CA 85* provided a company has authority in its articles, it may pass an *ordinary resolution* to alter the capital clause of its memorandum in any of the following ways:

a. *Increase*, ie an increase of nominal capital. This will only be necessary when all of the nominal capital has been issued.

b. *Consolidation*, i.e. the merging of a number of shares into one share of the nominal value of the aggregate, for example ten 5 pence shares are consolidated into one 50 pence share.

c. *Subdivision*. This is the reverse of consolidation. It has been held that a subdivision of shares does not vary the class rights of other shares even if voting equilibrium is altered.

In GREENHALGH V ARDERNE CINEMAS (**1946**) 10 pence ordinary shares ranked equally as regards voting with 50 pence ordinary shares. Each 50 pence share was then sub-divided into five 10 pence ordinary shares with one vote each. It was held that the voting rights of the original 10 pence shares had not been varied even though the holder of these shares had now lost his power to block a special resolution.

It is possible that such a decision could be successfully challenged under *S.459* if it is unfairly prejudicial to members generally or some part of the members.

d. *Conversion*. Fully paid shares may be converted into stock and vice versa.

Stock is basically a number of shares put in a bundle. The main difference between shares and stock is that a share cannot be split into fractions, whereas the stock of a company can be split into as many portions as is required. In practice stock is now extremely rare.

e. *Cancellation*. This refers to a decrease in the nominal capital of the company, ie un-issued shares are cancelled. Cancellation, which is also known as diminution, must be distinguished from reduction of capital, which is a decrease in the amount of issued share capital.

The registrar must be notified of an increase within 15 days. In other cases the registrar must be notified within one month.

Proposals for change contained in the Government's *White Paper, Company Law Reform 2005*, will remove the need for authority to reduce capital being required in the articles.

MAINTENANCE OF CAPITAL

11. *The Need to Maintain Capital*

The acceptance of limited liability has led to a need to protect the capital contributed by the members since the members cannot be required to contribute funds to enable the company to pay its debts once they have paid for their shares in full. The capital therefore represents a guarantee fund for creditors. It is protected in two basic ways:

a. Provisions designed to prevent the capital being 'watered down' as it comes into the company (12–16 below);

b. Provisions designed to prevent capital going out of the company once it has been received.

The *Company Law Reform 2005* proposes to repeal the special procedures in *S. 171–177*, because all private companies will have the option of making any kind of reduction of capital without court confirmation provided there is a directors' solvency statement.

12. *Underwriting Commission*

a. An underwriter is a person (or finance house) which, on a public issue of shares, agrees to purchase those shares which are not taken up by the public.

b. By *S.97* underwriters may be paid a commission not exceeding 10% of the issue price provided there is authority in the articles and compliance with any rules made by the Secretary of State under powers given in the FINANCIAL SERVICES ACT 1986. These rules include the requirement of disclosure in the listing particulars. The commission is charged on the number of shares underwritten and must be paid even if the issue is a success and the public take all the shares. The usual rate is 1¼%.

c. When a company has been in existence for some years it will probably be able to pay underwriting commission from its accumulated profits or its Share Premium Account. In contrast when a company makes its first issue of shares these funds will not exist. Underwriting commission must therefore be paid out of the proceeds of the issue, ie out of capital. This is why underwriting commission is subject to statutory control.

13. *Payment for Share Capital*

a. It is not possible for a company to make a gift of its shares to an allottee, the shares must always be paid for.

b. *S.99(1)* states that they may be paid for in money or in money's worth, including goodwill or know-how.

c. However, by *S.99(2)* a *public company* may not accept as payment an undertaking to do work or perform services for the company. This means that the shares of a public company must be paid up in *cash* or non-cash assets.

14. *The Issue of Shares at a Discount*

a. By *S.100* the issue of shares at a discount is prohibited. ie Shares may not be allotted as fully paid for a consideration of less than their nominal value. Today shares usually have a very low nominal value, for example 5 pence. Since there is no statutory obligation on a company to issue shares for the highest price it can get, it is possible for a person to obtain shares for a consideration of less than their full value.

b. This section applies to all companies.

15. *Minimum Payment for Allotted Shares*

a. By *S.101* a *public company* may not allot shares unless they are paid-up to the extent of one quarter of the nominal value plus the whole of the premium.

b. In practice the company will almost certainly require the shares to be paid up to the full nominal value plus all of the premium. The *share premium* is the difference between the nominal value and the issue price.

16. *Allotment for Non-cash Consideration*

a. By *S.102* where a *public company* allots shares which are fully or partly paid for by an undertaking to transfer to the company a non-cash asset at a future date, that asset must be transferred within five years of the date of allotment.

b. *Valuation of non-cash consideration, public companies.* By *S.103* a *public company* may not allot shares for a consideration other than cash unless the non-cash asset has been independently valued by a person qualified to be the auditor of the company. The report must state that the value of the consideration (including any cash payable) is not less than the nominal value of the shares plus any premium, ie that the shareholders are getting value for money.

c. *Valuation of non-cash consideration, private companies.* When a private company issues shares in return for a non-cash consideration the court will not usually inquire into the adequacy of consideration. For example although the valuation of Salomon's business at £39,000 was described by the House of Lords as 'a sum which represented the sanguine expectations of a fond owner rather than anything that can be called a businesslike or reasonable estimate of value', they were not prepared to set aside the transaction even though the correct valuation of the business was about £10,000. (See Chapter 39.4.)

There are three exceptional situations when the court is concerned with the adequacy of consideration

i.   Where the contract is fraudulent;

ii. Where the consideration is past; and

iii. Where the inadequacy appears on the face of the contract.

In HONG KONG AND CHINA GAS CO V GLEN (**1914**) the company agreed to allot to the vendor of a concession to supply gas to the city of Victoria in Hong Kong, 400 fully paid shares, plus one fifth of any future increase in capital, allotted as fully paid. It was held that the part of the agreement relating to future increases in capital was invalid because it meant that the company had agreed an unlimited value for the purchase of the concession.

17. *Serious Loss of Capital*

a. By *S.142* the directors of a *public company* must call an extraordinary general meeting when it becomes known to a director that the net assets have fallen to *half or less* of the company's called-up share capital.

b. The purpose of the meeting is to decide what action, if any, should be taken. In some cases the meeting will decide on a reduction of capital.

18. *Reduction of Capital*

    a.   By *S.135* a company may, if authorised by its articles (a requirement which will no longer be required if the proposed *Company Law Reforms 2005* are adopted), pass a *special resolution* and obtain the *consent of the court* to reduce its capital and alter its memorandum accordingly.

    b.   *S.135* enables a company to reduce its capital in any case but in particular it specifies:

        i.   To extinguish liability on share capital not paid up.

        ii.   To cancel paid-up capital which is lost and no longer represented by assets.

        iii.   To repay share capital in excess of the company's needs.

    c.   If the reduction affects creditors (ie i. or iii. above) the court will not confirm the reduction unless the creditors agree to it, or are paid off, or are given security.

    d.   In addition to the interests of the creditors the court will also ensure that the reduction is equitable between the various classes of shareholders involved. Note RE HOLDERS INVESTMENT TRUST (**1971**) (Chapter 43.13).

19. *The Issue of Shares at a Premium*

    a.   It is usual to issue shares at a price above their nominal value, ie at a premium. This may be because the net assets of the company exceed the nominal value of the shares, or because previously issued shares of the same class have a market value in excess of their nominal value.

    b.   By *S.130* when shares are issued at a premium (whether for cash or in exchange for property, goods or services) the premium must be paid into a *share premium account* which can only be used

        i.   To finance an issue of fully paid bonus shares to members;

        ii.   To write off preliminary expenses;

        iii.   To write off commissions paid, or discounts allowed, or the expenses of an issue of shares or debentures;

        iv.   To provide the premium payable on the redemption of any debentures of the company;

        v.   Where redeemable shares are issued at a premium, to provide the premium payable on redemption. This is subject to conditions (see paragraph 22 below).

    c.   *S.130* therefore requires that, except for the above purposes, share premiums are treated as capital, for example they cannot be distributed as dividends. In doing so it recognises that what is important is not the arbitrarily fixed nominal value, but the actual value received for the shares when issued.

20. *The Acquisition by a Company of its Own Shares*

    a.   For many years it was a fundamental case law principle of company law that a company may not purchase its own shares.

    b.   The basic rule is now contained in *S.143(1)* which states that(subject to the following provisions) a company shall not acquire its own shares. Any purported acquisition in contravention of this section is void.

    c.   There are a number of exceptions to the basic rule:

        i.   Where it acquires its own fully paid shares otherwise than for valuable consideration *(S.143(3))*.

        ii.   A purchase of redeemable shares *(S.159–160)*.

        iii.   A purchase of own shares under *S.162–178*.

        iv.   An acquisition as part of a capital reduction scheme.

        v.   An acquisition in pursuance of a court order under *S.5* (alteration of objects); *S.54* (re-registration of a public company as private); or *S.461* (unfair prejudice).

        vi.   Where shares are forfeited for non-payment of a call, or where shares are surrendered in lieu of forfeiture.

    d.   There are a number of reasons why it is undesirable for a company to be able to purchase its own shares:

        i.   It is a reduction of capital, ie if it pays shareholder A cash for his shares, less cash is available to satisfy the claims of creditors X, Y and Z;

        ii.   If it paid shareholder A too much for his shares this would dilute the value of the remaining assets, ie on winding-up there would be less cash available for shareholders B, C and D;

        iii.   If it paid shareholder A too little for his shares this would enhance the value of the remainder and could be used by the directors to increase the value of their own holdings;

        iv.   A method of frustrating a takeover bid is to buy shares on the open market. If the directors could use the company money to do this, no doubt they would do so, thus entrenching themselves in control of the company.

    e.   In recent years there has been increasing interest in relaxing the prohibition for the benefit of the company and its shareholders provided the position of creditors and other interested parties could be protected. The advantages of allowing a company to purchase its own shares are:

        i.   It facilitates the retention of 'family' control of a private company;

        ii.   It increases the marketability of a company's shares, since the company itself is a potential buyer. This in turn would increase interest in employee share schemes, and may therefore help the company to raise further capital;

iii. It enables both public and private companies to use surplus cash to the company's advantage. For example if redeemable shares have a market value of less than their redemption price, they could be redeemed immediately rather than waiting to pay the higher price on the redemption date;

iv. It may make it easier for companies to raise venture capital from merchant banks since the banks have the possibility of 'getting out' by selling their shares back to the company.

21. *Financial Assistance for Acquisition of Shares*

a. By *S.151* it is illegal for a company directly or indirectly to give any financial assistance for the acquisition of any of its shares or shares in its holding company. It is irrelevant whether the financial assistance is given before, at the same time as, or after, the acquisition. The purpose of *S.151* is to extend the rule in *S.143* in an attempt to prevent evasions of it.

b. *'Financial assistance'* is defined by *S.152* to include:

i. A gift;

ii. Provision of a guarantee, security, indemnity, release or waiver;

iii. A loan and related arrangements; and

iv Any other financial assistance by a company whose net assets are as a result reduced to a material extent or which has no net assets.

c. *S.151* can be illustrated by the following cases:

In HEALD v O'CONNOR (1971) the seller of the controlling shareholding in a company lent part of the price to the buyer. The loan was secured by a floating charge on the company's assets. In addition this debenture was guaranteed by the purchaser. It was held that the debenture amounted to financial assistance. Also the seller could not enforce the guarantee since it was not possible to guarantee an illegal transaction.

In BELMONT FINANCE v WILLIAMS FURNITURE (1980) Group 'A' wanted to buy Belmont from Group 'B' without paying for the shares with their own money. It was arranged that the purchase would be financed from Belmont's own assets, which were extracted by Group 'A' first selling to Belmont for £500,000 shares in another company which were worth only £60,000. The £500,000 was then used by Group 'A' to pay Group 'B' for Belmont's shares. It was held that the arrangement was illegal.

d. The effects of contravention of *S.151* are:

i. The financial assistance, for example the guarantee or security, is void;

ii. The company and any officer in default are liable to a fine and/or up to two years imprisonment;

iii. Every director who is party to a contravention of *S.151* is guilty of a breach of duty and is liable to recoup any losses which the company suffers as a result.

e. The exceptions to *S.151* are rather complex. Some straightforward examples include:

   i. Where the lending of money is part of the ordinary business of the company, and the loan is in the ordinary course of its business.

   For example a bank may lend to its customer so that he can buy shares in the bank.

   ii. Where the loan is provided in good faith in the interests of the company, for the purposes of an employees' share scheme.

   For example a company may give a guarantee or some other form of security to a bank that lends money to an employees' share scheme.

   iii. Where the loan is to employees (other than directors) to enable them to purchase fully paid shares to be held by them as beneficial owners.

f. In addition to the exceptions which apply to all companies, *S.151* is further relaxed for private companies. Thus, provided strict conditions are complied with, a private company may give financial assistance for the acquisition of its shares provided the company's net assets are not thereby reduced, or to the extent that they are reduced the financial assistance is provided out of distributable profits. This would allow a private company to arrange a *'management buyout'*, ie the disposal of a company to its management. The management could either buy shares in the company with a loan from company funds, or more usually, the management would buy the shares with a bank loan which would be secured by company assets. The main conditions are:

   i. A special resolution must be passed;

   ii. The directors must make a statutory declaration that in their opinion the company will be able to pay its debts immediately after, and during the 12 months following, the date on which the assistance is given;

   iii. A report by the company's auditors must be attached to the statutory declaration. It must state that they have enquired into the company's state of affairs and are not aware of anything to indicate that the opinion expressed by the directors is unreasonable.

Current *Company Law Reform* proposals 2005, will allow private companies to provide financial assistance for the purchase of their own shares.

22. *The Power to Issue Redeemable Shares*

a. By *S.159* a company may, if authorised by its articles, issue shares which are to be redeemed, or may be redeemed at the option of the company or the shareholder. The proposed *Company Law Reforms* 2005, will remove the need for authorisation from the articles.

b. The following conditions must be fulfilled:

   i. No redeemable shares may be issued unless there are shares in issue which are not redeemable;

   ii. Shares may not be redeemed unless they are fully paid;

    iii. The terms of the redemption must provide for payment on redemption;

    iv. Except for private companies which take advantage of the power to redeem shares out of capital (see 23.h. below) the shares may only be redeemed out of the company's distributable profits or out of the proceeds of a fresh issue of shares made for the purpose of the redemption *(S.160)*.

    v. The terms and manner of redemption must be specified at or before the time of issue, including the date on or by which (or dates between which) the shares will be (or may be) redeemed.

c. By *S.170* where shares are redeemed out of profits a sum equal to their nominal value must be transferred from profits to a capital redemption reserve. This reserve, like the share premium account, is a statutory capital reserve. Except for a reduction of capital under *S.135*, or a redemption or purchase of shares out of capital under *S.171*, the capital redemption reserve can only be applied in the allotment of fully paid bonus shares.

d. If the shares are redeemed out of the proceeds of a fresh issue, capital is automatically replaced and no capital redemption reserve is needed.

e. If the shares are redeemed at a premium the basic rule is that the premium must be paid out of distributable profits. There is an exception where the shares were originally issued at a premium. In such cases the premium on redemption may be provided out of the share premium account to the extent that it does not exceed the lesser of:

    i. The premiums received on the issue of the shares being redeemed; and

    ii. The balance on the share premium account.

f. Shares redeemed are treated as cancelled on redemption and the amount of the company's issued capital is reduced accordingly, but the company's authorised capital is not affected.

23. ***The Purchase by a Company of its Own Shares***

a. By *S.162* a company (public or private) may, if authorised by its articles, purchase its own shares (including redeemable shares).

b. The conditions that apply to the redemption of redeemable shares also apply to the purchase of own shares, for example the need for a capital redemption reserve.

c. A company may not purchase its own shares if, as a result, there would no longer be any member of the company holding shares other than redeemable shares.

d. The requirements for the authorisation of purchase of own shares depend on whether the transaction is an off-market purchase or a market purchase.

e. Before a company may make an *off-market purchase*, a *special resolution* must be passed authorising the purchase and its terms. The shares that are to be purchased *may not vote* on the resolution. Despite anything in the articles *any member* may demand a poll on such a resolution.

f. Before a company may make a *market purchase* an *ordinary resolution* must be passed. The resolution must:

    i. Specify the maximum number of shares to be purchased;

    ii. Specify the maximum and minimum prices which may be paid for those shares; and

    iii. Specify a date, not later than 18 months after the resolution, on which the authority is to expire.

    The shares to be purchased may vote on the ordinary resolution. Contrast a special resolution for the off-market purchase of own shares.

g. *All companies* must, within 28 days of a purchase of their own shares, deliver a return to the registrar stating the number and nominal value of the shares purchased and the date (or dates) of purchase. In addition a *public company* must state the aggregate amount paid by the company for the shares, and for each class of shares purchased, the maximum and minimum price paid.

h. *S.171–177* allow a *private company* to redeem or purchase its own shares out of *capital*. Since this potentially strikes at one of the basic functions of company law, ie to protect creditors by maintaining the capital fund, it is subject to extensive protective measures. Thus

    i. A *special resolution* must be passed. The shares to be purchased may not vote;

    ii. The directors must make a *statutory declaration* specifying, among other things, that they are of the opinion that the company will be able to carry on business as a going concern throughout the following year;

    iii. An *auditor's report* must be attached to the statutory declaration stating that, having enquired into the company's affairs they are not aware of anything to indicate that the opinion expressed by the directors is unreasonable;

    iv. Detailed *publicity requirements* must be complied with;

    v. Members and creditors have statutory rights to object;

    vi. If winding-up commences within one year, persons whose shares were purchased, or directors who signed the statutory declaration, remain liable to the extent that the payment out of capital relates to their shares.

DIVIDENDS

24. *Definition*

a. Dividends are payments made out of profits to the members of a company. Dividends paid to preference shareholders will be at a fixed rate, whereas dividends paid to ordinary shareholders will vary with the prosperity of the company. Shareholders do not have an automatic right to dividends even if profits are available. Directors may consider it more prudent to retain profits within the company. A dividend is therefore not a debt of the company until it is declared. Even then, on liquidation, it is not payable until after the outside creditors have been paid.

b.   Dividends must be distinguished from interest. Interest is paid to debenture holders. It is a debt and must be paid out of capital if no profits are available.

25. *The Requirement of Solvency*

Dividends cannot be paid if this would result in the company being unable to pay its debts as they fall due. All the rules are subject to this overriding condition of solvency. Clearly if a company did pay a dividend in this situation it would have to pay its debts out of capital.

26. *The Basic Rule*

By *S.263* no company, whether public or private, may make a distribution (ie pay dividends) except out of its accumulated realised profits less its accumulated realised losses. In addition unrealised profits may not be used in paying up debentures or amounts unpaid on issued shares. Note that:

a.   A '*distribution*' is defined as any distribution of a company's assets to its members (including preference shareholders) whether in cash or otherwise except:

  i.   The issue of fully or partly paid bonus shares;

  ii.   The redemption or purchase of any of the company's own shares out of capital (including the proceeds of any fresh issue of shares) or out of unrealised profits;

  iii. A reduction of capital;

  iv.   A distribution in a winding-up.

b.   '*Profits*' includes both capital and revenue profits and '*losses*' includes both capital and revenue losses.

c.   A provision (other than one arising as a result of a revaluation of all the fixed assets) must be treated as a realised loss. A provision is an amount set aside to meet a known liability the exact amount of which cannot be determined with accuracy.

d.   To avoid a company having to translate an unrealised surplus on the revaluation of a fixed asset into a realised loss as a result of depreciating the higher value of the fixed asset, it is provided that the part of the revaluation surplus that equals the excess depreciation which has been charged as a result of the revaluation may be treated as realised profit.

For example a company pays £10,000 for an asset and decides to write it off over 10 years (straight line method). The depreciation charge is therefore £1,000. After five years the asset is revalued at £15,000, but its useful life does not change. In future the depreciation charge will be £3,000 per year, ie £2,000 more than if the revaluation had not been made.

Thus £2,000 would have to be retained from realised profits but for *S.275* which allows this £2,000 to be distributed rather than retained.

e. The Act is not precise about what is to be regarded as realised profit. However, the courts will be guided by modern accounting practice. For example a profit will be regarded as realised when a sale is completed, even if the debtor has not paid.

The *Company Law Reforms 2005* proposals will make provisions for payment out of capital for the private company no longer necessary provided there is a statement of solvency.

27. *Public Companies*

a. By *S.264* a public company may not make a distribution if its net assets are less than the aggregate of its called-up capital plus undistributable reserves, or if the result of the distribution would be to reduce its net assets below the aggregate of called-up capital plus undistributable reserves.

b. *'Undistributable reserves'* means

i. The share premium account and the capital redemption reserve;

ii. Any other reserve which the company is prevented from distributing by law or by its memorandum or articles; and

iii. The excess of accumulated unrealised profits over accumulated unrealised losses.

c. The practical effect of *S.264* is that a public company must take into account an unrealised loss, whereas a private company need not do so. Such unrealised losses will usually arise from the writing down (other than by way of depreciation) of capital assets, since other unrealised losses will usually be charged to the profit and loss account.

28. *Relevant Accounts and Interim Dividends*

a. *S.270* requires the last annual accounts to be referred to when determining the legality and amount of any distribution.

b. *Interim dividends* are dividends which are paid between annual general meetings. Usually companies will try to make the interim dividend about the same amount as the final dividend and make the payment mid-way through the year.

c. Where a *public company* proposes to pay an interim dividend which would be unlawful if reference were made only to the last annual accounts then interim accounts will be necessary to justify the distribution. These must be properly prepared and a copy must be delivered to the registrar, but they do not have to be audited *(S.272)*.

29. *Consequences of Unlawful Distribution*

a. By *S.277* every shareholder who has received an unlawful distribution and who knew or ought to have known that it was paid out of undistributable funds is liable to repay it to the company.

b. Where dividends cannot be recovered from shareholders, every director who was knowingly a party to the unlawful distribution must pay to the company the amount lost plus interest.

30. *The Articles*

a. By *S.281* the above rules must be read subject to any provision in the articles which places further restrictions on the amount available for distribution. For example if the articles state that dividends may only be paid out of 'the profits of the business' then capital profits, ie realised profits on the sale of fixed assets, are not available for distribution.

b. Table A contains a number of provisions relating to dividends, for example

   i. The company declares the dividend by *ordinary resolution*, but the declaration cannot exceed the amount recommended by the directors, ie the shareholders can reduce the amount of the recommended dividend but they cannot increase it.

   ii. The directors may pay interim dividends if this is justified by the profits.

   iii. Dividends shall be paid proportionate to the amounts paid-up on shares.

   iv. Instead of payment in cash the directors may direct payment of a dividend by the distribution of specific assets or paid up shares or debentures of any other company.

   v. Any dividends payable in cash may be paid by cheque sent by post to the registered address of the holder.

   vi. Dividends do not bear interest.

31. *Capitalisation Issues*

a. A capitalisation issue is an allotment of fully or partly paid shares in the company to members in proportion to their existing shareholding. The money used to pay up the shares may have come from:

   i. The distributable profits of the company.

   ii. The share premium account or the capital redemption reserve; or

   iii. Any other reserve which is not available for distribution.

b. A capitalisation issue is sometimes referred to as a 'bonus' or 'scrip' issue. The term 'bonus issue' is rather misleading since it implies that the shares are free. This is not the case since if the funds had not been used to pay up the bonus shares, they could (if of type i. above) have been distributed as dividends.

c. If the shares are paid up from the funds referred to in ii. or iii. above this is not a true capitalisation issue since these funds must already be treated as capital. No profits have been capitalised.

d. In order to make a capitalisation issue:

    i. A company must have authority in its articles. Table A authorises such an issue provided an *ordinary resolution* is first passed;

    ii. The nominal capital must be sufficient. If it is not, it will have to be increased under *S.121*.

TYPES OF SHARES

32. *The Nature of Shares*

a. There are two basic types of company security, shares and debentures. The distinction is that a shareholder is a member of the company, whereas a debenture holder is a creditor of the company.

b. Ownership of shares does not constitute part ownership of the assets of the company. Since the company is a separate legal entity it owns its own assets. Ownership of shares amounts to ownership of certain rights (for example the right to attend and vote at meetings) and liabilities, ie the liability to pay for the shares.

c. Shares are personal property. They can be bought, sold, mortgaged or bequeathed. A fraction of a share cannot exist, but one share may be held by two or more people.

d. A share must be distinguished from the share certificate, which is merely evidence of title to the shares.

e. Both preference shares and ordinary shares may be issued as redeemable or irredeemable.

33. *Preference Shares*

a. Preference shares are designed to appeal to investors who want a steady return on their capital combined with a high level of safety. As their name implies, they confer on holders preference over other classes of shareholder in respect of either dividends, repayment of capital or both.

b. *Dividends*

    i. Preference shares have a fixed rate of dividend, for example 8%. This dividend must be paid before the ordinary shareholders receive anything.

    ii. Preference shares are *cumulative* unless the articles or terms of issue state otherwise. This means that if the company cannot pay a dividend in one year the arrears must be carried forward to future years and all the outstanding preference dividends must be paid before the ordinary shareholders receive anything. If preference shares are *non-cumulative* and the company cannot pay a dividend the arrears are not carried forward, so the preference shareholder will not receive a dividend for that year.

    iii.   Preference shares are normally *non-participating*, ie they are not enti-
tled to share in the surplus profits of the company after payment of a
specified dividend on the ordinary shares.

  c. *Voting*

    i.   Unless the articles otherwise provide, preference shares carry the same
voting rights as other shares.

    ii.   However, it is usual to restrict the preference shareholders' rights to
vote to specified circumstances which directly affect them, for example
when the rights of preference shareholders are being varied.

  d. *Rights on liquidation.* Preference shareholders do not automatically have a
right to prior return of their capital. If the articles are silent preference shareholders and ordinary shareholders rank equally. However, in most cases the
articles will give preference shareholders priority of return of capital.

34. *Ordinary Shares*

Ordinary shares are sometimes described as a residuary class, ie their rights are
the rights that remain after the rights of the other classes of shareholders (if
any) have been satisfied. Thus in good years ordinary shareholders take the
major share of the profits. Also since the preference shareholders' right to vote
is usually restricted, the ordinary shareholders control resolutions at general
meetings. The other advantages are that they have a statutory right of pre-
emption on the issue of new shares *(S.89)* and they usually take the surplus
assets if a profitable company is wound up. The disadvantage is that they take
the major share of the risk of failure.

Under the *Company Law Reforms 2005*, proposals:

    i.   members' register of past members will have to be kept for only 10 years
instead of the current 20 years;

    ii.   private companies will not be required to hold an Annual General Meeting
(AGM). A public company will have to hold its AGM within six months
after the end of each accounting reference period;

    iii.   the minimum notice period for shareholder meetings will be 14 days;

    iv.   extraordinary and elective resolutions will no longer be required;

    v.   the holder of a proxy vote will be able to vote on a show of hands;

    vi.   for private companies ordinary and special resolutions may be passed in writ-
ing if approved by a simple majority of those entitled to vote for the ordinary
resolution, and three-quarters of those entitled to vote for the special.

APPLICATION AND ALLOTMENT

35. *Application*

  a. When a person applies for shares he is offering to purchase new shares from
the company. He is not purchasing existing shares from a previous holder.

b. The general law of contract applies to an application for shares:

   i.   The prospectus is an invitation to treat;

   ii. The subscriber makes the offer when he sends in the application form;

   iii. The company accepts the offer by resolution of the board of directors. The acceptance becomes binding when a letter of allotment is posted to the allottee.

c. The rules of contract are, however, modified in three ways:

   i.   By *S.89* existing shareholders usually have a statutory right to be offered new shares before they are offered to outsiders;

   ii. The acceptance need not coincide precisely with the offer. Many issues are over-subscribed. In such cases the company will either ballot to decide to whom to allot the shares or it will allot only a proportionate part of those applied for. The company is able to do this because, on the application form, the subscriber agrees to take either the shares applied for or such lesser number as are allotted to them.

   iii. Further modifications result from rules issued by the Stock Exchange or the Secretary of State under powers given in the FINANCIAL SERVICES ACT 1986, for example an offer is irrevocable until several days after the closing date for applications. The reason for this is to inhibit '*stagging*', ie the revocation of an offer if it appears that the shares or debentures cannot quickly be re-sold at a profit.

36. *Statutory Restrictions on Allotment*

There are now numerous statutory provisions relating to the allotment of shares. The following were dealt with in paragraphs 15–16 above since they are concerned with maintenance of capital:

a. Minimum payment for allotted shares – *S.101*.

b. Allotment for a non-cash consideration – *S.102*.

c. Valuation of non-cash consideration – *S.103*.

The other main restrictions on allotment are dealt with below (37–39).

37. *Company Authority Required for the Allotment of Shares*

a. By *S.80* directors may not allot shares, except subscribers' shares or shares allotted under an employees' share scheme, without the authority of the company in general meeting or in the articles.

   (Subscribers' shares are shares shown in the memorandum to be taken by the subscribers to the memorandum.)

b. The authority may be general or specific, and it must state the maximum amount of shares which may be allotted, and must limit the time during which the authority may be exercised. This time limit must not exceed five years.

c. An *ordinary resolution* is necessary to grant authority to the directors, and since this may have the effect of altering the articles a copy of the resolution must be delivered to the registrar within 15 days. Registration of an ordinary resolution is not normally required.

38. *Private Companies*

By *S.170 FINANCIAL SERVICES ACT 1986* a private company must not issue any advertisement offering its shares for sale.

39. *Pre-emption Rights S.89–96*

a. A company may not allot *equity shares* unless it has made an offer to the existing shareholders to subscribe on the same or more favourable terms for such shares in proportion to their present holding *(S.89)*.

b. By *S.94* 'Equity shares' means shares other than:

   i. Shares which as respects dividends and/or capital distribution have restricted rights, ie preference shares; and

   ii. Shares held, or to be held, under an employees' scheme.

   The definition of equity shares basically means ordinary shares, however, it also includes the *right* to subscribe for, or convert to, shares.

c. Shareholders must be notified in writing and the offer must be open for at least 21 days. No allotment may be made until either 21 days has expired or every offer has been accepted or refused *(S.90)*.

d. By *S.95* these provisions do not apply:

   i. Where the shares are to be wholly or partly paid-up other than in cash;

   ii. To *private companies* who exclude the provisions in their memorandum or articles *(S.91)*;

   iii. Where the directors of *any company* have authorisation to allot shares under *S.80* they may be given authority, either by the articles or by special resolution, to exercise the power without complying with the pre-emption right provisions;

   iv. Where *any company* by special resolution resolves that the provisions shall not apply to a specific allotment, or shall only apply in a modified form. In such cases the directors must recommend the resolution, and circulate a written statement setting out the reasons for their recommendation.

40. *The Return of Allotments (S.88)*

a. When *any company* allots shares (including bonus shares) it must, within one month of the allotment, deliver to the registrar a return of allotments. This document must state:

   i. The number or nominal value of the shares allotted;

   ii. The names, addresses and descriptions of the allottees;

   iii. The amount paid and payable on each share; and

   iv. Details of any non-cash consideration.

   b.   The return must be accompanied by a payment of capital duty at the rate of 1% of the actual value of the consideration for the shares.

   c.   In the case of a public company the registrar must publish notice of receipt of the return of allotments in the Gazette *(S.711)*.

   d.   If *S.88* is contravened the allotment remains valid, but every officer in default is liable to be fined.

41. *The Share Certificate*

   a.   By *S.185* a share certificate must be made out by the company and delivered to the member within two months of allotment or the date when a transfer was lodged for registration. If the shares are quoted on the Stock Exchange the rules of the Exchange substitute a period of 14 days.

   b.   The certificate states that the person named is the holder of the shares and specifies the amount paid-up on them. It is not a negotiable instrument since an entry in the company's register of members is necessary to transfer ownership. However, by *S.186* it is *prima facie evidence of title*.

   c.   Since a share certificate is prima facie evidence of title it gives rise to *estoppels* (both as to title and as to the amount paid on the shares), as against the company in favour of a person who has relied on the certificate. Estoppel is a rule of evidence. It arises when a person has conducted himself in such a way that reasonable inferences as to his legal position may be drawn from his conduct. He cannot then give evidence to show that his legal position is not what it appeared to be, he is estopped (ie barred by his own conduct) from doing so.

   d.   Estoppel does not operate:

      i.   Where the share certificate is a forgery; or

      ii.   In favour of a person who lodged a forged transfer.

TRANSFER OF SHARES

42. *Validity of Agreement to Transfer*

There must be a valid agreement to transfer, either by contract or by gift.

In HARVELA INVESTMENTS v ROYAL TRUST COMPANY OF CANADA (**1986**) the House of Lords held that if the vendor of shares in a private company invited purchasers to submit sealed bids for shares the vendor could not accept a referential bid, ie one expressed as the amount above that submitted by another bidder. In this case the bid was as follows:

'2,100,000 Canadian dollars or 101,000 Canadian dollars in excess of any other offer which you may receive, whichever is higher'.

It was held that such bids were unacceptable since one party cannot win and the other party cannot lose. Also if more than one referential bid were to be submitted the process would be frustrated.

43. *Transfer of All of the Shares Comprised in One Certificate*

a. By *S.183* whenever shares are transferred a *proper instrument of transfer* must be delivered to the company, ie the transfer must be in writing. Thus an attempt to provide for the automatic transfer of a member's shares, for example to his wife on his death, is void.

b. A transfer form signed by the transferor is sent by the transferee, with the share certificate and the registration fee, to the company. If the articles restrict the right to transfer shares the transfer must be submitted to the board to ensure that the restrictions are complied with. After approval by the board the name of the transferee is entered on the register and that of the transferor deleted. The company must issue a new share certificate within two months, or 14 days if the company is listed on the Stock Exchange.

c. The procedure was introduced by the STOCK TRANSFER ACT 1963 and it applies despite anything in the articles.

44. *Transfer of Part of the Shares Comprised in One Certificate*

a. Here a different procedure is necessary because it would be unsafe for the transferor to give the transferee the certificate in return for a consideration in respect of only part of the shares. Similarly it would be unreasonable to expect the transferee to pay for the shares whilst allowing the transferor to retain the certificate.

b. The procedure is:

   i. The transferor executes the transfer and sends it with his share certificate to the company;

   ii. The company secretary indorses 'certificate lodged' on the transfer and returns it to the transferor, keeping the share certificate;

   iii. The transferor hands the certified transfer to the transferee who lodges it with the company for registration;

   iv. The company issues two new share certificates.

c. The indorsement of 'certificate lodged' on the transfer is known as *'certification of the transfer'*.

   i. *S.184* provides that certification of the transfer by the company is a representation by the company that documents showing prima facie evidence of title have been produced. It is not a guarantee that the transferor has title.

   ii. If the company fraudulently or negligently certifies the transfer when the transferor has not shown prima facie evidence of title the company is liable to anyone acting on the faith of it to his detriment.

   iii. However, if the company merely negligently returns the old certificate to the transferor the company is not liable to persons who deal with him. Their loss would be attributed to the transferor's fraud rather than the company's negligence.

45. *Forged Transfers*

The effects of a transfer of shares under a document on which the transferor's signature has been forged are as follows:

a. A forged document has no legal effect. Therefore the transferor's name must be restored to the register of members, even if he failed to reply to a letter advising him of the transfer.

b. The company is estopped from denying the title of a subsequent transferee who takes the transfer in good faith and for value. If such a person suffers loss due to the restoration to the register of the true owner the company must pay him compensation.

c. The person who lodged the forged transfer (the original transferee) is liable to indemnify the company for any loss it suffers as a result of having to pay compensation. The original transferee must pay this indemnity even if he was not aware of the forgery. He cannot rely on estoppel.

d. The above points were illustrated in the following case.

In RE BAHIA AND SAN FRANCISCO RAILWAY (1868) the holder of shares deposited the certificate with a broker. The broker forged the owner's signature and transferred them to X. When the certificate and the transfer were sent to the company for registration the secretary wrote to the owner advising of the transfer. The owner did not reply to this letter and X was registered as the new owner. X then transferred the shares to Y who was registered as owner, a new certificate being issued. When the forgery was discovered it was held:

i. That the original owner must be restored to the register;

ii. That the company was estopped from denying the validity of the certificate issued to Y, who was therefore entitled to damages;

iii. X, who lodged the forged transfer, had to indemnify the company for the loss it had incurred by compensating Y. The loss therefore fell on X, the original victim of the fraud.

46. *Restrictions on Transfer*

a. To retain control of private companies the articles usually contain either

i. A pre-emption clause, ie that no shares shall be transferred to an outsider as long as a member can be found to purchase them at a fair price, determined in accordance with the articles, or

ii. A power vested in the directors to refuse to register a transfer.

b. *Pre-emption clauses*

i. A member cannot exercise a pre-emption right in order to purchase the amount of shares that give voting control.

In OCEAN COAL CO v POWELL DUFFRYN STEAM COAL CO (1932) the plaintiff and defendant each held half of the shares of the Taff Merthyr Steam Co. The articles of this company stated that if a member wished to sell his shares to an outsider he must first offer them to other share-holders at the price at which it is proposed to sell to the outsider. The defendant wished to sell 135,000 shares, but the plaintiff only wished to buy 5,000 at the proposed price. It was held that he could not do so. The plaintiff either had to accept or reject the offer to sell the full 135,000 shares.

ii. Where the pre-emption provision is disregarded the directors cannot validly register the transfer since it is in breach of the articles. However, where the transfer is to a person who has paid for the shares, that person will acquire a beneficial (equitable) interest in the shares.

c. *The power to refuse to register transfers*

i. The directors must act bona fide in what they consider to be the best interests of the company.

ii. The directors must act on grounds personal to the transferee. They cannot for example refuse to register transfers merely because small numbers of shares are involved.

iii. The power to refuse must be exercised within a reasonable time. *S.183* provides that the company must give notice of refusal within two months. This statutory period now effectively determines what is a reasonable time.

The *Company Law Reforms 2005* proposals will require directors to provide information about reasons for refusing to register a share transfer.

CHAPTER 42

Loan Capital

1. *Borrowing by Companies*

a. *Power to borrow*

Trading companies have an implied power to borrow and give security. Although this power existed prior to the 1989 Act it has, in effect, been enacted by *S.110 CA 89 (S.3A CA 85)* which states that it will be sufficient for the memorandum to state that the object of the company is to carry on business as a general commercial company. The Act states that this will allow the company to do all such things as are incidental or conducive to carrying on any trade or business, clearly this will include borrowing. Non-trading companies still require an express power to borrow in the memorandum.

Private companies may borrow as soon as they are incorporated, but public companies must first obtain a certificate of compliance with the capital requirements of public companies *(S.117)*.

b. *Ultra vires borrowing*

Borrowing in excess of a limit stated in the memorandum, or borrowing for an ultra vires purpose, is itself ultra vires. However, *S.35(1)* has abolished the ultra vires rule in respect of outsiders by providing that the validity of an act done by the company shall not be called into question on the ground of lack of capacity by reason of anything in the company's memorandum. Consequently both the lender and the company will be able to enforce the contract, and the lender will have the full range of remedies available in the event of the company's failure to repay interest or capital.

S.35(2) preserves members' rights to restrain ultra vires acts. Therefore any member may bring proceedings to restrain borrowing which would be beyond the capacity of the company.

c. *Borrowing in excess of authority*

The 1989 Act has also improved the lender's position if borrowing is within the company's powers, but in excess of the authority of the person negotiating the loan on behalf of the company. *S.108 CA 89 (S.35A CA 85)* provides that in favour of a person dealing with a company in good faith, the power of the board of directors to bind the company or authorise others to do so, shall be deemed to be free of any limitation under the company's constitution. (See Chapter 44.11.)

In the unlikely event of the lender not being protected by the above provision, it would still be possible for the loan to be ratified by the company passing an ordinary resolution.

2. *The Nature of Debentures*

   a.   Strictly speaking a debenture is a document by which a company acknowledges its indebtedness under a loan, although the term is also used to describe the loan itself.

   b.   Debentures usually give a fixed or floating charge over the company's assets (or both) as security, although debentures may be unsecured.

       However, the Stock Exchange will not allow an issue of unsecured or 'naked' debentures to be listed as 'debentures'. The listing must indicate that they are unsecured, for example 'unsecured loan stock'.

   c.   A debenture may be an individual debenture evidencing a large sum lent by one person, or the company may create one loan fund known as 'debenture stock'. This is issued to create a class of debentureholders each of whom is given a debenture stock certificate evidencing the proportion of the total to which he is entitled. Whether the debenture is of the first or second type the basic rights of the holder against the company are contractual.

   d.   Not every type of company indebtedness can be described as a debenture, the loan must have some permanence although the precise extent is uncertain.

3. *Differences between Shares and Debentures*

   a.   A shareholder owns a bundle of rights in the company, for example the right to vote, attend meetings and receive a dividend (if declared). A debentureholder is a person who has lent money to the company. Debentureholders have a *claim against* the company rather than an *interest in* it. Shares (especially ordinary shares) carry a greater degree of risk than debentures, and ordinary shareholders may get a variable return on their investment. If profits are good this will probably exceed the fixed rate of interest paid to debentureholders. Debentures carry less risk, since interest is a contract debt and because debentures will be secured by a fixed and/or a floating charge on the company's assets.

   b.   The other main differences arise from the fact that debentures are not 'capital' in the company law sense. Thus:

       i.   A company's purchase of its own debentures is not subject to restrictions, in contrast to a company's purchase of its own shares;

       ii.   Interest on debentures may be paid out of capital, whereas dividends must be paid out of profits;

       iii.   Shares cannot be issued at a discount, whereas debentures may be issued at a discount, although these debentures cannot be exchanged for fully paid shares of an equal nominal value.

4. *Similarities between Shares and Debentures*

   a.   The typical debenture is one of a series or 'class' similar to a class of shares.

   b.   Debentures are transferable, the same form being used as for a transfer of shares.

c.   Debentures may be quoted on the Stock Exchange, and when debentures are issued to the public the same rules must be complied with.

d.   In theory it may appear that a debentureholder is only dependent on the prosperity of the company to the same extent as any other creditor. In practice this is not the case. Since the security is generally a floating charge the debentureholder will be as concerned about the success of the company as the shareholder, because if the company is unprofitable the security is placed in jeopardy.

e.   Usually a debenture is regarded as a more secure form of investment than a share. In times of high inflation this is not necessarily true. When the purchasing power of money is declining a debenture giving a fixed rate of interest and right to the future return of only the nominal value of the money advanced may well be an inadequate security. In contrast an ordinary share in a 'good' company may provide a better hedge against inflation since the nominal value of the assets is likely to appreciate as the value of money falls.

f.   *Conclusion*. In practice debentures are not regarded as differing significantly from shares. Potential investors are not really concerned with the choice of whether to be a member or creditor of a company.

They will be concerned with the potential for capital appreciation, the yield and the degree of risk. They will then make their basic choice between '*prior charges*' (ie debentures and preference shares) and '*equities*' (ie ordinary shares). From the company's point of view taxation considerations may be crucial, since debenture interest appears in the profit and loss account as an expense of running the business and therefore reduces the net profit of the company upon which corporation tax is assessed. In contrast dividends on shares are appropriations of profit after tax.

5. *Forms of Security*

a.   A *fixed charge* is a mortgage of freehold or leasehold land or fixed plant and machinery, although a fixed charge may be granted over other assets, eg book debts or uncalled capital. It prevents the company selling the assets charged without the consent of the debentureholders.

b.   A *floating charge* is an equitable charge which has the following characteristics:

   i.   It is a charge on some or all of the present and future assets of the company;

   ii.   That class is one which in the ordinary course of business changes from time to time;

   iii.   The charge envisages that, until some future step is taken by or on behalf of the charge holder, the company may carry on its business in the ordinary way.

c. A floating charge will '*crystallise*', ie convert to a fixed charge, when:

    i. The company defaults *and* the debentureholders take steps to enforce their security either by appointing a receiver or applying to the court to do so.

    ii. If winding-up commences.

    iii. If the company ceases business.

    iv. If an event occurs for which the charge deed provides for automatic crystallisation.

d. Advantages of floating charges (from the company's point of view):

    i. It can charge property which is unsuitable for a fixed charge.

    This is particularly useful if it has no fixed assets, but carries a large stock-in-trade; and

    ii. It can deal with the assets charged.

e. Disadvantages of floating charges (from the lender's point of view):

    i. Its value is uncertain since the value of the assets subject to the charge will fluctuate;

    ii. Where a seller of goods 'reserves title' until payment, a floating charge will not, on crystallisation, attach to those goods (see paragraph 6 below);

    iii. The charge may be avoided under *S.245 IA* (see paragraph 9 below);

    iv. If a creditor has levied and completed execution the debentureholders cannot compel him to restore the money, and prior to crystallisation he cannot be prevented from levying execution.

    v. The statutory preferential creditors must be paid out of assets subject to a floating charge unless there are other uncharged assets available for this purpose.

6. *Reservation of Title*

a. '*Simple*' *reservation of title clauses. S.17* SALE OF GOODS ACT *1979* provides the basic rule that in a contract for the sale of specific goods property passes when the parties intend it to pass. Consequently the parties can agree that the property will not pass until the goods are paid for. (In the absence of such agreement property will usually pass when the contract is made – *S.18 Rule 1 SGA 1979.*)

In ALUMINIUM INDUSTRIE VAASSEN V ROMALPA (**1976**) the following clause was the main provision in a detailed reservation of title clause.

'The ownership of the material to be delivered by AIV will only be transferred to the purchaser when he has met all that is owing to AIV no matter on what grounds'

Romalpa went into liquidation and AIV sought to enforce the above clause by recovering a quantity of aluminium. It was held that they could do so, own-ership had not passed to Romalpa, they were merely the bailee of AIV's goods.

b. *'Extended' clauses covering processed goods.* A reservation of title clause will not apply to goods which are subjected to a process under which they become a new product. The new product will be owned by the buyer, but subject to a charge created in favour of the seller by the reservation of title clause. Such a charge is not valid unless registered.

In BORDEN v SCOTTISH TIMBER PRODUCTS (**1981**) resin was sold on reservation of title terms. Both parties knew that the resin would soon be used to manufacture chipboard. It was held that the resin ceased to exist and the suppliers title was extinguished when the resin was made into chipboard, because this was a wholly new product.

c. *'Extended' clauses covering proceeds of sub-sales.* The situation becomes more complicated if the clause is extended to cover the proceeds of sale of goods subject to reservation of title clauses. Such an extension will be effective if it is drafted with sufficient care. The clause must make it clear that the buyer is made the agent of the seller when re-selling the goods and that he holds the proceeds as trustee for the seller. The position of the seller will be even stronger if the contract requires the buyer to store the goods in such a way as they are clearly the property of the seller and keep any sale proceeds in a separate account.

7. *Registration of Charges*

a. Since most companies obtain much of their finance from debentures secured by charges, it is important that people dealing with the company are able to find out which assets are subject to charges.

b. By *S.398* almost all charges created by a company must be registered within 21 days of creation. The particulars to be delivered include:

   i. The date of creation of the charge, or of the acquisition of the property subject to the charge.

   ii. The amount secured.

   iii. Short particulars of the property charged.

   iv. The persons entitled to the charge.

c. In general the 1989 Act abolished the doctrine of constructive notice (for example in connection with the memorandum and articles). However, one exception relates to a person taking a charge over a company's property. By *S.103 CA 89 (S.416 CA 85)* such a person shall be taken to have notice of any matter requiring registration and disclosed on the register at the time the charge is created.

d. If a charge is not registered within 21 days the security provided by the charge will only take effect in relation to events occurring after the date of registration. As under the 1985 Act, the company and its officers may be fined for failure to register in time.

e. If a charge is not delivered within the 21 day period, the charge will be void as against purchasers of an interest in, or a right over, property subject to the charge. Such protection is confined to the period before the charge is belatedly registered, ie once registered the charge will be valid as against persons subsequently acquiring an interest in the charged property.

f.   It is the duty of the company to effect registration, but any person interested in the charge may register it. In practice, since the consequences of non-registration affect the lender rather than the company, it is usually the lender's solicitor who deals with registration.

8. *Priority of Charges*

a.   Legal fixed charges rank according to their order of creation.

b.   If an equitable fixed charge is created first and a legal charge over the same property is created later, the legal charge ranks before the equitable charge, unless at the time when the legal charge was created, the person to whom it was given had notice of the existing equitable charge. Notice may be given by registration of the earlier charge.

NB. An equitable fixed charge is an informal mortgage created by depositing the borrower's title deeds or share certificate with the lender.

c.   If a floating charge (always equitable) is created and a fixed charge (legal or equitable) over the same property is created later, the fixed charge will rank first since it attaches to the property at the time of creation, whereas the floating charge attaches at the time of crystallisation. Once a floating charge has crystallised it becomes fixed and any subsequent fixed charge ranks after it. However, a floating charge will have priority over a later created fixed charge provided the floating charge prohibits the creation of later fixed charges with priority (known as a 'negative pledge' clause).

d.   If two floating charges are created over the general assets of the company they rank in order of creation. However, if a company creates a floating charge over a particular kind of asset, eg book debts, that will rank before an existing floating charge over the general assets.

9. *Avoidance of Floating Charges (S.245 IA)*

a.   It would be unjust to allow an unsecured creditor to obtain priority over other creditors by obtaining a floating charge when he realises that liquidation is likely. This applies in particular to directors who may have attempted to keep the company alive by making unsecured loans to it. When they realise their attempt has failed they may well wish to cause the company to execute a floating charge in their favour.

b.   By *S.245 1A* a floating charge may be invalidated if created in certain periods before either the commencement of liquidation or the presentation of a petition for an administration order. The periods are:

   i.   two years, if the charge is in favour of a connected person, for example a director or a relative, employee or business partner of a director.

   ii. one year, if the charge is in favour of any other person (but only if the company was insolvent at the time the charge was created, or became insolvent as a result of the transaction under which the charge was created).

    iii. At any time between the presentation of a petition for an administration order and the making of that order.

  c. *S.245* does not invalidate charges to secure money paid to the company at the time of, or subsequent to the creation of the charge, and in consideration for the charge.

10. *Transactions at an Undervalue and Preferences (S.238–241 IA)*

  a. A charge may also be avoided if it is a transaction at an undervalue or a preference.

  b. A *transaction at an undervalue* occurs when the company makes a gift, or enters into a transaction for no consideration, or for a consideration worth significantly less than the value of the benefit received by the company. However, transactions made in good faith, for the purpose of the business and in the reasonable belief that the company would benefit will not be invalid.

  c. A *preference* is any act that has the effect of putting one of the company's creditors in a better position in the event of the company going into insolvent liquidation. However, the court may not make an order unless it is satisfied that the company was influenced by a *desire* to put the creditor in a better position than he otherwise would have been.

  d. A transaction may only be invalidated if the company was insolvent at the time (or if it became unable to pay its debts as a result of the transaction). The transaction must also fall within the following periods either before liquidation or the presentation of a petition for an administration order:

    i. six months, where the transaction is a preference (not at an undervalue);

    ii. two years, where the transaction is a preference (not at an undervalue), given to a connected person;

    iii. two years, where the transaction is at an undervalue. (If the transaction was with a connected person the company is assumed to be insolvent unless proved to the contrary);

    iv. At any time between the presentation of a petition for an administration order and the making of that order.

  e. The court has power to make any order it thinks fit, for example that:

    i. Property transferred be returned to the company;

    ii. Security given by the company be discharged;

    iii. That any person pay to the liquidator or administrator such sum as the court directs in return for the benefit received.

  f. An important first case of the construction and application of *S.239 IA* (on preferences) occurred in 1990.

    In RE M.C. BACON (**1990**) the company got into difficulties following the sudden withdrawal of its main trading client. At the time its overdraft was unsecured, but when the bank became aware of the situation it required a debenture as a condition of the continued overdraft facility. Eight months after the start of the crisis and three months after the security was given, the company went into liquidation with a deficiency of approximately £330,000 as regards unsecured creditors and an overdraft of £235,500.

The Judge found in favour of the bank (ie the security was not regarded as a preference) because the decision to grant the security was not influenced by a desire on the part of the directors to improve the bank's position in the event of liquidation, but by a need to avoid the calling in of the overdraft, so that the company could continue trading.

The decision will be welcomed by companies and lenders since it enables a lender to nurse a company through economic difficulties without the risk that its security will be subsequently rendered voidable. Without such a decision many otherwise viable companies would find it almost impossible to obtain the necessary funds to enable them to overcome a temporary crisis.

11. *Company's Register of Charges*

    a.   In addition to registration at the Companies Registry, *S.411* requires all charges given by a company to be recorded in the company's own register of charges. The register must contain:

        i.   A short description of the property charged;

        ii.   The amount of the charge; and

        iii.   The names of the persons entitled to the charge.

    b.   Failure to register does not affect the validity of the charge, but officers of the company who knew of the omission are liable to a fine.

12. *Trustees for Debentureholders*

    a.   When debentures are issued to the public the company will enter into a trust deed with trustees (usually a trust corporation). The trustees are appointed and paid by the company to act on behalf of the debentureholders. Any charge is in favour of the trustees who hold it on trust for the debentureholders.

    b.   There are two main advantages of trustees:

        i.   It enables the security to be a legal mortgage of the company's land (unlike an equitable mortgagee the rights of a legal mortgagee will not be defeated by a transfer of mortgaged property to a bona fide purchaser for value). This would not be possible without trustees since under the LAW OF PROPERTY ACT 1925 a legal estate in land cannot be vested in more than four persons; and

        ii.   The trustees are available to exercise continuous supervision of the debentureholders' rights and take the necessary action if the company defaults.

c. The contents of the trust deed will depend on a number of factors. For example it will:

    i. Grant to the trustees a fixed charge over land and a floating charge over the rest of the assets;

    ii. Provide for the repayment of the principal sum borrowed plus interest;

    iii. Contain covenants by the company to insure and repair the property charged;

    iv. Specify the events in which the security becomes enforceable, and define the trustees' power to take possession of the property charged or appoint a receiver;

    v. Define the powers exercisable by the company only with the trustees' consent, for example leasing charged property;

    vi. Provide for meetings of debentureholders; and

    vii. Provide for the remuneration of the trustees.

13. *Remedies of Debentureholders*

The remedies of debentureholders are generally conferred by the trust deed. For example it may grant the power to appoint a receiver to sell charged property. In addition the debentureholders may:

a. Sue as creditors for arrears of interest;

b. Petition to wind up the company on the ground that it is unable to pay its debts; and

c. Apply to the court for the appointment of a receiver or for an order for sale if there is no power in the trust deed.

The usual first step is for the debentureholders or their trustees to secure the appointment of a receiver.

CHAPTER 43

Membership and Minority Protection

METHODS OF BECOMING A MEMBER

1. *The Basic Rule*

   A person becomes a member when:

   a.   He indicates that he has *agreed* to become a member; and

   b.   When his name is entered on the *Register of Members*.

2. *Methods of Indicating Agreement*

   a.   *Subscription to the memorandum.* By *S.22* the subscribers are deemed to have agreed to become members, and on registration must be entered on the register.

   b.   *Application and allotment.* Like subscribers, persons who have been allotted shares take them direct from the company.

   c.   *Transfer.* Here the member acquires his shares from an existing member, usually by purchasing them.

   d.   *Transmission.* This is a transfer which occurs when a member dies or becomes bankrupt.

   e.   *Estoppel.* If a person's name is entered on the register in error, or is not deleted when he transfers his shares, the person may be estopped from denying that he is a member if he knows of the error, but fails to take steps to rectify the register.

CAPACITY

3. *Minors*

   A person under the age of 18 may be a member, however:

   a.   If the company knows that a person is a minor it has the power to refuse to accept him as a member.

b. Where a minor is inadvertently registered as a member, the company, provided it acts promptly, can apply to the court to have the transfer set aside and the transferor restored to the register.

c. A minor who has been registered as a member may repudiate his membership before or within a reasonable time after reaching 18.

4. *Personal Representatives*

a. On a member's death his shares vest in his personal representative who may require registration of himself as a member. If a personal representative is registered as a member he is entitled to vote and is personally liable for calls, although he may claim an indemnity out of the deceased's assets.

b. A personal representative is not obliged to become a member since *S.183(3)* provides that he may make a valid transfer of the deceased's shares without becoming a member. If a personal representative does not register he is nevertheless entitled to all the benefits attaching to shares, such as bonuses and dividends, but the articles usually provide that he may not vote at meetings.

5. *Trustees in Bankruptcy*

The position of a trustee in bankruptcy is similar to that of a personal representative in that he can transfer the shares without being registered as a member, or he can require registration. If he does not register, the bankrupt must vote as the trustee directs.

6. *Trustees and Beneficiaries*

Shares may be held under a trust, and the trustee will be entered on the register of members. However, *S.360* states that no notice of a trust shall be entered on the register of members. The purpose of *S.360* is to avoid the involvement of the company in disputes where there are several equitable interests in one piece of property, and to relieve the company from liability to beneficiaries if a fraudulent trustee transfers the shares in breach of trust.

7. *Companies*

A company may be a member of another company, but by *S.23* a company cannot be a member of its own holding company.

THE REGISTER OF MEMBERS

8. *Contents of the Register*

a. By *S.352* every company must keep a register of members which must contain the following particulars:

i. The name and address of each member;

    ii.   A statement of the shares held by each member, with distinguishing numbers (if any). Where the company has more than one class of issued shares they must be distinguished by class;

    iii. The amount paid up on each share;

    iv. The date of entry on the register; and

    v.   The date of cessation of membership.

  b. If the number of members falls to one a statement to that effect must be entered in the register, together with the date of the occurence.

  c. By *S.361* the register is prima facie evidence of the matters it contains.

9. *Location of the Register*

S.353 requires the register to be kept at the registered office, unless it is made up at some other place in which case it can be kept at that other place. The registrar must be informed of where the register is kept and of any change in that place.

10. *Inspection of the Register*

By *S.356* members may inspect the register free of charge. Non-members may inspect the register on payment of a small fee. Any person may require a copy of the register. The fee is currently 10 pence per 100 words and the copy must be supplied within 10 days.

MAJORITY RULE

11. *The Rule in Foss v Harbottle (1843)*

  a. Where a wrong is done to a company, or there is an irregularity in the management of a company, and there arises a need to enforce the rights of the company, it is for the company to decide what action to take and it is the company which is the proper plaintiff in the action. For example:

In PAVLIDES v JENSEN (**1956**) the directors sold an asset of the company to a third party at a gross undervaluation. A minority shareholder commenced an action. It was held that he could not do so, it was up to the company to decide whether to sue the directors for negligence. Alternatively the company could decide to exonerate them.

  b. The reasons for the rule are:

    i.   It is the logical consequence of the fact that a company is a separate legal person. It is the company that has suffered a wrong, therefore it is the company which seeks a remedy.

    ii. It preserves the principle of majority rule.

    iii. It prevents multiple actions. If each shareholder were permitted to sue, the company might be subjected to many lawsuits started by numerous plaintiffs.

iv. It prevents futile actions. If the irregularity is one which can effectively be ratified by the company in general meeting, it would be futile to have litigation about it without the consent of the general meeting.

12. *Controlling Members' Duties*

The position of the controlling members (ie those possessing sufficient voting power to pass the appropriate resolutions at general meetings) is quite different from that of directors, since it is only directors who owe fiduciary duties to the company. In contrast shares are proprietary rights which members may exercise in their own self-interest, even to the detriment of the company. Thus directors who hold a majority of the shares may, in some cases, be able to disregard their fiduciary duties and duties of care and skill, provided they disclose what they propose to do and then pass a resolution allowing the action. Such a resolution may, for example:

a. Ratify directors' acts in excess of the powers conferred on them.

b. Resolve not to sue where a director has broken his duty of care and skill.

c. Allow a director to retain a secret profit provided:

i. The profit was not made at the expense of the minority; and

ii. The director acted in good faith and in the interest of the company.

MINORITY PROTECTION AT COMMON LAW

13. *Exceptions to the Rule in Foss v Harbottle*

The rule in Foss v Harbottle places the majority in such a strong position that minority shareholders would be at a serious disadvantage if the following exceptions were not allowed:

a. Where the company does an illegal or ultra vires act. However:

i. By *S.35(2)* if a company is required to carry out an ultra vires act in pursuance of an illegal obligation arising from a previous act of the company, the members cannot restrain the act.

ii. By *S.35(3)* a company may ratify an ultra vires act by special resolution.

b. Where the company acts on a resolution which has not been properly passed.

In BAILLE V ORIENTAL TELEPHONE CO (**1915**) a company was successfully restrained from acting on a special resolution of which inadequate notice had been given.

This exception has been severely curtailed by *S.35A* which provides that in favour of a person dealing with a company in good faith, the power of the board of directors to bind the company, shall be deemed to be free of any limitation under the company's constitution. 'Constitution' includes any resolution of the company and any agreement between the members, as well as the constitutional documents.

c. Where the individual rights of the plaintiff as a shareholder have been infringed, for example shareholder's right to vote.

d. Where the majority is committing a fraud on the minority. The word 'fraud' in this context does not mean deceit in the criminal sense as the following examples show:

i. *Expropriation of the company's property.*

In COOK v DEEKS (1916) the directors, whilst negotiating a contract on behalf of the company, took the contract in their own names. Then at a general meeting they used their votes to pass a resolution declaring that the company had no interest in the contract. It was held that the resolution was a fraud on the minority and was ineffective.

ii. *Expropriation of other members' property.*

In DAFEN TINPLATE v LLANELLY STEEL (1920) P was a member of D and used to purchase steel from them. When P started to purchase steel elsewhere a new article was inserted which conferred on the majority an unrestricted power to buy out any shareholders they might think proper. It was held that this power of expulsion went further than was necessary to protect the company's interests.

iii. *An issue of shares designed to harm the minority.*

In CLEMENS v CLEMENS LTD (1976) the plaintiff held 45% of the issued shares and her aunt, who was one of the directors of the company held 55%. The aunt's shares were used at a general meeting to pass resolutions to issue further shares to directors and to trustees of an employees' share ownership scheme. The resolutions were carefully designed to reduce the plaintiff's holding from 45% to about 24.5%. This deprived her of her power to block a special or extraordinary resolution. It also reduced the value of her rights under a pre-emption clause in the articles (a clause entitling her to first refusal if another member wished to sell shares). The court set aside the resolutions on the ground that they were oppressive to the plaintiff, since they were specifically designed (i) to ensure that she could never get control of the company and (ii) to remove her negative control.

iv. *A reduction of capital designed to harm a class of shareholders.*

In RE HOLDERS INVESTMENT TRUST (1971) a capital reduction scheme was not confirmed by the court because a resolution of the preference shareholders was only passed because trustees, who held a substantial number of ordinary shares, voted in favour of the scheme because it would be advantageous to their beneficiaries due to their larger holding of ordinary shares. It was held that the resolution had not been effectively passed because the majority had not considered what was best for the class of preference shareholders as a whole.

v. *A negligent act which benefits the majority at the expense of the company.*

In DANIELS v DANIELS (**1978**) the controlling directors and shareholders (Mr and Mrs Daniels) caused the company to sell a piece of land to Mrs Daniels at an undervalue. The plaintiff, a minority shareholder, did not allege fraud because he did not know all that had happened. His action was nevertheless successful and Mrs Daniels had to account for the profit. The strongest case against the plaintiff was PAVLIDES v JENSEN (**1956**), but this case was distinguished because the directors had not there benefited from their breach of duty since the sale had been to a third party.

14. *Personal, Derivative and Representative Actions*

a. *Personal actions.* Such an action can be brought when a person has been deprived of his individual rights as a shareholder.

b. *Derivative actions.* Where there is a dispute between the company and third parties (whether they are its directors or its controlling shareholders) and any person other than the company is allowed to appear as plaintiff on behalf of the company, then the action is called a *derivative action*. In such cases the right to sue is derived from the company since it is the company which has suffered as a result of the action of the majority. Where an action is successful the damages awarded belong to the company. Usually a derivative action is only appropriate where the wrongdoers have voting control and therefore prevent the company from making a claim.

c. *Representative actions.* Where individual shareholders have suffered personal loss in addition to the injury to the company one shareholder may bring a *representative action* on behalf of himself and all the other shareholders who have suffered similar injury. If a representative action is successful the plaintiff will obtain a declaration that the improper conduct has been proved. Each injured party may then claim damages without further need to prove improper conduct.

S.459–461 UNFAIR PREJUDICE

15. *Basic Rule*

a. By *S.459 a member* may petition the court for an order on the ground that the affairs of the company are being or have been conducted in a manner which is *unfairly prejudicial* to the interests of its members generally or some part of the members (including at least himself) or that any proposed act or omission of the company is or would be so prejudicial.

b. The reference to '*members generally*' was added by *CA 89*. This had the effect of overruling a much criticised 1987 case where it was held that failure to declare dividends would not be sufficient grounds for a petition. The judge's reasoning was that failure to declare a dividend was not directed against 'some part' of the members (as apparently previously required) since it affected all members.

c. Petitions under *S.459* have been successful in the following situations:

   i.   Where directors of a private company made incorrect statements to their shareholders regarding acceptance of an offer for their shares made by another company owned by the directors.

   ii. Where the majority made a rights issue with a view to altering the voting balance, because they knew that the minority shareholder could not afford to exercise his right to purchase.

   iii. Where the majority made a rights issue with a view to depleting the funds of a shareholder engaged in litigation with the company or with the majority shareholders.

   iv. Where the majority acted contrary to a person's 'legitimate expectation' to take part in the long-term management of a quasi-partnership company.

   In RE A COMPANY (No. 00477 of 1986) the petitioners (directors of A Ltd) sold their shares in A Ltd to O plc, relying on promises that O plc would develop A Ltd's business and that A Ltd's managing director (S) would be a director of O plc. In fact O plc sold A Ltd's assets to support its own business. S was also replaced as managing director of A Ltd and asked to resign from the board of O plc. The petitioners were successful and obtained an order that their shares be purchased at a price equivalent to the value of their shares in A Ltd at the date of the sale.

16. *The Powers of the Court*

The court may make any order it thinks fit. Thus it can

a. Regulate the future conduct of the company's affairs.

   In RE HARMER (**1959**) a successful family company was controlled by Mr H. He and his wife (who always voted with him) could control both ordinary and special resolutions at general meetings. The directors were Mr and Mrs H and their two sons. Mr H was the chairman and had a casting vote. The two sons brought an action under *S.210CA 1948* (similar, but narrower, previous legislation) on the ground that their father repeatedly abused his controlling power, particularly with respect to the appointment and dismissal of staff, and the opening of a branch in Australia. (This was opposed by the sons and proved to be an unsuccessful venture.) Mr H was generally intolerant of views contrary to his own, whether held by his sons or other shareholders. At the time of the hearing Mr H was 89 years old.

   The court granted an order that removed Mr H from the board and made him 'president' of the company for life at a salary of £2,500 per year. This post gave him no rights, and imposed no duties on him. It was directed that he should not interfere with the affairs of the company except in accordance with the decisions of the board.

b. Require the company to do or refrain from doing any act. Thus the court may require the company not to make any alteration either to its memorandum or articles, or to make a specific alteration.

c. Authorise civil proceedings to be brought in the name of, and on behalf of, the company by such persons and on such terms as it directs. This is important because if the court authorise proceedings a minority shareholder can sue a director on behalf of the company even if he cannot bring his claim within one of the exceptions to the rule in Foss v Harbottle.

d. Provide for the purchase of the shares of any member by other members or by the company.

In RE BIRD PRECISION BELLOWS (**1984**) the petitioners held 26% of the shares in a small 'quasi partnership' company. They suspected that the managing director was concealing bribes paid to secure contracts. After an unsuccessful attempt to secure the appointment of DTI inspectors the petitioners were removed from the board by the votes of the managing director, his wife and one other shareholder. The petitioners alleged unfair prejudice in that they had been wrongfully excluded from the company's affairs and they sought an order that the majority purchase their shares. It was held that exclusion from participation in the affairs of a 'quasi partnership' company was unfairly prejudicial and that in such companies a fair price for the purchase of the minority's shares should be calculated on a pro rata basis, not discounted because it was a minority shareholding.

17. *S.459 and Foss v Harbottle*

a. The rule in Foss v Harbottle and its exceptions have created several problems, in particular

   i. The extent of the 'fraud on the minority' exception; and

   ii. The procedural problems of personal, representative and derivative actions.

b. *S.459–461* has undoubtedly helped in both cases:

   i. It has the potential to supersede the concept of 'fraud on the minority' and replace it with the more flexible concept of fairness; and

   ii. It provides a simpler procedure than the common law since the court can give authority for legal proceedings in the company's name. It is likely that a dissatisfied minority shareholder would proceed in this way rather than attempt to sue under the common law rules.

c. *S.459–461* provide a practical and flexible remedy. They may be used, for example, to curtail excessive directors' remuneration, or to request an order that a dividend be declared. *S.459* also provides a remedy for an individual member. There is no minimum percentage of shares which must be held, nor minimum number of members who must join in the action. The conduct must, however, be unfairly prejudicial to members in their *capacity as members* and not, for example in their capacity as directors, creditors or employees.

CHAPTER 44

Directors and the Secretary

APPOINTMENTS AND REMOVAL OF DIRECTORS

1. *Position of Directors*

a. Directors are the persons to whom management of a company is entrusted. Together with the managers and the secretary they are the 'officers' of the company. It is not necessary that a natural person be appointed, a director may be another company. A person who acts as a director, eg by attending board meetings and taking part in board decisions will be a director even if he is called by another name such as 'governor' or 'trustee'.

b. The position of a director is similar to that of an agent in that he can bind his principal (ie the company) by his acts without incurring personal liability.

c. Directors have also been compared to trustees because they owe fiduciary duties to the company. However, they are not true trustees because the legal title to the company's property is vested in the company and not in the directors.

d. Directors are not servants of the company unless they have a separate contract of service with the company.

2. *Number of Directors*

a. By S.282 every public company must have at least two directors and every private company must have at least one. However, Table A provides that for all companies the number of directors shall not be less than two (unless otherwise decided by ordinary resolution).

Company Law Reform Proposals 2005 call for all plcs to have at least two directors, at least one director being a natural person. Also restrictions on people aged 70 or over being directors of public companies is to be abolished.

b. By S.283 every company must have a secretary, but a sole director cannot also be the secretary.

3. *Methods of Appointment*

a. *First directors*. By S.10 a statement of the first directors and secretary must be delivered with the application to register the company. The statement must contain their signed consent to act in the relevant capacity. These persons are, on the company's incorporation, deemed to have been appointed as its first directors and secretary.

b. *Subsequent directors*

    i. The usual method of appointment is by the company in general meeting, ie by *ordinary resolution*. Retiring directors are eligible for re-election and, if Table A is adopted, a retiring director who offers himself for re-election will be automatically elected unless a resolution not to fill the vacancy is passed or a resolution for his re-election is lost.

    ii. By *S.292* two or more directors of a *public company* cannot be appointed by a single resolution unless a previous resolution authorising this has been passed without dissent. This means that directors must be elected on their individual merits.

c. *Casual vacancies*

    i. A casual vacancy is one that occurs between general meetings, for example because of the death or resignation of a director.

    ii. Table A empowers the board to fill casual vacancies, and also to appoint additional directors up to the maximum specified in the company's articles.

    iii. A person appointed by the board holds office until the next AGM. He will then be eligible for re-election. His appointment will not be taken into account for determining who shall retire by rotation (see 5 below).

4. *Persons Who May Not be Appointed*

a. *Undischarged bankrupts.* By *S.11* COMPANY DIRECTORS DISQUALIFICATION ACT 1986 an undischarged bankrupt commits a criminal offence if he acts as a director without the permission of the court.

b. *Persons disqualified by the court* under *S.2–4* COMPANY DIRECTORS DISQUALIFICATION ACT 1986. Where a disqualification order is made the person concerned may not (without permission of the court) act as a liquidator, director, administrator, receiver or manager, nor may he take part in the promotion, formation or management of a company. A court of summary jurisdiction may make a disqualification order of up to five years, other courts up to 15 years. A disqualification order may be made in the following circumstances:

    i. Where a person is convicted of an indictable offence in connection with the promotion, formation, management, or liquidation or receivership of a company. (The maximum period for disqualification is 15 years.)

    ii. Where a person has been persistently in default in relation to filing documents with the registrar. (Maximum period five years.)

    iii. Where, in the course of a winding up, it appears that a person has been guilty of fraudulent trading *(S.458)* or, while an officer, liquidator, receiver or manager of a company, has been guilty of fraud or breach of duty to the company. (Maximum period fifteen years.)

c. *A person disqualified by the court* under *S.6–9* COMPANY DIRECTORS DISQUALIFICATION ACT 1986, because his conduct as a director, either considered in isolation or taken together with his conduct as a director of any other company, makes him unfit to be concerned with the management of a company. These sections are considered in more detail in paragraphs 33–34.

5. *Vacation of Office*

The office of director may be vacated by:

a. *Death of the director.*

b. *Dissolution of the company.*

c. *Retirement by rotation.* Table A states that at each AGM one third of the directors shall retire. Those to retire are those who have been longest in office. Retiring directors are eligible for relection.

d. *Retirement under an age limit.* By *S.293* a director of a public company or the subsidiary of a public company must retire at the first AGM after reaching the age of 70. *S.293* may, however, be excluded by the articles.

Company Law Reform Proposals 2005 will remove the over 70 restriction.

e. *Removal*

   i. By *S.303* despite anything in the articles or any agreement between the company and the director, a company can remove a director by *ordinary resolution.*

   ii. *Special notice* must be given of any resolution to remove a director.

   iii. On receipt of this notice the company must send a copy to the director. He may then make written representations to the company which must be sent to the members with notice of the meeting unless they are an attempt to gain needless publicity for defamatory matter. If the company receives the representations too late to send out with notice of the meeting the director may demand that his statement be read out at the meeting. In any case he may speak on the resolution at the meeting *(S.304)*.

   iv. Removal under *S.303* does not deprive the director of his right to damages for loss of appointment as managing director should such post be automatically terminated, see SOUTHERN FOUNDRIES v SHIRLAW (**1940**) (Chapter 40.28). A director will not, or course, be entitled to damages if he was removed as a result of his own breach of duty or breach of contract.

   v. *S.303* does not prevent the company from attaching weighted voting rights to a director's shares on a resolution for his removal.

   In BUSHELL v FAITH (**1970**) a company had an issued capital of 300 fully paid shares divided equally between F and his two sisters. The company's articles contained a provision that if a resolution were proposed to remove a director the shares held by that director would carry three votes each. The sisters wanted to remove F from his post as director, but he invoked the above article. The sisters disputed its validity. The House of Lords held that the article was not inconsistent with the terms of the Act and was therefore valid, although Lord Morris dissented on the grounds that the article made 'a mockery' of *S.303*.

vi. The removal of a director of a 'quasi-partnership' company may be so unfair that the court will grant a petition to wind the company up on the 'just and equitable' ground – *S.517(1)(g)*, RE WESTBOURNE GALLERIES (**1973**). (See Chapter 48.5.).

f. *Disqualification*. Table A provides that a director shall vacate office in the following circumstances:

i. If he ceases to be a director by virtue of a provision of the Act, eg *S.293* (age limits) or if he becomes prohibited by law from being a director;

ii. If he becomes bankrupt or makes a composition arrangement with his creditors;

iii. If he becomes of unsound mind;

iv. If he resigns by notice in writing; or

v. If he is absent from board meetings for more than six months without permission.

6. *Directors' Remuneration*

Since directors are not servants of the company they are not entitled as of right to remuneration. Table A empowers the company in general meeting to fix directors' remuneration. Directors cannot therefore vote remuneration to themselves, but if they appoint one of their number as managing director his remuneration may be fixed by the board. Once fixed, remuneration is a debt and must be paid out of capital if there are no profits.

POWERS OF DIRECTORS

7. *Relationship between the Board and the Company*

a. The extent of directors' powers is defined by the articles. Table A provides that 'The business of the company shall be managed by the directors who may...exercise all the powers of the company'. Also 'No alteration of the memorandum or articles and no such direction shall invalidate any prior act of the directors'.

b. Thus if the shareholders do not approve of the directors' acts they must either remove them under *S.303* or alter the articles to regulate their future conduct. (The alteration cannot have a retrospective effect.) They cannot simply take over the functions of the directors. For example:

In SCOTT v SCOTT (**1943**) the company in general meeting resolved, firstly to pay dividends to preference shareholders, and secondly that the financial affairs of the company be investigated by a firm of accountants. It was held that the resolutions were invalid as they usurped the powers which the articles had vested in the directors.

However, new wording in Table A, introduced in 1985, does make the directors' powers 'subject...to any direction given by special resolution'.

c. If directors exceed their powers, or exercise them improperly, their acts can be ratified by an *ordinary resolution* of the company.

In BAMFORD v BAMFORD (1970) in order to prevent a takeover bid the directors allotted 5,000 shares to another company. The articles provided that all unissued shares were to be at the disposal of the directors. Two shareholders sought a declaration that the allotment was void because it was not made bona fide for the benefit of the company. Soon afterwards an ordinary resolution approving the allotment was passed at a general meeting. Proceeding on the assumption that the directors had not acted for the benefit of the company, and had therefore acted improperly, the court had to decide whether the ordinary resolution had cured the irregularity. It was held that it had, and the allotment was valid.

8. Board Meetings

a. Subject to the provisions of the articles the powers conferred on the directors are conferred on them collectively as a board. Prima facie therefore their powers can only be exercised at a properly constituted board meeting. However, Table A provides that a resolution in writing signed by all the directors will be valid.

b. *Notice.* A board meeting may be summoned by a director at any time and directors must be given a reasonable period of notice. This may be days, hours or even minutes, depending on the circumstances.

c. *Quorum.* The quorum will be fixed by the articles. Table A provides that the quorum shall be fixed by the directors, and if it is not so fixed, shall be two. If a director has an interest in a contract to be considered at the meeting he does not count towards the quorum.

d. *Voting.* This is also governed by the articles. Usually directors have one vote each and a majority decision will prevail. If voting is equal the resolution is lost unless the chairman has a casting vote and exercises it in favour of the resolution.

e. *Delegation.* The board may, of course, appoint agents or servants of the company, but it must not delegate the exercise of its discretion. It is an application of the rule of agency that a person to whom power is delegated must not delegate further without the consent of his principal. This rule is usually modified in two ways:

    i. The directors may delegate any of their power to committees consisting of one or some of the directors; and

    ii. The board may appoint and delegate to a managing director. Today most companies are run by a managing director rather than by the board.

9. *The Managing Director*

a. Table A provides that the directors may appoint one of their number as managing director on such terms as they think fit. He therefore has no settled functions. His powers and duties depend on his service agreement.

In CADDIES v HOLDSWORTH (**1955**) the service agreement of the managing director of a holding company provided that he should perform the duties in relation to the business of the holding company and its subsidiaries as should be assigned to him by the board of the holding company. After policy disagreements the board directed him to confine his attention to the business of one of the subsidiaries. It was held that this was not a breach of his service agreement even though he had been deprived of the power the company which was employing him.

b. It is usual to provide that the managing director is not subject to retirement by rotation, but that his appointment as managing director will automatically end if he ceases for any reason to be a director.

In SOUTHERN FOUNDERS v SHIRLAW (**1940**) (see Chapter 40.28) it was held that a managing director's service contract contained an implied condition that the company would not make it impossible for him to act by removing him as a director. When he was removed damages for breach of contract were therefore payable.

10. *Unauthorised Acts by Directors*

Sometimes a company may wish to avoid a contract on the ground that either:

a. It was made by a person who was not a director (but who acted as such); or

b. It was made by the board, but in excess of the directors' collective authority as a board; or

c. It was made by an individual director without the required delegated authority of the board.

In such cases the outsider will be protected if he can persuade the company to ratify the contract. If the company will not ratify the outsider may be able to rely on *S.35A* or on the rules of agency.

11. *Power of directors to bind the company*

a. *S.35A* provides that in favour of a person dealing with a company in good faith, the power of the board of directors to bind the company, or authorise others to do so, shall be deemed to be free of any limitation under the company's constitution.

b. '*Constitution*' is defined to include any resolution of the company and any agreement between the members as well as the constitutional documents.

c. The Act also makes it clear that even a person dealing with a company with knowledge that the transaction is beyond the directors' powers will be protected. Such knowledge, by itself, does not amount to 'bad faith'. Bad faith will, however, exist if the person dealing with the company assists the directors in the abuse of their powers, or is party to fraud.

d. To prevent the new provisions being used as a vehicle for fraud *S.322A* contains measures invalidating certain transactions where directors have exceeded limitations placed upon their powers to bind the company. These are discussed in paragraph 18 below.

12. *The Rules of Agency*

Under the normal rules of agency where a person without actual authority contracts on behalf of a company, the other party can hold the company bound if he can show:

a. That he was induced to make the contract by the agent being represented as occupying a certain position in the company;

b. That the representation was made by persons with actual authority to manage the company; and

c. That the contract was one which a person in the position which the agent was held out as occupying would usually have authority to make.

In FREEMAN & LOCKYER V BUCKHURST PARK PROPERTIES (1964) a director who had never been appointed managing director assumed powers of management with the company's approval. He entered into a contract with the plaintiffs, who were architects. The company denied liability to pay the plaintiffs' fees, but were held bound to the contract because the act of engaging architects was within the scope of the authority of a managing director of a property company and the plaintiffs were not obliged to enquire whether the person was properly appointed. It was sufficient that under the articles there was a power to appoint a managing director, and that the board of directors had allowed him to act as such.

d. *S.35A* removes the need to rely on the rules of agency in almost all cases, for example Freeman's case, since the Act refers to the 'power of the Board of Directors to bind the company, or authorise others to do so'. There may, however, still be a few situations where a valid 'holding out' is done by someone other than the directors.

e. *S.36A* abolished the rule that a company must execute documents (this is different from making contracts) by affixing its common seal. It is now sufficient for a document to be signed by two directors or a director and the secretary, provided it is expressed to be executed by the company.

The Act also protects a bona fide purchaser by providing that if such a document is signed by persons purporting to be directors (or a director and secretary), but who in fact are not, the document is deemed to have been properly executed.

ENFORCEMENT OF FAIR DEALING BY DIRECTORS

13. *Introduction*

Part X of the Act deals with specific aspects of a company's relationship with its directors. It contains 30 sections of varying complexity dealing with situations where the interests of a director and his company may conflict, concerning for example service contracts, property transactions and loans. Before proceeding it is necessary to define several terms used in Part X.

a. *Shadow directors*

i. For the purpose of Part X the term 'director' generally includes a shadow director.

ii. A shadow director is a person in accordance with whose instructions the directors are accustomed to act unless the directors act on that person's advice only when it is given in a professional capacity.

b. *Connected persons.* Where the Act refers to 'a person connected with a director' the following are included (unless they are already directors):

i. The director's spouse;

ii. The director's child (whether legitimate or not) or step-child, so long as in either case the child is aged under 18;

iii. A company where the director, either by himself or in concert with others, controls more than 20% of the voting power or equity share capital;

iv. A person acting in the capacity of trustee of any trust (except one operating as an employees' share scheme or pension scheme), the beneficiaries of which include the director or any person in i., ii., or iii. above; and

v. A person acting in his capacity as partner of the director or of any person in i., ii., or iii. above.

c. *Relevant company.* A relevant company is either a public company or a private company in a group which contains a public company.

d. *Quasi-loan.* A quasi-loan is basically a payment or an agreement to pay a third party on behalf of a director or connected person where the company will be reimbursed in due course. For example where the company provides the director with credit card facilities, or pays for goods and services used by a director on terms that the director reimburses the company at some future date.

e. *Credit transaction.* A credit transaction may take any one of the following forms:

i. A sale of land or a supply of goods under a hire purchase or conditional sale agreement; or

ii. A lease of land or hire of goods in return for periodical payments; or

iii. A disposal of land or the supply of goods or services where payment is deferred.

14. *Compensation for Loss of Office*

By *S.312* it is unlawful for a company to pay a director compensation for loss of office or in connection with his retirement, unless particulars of the proposed payment (including the amount) have been disclosed to and approved by the members. If the payment is not disclosed and approved, the directors responsible for making it are liable to repay the sum misapplied. Rules on approval of compensation for directors' loss of office will be reformed under the *Company Law Reform Proposals 2005*.

15. *Disclosure of Interests in Contracts*

   a. By *S.317* a director who is in any way interested in a contract with the company must declare the nature of his interest at a board meeting. He must disclose his interest at the first board meeting at which the contract was discussed, or if he did not have an interest at that time, at the first board meeting after his interest arose.

   b. If disclosure is not made the director is liable to a fine of unlimited amount. In addition the contract is voidable by the company unless it is too late to rescind.

16. *Directors' Contracts of Employment*

   a. *S.319* provides that a company may not enter into an agreement for the employment of a director for a period exceeding five years (where the company's ability to terminate is limited) unless the agreement has been approved by the shareholders in general meeting.

   b. If the proper procedure is not followed the offending part of the contract is void. The remainder of the contract is valid, however, it is deemed to contain a term entitling the company to terminate the contract at any time by giving reasonable notice.

   c. There is however, nothing to stop a directors entering into a contract of employment with his company making him an employee of the company. Provided all the necessary ingredients are present for creating employee status, a director may become an employee of the company (see SECRETARY OF STATE FOR TRADE AND INDUSTRY V BOTTRILL (**1999**) and, CONNOLLY V SELLERS ARENASCENE LTD (**2000**)). This can have distinct advantages for a director, for example, entitlement to payment of wages as an employee upon insolvency, and a claim for unfair dismissal.

17. *Substantial Property Transactions*

   a. By *S.320* a company cannot transfer to or acquire from a director or any person connected with him any property the value of which exceeds the lesser of either £100,000 or 10% of the company's net assets without prior approval of the shareholders in general meeting. Arrangements to transfer the property through third parties to achieve the same objectives are subject to the same requirements.

   b. Some transfers are exempt, for example transfers between companies in the same group (ie where the transferee company is itself a director of the transferor company) transfers by companies in liquidation and transfers of less than £2,000 in value.

   c. If the transfer is not approved by the company beforehand, or affirmed within a reasonable time afterwards it is *voidable* by the company unless:

      i. Restitution of the subject matter is impossible; or

ii. A third party who is not aware of the contravention has acquired rights bona fide and for value.

In addition the director or connected person in question is liable to account to the company for any gain made and indemnify it against any loss resulting from the transfer.

18. *Invalidity of Certain Transactions Involving Directors*

   a. The provisions introduced by *S.35A* could be used as a vehicle for fraud where directors exceed the limits placed upon their powers and bind the company in a transaction where the other parties include either a director of the company or its holding company or a person connected with, or a company associated with, such a director.

   b. By *S.322A* such a transaction is voidable at the option of the company, and whether or not the transaction is avoided, any director who is a party to the transaction, or any person connected with him, or any director who authorised the transaction, is liable:

   i.   To account to the company for any gain, and

   ii. To indemnify the company for any loss or damage.

   Such persons will not be liable if they can show that, at the time of the transaction, they were unaware that the directors were exceeding their powers.

   c. The basic purpose of this section is to prevent dishonest directors misusing their power to bind the company in transactions from which they can benefit. Since the company can avoid the transaction it will usually be able to recover any money or property fraudulently transferred under the transaction.

   d. By *S.332B* where a private company with one member enters into a contract (which is not in the ordinary course of business) with the sole member who is also a director, the company shall (unless the contract is in writing) ensure that a written note of the contract is recorded in the minutes of the next board meeting.

19. *Dealings by Directors in Options*

   a. By *S.323* it is a criminal offence for a director to purchase for cash or otherwise a 'put' option, a 'call' option, or a 'put or call' option in the *listed shares or debentures* of any company in the group.

   b. A 'put' option is an option to buy. A 'call' option is an option to sell. A 'put or call' option allows the director to choose whether to buy or sell. The transactions are clearly objectionable because the director will certainly have inside information, and he may even be able to influence the future price of the securities.

   c. The term director includes a shadow director. The section also applies to a director's spouse or infant child unless the latter had no reason to know he was a director.

   d. *S.323(5)* permits a director to buy an option to *subscribe* for the unissued shares or debentures of a company.

20. *Loans to Directors. General Rules*

It would clearly be unfair to shareholders if money invested to generate business is used personally by the directors (especially if they do not re-pay the loan). The prohibition (with exceptions) of loans to directors is therefore a well established principle. However, to be really effective the rules must be extended to indirect arrangements, eg guarantees. There is also a need for careful anti-avoidance legislation designed to catch any scheme contrary to the general principle.

a. *Basic rule*

    i.   By S.330(2) a company may not make a loan to its directors or to a director of its holding company, nor may it enter into any guarantee or provide any security in connection with a loan made to such directors.

    ii.   Clearly a guarantee or provision of security on behalf of a director is not as directly harmful as a loan, since the company may never be called on to honour it, nevertheless it is an unacceptable risk for the company.

b. *Anti-avoidance provisions*

    i.   By S.330(6) a company may not arrange an assignment to it or assume any rights, obligations or liabilities under a transaction which contravenes these provisions. For example if a director borrows money from a bank, with a relative acting as guarantor, and then the relative assigns the guarantee to the company, S.330(6) will be contravened.

    ii.   By S.330(7) a company shall not take part in any arrangement whereby:

    a)   Another person enters into a transaction which if it had been entered into by the company would have contravened the above provisions; and

    b)   That other person, in pursuance of the arrangement obtains a benefit from the company or another company within the group. These widely drafted provisions will prevent for example:

        –   A loan by X Ltd to a director of Y Ltd in return for a loan by Y Ltd to a director of X Ltd.

        –   A loan by a company to a director of its subsidiary, the subsidiary making up the shortfall in interest by paying the holding company 'management fees'.

        –   A loan by an insurance company to a director of subsidiary A on the understanding that subsidiary B will place insurance business with the company.

c. *Relevant companies*

The Act draws a distinction between relevant companies and other companies because, in the past, most abuses have occurred in public companies where shareholders tend to be at greater risk from the directors. There are three basic differences:

    i.   The prohibition on loans and guarantees is extended to quasi-loans and credit transactions;

ii. The prohibitions apply not only to transactions with directors, but with a number of persons connected with directors, for example a spouse or business partner; and

iii. Directors of relevant companies, but not directors of other companies, commit a criminal offence if any of these rules are broken.

21. *Loans to Directors. Exceptions*

a. *Loans not exceeding £5,000 (S.334).* Any company may make a loan to a director of the company or of its holding company if the amount does not exceed £5,000.

b. *Loans to holding companies (S.336).* Loans or other borrowing assistance may be given by a company to its holding company. This exception is necessary because a holding company may be a director of the company making the loan or offering borrowing assistance. Alternatively a director of a subsidiary may control more than 20% of the voting power in the holding company, making the holding company a connected person. In either case prohibition of loans could interfere with proper inter-group lending.

Under the *Company Law Reform Proposals 2005* a company will be able to lend money to a director if shareholders approve.

c. *Loans, etc, to directors to enable them to perform their duties (S.337).*

Funds may be provided for a director to meet expenses incurred to enable him to perform his duties. However:

i. The transaction must have the prior authority of the company in general meeting; *or*

ii. The transaction must contain a provision that if it is not approved at the next general meeting the funds must be repaid within the following six months.

iii. In the case of a *relevant company* the value of the transaction must not exceed £20,000.

d. *Loans by money-lending companies and recognised banks (S.338).* In general the loan must be in the ordinary course of business and the terms must be no more favourable than those that would be offered to an independent person of similar financial standing.

e. *Inter-group loans, etc, by relevant companies (S.333).* Where a relevant company is a member of a group it may lend to other members of the group despite the fact that a director of the relevant company is associated with the other members of the group. Like (b) above the reason for this exception is to prevent interference with legitimate inter-group business.

22. *Civil Remedies for Breach of S.330. (S.341)*

a. The transaction is *voidable* at the instance of the company unless:

i. Restitution of the money or other asset involved is no longer possible; or

ii. A third party who is not aware of the contravention has acquired rights bona fide and for value.

b. In addition any director or connected person who benefited from the prohibited loan or assistance and any director who authorised the arrangement, is liable to account for any gain made directly or indirectly by the arrangement, and is liable to indemnify the company for any loss resulting from it, unless such person can show that he took all reasonable steps to secure the company's compliance or was not aware of the contravention.

23. *Criminal Penalties for Breach of S.330. (S.342)*

Directors of *relevant companies* who authorise a transaction in breach of *S.330* commit a criminal offence and are liable to a term of imprisonment not exceeding two years or a fine or both.

FIDUCIARY DUTIES AND DUTIES OF CARE AND SKILL

24. *Fiduciary Duties. Introduction*

a. The fiduciary duties owed by directors are basically similar to those applying to any other fiduciary, for example an agent or a trustee. They are based upon the principle that since the company places its trust in the directors they must display the utmost good faith towards the company in their dealings with it or on its behalf. The duties, however, only apply to what the directors undertake without the concurrence of the company in general meeting. For example directors may profit from their position, but they must not make a secret profit.

b. Note that:

i. Although the authority of the directors to bind the company usually depends on them acting collectively as a board, fiduciary duties are owed by each director individually.

ii. Fiduciary duties are owed to the company, not to individual shareholders.

In PERCIVAL v WRIGHT (1902) the directors purchased some shares from a member without revealing that negotiations were in progress for the sale of all shares in the company at a higher price. In fact no sale ever took place. The plaintiff nevertheless sought to have his sale to the directors set aside for non-disclosure. It was held that the sale should not be set aside since the directors owed no fiduciary duties to individual members.

This decision has been much criticised, and the directors involved would today be guilty of the criminal offence of insider dealing in a similar transaction involving *listed securities*. However, since PERCIVAL v WRIGHT was a private transaction the decision is not affected by the insider dealing legislation.

There may however, be occasions when directors owe a fiduciary duty to creditors, for example, where the company is insolvent or in severe financial difficulties. In COLIN GWYER & ASSOCIATES LTD v LONDON WHARF (LIMEHOUSE) LTD (2003) the directors, who agreed to compromise on a legal claim the company had against Colin Gwyer & Associates a compromise clearly to the detriment of the company, were found liable for breach of fiduciary duty not only to shareholders but also creditors of the company. The directors knew that the company was insolvent at the time.

25. *Directors' Duty in Relation to Employees*

a. *S.309* states that the directors are, in the performance of their functions, to have regard to the interests of the company's employees as well as the interests of the members. The section specified that the duty is *owed to the company* and is enforceable in the same way as any other fiduciary duty owed to a company by its directors.

b. Although directors' relationships with shareholders and employees are different they must have regard to the interests of both groups to discharge their duty to the company as a whole. Thus *S.309* allows directors to act in the interests of employees without fear of being in breach of their duty to the company. This does not mean that they can subordinate the interest of the company to that of employees by, for example, running the company at a loss to save jobs. It does, however, decrease the power of the members to object to an act which may not be beneficial to them, but would nevertheless be regarded as good industrial practice. For example a merger would have to be arranged to minimise loss of jobs provided this could be done without undue harm to the interests of the company as a whole.

26. *The Duty to Act Bona Fide and for the Benefit of the Company as a Whole*

a. The problem here is to define what is for the benefit of an artificial corporate entity. It is clear that directors do not have to maximise economic benefit to the company whilst disregarding the interests of members, since this would mean ploughing back all the profits to the exclusion of payment of dividends. The phrase 'benefit of the company' basically means that the directors must have regard to the interests of the present and future members of the company, ie they must view the company as a going concern and balance this long-term view against the interests of the present members.

b. It is not for the benefit of the company if they act in their own interest or the interest of a third party, without also considering the interest of the company.

In RE ROITH (**1967**) the controlling shareholder and director of a company wished to provide for his widow without leaving her his shares. Acting on legal advice he entered into a service agreement with the company whereby on his death she would be entitled to a pension for life. Since the sole object of the transaction was to benefit the widow the agreement was not held to be binding on the company.

A more recent illustration can be seen in, BRITISH MIDLAND TOOLS v MIDLAND INTERNATIONAL TRADING (2003). Here two directors about to resign and join a director who had previously resigned to set up a new rival company, were found to be in breach of their duty to act bona fide for the benefit of the company. They knew that the proposed new company was approaching existing employees to entice them to join the rival company (it had in fact already poached twelve employees) and they did nothing to discourage this.

c. Charitable and political donations of moderate value may be for the benefit of the company whilst it is a going concern, but if the company is about to cease then no commercial advantage can be gained by keeping outside interests happy. In such a case benefit of the company would be restricted to the economic interests of the present members.

d. If the breach of duty is a misapplication of company property, a person who receives such property and who knows of the breach holds the property as constructive trustee and must therefore return it to the company.

27. *The Duty to Use Their Powers for the Purpose for Which They Were Conferred*

a. If directors dishonestly use their powers for an improper purpose, for example to make a personal profit at the company's expense, they will not have acted bona fide and will therefore have broken the duty described in 26. above.

b. If, however, the directors act honestly in what they believe to be the best interests of the company they may still be liable if they do not use their powers for the purposes for which they were conferred.

In HOGG V CRAMPHORN (1967) in order to prevent a takeover bid which they believed would be bad for the company, the directors issued shares, carrying 10 votes each, to trustees of an employee pension fund. The shares were paid for by the trustees out of an interest free loan from the company. It was held that since the proper purpose of issuing shares is to raise capital, an issue made to forestall a takeover bid was a breach of the directors' fiduciary duties. However, the issue was within the power of the company and could therefore be ratified at a general meeting.

c. It is an improper purpose if shares are issued solely for the purpose of destroying the existing majority block of shares. Shares need not, however, be issued solely to raise capital, for example it may be proper to issue shares to a larger company to ensure the stability of the issuing company.

d. More recent use of director power for an improper purpose can be seen in the so called, 'poison pill' or 'shark repellent' instances. These are where the directors of a company put in place some defence mechanism against any unwanted or hostile takeovers, or attempts to alter the power of the board.

In CRITERION PROPERTIES PLC V STRATFORD UK PROPERTIES (2002), the managing director entered into an agreement with the holder of a substantial shareholding in the company, which required the company to buy back those shares at a high price should there be any change in the control or composition of the board. The managing director was later removed and the company was asking the court to set aside the buy back agreement on the basis of it being entered into through an improper use of the director's power. The High Court ruled that this was an improper use of the powers of the director and that the agreement would accordingly be set aside. The Court weighed up the advantages and disadvantages to the company in enforcing the agreement and found that the cost to the company in having to buy back the shares far outweighed any disadvantage caused by a shift in power within the board.

e. *S.80 COMPANIES ACT 1985* the company's authority is now required for the allotment of shares by directors, and this would have a bearing on many of the decided cases, for example HOGG v CRAMPHORN. The principles are nevertheless equally applicable to other powers vested in directors which do not require the company's authority. For example the power to make calls, forfeit shares or register transfers.

28. *The Duty to Retain Freedom of Action*

a. Directors cannot validly contract with each other or with third parties on the way which they will vote at future board meetings.

b. Sometimes a lender will insist that, as a condition of granting a loan, his representative sits on the board of the borrowing company. In theory the duty of such directors is owed to the company and not to the person responsible for their nomination.

29. *The Duty to Avoid a Conflict of Duty and Interest*

a. A director must not misuse corporate information or opportunity.

In INDUSTRIAL DEVELOPMENT CONSULTANTS v COOLEY (**1972**) the defendant was an architect who was employed as managing director of IDC. Whilst negotiating a contract with the Gas Board on behalf of IDC, Cooley realised that the contract probably would not be offered to IDC, but that if he left IDC he could obtain the contract himself. He therefore represented to IDC that he was ill and was allowed to terminate his contract. He then successfully obtained the contract with the Gas Board. IDC claimed the profit he made. It was held that Cooley was in breach of his duty as a director and must account to IDC with the profit made. It was immaterial that IDC might never have obtained the profit itself. What mattered was whether Cooley made a profit, not whether the company suffered a loss.

b. Thus a director must account for a profit even if it is not made at the company's expense. This is so even if the other party refused to contract with the company and even if the company is legally unable to acquire the benefit in question.

In BOSTON DEEP SEA FISHING CO v ANSELL (**1888**) directors of Boston had to pay to the company bonuses received as a result of placing contracts to purchase ice. These bonuses were only payable to shareholders who purchased ice. Boston's directors held shares in the ice-selling company, but Boston did not. The company therefore would not have been entitled to the bonus if the ice had been ordered direct.

c. There is Commonwealth authority for the proposition that a director does not misuse corporate opportunity if he enters into a transaction on his own account which the company has considered and rejected.

In PESO SILVER MINES V CROPPER (1966) (a Canadian case) the board of Peso considered and rejected the chance to purchase a number of prospecting claims near to the company's property. Peso's geologist then formed a company and it purchased the claims. Cropper, who was a director of Peso and a party to the original decision, was also a shareholder in the new company. The action was brought by Peso to claim from Cropper the profit he made on his shares in the new company. It was held that he did not have to account, he had acted in good faith and no information had been concealed from Peso's board when it made the decision not to purchase. There had not therefore been a misuse of corporate opportunity.

d. Although there is little case law on the subject it is clear that a director must not compete with the company. If he were to do so there would be an obvious conflict of personal interest and company interest.

30. *Duties of Care and Skill*

In contrast to their duties of utmost good faith and loyalty there is very little obligation on directors to display any skill and diligence.

Such duties as do exist were laid down by Romer J. in RE CITY EQUITABLE FIRE INSURANCE CO (1925). His statement can be analysed into propositions concerning skill, diligence and liability for others:

a. *Skill.* A director must exhibit the degree of skill which may reasonably be expected from a person of his knowledge and experience. This standard is objective in that the director must act as a reasonable man, but it is subjective in that the reasonable man is only regarded as possessing the knowledge and experience of the individual concerned. Thus in financial matters more would be expected of a director who is a qualified accountant than a director who has no accountancy training.

b. *Diligence.* A director is not bound to give continuous attention to the company's affairs, his duties are of 'an intermittent nature'. Directors are not bound to attend all board meetings, but must attend when they are reasonably able to do so (RE CARDIFF BANKING (1892)). The degree of diligence may, however, vary depending on the facts of the case, more would be expected from a director on whom the company relies than from one director among many, or from one who is given little effective power.

c. *Liability for others.* In the absence of suspicious circumstances directors are entitled to trust the company's officers to perform their duties properly. A director will not be liable for the acts of co-directors or other officers unless he participates in the wrong, for example by signing a cheque for an unauthorised payment.

d. Recently the courts have shown a tendency to move towards a more objective standard of care and skill than that laid down in RE CITY EQUITABLE FIRE INSURANCE. In RE D'JAN OF LONDON (1994) the judge made the recommendation that the general level of skill and care which a director is required to exhibit should be assessed through a two-stage process based upon the statutory requirement contained in *S.214* of the *INSOLVENCY ACT 1986* for wrongful trading. This is to, firstly, determine what it might be reasonable to expect in terms of knowledge and skills of a particular director when compared with a similar director (this will establish an objective minimum standard); then, secondly, take account of the particular experience, skills and knowledge of the director concerned (this will allow the court to take account of subjective factors of a particular director which may well raise the standard in one).

Under the *Company Law Reform Proposals 2005*, a statutory declaration of directors' duties will incorporate the dual objective-subjective standard of care and skill contained in *S.214* of the INSOLVENCY ACT 1986.

There has also been a recent development in the third element of the duty of care and skill laid down in RE CITY EQUITABLE FIRE INSURANCE CO, that of the ability of a director to entrust to others (delegate) his duties. Where director duties are delegated to other directors, officers, managers etc a director will not be able to evade responsibility for the wrongful acts of such persons. In RE BARINGS BANK (1999) the Court held that all directors should acquire and maintain sufficient knowledge and understanding of the company's business to enable them to properly discharge their duties: this will extend to any delegated tasks for although directors are entitled to delegate duties and responsibilities to others, the act of delegation will not absolve them of liability, they must supervise and keep themselves informed of the activities of those carrying out the tasks and duties delegated.

31. *Relief from Liability*

a. Under *S.727* the court has power in an action against an officer for breach of duty to grant relief where, although the officer is in breach, it appears that he has acted honestly and reasonably. The reasonableness of a director's conduct may depend on whether he has taken legal advice.

b. By *S.310* neither the articles nor any contract may exempt or indemnify any officer for the consequences of negligence, default, breach of duty or breach of trust. This probably invalidated insurance paid for by the company on behalf of such persons. However, *S.137 CA 89* (amending *S.310*) now enables companies to purchase for any of their officers or auditors, insurance against such liability. If a company does this, the fact must be disclosed in the directors' report.

32. *Statutory Statement of Directors' General Duties*

Under the *Company Law Reform Proposals 2005*, there will be a statutory statement of directors' duties which largely reflect the established common law principles but being in a statutory format it is felt that this will add clarity to the law in this area.

33. *Excuse Breach of Duty*

The *Company Law Reform Proposals* make it possible for the board of directors of a private company to ratify a breach of duty by one of their number, unless prevented by the company's articles and memorandum. It will be possible for the articles and memorandum of a public company to permit its board of directors to ratify a breach of duty by one of their number. The director concerned, and any other interested director, cannot vote on the issue.

DISQUALIFICATION OF DIRECTORS

34. *Introduction*

Paragraphs 33–34 describe various situations when, under the COMPANY DIRECTORS DISQUALIFICATION ACT 1986, a person may be disqualified from acting as a director.

35. *Mandatory Disqualification (S.6 CDDA 1986)*

a. A person may be subject to this procedure if he is, or has been, a director or a shadow director of a company which has gone into insolvent liquidation (whether voluntary or compulsory).

b. The court is required to make a disqualification order if the person's conduct as a director, either considered in isolation or taken with his conduct as a director of another company, makes him unfit to be concerned with the management of a company.

c. Since the Act came into force a number of disqualification orders have been made.

   In RE STANFORD SERVICES LTD (1987) a director was held to be unfit to hold office because the company owed considerable amount of PAYE, National Insurance and VAT. The director had used available funds to finance the company's business rather than arrange for the money to be set aside to meet the above liabilities. Although commercial morality may not have been infringed it was held that there had been a serious breach of the director's duties to the company's creditors and the public interest required that the misconduct should be recognised by two years' disqualification.

36. *Non-mandatory Disqualification*

This may arise in two situations:

a. By *S.8 CDDA 1986* an application for disqualification order may be made by the Secretary of State following a Department of Trade investigation.

b. By *S.10 CDDA 1986* the court may make a disqualification order on its own initiative when it makes a declaration that a person is liable to make a contribution to the company's assets. This may arise under *S.213–215 IA* which deal with wrongful trading and fraudulent trading.

37. *Director Undertakings*

A disqualification order can only be achieved by means of court proceedings, however, under the INSOLVENCY ACT 2000, the Secretary of State will have the power to accept an undertaking from a director where he agrees to a period of disqualification; this will achieve disqualification administratively more quickly.

38. *Acting While Disqualified*

A person who concerns himself with the management of a company while disqualified, or a person who acts in the management of a company on instructions given by a disqualified person, is personally liable for all debts incurred by the company during the period in which he acts. The liability is joint and several with that of the company.

THE SECRETARY

39. *Appointment*

a. S.283 states that every company must have a secretary, but a sole director cannot also be the secretary.

b. It is usual for the secretary to be appointed by the directors on such terms as they think fit. The directors may also remove the secretary.

40. *Qualifications*

S.286 stipulates minimum qualifications for secretaries of *public companies*. The directors must take all reasonable steps to ensure that the secretary is a person who appears to them to have the requisite knowledge and experience and who:

a. Already holds office as secretary, assistant secretary or deputy secretary of the company; or

b. For at least three out of the five years immediately preceding his appointment held office as secretary of a public company; or

c. Is a barrister, advocate or solicitor; or

d. Is a member of any of the following bodies:

   i.   The Institute of Chartered Accountants;

   ii. The Association of Certified Accountants;

   iii. The Institute of Chartered Secretaries and Administrators;

   iv. The Chartered Institute of Cost and Management Accountants;

   v.   The Chartered Institute of Public Finance and Accountancy; or

e. Is a person who, by virtue of having held any other position or being a member of any other body, appears to the directors to be capable of discharging the functions of secretary.

41. *Powers*

The secretary is the chief administrative officer of the company and on matters of administration he has ostensible authority to make contracts on behalf of the company. Such contracts include:

a. Hiring office staff;

b. Contracts for the purchase of office equipment; and

c. Hiring cars for business purposes.

In PANORAMA DEVELOPMENTS V FIDELIS FURNISHING FABRICS (1971) the secretary of the defendant company entered into a number of contracts for the hire of cars. The cars were ostensibly to be used to collect important customers from Heathrow Airport, but in fact the secretary used them for his own private purposes. The Court of Appeal held that the defendant company was liable. Lord Denning M.R. said:

'A company secretary is...an officer of the company with extensive duties and responsibilities...He is certainly entitled to sign contracts connected with the administrative side of a company's affairs, such as employing staff, and ordering cars and so forth.'

d. Although a secretary has 'extensive duties and responsibilities' there are a number of decisions where it has been held that he does not have authority for particular acts. Thus he may not:

i. Bind the company on a trading contract;

ii. Borrow money on behalf of the company;

iii. Issue a writ or lodge a defence in the company's name;

iv. Register a transfer of shares;

v. Strike a name off the register of members;

vi. Summon a general meeting on his own authority.

42. *Duties*

The secretary's duties include:

a. Ensuring that the company's documentation is in order, that the requisite returns are made to the Companies Registry, and that the company's registers are maintained;

b. Taking minutes of meetings;

c. Sending notices to members; and

d. Countersigning documents.

INSIDER DEALING

43. *Introduction*

Insider dealing concerns the duties of directors, officers, some members, and some outsiders when dealing in the company's securities with inside information which affects their value. It is controlled by provisions in the CRIMINAL JUSTICE ACT 1993.

44. *Definitions*

a. *Insider*. An insider is an individual who has information which

      i.   Is inside information; and

      ii.   Has come from an inside source.

    In each case the individual must *know* it is inside information and *know* it has come from an inside source.

  b. *Inside information.* This is information which

      i.   Relates to particular securities;

      ii.   Is specific or precise;

      iii. Has not been made public; and

      iv. Which would, if it were made public, be likely to have a significant effect on the price of the securities.

  c. *Inside source.* A person has information from an inside source if

      i.   He has it through being a director, employee or shareholder of an issuer of securities or through having access to the information because of his employment, office or profession; or

      ii.   The direct or indirect source of his information is one of the persons referred to in i. above.

  d. *Dealing.* A person deals in securities if

      i.   He acquires or disposes of securities either as principal or agent; or

      ii.   He procures, directly or indirectly, an acquisition or disposal of securities by another person.

    A decision not to deal, even if based on inside information, is not 'dealing'.

  e. *Price-affected securities.* The price of the securities would be likely to be significantly affected if information relating to the securities were to be made public.

45. *Prohibitions*

There are three offences which could be committed by an individual who has information as an insider

  a. Dealing in price-affected securities;

  b. Encouraging another person to deal in price-affected securities;

  c. Disclosing the information other than in the proper course of employment, office or profession.

46. *Defences*

  a. In relation to a. and b. above (dealing and encouraging to deal) an individual has a defence if he shows that

      i.   He did not expect the dealing to result in a profit; or

ii. He reasonably believed that the information had been so widely disclosed that none of those taking part in the dealing would be prejudiced by not having the information; or

iii. He would have dealt, even if he had not had the information

b. In relation to c. above (disclosing the information) an individual has a defence if

i. He did not expect any person, because of the disclosure, to deal in the securities; or

ii. Although he did expect the person to deal, he did not expect it to result in a profit attributable to the fact that the information was price-sensitive.

47. *Penalties and Remedies*

a. Insider dealing is a criminal offence, the maximum penalty being seven years imprisonment plus an unlimited fine. Prosecutions must be brought by the Secretary of State for Trade or the Director of Public Prosecutions. The Act does not provide for civil actions.

b. Contravention of the Act does not effect the validity of the transaction. This is rather unusual since criminal acts are normally void or voidable. The rule is, however, sensible since the chain of transactions may be complex and innocent parties could be affected if the transaction were held to be void.

48. *Investigations into Insider Dealing*

a. Prior to 1986 there was no mechanism for the investigation of suspected insider dealing other than investigation by the police. This was a serious drawback to the effectiveness of the legislation.

b. By *S.177 FINANCIAL SERVICES ACT 1986* as amended by the *CRIMINAL JUSTICE ACT 1993* the Secretary of State is empowered to appoint inspectors to investigate suspected insider dealing offences. The inspectors can require any person that may have relevant information to:

i. Produce documents in his possession. 'Documents' includes information recorded in any form;

ii. Attend before them;

iii. Otherwise give all reasonable help in connection with the investigation.

They also have powers to enter and search premises for evidence.

CHAPTER 45

Auditors and Investigations

THE AUDIT REQUIREMENT

1. *General Rule*

   By *S.384* (as amended) at each general meeting at which directors present the accounts, the company must appoint auditors to hold office from the end of that meeting until the end of the next such general meeting.

2. *Exemption for Certain Small Companies*

   a. Until 1994 it was a fundamental principle of company law that all companies would have their accounts audited by a properly qualified person who would report to the members. An important change was made by the COMPANIES ACT 1985 (AUDIT EXEMPTION) REGULATIONS 1994, which were enacted to reduce the administrative burden on small private companies while seeking to retain some degree of protection for members.

   b. The 1994 Regulations

      i. Allow for the abolition of the statutory audit for some small companies, and

      ii. Introduce an accountant's report instead of an audit report for other small companies.

   c. *Exempt companies*

      i. To be exempt from statutory audit and any audit report a company must

         – have a turnover not exceeding £90,000 in a particular year, and

         – qualify as a small company throughout the year.

         In addition it must not be, or have been, a public company, a bank, an insurance company, an insurance broker, an authorised person under the FINANCIAL SERVICES ACT 1986, an employers' association, a parent company or a subsidiary undertaking.

      ii. The abolition of the audit requirement is automatic for a company which satisfies the criteria and no action (eg resolutions) need be taken by the company. However, an exempt company may still need to have an external audit to satisfy conditions imposed by lenders who had previously placed trust in the statutory audit. In addition an exempt company must have an audit if required to do so by holders of not less that 10% of the issued shares. Such a request must be deposited in writing at the company's registered office at least one month before the company's year end.

There is a proposal that private companies should be automatically exempted from making an annual appointment of auditors unless a member requires a meeting to consider reappointing the auditors.

    iii.   The balance sheet of an exempt company must contain a statement by the directors:

- that it is entitled to the exemption,

- that no notice (referred to above) has been deposited by members, and

- acknowledging their responsibility for keeping accounting records and preparing accounts that give a true and fair view of the company's state of affairs.

   d.   *Companies requiring an accountant's report*

    i.   A company will be exempt from statutory audit, but will require an accountant's report if its turnover is more than £90,000 but less than £350,000. It must also qualify as a small company throughout the year and satisfy the other conditions set out in c.(i) above.

    ii.   The accountant's report must state that in the opinion of the reporting accountant

- the accounts for the year are in agreement with the accounting records kept by the company

- that based on these records the accounts have been drawn up in a manner consistent with the Act

- the company satisfies the criteria for exemption from audit.

    iii.   There has been no change in the law with regard to the entitlement of small companies to file abbreviated accounts. If an accountant's report is required it will be filed either with the full accounts or with abbreviated accounts.

3. Exemptions for Dormant Companies

   a.   A dormant company is one which has not made an accounting transaction in the preceding year or since incorporation.

   b.   A dormant company may pass a special resolution not to appoint auditors.

SUPERVISORY BODIES AND PROFESSIONAL QUALIFICATIONS

4. *Supervisory Bodies*

The 1989 Act introduced new rules to ensure that only persons who are properly supervised and appropriately qualified are appointed company auditors, and that audits are carried out properly and with integrity and independence.

5. *Types of Supervisory Body*

Two types of supervisory body were established under the Act.

a. *Recognised Supervisory Bodies* (RSBs) of which all company auditors must be members.

b. *Recognised Qualifying Bodies* (RQBs) which will offer the professional qualifications required to become a member of an RSB.

The same body can be both an RSB and an RQB. The existing professional bodies, for example the Chartered Association of Certified Accountants and the Institute of Chartered Accountants will fulfil both functions.

6. *Recognition of RSBs*

By *S.30 CA 89* each RSB must be a body established in the UK (this now includes a corporate body or an unincorporated association) which maintains and enforces rules as to

a. The eligibility of persons seeking appointment as company auditors, and

b. The conduct of company audit work.

Bodies wishing to be RSBs must apply to the Secretary of State, submitting their rules, any other written guidance, and any other information that the Secretary of State may reasonably require.

7. *Rules of RSBs (Schedule 11 CA 89)*

a. *Eligibility*. RSBs must ensure that only the following persons are eligible for appointment as auditors:

i. Individuals who hold appropriate qualifications;

ii. Firms controlled by qualified persons.

The RSB must ensure that such persons are 'fit and proper', taking into account the person's professional conduct, including the conduct of employees and close business associates.

b. *Professional integrity*. The RSB's rules must ensure that audit work is carried out properly and with integrity. A DTI consultative document on the implementation of the EC Eighth Directive considers that two areas must be addressed:

    i.   The standards of performance of the audit, including compliance with approved auditing standards and guidelines, and

    ii.   General ethical standards, such as rules to cover independence, objectivity and client confidentiality.

c.   *Technical standards.* The technical standards to be applied in company audits must be the subject of RSB rules. This is likely to be a reference to the need for auditing standards and guidelines rather than statements of standard accounting practice (SSAPs).

d.   *Maintenance of competence.* The rules of the RSB must ensure that eligible persons continue to maintain an appropriate level of competence.

e.   *Investigation and enforcement.* The RSB's rules must include provisions in respect of:

    i.   Monitoring and enforcement of compliance with its rules. The extent of monitoring is not yet clear and appropriate rules will be made after consultation between RSBs and the DTI. It may imply a regular examination of the activities of thousands of audit firms and individuals;

    ii.   Admission and expulsion of members;

    iii.   Grant and withdrawal of eligibility for appointment as an auditor;

    iv.   Disciplinary procedures.

    NB. The rules relating to ii.–iv. above must be 'fair and reasonable' and there must be adequate appeals procedures.

    v.   The investigation of complaints against members and against the RSB itself.

f.   *Liability of RSBs.* RSBs and their officers, employees and governors are exempt from damages in respect of the exercise of their statutory duties, unless it can be shown that they have acted in bad faith. This prevents them from being joined in any action taken against auditors for negligence.

8. *Appropriate Qualifications*

The 1989 Act makes it a requirement that auditors hold an 'appropriate qualification'. By *S.31 CA 89* a person will hold an appropriate qualification in the following cases:

a.   He satisfied the existing criteria for appointment as an auditor under the 1985 Act by being a member of one of the bodies recognised under that Act immediately before 1st January 1990.

b.   He holds a recognised professional qualification obtained in the UK (see 6 above). In future this will be the 'appropriate qualification' for all new auditors.

c.   He holds an approved overseas qualification and satisfies any additional requirements set down by the Secretary of State.

9. *Recognised Qualifying Bodies (S.32 and Schedule 12 CA 89)*

a. *Recognition.* To offer recognised professional qualifications bodies must be approved by the Secretary of State. The procedure for recognition is similar to that for recognition as an RSB. An RQB must have rules to ensure compliance with various entry, examination and training requirements.

b. *Qualifications*

i. The RQB's qualification must only be open to persons who have attained university entrance level (without necessarily having gone to university) or have a sufficient period of professional experience. 'Sufficient period of professional experience' means at least seven years in a professional capacity in finance, law or accountancy. Periods of theoretical instruction, up to a maximum of four years, count towards necessary experience so long as the instruction lasts for at least one year and is attested by an examination recognised for this purpose by the Secretary of State.

ii. The qualification must be restricted to persons passing an examination which tests theoretical knowledge and the ability to apply it in practice, although persons may be exempted from examination in subjects in which they already hold a recognised qualification, for example a university examination of equivalent standard.

iii. It is also a requirement that persons must have completed at least three years' practical training, although exemption from this requirement may be possible if the person has an approved diploma evidencing practical training. The practical training must be given by persons approved by the RQB as being suitable and at least two-thirds of it must be with a fully qualified auditor. A substantial part of the training must be in company audit work.

c. *Approval of overseas qualifications.* By *S.33 CA 89* the Secretary of State is empowered to consider professional qualifications obtained outside the UK as 'approved'. This will happen if he is satisfied that it gives a level of professional competence equivalent to a recognised professional qualification. Persons with overseas qualifications may be required to obtain additional educational qualifications to demonstrate that they have a sufficient knowledge of UK law and practice.

10. *Eligibility of Firms and Individuals*

a. Prior to the 1989 Act it was not possible for a corporate body to be an auditor. *S.25 CA 89* now provides that an individual or firm (defined to mean either a partnership or corporate body) may be appointed. Firms may only perform audits if they are controlled by qualified persons, ie a majority of those empowered to make the decisions are qualified persons.

b. *Appointment of partnerships.* Where a partnership is appointed *S.26 CA 89* makes it clear that it is the firm and not the partners that has been appointed (previously appointments were, strictly speaking, of individuals). The Act also provides that the appointment will continue despite any technical dissolution of the partnership when members join and leave. When a partnership ceases the appointment may go to any eligible partnership that succeeds the practice or any individual partner who has taken over the practice.

c. *Appointment of corporate bodies*. The Act provides that the majority of decision makers in such bodies must be qualified persons, but it leaves many of the detailed rules to be laid down by the RSBs.

d. *Ineligibility of auditors*

    i. By *S.27 CA 89* a person is ineligible to be a company's auditor if he is an officer or employee of the company, or a partner or employee of such a person. *S.27* also provides that a person will be ineligible if he is not sufficiently independent of the company, although it leaves lack of independence to be defined by regulations.

    ii. If an auditor ceases to be eligible under the rules of the RSB of which he is a member, he must immediately vacate office and give written notice to the company. If such a person continues to act, or fails to give written notice, he is guilty of an offence.

    iii. By *S.29 CA 89* if an auditor acts when ineligible the Secretary of State may direct the company to appoint another auditor to carry out a second audit or to review the first audit, stating (with reasons) whether a second audit is required.

APPOINTMENT, REMOVAL AND RESIGNATION

11. *Appointment*

a. *First auditors*. By *S.385* the first auditors may be appointed by the directors at any time before the first general meeting at which the accounts are laid. They then hold office until the end of that meeting. If the company has passed an elective resolution to dispense with the laying of accounts, the first auditors may be appointed within 28 days after the company's first annual accounts being sent to members. If the directors fail to make an appointment the general meeting may appoint.

b. *Subsequent auditors*

    i. At each general meeting at which accounts are laid the company may appoint one or more auditors. They then hold office from the end of the meeting until the end of the next meeting at which accounts are laid.

    ii. However, if the company chooses, by elective resolution, to dispense with the annual appointment of auditors, the auditors shall be deemed to be re-appointed annually for so long as the election remains in force *(S.386)*. During this time, any member may give written notice to the company proposing that the auditors' appointment be terminated.

The directors must then convene a general meeting, which must be held within 28 days of the notice being given *(S.393)*.

iii. If the company passes an elective resolution not to lay accounts before the general meeting, but does not elect to dispense with the annual appointment of auditors, it must still hold a general meeting each year for the purpose of re-appointing the auditors. This meeting must be held within 28 days of the dispatch to the members of the accounts. This 28 day period is defined as 'the time for appointing auditors'. Auditors appointed in this way hold office until the end of the time for appointing auditors in the next financial year. *(S.385A)*.

c. *Casual vacancies (S.388)*. The directors or the company in general meeting may appoint auditors to fill casual vacancies. The surviving auditor may continue to act during any vacancy. Special notice is required for a resolution:

i. Filling a casual vacancy; or

ii. Re-appointing as auditor a retiring auditor who was appointed by the directors to fill a casual vacancy.

On receipt of such notice the company must immediately send a copy to the person proposed to be appointed and (if the casual vacancy was caused by the resignation of an auditor) to the auditor who resigned.

d. *Appointment by the Secretary of State (S.387)*. If no appointment or re-appointment is made at a meeting at which accounts are laid, the company must inform the Department of Trade within one week. The Secretary of State may then make an appointment to fill the vacancy.

e. *Remuneration*. The term 'remuneration' includes sums paid by the company as auditors' expenses. By *S.390A*:

i. If the directors make the appointment they fix his remuneration.

ii. If he is appointed by the Secretary of State he fixes the remuneration.

iii. If the auditor is appointed by the company then the company fixes his remuneration, or determines the way by which it will be fixed.

12. *Removal*

a. By *S.391* the company may remove an auditor before the end of his period of office despite any agreement between it and him.

b. The registrar must be notified of the removal within 14 days.

c. An auditor who has been removed is entitled to attend the meeting at which his term of office would have expired and any general meeting at which it is proposed to fill a casual vacancy caused by his removal. He is entitled to receive all communications relating to the meeting which a member is entitled to receive, and he may speak on any matter concerning him as a former auditor.

13. *Resolutions to Appoint and Remove Auditors S.391A*

   a. Auditors may be appointed and removed by *ordinary resolution.*

   b. In the following cases *special notice* (see Chapter 46.5) is required:

        i. To appoint a person other than a retiring auditor;

        ii. To fill a casual vacancy;

        iii. To re-appoint as auditor a retiring auditor who was appointed by the directors to fill a casual vacancy; or

        iv. To remove an auditor before the end of his term of office.

   c. On receipt of the special notice the company must immediately send a copy to:

        i. The person proposed to be appointed or removed;

        ii. The retiring auditor where it is proposed to appoint another person; and

        iii. The resigning auditor where the appointment is to fill a casual vacancy caused by his resignation.

14. *Written Representations by Auditors S.391A*

   a. Where (b) (i) or (b) (iv) above apply the auditors may make written representations to the company and require the company (unless it receives them too late) to send a copy of these representations to the members with notice of the meeting.

   b. If for any reason these representations are not sent to the members the auditors can require them to be read out at the meeting. In any case he has a right to speak in his defence at the meeting.

   c. The representations need not be sent out, or read at the meeting, if the court is satisfied, on the application of the company or any aggrieved person, that the auditor is using his rights to secure needless publicity for defamatory matter.

15. *Resignation of Auditors S.392*

   a. An auditor may resign by giving written notice to the company at its registered office.

   b. The notice will not be effective unless it contains either:

        i. A statement that there are no circumstances connected with his resignation which he considers should be brought to the notice of the company's members or creditors; or

        ii. A statement of such circumstances.

   c. Within 14 days of receipt of an effective notice the company must send a copy to:

        i. The registrar; and

    ii.   If it contains a statement of connected circumstances, to every member and debentureholder of the company.

  d. Within 14 days of receipt of a notice containing a statement of connected circumstances the company or any aggrieved person may apply to the court if it is thought that the auditor is using the statement to secure needless publicity for defamatory matter. The court may then order that copies need not be sent to members and debentureholders. Within 14 days of the court's decision the company must send to every member and debentureholder:

    i.   A statement of the effect of the court order, if any; or if none

    ii.   A copy of the notice containing the auditor's statement of the circumstances connected with his resignation.

16. *Right of the Resigning Auditor S.392A*

  a. Where the notice of resignation contains a statement of connected circumstances the auditor may require the directors to convene an EGM to receive and consider the statement. This will be useful if the auditor wishes to resign mid-term.

  b. The auditor may require the company to send to the members before such an EGM, or before the AGM at which his term of office would otherwise have expired, a written statement of the circumstances connected with his resignation. Unless the company receives this statement too late, it must send it to the members with notice of the meeting. *S.392A* contains provisions relating to:

    i.   Reading statement at the meeting if for any reason it is not sent with the notice;

    ii.   Defamatory matter;

    iii. The auditor's right to attend and receive all communications relating to the meeting.

17. *Statements to Persons Ceasing to Hold Office as Auditor S.394*

Prior to 1989 the statement of circumstances connected with an auditor's resignation (or the statement that there are no circumstances that should be brought to the notice of members or creditors) only applied when an auditor resigned. This requirement has now been extended by the 1989 Act to all cases where an auditor ceases to hold office, for example if an auditor is removed from office or not re-appointed at a general meeting.

POWERS, DUTIES AND LIABILITIES OF AUDITORS

18. *The Auditors' Report S.235–236*

  a. It is the duty of the auditors to report to the members on the accounts laid before the company during their term of office. 'Accounts' includes the balance sheet, profit and loss account and group accounts (if any).

b. The report must be read before the company in general meeting, and must be open to inspection by any member.

c. The report must state whether, in the opinion of the auditors, the accounts have been properly prepared and whether a true and fair view is given:

   i. In the case of the balance sheet, of the state of the company's affairs at the end of its financial year;

   ii. In the case of the profit and loss account, of the company's profit and loss for its financial year; and

   iii. In the case of group accounts, of the state of affairs and profit or loss of the company and its subsidiaries so far as concerns members of the company.

d. In addition:

   i. If the accounts do not contain particulars of directors' emoluments and particulars of loan and other transactions favouring directors, the auditors must include in their report a statement giving the required particulars so far as they are reasonably able to do so.

   ii. The auditors must consider whether the information given in the directors' report relating to the financial year in question is consistent with those accounts. If they are of the opinion that it is not consistent they must say so in their report.

e. The auditors' report must state the names of the auditors and be signed by them.

19. *Auditors' Duties*

a. By *S.237* the auditors must carry out such investigations as will enable them to form an opinion as to whether:

   i. Proper accounting records have been kept by the company, and adequate returns received from branches not visited by them; and

   ii. The balance sheet and profit and loss account agree with the accounting records and returns.

   If they think that proper books or returns have not been kept or received by them they must say so in their report.

b. The auditors must also:

   i. Acquaint themselves with their duties under the articles and the Companies Act;

   ii. Report to the members, ensuring that the report complies with *S.235– 236;*

   iii. Act honestly and with reasonable care and skill (see below).

20. *Auditors' Powers S.389A*

a. The auditors have a right of access to the books, accounts and vouchers of the company.

b. The auditors may require from the officers of the company such information and explanations as they think necessary for the performance of their duties. If they fail to obtain such information they must say so in their report.

c. The auditors may attend any general meetings, they must be sent all notices and communications relating to general meetings, and they may speak at a meeting on any matter which concerns them as auditors.

21. *Power in Relation to Subsidiary Undertakings*

a. By *S.389A* it is the duty of a subsidiary and its auditors to give to the auditors of the holding company such information and explanation as they may reasonably require for the purposes of their duties as auditors of the holding company.

b. If the subsidiary is incorporated outside Great Britain, it is the duty of the holding company, if required by its auditors, to take reasonable steps to obtain such information from the subsidiary.

22. *False Statements to Auditors*

By *S.389A* it is a criminal offence for an officer of the company to knowingly or recklessly make, either orally or in writing, a statement to the company's auditors which is misleading, false or deceptive in a material particular.

23. *The Standard of Care and Skill*

a. The 1989 Act relates the legal standard of care and skill closely to the professional standards set by the RSBs, since RSB rules must:

   i. Ensure that only 'fit and proper' persons are appointed as company auditors. In determining whether someone is fit and proper the RSB has to take into account that person's professional conduct.

   ii. Ensure that audits are carried out with 'professional integrity'. One component of this will be compliance with technical standards, the other will cover independence, objectivity and confidentiality.

b. To some extent this formalises the present situation since the ICA and ACCA already require their members to act in accordance with rules enforced by disciplinary committees. However, the guidelines laid down by judicial decisions are still law and, to the extent that they are not covered by new RSB rules, they will still play a part in determining the required standard of care and skill. It has been held

   i. That they must ascertain that the books show the true financial position. To do this auditors must do more than merely verify the numerical accuracy, of the accounts (FORMENTO v SELSDON (**1958**)). If entries in or omissions from the books make the auditors suspicious they must make a full investigation into the circumstances. For example:

   In RE THOMAS GERRARD (**1968**) the managing director falsified the accounts by including non-existent stock and altering invoices. This caused the company's profits to be overstated. Dividends were declared that would not otherwise have been declared and too much tax was paid. The auditors became suspicious when they noticed that invoices had been altered, but they accepted the managing director's explanation and made no further investigation. The auditors were held liable to the company for the cost of recovering the excess tax paid and for dividends and tax not recovered.

ii. Auditors must check the cash in hand and the bank balance.

iii. Where payments have been made by the company, the auditors should see that they are authorised.

iv. Auditors should check that company borrowing has been authorised and is in accordance with the articles.

v. Auditors should satisfy themselves that the securities of the company exist and are in safe custody, either by making a personal inspection of the securities or checking that the securities are in the possession of a person who in the ordinary course of business keeps securities for customers, for example a bank.

vi. Auditors are not required to value stock or work in progress. They may accept the valuation of a responsible official of the company, unless they have reason to suppose it to be inaccurate. In practice auditors exceed this legal duty with regard to stock-taking.

vii. Auditors do not have a duty to comment on whether the management is running the business efficiently or profitably.

viii. If the directors do not allow auditors the time to conduct their investigations, the auditors must either refuse to make a report or make a qualified report. They must not make a report containing a statement the truth of which they have not had an opportunity to verify.

24. *To Whom are the Auditors' Duties Owed?*

a. The auditors have a contractual relationship with the company and it is therefore the company and to the members *as a whole* to whom the basic duty is owed. Even so auditors must, on occasions, disclose facts which may harm the company.

b. Since the decision in HEDLEY BYRNE v HELLER (1964) it has been clear that a person may be liable for financial loss resulting from a negligent statement even if there is no contract between the maker of the statement and the recipient (although a disclaimer of responsibility will exclude the defendant's liability).

As already noted, the duty of an auditor is owed to the company and its members as a whole, not to individual shareholders or members of the public. However, in CAPARO INDUSTRIES PLC v DICKMAN (1990) the House of Lords ruled that a wider duty might well be owed where the auditor is in a sufficiently close relationship with a particular person such that it can reasonably be inferred that such a person, upon receiving the information, will be likely to act upon it, here, a duty might well arise. But information put in general circulation is not, in itself, sufficient.

DEPARTMENT OF TRADE INVESTIGATIONS

25. *Types of Investigation*

    a. There are three basic types of investigation:

        i.   Investigation of the company's affairs;

        ii. Investigation of the company's ownership; and

        iii. Investigation of share dealings.

    b. In addition there are provisions for the inspection of a company's documents, and new powers under the FINANCIAL SERVICES ACT 1986 to investigate suspected insider dealing offences (Chapter 44.45).

26. *Investigation on the Application of the Members or the Company*

    a. By *S.431* the Department of Trade may appoint inspectors:

        i.   Where the company has a share capital, on the application of at least 200 members, or members holding at least 10% of the issued shares;

        ii. Where the company has no share capital, on the application of at least 20% of the members; and

        iii. In any case, on the application of the company. (An ordinary resolution would be sufficient to authorise an application.)

    b. The applicants (or applicant) must produce evidence in support of their application and may be required to give up to £5,000 security for costs.

    c. In the past *S.431* has not often been used. This is because it overlaps with *S.432.* This section is more flexible than *S.431* in that anyone can ask the Department to investigate and the Department may exercise their discretion to do so if there are circumstances suggesting:

        i.   That the affairs of the company have been conducted with intent to defraud its creditors, or in a manner unfairly prejudicial to some part of the members, or for an unlawful or fraudulent purpose; or

        ii. That the promoters or managers have been guilty of fraud or misconduct; or

        iii. That proper information has not been given to the members.

    d. The powers conferred by *S.432* are exercisable even if the company is in voluntary liquidation. Also the word 'member' includes persons who are not members but to whom shares have been transferred or transmitted by operation of law, for example personal representatives.

e. Application for a DTI investigation is a drastic step which dissatisfied shareholders will usually only consider after they have failed to obtain a remedy at a general meeting or through the courts. When an application is received the Department will call for the company to produce documents and records for internal examination by its staff. If the complaint is trivial or insubstantial it will go no further. An inspection will only be ordered if a strong case is made out since an appointment will attract publicity and cause damage to the company. If an inspection is ordered, two inspectors are usually appointed, normally a barrister and an accountant.

27. *Investigation by Order of Court*

S.432 also provides that the Department must appoint inspectors to investigate the company's affairs if the court orders it to do so.

28. *Powers of Inspectors*

a. Inspectors have extensive powers to:

   i. Require production of books and documents;

   ii. Question on oath any person, and administer the oath accordingly;

   iii. Obtain a warrant to enter premises and search for documents;

   iv. Take copies of any documents and require any person named in the warrant to provide an explanation of documents or state where documents may be found;

   v. Investigate the affairs of related companies;

   vi. Inform the Secretary of State of any matters coming to his knowledge as a result of the investigation.

b. The persons referred to under ii. above must give the inspector all assistance in the investigation that they are reasonably able to give. Refusal to comply with a request for documents or information is punishable as contempt of court. Intentional obstruction of an inspector is an offence.

29. *The Inspector's Report S.437*

a. The inspector presents his findings in a report to the Department. In some cases the inspector will also make interim reports. The Secretary of State has a discretionary power:

   i. To send a copy of the report to the company's registered office;

   ii. To provide copies to specified classes of persons, for example, members, auditors or persons referred to in the report;

   iii. To publish the report, unless inspectors were appointed subject to specific terms that the report would not be published (see 30.c. below).

b. When inspectors are appointed under a court order, the court must be sent a copy of the report.

30. *Consequences of the Report*

    a.   If, as a result of the report, it appears to be in the public interest that the company be wound-up the Department may present a petition that the company be wound-up because it is just and equitable to do so. An inspector's report may also be used as evidence to support a shareholder's petition under *S.122 IA* (the 'just and equitable' ground).

    b.   If it appears that there are grounds for a petition by a member under *S.459* (ie that the affairs of the company have been conducted in an unfairly prejudicial manner) the Department may, as well as or instead of petitioning to wind-up the company, present a petition for an order under *S.459*.

    c.   The Secretary of State may bring civil proceedings on behalf of the company when it appears from any report made or information obtained that it is in the public interest to do so.

    d.   The Department may also institute criminal proceedings against persons believed to be guilty of offences.

    e.   It may also apply to the court for an order disqualifying a person from acting as a director *(S.8* COMPANY DIRECTORS DISQUALIFICATION ACT *1986)*.

31. *Investigation of the Ownership of a Company*

    a.   By *S.442*

        i.   The Department must investigate the ownership of shares of a company on the application of 200 shareholders or holders of 10% of the issued shares, unless it considers the application is vexatious, or unless it considers it unreasonable to investigate any matter; and

        ii.   The Department may investigate share ownership if there appears to be good reason to do so.

    The Secretary of State, before appointing inspectors, may require the applicants to give up to £5,000 security for costs.

    b.   The inspector has the same general powers as in the investigation of the affairs of a company.

    c.   The provisions relating to the report are also similar, except that if, in the opinion of the Secretary of State, there is good reason for not divulging any part of the report, he may omit that part from the inspector's report.

    d.   The Secretary of State may disclose information relating to share ownership to the following persons:

        i.   The company whose ownership was subject to investigation;

        ii.   Any member of that company;

        iii.   Any person whose conduct was investigated;

        iv.   The auditors of the company;

        v.   Any person whose financial interests appear to be affected by matters covered by the investigation.

e. Powerful sanctions support *S.442*. In particular the Secretary of State may place restrictions on shares where there is difficulty in finding out relevant facts about any shares. For example no voting rights are exercisable in respect of the shares and any agreement to transfer the shares will be void unless approved by the court or the Secretary of State.

f. If the Secretary of State believes that there is good reason to investigate the ownership of a company, but that it is unnecessary to appoint inspectors for the purpose, he may require any person whom he reasonably believes to have information to give such information to him.

32. *Investigation of Share Dealings*

a. By *S.323* directors are prohibited from dealing in options to buy or sell the quoted securities of their company or associated companies. By *S.324* directors of all companies are required to disclose to their companies their interest in its shares or debentures.

b. By *S.446* if the Department suspects contravention of *S.323* or *S.324* it may appoint an inspector to establish whether this is the case.

33. *Inspection of Documents*

a. By *S.447* the Department, if it thinks there is good reason to do so, may give directions to any company requiring it to produce any specified books or papers. A similar direction may be made to any person who appears to be in possession of those books or papers. Copies or extracts of them may be taken and any person in possession of them, or a past or present officer or employee of the company, may be required to provide an explanation of them. There are also:

  i. Provisions enabling a search warrant to be obtained in respect of premises where the documents are believed to be;

  ii. Provisions allowing the Secretary of State to authorise 'any other competent person' (probably a lawyer or an accountant) to exercise his power to require the production of documents. The competent person will then report to the Secretary of State.

  iii. Provisions preventing publication or excessive disclosure.

b. It is an offence:

  i. For any officer of the company to be a party to the destruction, mutilation or falsification of any document relating to the company's property or affairs;

  ii. For any officer to fraudulently part with, alter or make an omission from any such document;

  iii. For any person to knowingly or recklessly make a false explanation or statement in response to the directions of the Department.

CHAPTER 46

Meetings, Resolutions and Publicity

TYPES OF MEETING

1. *The Annual General Meeting*

   a. Except for *private companies* that have taken advantage of the *elective resolution* procedure (see paragraph 17. below) every company must hold an AGM every calendar year with not more than 15 months between each AGM. However, provided the first AGM is held within 18 months of incorporation it need not be held in the calendar year of incorporation or the following year *(S.366)*.

   b. If a company fails to hold an AGM within the prescribed time the Secretary of State may, on the application of *any member*, order it to be held. He may give such directions as he thinks fit and may fix the quorum at one member only *(S.367)*.

   c. Prior to 1985 Table A prescribed following as the *ordinary business* of the AGM:

      i.   Consideration of the accounts, the directors' report and the auditors' report;

      ii. Declaration of a dividend;

      iii. Election of directors in place of those retiring; and

      iv. The appointment and remuneration of auditors.

      However, Table A now merely states that the notice shall specify the general nature of the business to be transacted.

2. *Extraordinary General Meetings*

   a. Any meeting which is not an AGM is an EGM. The articles usually provide that an EGM may be called by the directors.

   b. Members have a statutory right to require directors to convene an EGM. By *S.368* despite anything in the articles the directors must call an EGM if required to do so by holders of at least 10% of the paid-up capital with voting rights. If the directors do not convene the meeting within 21 days the requisitionists (or more than half their number) may do so, and recover their expenses from the company, which may then recover them from the directors.

c. In addition *S.370* states that unless the articles provide otherwise two or more members holding not less than 10% of the issued share capital may call a meeting.

d. By *S.371* if it is impractical to call or conduct a meeting in the manner prescribed by the Act or the articles the court may, on the application of any director or member entitled to vote, order a meeting to be called, giving such directions as it thinks fit.

e. Note also:

i. A resigning auditor may require the directors to convene an EGM *(S.392A)*.

ii. *S.142* – Which requires the directors of a public company to call an EGM when it becomes known to a director that the net assets have fallen to half or less of the company's called up share capital.

Company Law Reform Proposals 2005 call for the abolition of extraordinary resolutions.

CONVENING MEETINGS

3. *Length of Notice*

a. Every member is entitled to 21 days written notice of an AGM, although a shorter period is permissible if agreed by all the members entitled to attend and vote *(S.369)*. *Company Law Reform Proposals 2005* are that this should be reduced to 14 days.

b. *S.369* specifies a period of 14 days written notice for an EGM unless a special resolution is to be moved in which case 21 days notice is required.

4. *Contents of the Notice*

a. The notice must specify the date, place, and time of the meeting. It is not necessary to give details of ordinary business, but the nature of any other business must be specified. However, where a special or extraordinary resolution is to be moved, the notice must set out the full text of the resolution.

b. The notice must state that a member entitled to attend and vote may appoint a proxy to attend and vote on his behalf.

5. *Special Notice (S.379)*

a. It is important to distinguish special notice from *notice of a special resolution*.

b. Special notice is required for three types of *ordinary resolution*:

i. To remove a director or to appoint somebody in his place *(S.303)*;

ii. To appoint a director aged 70 or over, where the age limit applies under *S.293*; and

    iii. To remove an auditor or to appoint any auditor other than the retiring auditor *(S.391A)*.

c. Where special notice is required *the persons proposing the motion must give the company* 28 days notice of their intention to move the resolution. The company will then give the members notice of the resolution when it sends them notice of the meeting. If it is too late to include the resolution in the notice of the meeting it may be advertised or otherwise communicated to the members at least 21 days before the meeting.

6. *Members' Resolutions and Statements (S.376–377)*

Holders of at least 5% of share capital with voting rights *or* at least 100 members (whether entitled to vote or not) who have paid up on average £100 each can compel the company:

a. By six weeks' requisition to give the members notice of any resolution which the requisitionists intend to move at an AGM.

b. By one week's requisition to circulate to the members a statement of up to 1,000 words with respect to any proposed resolution at any general meeting.

7. *The Electronic Communications Order 2000*

a. Notices of meetings can be sent electronically on a individual basis or posted on a website.

b. A proxy may be appointed electronically.

c. With regard to the filing of resolutions and other documents with the Registrar of Companies, the Registrar may be delivered electronically.

e. Table A is amended accordingly to permit this.

CONDUCT OF MEETINGS

8. *The Quorum*

a. A quorum is the minimum number of persons who must be present to conduct a meeting.

b. The quorum for all company meetings is two members personally present, unless the company has only one member or the court directs that the quorum shall be one.

c. Table A states that if within half an hour a quorum is not present, the meeting will stand adjourned to the same day, time and place in the next week (or to such other day, time and place as the directors shall determine).

9. *The Chairman*

There must be chairman to preside over the meeting. The chairman must:

a. Act in good faith in the interests of the company as a whole;

b. Ensure that business is conducted in an orderly manner in the order set out in the agenda. Therefore he must ensure that members relate what they say to the items on the agenda and do not make irrelevant or provocative remarks;

c. Allow all points of view to be adequately expressed and then put the motion to the vote and declare the result. He has a casting vote only if given one by the articles;

d. Decide whether amendments to motions are admissible. He should reject an amendment if it is outside the scope of the business stated in the notice of the meeting;

e. Adjourn any meeting at which a quorum is present if so directed by the meeting; and

f. Sign the minutes of the meeting.

10. *Voting*

a. The usual practice is to vote by a show of hands, ie each member present has one vote regardless of the number of shares held.

b. However, if a poll is properly demanded, then a member's votes will depend on the number of voting shares he holds.

11. *Proxies*

a. The term proxy is used both to refer to the person appointed to act on behalf of the member and to the *instrument* which gives him the required authority.

b. Every member has the right to appoint a proxy to attend and vote for him. The proxy does not need to be a member.

    Company Law Reform Proposals 2005 are that in addition, a proxy will be able to vote on a show of hands.

12. *Minutes*

a. Every company must keep minutes of both company meetings and board meetings.

b. When the minutes are signed by the chairman they become evidence of the proceedings. In particular they are conclusive evidence that a resolution has been carried or lost. This prevents a later argument on a point which should have been challenged at the meeting.

c. A minute book of general meetings must be kept at the company's registered office and must be available for inspection by members for at least two hours on each working day.

RESOLUTIONS

13. *Ordinary Resolutions*

a. This is a simple majority of members present in person or by proxy entitled to vote and voting. For example a company has ten members holding an equal number of shares. Four do not attend the meeting (or appoint proxies), three abstain, two vote for the motion, and one votes against. The resolution is passed.

b. The period of notice depends on the type of meeting at which it is moved (21 days for an AGM and generally 14 days for an EGM).

c. An ordinary resolution is the type used whenever the law or the company's articles do not require a special or extraordinary resolution. In some cases the law specifies an ordinary resolution, for example *S.303* (removal of directors) and *S.122 CA 89 (S.391)* (removal of auditors). Where a section states that 'the powers conferred by this section must be exercised by the company in general meeting' for example *S.121* (alteration of capital) it means that an ordinary resolution is necessary.

d. In general copies of ordinary resolutions which have been passed need not be filed with the registrar.

14. *Special Resolutions (S.378)*

These require a three-quarter majority of members present in person or by proxy entitled to vote and voting. A period of 21 days notice is required but a shorter period is acceptable if a simple majority in number holding 95% in value of the voting shares agree. Because of this notice requirement amendments to special resolutions cannot be accepted at the meeting. A copy of every special resolution which is passed must be filed with the registrar within 15 days. Special resolutions are required for a number of important company decisions, for example:

a. To alter the objects clause of its memorandum.

b. To alter the articles.

c. To reduce its capital, subject to the consent of the court.

d. To commence a voluntary winding-up.

e. To change the company name, subject to approval by the Secretary of State *(S.28)*.

f. To ratify an ultra vires act.

15. *Extraordinary Resolutions*

An extraordinary resolution is similar to a special resolution with regard to the majority necessary to pass the resolution, the admissibility of amendments and the requirements of filing. The difference is that only 14 days notice is required, although a shorter period is acceptable as with a special resolution. An extraordinary resolution is required in the following circumstances:

a. To wind-up the company voluntarily on the ground that it is insolvent. The reason for an extraordinary rather than a special resolution is to dispense with 21 days notice when winding-up is urgent;

b. In a voluntary winding-up to sanction the exercise, by the liquidator of some of his powers, for example to pay any class of creditors in full or to make a compromise arrangement with creditors;

c. To sanction a variation of class rights at a class meeting. This is referred to as an 'extraordinary resolution' in the Act although it is a *class* resolution rather than a company resolution. As noted, *Company Law Reform Proposals 2005* would remove the need for extraordinary resolutions, requiring only a special resolution.

16. *Written Resolutions (S.381A–382A)*

a. The 1989 Act introduced new rules to simplify private company procedures. There are two main changes. *Firstly, a private company* can substitute the unanimous written agreement of its shareholders (or in the case of a company with one member a written record of the decision) for any resolution passed at a general meeting (written resolutions). *Secondly, a private company* can, by elective resolution, opt out of certain company law requirements, including the holding of an AGM.

   Company Law Reform Proposals 2005 will allow private companies to pass a written ordinary resolution if approved by a simple majority of those entitled to vote and a written special resolution will be passed if approved by three quarters of those entitled to vote.

b. Except as stated below, anything which can be done by resolution at a general meeting of a private company may, instead of the meeting being held, be done by a written resolution signed by or on behalf of all members of the company who would be entitled to attend and vote at such a meeting. Previous notice is not required and the signatures need not be on a single document, however, each must be on a document accurately stating the terms of the resolution. The date of the resolution is the date when the last member signed it.

c. *Exceptions.* A written resolution may not be used to remove a director or auditor before their period of office has expired.

d. *Rights of auditors.* To preserve the auditors' right to receive notices and other communications relating to general meetings and their right to attend and be heard on matters concerning them as auditors, the 1989 Act requires a copy of any proposed written resolution to be sent to the auditors. They have the right (to be exercised within seven days) to require the resolution to be considered by the company in general meeting if they consider that it concerns them as auditors.

e. A written resolution may be used whatever resolution would otherwise be required ie special, extraordinary, elective, ordinary, or ordinary requiring special notice.

   The court held in RE DUOMATIC (1969) that where all the shareholders of a company assent on a matter that should be brought into effect by a resolution in general meeting (or a written resolution) the unanimous consent of all the shareholders without a formal meeting or written resolution is enough to satisfy the law – referred to as the, '*Duomatic Principle*'.

   In DEAKIN v FAULDING (2001) bonus payments were made to a director which should have been approved by ordinary resolution. The payment was being challenged by the new owners of the company. The High Court found that at the time of the payment there was informal consent by all the shareholders to the payment; the transaction was held valid.

17. *Elective Resolutions*

    a. *S.116 CA 89 (S.379A CA 85)* has introduced a new procedure enabling private companies to dispense with or modify certain internal procedures. An elective resolution must be passed if the company wishes:

        i.   To extend beyond five years the duration of the directors' authority to allot shares.

        ii.   To dispense with the requirement to lay accounts and reports before the company in general meeting. (However, any member has the right to require that the accounts be laid before the meeting.)

        iii. To dispense with the requirement to hold an AGM. This is a major reform, it recognises that for many companies, where the directors are also the only shareholders, it is an unnecessary formality to hold an AGM. However, any member may, at least three months before the end of the year, serve a notice on the company requiring it to hold an AGM in that year.

        iv. To dispense with the obligation to appoint auditors annually, ie the existing auditors shall be deemed to be re-appointed.

        v.   To reduce the majority required to consent to the holding of a general meeting at short notice, from members holding at least 95% in nominal value of shares carrying right to attend and vote to 90%.

    b. If an elective resolution is proposed for a general meeting, at least 21 days notice of the meeting must be given in writing. The notice must give the terms of the elective resolution. At the meeting the resolution must be agreed by all members entitled to attend and vote, either in person or by proxy. Alternatively the written resolution procedure may be used.

    c. An elective resolution may be revoked at any time by passing an ordinary resolution. An elective resolution will also cease to have effect if the company re-registers as public. Elective resolutions and ordinary resolutions revoking them must be delivered to the registrar.

Company Law Reform Proposals 2005 call for a removal of the elective resolution.

PUBLICITY

18. *Introduction*

Protection by disclosure is one of the underlying principles of the COMPANIES ACT. The theory is that if members, creditors and the public can find out relevant information about a company they will do so and then conduct their affairs with it accordingly. It has, however, always been clear that disclosure alone is not sufficient protection and extensive protective measures therefore exist, for example *S.103* (which requires an independent valuation of non-cash assets received by a public company in consideration for an allotment of shares), and *S.459* (which enables any member to apply for a court order if the affairs of the company are being conducted in an unfairly prejudicial manner). Publicity nevertheless remains important and is achieved in four main ways:

a.　The requirement of official notification of certain matters in the *Gazette*;

b.　The registration of certain information at the Companies Registry;

c.　The compulsory maintenance of certain registers by the company; and

d.　The requirement to make an annual return and disclose the company's financial position in its published accounts and directors' report.

Although a. and b. above ensure that information is publicly available, *S.711A* provides that a person shall not be taken to have notice of the matter merely because it is disclosed in any document kept by the registrar or made available by the company for inspection, ie it abolishes, for most purposes, the doctrine of constructive notice. One exception is that a person taking a charge over a company's property is deemed to have notice of any matter requiring registration and disclosed on the register of charges at the time the charge was created. Note also that a private company may pass an elective resolution to dispense with the requirement to lay accounts and reports before the company in general meeting and/or dispense with the requirement to hold an AGM.

OFFICIAL NOTIFICATION IN THE GAZETTE

19. *The Requirement of Notification*

When various documents are issued by, or filed at, the Companies Registry the registrar must give notice to the public of the issue or receipt of such documents by means of a notice in the *London Gazette*. The notice merely records the name of the company, the nature of the document and the date of its receipt. The document itself is not reproduced. If a person wishes to see the document he must apply to the Registry or the company's registered office. Numerous matters require notification, for example:

a.　The issue by the registrar of a certificate of incorporation.

b.　The receipt by the registrar of:

　　i.　A resolution altering either the memorandum or articles;

　　ii.　A notice of any change among the directors;

　　iii.　Any documents required to be comprised in the accounts;

　　iv.　Any notice of a change in the situation of the registered office;

　　v.　Any order for the winding-up or dissolution of the company;

20. *The Effect of Official Notification*

The effect of notification is that the company cannot rely, as against third parties, on the happening of certain events unless their occurrence had been officially notified or the company can show that their occurrence was actually known to the third party. The events are:

a.   The making of a winding-up order;

b.   An alteration of the memorandum or articles;

c.   A change of directors; and

d.   A change of the address of the registered office.

MATTERS REQUIRING REGISTRATION AT THE COMPANIES REGISTRY

21. *Information on Record at the Companies Registry*

The following information is recorded on each company's file at the Companies Registry. Any member of the public may inspect the file. The fee is £1.

a.   The company's memorandum and articles;

b.   A statement containing the names and relevant particulars of the directors and the secretary;

c.   Any notice of the appointment of a liquidator or receiver;

d.   A statement of the address of the registered office;

e.   Details of the company's nominal, issued and paid-up capital;

f.   Details of charges over the company's property;

g.   The annual balance sheet, profit and loss account, directors' report and auditors' report (this requirement is modified in the case of certain small and medium-sized companies); and

h.   The annual return.

22. *Resolutions Requiring Registration*

a.   All special, extraordinary and elective resolutions must be registered within 15 days of passing the resolution.

b.   In general the fact that an ordinary resolution has been passed need not be registered. However, there are several exceptions, for example resolutions to:

i.   Appoint or remove directors.

ii.   Remove auditors.

iii. Change the address of the registered office.

iv.   Increase the authorised capital.

REGISTERS WHICH MUST BE MAINTAINED BY THE COMPANY

23. *The Registered Office*

   a. The documents and registers which must be kept by a company and the rights of inspection relating to them were set out in Chapter 40.10–11. In most cases no further explanation of their contents is necessary. However, the register of directors and secretaries, the register of directors' interests in shares and debentures and the register of substantial shareholdings merit further comment.

   b. Note that the register of members was discussed in Chapter 43.8 and the register of charges in Chapter 42.11.

24. *The Register of Directors and Secretaries*

   a. By *S.288* every company must keep a register of its directors and its secretary at its registered office.

   b. The register must contain the following particulars of each director:

   i.   Name and former name, (if any);

   ii. Address;

   iii. Nationality;

   iv. Business occupation, (if any);

   v.   Particulars of other directorships held, or which have been held, by him in the past five years, except for directorships of companies within the same group and directorships of dormant companies; and

   vi. Date of birth, where the company is subject to *S.293* (age limits). (See Chapter 44.5.).

   c. The company must notify the registrar within 14 days of any change in the particulars on the register. When a person becomes a director the notification must be accompanied by his signed consent to act.

25. *Directors' Names on Company Stationery (S.305)*

   A company may not state the name of any of its directors on its business letters (other than in the text or as a signatory) unless it states the christian name, or initials thereof, and the surname of every director who is an individual and the corporate name of every corporate director.

26. *The Register of Directors' Interests in Shares or Debentures*

   a. By *S.324* a director must notify the company in writing of any transaction involving his interest in the shares or debentures of the company. The notification period is five working days. By *S.328* the interest of a director's spouse or infant child must be treated as if it were the director's interest.

   b. There are detailed rules for determining when a director has an 'interest' in shares or debentures. Thus, for example a person holding a beneficial interest under a trust does have an interest in shares comprised in the trust, but the trustee (although on the register of members) does not have an interest. Also a person has an interest if shares or debentures are held by a company and

    i.   That company or its directors are accustomed to act in accordance with his instructions; or if

    ii.   He controls one-third or more of the votes at a general meeting of that company.

c.   By *S.325* every company must keep a register of directors' interests in shares or debentures. Information must be entered in the register within three working days of its receipt.

27. *The Register of Substantial Shareholdings*

a.   The rules are contained in *S.198–211* and *S.134 CA 89*. They only apply to *public companies*.

b.   A notifiable interest arises when a person knows that he has an interest in 3% or more of the company's voting shares. Notification must be in writing and must be made within two working days from when the obligation to notify arose.

c.   Notification is necessary on cessation or acquisition of an interest and also when *any change* in a notifiable interest takes place. For example, a company may issue new shares for the purpose of an acquisition. This could dilute a shareholder's interest from, say 6% to 2% without altering the total number of shares held. He would nevertheless be under an obligation to notify the company.

d.   The rules for defining the extent of an 'interest' are very detailed.

    For example a person is deemed to have an interest if:

    i.   His spouse or infant child has an interest;

    ii.   Shares are held by a company and that company or its directors are accustomed to act in accordance with his instructions, or he controls one-third or more of the votes in general meeting of that company; or

    iii. Another person is interested in the company's shares and he is *acting together* with that other person. This is discussed below.

e.   Persons acting together

    i.   When persons act in concert the Act attributes to each member of such a group (known as a 'concert party') the interests of the other members and places an obligation to notify on *all* members of the concert party, ie a person has an obligation to notify even if he does not have any shares himself but he is acting in concert with someone who has a notifiable interest.

    ii.   A concert party exists when there is an agreement (whether legally binding or not) under which at least one of the parties is to acquire an interest in the shares of a company. In addition there must be some understanding as to the way in which the interest acquired under the contract is to be used.

f. A public company must keep a register to record within three days the information notified. The register must be kept at the same place as the register of directors and secretaries. The register will also contain (in a separate part) the results of any investigations carried out under *S.212* (see below).

28. *Investigation by a Company of Interests in its Shares (S.212–216)*

a. If a *public company* knows, or has reasonable cause to believe, a person to be or have been interested in its voting shares within the past three years, it may make a written request of that person to indicate whether he holds or has held an interest in the shares. The request may require a written response within a specified time limit. When a company receives such information it must record it in the register of substantial shareholdings.

b. Members holding not less than one tenth of the paid-up voting shares may require the company to make an investigation by depositing a requisition at the registered office. The company must prepare a report on its investigation. The report must be available for inspection at the registered office within a reasonable period (not more than 15 days) after the conclusion of the investigation.

c. If a person fails to give information when requested to do so, the company may apply to the court for an order that the shares be sold or for an order imposing restrictions on the shares in question, for example:

   i.   That any transfer of the shares is void;

   ii. That no voting rights are exercisable is respect of the shares;

   iii. That (except in a liquidation) no payment shall be made in respect of sums due from the company on those shares.

The person is also liable to a maximum of two years imprisonment and an unlimited fine.

THE ANNUAL RETURN

29. *Making the Annual Return (S.363–365)*

a. *The return date.* The annual return will have to be made up to a date not later than the company's return date and filed within 28 days of the date to which it is made up. The return date will be either:

   i. The anniversary of the company's incorporation date or

   ii. If the company's previous return was made up to a different date, the anniversary of that date.

b.   The return must be signed either by a director or the secretary.

c.   If a company does not deliver its annual return within 28 days after the return date, or delivers a return which does not contain the required information, it is liable to a fine. Every director or secretary will also be liable unless they can show that they took all reasonable steps to avoid the offence.

30. *The Contents of the Annual Return*

The annual return must state the date to which it is made up and contain the following information:

a.   The address of the registered office and, if the register of members is not kept at that office, the address at which it is kept.

b.   A summary of share capital specifying for each class of share the total number of issued shares and the aggregate nominal value of those shares.

c.   The type of company and its principal business activities.

d.   A list of members on the date to which the return is made up showing individual shareholdings and changes that have taken place during the year. To avoid annual preparation of a lengthy list the company need only submit a full list of members every three years. In the intervening years only details of changes need be given.

e.   Particulars of directors and the secretary taken from the register, including the date of birth of each individual director.

f.   Where a private company has by elective resolution dispensed with the laying of accounts and reports before the general meeting, or with holding an AGM, a statement to that effect.

THE ACCOUNTING RECORDS AND THE ACCOUNTS

31. *Accounting Records*

a.   It is important to distinguish between the accounting records and the accounts.

   i.   The *accounting records* are the ledgers, cash book, order forms, receipts and other records maintained by the company to enable the accounts to be prepared.

   ii. The *accounts* (or financial statements) in the narrow sense consist of the balance sheet, the profit and loss account and the notes to the accounts, although other documents are comprised in the 'accounts' which are filed with the registrar.

b.   By *S.221–222* every company must keep accounting records which must:

   i.   Show with reasonable accuracy, at any time during the financial year, the financial position of the company at that time; and

ii. Enable the directors to ensure that any balance sheet prepared by them gives a true and fair view of the company's state of affairs and any profit and loss account gives a true and fair view of the company's profit or loss.

c. *In particular the records must contain:*

   i. A day-to-day record of money received by and spent by the company;

   ii. A record of the assets and liabilities of the company;

   iii. Statements of the stock held by the company at the end of each financial year; and

   iv. A record of goods sold and purchased, with details of the goods, buyers and sellers sufficient to enable them to be identified.

d. The accounting records must be kept at the registered office or such other place as the directors think fit. They must be open for inspection by officers at any time.

e. A private company must keep its accounting records for three years. Any other company must keep the records for six years from the date when they are made.

f. Failure to keep accounting records is an offence for which officers may be fined or imprisoned for a maximum of two years.

32. *The Accounting Reference Period and Accounting Reference Date*

By *S.226* the directors must prepare accounts based on an accounting reference period. This will commence on the day after the date to which the last annual accounts were prepared and will end on the last day of the company's financial year, known as the accounting reference date.

33. *Laying and Delivering Accounts*

a. By *S.241* the directors, in respect of each accounting reference period, must lay before the company in general meeting every document required to be comprised in the accounts.

b. In respect of each accounting reference period the directors must deliver to the registrar a copy of every document required to be comprised in the accounts.

c. By *S.252* a *private company* may decide, by *elective resolution*, to dispense with the laying of accounts before the company in general meeting. The accounts must still be sent to members and others entitled to receive notice of general meetings and filing requirements are not affected. While the election is in force any member, or the auditor can require the accounts to be laid for a particular financial year.

d. The documents required to be comprised in the accounts are:

   i. The profit and loss account;

   ii. The balance sheet. This must be signed by one director;

      iii. The auditors' report. The copy sent to the registrar must state the names of the auditors and be signed by them.

      iv. The directors' report.

      v. If the company has subsidiaries, group accounts.

e. Note that:

      i. An unlimited company is exempt from delivering accounts provided it is not in the same group as a limited company.

      ii. The requirements are relaxed for small and medium-sized companies. In particular a small company need not deliver a profit and loss account and a directors' report. Small and medium-sized companies are defined below.

      iii. The annual return is not annexed to the accounts, it is delivered to the registrar separately.

f. A *small company* is a private company which in respect of a particular financial year satisfies for that year and the preceding year at least two of the following conditions:

      i. A turnover not exceeding £2,000,000;

      ii. A balance sheet total not exceeding £975,000; and

      iii. An average number of persons employed per week not exceeding 50.

g. A *medium-sized company* is a private company which in respect of a particular financial year satisfies for that year and the preceding year at least two of the following conditions:

      i. A turnover not exceeding £8,000,000;

      ii. A balance sheet total not exceeding £3,900,000; and

      iii. An average number of persons employed per week not exceeding 250.

NB: Although small and medium-sized companies are permitted to file modified financial statements with the registrar, they must nevertheless prepare full financial statements for the members.

THE DIRECTORS' REPORT

34. *Introduction*

a. Consideration of the directors' report is one of the items of *ordinary business* at the AGM.

b. By *S.238* the balance sheet and every document which is required to be attached to it (the directors' report; the auditors' report; the profit and loss account; and group accounts, if any) must be sent to each member not less that 21 days before the AGM. They will therefore be sent to the members with notice of the AGM.

35. *Contents of the Directors' Report*

a. *General provisions*

   i. A review of the development of the business of the company during the year and of its position at the end of it;

   ii. A statement of the principal activities of the company and any significant changes in those activities during the year;

   iii. Particulars of any important events affecting the company;

   iv. An indication of likely future developments;

   v. An indication of the activities (if any) in the field of research and development.

b. *Dividends and reserves*

   i. The amount, if any, recommended for dividend; and

   ii. The amount, if any, proposed to be carried to reserves.

c. *Fixed assets*

   i. Any significant changes in the fixed assets during the year; and

   ii. An estimate of any substantial difference between the book value and the market value of the company's interests in land and buildings (if the directors consider this to be of significance to the members or debentureholders).

d. *Political and charitable donations.* If such donations together total more than £200 the report must show:

   i. Separate totals for each; and

   ii. The amount of each political contribution over £200, naming the recipient.

e. *Directors*

   i. The names of persons who were directors of the company at any time during the year; and

   ii. For persons who were directors at the end of the year, the interests of each (and the interests of any spouse or infant child) in the shares or debentures of the company and other companies in the group.

f. *Employees.* Except where the company has less than 250 employees the report must state the company's policy with regard to the employment, training, career development and promotion of disabled employees.

g. *Shares purchased.* Details of any shares of the company purchased by the company during the year.

h. *Shares otherwise acquired.* Details of any of the company's shares acquired by its nominee or with its financial assistance.

CHAPTER 47

Reconstructions, Mergers and Takeovers

RECONSTRUCTIONS AND MERGERS

1. *Introduction*

a. Several terms are used to describe the methods by which two or more companies join to form one. None of these terms have precise legal meanings. The terms are:

  i. *Merger*. This occurs when two companies join together under the name of one of them, or as a new company formed for the purpose. A merger may also be called an *amalgamation*. Mergers generally only take place when there is agreement between the directors of both companies.

  ii. *Takeover*. This term describes the acquisition by one company of sufficient shares in another company (sometimes referred to as the 'target' company) to enable the purchaser to control the target company. Sometimes takeover bids are contested by the board of the target company, and on some occasions rival bids are made for the control of the same company. A takeover differs from a merger in that both companies will remain in existence (at least for the time being). Takeovers are considered later in the chapter.

b. Sometimes a company will wish to reorganise in some way without involving other companies, it may wish for example:

  i. To transfer its assets to a new company, the persons carrying on the business remaining substantially the same. This is usually referred to as a *reconstruction*.

  ii. To make an *arrangement* with members and/or creditors because it is in financial difficulties, but where winding-up is not appropriate.

2. *Methods*

a. A merger, reconstruction or arrangement can be effected under *S.425* (schemes of arrangement).

b. A merger or reconstruction can be effected under *S.110 IA* (reconstruction by a company in voluntary liquidation). An arrangement with creditors cannot be effected under *S.110 IA*.

c. There is no particular section under which a takeover can be effected. It will, however, be seen that *S.428* enables a bidder who has purchased 90% or more of the shares in the target company to 'compulsorily purchase' the remaining shares.

3. *Mergers and Reconstructions Under S.110–111 IA*

a. *Basic procedure*

i. The members must pass a *special resolution* giving authority to the liquidator to sell the whole or part of its business or property to another company on terms that the consideration be divided among the members of the transferor company. The consideration may be cash, but it is usually shares in the transferee company.

ii. Only after the majority have ensured that there will be enough cash to pay dissentients should it pass a second special resolution, putting the company into voluntary liquidation.

iii. The effect of the scheme is that the shares in the transferee company then become the assets of the transferor company and must be distributed to its members in accordance with their rights on liquidation. The transferor company is then dissolved, its shareholders having become shareholders in the transferee company.

b. *Dissentient shareholders*

i. A dissentient shareholder is one who did not vote for the special resolution. He can require the liquidator to abstain from the sale or buy his shares. The right must be exercised by a written notice addressed to the liquidator and deposited at the registered office within seven days of the resolution.

ii. If the parties cannot agree on a price, the matter will be referred to arbitration. The price is likely to be based on the value before reconstruction was proposed rather than after.

c. *Dissentient creditors*

The creditors are not as directly affected by a reconstruction as the members. They have their usual rights on liquidation, although the funds from which they will be paid have changed. There is no legal obligation for the transfer agreement to provide for creditors, but in practice it will usually provide either:

i. That the transferee company takes over the debts of the transferor; or

ii. That the transferor company retains sufficient funds to pay its debts.

If the creditors feel that their position is jeopardised in that the new assets received by the transferor company will not be sufficient to pay their debts they can petition for the compulsory winding-up of the transferor company on the ground that it is unable to pay its debts.

4. Uses of S.110 IA

a. *For a reconstruction.* ie Company A transfers its assets to a new company, Company B, formed for the purpose, receiving in return shares in Company B. Companies may wish to reconstruct for several reasons, for example:

   i. The reconstruction will enable the transferee company to retain and realise cash assets, paying them to its members on liquidation.

   ii. It may be able to raise new capital by issuing the shares in the new company as partly paid-up.

   iii. To alter the objects where there has been a successful objection by a dissentient minority.

b. *For a merger.* There are two types of merger:

   i. Company A goes into voluntary liquidation, selling its assets to Company B (an established and successful company). In return the shareholders of Company A receive shares in Company B. Company A is then dissolved and the business of both companies is carried on by Company B. This is, in effect, a takeover by agreement.

   ii. Companies A and B both go into voluntary liquidation. The assets of both companies are then transferred to Company C, a new company formed for the purpose, the members of A and B receiving shares in Company C. Companies A and B are then dissolved. In order to retain their goodwill Company C may change its name to A B Ltd.

5. Schemes of Arrangement Under S.425–427

a. *S.425* can be used to effect any type of *compromise or arrangement* with creditors or members, for example changing their rights in or against the company, or transferring their rights to another company which then issues shares or takes over liabilities in return for cancellation of existing rights against the first company, ie it can be used for both reconstructions and mergers. There must, however, be a 'compromise' or an 'arrangement':

   i. A *compromise* can only be made when there has previously been a dispute.

   ii. An *arrangement* has a much wider meaning and does not depend on the presence of a dispute.

b. *Procedure under S.425*

   i. The first step is for the company, or any creditor, or any member or, if the company is being wound up, the liquidator, to ask the court to convene a meeting of creditors and meetings of each class of members.

   ii. By *S.426* the company must send out with the notice of any meeting called under *S.425* a statement explaining the effect of the scheme and in particular details of material interests of directors and its effect on them.

   iii. The compromise or arrangement must be agreed at each meeting by a *simple majority in number* representing *75% in value* of those voting in person or by proxy.

    iv. When the necessary meetings have been held and the required majorities obtained *the court must give its approval.*

  c. *The role of the court*

    i. It will ensure that the scheme is not ultra vires or an improper use of *S.425* (for example to reduce capital to which *S.135* should apply).

    ii. It will check that the meetings were properly convened and that the required majority approval was obtained.

    iii. Since the requirement is only for a majority of members voting rather than of all the members, the court will examine whether the class was fairly represented at the meeting. Probably the court will have already directed that a substantial percentage of the class constitute a quorum when the initial application was made to the court to hold the meetings.

    iv. The court will be very careful if the majority of one class of shares also hold the shares of another class since they may vote in favour of a scheme which harms the first class of shares but benefits the second class.

    v. The court will look at situations where creditors are also shareholders since a similar conflict of interest could arise.

    vi. In general the court will require disclosure of all relevant information, listen to any minority objections and finally only sanction the scheme if it is one that an honest and intelligent businessman would approve. Once the court has approved the scheme it binds all parties and cannot be altered.

6. *Voluntary Arrangements Under S.1–7 IA*

  a. The INSOLVENCY ACT contains procedures that provide an alternative to *S.425 CA 1985*. The procedures apply to any 'composition in satisfaction of debts' (ie all creditors agree to take a proportion of what is owed to them) or to a scheme of arrangement of the company's affairs.

  b. Meetings of members and creditors must be held to approve the scheme (as under *S.425*) but the main difference is that although the court receives a report on the results of the meetings, it is not directly involved unless the scheme is challenged by dissenting members or creditors on the grounds that it was unfairly prejudicial to them, or that there was an irregularity at either of the meetings.

TAKEOVERS

7. *Reasons for Takeovers*

The term takeover is usually used to describe a contested bid for the shares in one company (the 'target' company) by another company. Takeovers have become very common in recent years. They have also been the subject of increasing concern, because in some cases the interests of investors in general have suffered as directors and controlling shareholders have sought to further their own personal interests. Takeovers are not, however, undesirable as such. It may well be that larger size brings economies of scale and better management. Takeovers often take place for one of two reasons:

a. The target company may have been badly managed so that the market price of the controlling shares has fallen to less than the potential value of the company's assets. Thus even if the offeror pays slightly more than market value for the shares it will still obtain control of the assets for less than their true value.

b. A well-managed and successful company may be sufficiently attractive to a larger company that the larger company is prepared to pay the true value for its shares to secure control of its assets.

8. *Basic Procedure*

a. The bidding company will offer to purchase all the shares in the target company either for cash or in return for its own shares. Usually the offer will be conditional on acceptance in respect of a certain percentage of the shares.

b. In some cases the dissenting minority will not wish to sell their shares even at market value. This could be inconvenient for the offeror which may wish to acquire a wholly owned subsidiary. In such a situation the Act provides for the offeror to 'buy out' the dissenting minority of the target company, provided it acquires 90% of the shares to which the offer relates and complies with certain conditions. Such a purchase will not, however, be allowed if it is being used as a means of expropriating the minority interest when there is no genuine takeover.

In RE BUGLE PRESS (**1961**) persons holding 90% of the shares in a company formed a new company. The new company then made an offer for the shares of the old company. Clearly the 90% accepted the offer and the new company then served a notice on the 10% shareholder in the old company stating that they wished to purchase his shares. He opposed the scheme on the ground that it amounted to an expropriation of his interest in that the shareholders of the new company were the persons who held 90% of the shares in the old company. His claim succeeded. This is a good example of the court lifting the veil of incorporation of the companies and basing its decision on the actual identity of the members concerned.

c. The dissenting minority also have a right to change their minds and accept the offer when it becomes clear that the offeror has a substantial majority. It applies when the shares transferred under the scheme plus those already held by the offeror amount to 90% in value of the shares or class of shares in the target company. The offeror must then give notice of this fact to the remaining shareholders and any such shareholder can then require the offeror to buy his shares.

9. *The City Code on Takeovers and Mergers*

a. The first informal city guidelines on the conduct of takeovers were published in 1959. They were not very successful and 1968 the *City*

Code on Takeovers and Mergers was published. It has since been revised, the current edition being published in 1988. The Code was suggested by the Stock Exchange and the Bank of England and was prepared by the Executive Committee of the Issuing Houses Association in co-operation with other organisations, for example the Committee of London Clearing Bankers. The Code does not have the force of law, but it must be complied with by listed companies if they are to conform to Stock Exchange regulations.

b. The operation of the Code is supervised by the *Panel on Takeovers and Mergers*. The Panel is available for consultation at any time before or during a takeover or merger. It is not, however, concerned with the merits of the bid itself, this must be decided by the company and its shareholders. Occasionally the Panel has intervened in a takeover, for example by asking a party to pursue a particular course of action, or by investigating the conduct of an individual.

c. If the Panel discovers a breach of the Code and proposes to take disciplinary action an appeal may be made to an *Appeals Committee* chaired by a member of the House of Lords.

d. The basic purpose of the Code is to ensure that the boards of the companies involved and their advisers act in the best interests of their respective shareholders, in particular by providing them with full information and equal treatment. It also requires persons engaged in takeovers to be aware of and observe the spirit as well as the precise words of the code.

CHAPTER 48

Liquidation, Administration and Receivership

LIQUIDATION – INTRODUCTION

1. *Definition*

   a. *Liquidation* is the process by which the life of a company is brought to an end and its property administered for the benefit of its members and creditors.

   b. Liquidation or winding-up (the two terms mean the same) begins either by court order (compulsory liquidation) or by the members passing a resolution to wind-up (voluntary liquidation).

   c. This chapter starts with a description of insolvency practitioners, but it must be emphasised that although most voluntary and compulsory liquidations occur because a company cannot pay its debts, companies may be liquidated for reasons other than insolvency, for example a dissatisfied minority shareholder may petition to wind-up a company because he objects to the way in which the majority are running the company and he wants to recover his share of the assets.

2. *Insolvency Practitioners*

   a. Prior to 1985 neither liquidators nor receivers had to have any professional qualifications or practical experience. This no doubt contributed to some illegal and highly unethical practices by a minority of liquidators, usually to the detriment of creditors.

   b. Professional bodies must now incorporate into their rules provisions to ensure that such of their members who are permitted by its rules to act as insolvency practitioners are fit and proper persons so to act, and meet acceptable requirements as to education, practical training and experience. Professional bodies will be granted recognition by the Secretary of State and such recognition may be revoked if it appears to the Secretary of State that the body no longer satisfies the specified criteria.

COMPULSORY LIQUIDATION

3. Grounds

By *S.122 IA* there are seven grounds on which a company may be wound up by the court, although only two (f. and g. below) are of any importance:

a. The company has resolved by special resolution to be wound up by the court;

b. It has been formed as a public company but has not been issued with a certificate of compliance with the minimum share capital requirements;

c. Where an old public company has failed to re-register by 22nd March 1982, or a company incorporated as a public company has failed within one year to obtain a trading certificate;

d. It has not commenced business within a year of incorporation or has suspended business for a year;

e. The number of members has fallen below the statutory minimum of two, except in the case of a private company;

f. The company is unable to pay its debts; and

g. The court is of the opinion that it is just and equitable that the company should be wound up.

4. Inability to Pay its Debts (S.123 IA)

a. A company is *deemed* to be unable to pay its debts if:

   i. A creditor for more than £750 has served on the company a written demand for payment and within the next three weeks the company has neither paid the debt nor given security for its payment; *or*

   ii. Judgement has been obtained against the company for a debt (normally in excess of £750) and execution, ie payment out of the company's assets is unsatisfied; *or*

   iii. The court is satisfied that the company is unable to pay its debts as they fall due.

   iv. The court is satisfied that the value of the company's assets is less than the amount of its liabilities, taking into account its contingent and prospective liabilities.

b. The petition will of course be presented by a creditor. The company and creditors other than the petitioner are also entitled to be heard. If some creditors oppose the petition because they feel that the continued existence of the company is their best chance of payment, the court is likely to prefer the views of the creditors to whom in aggregate the largest amount is owing.

5. *The Just and Equitable Ground*

   a.   The court can make the order whenever the circumstances of justice or equity so demand. For example:

      i.   When the *substratum* of the company has gone, ie the main purpose for which the company was formed has been fulfilled or has become incapable of achievement.

      ii.   When there is *deadlock* in the management of the business because the directors cannot agree on vital matters or become personally antagonistic.

      iii.   Where the company is in substance a partnership and there are grounds for dissolving a partnership, for example the basis of mutual trust and confidence has been broken.

         In RE WESTBOURNE GALLERIES (**1973**) E and N had been business partners since 1945, taking an equal share in management and profit. In 1958 a private company was formed, E and N each holding one half of the shares (500 shares each). They were also the company's directors. Later it was agreed to admit N's son, G, to the business. E and N each transferred 100 shares to him and he was appointed a director. The company made good profits, but no dividends were paid, all the profit being distributed as directors' remuneration. Following a disagreement between E and N a general meeting was called and N and G removed E as a director and excluded him from management. E petitioned for an order that the company be wound up on the 'just and equitable' ground. It was held that the company must be wound up because when E and N formed the company it was clear that the basic nature of their personal business relationship would remain the same. Therefore N and G were not entitled, in equity, to use their statutory power to remove a director.

      iv.   Where there is justifiable lack of confidence in the management.

         In LOCH v JOHN BLACKWOOD (**1924**) the directors failed to call meetings, submit accounts or recommend a dividend. The reason was to keep the petitioners ignorant as to the value of the company, so that the directors could acquire their shares at an undervaluation. Winding-up was ordered.

   b.   An order will not be granted merely because the directors have exceeded their powers, or because they have refused to register a transfer, where a right of refusal exists under the articles.

6. *The Petition*

   a.   Proceedings are commenced by the presentation of a petition by a person qualified to do so on one of the above grounds.

   b.   The petition should be presented in the High Court, or if the paid-up capital does not exceed £120,000 in the County Court of the district where the registered office of the company is situated.

    c.   A petition may be presented by

        i.   *The company* or its *directors*.

        ii.   Any *creditor*.

        iii.   A *contributory*, ie any person liable to contribute to the assets of a company in the event of a winding up. This includes present and certain past members.

        iv.   The *Official Receiver*, where the company is already in voluntary liquidation.

        v.   The *Secretary of State*, usually only as a result of an investigation under *S.431* or *S.432*.

        vi.   The *Attorney-General*, when the company is registered as a charity.

7. Effects of a Compulsory Winding-up Order

    a.   The Official Receiver becomes the liquidator and continues in office until another person becomes liquidator.

    b.   Any disposition of the company's property, transfer of shares or alteration in the status of members is void unless the court orders otherwise.

    c.   No action can be commenced or proceeded with against the company without leave of the court, and any seizure of the company's assets to satisfy a debt after the start of winding-up is void.

    d.   The directors' powers cease and are assumed by the liquidator. Most of their duties also cease, one exception is the duty not to disclose confidential information, which continues after the winding-up order.

    e.   The company's employees are automatically dismissed, but they may sue for damages for breach of contract. The liquidator may of course re-employ the employees for the time being.

    f.   Floating charges crystallise, and there is a possibility that other charges and transactions may be invalidated.

    g.   The assets remain the legal property of the company, unless the court makes an order vesting them in the liquidator. The business may continue but only with a view to its most beneficial realisation.

8. Proceedings After a Winding-up Order

    a.   A copy of the winding-up order must immediately be sent by the company to the registrar, who must publish notice of its receipt in the *Gazette*.

    b.   The official receiver may require a *statement of affairs*. This would normally be submitted by the directors and/or the secretary, but may be required from, for example, company employees. It must contain:

        i.   Particulars of assets, debts and liabilities;

        ii.   Names and addresses of creditors;

        iii.   Details of security held by creditors and the date when given;

    iv. Any further information which may be prescribed or which the official receiver may require.

  c. The official receiver has a duty to investigate:

    i. The causes of failure (if the company has failed); and

    ii. The promotion, formation, business, dealings and affairs of the company.

    He must make such report (if any) to the court as he thinks fit. The report is prima facie evidence in any legal proceedings of the facts stated therein.

  d. Within 12 weeks of the winding-up order the official receiver must decide whether to summon meetings of creditors and contributories. If he decides not to do so he must inform the court, the creditors and the contributories. However, he must summon meetings of both creditors and contributories if required to do so by one quarter in value of the creditors. The purpose of the meetings is to choose a liquidator and to decide whether to appoint a *committee of creditors*. The purpose of this committee is to assist the liquidator and act as a link between him and the interests it represents. It also has a statutory power to sanction some of the liquidator's actions.

9. *General Functions of the Liquidator*

  a. To ensure that the company's assets are got in, realised and distributed to the company's creditors and, if there is a surplus, to the persons entitled to it.

  b. If the liquidator is not the official receiver he must:

    i. Furnish the official receiver with such information as he may reasonably require;

    ii. Produce and permit inspection of, books papers and other records;

    iii. Give such other assistance as the official receiver reasonably requires.

10. *Liquidator's Powers*

  a. *With the sanction* of the court or the committee of creditors he can:

    i. Bring and defend actions on behalf of the company;

    ii. Carry on the company's business to enable it to be wound up beneficially;

    iii. Pay any class of creditors in full; and

    iv. Make any compromises with creditors, contributories or debtors.

  b. *Without sanction* he can:

    i. Sell the company's property;

    ii. Draw, accept and indorse bills of exchange in the company's name;

    iii. Raise money on the security of its assets;

    iv. Appoint an agent;

v. Appoint a solicitor to assist him;

vi. Execute deeds, receipts and other documents, using the company seal when necessary;

vii. Prove in the bankruptcy or insolvency of any contributory; and

viii. Do all such other things as are necessary to wind-up the company and distribute its assets.

11. *Vacation of Office by the Liquidator*

The appointment will end when the liquidator

a. Is removed by order of the court, or by a general meeting of the company's creditors;

b. Resigns by giving notice to the court;

c. Ceases to be a qualified insolvency practitioner;

d. Is released after the conclusion of the winding-up.

12. *Dissolution*

When the registrar of companies receives notice from the official receiver that the winding-up is complete, or receives notice that the final meeting of creditors has been held, he notes this fact on the company's file and three months later the company is dissolved.

PROVISIONS APPLICABLE TO EVERY KIND OF LIQUIDATION

13. *Fraudulent Trading*

a. By *S.213 IA* if in a winding-up it appears that the company has been carrying on business with intent to defraud creditors or for any fraudulent purpose, the court can, on the application of the liquidator, order that persons who were knowingly parties shall be liable to make such contributions to the company's assets as the court thinks proper.

b. By *S.458* such persons may also be imprisoned or fined. Criminal liability may be imposed even if the company is not being wound-up, but winding-up is still a condition precedent to civil liability.

14. *Wrongful Trading (S.214 IA)*

a. If in a winding-up it appears to the liquidator that a *director* or *former director* has been guilty of wrongful trading he may apply to the court for an order that the person is liable to make a contribution to the company's assets.

b. The court must be satisfied that:

i. The company has gone into insolvent liquidation;

ii. At some time before the start of winding-up that person knew or ought to have concluded that there was no reasonable prospect that the company would avoid insolvent liquidation; and

iii. That person was a director of the company at the time.

c. The director will be deemed to know that the company could not avoid insolvent liquidation if that would have been the conclusion of a reasonably diligent person having:

i. The general knowledge, skill and experience that might reasonably be expected of a person carrying out that particular director's duties; and

ii. The general knowledge, skill and experience actually possessed by that director.

d. The court will not make an order if it is satisfied that, after the director became aware of the condition stated in b. ii. above, he took every step with a view to minimising the potential loss to the company's creditors as he ought to have taken in the circumstances.

In RE PRODUCE MARKETING CONSORTIUM (1989) the two directors of the company were aware of a serious drop in turnover and profits, and that insolvency was inevitable (despite the absence of accounts). They nevertheless continued to trade with the purpose of reducing secured indebtedness to their bank. They also ignored a warning by the auditor and made a number of untrue statements, indicating an unwillingness to acknowledge the serious state of the company's affairs. The company was eventually wound up and the liquidator claimed £108,000 compensation from the directors for wrongful trading. It was held that although there was no deliberate course of wrong doing, the directors had not taken every step to minimise potential loss, because they allowed the company to trade for over a year after they had become (or should have become) aware of insolvency. The court held that the provisions of S.214 were basically compensatory rather than penal, so the amount of personal liability was the loss caused to the company. The judge assessed this to be £75,000.

15. *Priority of Debts*

a. *Winding-up costs, charges and expenses*, for example the liquidator's remuneration.

b. *Preferential debts*. These rank and abate equally, ie if there are insufficient funds to satisfy all the preferential creditors, each gets an equal proportion of what is owed to him. The ENTERPRISE ACT 2002 abolished Crown preference and so debts owed to the Inland Revenue, to Customs and Excise for VAT and Social Security debts such as national insurance contributions are no longer preferential. They become unsecured creditors. Employees' wages owed for the previous four months up to a current maximum of £800 per employee gross, are a preferential debt.

Where assets are insufficient to pay all preferential debts in full, they rank equally and receive 'so much in the pound'.

    c. *Creditors secured by floating charges*. Under the ENTERPRISE ACT 2002 when assets of a company subject to a floating charge are realised, a certain proportion (not stated) must be set aside for the unsecured creditors; this is sometimes referred to as 'ring fencing' assets.

    d. *Ordinary unsecured creditors*. Their debts rank and abate equally.

    e. *Sums due to members* in their capacity as members, for example return of capital, and dividends declared but not paid before the commencement of the winding-up.

16. *Preferential Debts*

The main preferential debts are:

    a. 12 months pay as you earn (PAYE) deductions due from the company;

    b. Six months value added tax (VAT) due from the company;

    c. Social security (national insurance) contributions for the 12 months prior to the relevant date;

    d. Any sums owed in respect of occupational or state pension schemes;

    e. Employees' arrears of wages or salary (including commission and holiday remuneration) for four months prior to the relevant date subject to a financial limit to be set by delegated legislation. (At present the limit is £800);

    f. Loans by a third party to enable claims under d. and e. to be paid.

17. *Other Provisions*

There are numerous other provisions concerning for example:

    a. The delivery of property by the company officers, advisers, employees etc to the liquidator

    b. The re-opening by the court of extortionate credit bargains.

    c. Transactions at an undervalue and preferences (Chapter 42.10).

    d. Avoidance of floating charges (Chapter 42.9).

    e. Disclaimer by the liquidator of onerous property, for example unprofitable contracts.

    f. Publicity requirements throughout liquidation.

VOLUNTARY LIQUIDATION

18. *Types of Voluntary Winding-up*

Voluntary liquidations are far more numerous than compulsory liquidations. There are two types, *members' voluntary liquidations* (the more common type), and *creditors' voluntary liquidations*. Whether a liquidation is a members' or creditors' voluntary liquidation will depend on whether or not a declaration of solvency is filed.

19. *Members' Voluntary Winding-up*

    a. By *S.89 IA* a voluntary winding-up is a members' voluntary winding-up if, *within 5 weeks before* the resolution for voluntary winding-up (or on that date but before passing the resolution), the directors, or a majority of them made a *declaration of solvency*.

    b. It must contain the latest practicable statement of the company's assets and liabilities and must state that, after inquiry, in their opinion the company will be able to pay its debts within a stated period not more than 12 months after the resolution.

    c. If a director makes the declaration without having reasonable grounds for his opinion he commits a criminal offence and if, after the company is wound up, the debts are not paid in full within the specified period, it is presumed that the director did not have reasonable grounds for his opinion. He will therefore have to prove that his opinion was reasonable if he is to avoid liability.

    d. If the liquidator forms the opinion that the company will be unable to pay its debts in accordance with the declaration of solvency he must call a creditors' meeting to be held within 28 days. From the date of the creditors meeting the liquidation proceeds as if the declaration of solvency had never been made, ie as a creditors' voluntary liquidation. The main effects of this are that the creditors can replace the liquidator with their nominee and they can appoint a committee of inspection.

20. *Creditors' Voluntary Winding-up*

    a. The company must call a meeting of creditors to be held within 14 days of the resolution to wind-up. One of the directors must preside over the meeting and present a statement of affairs containing:

        i.   Particulars of the company's assets, debts and liabilities;

        ii. Names and addresses of the creditors;

        iii. Securities held by the creditors, with the dates when the securities were given.

    b. The company meeting may appoint the liquidator, but if the creditors meeting nominates a different person, the creditors' nominee will be the liquidator.

    c. At their meeting the creditors may appoint up to five persons to a *committee of inspection*. The members then have a right to do the same, but the creditors may by resolution exclude members' nominees unless the court orders otherwise.

21. *Consequences of Voluntary Winding-up*

    a. *After the commencement* of the winding-up (the time of the resolution, even if the company is later wound-up by the court):

        i.   The company must cease business except so far as is necessary for its beneficial winding-up;

    ii. Any transfer of shares without the liquidator's sanction, or alteration in the status of members is void;

    iii. If the company is insolvent the company's servants are automatically dismissed; and

    iv. If no liquidator has been appointed or nominated by the company the directors may not exercise any of their powers except as allowed by the court. However, they may dispose of perishable goods or goods that might fall in value and they may do anything necessary to protect the company's assets.

b. *On the appointment of the liquidator* the directors' powers cease except so far as sanctioned by the company in general meeting or the liquidator in a members' voluntary winding-up, or the committee of inspection or, if none, the creditors in a creditors' voluntary winding-up.

22. *Final Meeting and Dissolution*

a. In a members' voluntary winding-up the liquidator presents his final accounts to a meeting of members, sends to the registrar a copy of the accounts and a return of the holding of the meeting. Three months later the company is deemed to be dissolved unless the court orders otherwise.

b. The procedure is the same for a creditors' voluntary winding-up, except that the accounts must be presented to separate meetings of members and creditors.

ADMINISTRATION ORDERS

23. *Introduction*

The basic purpose of an administration order is to freeze the debts of a company in financial difficulties to assist an administrator to save the company or at least achieve the better realisation of its assets. It is not a procedure designed for creditors to enforce their security. The ENTERPRISE ACT 2002 made a number of changes to the administration procedure in order to try and make it an alternative to liquidation within the context of a rescue culture.

24. *The Power to Make an Appointment*

An administrator can be appointed by:

i. the court;

ii. the holder of a floating charge relating to the whole or substantially the whole of the company's property;

iii. the company itself;

iv. the directors.

The company itself and its directors cannot make an appointment where any insolvency or liquidation procedure is already in process (except for a voluntary arrangement) or there is a pending application.

The administrator is required within eight weeks of appointment to put forward a proposal for approval of the company's unsecured creditors. Administration is an insolvency procedure: it can be only be sought in a situation where a company is or is likely to become, insolvent. Administration is not a liquidation procedure. As noted the appointment of an administrator does not have to be through the court but any out-of-court appointment must be reported to the court.

The administrator must perform his or her functions with the objective of:

i.   rescuing the company as a going concern; or,

ii.   achieving a better result for creditors than would be the case if the company were wound up; or,

iii. realising assets in order to make a distribution to secured or preferential creditors.

An administration order cannot be made after the company has gone into liquidation.

25. *The Effect of an Application*

   a.   The company cannot be wound-up.

   b.   No charge, hire purchase or retention of title clause can be enforced against the company without the consent of the court.

   c.   No other proceedings can be commenced or proceeded with against the company without the consent of the court.

26. *The Effect of the Order*

   a.   The affairs, business and property of the company are managed by the administrator.

   b.   The restrictions on winding-up and legal proceedings continue.

   c.   Any administrative receiver vacates office.

   d.   Any receiver of part of the company's property must vacate office if required to do so by the administrator.

   e.   All company documents must indicate that an administration order is in force and must name the administrator.

27. *Administrator's Powers*

   a.   He has the general power to do all things necessary to manage the affairs, business and property of the company, for example:

      i.   To carry on the business;

      ii.   To deal with and dispose of assets;

      iii. To borrow money and grant security;

      iv.   To bring and defend legal proceedings on the company's behalf;

      v.   To employ and dismiss employees.

b. Further specific powers are given by the Act, for example:

    i. To appoint and remove directors;

    ii. To call meetings of members and creditors;

    iii. To deal with property subject to a floating charge as if there were no charge. When property is disposed of under this power, the sale proceeds become subject to a floating charge which has the same priority as the original security.

c. If the administrator wishes to dispose of other charged property or of goods subject to hire purchase or retention of title agreements, he must obtain the consent of the court.

d. In exercising his powers the administrator is deemed to be the agent of the company and any person who deals with him in good faith does not have to enquire whether he is acting within his powers.

28. *Administrator's Duties*

Although it is not referred to in the Act the administrator probably owes the same fiduciary duties to the company as a receiver. His main statutory duties are:

a. To take into custody or control all the property of the company.

b. To send notice of his appointment:

    i. To the company – immediately;

    ii. To the registrar – within 14 days;

    iii. To the creditors – within 28 days.

c. To require, within 21 days, a statement of affairs, from officers or employees, giving details of:

    i. Assets, debts and liabilities;

    ii. Names and addresses of creditors;

    iii. Securities held by creditors with the dates when given;

d. Within three months of the administration order, he must send to the registrar, the creditors and the members a *statement of his proposals* for achieving the purpose of the administration. He must lay this statement before a *meeting of creditors*. The purpose of the meeting is to approve the proposals.

29. *Protection of Members and Creditors*

a. If the creditors meeting does not approve the proposals the court may discharge the administration order, or make any other order it thinks fit.

b. If the meeting approves the proposals (with or without modifications) it may appoint a *committee of creditors*. The committee may require the administrator to attend before it and give such information as it may reasonably require.

c. *Any creditor or member* may apply to the court for an order on the ground that the company is or has been managed by the administrator in a manner *unfairly prejudicial* to the creditors or members or that any act or omission of the administrator is or would be so prejudicial. The court may make any order it thinks fit.

30. *Discharge or Variation of the Administration Order*

a. The administrator may apply to the court at any time to discharge or vary the order

    i. If it appears to him that the purpose of the administration order has been achieved or is incapable of achievement; or

    ii. If he has been instructed to apply to the court by the meeting of creditors.

b. The court may discharge or vary the order or make any other order it thinks fit. If the order is discharged or varied the administrator must, within 14 days, send a copy of the order of discharge or variation to the registrar.

31. *A Moratorium*

Under the INSOLVENCY ACT 2000, small companies, that is those:

a. with a turnover of not more than £2.8 million;

b. with a balance sheet total of not more than £1.4 million;

c. employing not more than 50 employees;

can, if in financial difficulties, seek a moratorium to enable a voluntary arrangement with creditors to be made; this will satisfy the company's debts through a legally binding agreement. The moratorium, which initially lasts for 28 days, will give the firm's management time to put a rescue plan to creditors.

During the period of the moratorium:

a. no petition may be presented to wind up the company;

b. no administrative receiver may be appointed;

c. no steps may be taken to enforce any security;

d. no legal proceedings can be commenced or continued.

The initial 28-day period is capable of extension or reduction by the Secretary of State. Also a meeting of the company and creditors held within the initial period may agree to extend the period of the moratorium by a further two months.

RECEIVERSHIPS

32. *Introduction*

The usual remedy for debentureholders when debenture interest has not been paid, or when some other term of the trust deed has been broken, is to secure the appointment of a receiver to realise the assets subject to the charge and repay the debentureholders.

a. *Receiver.* This is a general term and it applies to any person administering any type of receivership. The powers of a receiver may include the power to manage the business, in which case the person is called a receiver and manager.

b. *Administrative receiver.* This term was introduced by the Insolvency Act 1986. It basically means a person appointed as a receiver or manager under a floating charge over all or most of the company's assets.

It was found that the office of administrative receiver often inhibited any rescue attempted under an administration. This was because when a company or its creditors sought to appoint an administrator to try and save or better realise the company's assets, the holder of the power to appoint an administrative receiver under a floating charge – often a bank – would veto the application and appoint an administrative receiver whose prime interest was that of the floating charge holder and the need to manage the company in order to secure repayment of the floating charge holder. The ENTERPRISE ACT 2002 now prevents the holder of a floating charge from appointing an administrative receiver except in certain types of company. However, as the Act only came into force on 15th September 2003, any floating charges created before that date will not be affected and will be allowed to appoint an administrative receiver.

33. *Appointment*

The circumstances of the appointment of a receiver will depend on the terms of the trust deed and the nature of the security.

a. Where there is an appointment under a fixed charge it will indicate the circumstances when a power of sale will arise, for example if winding-up commences or if payment of interests is in arrears. In such cases a receiver can be appointed by the debentureholders to collect the income from the property from the time of default until sale.

b. *Appointment under a floating charge* (existing before September 2003). It will be remembered that a floating charge crystallises ie becomes fixed, either when winding-up commences or when the company defaults and the debentureholders take steps to enforce their security by appointing a receiver. If the trust deed specifies the circumstances when a receiver may be appointed no application to the court will be necessary. In any other case the court must make the appointment, which it will do when:

   i. The principal sum or interest is in arrear;

   ii. An event has occurred on which, under the terms of issue of the debentures, the security becomes enforceable; or

   iii. There has been no direct breach of the conditions under which the debentures were issued, but the security is nevertheless in jeopardy.

c. *Receiver and manager.* If it is necessary for a receiver to carry on the company's business until realisation of the security he must be appointed as *receiver and manager*, since appointment merely as receiver will not confer powers of management on him.

34. *Effect of Appointment*

a. Floating charges crystallise (prior to 2003).

b. The directors' powers of control are suspended, although they remain in office and are entitled to their fees. They are able to challenge the receiver's appointment. They may petition for the compulsory winding-up of the company and they may exercise their other powers provided that in doing so they do not interfere with the receiver's task of collecting in the assets.

c. If the receiver is an officer of the court (ie the appointment was made by the court) or if he was appointed by the debentureholders as their agent and not the company's agent, the company's servants are automatically dismissed, although the receiver may re-employ them. If he is an agent of the company all contracts of employment will continue.

35. *Receivers' Powers*

A receiver will have the power conferred on him by the trust deed under which he was appointed. An administrative receiver also has the powers specified in the INSOLVENCY ACT 1986 although references to 'property of the company' must be construed as references to that part of the property subject to the charge.

36. *Receiver's General Duties*

a. His preliminary duty is to acquaint himself with the terms of his appointment, for example his powers of selling property and the periods for presentation of accounts. He should also ensure that charges are not invalidated by S.398–400 (registration of charges), S.238–240 IA (transactions at an undervalue and preferences), or S.245 IA (avoidance of floating charges), since he may be held personally liable if he acts under an invalid charge.

b. His basic duty is to collect in the assets charged to collect rents and profits, and to exercise the debentureholders' powers of realisation, and to pay the net proceeds to them. However, if a receiver is appointed in respect of a debenture secured by a floating charge, the preferential debts must be paid as soon as the receiver has assets in his hands and before any payment is made to the debentureholders.

c. Where the receiver is also appointed as manager he should take a number of practical steps to ensure that nothing is done without his authority, for example:

    i. Contact the company's bankers and arrange for the bank account to be transferred into his name as receiver and manager;

    ii. Notify managers of branch offices of his appointment and instruct them that no goods are to be ordered or payments made without his authority;

    iii. Obtain a list of principal officers and employees, since it may be necessary in some cases to terminate their contracts of employment;

    iv.   Take an inventory of plant, machinery, fixtures, fittings, etc; and

    v.   Prepare a list of debts due to the company, noting the period of credit which has been allowed.

37. *Duties of an Administrative Receiver* (appointed prior to 2003)

    a.   On appointment the administrative receiver must send to the company and publish notice of his appointment.

    b.   Within 28 days he must notify all creditors.

    c.   He must immediately require a statement of affairs. This must be submitted within 21 days. The persons responsible and the contents are the same as when an administrator is appointed.

    d.   Within three months he must send a report to the registrar, secured creditors and trustees for secured creditors, containing information on the following matters:

        i.   The events leading up to his appointment, so far as he is aware of them.

        ii.   His disposal or proposed disposal of any of the company's property.

        iii.   His plans for carrying on the business.

        iv.   The amounts of principal and interest payable to the debenture-holders by whom he was appointed and the amounts payable to preferential creditors.

        v.   The amount, if any, likely to be available to pay other creditors.

        vi.   A summary of the statement of affairs and his comments, if any, on it.

    e.   He must also send a copy of the report to unsecured creditors or publish a notice giving an address to which the creditors can write for a free copy of the report. In either case he must lay a copy of the report before a meeting of unsecured creditors summoned for the purpose. The meeting of creditors may establish a committee. Like the committee of creditors in administration it may summon the administrative receiver on seven days notice and require reasonable information concerning the performance of his functions, but it cannot give him any directions nor is its consent required for any of his acts.

    f.   If the company has gone or goes into liquidation the administrative receiver must also send a copy of the report to the liquidator.

38. *The Receiver and the Liquidator*

    a.   In most cases when a receiver is appointed with a view to sale of assets the company will be forced into liquidation. On the other hand if the company is already in liquidation the debentureholders may seek to preserve their rights by the appointment of a receiver.

    b.   When the two functions are not vested in the same person the liquidator occupies the premier position since he is responsible for the interests of the creditors and contributories as well as the debentureholders. He must therefore:

i. See that the receiver confines his duties to the assets subject to the charge;

ii. See that he does not protract the receivership;

iii. See that he discharges the preferential debts; and

iv. Ensure that he accounts to the liquidator for any surplus after paying the debentureholders what is due to them.

c. The company's books remain with the liquidator, but the receiver must be allowed such access as is necessary to enable him to perform his duties.

Coursework Questions 36–42
(for answers see pages 682–90)

COMMERCIAL LAW

Typical Exam Questions

36. Explain the '*ultra vires*' rule as it applies to limited companies

(20 marks)
ICSA November 2004

37. *Multiple Choice*

In relation to E Ltd, a company limited by shares, which ONE of the following statements is correct?

A   The liability of the company and its shareholders is limited, but the directors are fully liable for the company's debts.

B   The liability of the company and its directors is limited, but the shareholders are fully liable for the company's debts.

C   The liability of the company, its directors and shareholders is limited.

D   The liability of the directors and shareholders is limited, but the company is fully liable for its own debts.

Adam, Ben and Carol have carried on business together in partnership since July 2001. In September 2001, they decided to enter into a formal partnership agreement. The partners agreed the terms of the agreement in October 2001 and signed the completed agreement in November 2001.

According to the law, when did the partnership commence?

A   July 2001. B September 2001. C October 2001. D November 2001.

Which of the following statements is correct?

(i)   It is not possible to register a company limited by shares with the same name as a company already on the register.

(ii) Once on the register, a company limited by shares cannot change its registered office.

A   (i) only. B (ii) only. C Both (i) and (ii). D Neither (i) nor (ii).

The authorised share capital of Wye Ltd is £250,000 divided into 250,000 ordinary £1 shares. The asset value of each share is £2.

Angela and Brian are the only shareholders. Each has taken 50,000 shares and each has, so far, paid £10,000.

Which ONE of the following statements is correct?

A   The issued share capital of Wye Ltd is £250,000, and the paid up capital is £20,000.

B   The issued share capital of Wye Ltd is £100,000, and the paid up capital is £20,000.

C   The issued share capital of Wye Ltd is £250,000, and the paid up capital is £100,000.

D   The issued share capital of Wye Ltd is £20,000, and the paid up capital is £20,000.

Which of the following statements is correct?

(i)   The Articles of Association of a company limited by shares contain the internal regulations of the company.

(ii) The Articles of Association form a contract between the shareholders and the company.

A   (i) only. B   (ii) only. C   Both (i) and (ii). D   Neither (i) nor (ii).

Which of the following resolutions may be used to increase a company's authorised capital?

(i)   Ordinary resolution.

(ii) Written resolution.

A   (i) only. B   (ii) only. C   Both (i) and (ii). D   Neither (i) nor (ii).

XYZ plc has issued shares on terms that they will be bought back by the company 12 months after the date of issue. What are these shares called?

A   Ordinary shares.

B   Bonus shares.

C   Preference shares.

D   Redeemable shares.

Which ONE of the following statements is INCORRECT in relation to elective resolutions?

A   An elective resolution may only be passed by private companies.

B   An elective resolution may be used to reduce the majority of votes necessary to authorise short notice to 90%.

C   An elective resolution may be used to authorise directors to issue shares for longer than the usual five years.

D An elective resolution may be used to dispense with the requirement to re-elect directors annually.

Which ONE of the following is INCORRECT?

A A public company must have at least two directors.

B A private company must have at least one director.

C Both public and private companies must have a qualified company secretary.

D A public company must have at least two shareholders.

Immediately before XY Ltd was placed in insolvent liquidation, Alex, the company's sole director, arranged for the company to make an early repayment of an unsecured loan of £15,000 which he had provided to the company.

Which ONE of the following is correct?

A The repayment may amount to a 'preference', and Alex may be required to hand back the £15,000 to XY Ltd.

B Alex may be fined.

C The repayment of the loan is valid so long as Alex was acting in good faith.

D XY Ltd and Alex may be guilty of fraud.

The court has decided that Jill, a director of Jay Ltd, has been wrongfully trading, in that she continued to carry on business at a time when she should have known that insolvency was inevitable. What are the possible consequences for Jill?

A Jill may be fined.

B Jill may be imprisoned.

C Jill may be required to contribute to the assets of Jay Ltd.

D Jill may be required to sell her shares in Jay Ltd.

Jack has acted in breach of his fiduciary duty as a director of JK Ltd. If the breach does not amount to fraud on the minority, which ONE of the following is correct?

A The breach cannot be ratified by the shareholders.

B The breach may be ratified by a written or ordinary resolution.

C The breach may be ratified by a provision in the company's Memorandum of Association.

D The breach may be ratified by a resolution of the board of directors.

Zed plc holds its board meetings on the fifteenth day of each month. At the meeting on 15 June 2001, the board discussed a potential contract with RST Ltd. On 1 July 2001, Lucy, a director of Zed plc, bought shares in RST Ltd. On 25 July 2001, Zed plc contracted with RST Ltd.

When should Lucy have declared her interest to the board of Zed plc?

A   15 June 2001. **B** 1 July 2001. **C** 15 July 2001. **D** 15 August 2001.

CIMA November 2001

38. Explain the differences between fixed and floating charges.

CIMA November 2001

39. In relation to company law explain:

  (a) the meaning of winding up;   (3 marks)

  (b) the procedures involved in:

  (i)   a members' voluntary winding-up;   (3 marks)

  (ii) a creditors' voluntary winding-up.   (4 marks)

(10 marks)
ACCA June 2004

40. Explain the meaning and effect of a company's articles of association, paying particular attention to the following issues:

  (a) the operation of Table A model articles of association;   (2 marks)

  (b) the effect of the articles on both members and non-members;   (4 marks)

  (c) the procedure for altering the articles of association.   (4 marks)

(10 marks)
ACCA June 2004

41. In relation to companies' loan capital explain the following terms:

  (a) debenture;   (3 marks)

  (b) fixed charge;   (3 marks)

  (c) floating charge.   (4 marks)

(10 marks)
ACCA June 2004

42. In relation to a private company explain:

  (a) the power to buy its own shares;   (6 marks)

  (b) the capital redemption reserve;   (2 marks)

  (c) the permissible capital payment.   (2 marks)

(10 marks)
ACCA June 2004

PART VI

EMPLOYMENT LAW

CHAPTER 49

Employees and Independent Contractors

1. *Distinguishing the Type of Relationship*

Where there is a contract of employment there is the relationship of employer and employee. This relationship imposes certain rights and duties on each party. It is important to distinguish whether a relationship is that of employer/employee or employer/independent contractor for several reasons. There are obligations at common law, eg an employer's vicarious liability for the torts of his employee. There are many statutory rights and liabilities which make the distinction important, eg redundancy and unfair dismissal under the EMPLOYMENT RIGHTS ACT 1996, and social security benefits under the SOCIAL SECURITY ACT 1975. Over the years certain 'tests' have been incorporated into common law which have arisen from particular cases in which the relationships were distinguished.

2. *The Control Test*

a. The first test that evolved to decide whether a person was an employee or an independent contractor was the *control test*. Under this test the greater the extent to which a person is under the direction and control of another person, the more likely he is to be an employee. Thus if a person controlled both what another did and how he did it the control test would clearly be satisfied.

b. However, as the size and complexity of businesses increased and employees became more skilled and professional, employment relationships became more impersonal. The control test was therefore less effective and even when a 'right to control' was substituted for actual control it was not possible to draw the correct distinctions with only one test. The courts therefore developed the integration test and the multiple test.

3. *The Integration Test*

Under this test (also called the organisation test) if the person doing the work and the work he does is an integral part of the business, rather than an accessory to it, then the person will be an employee. This test is useful in the case of professional employees, such as doctors who may be an integral part of the business without being under the direct control of their employer.

In WHITTAKER v MPNI (1976) a trapeze artiste engaged by a circus also performed other duties, eg acting as an usherette during other performances. Having fallen during her act she claimed industrial injury benefit. It was held that although the circus had no control over the artiste during the act, this was integrated into other duties and was therefore a contract of service.

Contrast WESTALL RICHARDSON v ROULSON (1954) where an 'outworker' in the cutlery industry who rented a workshop in a factory to polish cutlery manufactured in the factory was held to be self-employed in view of the independence he enjoyed, even though he formed an important part of the business carried on in the factory.

4. *The Multiple Test*

This test (also known as the economic reality test) will take into account control and integration as well as many other relevant factors. The following factors would indicate a contract of employment.

a. Remuneration by way of payment of wages or salary, net of tax.

b. Membership of company pension scheme.

c. Holiday pay.

d. Payment when absent for illness.

e. Prohibition on working for competitors.

f. Control by employer's disciplinary code.

g. Supply of uniform and/or equipment.

h. Work done on employer's premises rather than at home.

i. Lack of personal business risk on the part of the worker.

In READY-MIXED CONCRETE (SOUTH EAST) v MPNI (1969) each driver of the company was financially assisted to buy his own vehicle. The vehicle had to be painted in the company's colours. The drivers had to wear the company uniform and be available for work when required. They were paid a mileage rate for work done for the company. It was held that the drivers were not employees but independent contractors as they were operating at their own financial risk.

5. *Mutuality of Obligation Test*

This requirement that there exists a legal obligation on both sides to provide work and to do work in order for a contract of employment to exist, was originally put forward in O'KELLY v TRUST HOUSE FORTE (1983). Whilst over the years since that case the courts and tribunals have tended to adopt a fairly liberal approach to finding some mutuality of obligation where they thought justice required it, a recent decision in the House of Lords has brought the Trust House Forte criteria back to being a key essential ingredient.

In CARMICHAEL v NATIONAL POWER (2000), a case involving part-time tour guides who showed members of the public around a National Power facility who sought to be treated as employees for purposes of redundancy, the House of Lords, in over-ruling the Court of Appeal decision, stated that there must exist a formal legal obligation on both sides before a contract of employment and employee status can be founded. This is now firmly back as a requirement and was recently followed in MONTGOMERY v JOHNSON UNDERWOOD (2001).

6. *Other Considerations*

a. *What does the contract say?* If the employer does not want the contract to be construed as a contract of employment the contract should make it clear that the worker is an independent contractor and shall have rights and liabilities accordingly, for example personal liability to third parties for injury caused by negligent work.

However, the parties cannot change the true relationship by putting the wrong label on it.

In FERGUSON v DAWSON (1978) the worker was employed as part of the 'lump' labour force in the building industry. He gave a false name when signing on and no tax or insurance deductions were made by the contractor who engaged him. In order to claim compensation from his employer for an injury sustained at work the worker had to show that he was an employee. It was held that despite the contract which said he was self-employed, in reality he was an employee.

In WICKEN v CHAMPION EMPLOYMENT (1984) a woman had an agreement with an employment agency that was described as a 'contract of service'. However, she worked as a 'temp' for the agency's clients. It was held that she was not an employee because the agency exercised minimal control over her and there was no mutual obligation to provide and accept work.

b. *Part-time employees.* The amount of work given is not a deciding factor. A person working part-time may be an employee.

In MARKET INVESTIGATIONS v MINISTRY OF SOCIAL SECURITY (1969) a woman was intermittently engaged by a market research company to act as an interviewer for a fixed remuneration. She was given detailed instructions. It was held that she was an employee.

Contrast WILLY SCHEIDEGGER SWISS TYPEWRITING SCHOOL (LONDON) v MINISTRY OF SOCIAL SECURITY (1968) where a sales representative of typewriters and typewriting courses whose sole remuneration was a commission on sales with no expenses paid, was deemed to be an independent contractor.

c. *Effect of continuous service over a period of time.*

In NETHERMERE (ST NEOTS) v TAVERNA & GARDINER (1984) Mrs T and Mrs G were employed by N Ltd as 'homeworkers' manufacturing boys trousers. They worked whenever needed and let the company know when they were taking a holiday. They rarely refused work and gave warning when not wanting it. They submitted regular time-sheets and were paid the same rate of pay as the factory workers. The work was an essential part of the factory's production. The machines used were provided by the company. It was held that there may be a contract of service if, over a continuous period of regular giving and taking of work in accordance with the parties' expectation, obligations have been established on the part of the company to provide work and on the part of the homeworker to accept it.

7. *Statutory Employment Rights and Part-time Employees*

The *EMPLOYMENT PROTECTION (PART-TIME EMPLOYEES) REGULATIONS 1995* extended the same basic statutory employment rights to part-time employees as exist for full-time employees. Now part-time employees:

a. may bring a claim for unfair dismissal if employed for one year, and for redundancy if employed for two years (Chapters 56 and 57);

b. have a right to written particulars of the terms of employment if employed for one month or more (Chapter 50);

c. are entitled to a minimum period of notice after one month or more (Chapter 56);

d. have a right to maternity leave (Chapter 54);

e. have a right to an itemised pay statement (Chapter 53);

f. have a right to time off for public duties and for trade union duties and activities (Chapter 52).

8. *New rights for Employees on Fixed-term Contracts*

In order to comply with the *EC FIXED TERM WORKERS DIRECTIVE*, which was implemented in July 2002, the government has published a draft of the *FIXED-TERM (PREVENTION OF LESS FAVOURABLE TREATMENT) REGULATIONS* 2002, which came into effect on 10th July 2002. The Regulations' main provisions are: a right for fixed-term employees not to be treated less favourably than a comparable permanent employee, unless objectively justified. This does not require like-for-like pro rata entitlements – provided the fixed-term employee's contractual rights are as a whole at least as favourable as permanent employees' objective justification is deemed to be made out. There are also requirements that the employer advertise permanent vacancies to fixed-term employees and that a fixed-term contract will be converted to a permanent contract where the employee has been employed over four years unless the employer can demonstrate an objective justification for fixed-term employment. The ability to waive redundancy rights will be abolished.

9. *Agency Workers*

a. Judges have often had to decide which of two employers was responsible where one has lent an employee to the other. The general rule is that control remains with the original employer, because personal service contracts cannot be assigned.

In MERSEY DOCKS & HARBOUR BOARD v COGGINS & GRIFFITH (LIVERPOOL) LTD (**1946**) the Harbour Board lent the defendant company a crane plus an operator. The contract specified that the defendants would be the employer, but the Harbour Board retained ultimate right to employ, pay wages and dismiss. It was held that the Harbour Board was still the employer despite the terms of the contract. All of the circumstances should be considered.

b. The general rule can be rebutted, but the original employer must prove transfer of control. This transfer is more readily inferred when an employee is lent on his own, without equipment.

In GARRARD v SOUTHEY & CO (1952) G lent S two electricians for work on a factory. G retained right of dismissal and paid them. The electricians were supervised by S's foreman, a skilled electrician. One of the electricians was injured. It was held that control had passed to S who was thus responsible for provision of safe equipment.

c. *Agency worker and a potential implied contract of employment.* In a recent court of appeal decision, DACUS v BROOK STREET BUREAU (2004) the Court of Appeal ruled that a cleaner at a council hostel was not an 'employee' of the employment agency that has assigned her to the work and as such could not bring an action for unfair dismissal against the agency. The court gave general guidance on the employment status of agency workers who worked under the control of the client of the agency (the end-user) whilst having their salary paid by the agency who usually introduce them to the end-user. The guidance was that the employment tribunal should examine all the evidence relating to the relationships between the three parties – the worker, the agency, and the end user – including any written agreements and oral statements and also the conduct of the parties. There were certain key essentials of a contract of employment which had to be found to exist; these are:

  i. A mutual obligation to provide work and do work. It was found in the present case that this was lacking. As between the cleaner and the agency: the agency was under no duty to provide her with work and she was under no duty to accept any work offered.

  ii An obligation to remunerate the worker in return for that work – it making no difference whether the arrangements for payment were made directly or indirectly; and,

  iii. A sufficient degree of control over the worker.

Such an examination might well lead to the finding of an implied contract of employment with the end-user which should have been considered in the present case.

This was followed in a more recent case, MUSCAT v CABLE AND WIRELESS PLC (2006) here the court found that two contracts existed; a contract for services between agency and worker, and a contract of employment (a contract of service) between worker the client.

10. *The Importance of the Relationship between Employer and Employee*

There are numerous situations where the treatment of employees and independent contractors is different, including:

a. *Social Security.* Entitlement to benefits and rates of contributions payable depend on whether a person is an employee or an independent contractor.

b. *Employment protection.* The EMPLOYMENT RIGHTS ACT 1996 (ERA) provides employees with statutory protection in respect of minimum periods of notice, compensation for redundancy and unfair dismissal, maternity pay and so on.

c. *Taxation.* An employer is responsible for deducting income tax and national insurance contributions from the wages of an employee, and paying statutory sick pay.

d. *Common law duties.* An employer has duties under common law as outlined in Chapter 52.

e. *Employer's bankruptcy.* If an employer becomes bankrupt or, in the case of a company goes into liquidation, an employee will be a preferential creditor with regard to arrears of pay.

f. *Vicarious liability.* An employer is usually responsible for the wrongful acts of his employees, committed in the course of employment but not for the wrongful acts committed by independent contractors. Exceptions:

   i. *Negligent selection.* Where the employer is negligent in selecting the contractor, ie he does not ascertain the contractor's competence to do that particular job.

   ii. *Negligently gives instructions.* Where an employer issues, authorises or ratifies a negligent order or instruction, the third party has a good claim against the employer.

   iii. *Strict liability.* This usually refers to the employer's statutory duty in relation to the fencing of machinery under the HEALTH AND SAFETY AT WORK REGULATIONS 1992. Other instances where the employer is liable for the wrongful acts of independent contractors and cannot use the defence that he did not perform the task himself are as follows:

     (a) *Withdrawal of support from a neighbour's land.* Where the activities of a contractor working on the employer's land does something so as to cause subsidence on a neighbour's land.

     (b) *Work carried out on or near to a highway.* Because of the obvious danger to members of the public using the highway.

     (c) *The rule in Rylands v Fletcher.* Where dangerous or unpleasant substances escape onto a neighbour's land or property. In the above case water seeped onto Ryland's land through a mineshaft.

     (d) *Nuisance.* Where dust and noise inevitable from an extensive building or construction operation affect neighbouring property or persons.

     (e) *Acts causing fire or explosion.* Extra hazardous acts which, by their nature involve, in the eyes of the law, danger to others, eg where implements such as flame-bearing equipment or explosives are necessary or incidental to the work being performed.

     (f) *Contractor breaks the law.* If the employer engages a contractor to perform an unlawful task he cannot evade liability for any resultant damage.

     (g) *Safety of employees.* An employer cannot escape liability for a breach of his duty to provide safe working conditions by delegating this duty to an independent contractor.

CHAPTER 50

The Contract of Employment

1. *Formation of the Contract*

   To be legally binding a contract of employment must fulfil all the normal contractual requirements, ie

   a. *Offer and acceptance*. There must be offer and acceptance. The offer must contain the terms of the contract or indicate where they may be found. No particular form is required, the contract may be oral, or in writing.

   b. *Consideration*. The consideration is the employer's promise to pay the agreed wages in return for the employee's promise to perform a particular task. Generally speaking the courts would not be concerned with the adequacy of the consideration.

   c. *Capacity*. There is some restriction on the contractual capacity of minors. Protection is given both under common law and statute. Protection is also given to women, disabled persons and ethnic minorities.

   d. *Legality*. A contract of employment must not be tainted with illegality, eg a contract which deliberately seeks to defraud the Inland Revenue.

      In CORBY v MORRISON (**1980**) the employee received not only a gross wage in accordance with a wages council order but also an extra £5. This additional payment was not subject to income tax or social security deductions, neither was it shown on the pay envelope. It was held that the whole contract was illegal on the grounds of defrauding the Inland Revenue.

      Contrast DAVIDSON v PILLAY (**1974**) where Mrs D managed a shop and each week took her wages from the till without deducting tax. It was held that D was not aware of the illegality. Only if the employer is guilty of knowingly committing an illegal act to which the employee is not a party may the employee claim under the contract.

      However, a legal contract, performed illegally, eg where an employer contravenes the *WAGES ACT 1986*, will not be void on the grounds of illegality.

2. *Written Particulars*

   a. *S1* of the *EMPLOYMENT RIGHTS ACT 1996* (ERA) requires an employer to provide his employees with a written statement of the terms of his employment not later than two months after starting work. These statements are not contracts, but are taken into account by courts and tribunals. Employees are not required by the Act to sign anything in connection with these written particulars.

b. The written particulars must include:

i. Names of employer and employee;

ii. Date when the employment began;

iii. Date on which the employee's period of continuous employment began (taking into account employment with a previous employer);

iv. Scale or rate of remuneration or the method of calculating it;

v. Intervals at which remuneration is paid;

vi. Terms and conditions relating to hours of work;

vii. Terms and conditions relating to entitlement to holidays, including public holidays and holiday pay to enable these to be precisely calculated;

viii. Terms and conditions relating to incapacity for work due to sickness or injury, including any provision for sick pay;

ix. Pensions and pension schemes (not required if the pension rights depend on the terms of a pension scheme established under any Act of Parliament and the employee is employed by a body or authority which is required to give the new employee information concerning his pension rights or the determination of questions affecting his pension rights);

x. Length of notice to terminate employment (both employer and employee);

xi. Job title;

xii. For non-permanent employment – the expected period, or if for a fixed term, the date when it is to end;

xiii. Place of work, or an indication of the fact that the employee is expected to work at various places, and the address of the employer;

xiv. Any collective agreements directly affecting the terms and conditions of employment;

xv. Where the employee is required to work outside the UK for a period of more than one month – the length of period and the currency in which he is to be paid, any additional remuneration and benefits, and any terms and conditions in respect of his return to the UK.

c. The statement may refer the employee to the provisions of some other document which he has reasonable opportunities of reading in the course of employment or is reasonably accessible in respect of viii., and ix. above. The statement may refer an employee to the law or the provisions of any relevant collective agreement in respect of x., above.

Particulars of the other items must be included or referred to in a single document.

d.   The statement must include a note specifying any disciplinary rules applicable to the employee or referring to another document. The note should specify a person to whom the employee can apply if dissatisfied with any disciplinary decision, the person to whom he can apply for redress of grievance and the manner in which such application should be made.

New provisions have been introduced by the EMPLOYMENT ACT 2002, S.35 requires that all stages of the new minimum disciplinary and dismissal procedures be included in the written statement. These are contained in *Schedule 2* of the EMPLOYMENT ACT 2002. The employer may have his own procedures but if they do not comply with *Schedule 2* the statutory procedures prevail. *Schedule 2* provides for a series of steps to set out as a standard procedure –

Step 1: statement of grievance

The employee must set out the grievance in writing and send the statement or a copy of it to the employer.

Step 2: meeting

(a) The employer must invite the employee to attend a meeting to discuss the grievance.

(b) The meeting must not take place unless –

　　(i)   the employee has informed the employer what the basis for the grievance was when he made the statement under Step 1, and

　　(ii) the employer has had a reasonable opportunity to consider his response to that information.

(c) The employee must take all reasonable steps to attend the meeting.

(d) After the meeting, the employer must inform the employee of his decision if he is not satisfied with it.

Step 3: appeal

(a) If the employee does not wish to appeal, he must inform the employer.

(b) If the employee informs the employer of his wish to appeal, the employer must invite him to attend a further meeting.

(c) The employee must take all reasonable steps to attend the meeting.

(d) After the appeal meeting, the employer must inform the employee of his final decision.

In SHERGOLD v FIELDWAY CENTRE (2006) the Employment Appeal Tribunal took a very broad view of what can amount to a grievance requiring an employer to act. Provided the employee notifies his employer in writing and the general nature of what was complained of was the same as a subsequent claim, then that will be sufficient. There is no requirement that an employee invoke a formal grievance procedure or to state in any letter that it was a grievance.

e. An employee has the right to be given by the employer an itemised pay statement. This must include:

i. The gross amount of wages

ii. The amount of any deductions and the purpose of such deductions

iii. The net amount of wages payable

iv. Where different parts of the net amount are paid in different ways, the amount and method of payment.

f. *Exemptions*. The written statement shall not apply to an employee whose employment continues for less than one month.

g. *Changes to conditions of employment*. Any agreed changes to the conditions of employment must be notified to the employee within one month of the change taking place. The notification must be by means of a written statement. If a copy of the statement is not left with the employee the employer must preserve the statement and ensure that the employee has reasonable opportunities of reading it in the course of employment.

h. *Employees' remedies for failure to provide written particulars*. If an employee has not been given written notice as the Act provides or thinks that his notice is incorrect he can apply to an industrial tribunal. If it is necessary for the tribunal to imply a term they will consider all the circumstances particularly the way in which the parties had worked the contract since it was made. If the tribunal upholds a complaint they can state the particulars that should have been given and the employer will be deemed to have given such a statement. If the employer is in breach of any of those terms the employee can then commence an appropriate action.

S.38 of the EMPLOYMENT ACT 2002 provides for tribunals to award monetary compensation to an employee where the particulars received are incomplete or inaccurate. Where this is so, the tribunal may increase any subsequent award made against the employer by between two and four weeks' pay.

The Court of Appeal in ROBERTSON AND JACKSON v BRITISH GAS CORPORATION (1983) stated that the statutory statement of particulars contained in S.1 is neither the contract itself nor conclusive evidence of it.

3. *Part-time Employees and Fixed-term Workers*

Under THE PART-TIME WORKERS (PREVENTION OF LESS FAVOURABLE TREATMENT) REGULATIONS 2000 AND, THE FIXED-TERM EMPLOYEES (PREVENTION OF LESS FAVOURABLE TREATMENT) REGULATIONS 2002, part-time workers and employees on fixed-term contracts, are not to be treated less favourably than permanent employees, and as such, are entitled to the same information as permanent employees with regard to the statement of particulars required under S.1 of the EMPLOYMENT RIGHTS ACT 1996. In addition such persons must not be treated less favourably than full-time permanent employees with regard to:

i. Pay – that is normal and overtime rate. A lower rate may be justified on objective grounds other than the worker is part-time or on a fixed term contract, for example, where there is performance-related pay.

ii. Contractual sick pay and maternity pay.

iii. Occupational pensions and other benefits.

iv. Dismissal – where an employee is dismissed for reasons of being either part-time or on a fixed term contract, this would constitute an automatic unfair dismissal with no requirement for any qualifying period of employment to be shown.

v. Redundancy.

The Regulations also give to fixed-term employees a right to be informed of available vacancies for permanent employment and to apply for them. Also, in agreements entered into after 10th July 2002, where an employee on a fixed-term contract has had it renewed over an unbroken four year period then the renewal will convert the contract into a permanent one.

4. *Variation to the Contract of Employment.* Normally a contract cannot be varied unilaterally. *S.4* of the EMPLOYMENT RIGHTS ACT 1996 requires that changes to terms be notified to an employee with one month. However, this does not give an employer the right to unilaterally alter contract terms merely by giving notice. Contracts of employment have to be to some extent flexible and, in the absence of written terms the following may be implied:

i. *Implied in fact.* A term may be implied because it lends business efficacy to the contract.

In MCCAFFREY V JEAVONS LTD (1967) an employee described as a 'travelling man' in the construction industry was deemed contractually bound to work anywhere in the UK.

In BRISTOL GARAGE (BRIGHTON) LTD V LOWEN (1979) it was held that there was an implication that a garage employee would not have agreed to make up cash losses due to theft from his pay. Tribunals recognise the right of an employer to introduce, '*reasonable and necessary changes for the good of the organisation*'. In DRYDEN V GREATER GLASGOW HEALTH BOARD (1992) the introduction of a no smoking policy was deemed reasonable and necessary in the interests of health and safety. And in CRESSWELL V BOARD OF INLAND REVENUE (1984) the need to compel re-training due to the introduction of new technology was seen as reasonable and necessary by a tribunal.

ii. *Custom and practice.* These are terms implied by custom and practice in a particular trade, providing that these are well-known and reasonable.

iii. *Implied by law.* Some terms may be implied at common law or statute. Implied duties of employee and employer are outlined in subsequent chapters. There is an implied 'equality' clause in the EQUAL PAY ACT 1970 and a number of anti-discrimination clauses which are deemed to be read into all contracts of employment.

iv. There may be express terms in a contract of employment that seek to give management the right to impose changes on the employee. For example, 'Employees shall do whatever management from time to time deem necessary' or, 'employees shall work wherever management deems necessary' – a so-called 'mobility clause'. Such terms have to withstand the test of 'reasonableness', ie are the requests reasonable and necessary within the normal scope of an employee's existing contract?

v. *Implied through Collective Agreements*. Terms in collective agreements may be incorporated into contracts of employment:

In JOEL v CAMMELL LAIRD SHIP REPAIRERS LTD (**1969**) a collective agreement related to transfers of employees between ship repair and ship building. It was held to be incorporated into the contract of employment because the employees concerned had indicated that they were aware of the provision.

In ROBERTSON v BRITISH GAS (**1983**) meter readers and collectors employed by North Thames Gas received an incentive bonus of about £400 per month. The scheme was negotiated by their union and was referred to in the written statement of terms of each employee. Management gave the union six months notice to terminate the agreement. The union members successfully argued in the Appeal Court that this was a breach of contract.

vi. *Other documents*.

SECRETARY OF STATE FOR EMPLOYMENT v ASLEF (NO. 2) (**1972**). This case involved railwaymen 'working to rule' and by strict observance of the railway rules bringing the railways to a standstill. The court held that a work to rule was a breach of the individual employee's contract of employment because:

(a) There was an implied term that an employee should not wilfully disrupt his employer's undertaking.

(b) In this instance it involved refusal to work obligatory overtime.

(c) The employer's rule book contained instructions the employee was obliged by his contract to obey.

Contrast BRITISH LEYLAND (UK) LTD v MCQUILKEN (**1978**). An agreement with trade unions on closure of a department provided that employees should be interviewed to ascertain preference for future employment. It was held that the agreement was a long-term policy plan not incorporated into individual contracts of employment.

CHAPTER 51

The Common Law Duties of an Employee

INTRODUCTION

1. The duties of an employee are governed by the terms of his contract. In the absence of any express or implied terms his duties will be determined under common law. Contravention of any of these duties may give an employer the right to dismiss the employee.

IMPLIED DUTIES

2. The following are circumstances in which the courts have held employees to have implied duties towards their employers:

   a. *Indemnity*. Where the employer suffers some loss because of his liability for the wrongful act of his employee, the employee may be liable to indemnify (compensate) his employer.

   In LISTER v ROMFORD ICE & COLD STORAGE LTD (1957) P was a driver employed by the company. His father, a driver's mate, assisted P. Due to P's negligence his father was injured and claimed damages against the company. The company in turn claimed that P should indemnify it against the loss suffered. It was held that P should indemnify the company due to his negligence.

   Subsequently all members of the British Insurance Association agreed that they would not require the employer to claim indemnity from the employee unless there was evidence of collusion or wilful misconduct on the employee's part.

   b. *Misconduct*. The employee must not misconduct himself. The term misconduct includes insolence, persistent laziness, immorality, dishonesty and drunkenness. Misconduct will justify disciplinary dismissal if it directly interferes with the business of the employer, or the employee's ability to perform his services.

   In PEPPER v WEBB (1969) a gardener who behaved in a surly manner, showed disinterest in the garden, refused to perform certain tasks in the garden and was insolent to his employer was held to have been dismissed justifiably.

Contrast WILSON V RACHER (1974) a gardener was dismissed for swearing at his employer, on one occasion. It was held that this was an exceptional outburst from an otherwise competent and diligent employee who had been provoked by his employer. Therefore there were no grounds for dismissal.

c. *Personal service.* The employee must not allow others outside the scope of his employer's control to perform his tasks.

In ILKIW V SAMUELS (1963) a lorry driver allowed another person to drive his lorry. He did this against express instructions from his employer and without enquiry as to the other person's ability to handle his vehicle. As a result, a third party was injured. The employer was liable because of the negligence of his own driver (the person responsible for the operation of the lorry).

d. *Loyalty and good faith.* The employee must not accept bribes or make secret profits.

In BOSTON DEEP SEA FISHING CO V ANSELL (1888) whilst employed as managing director with the plaintiff company Ansell contracted with a shipbuilding company for supply of ships, taking a secret commission. It was held that Ansell's action was a breach of his duty to his employer.

e. *Interests of the employer.* The employee must do nothing to harm his employer's interests, even in his spare time:

In HIVAC V PARK ROYAL SCIENTIFIC INSTRUMENTS LTD (1946) employees of P worked for D (a rival firm) in their spare time. It was held that P would be granted an injunction restraining them from working for D.

In BARTLETT V SHOE LEATHER RECORD (1960) P, an editor, worked for a newspaper and a fashion trade journal in his spare time. Although not writing on the same subject it was held that he would not be able to give of his best by reason of his spare-time activities.

However, in NOTTINGHAM UNIVERSITY V FISHEL (2000) the court found where an employee pursued outside activities which might affect his employer's interests, the duty of loyalty would only be broken where there is an express contractual term forbidding an employee from such conduct. As a general proposition, it was not a requirement that an employee place his employer's interests above his own.

An employee should do nothing to cause his employer to lose confidence in him:

In SINCLAIR V NEIGHBOUR (1967) a betting-shop manager 'borrowed' £15 from the till, intending to replace it the following day, although he knew his employer would not approve. The employer discovered the employee's act and dismissed him without notice. It was held that dismissal was justified.

f. *Careful service.* An employee must exercise due care and skill in the performance of his duties. Where he claims that he has the ability to do the work undertaken, besides having the ability, he must also perform the tasks diligently and efficiently.

In HARMER v CORNELIUS (**1858**) a person who was given a job as a scene painter had never painted scenes and was incompetent. He was held to have been justifiably dismissed without notice.

In SUPERLUX v PLAISTED (**1958**) D, a vacuum-cleaner salesman left his van outside his home overnight. Several cleaners were stolen. It was held that his breach of the duty of careful service justified dismissal.

An employee who is negligent can be sued for his negligence by his employer or by a third party who suffers loss as a result. However, some relief may be granted under the *LAW REFORM (CONTRIBUTORY NEGLIGENCE) ACT 1945.*

In JONES v MANCHESTER CORPORATION (**1948**) a doctor and anaesthetist, both very inexperienced, were left in charge of an emergency ward with no one to supervise them. A patient suffered an injury as a result and was awarded damages which were apportioned, 20% against the doctor and anaesthetist and 80% against the hospital.

g. *Account for property and gain.* An employee must account for any money or property belonging to his employer, and any gains made thereon.

READING v ATTORNEY GENERAL (**1951**). (See Chapter 30.10.)

h. *Trade secrecy.* The employee must maintain secrecy over his employer's affairs during the time of his employment. If the employer wishes to extend this beyond the period of employment it would be advisable to insert a suitable clause in the contract of employment. The employee is under an obligation to his employers not to disclose confidential information obtained by him in the course of, and as a result of his employment. This duty applies both during employment and afterwards if the employee seeks to use such information to the detriment of his employer.

In ROBB v GREEN (**1895**). An employee who copied down a list of customers intending to use it after leaving employment, was restrained from doing so.

Restraint of trade clauses. Often an employer will wish to protect his trade secrets from disclosure by an employee when the employee leaves his service, and not leave it to the employee's common law duty of fidelity. The employer will do this by including in the contract of employment a clause placing some restriction on future employment, ie a restraint of trade clause. This important aspect of employment law is discussed in Chapter 17.19.

In BENTS BREWERY CO LTD v HOGAN (**1945**) a trade union official invited certain employees to disclose particulars of the total amount of the sales made and the wages paid at the branches of the company in which they were employed. It was held that if any employee gave that information he would commit a breach of contract, and the trade union official would be liable for inducing such breach.

However, an employee may disclose information if it is such that it is in the public interest to disclose it. Furthermore it should be disclosed to one who has a proper interest to receive it:

In INITIAL SERVICES LTD v PUTTERILL (1968) D was sales manager of the company which operated a laundry. He left their employment and took with him some documents relating to the company which he passed on to a national newspaper. The newspaper subsequently published articles alleging that there was profiteering in the laundry industry. The company sought an injunction against their former employee, but were unsuccessful since if the allegations were true there were arrangements in the industry which should have been registered under the RESTRICTIVE TRADE PRACTICES ACT 1976.

The PUBLIC INTEREST DISCLOSURE ACT 1998 prevents a worker suffering any form of detriment where he discloses information about the employer – a protected disclosure – believing that:

i.   A criminal offence is being, or has been, or is about to be committed;

ii.   Some legal obligation is likely to be avoided;

iii. A miscarriage of justice has occurred, is occurring or is likely to occur;

iv.   The health and safety of an individual is put in danger;

v.   Damage to the environment is occurring, or is likely to occur or has occurred;

vi.   Information relating to any of the above is likely to be concealed.

This right not to suffer a detriment where a protected disclosure has occurred extends to all workers, there is no requirement for a one year qualifying period or to be under 65 years of age.

In FERNANDES v NETCOM CONSULTANTS (UK) LTD (2000) an employee was awarded £290,000 by an employment tribunal when he was pressured to resign after informing the parent company that his boss was submitting expense claim forms without receipts to evidence his claims. The tribunal found that the dismissal was automatically unfair under the 1998 Act.

i.   *Inventions.* It is the duty of the employee to disclose all inventions made using the facilities of the employer.

In BRITISH SYPHON COMPANY LTD v HOMEWOOD (1956) D was employed as a technical adviser and was asked to design a soda syphon, which he did, but he patented the syphon in his own name. It was held that the patent right belonged to the employer.

Statutory provision has been made with regard to employees' inventions by the PATENTS ACT 1977, which largely restates the common law position. This is that an invention belongs to the employer if made in the normal course of duties under the circumstances in which it might be expected an invention to result. In addition it is deemed to belong to the employer if the invention results from special duties assigned to the employee under circumstances in which an invention might reasonably be expected to result. However, in all other cases, even where the invention occurs in the course of employment, using the employer's materials but where an invention cannot reasonably be expected it will be deemed to belong to the employee.

j. *Obedience.*

    i.   The employee must obey all lawful and justifiable orders given by his employer in the ordinary course of business, but only undertakes to perform those tasks to which he has agreed in his contract of employment. An employer may not require him to do other tasks, however reasonable, unless the contract is wide enough to permit this. This applies to both the nature of the work and to the location.

        In PRICE v MOUAT (1862) a lace dealer was asked to card lace. This was not a task he had undertaken and he was justified in refusing, as it would have involved a lowering of his status.

        In O'BRIEN v ASSOCIATED FIRE ALARMS (1968) an employee in a Liverpool factory was required to work in Barrow. It was held that such a request was outside the scope of the contract.

    ii.   In some circumstances an employee will be justified in refusing a task, even though it is in the contract of employment:

        In OTTOMAN BANK v CHAKARIAN (1930) D refused to move to a branch of the bank situated in a country in which his life would have been in danger. It was held that his refusal was justified.

    iii. The duty of obedience is mitigated where the employee does not show a wilful flouting of the essential conditions of the contract:

        In LAWS v LONDON CHRONICLE (1959) P was secretary to an advertising manager. She followed him when he walked out of an editorial conference despite an order from the managing director to remain. It was held that P could not be summarily dismissed because her disobedience was an isolated instance and did not show an intention to repudiate her contract of service.

k. *Notice.* The employee must give proper notice of termination of his services according to the terms of his contract, the custom of the trade or statute (EPCA 1978).

Note: The foregoing are examples of occasions where an employee's duties to his employer have been implied at common law. However, it is not necessarily an exhaustive list. Generally courts will not imply unreasonable terms and will justify the implication of any terms they do imply, eg in SECRETARY OF STATE FOR EMPLOYMENT v ASLEF (1972) Lord Denning concluded that every contract of employment should contain an obligation on the employee not to wilfully disrupt his employer's undertaking.

CHAPTER 52

Duties of an Employer

INTRODUCTION

1. This chapter is concerned with an employer's duties implied under common law and expressed in statutes. In addition, an employer's duties to persons other than employees is considered, eg visitors and third parties who suffer loss due to the acts of the employees.

COMMON LAW DUTIES

2. *Work*. The employer is not obliged to provide work for his employees except in the following circumstances:

   a. Where employment is essential to provide a reputation for future employment. This was originally considered to be in the case of actors:

   In CLAYTON & WALLER v OLIVER (**1930**) an actor was engaged for the leading role in a show. The management engaged someone else but agreed to pay the actor for his lost wages; however, he also sued for loss of reputation. It was held that he was entitled to damages.

   This principle was also extended to journalists and skilled workers.

   In COLLIER v SUNDAY REFEREE (**1940**) P, a sub-editor was able to claim damages in accordance with the ruling given in the Clayton & Waller v Oliver case.

   In LANGSTON v AUEW (**1974**) P resigned from the AUEW in 1972 and was suspended on full pay for nearly two years. He succeeded in his claim, as a skilled man, for the right to work.

   b. Where remuneration depends on the amount of work, eg sales commission, the employer will be obliged to provide the work to enable commission to be earned:

   TURNER v GOLDSMITH (**1891**). (See Chapter 32.25.)

   In DEVONALD v ROSSER & SONS (**1906**) the court decided that an employer was obliged to provide work for pieceworkers whose pay depended upon performance.

3. *Pay*. The employer's common law duties with regard to pay are considered in Chapter 53.

4. *Indemnity*. An employer must indemnify his employee where the employee has incurred a liability whilst acting on the employer's behalf, except where:

    a.   The employee knew that he was doing an unlawful act.

    b.   The employee knew that the employer had no right to give the order in question.

In BURROWS v RHODES (1899) D were the organisers of the Jameson raid. They induced P to re-enlist in the armed forces of the British South Africa Company, this they did by means of a fraudulent statement. P believed that the venture in which he was to take part was lawful. It was held that he was entitled to damages from his employers for injuries received.

5. *Equipment and Premises (Safety)*. The employer must take reasonable care to make his premises safe. Examples of unsafe premises include structural defects, bad ventilation, unsafe insulation, slippery floors or staircases etc. Some specific areas are covered by statute, eg the necessity to maintain safe means of access (HSAW Regulations 1992).

Equipment includes plant, tools and materials, ie all those things with which a person may be expected to work must be of a safe nature. Many of these things are governed by various statutes, eg the *HSAWA 1974*, and *HEALTH AND SAFETY AT WORK REGULATIONS 1992*. Plant, tools and equipment supplied by the employer must be reasonably safe and the employer fails in this duty in the following circumstances:

    a.   He fails to supply suitable equipment and the employee is forced to improvise:

        In LOVELLS v BLUNDELL (1944) workers overhauling a ship's boiler needed planks, none were provided and there was not a supervisor to advise. They found a plank lying about and used it. The plank broke and they sued the firm for not providing a safe system of work. It was held that the firm was liable.

    b.   He provides defective equipment knowingly, or which he should have known on a reasonable examination. The onus is on the employer to inspect equipment.

        In BAXTER v ST HELENA GROUP HOSPITAL MANAGEMENT COMMITTEE (1972) a nurse sat on a chair which collapsed due to woodworm and she suffered a back injury. It was held that the hospital was liable as the chair should have been inspected.

    c.   He fails to remedy defects which have been brought to his notice.

        In MONAGHAN v RHODES (1920) a stevedore's labourer fell off an unsafe rope ladder leading to the hold of a ship. He had already drawn the foreman's attention to its danger.

    d.   But 'reasonableness' is all that is required:

        In LATIMER v AEC (1953) a factory floor became flooded owing to a storm, and the water, when mixed with oil, made the floor slippery. The employer dried the floor and spread sawdust, but P slipped and was injured. It was held that the employer had taken all reasonable precautions and was not liable for the injury.

Note: The employer's failure to take reasonable steps to ensure the safety of an employee may be a breach of a fundamental term of the contract entitling the employee to resign and claim constructive dismissal.

In BRITISH AIRCRAFT CORPORATION LTD v AUSTIN (1978) it was held that there was an implied term in the contract of employment that the employer would not behave intolerably. In this case it was regarded as intolerable that the employer failed to investigate the possibility of purchasing special eye protectors which would accommodate the employee's own spectacles.

6. *Disciplinary and grievance procedure*

We have noted that *S.1* ERA provides that details of any grievance procedure be notified to employees and any failure to observe such a procedure would result in a breach of contract; however, in a recent case the duty to provide all employees with some means of redressing grievances was established as being a common law implied duty: in WA GOOLD (PEARMACK) LTD v MCCONNELL (1995) the claimant had suffered a reduction in salary due to changes introduced by the employer; on a number of occasions he sought to take up his grievance with management but was repeatedly put off. The court held that the treatment he received was a breach of contract which he was entitled to treat as a breach and constructive dismissal and went on to say that the employer must reasonably and promptly afford an opportunity to employees to obtain redress of a grievance.

'REASONABLE' SAFETY

7. The employer must take reasonable care not to subject his employees to unnecessary risk. The requirements of safety on one hand and production on the other must sometimes conflict. By the test of 'reasonableness' judges have brought widely accepted ideas of fairness to assess the merits of a case. The standard of reasonableness indicates that there cannot be a guarantee of absolute safety. Some considerations which would be taken into account are:

a. *Inherent risk*. All work carries some risk and an employer would not be liable for events outside his control provided he had not been negligent.

(MITCHIE v SHENLEY (1952) a case involving a nurse who was injured by a mental patient.)

b. *Reasonably foreseeable*. If the danger could be reduced or eliminated the question is whether or not the employer was negligent in failing to do so.

In DOUGHTY v TURNER MFG CO (1964) an asbestos cover fell into a cauldron of molten metal. There was an explosion and the plaintiff, an employee standing by, was injured by molten metal. It was held that the explosion and hence the injuries were not reasonably foreseeable, therefore the employer was not liable.

c. *Obviousness of risk*. The more obvious the danger the more likely the law is to impose liability on the employer for failing to prevent the accident.

d. *Seriousness of risk*. This depends partly on the probability of an accident occurring but partly also on the gravity of the results if it does occur. The greater the risk the greater is the liability of the employer, and the more thorough are the precautions he should take.

e. *Cost.* The magnitude of the risk has to be weighed against other factors, particularly against the expense involved in safety measures and the necessity of carrying out the work in hand. The law would think it unreasonable to force employers to spend vast sums avoiding some slight chance of an accident.

In HAWES v RAILWAY EXECUTIVE (1952) an employee was electrocuted while carrying out repair work. It was held that the only foolproof safe system was for the current to be turned off in the region, the cost of which was too great compared with the risk of injury.

A REASONABLE SAFE SYSTEM OF WORK

8. There is the requirement for an employer to provide a 'reasonably safe system of work'. Formerly just a common law duty, the duty is now incorporated into the *HEALTH AND SAFETY AT WORK ACT 1974.* A safe system consists of:

a. *Reasonably safe work-fellows.* If an employer knows or ought to know (perhaps because of complaints) that employees are a danger to others he is obliged to remove the danger. Employers are held liable for the conduct of known bullies or practical jokers.

In HUDSON v RIDGE MFG CO LTD (1957) an employee of a firm was known for his practical jokes. A fellow employee suffered injury as a result of one of these practical jokes, and sued the firm for damages. It was held that the firm was liable for not providing a safe system of work.

Contrast SMITH v CROSSLEY BROTHERS LTD (1951) where two apprentices, by way of a practical joke, injected compressed air into the body of a third apprentice. It was held, on the evidence, that such an action could not reasonably be foreseen, there was no failure in the duty of supervision, and the employers were not liable.

b. *Training of employees.* Employees must be instructed in the choice of proper equipment and the correct method of working.

In BROWN v JOHN MILLS & CO LTD (1970) P was new at his job, of polishing brass nuts, which he did by the use of emery cloth wrapped around his finger whilst the nuts were secured in a lathe turning at high speed. He was injured. He had not been properly instructed in the correct method of working. It was held that the company was liable.

c. *Effective arrangements with regard to safety apparatus.*

i. Arrangements must be made for the provision and use of safety apparatus which will reduce the danger to the absolute minimum. No employee, even though experienced, must be left to look after his own safety.

In GENERAL CLEANING CONTRACTORS v CHRISTMAS (1953) a window cleaner employed by a firm fell from a ledge while attempting to clean the windows, it was normal practice to stand on the ledge to clean windows. It was held that even though normal practice, this method was not a reasonably safe system of work, and the firm was liable.

ii. Safety apparatus must be available at the place it is required.

In FINCH v TELEGRAPH CONSTRUCTION & MAINTENANCE CO (**1949**) P was injured when metal flew into his eye from a grinding operation. Goggles were provided but the workman did not know where to find them. It was held that the company was liable.

iii. It is not necessary to stand over experienced workers instructed in safety systems to ensure they are used.

In WOODS v DURABLE SUITES (**1933**) P contracted dermatitis due to working with glue. He had been instructed in the safety precautions. It was held that the employer was not liable as the employee was experienced, and the employer was not bound to stand over such a worker of full age to ensure that he took the precautions.

However, the employer must take all reasonable measures, including warning of dangers, and persuasion to ensure the use of the safety equipment.

In QUALCAST LTD v HAYNES (**1959**) molten metal splashed onto the foot of an experienced moulder. He knew that protective clothing was available but did not wear it. It was held that the employer was not responsible for failing to bring pressure to bear on his employee.

Contrast BUX v SLOUGH METALS LTD (**1970**) where P, a die caster, was injured when molten metal flew into his eyes. The company had complied with statutory safety regulations in providing suitable goggles for its foundry workers, but P was not wearing goggles at the time of the accident. The court held that the company were in breach of their common law duty to take reasonable steps for P's safety. They should have made a rule, enforced by supervision, that goggles should be worn. The non-use of goggles by workers had been reported but no management action taken. There were posters in the factory, but no campaign to enforce their use.

Contrast JAMES v HEPWORTH & GRANDAGE LTD (**1967**) where P, who could neither read nor write, had been employed by the defendants for four years, the last six months of which he had been working at a job involving molten metal. In an accident he had molten metal splashed on his foot and claimed damages, alleging the non-provision of safety spats. A prominent notice stated that spats were available and should be used. It was held that there was no additional legal obligation upon the employers of an illiterate workman.

d. *Proper co-ordination.* When safety depends on co-ordination of the work of a number of departments the employer must ensure that such co-ordination exists.

In SWORD v CAMERON (**1839**) employees were working in a quarry in which blasting operations were being carried out. They were not given sufficient time to get clear before an explosion took place. It was held that the employer had failed in his duty to provide proper co-ordination.

e. *Suitable working conditions.* Suitable working conditions must be provided. General conditions under which work is carried on must, so far as reasonable care can ensure, be such as are consistent with safety.

In MCGHEE v NCB (**1971**) P worked in a brick-making plant. No washing facilities were provided and he had to cycle several miles to his home after work. He contracted dermatitis. It was held that the ailment was mainly attributable to the employer's failure to provide suitable working conditions.

But the employer is not liable when he does not control the premises:

In CILIA v H.M. JAMES & SONS (**1954**) during the installation of plumbing a plumber's mate was electrocuted due to defective electrical wiring in the building. It was held that the employer was not liable as he was not in occupation of the building.

f. *Sufficient men for the task.* It is the employer's duty to ensure that there are sufficient employees to perform a task.

In HARDAKER v HUBY (**1962**) the employer was liable for not providing a plumber with a mate to help in carrying a bath upstairs.

g. *Hours of work and stress-related illness.*

It is now recognised that a foreseeable risk to the health and safety of employees will include hours of work, shift patterns and how work is organised by the employer. Employees working long possibly unsociable hours with over-burdensome workloads can suffer ill health and employers must recognise this as a risk factor in modern day work practices and plan accordingly to manage that risk.

The *WORKING TIME REGULATIONS 1998* set out broad criteria for employers as to hours and patterns of work for all employees both full time and part time, these include:

i. A maximum working week of 48 hours calculated over a 17 week period;

ii. A minimum of four weeks paid annual leave;

iii. Daily rest periods of at least 11 hours between each working day;

iv. A weekly rest period of 24 hours in each seven-day period of work. This may be averaged over a two-week period;

v. An in-work rest break of 20 minutes for employees working more than six hours a day;

vi. The hours which night shift workers do should not exceed an average of eight hours for a 24-hour period of the 17 week 'reference period'.

h.   *THE ASYLUM AND IMMIGRATION ACT 1996* requires that employers take steps to check the existence of certain key documents of potential employees. Failure to carry out the checks may result in a fine on the employer of up to £5,000. The Act does not apply to employees under the age of 16 or to self-employed or agency workers.

LIMITATIONS ON THE EMPLOYER'S DUTIES

9. The following show the extent of the employer's duties with regard to safety provisions.

a.   *Reasonable safety is all that is required.*

i.   Where there are generally accepted safety measures in a particular trade there would be a prima facie breach of duty if the employer failed to take them. However, it may well be that an accepted trade practice is a bad practice and the employer may be liable if he neglects to take precautions even though trade practice has been complied with.

In POTEC v EDINBURGH CORPORATION (**1964**) P's job was to stand on a platform at a refuse depot over a deep trench keeping the refuse moving with a long pole. He fell into the trench and contended that there should have been a guard rail. Such rails were not provided at other depots because of overwhelming evidence that a guard rail would impede the use of the pole. It was held that the employer was not liable.

Contrast CAVANAGH v ULSTER WEAVING CO LTD (**1959**) where P fell whilst going down a ladder on a sloping roof. Common practice was that no handrail was provided. It was held that although trade practice had been complied with, it was not conclusive proof that the employer had met his obligations at law and he was liable.

ii.   Where there are unusual circumstances special safety measures should be taken:

In PARIS v STEPNEY BOROUGH COUNCIL (**1951**) P a garage mechanic with one eye, lost his other eye in an accident. No goggles had been provided. It was held that whilst goggles were not usually provided, the employer should have provided them in this case because of the greater risk to eyesight involved.

Contrast CORK v KIRBY MACLEAN LTD (**1952**) P suffered injury caused partly by a breach of statutory duty by his employers and partly by reason of a fall caused by an epileptic fit. It was held that he was contributorily negligent by failing to notify his employer that he suffered from epilepsy. Consequently his damages were reduced by half.

iii.   Whilst the employer must do everything reasonable to protect the employee from injury he need not go so far as to dismiss an adult worker because the work is likely to endanger him. If an employer were to conceal risk or fail to give an employee enough information for him to assess the risk, then there may be liability.

In WITHERS v PERRY CHAIN CO LTD (**1961**) P contracted dermatitis due to working in greasy conditions. She was moved to another job considered free from this hazard. However, she continued to suffer attacks of the ailment and was off work for long periods. It was held that the employer was not negligent in allowing P to continue at work as the only alternative would have been to dismiss her.

iv. The burden of proof is on the plaintiff who must show that:

(a) The defendant (employer) was in breach of his duty to take care, and

(b) This breach was the direct cause of the plaintiff's (employee's) injuries:

In MCWILLIAMS v SIR WILLIAM ARROL (**1962**) the employer failed to provide safety harness for the employee who fell to his death because of the lack of a harness. Evidence was produced to show that the employee would not have worn his safety equipment even if it had been provided. The employer was not liable.

b. *Provision of tools.* Under the *EMPLOYERS' LIABILITY (DEFECTIVE EQUIPMENT) ACT 1969*, should any tools supplied to the employee prove to be defective in any way, thus causing injury to the user, the employer shall be liable to the employee. The employer's remedy is to sue the manufacturer.

c. *Protection of the employee's property.* The employer's common law duty for safety extends only to the employee's person and not his property. There may, however, be a tortious liability on the basis of a duty owed by occupiers to lawful visitors. Tucker L J said in DEYONG v SHENBURN (**1946**) that there is no reason why an employer knowing his servant has placed property in his care shall not be under a duty, as a neighbour, to take reasonable care of it. Furthermore there may be an express contractual duty.

In EDWARDS v WEST HERTS HOSPITAL COMMITTEE (**1957**) a resident surgeon had personal property stolen from his room at the hostel where he lived. There were no security arrangements at the hostel. It was held that the employers had no liability for the safety of employees' personal possessions.

Contrast MCCARTHY v DAILY MIRROR (**1949**) where an employee had clothing stolen from a peg. It was held that this was not 'adequate accommodation' which was required to be provided for employees' clothing under the *FACTORIES ACT*.

REFERENCES AND TESTIMONIALS

10. *Obligation to Give References*

An employer is not obliged to give references to his employees:

In GALLEAR v J.F. WATSON & SON LTD (**1979**) a dismissed employee claimed compensation for the failure of his employers to give him a reference. It was held that there is no implied duty to provide a reference and therefore there was no entitlement to compensation.

However, if an employer does give a reference he may be liable to a charge of defamation of character if any statement tends to lower the employee 'in the eyes of right-thinking people'.

11. *Action by the Plaintiff and Defendant*

The law relating to defamation including the action to be taken by the plaintiff and the defences open to the defendant, is outlined in Chapter 28. Also, there may be an alternative remedy in *negligence*.

In SPRING V GUARDIAN ASSURANCE (**1994**) S failed to get a number of jobs for which he applied because of an unfavourable and inaccurate reference given to him by the defendant employer. The judge found that there was a duty of care owed to S and that a case could be based in negligence. (See Chapter 24.)

12. *Qualified Privilege*

Generally an employer would claim that a reference he gave was subject to qualified privilege, ie, being made in good faith by a person who has a legal, social or moral duty to make it, to a person who has a similar interest or duty to receive it (ie a subsequent employer). The success of this defence depends on the statement having been made carefully, honestly and without malice.

13. *Untrue References*

   a. If an employer knowingly recommends an employee in terms which he knows to be false, the subsequent misconduct of the employee may render his former employer liable for damages in the tort of deceit.

   b. However, if the misstatement is negligent the employer may be liable to the recipient and the employee for negligent misrepresentation if either suffers consequential loss. HEDLEY BYRNE & CO LTD V HELLER & PARTNERS LTD (**1964**).

   In MCNALLY V WELLTRADE INTERNATIONAL LTD (**1978**) the employer was held liable in damages for negligent misrepresentation when he led the employee to believe that the job in Libya to which the employee was being sent was within the employee's capabilities.

14. The *SEX DISCRIMINATION ACT 1975* (as amended by the Regulations 2003) prohibits discrimination after the end of an employment relationship, eg an unreasonable refusal to supply a reference. Other anti-discrimination legislation deals in a similar way with regard to: race, religion and belief, sexual orientation and disability.

15. *REHABILITATION OF OFFENDERS ACT 1974*. Under this Act a person's convictions will not be subject to disclosure after a lapse of time. Some more serious offences are not subject to non-disclosure. The effect of this in regard to references is that an employer is not bound to disclose a spent conviction to another subsequent employer, and will therefore incur no liability.

16. The *TELECOMMUNICATIONS (LAWFUL BUSINESS PRACTICE) (INTERCEPTION OF COMMUNICATIONS) REGULATIONS 2000*, provide employers with lawful no-consent access to their employees' use of email and other communications in order to establish whether the use is related to the employers' business.

In addition, the employer can record employee communications without consent where:

i. It is necessary to establish the existence of facts relevant to the business of the employer, for example, keeping records of transactions and other communications where it is necessary to know the specific facts of a particular conversation;

ii. To ascertain compliance with regulatory or self-regulatory practices that apply to an employer's business;

iii. To demonstrate that certain standards are being achieved using the telecoms system, for example, quality control and/or staff training;

iv. To prevent or detect crime;

v. To detect and investigate unauthorised use of the employer's telecoms systems;

vi. To ensure the effective operation of systems as by monitoring for viruses or other matters that threaten the system.

The Act also allows monitoring, but not recording, without consent where:

i. It is necessary to determine whether or not communications are relevant to the business, for example, checking email accounts;

ii. In regard to communications that are to a confidential, anonymous counselling or support helpline.

Where an employer wishes to rely on the Act he is required to make all reasonable efforts to bring to the attention of employees that their communications might be intercepted.

EMPLOYER'S DUTY TO PERSONS OTHER THAN EMPLOYEES (see also Chapter 24.10–24.14)

15. The employer (as occupier of premises) has only the duty of common care to see that a visitor will be reasonably safe in using the premises for the purpose for which he is invited or permitted by the owner to be there. 'Common care' is a duty to take such care as in all the circumstances is reasonable. A 'visitor' is anyone who has express or implied permission of the occupier to be on the premises. This is in contrast to a 'trespasser', one who enters premises or land without permission (if continued acts of trespass are ignored it could be implied that the person was a 'visitor').

However, there is also a statutory duty under the *HSAWA 1974* for an employer to give information about potential dangers on his premises to all persons working on the premises.

In R v SWAN HUNTER SHIPBUILDERS LTD (**1981**) eight men were killed when a fire broke out on HMS *Glasgow*. The fire was especially intense because the vessel was badly ventilated and oxygen had escaped from a hose kit left by an employee of a firm of sub-contractors. It was held that the subcontractors had not been given sufficient information about the dangers of oxygen enrichment in confined spaces, nor, such instruction as was necessary to ensure the safety of all the workers on the vessel, no matter by whom they were employed.

NB. Contravention of the HSAWA 1974 gives rise to criminal liability.

a. The occupier is entitled to assume that the visitor will guard against the normal hazards of his own trade, ie where the visitor is performing work on the premises, ROLES v NATHAN (1963). In this case a sweep was poisoned by dangerous fumes in a chimney.

b. The occupier must, however, give suitable warnings of 'traps', ie slippery floors, steep staircases, etc.

c. The occupier will be liable if the visitor's possessions are stolen, only where the occupier can be proved to be negligent.

d. Where a visitor is injured through the negligence of an independent contractor working on the premises, the contractor will be liable. However, the burden of proof is on the occupier to give 'beyond reasonable doubt' facts to show that it was the fault of the contractor (O'CONNOR v SWAN & EDGAR (1963). The contractors were liable when a ceiling under repair fell and injured a shopper).

e. The position of a person other than a 'visitor' is covered by the OCCUPIERS LIABILITY ACT 1984 (see Chapter 24.10).

VICARIOUS LIABILITY (see Chapter 24)

16. Where a person is injured by another the rule at common law is that the injured party may sue the actual wrongdoer. Where the wrongdoer is an employee the injured party may also have an action against the employer. This is 'vicarious liability', ie although the employer did not personally commit the wrong, he may be held responsible for all those who are employed by him. The third party will usually sue the employer as he is usually in a better financial position to meet a claim for damages.

17. Vicarious liability arises in two ways. Firstly, by an employer authorising a wrongful act. Secondly, although the employer did not authorise the act the employee performed it in the course of employment. This may appear to be unfair, but the view is taken that, by employing a person, the employer makes it possible for him to commit the wrong. It is regarded as a normal business risk undertaken by the employer for which he would be wise to take out insurance.

18. *Circumstances of Vicarious Liability.* The following are cases in which attempts have been made to clarify the position. Generally speaking the employer is deemed to be liable for the acts of an employee committed in the

course of employment during contractual hours of work and whilst he is performing a task for which he is employed:

a. The employee carries out an authorised task, but in a *wrongful manner*:

    In LCC v CATTERMOLES GARAGE (**1953**) an employee was employed to remove vehicles that blocked the garage entrance. As he had no licence he was instructed to push them by hand. On one occasion he drove a vehicle and caused an accident. It was held that the employers were liable for the damages as the employee had done what he was employed to do, albeit in an unauthorised manner.

b. The employee commits a wrongful act that was *expressly forbidden*: LIMPUS v LONDON GENERAL OMNIBUS CO (**1862**). The court found the employer liable: the employee was acting within the scope of his employment and it did not matter that the employer had expressly forbidden the wrongful act.

c. The employee commits a *wilful wrong*, even though it was a *criminal offence*: LLOYD v GRACE, SMITH & CO (**1912**). Here the employer would be vicariously liable even though the act was done for the benefit of the employee not his employer.

    In LISTER v HESLEY HALL LTD (**2001**) a warden employed by the defendant systematically abused children with emotional difficulties in the care of a special school. The House of Lords held the employer liable; the criminal acts were carried out within the scope of his employment; the employer had placed him in the position that enabled him to carry out the abuse.

    In so finding the House of Lords overruled an earlier decision in TROTMAN v NORTH YORKSHIRE CC (**1998**) where it was held that acts of sexual abuse were beyond the scope of employment so that the employer was not liable.

d. The employee acts *negligently*:

    In CENTURY INSURANCE v N IRELAND ROAD TRANSPORT BOARD (**1942**) a lorry driver was smoking whilst transferring petrol from his tanker to a store. A fire resulted. It was held that the driver's employer was vicariously liable.

    Contrast WILLIAMS v JONES (**1865**) where the defendant's employee was making a sign-board in a shed the floor of which was littered with wood-shavings. He lit his pipe and the shed burned down. It was held that the employer was not liable as the act was not deemed to be negligent.

    In the Century Insurance case there was an element of danger and lighting a cigarette amounted to negligence. In the second case lighting a pipe was not necessarily negligent in relation to the making of a sign-board.

e. The employee *wrongfully permits another* to perform his duties: ILKIW v SAMUELS (**1963**).

f. The employee makes a mistake.

    In BAYLEY v MANCHESTER, SHEFFIELD & LINCOLNSHIRE RAILWAY CO (**1872**) P, a passenger, was forcibly ejected from a train onto the platform by a zealous porter who believed him (wrongly) to be on the wrong train. It was held that the company was vicariously liable for the injury caused by their employee's mistake.

19. Acts committed in an emergency, in the protection of the employer's property, are classed as being in the course of employment.

   In POLAND v JOHN PARR & SONS (1927) an employee struck a boy whom he thought was stealing from his employer's wagon. The employer was liable. He would not have been liable if the carter's act had been so excessive as to take it out of the class of authorised acts.

20. Employers are not liable for the acts of their employees which are done outside the course of employment, even though they are closely connected with employment:

   In WARREN v HENLYS LTD (1948) a petrol pump attendant engaged in a fight with a customer over payment. It was held that the employer was not liable as the matter had become personal, outside the course of employment.

21. When an employee uses his employer's property for purposes of his own unconnected with his employment the employer will not be liable even though he gave consent for the use of his property.

   In HILTON v THOMAS BURTON LTD (1961) employees who were allowed to use their employer's van for reasonable purposes used it to drive to a cafe whilst awaiting their normal finishing time. On the way back there was an accident due to negligent driving. It was held that the employer was not liable as the employees were acting outside the course of employment 'on a frolic of their own'.

22. *Lifts Given in Employer's Vehicle*. The following cases are examples of court decisions on this matter:

   In TWINE v BEAN'S EXPRESS (1946) a driver employed by the defendants gave a lift to a person who was killed due to the employee's negligent driving. The employee had been expressly forbidden to give lifts and a notice to this effect was displayed in the vehicle. It was held that the employer was not vicariously liable as the driver's action was outside the scope of his employment and the injured person was deemed to be a trespasser.

   In YOUNG v EDWARD BOX & CO LTD (1951) P was a workman employed by the defendants. He was responsible for getting himself to and from his workplace. However, due to the inadequacy of public transport on Sundays it had become the practice to get a lift in his employer's vehicle. Young was injured in the course of one of these journeys.

   It was held that the employer was liable as the plaintiff's driver and foreman had concurred to the lifts and this was within the ostensible authority of the foreman. Thus the plaintiff had become a licensee and was not a trespasser.

   However, Denning, L J dissenting said

   'The liability of the owner does not depend on whether the passenger was a trespasser or not; it depends on whether the driver was acting within the scope of his employment.'

   Contrast ROSE v PLENTY (1976) (Chapter 23.13).

23. *Acts for the Exclusive Benefit of the Employee*. If an act is not only forbidden but done for the exclusive benefit of the employee, the employer is not liable.

In RAND v CRAIG (1919) carters employed by the defendant took rubbish to land owned by the plaintiff and tipped it there, instead of onto a dump provided by their employer which was further off. They did this as they were paid per load.

Contrast PERFORMING RIGHTS SOCIETY v MITCHELL & BOOKER LTD (1924) where P accused D of infringing copyrights by performance of certain dance music in their dance hall. The band had a clause in its contract forbidding the infringement of copyright and D tried to claim that they did so for their own benefit. It was held that the band infringed the copyright in the course of employment and for the benefit of the dance hall.

TIME OFF WORK

24. *Trade Union Duties.* Under the TULR(C)A an employer is obliged to permit an employee who is an official of an independent trade union recognised for collective bargaining purposes to take reasonable time off, with pay, during working hours. This is to enable the employee to carry out official duties concerned with industrial relations and to undergo relevant training in respect of these duties.

25. *Trade Union Activities.* An employer is similarly obliged to allow reasonable unpaid time off for the purpose of taking part in certain trade union activities. The activities are those in which the employee takes part as a member or in his capacity as a representative, but not activities classed as industrial action.

26. *Public Duties.* Under *S.50* ERA and employer is obliged to permit time off, without pay, during working hours for the purpose of performing certain public duties, including Justice of the Peace, member of a local authority or a statutory tribunal etc. The amount of time off allowed must be reasonable taking into account the length of time for the duty, time off already taken and the effect on the business of the employee's absence.

27. *To Look for Work or Make Arrangements for Training.* S.52 ERA gives a right to an employee who is dismissed for redundancy, and has at least two years service, to reasonable time off with pay to look for new employment or to make arrangements for training.

28. *Safety Representatives.* An employer shall permit a safety representative to take such time off with pay during the employee's working hours as shall be necessary to enable the safety representative to:

   a. Perform his functions under the Act.

   b. Undergo training to enable him to perform these functions.

29. *For Ante-Natal Care.* An employee has a right not to be unreasonably refused paid time off during working hours to keep an appointment for ante-natal care prescribed by a registered medical practitioner, registered midwife or registered health visitor. This right is accorded to all pregnant employees irrespective of hours worked weekly or length of service. Except in the case of the first appointment the right to time off is specifically linked with attendance at appointments

and the employer may require the employee to produce a certificate stating that she is pregnant and documentary evidence that an appointment has been made.

30. ***Complaints for refusal to give time off.*** In all cases where a complaint is made to an industrial tribunal relating to an employer's duty to permit time off, the complaint must be presented within three months of the date when the alleged failure occurred, or within a reasonable time when the tribunal is satisfied that it was not reasonably practicable to present the complaint within three months.

DISCLOSURE OF INFORMATION

31. ***Trade Union & Labour Relations (Consolidation) Act 1992***

   a. *Duty to disclose.* An independent trade union recognised by an employer for collective bargaining purposes may request either orally, or if required by the employer, in writing:

      i. Information without which the trade union representative would be materially impeded in carrying on the collective bargaining, and

      ii. Information which it would be in accordance with good industrial relations practice that the employer should disclose to the trade union representative for the purpose of collective bargaining.

   b. *Exceptions.*

      i. Against the interests of national security

      ii. In contravention of a statutory prohibition

      iii. Communicated to the employer in confidence

      iv. Relating to an individual without his consent

      v. Likely to cause substantial injury to the business

      vi. Information concerned with legal proceedings.

   c. *Failure to disclose.* If an employer fails to disclose information the matter may be referred to ACAS. Alternatively and when the ACAS has failed in its attempt at a conciliation the CAC will hear and settle the complaint. If the CAC finds the complaint wholly or partly justified it may make a declaration, specifying:

      i. The unfounded information

      ii. The date the employer failed to supply the information

      iii. A period (being not less than one week after the declaration) within which the information must be disclosed.

32. ***Health & Safety At Work Act 1974***

   a. *Employees.* To provide the employees with such information as is necessary to ensure their health and safety at work (this requirement is tested on the basis of what information could have reasonably been discovered or known by the employer and therefore disclosed); and

To prepare, and bring to the notice of all their employees, a written statement of their general policy regarding health and safety at work of their employees and the organisation and arrangements for the implementation of that policy. Moreover, any revision of this written statement must also be brought to the notice of employees.

b. *Safety Representatives.* Additionally, safety representatives under the Safety Representatives and Safety Committees Regulations 1977 are entitled to inspect and take copies of any document which their employer is legally obliged to keep (except health records of identifiable individuals). Moreover, the employer is obliged to provide safety representatives with any information in his possession relating to health, safety or welfare which will enable the representatives to fulfil their functions except:

i. Any information the disclosure of which would be against the interests of national security; or

ii. Any information which he could not disclose without contravening a prohibition imposed by or under some enactment; or

iii. Any information relating specifically to an individual, unless the individual has consented to the disclosure; or

iv. Any information the disclosure of which would, for reasons other than its effect on health, safety or welfare at work, cause substantial injury to the employer's undertaking or, where the information was supplied to the employer by some other person, to the undertaking of that other person; or

v. Any information obtained by the employer for the purpose of bringing, prosecuting or defending any legal proceedings.

CHAPTER 53

Wages

INTRODUCTION

1. The contract of employment usually gives details of the amount to be paid, payment during absence from work, method of payment, etc. In the absence of express terms other terms have been implied by the courts. In addition a body of statute law has arisen governing such things as deductions from pay etc. The *NATIONAL MINIMUM WAGE ACT 1998* empowers the Secretary of State to set a minimum wage which all employers must pay (this is currently set at £5.05 for workers with a lower rate for young workers and those undergoing training. The rate will rise to £5.35 in October 2006).

S.27 EMPLOYMENT RIGHTS ACTS 1996 provides a statutory definition of the meaning of wages, it includes: any fee, bonus, commission and holiday pay.

The common law duties of an employer to an employee and the statutory requirements with regard to pay are considered in this chapter.

PAY – COMMON LAW

2. The following are the employer's duties to his employees in the absence of express provision in the contract of employment.

a. *Amount of pay.* The employer must pay the agreed remuneration or what is reasonable in the circumstances.

b. *Availability of work.* There is an entitlement to pay even though employees cannot work because no work is available. Time workers are paid for being ready, willing and able to work for their agreed hours.

In TURNER v SAWDON & CO (1901) it was held that the employer had a duty only to pay wages, not to provide work to a man employed as a salesman.

c. *Piece workers.* Piece workers are also paid for being ready, willing and able. It is up to the employer to find them work. (DEVONALD v ROSSER (1906).)

In MINNEVITCH v CAFE DE PARIS (LONDRES) LTD (1936) musicians were employed under a contract including a clause to the effect that they would not be paid if they did not play. It was held that the clause implied that they were not entitled to receive pay for such performances their employer thought fit to cancel. This was not valid – it was up to the employer to find the musicians work to enable them to earn their remuneration.

d. If there is no work available due to circumstances outside the control of the employer, then he is under no obligation to pay his employees. Each case must be examined in the light of the circumstances:

In BROWNING V CRUMLIN VALLEY COLLIERIES LTD (1916) a mine became unsafe due to flooding and work stopped. It was held that the circumstances were outside the employer's control and there was therefore no need to pay wages.

Contrast JONES V HARRY SHERMAN (1969) where due to an outbreak of foot and mouth disease racing was cancelled and a turf accountant did not need so many employees. It was held that the right to 'lay-off' could not be implied into a contract of employment at fixed or guaranteed periodic wages.

e. *Overtime*. Overtime is payable when expressly agreed in the contract, or is customary. Where the overtime is expressed as obligatory the employer must provide overtime and the employee must serve it.

f. *Discretionary payments*. An employee cannot claim, as a right, a payment which has always been stated 'to be within the management's discretion' however often and regularly it may have been paid:

In GRIEVE V IMPERIAL TOBACCO CO LTD (1963) part of an annual gift was withheld from P after he took part in a strike. It was held that the company was entitled to withhold a gratuitous payment, despite the argument that it had become a term of the contract.

However, a contractual bonus which has been earned cannot legally be withheld.

g. *Payment during illness*. Payments during periods when an employee is absent due to illness will depend on the custom of the trade or industry, or of individual firms. In the absence of any agreement or custom the following will apply:

i. There is an implied right to receive payment:

In ORMAN V SAVILLE SPORTSWEAR LTD (1960) P, a production manager, had been off work ill for ten weeks. It was held that there was an implied term in his contract that he should be entitled to pay during sickness. It was considered that if there had been an express term that he would not be entitled. P would not have accepted the contract.

ii. The implied right can successfully be rebutted where the conduct of the employee shows that his right has been foregone.

In O'GRADY V SAPER LTD (1940) P, a doorman at a cinema, had never previously received pay during illness. He claimed pay after seeing the report of another case. It was held that he was not entitled, as the conduct of the parties showed that there was an implied term excluding payment during illness.

iii. An employer may expressly exclude his liability from paying wages during sickness:

In PETRIE V MACFISHERIES LTD (1940) a notice on the wall stated that payments made during sickness were ex-gratia payments, and indicated the amounts usually paid. It was held that the clause showed that payments were not made as of right during sickness.

h. *Suspension without pay*. The power to suspend an employee without pay must be provided for expressly or implicitly by contract. Suspension without pay in the absence of contractual power will amount to a repudiatory breach of contract of employment (ie constructive dismissal).

UNAUTHORISED DEDUCTIONS FROM WAGES

3. *S.2 EMPLOYMENT RIGHTS ACT 1996* introduced new protection for employees. The Act simplified the law and put manual and non-manual workers on the same basis.

4. **Deductions from Pay**. Deductions from an employee's pay will be unlawful unless:

   a. Authorised by statute, eg income tax, national insurance contributions.

   b. Agreed in the contract of employment, or,

   c. Agreed in advance by the employee in writing.

   d. An employer may not receive payment from an employee unless in accordance with a, b and c above.

   e. An employer may make deductions from wages or receive payments in respect of:

      i. Overpayment of wages or expenses

      ii. Disciplinary proceedings in respect of a statutory provision

      iii. Payment to a third person if agreed in writing by the employee

      iv. The employee's participation in a strike or other industrial action

      v. An order by a court or tribunal.

   f. 'Check-off' – authorisation

      An employer may not deduct union subscriptions from a worker's wages in respect of check-off arrangements unless the worker has authorised these deductions in writing within the last three years, and has not withdrawn his authorisation. If the subscriptions are increased the employer must give at least one month notice before deductions are made at the higher rate. At the same time the worker must be reminded that he has the right to withdraw authorisation at any time. Any contravention of these rules gives the worker the right of complaint to an industrial tribunal.

5. **Retail Employment**. In the event of employees in the retail trade who suffer deductions from their pay on account of stock or cash deficiencies, any deduction will be limited to 10% of wages. The same limit will apply to any payment required by an employer.

6. **Complaints to an Employment Tribunal.** An employee who considers he has been subjected to an unlawful deduction may go to an industrial tribunal.

EQUAL PAY ACT 1970

7. **Purpose.** The EQUAL PAY ACT 1970 (as amended by the SEX DISCRIMINATION ACT 1975) has the object of eliminating discrimination between men and women in regard to pay and other conditions of employment (eg overtime, bonus, output and piecework payments, holidays and sick leave entitlement). Pay is given a broad definition and includes male travel concessions not given to females; part-time employees not receiving sick pay when it was paid to full-time employees; differing redundancy payments; denial of access to compensation from a tribunal.

8. **Persons Covered.** The Act extends to all persons under a contract of employment, full or part-time, irrespective of age or length of service. Sex discrimination is forbidden in regard to all terms of employment, except:

   a.   Where the work is wholly or mainly outside Great Britain,

   b.   Members of the armed forces,

   c.   Where statute law requires discrimination,

   d.   A woman may enjoy privileges in respect of pregnancy and childbirth,

   e.   In provisions for death or retirement.

9. **Right to Equal Treatment.** The Act requires that every term in an employee's contract must not be less favourable than the terms in the contract of an employee of the opposite sex with regard to pay or other terms. This applies providing the work they are doing is:

   a.   Like work with a man in the same employment;

   b.   Of a broadly similar nature, or

   c.   Although the work is different has been rated of equal value under a job evaluation exercise.

   In DUGDALE & OTHERS v KRAFT FOODS LTD (**1976**) P and other women claimed unfair discrimination under the Equal Pay Act as they received lower basic rates of pay than men who worked on a night shift and on Sundays (women precluded under the Factories Act). The woman did work which was broadly similar to the men. The tribunal held that merely because the men worked at a different time did not constitute a difference of practical importance. Therefore the women should receive the same basic pay as men.

   d.   Employed on work which in terms of the demands made, is of equal value to that of a man in the same employment.

   In HAYWARD v CAMMEL LAIRD (**1984**) P was a cook employed in a shipyard. An industrial tribunal held that her work was of equal value to the company as men employed at the yard in other trades and she was therefore entitled to equal pay.

10. An 'equality clause' is written into every contract of employment. If a term in a contract is inconsistent with the 'equality clause' then that term is ineffectual.

11. The comparison of jobs may be made only with an employee of the opposite sex employed with the same employer or another establishment owned by the same employer, or which is a member of the same group of companies.

In BRITISH COAL CORPORATION v SMITH (1996) female canteen workers and cleaners employed at 47 different establishments of British Coal were allowed to compare themselves with male surface workers and clerical staff working at four different establishments; the court finding that common terms and conditions for purposes of the Act would be found where they were substantially comparable on a broad basis. They did not have to be identical.

12. *Difference in Rate of Pay.* Where it has been established that an employee is entitled to equal treatment under paras 9. a. b. c. and d. above, the employer would be liable unless he could prove that the variation in pay was genuinely due to a 'material difference'. For example, the higher pay may be due to longer service or higher productivity or because an employee has moved from a higher paid job to a lower, but his higher rate of pay has been preserved (this is known as 'red circling').

In METHUEN v COW INDUSTRIAL POLYMERS LTD (1980) a female employee sought equality with a man who was performing the same clerical job as herself, although receiving higher pay. The employers established that the man had been transferred from the shop floor because of age and sickness but his previous income and status had been preserved. It was held that the difference was due to a 'material difference', ie the protection of his income and position, and nothing to do with sex.

In COOMES (HOLDINGS) LTD v SHIELDS (1978) the employer owned a string of betting shops. In some shops the male employees were paid more than female employees, because of anticipated trouble from customers. It was held that the deterrent function of the male staff was not a genuine difference as all males received the higher rate regardless of performance of this function.

In CAPPER PASS LTD v LAWTON (1977) a female cook sought equal pay with male chefs. She worked in the directors' dining room preparing up to 20 lunches a day, whilst the male chefs worked in the company's canteen preparing 350 meals a day. It was held that she was employed on 'like work' and should therefore receive equal basic pay for a 40 hour week. The Act did not intend that too minute an examination of comparative work should be done.

In SHARP v CALEDONIA GROUP SERVICES LTD (2005) the Employment Appeal Tribunal ruled that any material factor defence put forward by an employer, must be objectively justified.

13. Reference to an Industrial Tribunal

a. A woman believing that she has a right to equal treatment for any of the reasons under the Act may refer her claim to an industrial tribunal. If the tribunal finds the complaint well-founded, it can make an order.

In addition the Secretary of State may apply for an order where it appears to him that an employee has a claim for equal treatment but it is not reasonable to expect the employee to make a complaint.

b.   Reference may be made, either during employment or within six months of termination.

c.   Arrears of pay may be claimed for up to two years before the date of reference to the tribunal. Damages in respect of non-cash benefits may be claimed for the same period.

14. *European Community Law.* Article 141 of the Treaty of Rome provides that women shall be accorded equal treatment for like work with men. This is superimposed on our own legislation. Where there is a conflict or where there is a gap in our own legislation the European Community law takes precedence. The interpreter of EEC law is the European Court, it is then incumbent on our own courts to apply that law.

In MCCARTHYS LTD v SMITH (NO. 2) (1980) a female worker claimed equal pay with her predecessor, a man. The case went to the European Court which ruled that, under Article 119, provided there is not a long gap between the end of one and the beginning of the other, a woman is entitled to equal pay with her predecessor.

15. *Part-Time Workers.* Discrimination against part-time workers was challenged in the European Court.

In JENKINS v KINGSGATE (1981) in a textile factory all the men worked 40 hours a week and all except a few women worked 30 hours. The part-timers got an hourly rate of pay 10% less than those on full-time. They claimed equality. The employers said the differential was justified by the need to discourage absenteeism, increase productivity and use the plant to the full. The European Court held that working shorter hours is not itself a material difference justifying unequal pay. However, a differential can be justified if it fulfils the stated needs of the employer (productivity etc) which are non-discriminatory.

GUARANTEE PAYMENTS (*ERA S.28–34*)

16. *Guarantee Payments.* These ensure that employees who are laid-off will receive some payment during that time.

17. *Entitlement.* Employees will be entitled to five days payment in any three month period at a maximum daily rate specified from time to time (£18.40). This is paid when an employee is laid off work for a whole day.

18. *Eligibility.* To be eligible an employee must:

a.   Have at least one month continuous service when the lay-off occurs.

b.   Be laid-off for the whole of his normal working hours.

c.   Be laid-off because of an occurrence preventing his employer providing him with work (apart from a dispute involving employees of the same or an associated employer).

d. Not have unreasonably refused an offer of alternative employment.

e. Be available for work.

19. *Exemption*. Employees who are covered by a collective agreement or a wages order with a provision for guaranteed pay may be exempted from the statutory requirements.

20. *Failure to Make Payment*. Where an employer fails to make an entitled guarantee payment an industrial tribunal can order him to make it.

MEDICAL SUSPENSION (*ERA S.64–65*)

21. Payment during medical suspension enables an employee to receive compensation when not actually sick or disabled.

22. *Entitlement*. An employer may suspend an employee on medical grounds (eg when he may be exposed to radiation or lead poisoning). During such suspension an employee is entitled to receive his pay, and may do so for a maximum period of 26 weeks.

23. *Eligibility*. To be eligible an employee must:

a. Have at least one month continuous service

b. Have not refused reasonably suitable alternative employment

c. Be available for work should he be required.

24. *Dismissal*. If the employer dismisses an employee instead of suspending him on medical grounds the employee will have the right to a claim for unfair dismissal. He need have only four weeks' continuous service to qualify (not the normal one year).

25. *Temporary Replacements*. An employer may engage temporary replacements for those medically suspended. However, he must make the temporary nature of the employment clear at the outset and offer alternative employment on termination if that is possible.

26. *Failure to Make Payment*. Where an employer fails to make an entitled medical suspension payment an industrial tribunal can order him to make it.

INSOLVENCY (*ERA S.182–188*)

27. The *ERA 1996* provides protection for employees in respect of amounts owing to them at the time an employer goes bankrupt or into receivership.

28. Amounts due under the Act eg for time-off or medical suspension will also be regarded as wages for preferential payment.

29. If the sum owed cannot be met by the liquidator or receiver the employee may apply for payment to be made from the National Insurance Fund.

30. The maximum recoverable from the liquidator is limited to eight weeks arrears of wages subject to a maximum at present of £280 per week. If the amount owing cannot be met by the liquidator the excess (plus other sums, ie wages in lieu of notice, holiday remuneration (maximum six weeks) and unfair dismissal compensation) may be claimed from the National Insurance Fund up to a maximum £280 per week (subject to review by the Secretary of State).

31. Unpaid employer contributions to occupational pensions funds up to a maximum of twelve months may be paid from the National Insurance Fund.

32. Any amount due in respect of a maternity payment may be obtained from the National Insurance Fund.

PAY STATEMENTS (*ERA S.8*)

33. The ERA 1996 gave every employee the right to a written itemised pay statement. The statement must include:

    a. Gross amount of wages.

    b. Deductions which vary with the wage, eg Income Tax.

    c. Total fixed deductions, eg trade union subscriptions.

    d. Net wages payable.

34. Failure to notify deductions makes the employer liable to pay the employee a sum equal to the amount of 13 weeks deductions, on a tribunal finding.

35. In MILSON V LEICESTERSHIRE CC (**1978**) P was advanced £111 for exam fees on the basis that if he failed or resigned within a year he would pay the money back in a lump sum. He gave notice but objected to paying back the money all at once. His employers deducted the £111 from his salary under the heading of 'miscellaneous deductions'. This was deemed not to be a properly itemised pay statement and therefore the deduction was unlawful. As P suffered no financial loss the employers were ordered to pay him a nominal sum of £25.

36. *Standing Statement.* Provided that the employer has given in writing a standing statement of fixed deductions, there is no need to itemise fixed deductions on an employee's pay statement, but simply to state the total amount of the deductions. The standing statement should give the following information:

    a. The amount of each deduction,

    b. The intervals at which the deduction is to be made, and,

    c. The purpose for which it is made.

This statement must be renewed after a period of 12 months.

CHAPTER 54

Maternity Rights

INTRODUCTION

1. The *ERA 1996* gives employees the right not to be dismissed by reason of pregnancy, a right to maternity pay and leave, and a right to return to work after maternity leave. The chapter outlines the main statutory provisions.

DISMISSAL

2. Dismissal of an employee for reasons of pregnancy, childbirth, or the fact that she took or asked for maternity leave is an *automatic unfair dismissal*.

MATERNITY LEAVE

3. The MATERNITY AND PARENTAL LEAVE REGULATIONS *1999*, as amended in 2002, provide for three types of maternity leave:

   a.   Ordinary maternity leave;

   b.   Compulsory maternity leave;

   c.   Additional maternity leave.

   These are periods of leave, before and after childbirth to which a pregnant employee is entitled. The dates of leave are calculated as being periods before or after the *expected week of childbirth*.

4. *Ordinary Maternity Leave*. An employee may be entitled to ordinary maternity leave if she satisfies certain conditions. These are.

   i.   No later than fifteen weeks before the expected week of childbirth, she notifies her employer:

      a.   That she is pregnant;

      b.   The expected week of childbirth;

      c.   The date on which she intends to start her ordinary maternity leave.

ii. The employee must give this notice in writing if requested by her employer. She is entitled to change her mind about the date for commencement of her maternity leave provided she notifies the employer at least 28 days before the new date.

iii. The employer is entitled to request medical confirmation of the expected week of childbirth and the employee is required to provide it. Failure to provide this information will remove the right to ordinary maternity leave.

iv. As a response to the notice the employer must, within 28 days, notify the employee of the date when ordinary maternity leave will end.

Ordinary maternity leave runs for a period of 26 weeks.

5. *Compulsory maternity leave.* An employer must not allow a woman who is entitled to ordinary maternity leave to work during the compulsory leave period. Compulsory leave is for two weeks commencing with the day on which childbirth occurs. These two weeks form part of the 26 week ordinary maternity leave period.

6. *Additional maternity leave.* An employee is entitled to additional maternity leave where she can show:

   a. Entitlement to ordinary maternity leave;

   b. At the beginning of the 14th week before the expected week of childbirth, she has been continuously employed for a period of not less than 26 weeks.

Additional maternity leave commences on the day after the last day of her ordinary maternity leave period and is for an additional period of 26 weeks.

7. *Maternity pay.* If a woman has been employed by her employer for at least 26 weeks, ending with the 15th week before the expected week of childbirth, and earns more than £82 per week, then, although she is not entitled to be paid her salary, she will receive *Statutory Maternity Pay (SMP)* during the ordinary maternity leave 26 week period. There are two levels of *SMP*:

   a. *The higher rate* is paid for the first six weeks. This is equivalent to 90% of the woman's salary. After this she is paid;

   b. *The lower rate*, which is £106 per week.

SMP is payable by the employer, but is partly (for small firms wholly) reimbursed by the state through reduced employer national insurance contributions.

8. *Redundancy during maternity leave.* Where redundancy occurs during maternity leave an employee is entitled to be offered any available suitable alternative employment with her employer, his successor or associated employer. This would take effect immediately on the ending of her employment under the previous contract. The new contract must be one which is suitable and the provisions of which not substantially less favourable than if she had continued to be employed under the previous contract.

9. *Unfair dismissal.* Dismissal for reasons of pregnancy is an unfair dismissal.

RIGHT TO RETURN TO WORK

10. There is no requirement for the employee to notify her employer of her return to work after *ordinary maternity leave*, unless she wishes to return early when she must give at least 28 days notice. The employee is entitled to return to the job she was previously employed to do, this means the same seniority, pension and other rights intact with terms and conditions no less favourable than those which applied before her absence.

11. *Flexible Working*

SECTION 47 of the EMPLOYMENT ACT 2002, amended the EMPLOYMENT RIGHTS ACT 1996, to make provision for flexible working arrangements. A qualifying employee may apply to his employer for a change in the terms and conditions of employment in relation to:

a. Hours of work;

b. Time when work is carried out;

c. Whether work should take place at home or in the place of business;

The purpose of the application must be the care of a child. The application must be made at least 14 days before the child's sixth birthday. No more than one application every 12 months can be made and agency workers are expressly excluded. An employee may request a contract variation where he or she has been continuously employed for a period not less than 26 weeks and be either, the mother, father, adopter, guardian or foster parent of the child, or is married to one of these. The request must be in writing. Within 28 days of the request, the employer must hold a meeting with the employee to discuss the application. The employee has the right to be accompanied by a fellow employee. After the meeting there is a further period of 14 days for the employer to notify the employee of his decision. The decision must be in writing either agreeing to the request or rejecting it. Where the request is refused, the employer must state the grounds for the refusal.

SECTION 80G(1)(B) of the EMPLOYMENT RIGHTS ACT 1996, provides the grounds for an employer refusal. There must be one or more of the following:

a. The burden of additional cost;

b. Detrimental effect on ability to meet customer demand;

c. Inability to reorganise work among existing staff;

d. Inability to recruit additional staff;

e. Detrimental impact on quality;

f. Detrimental impact on performance;

g. Insufficiency of work during the periods the employee proposes to work;

h. Planned structural changes;

i. Such other grounds as may be specified by regulations.

The employee is entitled to appeal against any refusal by the employer. This has to be made in writing, within 14 days after the refusal, giving the grounds for the appeal. The employer then has 14 days to respond. The final step would be to make a complaint to an employment tribunal.

SUSPENSION FROM WORK ON MATERNITY GROUNDS

12. An employee is suspended from work on maternity grounds where in consequence of any requirement by statute, regulation or a code of practice issued under the HSAWA *1974* she is suspended from work on the ground that she is pregnant, has recently given birth or is breastfeeding a child. *S.66–68 EMPLOYMENT RIGHTS ACT 1996*, provides that an employee so suspended is entitled to be paid during the suspension or offered *suitable alternative work* (see 15 below). She will not be entitled to pay for any period during which she was offered suitable alternative work and unreasonably refused it.

13. She is suspended if she continues to be employed by her employer but is not provided with work or does not perform the work she normally performed.

14. The *MANAGEMENT OF HEALTH AND SAFETY AT WORK REGULATIONS 1999* requires that an employer carries out an assessment of risks to the health and safety of employees and others. The Regulations require special attention in the event of there being female employees of childbearing age.

15. *Offer of suitable alternative work.* Where alternative work is available an employee has a right to be provided with it before being suspended on maternity grounds.

16. 'Suitable' work is suitable and appropriate for her in the circumstances and the terms and conditions not substantially less favourable than those of her usual work.

17. An employee may present a complaint to an employment tribunal that she has not been offered suitable alternative work. The complaint must be submitted not later than three months from the first day of suspension.

18. An award of compensation may be made such as the tribunal considers just and equitable in the circumstances.

19. The amount of remuneration will be a week's pay in respect of any week of suspension.

20. A complaint that an employer has failed to pay the whole or any part of her entitlement to remuneration must be made to a tribunal within three months.

BRITISH AIRWAYS (EUROPEAN OPERATIONS AT GATWICK) LTD v MOORE AND BOTTERILL (**2000**) concerned cabin crew who could not fly during their pregnancies who were successful in their claim for full flying allowances whilst employed on ground-based alternative work.

ANTE-NATAL CARE

21. *Contractual Remuneration.* Where an employee receives any payment by way of contractual remuneration for a period when she would have received maternity payment, any sum paid reduces her entitlement to maternity pay.

22. Pregnant employees can have time off with pay during working hours to attend ante-natal clinics.

23. Apart from the first appointment, the employer can require the employee to produce a certificate of pregnancy and appointment card.

24. If the employer fails to comply with his obligations the employee can apply to an employment tribunal which can grant her compensation. If time off has been refused the amount of compensation will be the sum she would have received if the time off had been granted. If the time off has been granted but without pay the compensation will be the pay which ought to have been paid to her.

25. This right is not dependent on the employee's length of service, ie she can have time off on the first day of her employment. It also does not depend on the number of hours per week that the employee works.

26. *Parental Leave.* The MATERNITY AND PARENTAL LEAVE REGULATIONS 1999 gives to employees the right to unpaid leave, after one year's continuous employment, of up to 13 weeks per child, to care for their children under the age of five (18 weeks for a disabled child). The employee is required to give at least four weeks notice to the employer of the intention to take parental leave.

27. *Time Off for Dependants.* Employees are entitled to unpaid time off work to help a dependant who has given birth, is ill, has been injured or assaulted or who has died. In addition an employee is entitled to time off to deal with an incident involving their child which occurs unexpectedly during school hours. A dependant is widely defined as being a spouse, child, parent or live-in-lover or any person who relies on the employee to make child care arrangements.

The employee is required to inform the employer as soon as is reasonably practicable. Where an employee is denied this right a complaint can be made to an employment tribunal within three months of the refusal; the tribunal has the power to extend leave and/or award compensation.

28. *Adoption Leave.* Adoption leave was introduced as part of the same legislation as paternity leave. It applies to 'an employee (whether male or female and whether married or single) who is the adoptive parent of a child newly placed for adoption'. It does not apply to step-family adoption or adoption by a child's existing foster carers. To qualify the employee has to meet the same requirements as for paternity leave. The leave is the same as that for maternity leave. Where a couple adopt a child, only one of them is entitled to take adoption leave.

CHAPTER 55

Discrimination

INTRODUCTION

1. The problems of discrimination against certain classes of employees are tackled by the *SEX DISCRIMINATION ACTS 1975* and *1986*, the *RACE RELATIONS ACT 1976* and the *DISABILITY DISCRIMINATION ACT 1995*. In addition European Community law exists in this field. Although the scope of these statutes is greater than merely that of employment this chapter outlines the main provisions of the Acts only insofar as they affect discrimination in the matter of employment.

SEX DISCRIMINATION ACT 1975

2. *Forms of Discrimination.* There are three basic forms of discrimination covered by the Act. They are direct discrimination, indirect discrimination and discrimination by way of victimisation. Discrimination arises where an employer or prospective employer treats a woman less favourably than he treats or would treat a man (or vice versa). The Act also relates to discrimination against married persons.

Positive Discrimination. There have been recent developments with regard to a particular form of discrimination, 'positive discrimination'. This occurs where an employer positively discriminates in favour of women where there exists an under-representation of them in some particular area, eg women engineers.

Initially in KALANKE V FREIE HANSESTADT BREMEN (**1996**) the European Court of Justice ruled that for an employer to 'positively discriminate' in favour of women was unlawful. However, in recognition of the problems of redressing historical imbalances in certain job categories, the *TREATY OF ROME* was amended so that from May 1999, Member States can maintain and adopt measures that provide specific advantages for an under-represented sex in employment. This was applied in APPLICATION BY BADECK AND OTHERS (**2000**) in the public service sector allowing 'positive discrimination' where (a) there was no automatic preference for a women in that both sexes were considered equally, and (b) there was an objective assessment which considered both sexes' personal situations. If this resulted in a man and women being equally qualified for the job, the woman could be selected.

a. *Direct discrimination.* This has been equated with 'intentional' discrimination. Intention is most difficult to prove, but complainants need only provide facts which show prima facie evidence of intentional discrimination. If the inference of direct discrimination can be arrived at from the evidence produced by the complainant then the motive for the discrimination is immaterial:

In GRIEG V COMMUNITY INDUSTRY (**1979**) a young girl applied for a job with an organisation whose purpose was to relieve unemployment amongst juveniles. She was refused employment in a particular activity because she would have been the only girl in a group of men, and emotional problems were anticipated. It was held to be sex discrimination, even though the motives were honourable.

In JAMES V EASTLEIGH BOROUGH COUNCIL (**1990**) the House of Lords ruled that discrimination was simply an objective assessment of the facts and the motives of the discriminator were irrelevant; in this case a local authority gave concessions to those in receipt of a state pension to cheaper entrance to its swimming baths. James successfully brought an action claiming sex discrimination in the provision of public services (also outlawed under the 1975 Act) in that his wife could gain cheap entry but he could not. The House of Lords ruled that the question to be asked was whether a man would have received the same treatment as a woman but for his sex (sometimes referred to as the 'but for' test).

In GUBALA V CROMPTON PARKINSON LTD (**1977**) P was made redundant in preference to a male colleague of the same seniority. The employer admitted that he had been influenced by the fact that the man was older and had a mortgage whereas P's husband worked. It was held that this was a case of unlawful discrimination.

In PEAKE V AUTOMOTIVE PRODUCTS LTD (**1977**) a male employee complained that there was sex discrimination as women were allowed to leave work five minutes earlier than men to avoid the crush at the factory gates. His complaint was, at first upheld. On appeal the decision was reversed on the grounds that this was a minor act of chivalry. Furthermore it was in the interests of safety and therefore there was no unlawful discrimination.

b. *Indirect discrimination.* This occurs where the same conditions apply equally to both sexes, but because of the nature of the conditions it is more difficult for one group to qualify than the other and this discrimination cannot be justified. For example, if a height requirement were to be fixed at six feet there would be relatively few women capable of qualifying. Similarly if a shoe size of five should be set, few men would qualify.

In STEEL V UNION OF POST OFFICE WORKERS AND GPO (**1978**) prior to the Sex Discrimination Act women could only be 'Temporary' full-time postmen. After the Act was passed women could become full-time postmen but walks and rounds were allocated on the basis of service as a full-time postman. It was held that failure to make the allocation on length of service irrespective of whether it was temporary or not was discriminatory.

In PRICE v CIVIL SERVICE COMMISSION (1977) the requirement that applicants for employment should be between the ages of seventeen and half and twenty-eight was held to be unlawful discrimination because, in practice, the demands of maternity prevented a considerable proportion of women from availability.

In POWELL v ELY-KYNOCH LTD (1981) an agreement was in existence whereby the first employees to go if redundancies were needed would be the part-time employees. This was held to be discriminatory as family commitments meant that all the part-time workers were women who would be unable to comply with the condition of full-time work in order to keep their jobs.

In MACGREGOR WALLCOVERINGS LTD v TURTON (1977) a scheme whereby employees over 60 who were made redundant received an extra 10 weeks pay was held to contravene the Sex Discrimination Act as it precluded women (who retired at 60) from qualifying. It therefore did not give women equal rights with men to benefits.

In WRIGHT v RUGBY CC (1984) Rugby Council refused to allow P to work times which fitted in with care of her baby. It was held to be sex discrimination as it was a circumstance under which a far greater proportion of women than men would be affected.

c. *Victimisation.* This occurs when less favourable treatment is given to a person because that person has brought proceedings under the Sex Discrimination Act or Equal Pay Act, or has given evidence or made allegations with regard to these Acts. This does not apply when the person who is victimised does not act in good faith (for example, makes false allegations) or where the conduct of the employer was an honest and reasonable attempt to compromise the proceedings. This was shown in ST HELENS METROPOLITAN BOROUGH COUNCIL v DERBYSHIRE AND OTHERS (2005). Here the council wrote a letter to claimants warning them of the consequences of continuing their equal-pay claims. The Court of Appeal followed an earlier House of Lords decision in, CHIEF CONSTABLE OF WEST YORKSHIRE POLICE v KHAN (2001) where it was stated that an employer may take honest and reasonable steps to safeguard its position in proceedings without infringing the victimisation provisions, and found that the tribunal should have considered whether the actions of the Council were reasonable steps taken to try and persuade claimants to settle their claims.

3. *Scope of the Act.* The Act makes discrimination on the grounds of sex unlawful in employment, training and related matters. It is unlawful for an employer to discriminate against a person on the grounds of sex or marital status in relation to employment with regards to contracts of employment and in contracts for services. This covers all contracts, irrespective of an employee's age or service, apart from:

a. Employment wholly or mainly outside Great Britain.

b. Employment in a private household if there could be a reasonable objection to someone of a particular sex having the degree of physical or social contact with a person living in the home, or the knowledge of such a person's private affairs, which the job is likely to entail.

4. *Recruitment.* It is unlawful to discriminate when recruiting employees:

   a. In the arrangements an employer makes for deciding who should be offered a job, for example, instructions given to a personnel officer.

   b. In relation to terms offered, for example, pay and holidays.

   c. By deliberately refusing employment, on the grounds of sex.

5. *Treatment of Present Employees.* Discrimination against employees on the matter of opportunities for promotion, transfer, training and any other benefits is unlawful.

6. *Pregnancy, Childbirth, Death and Retirement.* In these matters it is not unlawful to discriminate by:

   a. Giving a special treatment to women in respect of pregnancy and childbirth, and,

   b. An employer making special provisions in regard to death or retirement, unless the employer discriminates against a woman in respect of opportunities for promotion, transfer or training.

7. *Burden of Proof.* The SEX DISCRIMINATION – BURDEN OF PROOF REGULATIONS 2001 add a new section to the SEX DISCRIMINATION ACT 1975 (S.63A) this states that where an applicant proves facts giving rise to an apparent case of discrimination, the tribunal *shall* uphold the complaint of discrimination unless the respondent proves he did not commit the act. This will shift the burden of proof onto the respondent. Also the regulations will alter the words contained in *S.1* on indirect discrimination from, 'requirement or condition' to any 'provision, criterion or practice'. It is thought that this will make it easier for an applicant to allege an act of indirect discrimination.

In BARTON v INVESTEC HENDERSON CROSSWAITE SECURITIES (2003) the Employment Appeal Tribunal laid down guidelines on the operation of S63A. The case concerned a media analyst who brought a claim for sex discrimination and equal pay. She contended that over a period of four years she had received less basic pay and bonuses and fewer benefits in the form of share options than her two male comparators. The EAT, in finding for the claimant, stated:

   i. The burden of proving the facts from which a tribunal could conclude that, in the absence of an adequate explanation, the employer had committed an act of sex discrimination, rested with the claimant. She had in the present case succeeded in doing that;

   ii. Once this had been achieved, the burden then shifted to the employer to show a material difference in the work carried out and/ or some objective reason for allowing the disparity in pay. This the employer had failed to do.

In order to assist with determination of the facts a form of questionnaire has been prepared by the Secretary of State. This can be served on the employer for answering. The reply should enable the person with the grievance to decide whether or not he has a reasonable case. Although the employer is not bound to reply to the questionnaire if he fails to do so an adverse inference may be taken by a tribunal.

8. *Genuine Occupational Qualification.* Discrimination is not unlawful where a person's sex is a genuine occupational qualification for a job. A person's sex is regarded as a genuine occupational qualification where:

   a. The essential nature of the job calls for a man (or woman) for reasons of physiology (excluding physical strength or stamina), for example modelling clothes, bunny-girls.

   b. Considerations of decency or privacy, for example because of likely physical contact (clothing sales assistant), or because it involves use of sanitary facilities (lavatory attendant).

   c. The nature of location of the establishment makes it impracticable, for example on an oil rig, or ship where separate sleeping and sanitary facilities do not exist.

   d. In a single-sex establishment, for example a single-sex hospital. It is reasonable to restrict employment to persons of the same sex as that of the establishment.

   e. The job-holder provides a personal service, for example where a person of a particular sex is more acceptable, for example social worker, masseuse.

   f. Where the law requires it, for example the restriction on a woman resuming work within four weeks of giving birth, and exposure to lead.

      In PAGE v FREIGHT HIRE (TANK HAULAGE) LTD (**1981**) the applicant, a 23 year-old divorcee was removed by her employer from haulage work involving the chemical dimethylformide on the ground that the substance was a danger to women of child-bearing age. The employer claimed that he was required to do this under the general duty to safeguard the health and safety of his employees imposed by *S.*2 of the HSAWA *1974*. The EAT held that the employer had acted lawfully.

9. *Sexual Harassment.* Direct discrimination may also be found in a particular form of treatment to which a woman is generally regarded as being more vulnerable to, 'sexual harassment'. In PORCELLI v STRATHCLYDE REGIONAL COUNCIL (**1986**) a female laboratory technician was subjected to continuing unpleasant behaviour of a sexual nature by her fellow male employees. The Court found that whilst a male employee who was also disliked by fellow workers would have received similar treatment, the nature of this particular treatment was of a sort which a woman would find particularly offensive and was therefore, direct discrimination.

This subjective approach that takes account of the particular feelings and attributes of the victim, was confirmed in a Code of Practice issued by the European Commission in 1991 on protecting the 'dignity of women at work'.

This requires that employers stop behaviour which an employee makes clear she regards as unwanted, unreasonable and offensive.

A new statutory definition outlawing sexual harassment is contained in an amendment to the SEX DISCRIMINATION ACT 1975, S.4A. It states that a person subjects a woman to harassment if:

> on the ground of her sex he engages in unwanted conduct that has the purpose or effect of violating her dignity, or creating an intimidating, hostile, degrading or offensive environment for her.
>
> or
>
> He engages in any form of unwanted verbal, non-verbal or physical conduct of a sexual nature that has the same effect.

In order to give tribunals some discretion when dealing with persons who might be seen as being unreasonable or unduly sensitive, the new section goes on to state:

> conduct shall be regarded as having the effect of violating dignity or creating an intimidating, hostile, degrading or offensive environment, only if, having regard to all the circumstances, including in particular the perception of the woman, it should reasonably be considered as having that effect.

In DRISKEL V PENINSULAR BUSINESS SERVICES LTD (2000), Mrs Driskel claimed that she had been sexually harassed by her boss. She alleged that she had been subject to sexual banter and comments and that at an interview for promotion he had suggested that she wear a short skirt and a see-through blouse showing plenty of cleavage. She refused to return to work unless her boss was moved elsewhere. She was then dismissed and made a claim to an employment tribunal. At the initial employment tribunal hearing, the tribunal dismissed her claim finding that each incident considered in isolation, did not amount to sexual harassment. The Employment Appeal Tribunal held that this was the wrong approach and that sexual harassment had occurred:

a. The original tribunal should have looked at the total overall effect of the acts complained of, not each individual act;

b. A woman's failure to complain at times throughout the conduct should not necessarily be taken as significant;

c. Sexual banter between heterosexual men is not the same as similar comments towards a woman.

The same definition is contained in the RACE RELATIONS ACT 1976 S.3A (see below) in the form of racial harassment where on grounds of race, ethnic or national origins, he engages in unwanted conduct which has the same effect on dignity and environment stated above for sexual harassment. The same definition applies for *sexual orientation* and *disability* (see below).

There exist other legislation relating to harassment. The CRIMINAL JUSTICE AND PUBLIC ORDER ACT 1994, creates a criminal offence of intentional harassment – covering harassment in the workplace. The penalty on conviction is imprisonment for up to six months and/or a fine up to £5,000.This means that an employee who is harassed at work is able to report the matter to the police. The PROTECTION FROM HARASSMENT ACT 1997 is also relevant. The Act covers wide ranging acts of harassment and bullying at work, and provides the possibility of bringing civil proceedings against offenders.

10. *Ageism.* The EMPLOYMENT EQUALITY (AGE) REGULATIONS 2006 come into force on 1st October 2006. The Regulations set out law, making it unlawful directly or indirectly to discriminate in the employment sphere on the grounds of age. Enforcement will be through tribunals and compensation potentially will have no maximum limit. Under age discrimination law, there will be an employer defence of justification for both direct and indirect discrimination, if he can show that the action was a proportionate means of attaining a legitimate aim. The Regulations will permit discrimination against job applicants whose age is already above the normal retirement age (or 65 if there is no stated age of retirement).

11. *Sexual orientation.* The EMPLOYMENT EQUALITY (SEXUAL ORIENTATION) REGULATIONS 2003, outlaw direct or indirect discrimination, harassment and victimisation on grounds of sexual orientation. Sexual orientation is given a broad definition to include heterosexual, homosexual and bisexual prefer- ences. However, the Regulations do not extend protection to those discrim- inated against because they have a particular type of sexual preference, for example, paedophilia. The words 'on grounds of' means that the Regulations would protect third parties discriminated against, for example, a man harassed at work because his son is homosexual, or someone is discriminated against because they have gay friends. The Regulations also cover 'perceived' sexual orientation by the employer; so if an employer believes a particular employee is bisexual and discriminates against them for that reason, then it does not matter if the employee is in fact not bisexual. To bring an action a claimant does not have to declare his sexual orientation; all he has to show is that he was treated less favourably than a heterosexual person by his employer because the employer believed the claimant to be bisexual.

12. *Religion or belief.* The EMPLOYMENT EQUALITY (RELIGION OR BELIEF) REGULATIONS 2003, like sexual orientation above, cover employer 'percep- tions' and discrimination against third parties because, for example, of their connection with persons of a certain religion or holding a certain belief. The Regulations do not contain a definition, merely a statement that they apply to, 'any religion, religious belief, or similar philosophical belief', it will be left to the courts to build up a body of case law as to what counts as a religion or belief.

13. *Gender reassignment.* S.82 SEX DISCRIMINATION ACT 1975, defines gender reassignment as:

> a process which is undertaken under medical supervision for the purpose of reassigning a person's sex by changing physiological or other charac- teristics of sex.

S.2A of the Act provides that a person unlawfully discriminates against another by treating them less favourably on the grounds that they intend to undergo, is undergoing or has undergone gender reassignment. In CHESSINGTON WORLD OF ADVENTURE LTD V REED (1997) an individual announced a change of gender from male to female and, as a result, was subjected to continuous harassment from fellow workers. She eventually was absent through sickness and was dismissed. The Employment Appeal Tribunal held that the employer, who had known of the harassment, was directly liable for the sex discrimination that had taken place.

14. *Discrimination Against Contract Workers.* It is unlawful to discriminate against the employees of an independent contractor. The contractor himself is liable in regard to the selection of his employees. The 'principal' is liable for discrimination in the terms of the contract with the independent contractor or the provision of facilities to contract workers.

In RICE V FON-A-CAR (1980) taxis were owned and maintained by the driver but run by a firm to whom the owner paid a weekly sum in return for business. The driver obtained permission to employ a relief driver for his night shift but, when the firm learned it was a woman, they told him to dismiss her, which he did. It was held that the driver did not supply contract labour nor provide services for the purpose of finding employment for women, and consequently the Act did not apply.

15. *Collective Agreements.* Any term in a collective agreement or in an employer's rules for his employees which would result in a breach of the SDA or Equal Pay Act will be void. The same applies to any rule made by an organisation of employers or workers or trade association or body which confers qualifications. The voiding of discriminatory terms and rules will not impair employees' rights under their contracts of employment.

16. *Miscellaneous.* The Act also applies to partnerships, trade unions and employers organisations, professional and trade bodies. It also applies to vocational training bodies apart from midwifery, to the police and prison service.

17. *Complaints.* A person who has been discriminated against may apply to an industrial tribunal where the employer must attempt to justify his action. Application must be made within three months of the act of discrimination, or if it is a continuing discrimination, from when it ceases. The time limit may be extended by the tribunal if it is considered just and equitable to do so.

18. *The Equal Opportunities Commission.* This body is required to work towards the elimination of discrimination, to promote equality and to keep the Sex Discrimination Act under review. It has the following functions:

   a. Conduct formal investigations into cases where it believes that conduct contravenes either the Sex Discrimination Act or the Equal Pay Act. It may issue a 'non-discrimination notice', requiring the employer to act in accordance with its terms.

   b. Seek a declaration from the tribunal that an employer is engaging in discriminatory practices, or an advertisement is discriminatory, or that he has instructed someone over whom he has control to discriminate, or he is pressurising another to discriminate.

   c. Assist an individual in preparing or presenting her case.

19. *European Community Law*. Article 141 TREATY OF ROME provides that women shall be accorded equal treatment for like work with men. This is super-imposed on our own legislation. Where there is conflict or where there is a gap in our own legislation the European Community law takes precedence. The interpreter of EC law is the European Court, it is then incumbent on our own courts to apply that law.

RACE RELATIONS ACT 1976

20. Under this Act it is an offence for an employer to directly or indirectly dis-criminate against an employee on account of his colour, race, nationality or ethnic or national origins. Discrimination consists of treating an employee less favourably than he treats other employees.

21. *Scope*. The Act covers discrimination in advertising for an employee, engaging or dismissing him or in his conditions of employment (for example opportun-ities for training and promotion).

In ZARCZYNSKA V LEVY (1978) a white student got a part-time job in an East London public house. She was told not to serve blacks. She objected to this and was sacked. She complained to the CRE which supported her appeal. The EAT said she was treated less favourably than a person who went along with the colour bar and was therefore discriminated against on racial grounds.

22. *Exceptions*. It is lawful in certain circumstances to discriminate, they are:

   a. Where authenticity in drama or other entertainment requires a person of a particular racial group;

   b. Where the production of visual imagery in art or photography requires a person from a particular racial group for reasons of authenticity;

   c. Where the job involves working in a place where food and drink is served to the public and membership of a racial group is required for authenticity;

   d. Where the job holder provides persons of that racial group with personal services promoting their welfare, and where those services can be most effectively performed by a person of that racial group.

   In TOTTENHAM GREEN UNDER FIVES' CENTRE V MARSHALL (NO 2) (1991) it was held that the desirability of having a nursery worker who could read and talk in a dialect of children and parents was sufficient to justify a gen-uine occupational qualification exception.

   The RACE RELATIONS (AMENDMENT) ACT 2000 amended the 1976 Act (S.71) and placed a statutory duty on public authorities to promote racial equality and to prevent racial discrimination.

23. *Racial harassment*. S.3A RACE RELATIONS ACT 1976 makes unlawful harass-ment on grounds of race ethnic or national origins. This occurs when a person

engages in unwanted conduct which has the purpose or effect of violating that other person's dignity, or creating an intimidating, hostile, degrading, humiliating or offensive environment. Like sexual harassment, conduct will only be regarded as having this effect if having regard to all the circumstances, including in particular the perception of that other person, it should reasonably be considered as having that effect.

24. *Trade Unions, Employers' Organisations, etc.* Trade Unions, Employers' Organisations and others concerned with trades or professions must not discriminate in the following ways:

   a. Admission to membership.

   b. Grant of benefits to members.

   c. Expulsion.

25. *Liability for Employee's Discrimination.* An employer is vicariously liable for racial discrimination by an employee done in the course of his employment. This is regardless of whether or not the employer approved or had knowledge of it. In court proceedings the employer would have to show that he took all such steps as were reasonably practicable to prevent such discrimination.

26. *Burden of Proof.* The burden of proof is upon the applicant, however, as with sex discrimination a questionnaire may be served on the employer. Also, where a complainant proves facts from which the tribunal could conclude in the absence of an adequate explanation that the respondent has committed an act of discrimination against the complainant, the tribunal will uphold the complaint unless the respondent proves that he did not commit the act.

27. *Commission for Racial Equality.* This body has the same duties and powers as the Equal Opportunities Commission.

DISABILITY DISCRIMINATION ACT 1995

28.a. The purpose of the DISABILITY DISCRIMINATION ACT 1995 (DDA 1995) is to enable disabled people to live independently in society by enjoying equal opportunities at work, in access to goods and services and by way of educational facilities. The Act was amended by the DISABILITY DISCRIMINATION ACT 1995 (AMENDMENT) REGULATIONS 2003 and the DISABILITY DISCRIMINATION ACT 2005, which imposed a duty on public authorities to have regard to the need to eliminate disability discrimination in the carrying out of their functions. SECTION 53A provides for the Disability Rights Commission (DRC) to give practical guidance on prevention of disability discrimination and to promote equality of opportunity. The DRC have issued a Code of Practice to guide employers and others.

   b. Disability is defined as physical or mental impairment which has a substantial and long-term effect on a person's ability to carry out normal day-to-day activities.

The determination of disability involves a four stage test:

i. A finding of a physical or mental impairment;

ii. That impairment must have a substantial adverse effect;

iii. It must have a long-term adverse effect;

iv. The adverse effect must relate to the ability to carry out normal day to day activities.

Certain addictions and conditions are not to be treated as impairments for purposes of the Act. These include:

i. Addictions to alcohol, nicotine or any other substance, unless the addiction was originally the result of medically prescribed drugs or treatment;

ii. A tendency to set fires, to steal or to physically or sexually abuse other persons;

iii. Exhibitionism and voyeurism;

iv. Seasonal allergic asthma, although this may be taken into account where it aggravates other conditions;

v. Severe disfigurement which results from tattooing or piercing.

c. The *DDA 1995* makes a number of forms of discrimination unlawful. These are:

i. *Direct discrimination.* This occurs where a disabled person, on the grounds of their disability, is treated less favourably than another person not having that particular disability, and the relevant circumstances, including the abilities of the person being used as the comparator, are the same as, or not materially different from those of the disabled person.

ii. *Disability related discrimination.* This occurs where less favourable treatment is given to a disabled person for a reason related to his or her disability, and the employer cannot show that the treatment can be justified. Any justification must be material to the circumstances and substantial. The justification defence cannot be used in cases of direct discrimination or for failures to make reasonable adjustments (see below). The employer would need to show that material and substantial circumstances would have applied even if the adjustments had been made.

iii. *Victimisation.* Unlawful victimisation will occur where an employer treats an employee less favourably than another employee because they have brought proceedings against the employer under the *DDA 1995* or has given evidence in any such proceedings.

iv. *Failure to comply with the duty to make reasonable adjustments. SECTION 3A DDA 1995* places a duty on employers to make reasonable adjustments in relation to the disabled persons. The employer has to take all reasonable steps to ensure that no provision, criterion or practice employed on his behalf or any physical feature of premises occupied by him, leads to discrimination against a disabled person. The obligation applies to not only existing employees but also applicants for employment. There is no obligation placed upon the employer if the employer does not know, or could not have reasonably been expected to know, that the applicant or employee had a disability.

Provision criteria or practice includes arrangements for:

i   Determining who should be offered employment;

ii Any term, condition or arrangements on which employment, promotion, transfer, training or any other benefit offered.

In NOTTINGHAM COUNTY COUNCIL v MEIKLE (2004) A local authority school teacher experienced a deterioration in her sight to the point where she lost sight in one eye and some vision in the other. She made a number of requests to her employer for adjustments to be made in her workplace; these included: a different classroom location, an increase in time allowed for preparation and enlarged notices and written materials. There were delays in response from the employer and eventually she resigned. The Court of Appeal found that the continuing failure of her employer to make the requested adjustments, amounted to disability discrimination causing a fundamental breach of contract leading to a constructive dismissal (see Chapter 56).

29. *EC Directive 2000/43* will extend the EU's involvement in promoting equal treatment to race or ethnic origin requiring that there be equal treatment between persons irrespective of racial or ethnic origin. This will allow UK courts and tribunals to be subject to scrutiny by the Commission and ultimately the European Court of Justice. Previously, promoting equal treatment between different races and ethnic minorities had been left to Member States.

CHAPTER 56

Termination of Contracts of Employment

INTRODUCTION

1. Termination of a contract of employment can arise in several ways.

   a. By agreement between the employer and employee;

   b. By an act of either party of sufficient gravity to terminate the contract without notice;

   c. By operation of the law, for example, death, dissolution of a partnership, appointment of a receiver, compulsory winding-up of a company or frustration;

   d. By an act of either party terminating the contract with notice.

   In this chapter we will consider termination with notice, termination by operation of the law, wrongful dismissal and unfair dismissal.

TERMINATION WITH NOTICE

2. The usual method of terminating a contract is for the employer to give a period of notice, determined as follows:

   a. Where the contract is for a fixed term – on completion of that term.

   b. It may be ascertained by custom of the trade.

   c. The contract may state the period – subject to the minimum under *S.86 ERA 1996*.

NOTICE – S.86 EMPLOYMENT RIGHTS ACT 1996

3. The notice required to be given by an employer to terminate the contract of employment of a person who has been continuously employed for four weeks

or more shall be:

    a.   Not less than one week if his period of continuous employment is less than two years;

    b.   Not less than one week for each year of continuous employment if his period of employment is two years or more but less than twelve years; and

    c.   Not less than twelve weeks if his period of continuous employment is twelve years or more.

4. The employment must be of a continuous nature; periods of sickness are reckonable, but not periods of strikes.

5. The following categories of employee have no right to the statutory minimum period of notice:

    a.   Employees engaged in work wholly or mainly outside Great Britain. However, such periods, whilst not counting towards service, do not break its continuity.

    b.   Employees in employment under a contract made in contemplation of the performance of a specific task which is not expected to last for more than three months and which in fact lasts no longer than that time.

    c.   Certain seamen.

6. The employee, in the absence of any other term in the contract, is required to give one week's notice after he has been employed for four weeks or more. When an employee has contracted to give a longer period of notice and fails to do so, the employer cannot seek a court order to compel him to continue working. However, in rare cases, an employer may claim damages for any loss caused by the employee's premature departure.

7. Any employer may generally pay wages in lieu of notice unless the employee's reputation is involved. (CLAYTON & WALLER v OLIVER (1930).)

BY OPERATION OF THE LAW

8. a.   *Death*. Death of either the employer or the employee will end the contract.

   b.   *Dissolution of a partnership*. Such an event will end a contract of employment and may give rise to wrongful dismissal, but:

     In BRACE v CALDER (1895) P was employed by a partnership. There was a change in the membership of the partnership which automatically results in dissolution. The plaintiff was offered re-engagement on the same terms by the remaining partners but refused. It was held that he was entitled to nominal damages as he had failed to mitigate his loss.

   c.   *Sale of a business*. As contracts of employment (ie of personal service) cannot be assigned, the sale of a business constitutes the 'death' of one employer and the 'birth' of another. An employee cannot be transferred to the new employer against his will.

If he wishes to treat the contract as terminated he will only be awarded nominal damages for dismissal. It is because of this fundamental principle of English law that statutory rules have been devised to safeguard the continuity of employment and other statutory rights of employees in the event of the transfer of a business, or the transfer of an employee to an associated employer. (See Transfer of Undertakings (Protection of Employment) Regs 2006.)

d. *Liquidation of a company*. An order for compulsory winding up will operate to terminate the contracts of employment of all the company's employees (employees may have a right to claim damages for wrongful dismissal). However, a resolution for voluntary winding up does not automatically terminate employees' contracts of employment. The liquidator may carry on the business or he may close it down and thus terminate the employment contracts. In these circumstances an employee has no right to terminate his contract without notice and claim damages unless it is obvious that the company will be unable to fulfil its obligation under the contract.

e. *Bankruptcy*. Bankruptcy or insolvency of either party will terminate the contract if the solvency of the party concerned is an essential element of the relationship.

f. *Frustration*. A contract of employment will be frustrated when either party is incapable of performing his part of the contract due to circumstances beyond his control. Frustration is not dependent upon the conduct of the parties to the contract and therefore there is no dismissal. The employee cannot claim wrongful or unfair dismissal. Frustrating events are:

   i. *Illness*. Sickness may be a frustrating event if it renders future performance impossible or fundamentally different from that envisaged by the parties when they entered into the contract:

   In CONDOR v BARRON KNIGHTS (**1966**) P was the drummer in a pop group. Owing to illness he was forbidden by his doctor from performing more than a few nights per week. Since the nature of the work required him to be present seven nights a week the contract was held to be frustrated.

   Contrast STOREY v FULHAM STEEL WORKS (**1907**) where a manager on a five years contract was absent owing to illness for five months and was dismissed. It was held that in this case the period of illness did not frustrate the contract because of the nature of the contract. However, an employer would not be expected to keep a job open indefinitely.

   Further indication as to the criteria to be applied in deciding whether or not a contract of employment is frustrated has been given in more recent cases, as follows:

   In MARSHALL v HARLAND & WOLFF LTD (**1972**) the Court held that the industrial tribunal should take the following points into account when considering whether or not a contract of employment is frustrated by sickness or injury:

(a)   Terms of the contract (including sick pay),

(b)   Duration of the contract in the absence of sickness,

(c)   Nature of the employment,

(d)   Nature of the incapacity, its duration and the prospects of recovery.

(e)   Period served in employment up to the time of the sickness.

In addition, when considering whether it is reasonable for an employer to keep open an employee's position the following should be taken into account (EGG STORES (STAMFORD HILL) LTD V LEBOVICI (1977)):

(a)   The need for the work to be done and the requirement for a replacement,

(b)   Whether wages have continued to be paid,

(c)   The acts and statements of the employer, including dismissal or failure to dismiss the employee,

(d)   Whether it is reasonable for the employer to wait longer before replacing the employee.

ii.   *Imprisonment.* A contract of employment may be frustrated by a period of imprisonment, dependent on the length of service and the nature of employment.

In HARE V MURPHY BROS LTD (1974) P received a 12 months' prison sentence for an assault not connected with his employment. It was held that although the offence may not be a frustrating event (being self- induced) the prison sentence frustrated the contract, being an unforeseen event and delaying return to work for so long that the contract was brought to an end.

The contract is frustrated from the time of the sentence regardless that the employee appeals against the sentence and even if the appeal is successful.

WRONGFUL DISMISSAL

9. If an employee is unjustifiably dismissed he has a claim in damages at common law. A claim for wrongful dismissal may be carried on concurrently with a claim for unfair dismissal under the *EMPLOYMENT RIGHTS ACT 1996*.

10. *Contract of Indefinite Duration*. Where a contract is of an indefinite duration it may be terminated by notice on either side. Notice must be at least as long as that laid down in the *EPCA*. If the parties intend the period of notice to be greater than the statutory period and this is not expressly stated in the contract, the courts may decide on what is reasonable in the circumstances. This depends on, for example the status, skills and length of service of the employee. Some examples of court decisions in the past in this respect

are: twelve months for the chief engineer of an ocean liner (SAVAGE V BRITISH INDIA STEAM NAVIGATION CO LTD (1930)), six months for a journalist (BAUMAN V HULTON PRESS LTD (1952)), three months for a company director (JAMES V THOS H KENT & CO LTD (1951)) and one month for an advertising and canvassing agent (HISCOX V BATCHELOR (1867)).

11. If the employer dismisses an employee without notice the employee may take action for wrongful dismissal, unless the dismissal results from certain actions of the employee.

12. *A Fixed Term Contract.* A contract of employment will be regarded as one of a fixed term if it states the maximum duration of the contract, even if provision is made for notice to be given before this by either party. It is not a fixed contract if it has no definite end, that is based upon some uncertain future event. A contract for the completion of a particular task is not a fixed term contract.

13. *Action by the Employee.* The employer may terminate a contract of employment without notice if the employee acts in such a manner as to show repudiation of the contract. The circumstances can be summarised as being:

   a. *Misconduct.* Where the conduct of the employee interferes with the proper performance of his duties, even outside working house, eg drunkenness, immorality, insubordination.

   b. *Disobedience.* Disobedience of a lawful order may justify dismissal, but this may be mitigated if it is only a single act which is not a wilful flouting of authority.

   c. *Negligence.* Negligence, to warrant dismissal, must be a single act of a serious nature, or habitual minor acts.

Details of the above circumstances, with case law, are outlined in Chapter 51.

Since the introduction of statutory unfair dismissal employees must be given a clear indication of the type of conduct which the employer regards as warranting summary dismissal. Moreover the misconduct must be gross or grave, seen in the light of all the circumstances of the case.

In MARTIN V YORKSHIRE IMPERIAL METALS LTD (1978) dismissal was for tying down one of two levers (designed as a safety device to occupy both hands of an operative) which activated a machine. The operative admitted to being aware that interference with the safety device would lead to dismissal without warning. It was held that the dismissal was fair.

Contrast LADBROKE RACING LTD V ARNOTT (1979) where the Employment Appeal Tribunal (EAT) held that warning of liability to summary dismissal could not be justification for summary dismissal for a minor offence.

CONSTRUCTIVE DISMISSAL

14. A contract of employment may be terminated by an employer's repudiatory conduct. For there to be a repudiation by the employer he must by his act

or omission be guilty of either a fundamental breach of the contract or a breach of a fundamental term of the contract. The term may be express or implied:

In MARRIOTT V OXFORD AND DISTRICT CO-OPERATIVE SOCIETY LTD (**1970**) P (an electrical supervisor) was informed that because of a reduction in the size of his department his post had been made redundant and his salary and status would be reduced. P protested but continued to work under the new conditions for a few weeks until he found alternative employment. It was held that his contract had been terminated unilaterally by his employer. The fact that he had stayed on for a few weeks did not signify his agreement to the change.

In COLEMAN V BALDWIN (**1977**) the buyer in a green-grocery business had the bulk and the most interesting part of his work removed from him, which left only repetitive and boring duties. This occurred without any agreement. It was held that there was a fundamental breach of contract entitling the employee to leave. It was unfair because no attempt had been made to negotiate with him.

15. For the purposes of redundancy and unfair dismissal the ERA 1996 (*S.95*) gives statutory force to the doctrine of constructive dismissal by declaring that an employee shall be treated as dismissed by his employer if the employee terminates the contract, with or without notice, in circumstances such that he is entitled to terminate it without notice by reason of the employer's conduct. Examples of the courts interpretation are given below:

In WESTERN EXCAVATING (EEC) LTD V SHARP (**1978**) an employee left his employment because his employer would not give him an advance of pay. It was held that this was not a fundamental breach of contract. The employee could not leave on some 'equitable test' based on the employer's 'unreasonable conduct'.

However, in BRITISH AIRCRAFT CORPORATION LTD V AUSTIN (**1978**) it was suggested that a term might be implied in a contract of employment that employers shall act in accordance with good industrial relations practice.

In WIGAN BOROUGH COUNCIL V DAVIES (**1979**) D, an employee at an old people's home was 'sent to Coventry' by fellow employees following her impropriety. It was not possible to move her to another job. D left and claimed constructive dismissal. It was held that the employer had been in breach of the contractual obligation to give her support to enable her to carry out her duties free from harassment.

In ISLE OF WIGHT TOURIST BOARD V COOMBES (**1976**) a director made a remark to his secretary about another employee that she was an intolerable bitch on a Monday morning. The employee left and claimed constructive dismissal. It was held that there was a fundamental alteration to the trust and respect the relationship required.

REMEDIES FOR WRONGFUL DISMISSAL

16. *Damages.* To claim damages for wrongful dismissal the employee must prove that:

   a. He was engaged on a fixed term – and that he was dismissed before the expiry of the term.

   b. The contract stipulates a period of notice – and that the dismissal was without such notice.

   c. The notice given was less than that required by the ERA 1996.

   d. Dismissal was without just cause.

17. *Assessment of Damages*

   a. Damages should cover such loss as may be fairly considered to arise naturally from the breach and also for any loss which was reasonably foreseeable as likely to arise from the breach. Generally the amount awarded should compensate for the monetary loss for the period of notice entitlement.

   b. The amount should cover the following:

      i. Wages,

      ii. Gratuities,

      iii. Commission,

      iv. Publicity and reputation (actors, etc),

      v. Difficulty in obtaining future employment in cases where narrow specialisation has occurred.

Damages are not recoverable for the manner in which the dismissal took place (ADDIS v GRAMOPHONE CO (1909)), nor for hurt feelings, in BRITISH GUIANA CREDIT CORPN v DA SILVA (1965) the employee unsuccessfully claimed additional damages in respect of 'humiliation, embarrassment and loss of reputation'.

18. *Deductions from Damages.* A dismissed employee must mitigate his loss, (BRACE v CALDER (1895)). In assessment of damages the court would take the following into account:

   a. Income tax liability,

   b. Unemployment benefit received by the employee,

   c. National insurance contributions payable,

   d. Unfair dismissal compensation received,

   e. Redundancy payment received.

19. *Other Remedies.* Other remedies, apart from damages are:

   a. *Quantum meruit.* This is an equitable remedy compelling the defendant to pay for performance done and already accepted.

b. *Injunction.* A court will not normally grant an injunction which has the effect of requiring specific performance of a contract for personal services owing to the voluntary nature of contracts of employment and the difficulty of the supervision of the enforcement of this remedy.

In PAGE ONE RECORDS v BRITTON (1968) an injunction was sought against a pop group (the 'Troggs') which would require the group to honour a promise to employ a certain person as manager. The injunction was refused as it was held that a manager had duties of a 'personal and fiduciary' nature and in this particular case the pop group had lost confidence in the person.

However, sometimes an injunction will be granted restraining an employee from working for a rival employer, eg WARNER BROTHERS v NELSON (1937). (See Chapter 19.11.)

An injunction may be granted in exceptional cases:

In HILL v C.A. PARSONS LTD (1972) the court granted the employee an injunction restraining his employer from terminating his employment. The employer had been influenced by union pressure to dismiss the employee, and the court considered it a 'highly exceptional case'.

UNFAIR DISMISSAL

20. The law relating to unfair dismissal is contained in the *S.94,* EMPLOYMENT RIGHTS ACT *1996 (ERA).* The rights apply to those working on a contract of service.

21. *Excluded Categories.* The following categories of employees are excluded from the unfair dismissal provisions:

a. Those with less than one year's continuous service.

b. Those who have reached the recognised retirement age of the undertaking, or the statutory retirement age, or, in the event of the absence of a normal retirement age, the age of 65 (this applies to both men and women).

Note: categories a. and b. will not be excluded from claiming compensation if the dismissal was as a result of the exercise of their individual rights (joining or refusing to join a trade union).

c. Ordinarily working outside Great Britain;

d. On fixed term contracts of two years or more which contain a clause waiving these rights;

e. Employees covered by an approved scheme (collective agreement) relating to compensation for unfair dismissal.

22. *The Meaning of 'Dismissal'.* 'Dismissal' is deemed to have occurred in the following situations: *(S.95)*

a. The employee's contract of employment is terminated, with or without notice (ie voluntary resignation is not 'dismissal');

b. The employee is employed under a fixed term contract which is not renewed;

c. The employer is in breach of contract, in circumstances such that the employee is entitled to regard the contract as repudiated, ie 'constructive dismissal'.

d. Failure to permit a female employee to return to work after confinement.

Note: The employee must prove 'dismissal'.

23. *Compensation for Unfair Dismissal*. The right not to be 'unfairly' dismissed is applicable regardless of whether or not the employer has given the statutory amount of notice. The concept of unfair dismissal goes some way towards acknowledging the property right an employee has in his job.

The onus is on the employer to prove that the dismissal was fair. He must satisfy the tribunal that there was a valid reason for the dismissal, ie any one of the following reasons:

a. *Lack of capability or qualifications*. Capability is assessed by reference to skill, aptitude, health or any other physical or mental quality. Qualification refers to any degree, diploma or other academic, technical or professional qualification relevant to the position which the employee held.

In WINTERHALTER GASTRONOM v WEBB (1973) a sales director was held to have been fairly dismissed where his employers established that he had not achieved the standard of sales which the company was entitled to expect from its sales director, notwithstanding the difficulties under which he was working.

Contrast EARL v SLATER & WHEELER (AIRLYNE) LTD (1972) where a planning and estimating engineer was dismissed, after several warnings, for inadequate performance. He was dismissed after a spell of absence when it was discovered that contracts were behind time. On his return to work he was handed a letter dismissing him summarily. The court found the dismissal to be unfair as the employee was not given an opportunity to explain the deficiencies in his work.

Generally an employee should be given an opportunity to state his case, but failure to do so does not necessarily render dismissal unfair:

In TAYLOR v ALIDAIR LTD (1978) an airline pilot made one single but serious mistake on landing his aircraft. His dismissal was held to be fair even though he had been given no opportunity to state his case prior to dismissal.

b. *The conduct of the employee*. Examples of misconduct which have been held to justify dismissal include: dishonesty (even suspected dishonesty), breach of safety regulations, conviction for a criminal offence, sexual aberrations, fighting with fellow-employees, disclosing information to a competing firm and rudeness to customers.

In NEEFJES v CRYSTAL PRODUCTS CO LTD (1972) the employee assaulted a fellow-employee and was dismissed. He had been warned in writing several months earlier that he would be dismissed in the event of further complaints as to his conduct. It was held that he was fairly dismissed. For crimes committed outside of employment the employer would have to show some damage to the organisation. In POST OFFICE V LIDDIARD (2001), an employee was involved in football violence overseas, he was dismissed. A tribunal found the dismissal unfair, there was no evidence of any adverse effect on the business of the employer.

An employee may refuse to obey an unreasonable order:

In MORRISH V HENLYS (FOLKESTONE) LTD (1973) a stores driver objected when the manager altered the record of the amount of diesel oil drawn by the employee. The manager explained that alteration of the record was done in order to cover any discrepancies in the account. He was dismissed when he continued to object. It was held that the dismissal was unfair, as his objection to the falsification of the account was not unreasonable.

Conduct outside working hours may also amount to a valid reason for dismissal if it affects his employer's business adversely:

In SINGH V LONDON COUNTY BUS SERVICES LTD (1976) the employee drove a one-man-operated bus. He was convicted of offences of dishonesty committed outside his employment. It was held that misconduct does not have to occur in the course of employment, or at the employee's place of work, or even connected with work to justify dismissal, so long as it somehow affects the employee when he is doing his work or is thought likely to do so.

In CREFFIELD V BBC (1975) a film cameraman was dismissed following his conviction of indecently assaulting a thirteen-year-old girl. His dismissal was held to be fair as the employer could not be selective in allocation of assignments to the employee, and might justifiably fear a recurrence of the employee's behaviour.

c. *If the employee is redundant.* Provided there is no unfair discrimination and the proper procedures are carried out, an employee who is dismissed because of redundancy will not succeed in a claim for unfair dismissal.

In HEATHCOTE V NORTH WESTERN ELECTRICITY BOARD (1974) the employee held the position of driver's mate, classed as a labourer. He was dismissed for redundancy because the board decided there was no longer any need for drivers' mates. Selection was made on the basis of last in, first out. However, selection was confined to the transport section and not the whole of the business. It was held that this was not the correct approach. As the employee was in a class of lesser-skilled worker selection should have been made from the whole concern.

d. *If the employee could not continue to work in that position without contravening a statutory restriction.*

In FEARN V TAYFIELD MOTOR CO LTD (1975) the employee was engaged as a vehicle supervisor, part of his duties including the requirement to drive vehicles. He was convicted of careless driving and failing to stop after an accident and was disqualified from driving for twelve months. His dismissal was held to be fair as he could no longer legally do the job he was employed to do.

e. *Some other substantial reason.* In considering the case of RS COMPONENTS LTD V IRWIN (1973) it was said

'There are not only legal but also practical objections to a narrow construction of "*some other reason*". Parliament may well have intended to set out the common reasons for a dismissal but can hardly have hoped to produce an exhaustive catalogue of all the circumstances in which a company would be justified in terminating the services of an employee'.

Some examples are:

i. Where personality conflicts gave rise to hostility and tension between employees began to have a detrimental effect on the employer's business TREGANOWAN v ROBERT KNEE & CO LTD (**1975**);

ii. Failure to accede to a request by the employer to work at times other than those provided in the contract KNIGHTON v HENRY RHODES LTD (**1974**);

iii. Where an employee refuses to sign an undertaking that on leaving the employment he would not compete with the employer GLENDINNING v PILKINGTON BROS LTD (**1973**);

iv. Where an employee moves to an unreasonable distance from his work, despite a company rule that employees must live within reasonable travelling distance FARR v HOVERINGHAM GRAVEL LTD (**1972**).

v. When an employee is a danger to other workers MORTIBOY v ROLLS ROYCE (**1983**).

Even if the employer can show that an employee was dismissed for any of the above reasons, or some other substantial reason he must have acted 'reasonably' in dismissing the employee.

The decision is left to the tribunal which would take into account all circumstances including the size and administrative resources of the undertaking, and decide the question on the grounds of equity and the substantial merits of the case. The tribunal's assessment of whether a particular employer has acted reasonably or not will require that he be compared with what a similar employer might reasonably have done in a similar situation. This was laid down in ICELAND FROZEN FOODS v JONES (**1983**) where the court held that if a tribunal found that a similar employer might reasonably dismiss, then the dismissal is fair, it is not for the tribunal to decide alone. This has been referred to as the 'range of reasonable employer response' test. In FOLEY v POST OFFICE AND HSBC BANK v MADDEN (**2000**), The Court of Appeal reaffirmed the approach to the assessment of reasonableness. Tribunals were not to approach the matter of reasonableness or unreasonableness of a dismissal by reference to their own judgement of what would have been done if they had been the employer. A tribunal should conclude that a dismissal is fair if it is within the range of reasonable responses an employer might make, even though the tribunal would not have regarded the response of an employer as reasonable.

24. *Codes of Practice.* In determining whether or not an employer has acted reasonably or not the tribunal may examine the procedures followed by the employer. Guidance as to the fairness of a procedure can be obtained from the ACAS Code of Practice on Disciplinary and Grievance Procedures. The current version is dated 2004. The Code is a guide with the purpose of promoting good industrial relations. If an employer fails to observe any provision of the codes he

will not be thereby liable to any proceedings, but the employment tribunal can take the codes into account in any proceedings brought against the employer.

25. *Procedural fairness* requires the employer to:

   a. A set of rules attempting to set out the circumstances that may give rise to disciplinary procedures.

   b. Employees must be made aware of the likely consequences of breaking the rules. They should in particular clearly identify those acts which can result in dismissal without notice.

   c. Disciplinary procedures should not be seen as primarily a means of imposing sanctions; they should help and encourage an improvement in performance.

   d. Due regard should be paid to the rules of natural justice, that is;

   > advanced warning to the employee of the hearing and allegations alleged with evidence;

   > an opportunity to challenge the allegations and evidence before a decision is reached;

   > a right of appeal against the decision;

   > provision for a brief period of suspension with full pay, where relationships have broken down or there is a risk to property, should be available;

   > conditions applying for oral or written warnings should be clearly stated.

The EMPLOYMENT RELATIONS ACT 1999 introduced the right for employees to be accompanied by a single person if the employee requests it.

The EMPLOYMENT ACT 2002 introduced new statutory dismissal and disciplinary procedure and a statutory grievance procedure. *S.98A ERA 1996*, provides that an employee who is dismissed without the relevant statutory procedure being completed will be regarded as unfairly dismissed. This is provided that the non-completion is wholly or mainly attributed to the employer's failure to comply with its requirements. These statutory procedures set a minimum standard. For both the dismissal and disciplinary procedure and the grievance procedure, there is a three step process:

1. *The statement.* The employer is required to set out in writing the employee's alleged conduct or other circumstances which have led to the employer contemplating dismissal or disciplinary action. A copy of the statement must be sent to the employee. For a grievance procedure, it is for the employee to set out a statement of grievance for the employer.

2. *The meeting.* In a disciplinary or dismissal procedure, there is an obligation for a meeting to take place before any action, short of suspension, is taken. The employee must take all reasonable steps to attend the meeting, after which the employer must inform the employee of the decision. The employee must be informed at this point of the right to appeal if unhappy with the decision. Similar requirements exist for a grievance procedure.

3. *The appeal.* If the employee wishes to appeal then he or she must inform the employer, after which the employee is invited to attend a further meeting. Again, the employee must take all reasonable steps to attend the meeting and after which be informed of the final decision.

There are penalties for not using the statutory procedures. If the failure to complete is the fault of the employer, then the employment tribunal may increase the award by between 10% and 50%. The reverse will apply where the fault is that of the employee.

25. *Presumption of Unfair Dismissal.* Dismissal is presumed to be unfair in the following circumstances:

   a. The employee was selected for redundancy whilst other employees in a similar position were retained and either:

      i. Selection was in contravention of an agreed or customary arrangement relating to redundancy (eg last in, first out) or

      ii. Reason for the selective dismissal was in connection with the trade union membership or activities of the employee;

   b. *Dismissal on the ground of pregnancy and childbirth.* An employee shall be treated as unfairly dismissed if the reason, or principal reason is:

      i. Pregnancy or a reason connected with pregnancy

      ii. Maternity leave period is ended by dismissal and the reason is that she has given birth to a child

      iii. She took or availed herself of the benefits of maternity leave

      iv. Before the end of maternity leave she notified her employer that by reason of disease or bodily or mental disablement she would be incapable of work after the end of her leave, or her contract was terminated within four weeks of the end of her leave when she continued to be incapable of work and the reason for dismissal was that she had given birth to a child.

      v. Her maternity leave is ended by dismissal on account of redundancy and the employer has not complied with the statutory requirements (offer of alternative employment).

   c. If the employee was selected for dismissal on grounds of race or sex.

   d. *TRANSFER OF UNDERTAKING (PROTECTION OF EMPLOYMENT) REGULATIONS 2006.* When an undertaking is transferred from one person to another every contract of employment is automatically transferred. A relevant transfer will be found where, pre-transfer, there is an undertaking consisting of an organised group of employees which has as its principal purpose the carrying out of the activities concerned on behalf of the transferor, and the transferee carries out the same activities. However, an organised grouping of employees will include a single employee. There has to exist an *economic entity* by which is meant an organised grouping of resources (including employees) which has the objective of pursuing an economic activity, whether or not that activity was central or ancillary to the employer. The Regulations will not apply where there exists a single specific event or task of short term duration. Where the Regulations apply, if either the transferor or transferee dismisses any employee for a reason connected with the transfer the dismissal is unfair. Dismissal, however, will not be unfair if it is caused by economic, technical or organisational reasons incidental to the transfer and these reasons entail changes in the workforce of either the transferor or transferee. On the other hand an employee need not accept a transfer if there is a substantial change in his working conditions or the change of employer leads to a significant change, to the detriment of the employee.

In SHIPP v D.J. CATERING LTD (1982) dismissal in order to reduce manning levels under new management was held by an industrial tribunal to be fair – the dismissal being economic grounds for changes in the workforce.

e. *Dismissal for claiming a statutory right*. It will be an automatic unfair dismissal where an employee is dismissed for bringing proceedings against the employer to enforce a statutory right.

f. *Cases of health and safety*. Dismissals will be automatically unfair where the reason for dismissal was an employee carrying out health and safety duties.

g. *Working time*. Dismissal will be automatically unfair where the reason for the dismissal is an employee insisting on his rights under the WORKING TIME REGULATIONS 1998.

h. Dismissal for a spent conviction under the REHABILITATION OF OFFENDERS ACT 1974.

26. **Dismissal in Other Circumstances**. The following are the rules of unfair dismissal in other situations:

a. Unfair dismissal in connection with trade union membership or activities.

The dismissal of an employee shall be regarded as unfair if the reason for dismissal is that the employee:

   i. Was or proposed to become a member of an independent trade union, or

   ii. Had taken part or proposed to take part in the activities of an independent trade union, or

   iii. Was not a member of any trade union or had refused or proposed to refuse to become or remain a member.

b. *Dismissal during a strike*. If an employee is dismissed for taking part in a strike the tribunal has no jurisdiction to decide whether the dismissal was fair or unfair unless it was a case of selective dismissal, ie

   i. Others taking the same action were not dismissed, or

   ii. Any of the strikers has, within three months, been offered re-engagement, but the complainant has not been offered re-engagement, and the reason is the complainant's membership or non-membership of a trade union or union activities.

Note: There may be selective dismissal of employees taking part in an unofficial strike or other unofficial action.

c. *Dismissal during a lock-out.* Dismissal following a lock-out is fair if the employee is offered re-engagement from the date of resumption of work, and refuses. Dismissal is unfair if re-engagement is not offered.

d. *Industrial pressure.* If an employer dismisses an employee because of threats of strike action by other employees no account shall be taken of this factor in deciding whether the dismissal was fair or unfair.

e. *Dismissal on grounds of health and safety.* (See Chapter 60, paragraph 42–44.)

27. ***Written Statement of Reasons for Dismissal.*** Employees with one year's service have a right to a written statement of the reasons for their dismissal, subject to the following conditions: (*S.92*)

a. The entitlement to a statement does not depend on whether or not the dismissal is fair;

b. It must be supplied by the employer within 14 days of the request;

c. Failure to provide a statement within 14 days, or the provision of one with 'inadequate or untrue' reasons gives the right of a complaint to an industrial tribunal within three months of dismissal;

d. The statement has the protection of 'qualified privilege', ie the employer will not be liable for defamatory statements unless malice can be proved.

REMEDIES FOR UNFAIR DISMISSAL

28. ***Reinstatement and Re-engagement.*** An unfairly dismissed employee has the right to state whether he wishes to be reinstated or re-engaged. In reinstatement the employee is treated in all respects as if he had not been dismissed. Any pay, pension and seniority must be restored to him and he must be given any pay arrears and any other lost benefits. In re-engagement the employee may be employed in a different job provided it is suitable. The terms and conditions may differ from the previous ones. Re-engagement may be by a new employer, eg a successor to the former employer. Damages may be awarded in respect of loss of benefits arising between the dismissal and re-engagement (*S.117, 118*).

29. The tribunal may make a recommendation to reinstatement taking into account the extent to which the employee contributed to his own dismissal and the practicability of reinstatement (eg his fellow-employees' attitude). Alternatively the tribunal can recommend re-engagement.

30. If an employer fails to comply with a recommendation for reinstatement or re-engagement he may be liable to pay 'punitive' compensation in addition to compensation based on actual loss suffered by the employee.

31. ***Compensation.*** Any compensation which may be awarded is based on the following factors:

a. The immediate loss of wages, if any;

b. Compensation for future loss of wages;

c. The loss of statutory protection from unfair dismissal and redundancy as the employee will need to complete a further two years with another employer to qualify again for such protection.

32. Compensation may be reduced if there is contributory fault on the part of the employee:

In ROBERTSON V SECURICOR TRANSPORT LTD (**1972**) an employee was dismissed for carelessness in signing a receipt for a missing container. It was held that he was unfairly dismissed as his employer had not acted reasonably by treating this one act of negligence as sufficient to justify dismissal. However, the employee's compensation was reduced by 50% because of his contributory fault.

33. *Reduction in Basic Award*. There are two circumstances under which a tribunal could reduce the basic award of compensation:

a. Where the employee has unreasonably refused an offer of reinstatement which would have had the effect if accepted of reinstating him in all respects as if he had not been dismissed;

b. Where the tribunal considers that the employee's conduct before the dismissal was such that it would be just and equitable to reduce the basic award. The conduct referred to was not the reason for the dismissal, but came to light afterwards.

In DEVIS & SONS LTD V ATKINS (**1977**) the employee was dismissed for alleged incompetence, receiving six weeks notice and £6,000 compensation. Afterwards, it came to light that he had been accepting secret commissions. His employers refused to pay the compensation and treated him as summarily dismissed. It was held that this was unfair dismissal as only information known at the time of dismissal is relevant to determine whether it is fair.

34. *Amount of Compensation*

a. *The basic award*. This is calculated on a formula set out in the Act (*S.119*). It is based upon an employee's length of service within certain age categories. For each year worked under 22 years of age the employee is awarded half a week's pay. From 22 to 41 years of age, one week's pay, and above 41 years of age, one and a half week's pay. It is calculated on a normal week's pay excluding overtime, unless there is a contractual term entitling the employee to work overtime. There are limitations on the overall amount claimable; firstly, only a maximum of 20 years service can be claimed; secondly, the amount of weekly pay is a maximum of £290. When a complainant reaches the age of 64 the basic award is reduced by one twelfth for each month over 64.

The basic award can be reduced where:

i. Re-engagement or reinstatement is offered and unreasonably refused by the claimant;

ii. The conduct of the employee before the dismissal makes it reasonable to do so;

    iii. Where it is found that the true reason for the dismissal was redundancy, the redundancy entitlement will be reduced from the basic award.

  b. *Compensatory award.* This is an amount left to a tribunal to determine based upon what it considers to be just and fair, the current maximum under this head is £58,400. (In cases of dismissal founded upon discrimination, there is no upper limit.) Factors covered here will include:

    i. Immediate and future loss of earnings;

    ii. Expenses and loss of statutory rights;

    iii. Loss of pension rights;

    iv. Failure of the employer to go through a laid down appeal procedure.

The employee is required to mitigate his loss and the amount awarded will be reduced where he fails to do so.

  c. *Additional award.* Where an employer unreasonably refuses to re-engage or reinstate an employee an additional award may be made; this will be between 13 and 26 weeks' pay, but if dismissal is on grounds of sex or race this will increase to 26 and 52 weeks' pay. (The week's pay being subject to the £290 maximum.)

35. ***Complaints to Employment Tribunals.*** An employee who considers that he has been unfairly dismissed may complain to an employment tribunal from the time he receives notice. An appeal lies from an industrial tribunal on a point of law to the Employment Appeal Tribunal. Appeals lie from the EAT to the Court of Appeal, and from there to the House of Lords.

36. ***Interim Relief for Unfair Dismissal.*** An employee may apply to a tribunal for interim relief. He must apply within a period of seven days following termination of employment. The tribunal must notify the employer of the application, and time of the hearing within seven days. The tribunal will announce its findings and ask the employer if he will reinstate or re-engage the employee and treat him as if he had not been dismissed. If the employer will not comply with the tribunal's request or the employee reasonably refuses to accept re-engagement on the employer's terms, the tribunal will make an order for continuance of the employee's contract of service. This is for the purposes of pay and other benefits derived from employment and his period of continuous employment. This order will also specify the amount to be paid by the employer between the date of dismissal and final determination of the complaint. The sums paid will be taken into account in discharging the employer's liability for breach of contract for that period.

CHAPTER 57

Redundancy

INTRODUCTION

1. In certain circumstances an employee may receive compensation for the loss of his job. The amount of compensation is related to the age, length of service and average weekly earnings of the redundant employee. The purpose of the redundancy payments scheme is to compensate for loss of security and to encourage employees to accept redundancy without damaging industrial relations. A Redundancy Fund is established, financed by contributions collected with the employers' National Insurance payments. The fund is used to make redundancy payments in the event of an employer being unable to pay due to insolvency. Disputes about entitlement to payment etc are settled by employment tribunals. The law relating to redundancy payments is contained in the *EMPLOYMENT RIGHTS ACT 1996 S.135*. References in this chapter are to the ERA unless otherwise stated.

CONDITIONS FOR PAYMENT

2. For a person to be entitled to redundancy payment he must have been:

   a. An employee;

   b. Continuously employed for the requisite period;

   c. Dismissed; and

   d. Dismissed by reason of redundancy.

3. *'Employee'* is defined as 'an individual who has entered into or works under (or, where the employment has ceased, worked under) a contract of employment'. In cases where the employer disputes that the applicant was an employee, it is for the applicant to prove that he was in fact an employee.

4. *Continuous Employment for the Requisite Period.* The applicant must have been continuously employed for a period of two years ending with the relevant date. The following events do not break continuity:

   a. *Change in job with the same employer.*

   b. *Change in ownership of the business.* When a business that is wholly or partly carried on in the UK is transferred from one person to another the

TRANSFER OF UNDERTAKINGS (PROTECTION OF EMPLOYMENT) REGULATIONS 1981 impose the following obligation on the transferor and transferee:

    i.   Every contract of employment is automatically transferred to the transferee employer. Thus the employee cannot claim that he has been dismissed or made redundant.

    ii. Dismissal by reason of the transfer of the business will be unfair unless it is caused by economic, technical or organisational reasons (ETO) incidental to the transfer. A true redundancy situation might well establish grounds for an ETO justification. (See Chapter 56, 25. d.)

c.   *Engagement by an associated employer.* Where an employee is taken into the employment of an associated company his period of employment with the first company counts as a period of employment with the associated company. Two companies are associated if one has control (directly or indirectly) of the other or if both are controlled (directly or indirectly) by a third person.

In ZARB v BRITISH & BRAZILIAN PRODUCE CO LTD (1978) P was a canteen worker employed by Total Staff (Recruitment) Ltd. D took over the running of the canteen and P became employed by them. It was held that the two companies were associated employers. The same two people controlled more than 50% of shares in each company. The case brought out the fact that a group of persons who act together can share control.

d.   *Absence.* Periods of absence from work for reasons of sickness, injury, absence due to pregnancy or confinement of less than 26 weeks, or temporary cessation of work count as periods of employment. Additionally, where an employee exercises her right to return to work after an absence due to pregnancy or confinement, the whole period of absence will count as continuous employment notwithstanding that it is longer than 26 weeks.

e.   *Strikes.* The continuity of employment is not destroyed by participation in a strike. However, any week during any part of which the employee is on strike is not counted in the computation of the number of weeks of employment.

f.   *Lock-outs.* A period in which an employee is locked out by his employer does not break continuity of employment.

g.   *Working temporarily abroad.* An employee may work abroad temporarily for up to 26 weeks without breaking his contract of employment, but the time abroad does not count towards computation of the length of continuous service.

h.   *Dismissal followed by re-instatement or re-engagement.* Where an employer reinstates or re-engages an employee after he has been dismissed the continuity of employment is maintained if the action was taken as a result of an application to an industrial tribunal by the employee or as a result of an agreement brought about by a conciliation officer.

The 'relevant date' is generally the date on which the employee actually ceased to work. However, where less than the statutory minimum period of notice is given, the relevant date is calculated as the date on which the minimum period of notice would have expired had it been given. If an employee is given pay in lieu of notice the relevant date is the day of dismissal.

In SLATER v JOHN SWAIN & SON LTD (**1981**) P was made redundant at the age of 64 years and 8 months with 12 weeks' pay in lieu of notice. His redundancy payment was reduced by 11/12 to take into account the period between his 64th birthday and the end of the last week for which he was paid. He claimed that only 8/12 were deductible. It was held that the date of actual termination was the 'relevant date' for this purpose and not the date at which any notice given would have expired. P's claim was upheld.

But an employer cannot prevent an employee from having the necessary qualifying period by dismissing him without notice, or with pay in lieu of notice, where to have given him proper notice would have given him the qualifying length of employment. Additionally, an employee exercising her right to return to work after a pregnancy will be deemed to have been continuously employed up to her notified date of return if she is not permitted to return to work by the employer.

Temporary cessation of work is a matter of fact in each case:

In BENTLEY ENGINEERING CO LTD v CROWN (**1976**) C was employed by X Co from 1948 to 1963 when he became redundant. He obtained employment elsewhere. In 1965 he became employed by Bentley Eng Co (an associated company of X Co) C was subsequently made redundant again and claimed payment on the basis of continuous employment from 1948. It was held that the period 1963 to 1965 should be regarded as temporary cessation of work. Regard was especially taken of the length of service before and after the cessation.

Contrast WISHART v NATIONAL COAL BOARD (**1974**) where P was employed by D. He left and subsequently returned. During his absence he remained a member of D's pension scheme (for D employees only). It was held that P was regarded as in D's employment by custom or arrangement for the purposes of the pension scheme. He was therefore to be regarded as in continuous employment for redundancy payments.

5. *The Meaning of Dismissal.* By *S.136* an employee will be taken to be dismissed by his employer if:

   a. The contract under which he is employed by the employer is terminated by the employer, whether it is terminated by notice or not; or

   b. Where under that contract he is employed for a fixed term which expires without being renewed under the same contract; or

   c. The employee terminates the contract with or without notice where his employer's conduct is such as to justify the employee leaving without notice (constructive dismissal).

There is no dismissal, and therefore no redundancy payment where an employee leaves voluntarily or where the contract is frustrated:

In MORTON SUNDOUR FABRICS LTD v SHAW (**1966**) S was employed in the company's velvet department. He was notified that his job in that department was likely to end in some months time. S found a job elsewhere and left MSF Ltd. It was held that S was not entitled to a redundancy payment as he had left voluntarily without having had notice from his employer.

6. *Redundancy Must be the Reason for Dismissal*. Redundancy is defined by S.139 as the dismissal of an employee wholly or mainly on account of:

   a. The fact that his employer has ceased, or intends to cease, to carry on the business for the purposes of which the employee was employed by him, or he ceased, or intends to cease, to carry on that business in the place where the employee was so employed; or

   b. The fact that the requirements of that business for employees to carry out work of a particular kind in the place where he was so employed, have ceased or diminished or are expected to cease or diminish.

7. The following cases illustrate how the statutory definition of 'redundancy' has been interpreted:

In EUROPEAN CHEFS v CURRELL LTD (**1971**) a pastry cook was dismissed because the requirement for his speciality (eclairs and meringues) had ceased and there became a requirement to produce Continental pastries, for which another person was taken into employment. It was held that the pastry cook was entitled to redundancy payment as *the need for a cook of his type had ceased.*

In VAUX & ASSOCIATED BREWERIES v WARD (**1969**) a quiet public house was converted into a discotheque. The landlord dismissed the 57-year-old barmaid as he required a younger person (a 'Bunny Girl') to attract customers. It was held that there was no entitlement to redundancy payment as there had been no change in the nature of the particular work being done.

In LESNEY PRODUCTS & CO LTD v NOLAN (**1977**) a reorganisation entailed elimination of the night shift. The night shift employees received redundancy payments. A double day shift system was introduced and all day shift workers were offered employment on it. Those who refused the offer were dismissed. It was held that they were not entitled to redundancy payments as *there had been no diminution in requirement for a type of worker, just a reorganisation in the interests of efficiency.*

In UK ATOMIC ENERGY AUTHORITY v CLAYDON (**1974**) the employee was obliged by his contract to move anywhere in the UK as required by his employer. *The need for fewer employees at one plant did not constitute a diminution at his place of employment* as his place of employment was 'anywhere in the UK'.

In NORTH RIDING GARAGES v BUTTERWICK (**1967**) B had been employed at a garage for 30 years as a workshop manager, which mainly involved a mechanic's work. When the garage came under new ownership B was required to deal with administrative as well as technical matters. B found that he could not adapt to the new situation, and was dismissed. He claimed redundancy payment but failed as it was held that there had been no diminution in requirement for a workshop manager.

In HINDLE v PERCIVAL BOATS LTD (1969) P was dismissed on the ground that his work was too thorough to be economical. He was a highly skilled carpenter who had spent his working life building boats and his employer's business had moved from wooden hulled to fibreglass boats. The company still employed woodworkers to install wooden furniture. It was held that dismissal was not due to redundancy as the employers still required woodworkers.

In O'HARE v ROTOPRINT LTD (1980) in anticipation of increased sales the employers took on additional personnel. The increased work failed to materialise and the staff was reduced back to its original level. It was held that *there was no cessation or diminution of work*, and a redundancy payment was inadmissible.

In CHAPMAN v GOONVEAN AND ROSTOWRACK CHINA CLAY CO LTD (1973) the company provided free transport for employees living 30 miles from the works. The transport was discontinued when demand fell so as to make it uneconomical. Employees who could not then get to work gave notice. It was held that there was no redundancy as the *requirement for employees had not diminished*.

In BROMBY & HOARE LTD v EVANS (1972) the company's business had been increasing but found it more economical to use self-employed workers rather than its own men. As a consequence two workers were dismissed. It was held that they were entitled to redundancy payments as the company's need for employees had diminished.

In EXEC OF EVEREST v COX (1980) a canteen manageress of a firm with a concession at a police station was offered suitable employment elsewhere when the concession came to an end. She refused because the company taking over the work led her to believe she would be employed by them, but in the event she was not. It was held that she was entitled to redundancy payment as her conduct was not unreasonable at the time she took the decision.

In J STOTT & SON LTD v STOKES (1971) the employee, an alleged troublemaker was sacked for absenting himself from a site when he should have been working. He claimed it was a cover-up for redundancy. It was held that as it was proved the dismissal was due to conduct entitling the employer to sack him summarily, then even though a redundancy situation existed, the employee was not entitled to redundancy pay.

In HIGH TABLE LTD v HORST (1997) the question arose as to whether an employee could truly be regarded as being redundant where there was an express term in the contract of employment stating that the employee could be required to work anywhere within the UK (a mobility clause). The employer claimed that the employees were no longer needed at the place where they worked and were therefore, redundant. The employees claimed that they could have been relocated to another branch. The Court of Appeal ruled that the correct approach was a factual investigation into whether employees had in fact been required to work at one location and not what the strict contractual terms stated.

In SAFEWAY STORES PLC v BURRELL (1997) a petrol station manager was dismissed following a re-organisation of the workforce; a new post, at a reduced salary, of petrol station controller was introduced. There were insufficient vacancies in the new post and redundancies were inevitable. The claimant argued that he had not been made redundant as the new post was essentially the same as his old job. The court laid down a three stage test as to whether a redundancy situation existed:

  i.   Was the employee dismissed? if so;

  ii.   Had the requirements of the employer's business for employees to carry out work of a particular kind ceased or diminished?

  iii. Was the dismissal of the employee caused wholly or mainly by the state of affairs identified at stage ii?

Whether the claimant was no longer needed was to be assessed by reference to the needs of the business; here the claimant was no longer required and was redundant. This statutory test approach was affirmed in a recent House of Lords decision MURRAY v FOYLE MEATS (**1999**). The current situation now appears to be that the employer only needs to show some reduction in the need for work of a particular kind in his business and that this situation led to the dismissal of the claimant. For example, an employer who employs two chefs and one receptionist may show redundancy where the requirements of the business for chefs is reduced (as in a fall in demand) and selects the receptionist for redundancy (being the last to join the business) and gives that job to one of the chefs (sometimes referred to as 'bumping').

SPECIAL CONDITIONS FOR LAY-OFF AND SHORT-TIME

In NEEPSEND STEEL & TOOL CORPN v VAUGHAN (**1972**) in order to cancel the effect of lay-offs or short time an employee must be offered work of a kind he is employed to do. This is not a case of a 'suitable alternative offer' of work.

EXCLUSIONS FROM THE RIGHT TO A REDUNDANCY PAYMENT

8. The following employees are not entitled to a redundancy payment:

  a.   Employees who have not completed at least two years' continuous employment with their employer.

  b.   Employees who have reached the age of 65.

  c.   Civil servants and other public employees.

  d.   Persons employed as a domestic servant by someone to whom they are related.

  e.   Share fishermen.

f. Persons on a fixed term contract who have agreed in writing to exclude any right to a redundancy payment. (This is the only circumstance in which the statutory right to a redundancy payment may be excluded by a term in the contract of employment.)

g. Employees who are summarily dismissed for misconduct or if notice is given and is accompanied by a statement in writing that the employer would be entitled to terminate the contract without notice by reason of the employee's conduct. This provision does not apply where the dismissal is for taking part in a strike.

h. Employees who, after having been given notice of dismissal for redundancy, accept oral or written offers of further employment on the same or similar conditions.

i. Employees who unreasonably refuse oral or written offers of further employment on the same or similar conditions. Where the offer of continued employment is on different terms and conditions, the employee must be permitted a trial period of up to four weeks in which to decide whether the job is suitable.

j. Persons outside Great Britain on the relevant date, unless they are ordinarily employed in Great Britain.

k. Persons ordinarily employed outside Great Britain unless they are at the relevant date in Great Britain in accordance with their employer's instructions.

(The non-entitlement to persons outside Great Britain does not apply to persons employed as master or seamen in a British ship who are ordinarily resident in Great Britain.)

Note: *Suitable Alternative Offer and Reasonable Rejection.* Whether an offer of alternative employment is suitable or not must be determined objectively. If an employee's wages or status are considerably reduced, this will not normally amount to a suitable alternative. Even if the offer is suitable, an employee may not be barred from compensation if he can show that his refusal to accept it was not unreasonable in the circumstances. The latter is a subjective test, and may depend on personal or financial circumstances.

In TAYLOR v KENT COUNTY COUNCIL (1969) P was headmaster of a boys' school. The school was amalgamated with a girls' school and new head appointed over the combined school. P was offered employment in a pool of teachers, standing in for short periods in understaffed schools. He would retain his current salary. It was held that P was entitled to redundancy pay as he was being offered something substantially different, particularly in regard to status.

CALCULATION OF REDUNDANCY PAYMENTS

9. The amount of the payment is related to the employee's length of continuous employment, age and gross average wage.

10. *Continuous Employment*. This is employment on a contract of employment excluding the following:

   a. Any week when the employee was on strike.

   b. Any week before the employee's 18th birthday.

   c. Any week when the employee was employed outside Great Britain and no employer's contribution was payable in respect of that week.

11. *Employee's Age*. The amount of redundancy payment is calculated in the same way as the basic award for unfair dismissal, see Chapter 56.34.

   Where an employee is made redundant in the year of retirement, the amount payable is reduced by one-twelfth for each month by which the age of the employee approaches retirement, this lower age limit does not count for calculation of the basic award for unfair dismissal.

NOTIFICATION OF REDUNDANCIES UNDER TULR(C)A 1992

12. *Introduction*. The employer has a duty under the EPA to notify both recognised trade unions and the Secretary of State for Employment of forthcoming redundancies.

13. *Notification to Trade Unions*. An employer proposing to dismiss as redundant any employee of a class in respect of a trade union recognised for collective bargaining purposes must consult with the representatives of that union at the earliest opportunity, and in any event comply with the following timings:

   a. Where it is proposed to dismiss 100 or more employees at one establishment within a period of 90 days or less, notification must be given at least 90 days before the first of the dismissals takes effect.

   b. Where it is proposed to dismiss 10 or more, but less than 100 within a period of 30 days or less, notification must be given at least 30 days before the first of the dismissals takes effect.

   The employer must begin consultations with the trade union representatives before giving individual notices of dismissal.

   In NATIONAL UNION OF TEACHERS v AVON COUNTY COUNCIL (1978) the employers issued dismissal notices to some of their teachers on 28th October 1976. Consultation over redundancies with the recognised independent union was not started until 29th October 1976. It was held that the employer failed to comply with the rules, in that individual notices of dismissal should not have been issued before consultations began.

14. *Consultation*. For the purposes of consultation, the employer must disclose in writing to the trade union representatives the following:

   a. Reasons for the proposed redundancies.

   b. Number and description of the employees involved.

c. Total number in that category employed at the establishment.

d. Proposed method of selection for redundancy.

e. Proposed method of carrying out the dismissals.

The employer must consider any representations made by the trade union, reply to those representations and where he rejects any of them, state his reasons.

Failure to consult may render the employer liable to a claim for unfair dismissal and a complaint by the trade union to an employment tribunal. A Bill before Parliament at the time of writing, the EMPLOYEE CONSULTATION RIGHTS BILL 2001, will require, if it becomes law, all employers with more than 50 employees to consult the workforce representatives on large business issues which directly affect employees.

15. *The Protective Award*. Where a trade union makes a complaint, which is upheld by the tribunal, the tribunal may make a protective award. In this case the employer will have to pay remuneration to the specified employees for a protected period. This is the period beginning with the date on which the first of the dismissals take effect, or the date of the award whichever is the earlier.

The maximum awards permitted are:

a. Up to 90 days' pay where a minimum of 90 days' notice should have been given;

b. Up to 30 days' pay where a minimum of 30 days' notice should have been given; or

c. Up to 28 days' pay in any other case.

In JOSHUA WILSON & BROS v USDAW (1978). The EAT made a protection award of 40 days because it found that on 31st January 1977 the employees were told that they were being made redundant as from 26th February, since the warehouse in which they were working was closing down. The employers recognised the independent union for collective bargaining purposes and there were no special circumstances in which the employers could claim exemption from their duty to consult the union.

Any payment of wages made by an employer to an employee in respect of any period covered by a protective award will offset the protective award.

An employer who fails to consult with the trade union may use as a defence that special circumstances existed which made it impracticable to consult. Nevertheless he must show that he has taken such steps to comply as are reasonably practicable. An employee himself cannot apply for a protective award but may complain to an industrial tribunal if he fails to receive full payment of any such award.

16. *Notification to the Department of Employment*. The employer also has a duty to notify the D of E when redundancies are proposed. The requirements are as for trade unions. Failure to notify the D of E may lead to a fine.

MISCELLANEOUS PROVISIONS

17. *Death of Employer.* Where the employer dies the employee is deemed to be dismissed and may claim a redundancy payment from his employer's personal representative, unless the business is carried on and re-engagement is offered and takes effect within eight weeks.

18. *Death of Employee.* Where the employee dies, any unresolved claims which are pending will survive him.

19. *Insolvency of Employer.* A redundant employee may claim payment out of the Redundancy Fund where his employer is unable to make payment on the grounds of insolvency.

20. *Employee Leaving Before Expiry of Notice.* A redundant employee wishing to leave before expiry of his notice may do so if he notifies his employer in writing and the employer has no objection. If the employer objects he must notify the employee of his objection and his intention to contest the redundancy payment.

21. *Strikes During Notice.* If, whilst serving notice due to redundancy, an employee is dismissed for going on strike he is still entitled to a redundancy payment. The employer may require him to return to work to complete the days lost due to the strike.

22. *Written Statement.* On making any redundancy payment, except as a result of a tribunal decision, the employer must give the employee a written statement indicating how the payment has been calculated.

23. *Time Limit for Claims.* Employees are not entitled to a redundancy payment after six months from the date of redundancy unless:

    a. The payment has been agreed and paid;

    b. The employee has made a claim for payment in writing;

    c. A question as to the right of the employee to the payment, or to the amount, has been referred to an industrial tribunal;

    d. A complaint of unfair dismissal has been presented by the employee to an industrial tribunal.

    An industrial tribunal may order a redundancy payment in respect of a late claim if it considers it 'just and equitable'. However, after one year has elapsed a claim will not be considered.

24. *Exemption Orders.* The Secretary of State for Employment may exempt employers from liability to make redundancy payments under the ERA where they have similar or more advantageous agreements with their employees or with trade unions representing them.

CHAPTER 58

Social Security

INTRODUCTION

1. The law in respect of Social Security benefits is mainly contained in the *SOCIAL SECURITY ACT 1975* and the *SOCIAL SECURITY & HOUSING BENEFIT ACT 1982*. The employment-related benefits covered in this study are in respect of disablement benefits, unemployment, sickness and invalidity. The right to unemployment and sickness benefit depends on payment of a minimum number of weekly national insurance contributions.

INDUSTRIAL INJURIES

2. Where an employee suffers injury at work he may claim damages for his employer's negligence. If, however, the injury results without negligence on the part of his employer, apart from private insurance his only avenue for compensation may be through the Social Security Act in the form of sickness or disablement benefit. Prior to the *SOCIAL SECURITY & HOUSING BENEFIT ACT 1982* industrial injuries benefit was payable if an employee was absent from work due to an industrial injury which complied with the rules. The current position is that an industrial injury resulting in absence from work will give entitlement to sickness benefit. However, the criteria for determining whether or not an injury is resulting from an accident in the course of, and arising out of employment is important for the purpose of disablement benefits and, where the claimant has insufficient contributions for entitlement to sickness benefit within the normal rules.

3. *Exemptions from the Scheme.* In the following circumstances there is no entitlement to claim benefits for injuries under the Act.

   a. Where employment is of a casual nature, eg, assistance to a farmer at harvest-time. (This does not refer to part-time work.)

   b. Employment by one's spouse, or employment on household duties by a near relative.

   c. Self-employed persons.

Risks Insured Against. The Act insures against the following risks:

a.   Personal injury caused by an accident 'arising out of employment.

b.   A disease, or personal injury, not caused by accident, but arising from the nature of the person's employment. (The distinction between a. and b. is between an unforeseen single event and exposure to conditions over a period of time.)

'Injury' includes mental as well as physical injuries. In YATES v SOUTH KIRBY COLLIERIES LTD (**1910**) it was stated that 'Nervous shock due to an accident which causes incapacity is as much personal injury by accident as a broken leg'.

4. The term 'accident' is construed as being an unlooked-for mishap or an untoward event which is not expected or designed. Over-exertion causing a rupture was held to be an accident, and a draught causing a chill.

Where there has been a progressive deterioration of health resulting in personal injury it will not generally be regarded as an accident, eg a doctor who contracted tuberculosis as a result of prolonged exposure to bacilli over a long period of time. However, a trainee nurse who contracted infantile paralysis within seven days of nursing a patient was held to have suffered an industrial accident.

Other court decisions are as follows:

In BRINTON v TURVEY (**1905**) a workman was sorting out wool when a bacillus entered his eye and resulted in anthrax from which he died. It was held to be an accident although the employee actually died from a disease.

In TRIM JOINT DISTRICT SCHOOL BOARD OF MANAGEMENT v KELLY (**1914**) a schoolmaster at an industrial school was killed by the premeditated act of pupils he was supervising in the school yard. It was held to be an 'accident' even though it was a premeditated act by third parties.

Even suicide may be regarded as an industrial accident if it can be shown to be causally related to the injury, eg a miner who was almost blinded and in great pain committed suicide; it was held that he died as a result of an industrial accident. However, an employee who committed suicide because he was told he would have to remain off work for a lengthy period was held not to have died as a result of an accident.

5. *'In the Course of Employment'*. This refers to the time element of employment and includes:

a.   The contractual hours of work and reasonable periods before and after those hours, eg, time to change clothes at the beginning and end of work.

b.   Interruptions in contractual hours, eg, authorised breaks for meals eaten on the premises, tea breaks, etc.

In R v INDUSTRIAL INJURIES COMMISSION EX PARTE AEU (**1966**) smoking was prohibited in a factory except in booths provided, during the 10 minutes tea break. An employee was injured while waiting outside a booth, but after the tea break had finished. It was held that the injury was outside the course of employment.

c.   Travelling to and from work as a passenger in a vehicle supplied by the employer. However, it was decided in VANDYKE v FENDER (**1970**) that such a claim will only succeed where the employee is obliged to travel by this method, ie, where such travel is part of the contract of service.

6. *'Arising Out of Employment'*. This refers to reasons for the accident

a. Performing a task for which he was employed, or one which is incidental to his employment, ie if an employee is injured whilst working on a different machine, without authority, he would not be entitled to benefit.

b. A task performed in an unauthorised manner, but for the benefit of the employer, will be deemed to arise out of employment. A miner, injured whilst travelling to the coal-face on a coal wagon, contrary to regulations, was entitled to benefit.

c. Accidents occurring during emergencies are deemed to have arisen out of employment, eg, an employee injured whilst fighting a fire.

d. Accidents to which the claimant has not contributed are deemed to have arisen out of employment when due to:

   i. *Another person's conduct*, ie sky-larking, negligence or a criminal act. A collector of insurance premiums was robbed and injured, a foreman was struck by an employee whom he reprimanded, and both were deemed to be accidents in the course of employment.

   ii. *The presence of an animal* (including bird, fish or insect).

e. Events not arising out of employment include:

   i. *Assault*, as a result of a quarrel not connected with work, eg a workman who asked another for assistance which was refused called the other a 'lazy swine' and had some teeth knocked out as a result. It was held that the truculent attitude of the injured workman converted the dispute into a personal quarrel.

   ii. *Common risks* (eg street accidents), eg an employee who is injured in a street accident after leaving work is regarded as a member of the public. However, a person employed as a messenger injured in this manner whilst on his employer's business would be regarded as having suffered an injury in the course and arising out of his employment. This would be the case also, where an employee was injured whilst travelling to or from work in a manner prescribed in his contract of employment where the vehicle is operated by or on behalf of his employer and not in the ordinary course of a public transport service.

   iii. *Unauthorised acts*, where an employee carries out a task he is not employed to do, eg a Post Office worker was injured whilst putting up Christmas decorations at a post office. He had been asked to do this task by his immediate superior, and there was no objection from his employers. Nevertheless he was not entitled to benefit.

   However, a colliery worker injured whilst going to the canteen to buy a replacement bootlace, necessary before he could start work, was entitled to benefit.

iv. *Games*, even authorised games, eg a police constable who was injured whilst playing for his county police team on his rest day, was not entitled to benefit, even though his participation was beneficial, eg to the police 'image'. However, the member of a fire brigade injured during recreational training would be regarded as having suffered an injury arising out of his employment, as recreational training is a normal part of a fireman's duty.

7. *Industrial Diseases*. In addition to accidents, the following may be included in the scheme:

a. Selected diseases, eg asbestosis, and,

b. Personal injuries arising from the nature of the employment, ie, prolonged exposure to certain working conditions.

c. To claim the benefit the employee must prove:

i. He has the disease;

ii. That he was employed in the particular occupation during the time the disease was contracted.

8. a. *Industrial disablement benefit.*

i. There is no maximum period of payment.

ii. The benefit is claimed where:

(a) The employee will be capable of work despite some permanent injury suffered (eg lost fingers).

(b) Sickness benefit having expired, there remains some lasting effect of the injury, and the employee is still incapable of work.

b. *Industrial death benefit.*

i. Paid to the widowed dependant spouse (male or female) or exceptionally to parents.

ii. Death must have resulted from an accident or industrial disease.

c. *Disqualification from benefit.* An employee may be disqualified from receiving benefit for a maximum of six weeks under the following circumstances:

i. Industrial Injury Benefit (now sickness benefit) may be withheld where the claimant does not attend for medical examination and treatment when required to do so.

ii. Disablement Benefit may be withheld where the claimant does not attend:

(a) For medical examination and treatment when required to do so, or

(b) A suitable course of vocational training or rehabilitation approved by the Department of Employment.

UNEMPLOYMENT BENEFIT

9. The *SOCIAL SECURITY ACT 1975* gives the rules under which an employee who loses his job may be entitled to unemployment benefit provided he is not in gainful employment, is available for work if required and has satisfied the rules in respect of national insurance contributions.

10. *Disqualification*

a. *Trade disputes.* A claimant is disqualified from benefit when he is unemployed owing to a trade dispute (eg a strike) at his place of employment, unless he can show that:

    i. He was not participating in the dispute, or,

    ii. He had obtained employment elsewhere and was subsequently unemployed for a reason other than a trade dispute. Benefit is payable only from the date of subsequent unemployment.

In **PUNTON AND ANOTHER v MPNI (1963)** the case involved a demarcation dispute in a shipyard between platers and shipwrights (skilled workers belonging to different trade unions). The plaintiffs were semi-skilled platers' assistants belonging to a different union. Their claim for unemployment benefit for the period of the dispute was rejected. It was held that the plaintiffs had failed to prove that they were not directly involved in the dispute. Since a plater and a plater's assistant work as a team the platers' assistants had as great an interest in the type and volume of work as the platers themselves.

b. *Other causes.* Disqualification for a maximum of six weeks may occur under the following circumstances:

    i. Leaving employment voluntarily, without 'just cause' (the onus is on the employee to establish that he had just cause for leaving). Examples of just cause would be serious domestic problems, difficulties in travelling to work and leaving to go to another job which fails to materialise. Leaving employment on voluntary redundancy is regarded as a 'just cause'.

    ii. Dismissal owing to misconduct. The test of misconduct is whether it would lead a reasonable employer to terminate the claimant's employment. However, proceedings at an industrial tribunal or court are not conclusive as far as determining social security benefits are concerned. For example, in one case a shop manager was acquitted for embezzlement yet was disqualified from unemployment benefit. He had been dismissed when the cash was found to be missing from the till, but despite the acquittal, the loss showed that he was incompetent to handle money.

    iii. Failure (without just cause) to apply for employment of which he had been informed, or to accept employment offered to him.

    iv. Neglect to take 'reasonable opportunity of suitable employment'.

    v. Failure to take a recommended course of training.

   c.   *Suitable employment*. The following are not regarded as being suitable employment:

      i.   A vacancy arising from a trade dispute (ie, an unemployed person cannot be expected to take over the work of a striker).

      ii.   Where conditions of employment are less favourable than those generally observed, or to which the claimant is accustomed.

      iii.   Work of a different kind, unless a reasonable time has elapsed since his last employment.

      iv.   Work which may cause deterioration to health.

      v.   Work involving excessive travelling, thus causing financial hardship to his family.

As the period of unemployment increases the claimant has a greater obligation to accept employment of a different kind.

SICKNESS BENEFIT

11. *Entitlement*. Employees are entitled to sickness benefit subject to the same conditions as for unemployment benefit.

A person is entitled to claim if he is incapable of work through illness or disablement.

12. *Disqualification*. A maximum of six weeks disqualification may be imposed for the following reasons:

   a.   Incapable of work because of own misconduct.

   b.   Refusal or failure to undergo medical treatment without 'just cause'.

   c.   Retarding recovery owing to own misconduct.

   d.   Following gainful employment on medical advice.

13. *State Incapacity Benefit*. State Incapacity Benefit replaced invalidity benefit. It is paid to people who are absent from work by reason of illness or injury for more than 28 weeks and the incapacity continues. The reason for the change was to bring the cost of such benefits under control by switching the medical reporting from the claimant's general practitioner to an independent test on a scored basis. The medical test measures functional capacity in relation to 15 functional categories including, for example, walking, speech, bending, kneeling and standing. For each of the tests a score is assigned, zero for no impairment to 15 for extreme impairment. This benefit is liable to tax. The benefit is paid until the statutory retirement age, or the incapacity ceases, whichever is sooner.

ADMINISTRATION OF BENEFITS

14. The Secretary of State for Health and Social Security has overall responsibility for the administration of Social Security benefits. However, the day-to-day administration falls upon the local officers of the DHSS. The system for claims is outlined below:

   a. All claims are dealt with initially by local insurance officers of the DHSS. All claims are against the State, not the employer, and there is no appeal to the courts of law except as indicated below.

   b. The claimant may appeal against the local insurance officer's decision to the Local Appeal Tribunal, and thence to the National Insurance Commissioner.

   c. The local insurance officer may refer medical questions to the Local Medical Board and, if rejected, the claimant may appeal to the Medical Appeal Tribunal. Industrial Injuries cases may be referred to the Industrial Injuries Commission.

   d. The local insurance officer must refer 'special questions' to the Secretary of State, eg,

      i. Whether a person is or was in insurable employment.

      ii. Whether a person is exempt from paying contributions.

      iii. Who is liable to pay the employer's contributions.

      iv. Rate of contribution payable.

STATUTORY SICK PAY

15. Under the *SOCIAL SECURITY AND HOUSING BENEFIT ACT 1982* employers took over almost total responsibility for payment of sickness benefit to employees. The employer will pay the employee direct for the first 28 weeks of sickness in each tax year. It is illegal to pay SSP on top of a contractual payment. Under the *STATUTORY SICK PAY ACT 1994* the whole burden of the cost of statutory sick pay was transferred from the State to individual employers. The small employer whose National Insurance Contribution is less than £20,000 per annum can continue to reclaim money. For the rest SSP payments come wholly from the employer who cannot recoup anything from the DSS.

16. Entitlement to SSP will depend on three tests as follows:

   a. *Incapacity for work.*

      i. The employer must be satisfied that the employee is incapable of doing work under the contract of employment.

      ii. There must be a period of incapacity of at least four consecutive days including Sunday.

b. *Entitlement to SSP*. The following are excluded in respect of SSP:

    i. Employees over state pensionable age.

    ii. Employees with contracts of less than three calendar months.

    iii. Employees with earnings less than lower earnings level set for payment of NI contributions.

    iv. Employees who are sick within eight weeks of receiving other State benefits.

    v. New employees who have done no work for the new employer.

    vi. If there is a trade dispute and the employee cannot prove that he was not involved in the dispute.

    vii. During the 11 weeks before the expected date of confinement (maternity) and six weeks after.

    viii. Maximum entitlement already reached (28 weeks in each tax year).

    ix. Illness in a European Community country counts as for the UK.

    x. If the employee is detained in legal custody.

c. *Days which count*. SSP is only payable for qualifying days. The first three qualifying days are 'waiting days'.

d. A person excluded from SSP may be able to claim sickness benefit.

e. Anyone who is still incapacitated after 28 weeks will transfer to incapacity benefit.

CHAPTER 59

Industrial Injuries: Employer's Liability

INTRODUCTION

1. An employer has a responsibility for the safety of his employees whilst at work. This responsibility includes common law and statutory duties. If an employee suffers injury at work he may be entitled to claim compensation from his employer. In this chapter we consider the courses and remedies open to an employee injured at work, and an employer's defences. In addition the subjects of fatal accidents and limitation of action by lapse of time are covered.

COMMON LAW

2. *Action by an Employee.* If an employee suffers injury as a result of the failure of his employer's common law duties of safety the employee must prove the following if he wishes to claim damages:

   a. There was a duty imposed on the employer, ie, the common law duty to provide a safe system of work, safe premises, etc, and

   b. The employer failed to carry out his duties in a reasonable manner. This action is on the grounds of negligence, and

   c. The employee suffered an injury as a *direct* result of the breach. It is possible that an injury suffered by an employee may not be as a direct result of his employer's breach of duty, ie the fault may lie with the employee (MCWILLIAMS v SIR WILLIAM ARROL (1962)) or the chain of causation may have been broken QUINN v BURCH BROTHERS LTD (1966). A breach of contract to supply plant to a sub-contractor was not a 'cause' of the sub-contractor being injured by using makeshift equipment, but just the 'opportunity' or 'occasion'.

   If there are several reasons for the occurrence of an accident the court will single out the root cause and base judgement on this.

3. *Employer's Defences*. An employer may attempt to refute his employee's action by raising the following defences:

   a. *Deny the breach of duty.* For example the employer may show that the claimant was acting outside the course of employment when injured, eg he was on 'a frolic of his own'. Or he may show that he had used all reasonable care, eg in making all efforts to persuade his employee to use safety equipment. WOODS V DURABLE SUITES LTD (**1933**).

b. *Plead 'Volenti non fit injuria'.* Literally this means 'That to which a man consents cannot be considered an injury'. The nature of this defence is that in a dangerous employment situation the employee is not only aware of the risk, but freely takes the risk. This defence is normally applicable to jobs with high inherent dangers. There must be no pressure on the employee to take the risk (eg the threat of loss of his job), and the employer must prove that the employee willingly agreed to the risk.

BOWATER V ROWLEY REGIS CORPORATION (**1944**) (See Chapter 22.3c.).

Contrast BOLT V WM MOSS & SONS LTD (**1966**) where a workman, expressly informed of the danger, persisted in performing a task in a dangerous manner (having a painter's moveable scaffold moved whilst remaining on it). It was held that volenti was a good defence because the task was undertaken entirely with full knowledge of the risk.

ICI LTD V SHATWELL (**1965**) (See Chapter 22.3b.).

c. *The injury was the sole fault of the employee.* It is a good defence if it can be shown that the employee was solely responsible for his injury. In BROPHY V BRADFIELD & CO (**1955**) the body of a lorry driver was discovered in a boiler house. He had been overcome by fumes. The employer knew of no reason why the driver should have been there and could not have known of his presence. The employer was not liable.

d. *Plead contributory negligence.* This defence, whilst admitting a breach of duty, attempts to secure a reduction in any damages awarded because of the employee's own negligence. 'Contributory negligence' was introduced by the *LAW REFORM (CONTRIBUTORY NEGLIGENCE) ACT 1945*. This is not merely carelessness or inadvertence as an employer has a greater degree of responsibility for the employee's safety than he does for himself. It is more in the nature of a deliberate flouting of safety regulations.

In awards of contributory negligence the motive would be taken into account, eg, if the employee was acting in the employer's best interest the negligence attributable to the employee would tend to be lower.

In SHILTON V HUGHES-JOHNSON (**1963**) an employee was injured whilst investigating a fault in a press without first switching off the machine, as to do so would have stopped all production. It was held that the employee was contributorily negligent, but as he had acted in the best interest of the employer by not causing a stoppage of production, the amount of contributory negligence was reduced.

e. *Deny the existence of an employer/employee relationship.* This would generally be a good defence unless the injury arose as a result of the employer's breach of duty of common care to visitors, as the occupier of premises.

f. *Rely on an exemption clause in the contract of service.* This would be extremely rare, relating only to very risky jobs, eg circus acts.

An exemption clause for accidents which are no fault of the employer is still valid. However, a clause which purports to exempt an employer for liability for an accident caused by his own or the employee's negligence is invalid under the UNFAIR CONTRACT TERMS ACT 1977. The Act states that liability for personal injury through negligence cannot be excluded or restricted by any contract term or notice.

g. *Stress-related personal injury.* Recent case law, to be now considered, allows the employer to show that he took all reasonable steps to manage risk associated with stress at work. The Court of Appeal in HATTON v SUTHERLAND (2002) set out guidance for employers which if followed, would lead to a defence against any claim for alleged stress related illness at work. These are:

i   Employers are not obliged to make searching enquiries to establish whether an individual is at risk:

ii.   Where an employee voluntarily agrees to stay in a stressful job, then without more he will bear the burden of any subsequent stress related harm:

iii. Any impending harm arising from workload must be clearly foreseeable by the employer;

iv. There are no occupations that should be regarded as intrinsically harmful to mental health;

v.   Employers who offer confidential counselling services with access to treatment are unlikely to be found in breach;

vi   Any illness must be caused by the employer breaching his duty and not be just occupational stress;

vii. Any compensation awarded must take account of any pre-existing condition or factors indicating that an employee would have become ill anyway.

More recently the House of Lords endorsed the above principles in BARBER v SOMERSET COUNTY COUNCIL (2004).

STATUTE

4. In order to claim damages for an employer's breach of a statutory duty, eg under the HSAW REGULATIONS 1992, the employee must prove:

a. The employer failed to comply with the statutory duty, eg failure to fence a dangerous piece of machinery,

b. The employee was injured as a result of the breach, and

c. The injury was of a class the duty was designed to prevent.

Generally statutory duties are specific and well defined, and are thus easier to prove than breaches of common law duties. In some cases statutory duties of care are 'absolute' whereas the common law duties tend to require only 'reasonable' care.

5. **The Employer's Defences**. An employer may bring the following defences to counter an allegation of breach of statutory duty:

    a.   Deny the breach.

    b.   Allege contributory negligence.

    c.   Deny employer/employee relationship. This defence would not be valid against all breaches of statutory duty as some sections of, eg, the Factories Act make an employer liable to 'all persons working on the premises', ie, including independent contractors.

        i.   The employer cannot exclude statutory duties in a contract of service.

        ii.   The statutes exist to protect the employee, therefore *volenti non fit injuria* cannot be pleaded.

FATAL ACCIDENTS

6. The FATAL ACCIDENTS ACT 1976 (amended by the ADMINISTRATION OF JUSTICE ACT 1983) gives certain rights to the dependants in the circumstances where an employee dies due to an employer's breach of duty such as would have given the deceased employee a right to an action for damages if he had lived.

7. **Definition of 'Dependant'**. In the Act a dependant means:

    a.   The wife or husband of the deceased.

    b.   The parent or grandparent of the deceased.

    c.   A child or grandchild of the deceased.

    d.   A brother, sister, aunt or uncle of the deceased.

    e.   A son or daughter of the brother, sister, aunt or uncle of the deceased.

The Act also includes step-children and illegitimate children.

8. **Persons Entitled to Bring the Action**. In the first place action should be taken by the executor or administrator of the deceased. In the event of there being no executor or administrator or if the action is not commenced within six months after death the action may be taken by, and in the name of, all or any of the dependants. However, only one action may be taken in respect of the subject matter of the complaint.

9. **Assessment of Damages**

    a.   Damages awarded may be divided amongst the dependants as directed.

    b.   In the case of damages awarded to a widow, no account shall be taken of her remarriage or her prospects for remarriage.

c.   Damages may be awarded in respect of funeral expenses.

d.   Damages may be awarded in respect of bereavement, which may only be paid for the benefit of the wife or husband of the deceased or in the case of an unmarried child, his parents.

e.   Damages will not be reduced by any financial benefits received by the dependants on account of insurance money, pensions, or benefits received in respect of social security or payment by a trade union or friendly society.

f.   Any saving to the injured person attributable to his maintenance at public expense in a hospital or other institution shall be set off against loss of income attributable to his injuries.

Note: The estate may claim for other than loss of earnings under the LAW REFORM (MISCELLANEOUS PROVISIONS) ACT 1934, eg, pain and loss of amenities. However, any damages awarded under this Act would be subject to reduction for contributory negligence.

THE LIMITATION ACT 1980

10. The LIMITATION ACT 1980 lays down time limits and other rules for the bringing of actions in respect of wrongs causing personal injuries or death.

a.   No action may be brought after the expiration of three years from:

   i.   The date on which the cause of action arose; or,

   ii.   The date of the plaintiff's knowledge, if the extent of the injury is not immediately apparent.

b.   If a claim is made under the FATAL ACCIDENTS ACT 1976 no action may be brought after the expiration of three years from:

   i.   The date of death; or,

   ii.   The date of knowledge of the person for whose benefit the action is brought, whichever is the later.

11. Reference to a plaintiff's date of knowledge is a reference to the date on which he first had knowledge of the following facts:

a.   The injury was significant (sufficiently serious to justify proceedings).

b.   The injury was attributable to the act of alleged negligence or breach of duty.

c.   The identity of the defendant (eg, in the case of vicarious liability or, for example, a 'hit and run' driver).

A person's knowledge includes his own observable knowledge or facts ascertainable with the help of medical or other expert advice.

12. The court may override the time limit if it considers it equitable to do so, taking into account, eg, the reasons for the plaintiff's delay, eg, the nature of the injury being such that the plaintiff is incapable of making judgements.

ASSESSMENT OF DAMAGES

13. Damages may be awarded under two general headings, ie Special and General damages.

    a. *Special damages*. These are awarded on the basis of an estimated loss of earnings. This includes not only loss of present earnings, but an estimate of future loss. It would take into account the employee's age, his position and his earnings potential.

    b. *General damages*. These are at the discretion of the court and include such things as, loss of expectation of life, pain and suffering, expenses, loss of faculties and loss of enjoyment of life. In past cases general damages have been awarded where an employee has become sexually impotent due to an accident, and where an employee has lost the ability to enjoy his recreational pursuits, eg, darts playing or dancing.

14. Any damages awarded will be reduced by, eg, contributory negligence, a proportion of any benefits received under the Social Security Acts and an estimated amount of income tax which would have been payable on future earnings.

CHAPTER 60

Health and Safety at Work

INTRODUCTION

1. This chapter deals with two pieces of legislation, namely, the *HEALTH & SAFETY AT WORK ACT* and the *HEALTH & SAFETY AT WORK REGULATIONS 1999*. The former lays down a requirement for reasonable safety at all places of work and is couched mainly in general terms. The intention is that most of the health and safety legislation will be replaced by a system of Regulations and Codes of Practice. The HSAW Regulations 1999 introduce more detailed rules with appropriate Codes of Practice.

HEALTH & SAFETY AT WORK ACT 1974

2. *Introduction*. The *HSAWA 1974* is to provide for reasonable safety at all places of employment. The Act covers not only persons at work (including self-employed) but also the general public. The only excluded category is that of domestic employment.

GENERAL DUTIES OF EMPLOYERS TO THEIR EMPLOYEES

3. *Health, Safety and Welfare*. Under *S.2* of the Act it is the duty of an employer to ensure, so far as is reasonably practicable the health, safety and welfare at work of all his employees. This duty covers the following aspects:

   a. The provision of plant and systems of work that are safe and without risks to health.

   b. Arrangements for ensuring safety and absence of risks to health in connection with the use, handling, storage and transport of articles and substances.

   c. The provision of such information, instruction, training and supervision as is necessary to ensure the health and safety at work of his employees.

   d. With regards to any place of work under the employer's control. He must maintain it in a safe condition and without risks to health, and provide safe means of access to and egress from his premises.

e. The provision and maintenance of a working environment that is safe, without risk to health and with adequate facilities and arrangements for his employees' welfare.

The above duties are not absolute but require the employer to exercise 'reasonable care'. Thus they accord with an employer's common law duties toward his employees.

4. *Information and Consultation.* An employer must comply with the following provision with regard to the supply of information and consultation with trade unions:

a. Provide a written statement of safety policy, eg, accident procedure, action on outbreak of fire, safety training. An establishment with fewer than five employees is exempt from this provision.

b. Where the appointment is made of a safety representative by a recognised trade union or other employees he shall represent the employees in consultations with the employer.

c. The employer must consult any such representatives with a view to the making and maintenance of arrangements for enabling their effective co-operation in promoting, developing and monitoring measures to ensure the health and safety at work of the employees.

d. Appoint a safety committee on the request of two or more safety representatives.

DUTIES TO PERSONS OTHER THAN EMPLOYEES

5. The following duties are imposed on employers and self-employed persons for the safety and health of their employees *(S.3)*:

a. An employer and a self-employed person shall conduct his undertaking in such a manner that persons other than employees are not exposed to risks to their health or safety.

b. The also have the duty to give information to persons other than employees, who may be affected by the way the business is carried out. Such information will detail aspects of the way in which the business is carried out which may affect their health or safety.

DUTIES OF PERSONS IN CONTROL OF PREMISES (S.4, 5)

6. *Health and Safety.* The Act provides that a person who has control of any work premises owes a general duty of care to persons other than his employees who are working there.

7. His duty shall be to ensure, as far as is reasonably practicable that the premises and means of access to and egress from, and any plant or substance in the premises are safe and without risks to health.

Similar provisions are laid down in the OCCUPIERS LIABILITY ACT 1957. However, contravention of the Occupiers Liability Act is a civil offence, contravention of the *HSAWA* is a criminal offence.

8. *Harmful Emissions*. A person who has control of a business where noxious or offensive fumes are involved must do his best to prevent these fumes from entering the atmosphere, and to render them harmless if they are emitted.

DUTIES OF MANUFACTURERS AND INSTALLERS (S.6)

9. The Act requires anyone who designs, manufactures, imports or supplies an article or substance for use at work to ensure that such article or substance is safe when used in accordance with the instructions issued by them.

10. The duty extends to the provision of instructions for the user and the carrying out of any necessary testing, inspection and research to ensure compliance with the obligations of safety.

11. Those who install plant have a duty to ensure it is safely installed.

DUTIES OF EMPLOYEES (S.7)

12. An employee has the following duties:

   a. To act, in the course of employment, with due care for the health and safety of himself, other workers and other persons who may be affected by his acts or omissions at work (ie, the general public).

   b. To observe the provision of the Act insofar as it concerns him and is under his control.

   c. To co-operate with his employer to enable compliance with the requirements of the Act.

GENERAL DUTIES

13. The Act makes provision for the following general duties:

   a. No person shall interfere with or misuse anything provided under any statutory provision in the interests of health, safety and welfare, eg safety clothing, washing facilities. *(S.8)*

   b. An employer shall not levy a charge on his employees for anything provided to meet the legal requirements. *(S.9)*

HEALTH AND SAFETY COMMISSION (S.10–14)

14. The Act made provision for the setting up of two corporate bodies, the Health and Safety Commission and the Health and Safety Executive.

15. *Composition of the Commission*. The Commission is comprised of a Chairman and not less than six but not more than eight members appointed by the Secretary of State: three after consultation with employers' organisations, three after consultation with the TUC and two others appointed from local authorities.

16. *Composition of the Executive*. The Executive will consist of three persons: the Director is appointed by the Commission and approved by the Secretary of State and the two others are appointed by the Commission after consultation with the Director.

17. *Functions of the Commission*. The Commission has the following functions:

   a. To ensure provision for the health, safety and satisfactory working environment of persons during the course of work. This excludes domestic and agricultural operatives work and certain activities of transport workers.

   b. To secure provision against hazards to the safety and health of the public from industrial, etc activities.

   c. To advise Government Departments and to promote safety education and training.

   d. To prepare and enforce regulations and codes.

   e. To investigate any hazardous situation, accident or occurrence.

   f. To delay inquests pending investigation of fatal accidents, to authorise a representative to be present at inquests, with the power to examine witnesses and request a report from the coroner.

   g. To charge fees for, eg, providing advisory work.

   h. To appoint independent persons or committees if considered necessary, to assist and advise the Commission in its work.

18. *Functions of the Executive*. The Executive has the following duties:

   a. To exercise such of the Commission's functions as it delegates to it,

   b. To make adequate arrangements for the enforcement of the relevant statutory provisions except insofar as the Secretary of State has conferred the duty of enforcement upon some other authority.

REGULATIONS AND CODES OF PRACTICE (S.16, 17)

19. The Secretary of State, after consultation with the Commission, has the power to make 'health and safety regulations'. Such regulations may:

   a. Repeal any of the existing statutory provisions, eg the FACTORIES ACT 1961.

   b. Exclude or modify any of the foregoing duties, or statutory provisions.

   c. Impose requirements by reference to the approval of the Commission.

   d. Provide for exceptions from any of the relevant statutory provisions.

Note: see Health and Safety at Work Regulations 1992. (Paragraphs 42–48)

20. If a person does not observe any particular approved code of practice it does not mean he will be open to criminal proceedings, but a relevant code of practice is admissible as evidence where there are criminal proceedings.

21. *Authorities Responsible for Enforcement.* The Secretary of State may make local authorities responsible for enforcement of the Act, including the current Acts, scheduled for replacement. *(S.18)*

22. Local authorities already have safety and health enforcement duties under existing regulations.

23. Guidance will be given by the Commission. Where technical assistance is required it will be provided, as far as possible by the central organisation.

24. Provision is made for closer and more effective co-operation between the health and safety organisation and other bodies, ie, the local authorities, the fire authorities and the local planning authorities.

HEALTH AND SAFETY INSPECTORS

25. Enforcing powers have authority to appoint inspectors, who have the following powers: *(S.19, 20)*

   a. To enter (accompanied by any person he considers necessary) any place where it is considered the Act will apply. This includes any premises on which he has reason to believe activities are being carried out which could endanger public safety.

   b. To enquire into the causes and assist enquiries on any safety situation. He can demand either oral or written information.

   c. If a qualified medical practitioner he may carry out medical examinations he considers necessary.

   d. To examine, search any premises, plant, materials, equipment, records or any other documents and take samples, measurements, recordings, copies and conduct tests.

   e. To demand facilities and assistance from any person if it is considered necessary.

26. *Enforcement.* An inspector is empowered to issue:

   a. *Improvement notices.* These are to meet a situation where there is contravention of a regulation but no imminent, serious risk of injury is involved. They require remedial action to be taken within a specified time, to comply with the requirements of the Act or to implement non-statutory codes and standards where the inspector considers this to be appropriate.

   b. *Prohibition notices.* An inspector may serve a prohibition notice upon a person who is in control of activities which, in the inspector's opinion, involve a risk of serious personal injury. The prohibition notice will state the inspector's opinion that there is a risk of this nature, specify the matters which in his opinion give rise to the risk, and direct that the activities to which the notice relates shall not be carried on, by or under the control of the person on whom the notice is served unless the matters specified in the notice have been remedied. A direction contained in a prohibition notice when the risk of personal injury is imminent shall take effect:

i.   at the end of the period specified in the notice, or

ii.   if the notice so declares, immediately.

27. **Right of Appeal.** There is a right of appeal against an improvement or prohibition notice. This should be made to an industrial tribunal within 21 days. Pending the appeal, improvement notices will be held in abeyance but prohibition notices will remain in force unless the employer satisfies the tribunal by an application prior to the hearing that it should not do so. *(S.24)*

OFFENCES (S.33)

28. It is an offence for a person:

a.   To fail to discharge a duty as outlined in paragraphs *4.* to *14.* above.

b.   To wilfully interfere with anything provided for health, safety and welfare.

c.   To contravene any health and safety regulation.

d.   To contravene any requirement imposed by an inspector.

e.   To contravene any requirements made by an improvement or prohibition notice.

f.   To intentionally obstruct an inspector in the performance of his duties.

g.   To intentionally make a false entry in any book, notice or document required to be kept by law.

29. **Penalties.** For most of the offences the maximum penalty is £1,000. However, some offences are triable by the Crown Court and a convicted person is liable to imprisonment for a term not exceeding two years or an unlimited fine or both.

30. **Offences Due to the Fault of Another Person.** Where a person is accused of an offence, but this is due to another person, the other person shall be guilty of the offence. *(S.36)*

31. **Offences by a Body Corporate.** Where an offence committed by a body corporate is proved to have been committed with the consent, agreement or neglect of any company officer, then the officer as well as the body corporate shall be guilty of the offence. *(S.37)*

32. **Onus on Proving Limits of 'Practicability'.** If a person is accused of an offence involving failure to comply with statutory provisions of the Act as far as is reasonably practicable he has to prove that it was not practicable to do more than he had done in the situation and he had been as practicable as possible to meet the duty, ie, the onus is on the employer. *(S.40)*

SAFETY REPRESENTATIVES

33. *Appointment*. A recognised trade union:

    a. Appoints safety representatives where one or more members are employed. Normally more than two years' service with the company or with a similar industry is required.

    b. Notifies the employer in writing of the names.

    c. Notifies employers when an appointment is terminated.

34. *Functions*. The functions of a safety representative are:

    a. To represent employees in discussions with management.

    b. Investigate potential hazards.

    c. Investigate complaints.

    d. Inspect the workplace at three-monthly intervals, or more often after agreement with the employer.

    e. Carry out inspections after an accident, dangerous occurrence or notifiable industrial disease.

    f. Receive information from Health and Safety Inspectors.

    g. Attend meetings of safety committees.

35. *Inspections*. Safety representatives have the authority to inspect the workplace:

    a. After giving the employer reasonable written notice and a three-month interval has passed.

    b. If there has been a substantial change of work within the three-month interval.

    c. If there has been a notifiable accident, dangerous occurrence or industrial disease in the workplace.

    d. Inspect any document which is required to be kept by law except a medical examination report of an identifiable employee.

36. *Notifiable Accidents, Dangerous Occurrences and Notifiable Diseases.*

    a. An immediate inspection takes place when there has been a notifiable accident or dangerous occurrence.

    b. Written or verbal notification to be given to management by the safety representative.

    c. Employer shall provide all facilities.

    d. Although independent inspections are allowable, nothing shall prevent the employer or his representative from being present at the workplace.

Note: *'Accident and Dangerous Occurrences'*. Accidents and dangerous occurrences are those which are listed in the Notification of Accidents and

Dangerous Occurrences Regulations 1980, and which are notifiable to the Health and Safety Executive. They include, inter alia, accidents involving personal injury which result in employees being absent for more than three days, and such occurrences as the overturning of cranes, boiler explosions, building collapses, explosions or fires causing damage and leading to suspension of work for at least five hours, and gassing accidents.

37. ***Information from an Employer.*** Safety representatives have the right to inspect any relevant document kept under the Act for health, safety and welfare. The exceptions are:

    a.   Information against the interests of national security.

    b.   Information relating specifically to an individual without his consent.

    c.   Information, the disclosure of which, for reasons other than health and safety at work could cause substantial injury to the employer's undertaking.

    d.   Information obtained for legal proceedings.

38. ***Payments and Time Off for Safety Representatives.*** An employer shall permit a safety representative to take such time off with pay during the employee's working hours as shall be necessary to enable the safety representative to:

    a.   Perform his functions under the Act.

    b.   Undergo training to enable him to perform these functions.

39. ***Industrial Tribunals.*** Complaints may be made to an industrial tribunal if the safety representative is not paid or is not given time off for safety matters. The complaint must be made within three months of the date the failure took place. If the complaint is justified, the tribunal can order the employer to pay compensation.

SAFETY COMMITTEES

40. ***Establishment.*** An employer must establish a safety committee conforming to these requirements:

    a.   Safety representatives have been appointed and at least two request a safety committee in writing.

    b.   Employer and safety representatives and trade union representatives consult to determine the composition of the committee.

    c.   A notice must be posted in a place where it can be read.

    d.   The committee shall be formed within three months.

41. ***Functions.*** The committee will meet for discussion. Topics for discussion may include:

    a.   The investigation of individual accidents and cases of notifiable diseases.

    b.   The study of accident statistics and trends.

c. Examination of safety audit reports.

d. Consideration of safety representatives' reports.

e. Assist in the development of works safety rules and safe systems of work.

f. Periodic inspection of the workplace, its plant, equipment and amenities.

g. Publicity and communication effectiveness.

h. Keeping adequate records of the proceedings and activities of the committee.

HEALTH & SAFETY AT WORK REGULATIONS 1992

42. *Introduction*. The HASAW Regulations 1992 implement EC Directives on health and safety at work. They are part of a continuing modernisation of existing UK law and part of the European Commission's programme of action on health and safety. They have been developed under Article 118A which has been added to the Treaty of Rome for this purpose. The duties outlined in the regulations clarify and make more explicit the current health and safety law. Much old law is repealed by the new regulations. The emphasis is on sound health and safety management and duties to assess risk and choose matching protective measures. The regulations cover: General Health & Safety Management, Work Equipment Safety, Manual Handling of Loads, Workplace Conditions, Personal Protective Equipment and Display Screen Equipment. For each of these regulations the Health and Safety Executive has issued a Code of Practice. The Regulations came into effect on 1st January 1993. In this Chapter the regulations are covered in outline only. Copies of the full regulations and Codes of Practice may be obtained from HMSO bookshops.

43. *Health & Safety (General Provisions) Regulations*

The Health and Safety (General Provisions) Regulations set out some broad general duties which will apply to almost all kinds of work. They are aimed mainly at improving health and safety management.

The regulations will require and employer to

a. Assess the risk to the health and safety of his employees and to anyone else who may be affected by his work activity. This is so that the necessary preventive and protective steps can be identified. Employers with five or more employees will have to write their risk assessments down. (The same threshold is already used in the HSAWA. Employers with five or more employees have to prepare a written safety policy);

b. Make arrangements for putting into practice the preventive and protective measures that follow from his risk assessment. They will have to cover planning, organisation, control, monitoring and review, ie the management of health and safety. Again, employers with five or more employees will have to put their arrangements in writing;

c. Carry out health surveillance of his employees where it is appropriate;

    d.   Appoint competent people to help him to devise and apply the protective steps shown to be necessary by the risk assessment;

    e.   Set up emergency procedures;

    f.   Give his employees information about health and safety matters;

    g.   Work together with other employers when he shares a workplace;

    h.   Make sure that his employees have adequate health and safety training and are capable enough at their jobs to avoid risk; and

    i.   Give some particular health and safety information to temporary workers, to meet their special needs.

The regulations will also:

    j.   Place duties on employees to follow health and safety instructions and report danger; and

    k.   Extend the current law which requires an employer to consult employees' safety representatives and provide facilities for them.

44. *Provision and Use of Work Equipment Regulations*

These regulations are designed to consolidate the laws governing equipment used at work. Instead of piecemeal legislation covering particular kinds of equipment in different industries they will:

    a.   Place general duties on employers; and

    b.   List minimum requirements for work equipment to deal with selected hazards whatever the industry.

In general, the regulations will make explicit what is already somewhere in the law or is good practice. Some older equipment may need to be upgraded to meet the minimum requirements. 'Work equipment' is broadly defined to include everything from a hand tool, through machines of all kinds, to a complete plant such as a refinery. 'Use' will include starting, stopping, installing, dismantling, programming, setting, transporting, maintaining, servicing and cleaning.

The general duties will require an employer to:

    a.   Take into account the working conditions and hazards in the workplace when selecting equipment;

    b.   Make sure that equipment is suitable for the use that will be made of it and that it is properly maintained; and give adequate information, instruction and training.

Specific requirements will cover:

    c.   Guarding of dangerous parts of machinery (replacing the current law in the FACTORIES ACT *1961*);

    d.   Maintenance operations;

    e.   Danger caused by equipment failure;

    f.   Parts and materials at high or very low temperatures;

g.   Control systems and control devices;

h.   Isolation of equipment from power sources;

i.   Stability of equipment;

j.   Lighting; and

k.   Warnings and markings.

The regulations implement an EC directive aimed at the protection of workers. There are other directives setting out conditions which much new equipment (especially machinery) will have to satisfy before it can be sold in EC member states. They will be implemented in the UK by regulations made by the Department of Trade and Industry. Equipment which satisfies those other directives will satisfy many of the specific requirements listed above.

45. *Manual Handling Operations Regulations*

The regulations apply to any manual handling operations which may cause injury at work. Those operations will be identified by the risk assessment carried out under the Health and Safety (General Provisions) Regulations. They include not only the lifting of loads, but also lowering, pushing, pulling, carrying or moving them, whether by hand or other bodily force.

An employer has to take three key steps:

a.   Avoid hazardous manual handling operations where reasonably practicable. Consider whether the load must be moved at all. And if it must, whether it can be moved mechanically, for example, by fork-lift truck;

b.   Assess adequately any hazardous operations that cannot be avoided. An ergonomic assessment should look at more than just the weight of the load. He should consider the shape and size of the load; the way the task is carried out (eg the handler's posture); the working environment (eg is it cramped or hot?); the individual's capacity (eg is unusual strength required?). Unless the assessment is very simple a written record of it will be needed.

c.   Reduce the risk of injury as far as reasonably practicable. A good assessment will not only show whether there is a problem but will also point to where the problem lies. That is the starting point for improvements. For example, if the load is bulky or heavy it may be possible to use mechanical handling aids or break down the load. If handlers have to adopt an awkward posture he may be able to rearrange the task. Additional training may be required.

46. *Workplace (Health, Safety and Welfare) Regulations*

These regulations replace much old law including parts of the FACTORIES ACT 1961 and the OFFICES, SHOPS AND RAILWAY PREMISES ACT 1963.

The regulations cover many aspects of health, safety and welfare in the workplace. Some of them are not explicitly mentioned in the current law though they are implied in the general duties of the HSW ACT. The regulations will apply to all places of work except: means of transport, construction sites, sites where extraction of mineral resources or exploration for them is carried out and fishing boats. Workplaces on agricultural or forestry land away from main buildings will also be exempted from most requirements.

The regulations will set general requirements in four broad areas:

a. *Working environment*

    i. Temperature

    ii. Ventilation

    iii. Lighting including emergency lighting

    iv. Room dimensions

    v. Suitability of workstations

    vi. Outdoor workstations (eg weather protection)

b. *Safety*

    i. Safe passage of pedestrians and vehicles (traffic routes, for example, must be big enough and marked where necessary, and there must be enough of them)

    ii. Windows and skylights (safe opening, closing and cleaning)

    iii. Glazed doors and partitions (use of safe material and marking)

    iv. Doors, gates and escalators (safety devices)

    v. Floors (construction and maintenance, obstructions and slipping and tripping hazards)

    vi. Falls from heights and into dangerous substances

    vii. Falling objects

c. *Facilities*

    i. Toilets

    ii. Washing, eating and changing facilities

    iii. Clothing storage

    iv. Seating

    v. Rest areas (and arrangements in them for non-smokers)

    vi. Rest facilities for pregnant women and nursing mothers

d. *Housekeeping*

    i. Maintenance of workplace, equipment and facilities

    ii. Cleanliness

    iii. Drainage

An employer will have to make sure that any workplace within his control complies with the regulations. Other people concerned with the workplace, such as the owner of a building which is leased to one or more employers or self-employed people, will also have to make sure that requirements falling within their control are satisfied.

47. *Personal Protective Equipment at Work (PPE) Regulations*

Personal protective equipment is defined as all equipment designed to be worn or held to protect against a hazard. It includes most types of protective clothing and equipment such as eye, foot and head protection, safety harnesses, life jackets and high visibility clothing. There are some exceptions, for example, ordinary working clothes and uniforms (including clothing provided for food hygiene).

Personal protective equipment should be relied upon only as a last resort. But where risks are not adequately controlled by other means an employer will have a duty to provide suitable PPE, free of charge, for employees exposed to those risks.

The regulations say what is meant by 'suitable' PPE, a key point in making sure that it effectively protects the wearer. Personal protective clothing will be suitable only if it is appropriate for the risks and the working conditions; takes account of workers' needs and fits properly; and gives adequate protection. An employer will have to assess the risks and the PPE he intends to issue to make sure that these conditions are satisfied.

An employer will also have duties to:

a. Maintain, clean and replace PPE;

b. Provide storage for PPE when it is not being used;

c. Ensure that PPE is properly used; and

d. Give training, information and instruction on its use to his employees.

New PPE will also have to comply with an EC directive on design, certification and testing. It will be implemented in the UK by regulations made by the Department of Trade and Industry. PPE brought before these regulations came into force may still be used.

48. *Health and Safety (Display Screen Equipment) Regulations*

Unlike some of the other regulations the Health and Safety (Display Screen Equipment) Regulations will not replace old legislation but will cover a new area of work activity for the first time. Work with display screen equipment is not generally high risk, but it can lead to muscular and other physical problems, eye fatigue and mental stress.

The regulations apply to display screens where there is a 'user', that is, an employee who habitually uses display screen equipment as a significant part of normal work. They cover equipment used for the display of text, numbers and graphics regardless of the display process used. There are some specified exclusions, such as systems on board a means of transport, systems mainly for public use, portable systems, cash registers and window typewriters.

An employer will have duties to:

a. Assess display screen equipment workstations and reduce risks which are discovered;

b. Make sure that workstations satisfy minimum requirements which are set for the display screen itself, keyboard, desk and chair, working environment and task design and software;

c. Plan display screen equipment work so that there are breaks or changes of activity; and

d. Provide information and training for display screen equipment users.

Display screen equipment users will also be entitled to appropriate eye and eyesight tests, and to special spectacles if they are needed and normal ones cannot be used.

CHAPTER 61

Institutions and Tribunals

INTRODUCTION

1. The *EMPLOYMENT PROTECTION ACT 1975 (EPA)* set up a number of statutory bodies described as the 'machinery for promoting the improvement of industrial relations'. The constitution and functions of these statutory bodies, which are now set out in the *TULR(C)A 1992* as amended by the *TUR & ERA 1993*, are explained in this chapter. The jurisdictions of the Employment Tribunal and the Employment Appeal Tribunal are also explained for the purpose of completing the students' overall view of the machinery available for settling employment disputes.

THE ADVISORY, CONCILIATION AND ARBITRATION SERVICE (ACAS)

2. ACAS is charged with the general duty of promoting the improvement of industrial relations, and in particular of encouraging the extension of collective bargaining and the development and, where necessary, reform of collective bargaining machinery. ACAS is directed by a council appointed by the Secretary of State for Employment. The council consists of a full-time chairman and nine other members. In appointing six of the nine members the Secretary of State is required to consult employers' organisations as regards three appointments and workers' organisations as regards three. This ensures that a balance between workers' and employers' interests is maintained.

3. *Principal Functions.* ACAS has five principal functions:

   a. *Conciliation*

      i.   Where a trade dispute exists or is anticipated, ACAS may offer to assist in bringing about a settlement either with or without the consent of the parties.

      To achieve this, ACAS may either appoint an independent person or one of its own officers as a Conciliation Officer. No charge may be made for such assistance. Moreover, during the course of conciliation the parties should be encouraged to use any existing procedures for the resolution of the dispute.

ii. Conciliation Officers appointed by ACAS are required to endeavour to promote a settlement of any complaint presented to an industrial tribunal in respect of:

(a) Unfair Dismissal

(b) Sex, Race or Disability Discrimination

(c) Itemised Pay Statements

(d) Guarantee Payments

(e) Medical Suspension Payments

(f) Trade Union Membership and Activities

(g) Time off work

(h) Maternity Rights

(i) Written Statement of Reasons for Dismissal

(j) Redundancy Consultations

(k) Protective Awards

Where a conciliation officer succeeds in bringing about an agreement between the parties, it is recorded in writing and is legally binding on the parties. The Court of Appeal has held that where the conciliation officer has formally recorded any agreement and the parties have signed it, the employee is precluded from presenting a complaint to an Industrial Tribunal. MOORE V DUPORT FURNITURE PRODUCTS LTD AND ACAS (1980).

b. *Arbitration.* The EPA provides for ACAS, at the request of one or more - parties to a dispute and with the consent of all the parties in dispute, to refer any or all of the matters in dispute for settlement by arbitration of:

i. An independent arbitrator who may not be an officer or servant of ACAS; or

ii. The Central Arbitration Committee.

It is the duty of ACAS to ensure that existing conciliation procedures have been exhausted before referring a matter for arbitration, unless there is some special reason which justifies arbitration. The report of the arbitrator may be published by ACAS providing all the parties consent.

c. *Advice.* ACAS has the discretionary power to offer advice to employers, workers and their organisations on any matter concerned with industrial relations or employment policies, including the following:

i. The organisation of workers or employers for the purpose of collective bargaining;

ii. The recognition of trade unions by employers;

iii. Machinery for the negotiation of terms and conditions of employment, and for joint consultation;

iv. Procedures for avoiding and settling disputes and workers' grievances;

v. Questions relating to communication between employers and workers;

vi. Facilities for officials of trade unions;

vii. Procedures relating to the termination of employment;

viii. Disciplinary matters;

ix. Manpower planning, labour turnover and absenteeism;

x. Recruitment, retention, promotion and vocational training of workers;

xi. Payment systems, including job evaluation and equal pay.

Such advice may be given either on the initiative of ACAS itself or upon the request of an interested party. The advice so given may be published by ACAS without the consent of any other party, but it must be of a general nature and without reference to specific employers or employees.

d. *Inquiry*. ACAS may, if it thinks fit, inquire into any question relating to industrial relations generally or to industrial relations in any particular industry or in any particular undertaking or part of an undertaking. The findings of such an inquiry may be published if ACAS consider publication to be desirable for the improvement of industrial relations, but only after consulting all the parties concerned and taking account of their views.

e. *Codes of practice*. The original code of practice was published by the Secretary of State for Employment under powers conferred by the INDUS-TRIAL RELATIONS ACT 1971 with the specific purpose of giving practical guidance upon the four general principles set out in Section I of that Act, namely:

i. Freely conducted collective bargaining;

ii. Orderly procedures for settling disputes;

iii. Free association of workers and employers;

iv. Freedom and security for workers.

This code of practice has been retained, and in addition the following codes have been issued by ACAS, under the EPCA.

i. Disciplinary Practice and Procedures in Employment;

ii. Disclosure of Information to Trade Unions for Collective Bargaining Purposes;

iii. Time off for Trade Union Duties and Activities.

Additionally ACAS has a general power to issue codes of practice to give practical guidance for promoting the improvement of industrial relations.

The Secretary of State is also empowered, after consulting ACAS and gaining the approval of both Houses of Parliament, to issue Codes of Practice. Two codes have been issued by the Secretary of State on:

i. Picketing; and

ii. The Closed Shop.

Codes issued under the HSAWA are:

i. Time off work with pay for safety representatives to carry out their statutory functions and undergo training.

ii. Disclosure of relevant information to safety representatives on matters such as dangers relating to machinery used at work.

The provisions of a code of practice are not legally binding upon employers. Failure to observe provisions cannot of itself lead to a criminal penalty or civil liability. Nevertheless, in any proceedings before an industrial tribunal or the CAC a code of practice is admissible in evidence. The employer's compliance or otherwise is taken into account.

THE CENTRAL ARBITRATION COMMITTEE (CAC)

4. The Secretary of State is responsible for appointing the members of the CAC and its chairman and deputy chairman. ACAS must be consulted with regard to the appointment of the chairman and his deputies. ACAS nominates persons as members who are experienced in industrial relations, ensuring that both employers' and workers' representatives serve on the Committee.

5. *Jurisdiction*. The main jurisdictions of the CAC are as follows:

   a. Voluntary jurisdiction in matters referred by ACAS in connection with a trade dispute. An award under this jurisdiction will only be binding upon the parties insofar as it is incorporated into individual employment contracts with the agreement of the parties.

   b. Statutory jurisdiction regarding a complaint that an employer has failed to disclose to a trade union information under the EPA in respect of the findings of a Statutory Joint Industrial Council.

   c. Statutory jurisdiction derived from the EPA in respect of the findings of a Statutory Joint Industrial Council.

   d. Jurisdiction arising from various statutes where financial assistance or licence is provided by central or local government.

6. *Appeals*. There is no procedure for appeal against an award made by the CAC but if it can be shown to have exceeded its powers or acted in breach of natural justice, its decisions may be challenged in the High Court.

THE CERTIFICATION OFFICER (CO)

7. The CO is appointed by the Secretary of State and its principal functions are:

   a. Duties in connection with the listing and certification of independent trade unions and the monitoring of their annual returns and accounts.

   b. The exercise of powers concerning the political fund rules of trade unions.

   c. The handling of complaints relating to amalgamations of trade.

   Provision is made for appeal from certain decisions of the CO to go before the Employment Appeal Tribunal (see paragraph 12 below).

COMMISSIONER FOR THE RIGHTS OF TRADE UNION MEMBERS

8. The Secretary of State appoints the Commissioner, who holds office for five years, and then is eligible for re-appointment. An annual report of the Commissioner's activities will be laid before Parliament.

9. The Commissioner is empowered to assist a trade union member who is taking (or contemplating) the following types of action against his trade union:

   a. An application to the court in respect of:

      i. Failure to call a ballot on industrial action

      ii. Failure to permit the member to examine the union's accounts, etc

      iii. Unlawful application of the union's property by trustees

      iv. Failure to hold a ballot on the use of the union's funds for political purposes.

   b. That a trade union has failed to bring or continue proceedings to recover funds or property used unlawfully to indemnify an individual

   c. Failure to hold secret ballot for election to the principal executive committee

   d. To restrain the use of trade union funds for unlawful political purposes

   e. Proceedings arising out of an alleged breach or threatened breach of a union's rules in relation to:

      i. Appointment or election of a person to, or removal from, any office.

      ii. Disciplinary proceedings by the union (including expulsion)

      iii. Authorising or endorsing industrial action

      iv. The balloting of members

  v.   Application of union funds or property

  vi. In respect of any levy for the purposes of industrial action

  vii. The constitution or proceedings of any committee conference or other body.

10. Assistance in respect of e. may only be given if the breach in question affects a member of the union other than the applicant.

11. In determining whether or not to grant the application for assistance, the Commissioner may consider:

  a.   Whether the case raises a question of principle

  b.   Whether it is unreasonable, with respect to the complexity of the case, to expect the applicant to deal with it unaided; and

  c.   Whether the case involves a matter of substantial public interest.

The Commissioner is not empowered to provide assistance in the making of an application to the Certification Officer, in industrial tribunals or before the EAT.

COMMISSIONER FOR PROTECTION AGAINST UNFAIR INDUSTRIAL ACTION

12. The Commissioner is appointed under the *TUR & ERA* 1993 (S.21) to consider requests for assistance in proceedings taken by persons suffering from industrial action affecting the supply of goods or services. The matters taken into consideration by the Commissioner are:

  a.   Whether the case is so complex as to make it unreasonable for the applicant to deal with it unaided,

  b.   Whether it is a matter of public concern.

13. If the Commissioner decides not to provide assistance he must notify the applicant as soon as is reasonably practicable with the reasons. If assistance is to be provided the applicant must be notified giving a choice as to financial arrangements in connection with the provision of the assistance.

14. The assistance provided may include arrangements for the Commissioner to bear the costs of:

  a.   Giving of legal advice, and

  b.   The legal representation of the applicant in preliminary steps to the proceedings or in arriving at a compromise to bring an end to the proceedings.

EMPLOYMENT TRIBUNALS

15. Employment tribunals were established for the purpose of resolving disputes between employers and Training Boards arising out of the liability to pay a training levy. Since 1964 the industrial tribunal has assumed many other statutory jurisdictions and have emerged as 'labour courts'. The tribunals have some 30 separate statutory jurisdictions covering virtually every individual employment right which has been created by statute.

16. *Advantages*. The advantages of bringing a case before an employment tribunal are:

   a. The procedure is far simpler than for a case in the County Court.

   b. The interval of time between commencing proceedings and the hearing is much shorter in comparison with ordinary courts.

   c. The formality of tribunals is considerably relaxed being designed to put the parties at ease; procedural rules are interpreted flexibly and the rules of evidence which apply in the ordinary courts are not binding on the tribunal.

   d. They are relatively inexpensive, in comparison with the ordinary courts since legal representation is not encouraged by the rule that costs may only be awarded to the losing party where the complaint is frivolous or vexatious.

17. *Claims*. A person wishing to bring a claim before an employment tribunal is called the 'applicant' and he commences proceedings by lodging an Originating Notice of Application at the Central Offices of employment tribunals (COET). The COET then serves a copy of the application on the defendant who is known as the Respondent who has 14 days in which to return his answer in the form of a Respondent's Notice of Appearance. The COET is also required to notify Conciliation Officers, designated by ACAS, of the claim. These officers have a statutory duty to endeavour to promote a settlement even in the absence of a request from either party, providing there is a reasonable prospect of success. In cases where the CO has been unable to achieve a settlement, the tribunal chairman has powers to order the giving of particulars by one party to the other, the attendance of witnesses and the production of documents. A tribunal may order an applicant to pay a deposit of up to £1,000 as a condition of proceeding with his claim. The *EMPLOYMENT TRIBUNALS (CONSTITUTION AND RULES OF PROCEDURE) REGULATIONS 2001* in attempting to speed up tribunal claims and reduce the number of frivolous claims puts the parties under a duty to assist the tribunal in ensuring that both parties deal on an equal footing, saving expense and dealing with cases in a way that is proportionate to the issues. In addition tribunals have the power to award costs (up to £10,000) where they believe that a party has acted 'vexatiously, abusively, disruptively or otherwise unreasonably, or the bringing or conducting of the proceedings has been misconceived'.

18. *Composition.* Employment tribunals sit in about 80 different centres through Britain, each tribunal consisting of a chairman, who must be a barrister or solicitor of not less than seven years' standing, and two panel members one representing employees' interests and the other employers' interests. Panels of each category of member are nominated; the chairman being appointed by the Secretary of State after consultation with employers' and employees' organisations.

EMPLOYMENT APPEAL TRIBUNAL (EAT)

19. The EAT was established to hear appeals from industrial tribunals. An appeal to the EAT may be made on a question of law arising from any decision of an industrial tribunal under:

   a. The Equal Pay Act 1970;

   b. The Sex Discrimination Acts 1975 and 1986;

   c. The Employment Protection Act 1975;

   d. The Race Relations Act 1976;

   e. The Employment Rights Act 1996;

   f. The Wages Act 1986.

   Additionally, the EAT hears appeals on questions of law from decisions of the CO concerning the political fund rules and amalgamations and on questions of fact and law under the *TULR(C)A 1992* (relating to listing and independence of trade unions), and unfair exclusion or expulsion from a trade union.

20. *Appeals.* An appeal generally lies only on an error of law. In order to succeed the appellant must show:

   a. The tribunal misdirected itself in law, or misunderstood the law or misapplied the law; or

   b. That there is no evidence to support the tribunal's findings of fact; or

   c. That the decision was 'perverse' (ie no reasonable tribunal could have reached such a decision).

21. *Composition.* The EAT is composed of High Court and Court of Session Judges and appointed members who must have industrial relations knowledge or experience. Each appeal is heard by one judge and between two and four appointed members.

22. *Further Appeals.* A decision of the EAT may, with leave, be appealed to the Court of Appeal, and with further leave, to the House of Lords. Such appeals must, however, be on a point of law. On some matters, eg sex discrimination, cases may be referred to the European Court of Justice.

23. *The Employment Rights (Dispute Resolution) Act 1998.* Under this Act, Employment Tribunals are to be allowed to determine proceedings without a

hearing and in private where the parties give their written consent. ACAS conciliation officers may be used for statutory redundancy claims. The Act seeks to facilitate compromise agreements outside of ACAS, encouraging employer 'in house' disciplinary and grievance procedures to be used, with power given to tribunals to reduce or increase compensation awards where an employee refuses to use them or an employer denies access to them.

CHAPTER 62

Trade Unions

INTRODUCTION

1. In this chapter we shall consider the status of trade unions and the liabilities and rights of unions and their members under current legislation which is the *TULR(C)A 1992* as amended by the *TUR 1993, ERA 1996* and *1999*.

DEFINITION

2. A trade union is an organisation (whether permanent or temporary) which either:

   a. Consists wholly or mainly of workers and is an organisation whose principal purposes include the regulation of relations between workers and employers or employers' associations; or

   b. Consists wholly or mainly of:

      i. Constituent or affiliated organisations which fulfil the conditions specified in 2. a. or

      ii. Representatives of such constituent or affiliated organisations; and in either case is an organisation whose principal purposes include the regulation of relations between workers and employers or between workers and employers' associations, or include the regulation of relations between its constituent or affiliated organisations.

LEGAL CAPACITY

3. A trade union is not a body corporate but nevertheless has been given some characteristics of legal personality, so that it can:

   a. Make contracts;

   b. Own property, though it must be vested in trustees;

c. Sue or be sued in its own name in proceedings relating to property or founded in contract or tort or any other cause of action (subject to statutory immunity in tort).

d. Be subject to judgements, orders or awards, in proceedings brought against it.

LIABILITY IN TORT

4. Action in tort may be brought against a trade union if a person suffers loss due to unlawful industrial action organised by its officials. It will be liable for actions inducing breach of contract (or threats to do so) or actions for conspiracy not in contemplation or furtherance of a trade dispute if that action is authorised or endorsed by a responsible person of the union, ie the principal executive committee, any other person empowered by the rules of the union to authorise or endorse such action, the president or general secretary, an employed official, or any committee to whom an employed official regularly reports. The Act makes provision for exemption from liability if the action is repudiated.

TRADE UNION AFFAIRS

5. *Listing of Trade Unions*. An association of employees which falls within the statutory definition of a trade union is entitled to have its name entered on a list of trade unions. This list is maintained by the CO. In order to be listed a trade union must:

a. Pay the requisite fee;

b. Submit a copy of its rules;

c. State the address of its head or main office;

d. Submit a list of its officers; and

e. State the name under which it is known.

6. The CO has the following powers in relation to the list, subject to a right of appeal on questions of both fact and law to the EAT:

a. To prevent the use of a misleading name;

b. Removal of a trade union if it no longer appears to be a union within the statutory definition;

c. Removal of a trade union from the list upon the specific request of that union;

d. Removal where a trade union has ceased to exist;

e. The issue of a certificate of listing, which is evidence of trade union status.

7. The purpose of the certificate of listing is twofold:

    a. It is proof of the trade union's status without which it would be unable to obtain tax relief on its provident fund income; and,

    b. It is a prerequisite for obtaining a certificate of independence.

8. *Certificate of Independence*. A listed trade union may apply to the CO for a certificate that it is independent. The certificate is conclusive evidence of a trade union's independence.

9. *Definition of Independence*. An independent trade union is one which:

    a. Is not under the domination or control of an employer or a group of employers or of one or more employers' associations; and

    b. Is not liable to interference by an employer or any such group or association (arising out of the provision of financial of material support or by any other means) tending towards such control.

10. The importance of the certificate of independence lies in the statutory requirement that a union must be independent in order to:

    a. Enforce rights to information;

    b. Allow individuals to claim protection for trade union membership and activities;

    c. Allow individuals to claim time off for union activities;

    d. Claim consultation in respect of redundancies;

    e. Obtain planning information under the INDUSTRY ACT *1975*;

    f. Appoint safety representatives under regulations issued under the HASAW *1974*.

    g. Be consulted about contracting-out of occupational pension schemes under the SOCIAL SECURITY PENSIONS ACT *1975*;

    h. Take advantage of the financial assistance available for conducting union ballots;

    i. To be able to use employer's premises for the purpose of a secret ballot.

    The absence of a certificate of independence will not in itself prevent a trade union exercising the above rights, but in the event of the union's independence being challenged any proceedings would be stayed until the CO had issued or refused a certificate.

11. Additionally, the CO may withdraw a certificate at any time if he is of the opinion that the union is no longer independent. The CO must, in coming to such a decision, take into account any relevant information submitted to him by any person. Appeal lies to the EAT.

12. The CO is also required to keep a register of independent trade unions which is open to inspection by the public, free of charge, at all reasonable hours.

RECOGNITION

13. For an independent trade union to exercise the rights set out in 10. a. c. d. f. g. and i., it must be one which is 'recognised' by the employer for the purposes of collective bargaining. Recognition must now be achieved voluntarily through the conciliation procedures of *S.2, EPA* may still be exercised by ACAS on application of either party, or otherwise if in the view of ACAS it can achieve a settlement to a dispute.

14. Recognition for collective bargaining purposes may be either express or implied. For recognition to be implied the alleged acts of recognition must be clear and unequivocal and involve a course of conduct or a period of time. NATIONAL UNION OF GOLD, SILVER AND ALLIED TRADES v ALBURY BROS (**1979**).

ANNUAL RETURNS AND ACCOUNTS

15. Detailed requirements with regard to the keeping of accounts, making of annual returns, appointment of auditors and the qualified examination of a report on members' superannuation schemes are contained in the TULR(C)A.

   a. *Duty to keep accounting records.* Every trade union must keep proper accounting records so as to give a true and fair view of the state of its affairs and to explain its transactions, and in particular:

   i. Cause to be kept proper accounting records with respect to its transactions and its assets and liabilities; and

   ii. Establish and maintain a satisfactory system of control of its accounting records, its cash holdings and all its receipts and remittances.

   b. *The Annual Return.* A return must be made in each calendar year to the CO, containing:

   i. Revenue accounts indicating the income and expenditure of the trade union for the period to which the return relates;

   ii. A balance sheet as at the end of that period;

   iii. Such other accounts (if any) as the CO may require;

   iv. A copy of the rules of the trade union as in force at the end of the period;

   v. A note of all changes in the officers of the union and any change in the address of the head or main office of the union during the period to which the return relates;

   vi. A copy of the auditors' report.

   vii. Details of the salary paid to and other benefits provided to each member of the executive, the president and general secretary by the trade union.

   viii. The number of names on the union register and the numbers not accompanied by an address.

c. *Appointment of auditors.* Trade unions must appoint auditors to audit the annual accounts. Generally, such auditors must be qualified to act as auditors of a company incorporated under the Companies Acts. The auditors are required to report on the accounts stating whether, in their opinion, the accounts give a true and fair view of the matters to which they relate.

d. *Members' superannuation schemes.* Before such a scheme is commenced:

    i. The proposals for the scheme must have been examined by an appropriately qualified actuary; and

    ii. A copy of a report made to the trade union by the actuary on the results of his examination, signed by the actuary, must have been sent to the CO.

The CO must keep available for public inspection copies of all annual returns. Every trade union must, on the request of any person supply a copy of its rules and latest annual return, for which it may make a reasonable charge.

AMALGAMATION

16. There are two methods by which a merger of trade unions can be achieved:

a. By an agreed instrument of amalgamation must contain certain matters (a guidance pamphlet is available from the CO) and obtain a simple majority of the members of each union voting by ballot.

b. By a transfer of engagements which involves the transference by one union of all its obligations and assets to the other whilst still retaining its nominal identity. In this method only the members of the transfer union are required to vote and a simple majority of those voting by ballot will suffice.

17. The Act lays down procedural requirements, which in some cases must first be approved by the CO, for the notice informing members of the proposals and for the conduct of the ballot. Additionally there are grounds for complaint, by any member of the unions concerned, to the CO and a right of appeal on questions of law to the EAT. Union merger ballots are to be fully-postal and subject to independent scrutineer. The notice sent out with voting papers for union merger ballots must not make a recommendation or express an opinion about the proposed merger.

THE POLITICAL FUND

18. The procedure for the maintenance and conduct of a political fund, for the protection of the minority is as follows:

a. There must be a secret ballot of the membership of the trade union to approve the establishment of a political fund.

b. Any trade union which has adopted a political fund resolution must pass a new resolution by means of a secret ballot of all its members if it wishes to spend money on political matters. The ballot must be carried out at intervals of not more than 10 years.

c. It is the duty of the union to provide the independent scrutineer with an up to date copy of the membership register and the duty of the scrutineer to inspect it.

d. The union must also ensure an independent count of the votes on the ballot and safe-keeping of the ballot papers.

e. The fund must be financed by a political levy and in no other way.

f. After approval by a simple majority of those voting in the ballot at a. the union must incorporate in its rules special rules, approved by the CO for the conduct of the fund.

g. Members of the union must have the right to contract out and to suffer no discrimination by doing so, except in the control of the fund.

h. The political fund may only be used to promote certain political objects:

   i. Payment of expenses incurred by a candidate or prospective candidate for election to Parliament or any other public office.

   ii. Holding of meetings and the distribution of literature in support of such candidates or prospective candidates;

   iii. Maintenance of a person who is a Member of Parliament or holds any other public office;

   iv. Registration of electors or the selection of a candidate for Parliament or any other public office;

   v. Holding of political meetings of any other kind or the general distribution of political literature, unless the main purpose of these is the furtherance of the statutory objects of the union.

   vi. Complaints regarding any breach of the political fund provisions are dealt with by the CO with a right of appeal to the EAT.

TRADE UNION BALLOTS

19. Specific provision is made for the financing and holding of secret ballots by trade unions.

    a. *Financial assistance in respect of secret ballots.* The Secretary of State is empowered to make regulations providing for financial assistance to be given to independent trade unions holding a secret ballot within the following purposes:

       i. Obtaining a decision or ascertaining the views of members as to the calling or ending of a strike or other industrial action;

    ii. Carrying out an election provided for by the rules of the union;

    iii. Electing a worker who is a member of a trade union to be a representative of other members also employed by his employer;

    iv. Amending the rules of a trade union.

b. *Secret ballots for election of principal executive committees*. The Act requires that all voting members of a trade union's executive committee will be elected by secret postal ballot at least once every five years. All members of the trade union in question must be given a voting entitlement except those who are precluded by the union rules and those in the following classes:

    i. Members who are not in employment

    ii. Members in arrears with union subscriptions

    iii. Apprentices, trainees, students or new members.

c. *Workplace ballot*. Alternatively a workplace ballot may be allowed if it is:

    i. Secret and free from interference or constraint

    ii. Provides a convenient method of voting to members without incurring cost to themselves (eg by forfeiting overtime in order to vote)

    iii. Voting is by ballot paper and votes are fairly and accurately counted.

d. *Secret ballot before industrial action*. A trade union must hold a secret ballot not more than four weeks before taking strikes or other industrial actions to ascertain the wishes of the majority of their members. In the event of failure to do so the union will lose any immunity in tort. The ballot must be conducted by post and involve the marking of a ballot paper. The ballot must be secret and followed by announcement of the voting figures to the members concerned. Entitlement to vote must be given equally to trade union members who it is believed will be called upon to take industrial action, and to no others. Written notice of intent to ballot must be given to an employer at least seven days before the opening of the ballot. The notice includes details of the employees and includes a sample voting paper.

e. *Secret ballots on employer's premises*. An employer with more than 20 workers, has a statutory duty to permit the use of his premises, so far as is reasonably practicable, for the purpose of giving those workers employed by him and who are member of the union, a convenient opportunity of voting. This duty only exists where the request is made by an independent trade union recognised by the employer for the purpose of collective bargaining and where the ballot is in respect of at least one of the questions set out in a. above. Moreover, the proposals for the conduct of the ballot must be such as to secure so far as reasonably practicable, that those voting may do so in secret. Where an employer is in breach of this duty the trade union concerned may complain to an industrial tribunal which has the power to award compensation to be paid by the employer to the union. Appeal on the question of law lies to the EAT. This provision will cease on 31st March 1996 under a provision of the *TUR & ER ACT 1993*.

20. *Postal ballot.* The regulations so far issued only provide for financial assistance to be given in the case of a postal ballot and contain detailed conditions to ensure that payment is not made if the CO is not satisfied that the ballot was properly and fairly held.

    a. The ballot must be conducted so as to secure as far as reasonably practicable, that those voting may do so in secret;

    b. Those voting must be required to do so by marking a voting paper;

    c. Those voting must be required to return the voting papers individually by post to the union or to a person responsible for counting the votes;

    d. The voting paper must contain only questions within the prescribed purposes. Moreover, as regards election of officers, only the positions of president, chairman, secretary, treasurer, executive committee members or other positions whereby the person becomes an employee of the union are permitted under heads ii. and iii.

    e. Payments under the scheme will generally cover the cost of printing stationery and postage and will be made by the CO upon application of the union after the expenditure has been incurred.

TRADE UNION MEMBERSHIP

21. *Rules.* The statutory regulation of trade union rules is as follows:

    a. No rule of a trade union shall be unlawful or unenforceable by reason only that it is in restraint of trade.

    b. Where a union membership agreement exists, an actual or prospective employee is entitled not to have his application for union membership unreasonably refused, and not to be unreasonably expelled from the union. This right is in addition to any common law right that may exist. The question as to whether the trade union has acted reasonably is to be tested in accordance with equity and the substantial merits of the case. Compliance with the rules does not of itself establish reasonableness, nor does a breach automatically demonstrate unreasonableness.

22. *Compensation for Unreasonable Exclusion or Expulsion.* In addition to any common law action a complaint may be made to the employment tribunal in a situation where a person is unreasonably excluded or expelled from a trade union in circumstances where he either is, or is seeking to be, employed by an employer who has entered into a union membership agreement and it is the practice for the employees to belong to a union in accordance with that agreement. The ultimate remedy of the industrial tribunal will of course be compensation since a person could not be forced upon any particular trade union.

23. When a tribunal finds an applicant's case well founded it makes a declaration that the exclusion or the expulsion was unreasonable. There is a right of appeal from the tribunal's decision to the EAT on the question of both law and fact.

24. For the applicant to obtain compensation a further application to either the employment tribunal or the EAT must be made at least four weeks after and within six months after the declaration as follows:

   a. *Industrial Tribunal.* If at the time of the application for compensation the applicant has been admitted or re-admitted to membership of the union against which he made the complaint, the industrial tribunal may award such amount as it considers appropriate for the purpose of compensating the applicant for the loss sustained by him in consequence of the exclusion or expulsion which was the subject of the complaint. Such compensation is payable by the trade union concerned and may not exceed an amount equal to thirty times the current maximum amount of a week's pay for the purposes of calculating the basic award in unfair dismissal cases plus an amount equal to the current maximum compensatory award.

   b. *Employment Appeal Tribunal.* On the other hand, if the applicant has not been admitted or re-admitted to trade union membership at the time of the application for compensation it will be made to the EAT which can award compensation of such amount as it considers just and equitable in all the circumstances. The maximum compensation that the EAT can award is the limit of the industrial tribunal plus a sum equal to fifty-two times the maximum amount of a week's pay for the purposes of calculating additional awards of compensation in unfair dismissal cases.

25. *Exclusion or Expulsion from Membership.* An individual may not be excluded or expelled from a trade union unless it is for a permitted reason. These are:

   a. Not qualified because the union's rules restrict membership to a specified trade or industry, of a particular occupation or in possession of specified qualifications or work experience

   b. The individual's conduct.

   Any individual who claims to have been unreasonably excluded or expelled from a trade union has the right of complaint to an employment tribunal.

26. *Participation in Trade Union Affairs.* The right of the individual member to participate in the affairs of his trade union may be conveniently classified under two headings.

   a. *Positive rights.* Other than the two statutory rights (of voting where a trade union proposes to establish a political fund and where it proposes to amalgamate with another trade union) the positive right of the trade union member to participate in his trade union affairs by attending meetings, voting, seeking office, attending delegate conferences etc, is merely a matter of construction of the contract established by the rules of the trade union.

   In BREEN v AEU (1971) the plaintiff sought a declaration that the decision of a union's district committee to refuse to endorse his election as a shop steward was void as being contrary to the requirements of natural justice. The union claimed that natural justice was inapplicable as the committee's function was not judicial. It was held that natural justice, ie the need to act fairly was applicable. However, in this particular instance the facts indicated that the committee's decision was not biased.

b. *Negative rights.* The member also has a right to restrain any trade union action which is not permitted by its constitution subject to the rule in FOSS v HARBOTTLE (1843). This again is a question of the individual enforcing his right under the contract of membership to prevent the trade union acting in breach of its rules.

In EDWARDS v HALLIWELL (1950) an ultra vires resolution to increase members' subscriptions.

In HODGSON v NALGO (1972) an executive council instruction to delegates attending a TUC conference to vote in favour of Britain joining the EEC contrary to NALGO policy.

Note: The rule in FOSS v HARBOTTLE in this context provides for a minority to restrain a trade union action where it is acting ultra vires. The courts will not permit a minority action to proceed where the action is intra vires though lacking some formality which can be ratified by the appropriate body.

COLLECTIVE AGREEMENTS

27. *Statutory Definition.* A collective agreement as any agreement is defined or arrangement made by or on behalf of one or more trade unions and one or more employer or employers' association and relating to one or more of the following matters:

a. Terms and conditions of employment, or the physical conditions in which any workers are required to work;

b. Engagement or non-engagement, or termination or suspension of employment or the duties of employment, of one or more workers;

c. Allocation of work or the duties of employment as between workers or groups of workers;

d. Matters of discipline;

e. The membership or non-membership of a trade union on the part of a worker;

f. Facilities for officials of trade unions; and

g. Machinery for negotiation or consultation, and other procedures, relating to any of the above matters, including the recognition by employers or employers' associations of the right of a trade union to represent workers in any such negotiation or consultation or in the carrying out of such procedures.

28. *Enforceability.* A collective agreement shall be presumed not to have been intended by the parties to be a legally enforceable contract unless the agreement is in writing, and contains a provision which (however, expressed) states that the parties intended that the agreement shall be a legally enforceable contract.

29. If a collective agreement contains a provision which states that the parties intend that only one or more parts of the agreement shall be a legally enforceable contract, then it will have this effect.

30. The extent to which a collective agreement may be enforced by or against those workers who are covered by it is a question of whether it has been expressly incorporated, in whole or in part into the contract of employment.

31. *The Collective Agreement and Common Law.* The collective agreement is the product of a generally voluntary system of negotiation of terms, and conditions of employment. This is reflected in the presumption as to non-enforceability unless the parties take positive steps to make the agreement legally binding. This presumption, however, applies only to those agreements which fall within the statutory definition. The common law will apply in the case of agreements not conforming to the statutory definition, but it is uncertain what provision is made under common law. There are three possibilities:

    a. It is suggested that there is a general presumption of legal enforceability as there is with any other commercial agreement.

    b. There is the view of the Donovan Commission that collective agreements are not enforceable because the parties do not intend to create legal relations.

    c. In the only recent case raising the issue of enforceability, the Court held that the particular agreements were not enforceable because of the nature and wording of the agreements. The case is no authority, therefore, for adopting a general view of non-enforceability.

    It rather suggests that collective agreements are of such a diverse nature that it is impossible to adopt a universal rule and that each must be considered on the facts at the time. Moreover, some collective agreements do not fulfil a contractual function, and others are too vague to be enforceable.

32. *'No Strike' Clauses.* Any terms of a collective agreement which prohibit or restrict the right of workers to engage in a strike or other industrial action, or have the effect of prohibiting or restricting that right, shall not form part of any contract between any worker and the person for whom he works unless the agreement:

    a. Is in writing; and

    b. Contains a provision expressly stating that those terms shall or may be incorporated in such a contract; and

    c. Is reasonably accessible at his place of work to the worker to whom it applies and is available for him to consult during working hours; and

    d. Is one where each trade union which is a party to the agreement is an independent trade union; and unless the contract with the worker expressly or impliedly incorporates those terms in the contract.

33. The effect of this provision is that no court shall, whether by way of an order for specific performance or an injunction restraining a breach of, or threatened breach of a contract of employment, compel an employee to do any work or attend at any place for the doing of any work.

34. The effect of a 'no strike' clause complying with the statutory provisions is therefore limited to circumstances where, for example, procedural requirements like consultation must be exhausted before taking strike action. In such circumstances an injunction could be granted in order that the proper procedure be followed.

35. Right to challenge the validity of the terms of a collective agreement. An employee may present a complaint to an industrial tribunal that a term in a collective agreement is void as being discriminatory under the terms of the Sex Discrimination Act 1975 if he has reasons to believe that:

   a. The terms may at some future time have effect in relation to him, and

   b. An act provided by the term may at some time be done in relation to him and the act would be unlawful.

36. *The Present Law Relating to Immunity in Tort.* An act done by a person in contemplation or furtherance of a trade dispute shall not be actionable in tort on the ground only,

   a. That it induces another person to break a contract or interferes or induces any other person to interfere with its performance; or

   b. That it consists in his threatening that a contract (whether one to which he is a party or not) will be broken or its performance interfered with, or that he will induce another person to break a contract or to interfere with its performance.

   Note: An agreement or combination by two or more persons to do or procure the doing of any act in contemplation or furtherance of a trade dispute shall not be actionable in tort if the act is one which, if done without any such agreement or combination, would not be actionable in tort.

37. *Trade Dispute.* This is defined as a dispute between workers and their employer which is connected with one or more of the following:

   a. Terms and conditions of employment, or the physical conditions in which any workers are required to work;

   b. Engagement or non-engagement, or termination or suspension of employment or the duties of employment, of one or more workers;

   c. Allocation of work or the duties of employment as between workers or groups of workers;

   d. Matters of discipline;

   e. The membership or non-membership of a trade union on the part of a worker;

   f. Facilities for officials of trade unions; and

   g. Machinery for negotiation or consultation, and other procedures, relating to any of the above matters, including the recognition by employers or employers' associations of the right of a trade union to represent workers in any such negotiation or consultation or in the carrying out of such procedures.

38. *Acts in Contemplation of Furtherance of a Trade Dispute*. The statutory immunity only applies where industrial action is taken in contemplation or furtherance of a trade dispute. This is traditionally called the '*Golden Formula*' and has recently been subjected to considerable scrutiny by the courts. The following criteria must be satisfied in order to gain the protection of the golden formula:

a. There must be a dispute.

In BBC v HEARN (**1977**) the refusal of technicians to transmit television pictures of the FA Cup Final to South Africa was held not to be a trade dispute.

b. The dispute must fall within the statutory definition of a trade dispute.

In JT STRATFORD & SONS LTD v LINDLEY (**1965**) the plaintiffs hired out barges. A trade union imposed an embargo on the company because one of the company's subsidiaries refused to recognise the union. Members of the union would not return the barges which had been hired out thus rendering the hirers in breach of contract. The company's business was brought to a standstill. The company was granted an injunction against the union as no trade dispute as then defined was shown to exist.

c. The dispute must be between the parties mentioned in 37. above. BEAVER-BROOK NEWSPAPERS LTD v KEYS (**1980**).

d. The action must be in contemplation or furtherance of the dispute. EXPRESS NEWSPAPERS LTD v MACSHANE (**1980**).

39. *Strikes*. A strike is defined for the purpose of computing continuous employment as a cessation of work by a body of persons employed acting in combination, or a concerted refusal of any number of persons employed to continue to work for an employer in consequence of a dispute, done as a means of compelling their employer or any person or body of persons employed, or to aid other employees in compelling their employer or any person or body of persons employed, to accept or not to accept terms or conditions of or affecting employment.

40. In TRAMP SHIPPING CORPN v GREENWICH MARINE INC (**1975**) Lord Denning defined a strike as a concerned stoppage of work by men done with a view to improving their wages or conditions of employment, or giving vent to a grievance or making a protest about something or other, or supporting or sympathising with other workmen in such endeavour.

41. There is no right to strike recognised by British law, though immunity from the consequences is conferred under the law, provided the strike is for a proper purpose. There would seem little argument to contradict the view that a strike is merely one form of industrial action.

42. *Picketing*. Lawful picketing must be:

a. In contemplation or furtherance of a trade dispute; and

b. Only at the following specified places:

i. At or near his own place of work, or

ii. If his last employment was terminated in connection with a trade dispute, at or near his former workplace, or

   iii. If he does not work at any one place or if the place is in a location such that attendance there for picketing is impracticable, any premises of his employer from which he works or from which his work is administered, or

   iv. If he is an official of a trade union, at or near the place of work or former place of work of a member of that union whom he is accompanying and whom he represents; and

  c. For the purpose only of peacefully obtaining or communicating information or peacefully persuading any person to work or abstain from working.

43. Where picketing extends outside the legal limits the persons concerned may not claim the immunity from actions in tort.

44. Additionally, even where picketing falls within the conditions described in 42 above immunity will only be effective if:

  a. The picketing does not constitute secondary industrial action; or

  b. The employer of the pickets is a party to the trade dispute, or, if not, the actions of the pickets fall within the rules of lawful secondary action.

45. *Secondary Action.* Immunity from legal proceedings in tort is not available when the industrial action consists of secondary action which is not lawful picketing. There is secondary action in relation to a trade dispute when a person:

  a. Induces another to break a contract of employment interferes or induces another to interfere with its performance, or

  b. Threatens that a contract of employment under which he or another is employed, will be broken or its performance interfered with, or that he will induce another to break a contract of employment or to interfere with its performance if the employer under the contract of employment is not a party to the trade dispute. Contracts of employment include self-employed and persons employed from an employment agency.

  In MARINA SHIPPING LTD v LAUGHTON AND ANOTHER (**1981**) a blacking action by officials of the International Transport Workers Federation against a Maltese ship was declared unlawful in the Court of Appeal. The court held that for such secondary action to be lawful under the EA 1980 a contract would have to exist between the shipowners and the port authority supplying the services. No such contract had been entered into by the owners, or by the ship's master on their behalf.

  In SHAH v SOGAT 82 (1984) members of SOGAT picketed the premises of the 'Stockport Messenger' a place which was not the pickets' place of work. It was held that the action was unlawful; secondary picketing and an injunction was imposed. The plaintiff also successfully claimed damages for loss of revenue.

46. *Acts to Compel Trade Union Membership.* There is no immunity from liability in tort:

  a. Where a person induces or threatens to induce an employee to break his contract of employment, or interferes with or threatens interference with performance by an employee of his contract of employment, for the purpose of compelling workers to join a particular trade union, where the workers being compelled are employed neither by the same employer nor at the same place of work as that employee.

b. Any term in a contract for the supply of goods or services is void in so far as it purports to require that the whole or part of the work is to be done by persons who are members of a trade union. Thus, union-only or non-union-only labour contracts are void.

47. *Employers' Remedies*. The rights and remedies of an employer who is or has been the target of industrial action are discussed under the following headings:

a. *Remuneration of employees*. Industrial action by employees may constitute a breach, termination or suspension of the contract of employment dependent upon the terms of the contract. Similarly, the giving of notice of intention to take industrial action may be construed as anticipatory breach or repudiatory action or merely as an intention to suspend the contract. In any event it would seem that the employer has no duty to remunerate employees participating in industrial action unless he has expressly or impliedly contracted to do so.

b. *Dismissal of employees*. Where industrial action may be construed as a breach of the contract of employment, the employer may dismiss all employees participating in the industrial action. For unfair dismissal provision see Chapter 56, 26.

c. *Damages*. The employer may have a right to claim damages in tort against workers participating in industrial action for which immunity is not provided by statute. Moreover, a claim for damages in tort may also be impossible against trade unions and their officials. Damages may be awarded against trade unions for certain torts. The limits depend on the total membership of a particular union, eg, £10,000 for less than 5,000 members to £250,000 for 100,000 or more. These limits do not apply in cases of personal injury caused by negligence, nuisance or breach of duty, nor for breach of duty connected with the ownership, occupation, possession, control or use of property.

d. *Injunction*. Where the industrial action is not in contemplation or further-ance of a trade dispute the employer can seek an injunction to restrain such action. The courts, however, will not grant an injunction where its effect is to compel employees to work.

e. *Conciliation*. In the interests of promoting good industrial relations the best solution to industrial action that the employer has available is concil-iation and if necessary with the assistance of ACAS.

48. *Effect of Industrial Action on Employees' Rights*. The consequences for employees participating in industrial action (whether or not in furtherance of a trade dispute) are discussed under the following headings:

a. *Remuneration*. As indicated in the preceding paragraph the employee loses his right to receive remuneration during the industrial action.

b.   *Social security benefits*. An employee is not entitled to unemployment benefit for any period during which he is participating in industrial action. He may, however, be entitled to supplementary benefit in respect of his dependants.

c.   *Guarantee payments*. Employees engaged in industrial action are not entitled to guarantee payments under the terms of the ERA 1996.

d.   *Unfair dismissal*. An employee dismissed because of his participation in industrial action will only be considered as unfairly dismissed in the circumstances outlined in Chapter 56, 26.

e.   *Continuous employment*. For the purposes of redundancy and unfair dismissal, absence due to participation in a strike does not break the continuity of employment, but the period of absence does not count in the computation of the period of continuous employment.

Coursework Questions 43–46 (for answers see pages 690–2)

Typical Exam Questions

43. (a) Ronald, a male employee at Mac's Garage Ltd, left his job without giving any notice to his employer. He had been employed for fifty-one weeks. He has confided to you that the reason he left was because of persistent, and sometimes dangerous, practical jokes against him by a number of employees. Despite addressing his grievances to Mac, the garage owner, the problem had persisted for a further six months without any direct action by Mac.

Mac is threatening to sue Ronald for breach of contract, and Ronald seeks your advice as to whether he has a claim against the garage, or whether he is liable for breach of contract.

Advise Ronald. (8 marks)

(b) You have been asked by the board of directors to prepare a report regarding the proposed redundancy of some fifty employees.

Your report should consider the procedures they need to follow: selection criteria, entitlement based on age and length of service, and whether re-deployment is to be considered.

(12 marks)

(20 marks)

ICSA November 2004

44. Explain in detail the main duties owed by employers to employees under legislation, and those implied, in the context of health and safety in the workplace.

(20 marks)

ICSA November 2004

45. When must an employer must provide an employee with a written statement of particulars of the employment

A within one month of the employment commencing;

B as soon after the commencement of employment as possible;

639

    C within two months of the employment commencing;

    D within a reasonable time of the employment commencing;

CIMA November 2001

46. Which ONE of the following statements is *correct*?

    A An employer is obliged to provide a careful and honest reference.

    B An employer is obliged to provide a safe system of work.

    C An employer is obliged to provide employees with smoking facilities during authorised breaks at work.

    D An employer with fewer than 20 employees is obliged to provide an itemised written pay statement.

CIMA November 2001

Suggested Answers to Coursework Questions

Introduction

1. The answers in this appendix serve three purposes:

   a. They illustrate the style and structure of legal answers.

   b. They are a valuable means of self-testing.

   c. They provide an incentive to practise.

2. The way to use these answers is:

   a. First attempt the question. Your attempt may be a 'timed' answer, ie written in 30–35 minutes without the aid of notes or textbooks, or a 'model' answer, ie an examination-length answer prepared in as much time as necessary, using all available resources.

   b. Then, and only then, read the suggested answer. You can then critically assess your own answer, perhaps awarding yourself a mark, or even rewriting the answer if you consider your attempt very poor.

3. The authors would like to make it clear that although many of the questions have been selected from past ACCA, CIMA and ICSA examination papers, the solutions have been prepared by the authors and do not represent the official solutions of the examining boards concerned.

SUGGESTED ANSWERS TO COURSEWORK QUESTIONS 1–7, PAGES 92–3

THE ENGLISH LEGAL SYSTEM

1. Precedent

The doctrine of binding precedent, or *stare decisis*, lies at the heart of the English legal system. The doctrine refers to the fact that within the hierarchical structure of the English courts, a decision of a higher court will be binding on a court lower than it in that hierarchy. When judges try cases they will check to see if a similar situation has come before a court previously. If the precedent was set by a court of equal or higher status to the court deciding the new case then the judge in the present case should normally follow the rule of law established in the earlier case.

(a) The Hierarchy of the Courts

The House of Lords stands at the summit of the English court structure and its decisions are binding on all courts below it in the hierarchy. As regards its own previous decisions, up until 1966 the House of Lords regarded itself as bound by its previous decisions. In a Practice Statement ([1966] 3 All ER 77) of that year, however, Lord Gardiner indicated that the House of Lords would in future regard itself as free to depart from its previous decisions where it appeared right to do so. There have been a number of cases in which the House of Lords has overruled or amended its own earlier decisions (eg CONWAY v RIMMER (**1968**); HERRINGTON v BRITISH RAIL BOARD (**1972**); MILIANGOS v GEORGE FRANK (TEXTILES) LTD (**1976**); R v SHIVPURI (**1986**)) but this is not a discretion that the House of Lords exercises lightly. It has to be recognised that in the wider context the House of Lords is no longer the supreme court and its decisions are subject to decisions of the European Court of Justice in terms of European Community law, and, with the implementation of the Human Rights Act 1998, the decisions of the European Court of Justice in matters relating to human rights.

The Court of Appeal. In civil cases the Court of Appeal is generally bound by previous decisions of the House of Lords and its own previous decisions. There are, however, a number of exceptions to this general rule. The exceptions arise where:

(i)   there is a conflict between two previous decisions of the Court of Appeal;

(ii) a previous decision of the Court of Appeal has been overruled by the House of Lords. The Court of Appeal can ignore a previous decision of its own which is inconsistent with European Community law or with a later decision of the European Court;

(iii) the previous decision was given *per incuriam*, ie in ignorance of some authority that would have led to a different conclusion (YOUNG v BRISTOL AEROPLANE CO LTD (**1944**)).

Courts in the criminal division, however, are not bound to follow their own previous decisions which they subsequently consider to have been based on either a misunderstanding or a misapplication of the law. *The Divisional Courts of the High Court* are bound by the doctrine of *stare decisis* in the normal way and must follow decisions of the House of Lords and the Court of Appeal. They are also normally bound by their own previous decisions, although in civil cases it may make use of the exceptions open to the Court of Appeal in YOUNG v BRISTOL AEROPLANE CO LTD, and in criminal appeal cases the Queen's Bench Divisional Court may refuse to follow its own earlier decisions where it feels the earlier decision to have been wrongly made.

The High Court is bound by the decisions of superior courts. Decisions by individual High Court judges are binding on courts inferior in the hierarchy, but such decisions are not binding on other High Court judges although they are of strong persuasive authority and tend to be followed in practice.

Crown Courts cannot create precedent and their decisions can never amount to more than persuasive authority. County courts and *Magistrates' courts* do not create precedents. It is important to establish that it is not the actual decision in a case that sets the precedent; that is set by the rule of law on which the decision is founded. This rule, which is an abstraction from the facts of the case, is known as the *ratio decidendi* of the case. Any statement of law that is not an essential part of the *ratio decidendi* is, strictly speaking, superfluous; and any such statement is referred to as *obiter dictum*, ie said by the way. Although *obiter dicta* statements do not form part of the binding precedent they are persuasive authority and can be taken into consideration in later cases.

Advantages of Case Law

There are numerous perceived advantages of the doctrine of *stare decisis*, such as:

(i) *Time saving*. This refers to the fact that it saves the time of the judiciary, lawyers and their clients for the reason that cases do not have to be re-argued. In respect of potential litigants it saves them money in court expenses because they can apply to their solicitor/barrister for guidance as to how their particular case is likely to be decided in the light of previous cases on the same or similar points.

(ii) *Certainty*. Once the legal rule has been established in one case, individuals can act with regard to that rule relatively secure in the knowledge that it will not be changed by some later court.

(iii) *Flexibility*. This refers to the fact that the various mechanisms by means of which the judges can manipulate the common law provides them with an opportunity to develop law in particular areas without waiting for Parliament to enact legislation.

The main mechanisms through which judges alter or avoid precedents are:

Overruling, which is the procedure whereby a court higher up in the hierarchy sets aside a legal ruling established in a previous case. Distinguishing, on the other hand, occurs when a later court regards the facts of the case before it as significantly different from the facts of a cited precedent. Consequently it will not be bound to follow that precedent. Judges use the device of distinguishing where, for some reason, they are unwilling to follow a particular precedent.

Disadvantages of Case Law

(i) *Uncertainty*. This refers to the fact that the degree of certainty provided by the doctrine of *stare decisis* is undermined by the absolute number of cases that have been reported and can be cited as authorities. This uncertainty is increased by the ability of the judiciary to select which authority to follow through use of the mechanism of distinguishing cases on their facts.

(ii) *Fixity*. This refers to the possibility that the law in relation to any particular area may become set on the basis of an unjust precedent with the consequence that previous injustices are perpetuated. An example of this is the long delay in the recognition of the possibility of rape within marriage, which has only been recognised relatively recently.

(iii) *Unconstitutionality*. This is a fundamental question that refers to the fact that the judiciary are in fact overstepping their theoretical constitutional role by actually making law rather than restricting themselves to the role of simply applying it.

2. Parliamentary 'sovereignty' is a fundamental principle of English law and means that each Parliament can make such law by statute or by delegated powers as it thinks necessary. Earlier statutes may be repealed; case law may be overruled eg the *WAR DAMAGE ACT 1965* (BURMAH OIL v LORD ADVOCATE); new law can be made; existing law altered; common law can be put on a statutory basis by means of a codifying statute eg the *SALE OF GOODS ACT 1979*; consolidating statutes can be passed eg the *COMPANIES ACT 1985*. No one Parliament can pass legislation which will bind a future Parliament to any particular course of action eg VAUXHALL ESTATES v LIVERPOOL CORPORATION.

Whilst the courts must apply the law as laid down by Parliament, they do have some control over the matter by way of their constitutional role of interpreting statue law (see the rules of Statutory Interpretation); this can lead to some meaning being given to a statute which was not intended by Parliament.

However, the essential validity of statute cannot be questioned, eg CHENEY v CONN; BRITISH RAILWAYS BOARD v PICKIN. In countries with a written constitution (eg the USA), on the other hand, 'unconstitutional' legislation made by the statutory law-making body can be challenged in court.

The entry of the United Kingdom into the European Community in 1973 has placed some fetters on the complete sovereignty of Parliament. Under the *TREATY OF ROME* there is an obligation to bring United Kingdom law into line with the Treaty. Regulations may be made and these have the force of law in member states. See eg COSTA v ENEL; MINISTER OF FINANCE v SIMMENTHAL.

The *HUMAN RIGHTS ACT 1998*, which came into focus in 2000, provides that English law must comply with the provisions of the European Convention on Human Rights. English courts now have the power to declare that laws passed by parliament are inconsistent with the provision of the Convention. (This is not the power to strike down such laws as being unconstitutional.)

Examiner's comments

Quite a popular question. In general, there were a small number of reasonable answers and many below the required standard.

A lot of candidates displayed a disappointing lack of knowledge of the subject matter as a whole, with some launching into a detailed description/explanation of parliamentary *procedure*, which meant that they had strayed off the point of the question. The question required a detailed and precise answer containing authority from the case law, being another routine question on parliamentary *legal* authority.

3. 'Direct applicability' and 'direct effect' are key concepts of European Community Law. Direct applicability means that some provision of European Community Law is directly, ie automatically, part of the domestic (national) law of a member state of the European Union. It is not necessary for a member state to incorporate the provision in domestic legislation.

Direct effect, on the other hand, means that some provision of European Community Law creates individual rights, which can be enforced in national (domestic) courts. In fact, direct effect takes two forms viz 'vertical direct effect', ie individual rights which can be enforced against a national (member) state and 'horizontal direct effect', ie individual rights, which can be enforced against other individuals.

The distinction between direct applicability and direct effect forms the background to European Union 'secondary' legislation, ie Regulations, Directives and Decisions. It is necessary, therefore, to examine each of these in turn.

Regulations

These are 'self executing' (ie have direct applicability) in each European Community State, to achieve uniformity of law throughout the European Community and are used generally to implement the basic aims of the Treaty of Rome, eg establishing a single, unrestricted market in the European Community in manufactured goods. Indeed, national (domestic) acts of incorporation are usually prohibited so that member states will not advertently or inadvertently alter the Regulations in any way. Domestic legislation may be needed on occasion. See, eg EC COMMISSION V UK (TACHNOGRAPHS). Since Regulations are meant to be directly applicable they are also directly effective vertically and horizontally.

Directives

These are issued to member (national) States and must be incorporated into their national laws within some specified time limit (usually two years). See, eg the *COMPANIES ACT 1989*, which gives effect to the 8th Directive. Individuals are usually affected in the UK when Parliament passes the relevant statute or executes a statutory instrument. Directives give rights to individuals only, they do not impose on individuals obligations to the state. They constitute the most significant form of incorporation of EU laws into UK system of law. Directives have direct effect vertically; it is not yet clear whether they have direct effect horizontally before incorporation into domestic law, other than in some indirect way.

See, eg MARSHALL V SW HAMPSHIRE AHA; VAN COLSON; MARLEASING; FRANCOVICH; FACTORTAME 4.

Decisions

These are individual Acts, addressed by the EC Commission, to a specific specified person or persons, company or companies, state or states; they are of an administrative nature and have the full force of law, ie are immediately binding on the particular addressee(s). Decisions have effect without further expansion.

Examiner's comments

This was quite a popular question. Generally, there was a fair balance between competent and incompetent answers, with a small number of good ones.

In some instances candidates were confused and discussed the differences between common law and equity.

This was a fairly straightforward question requiring a description/explanation of the differences between the two types of legal 'effect'. The use of clear, unambiguous language, with no waste of precious time on excess verbiage, is essential.

4. The English legal system is one of only three in the world to have a *formally* divided legal profession, in which a lawyer is either a solicitor or barrister. (In some countries, eg the USA, there is an *informal* division of lawyers into 'trial' and 'desk' lawyers.) Each branch has its own separate traditions, training requirements and customs of practice.

Solicitors. In broad terms, a solicitor is a general practitioner: he will deal with clients directly and will engage the services of a barrister when a particular specialism or litigation is required – but many solicitors are themselves experts in their field and many engage in advocacy. Many barristers also engage in a wide variety of work, so the distinction is today not universally clear-cut. The Law Society is the professional body for solicitors. Many 'paralegals' work in solicitors' offices. They are known as 'legal executives' and are regulated by the Institute of Legal Executives. There are also some 'licensed conveyancers'.

Barristers. A barrister is often thought of as being primarily the court advocate/specialist/expert, but many barristers spend as much, if not more, time on drafting, pleadings and writing advice ('opinions') for solicitors.

Barristers work together in 'chambers', but singly and not in partnership; unlike solicitors. The majority of barristers practise in London; solicitors are much more widely dispersed throughout the country.

Only 'professional' clients (eg surveyors, accountants, chartered secretaries) can deal directly with barristers; other clients must deal through solicitors.

The General Council of the Bar is the barristers' governing body, and the Council of Legal education is responsible for education and training. Arguments advanced for retaining a divided profession in formal terms include:

- barristers are allowed thereby to be 'real' specialists (solicitors having identified the basic issues in advance);

- there is a need for advocates experienced in handling juries; if fusion took place barristers would join big firms of solicitors, then there would be fewer barristers (ie advocates) for other solicitors to call upon;

- there would be a loss of quality in advocacy because the specialist knowledge of barristers would be watered down;

- solicitors' overheads are higher then those of barristers;

- there is a need for real specialists in the oral presentation of cases and specialist knowledge of procedures is also important;

- barristers have a special duty to instruct and advise the court.

Arguments used against the present system (ie in favour of fusion) include:

- expense to client;

- inefficiency and delay caused by the 'distance' between solicitors and barristers;

- solicitors' instructions are not always clear enough;

- there is often a problem with 'returned briefs', ie barristers are often too busy to accept work and solicitors have to look elsewhere for a barrister;

- the present system can lead to a waste of talent because people have to specialise too early on in their careers;

- other countries manage without such a formal distinction.

It should also be pointed out that the COURTS AND LEGAL SERVICES ACT *1990* and the ACCESS TO JUSTICE ACT *1999* have eroded the traditional monopolistic split in the profession; there is now an increased advocacy role for solicitors (wider rights of audience, etc) and more of them are becoming judges (traditionally judges have been drawn from the ranks of barristers). Is this a slow move towards 'de facto' fusion?

Examiner's comments

Not a very popular question. Overall, candidates produced unsatisfactory answers to this question.

In some cases candidates wrote about civil and criminal law or common law and equity rather than the legal *profession*.

This was a routine question on the structure of the English legal *profession*. Candidates should have discussed the division between barristers and solicitors.

5. Property is anything that can be owned. English law recognises two basic kinds of property namely real property, which consists of freehold land, and personal property, which is any other property, including leasehold land. Property is classified as real or personal according to the right of action that used to have to be followed to claim a right to such property. If a person was dispossessed of freehold land he had a right 'in rem' (ie in 'the thing') and he could claim back the thing lost by bringing a real action. If a person was dispossessed of any other property he only had a right 'in personam', ie he only had a right against the person who dispossessed him which he could enforce by means of a personal action. The distinction between real and personal actions has long since ceased to exist but the method of classification that it gave rise to is still used.

Real property, ie freehold land, is one of only two legal estates which may exist in land (the other being a term of years absolute, ie a lease). The correct name for this legal estate is the fee simple absolute in possession. This means an estate capable of being inherited, and able to pass to any person under a will or on an intestacy. It must not be subject to any conditions and the owner must be entitled to physical possession.

There are several types of personal property. Leasehold interests in land are known as chattels real, whereas all other personal property is known as chattels personal or pure personalty. (The word 'chattel' is derived from cattle.)

Chattels personal are further sub-divided into choses in action and choses in possession. A chose in action is a property right which can only be protected by legal action, for example a patent, copyright, or shares in a limited company. A chose in possession is property which can be protected by physical control, for example a car, book, or pen. It is interesting to note that although leasehold land has been classified as personal property, the courts since the 15th century have allowed a person dispossessed of such land to bring a real action to eject the trespasser. Thus leasehold land was in this respect similar to freehold land and became known as chattels real. Since the LAW OF PROPERTY ACT 1925 leasehold property has been treated in all respects as real property. An important modern distinction between real property (and leasehold land) and personal property, is the method by which such property must be transferred. Freehold land must be transferred by deed. Leases for more than three years must be granted by deed, even a gift of land must be by deed. In contrast ownership of a chose in possession can usually be transferred by mere delivery, either actual delivery, ie handing over the thing itself, or constructive delivery, for example handing over the keys to a warehouse where the goods are kept. Choses in action may be assigned at law under S.136 LAW OF PROPERTY ACT 1925. This section requires that the assignment is in writing and signed by the assignor. The whole of the interest must be transferred to the assignee and where a debt is assigned written notice must be given to the debtor. There is also a distinction with regards to the creation of real and personal property. Personal property can be created in various ways, for example an artist may paint a picture, a cat may have a kitten or an inventor may be granted a patent. Real property cannot really be created at all. Freehold land may be split and transferred to several people to create new legal estates and leasehold land may revert to freehold at the end of the term of the lease, but the historical origin of freehold land precludes the creation of real property in any literal sense.

6. As the 20th century has progressed the activities of government have widened into more and more new areas, for example the payment of State pensions and Social Security benefits, the compulsory acquisition of land, town and country planning and, more recently, the area of data protection. This has resulted in so many disputes between individuals and the State that it would be impossible to deal with them through the court system. There are also an increasing number of disputes between individuals that are better suited to resolution by administrative tribunals, for example disputes between landlord and tenant over fair rents and disputes between employer and employee over, for example, dismissal or redundancy. Although they are called 'administrative tribunals' their function is judicial and they carry out a significant proportion of the country's judicial work. They generally consist of a legally qualified chairman

and two lay members. Some of the more important tribunals are:

a. *The Lands Tribunal*, established in 1949 to determine, among other things, the level of compensation to be paid when land has been compulsorily purchased.

b. *Social Security Tribunals*, which primarily hear appeals from the decisions of Social Security Adjudication officers.

c. *Rent Tribunals*, to resolve disputes between landlords and tenants in the context of rent legislation which is designed to reduce the unfairness that could arise from an unrestricted free market in rented property.

d. *The Data Protection Tribunal*, to consider, for example, appeals by data users or computer bureaux against the decisions of the Data Protection Registrar, for example a decision to refuse to register a data user.

e. *Industrial Tribunals*, with jurisdiction over disputes concerning statutory employment rights, for example the right to a redundancy payment.

The advantages of tribunals are:

i. They specialise in a particular field and thus have a detailed knowledge of all the issues.

ii. Procedure is simple and informal, so persons appearing at the tribunal are usually more relaxed and better able to present their case.

iii. They are cheaper and quicker than the courts, since there are no court fees and costs, unless one of the parties employs their own lawyer.

iv. Tribunals are usually local so they will have knowledge of local conditions and, if relevant, will be able to inspect local property.

The disadvantages are that some tribunals do not give reasons for their decisions and others sit in private. Also legal aid is generally not available (with the exception of the Lands Tribunal and Employment Appeal Tribunal), consequently some unrepresented persons may not take full advantage of their rights.

The small claims procedure in the county court is referred to as arbitration, but here we are concerned with arbitration arising from commercial contracts under which the parties agree to submit disputes to an arbitrator, who will either be a lawyer or a specialist in a relevant field.

The main advantages of arbitration are that (i) there need not be any publicity and (ii) the arbitrator will have specialist knowledge that a judge would not possess. Arbitration may also be quicker and cheaper than court procedure, but this is not necessarily the case, since both arbitrators and the parties' lawyers can command high fees.

Where the parties have previously agreed in writing to submit the dispute to arbitration, the procedure will be governed by the Arbitration Acts of 1950 and 1979. This means that the arbitrator will have the power to examine witnesses, order the inspection of documents, and take evidence on oath. It is also provided that the award of an arbitrator can be enforced in the same way as a judgement of the court.

The *CONSUMER ARBITRATION AGREEMENTS ACT 1988* regulates the use of arbitration clauses in consumer contracts, by providing that such clauses cannot be enforced against a non-consenting consumer where the amount involved is less than £1,000.

Other forms of Alternative Dispute Resolution are becoming popular. These include:

Early Neutral Evaluation. Where a neutral person, perhaps a lawyer or an expert in a particular field, gives a non-binding opinion on the merits of the case. This can then be used by the parties to negotiate or reach agreement.

Expert Determination occurs where an expert is agreed upon by the parties to settle the dispute which is legally binding.

Mediation involves a mediator working with the parties to reach a settlement or agreed position. Mediation takes two forms: 'evaluative'; where the mediator assesses the strengths and weaknesses of the case, or 'facilitative', where his role is to facilitate/broker an agreement. Mediation has significant advantages in that costs and conflict can be much reduced. If agreement is reached the parties may set out their agreement in a binding contract.

Conciliation is similar to mediation with the conciliator – an outside person actively seeking and putting forward a suggested basis for agreement between the parties. For example ACAS (the Advisory Conciliation and Arbitration Service) has a role in relation to proceedings that may be brought before an Employment Tribunal. The procedure is that when a complaint is presented to an Industrial Tribunal, a copy is sent to the Conciliation Officer. He may try to settle the dispute if asked to do so by either party, or if in his opinion there is a good chance of a settlement. The parties should feel able to speak openly to the Conciliation Officer, since a person's statement is not admissible in evidence in an Industrial Tribunal without that person's agreement.

Med-AB is a procedure that combines mediation and arbitration. Mediation is first tried, if this fails, the dispute is referred to arbitration. It is not unusual for the same independent person to act as both mediator and arbitrator.

Neutral fact finding is a process commonly used in cases where there are complex technical issues to be determined. An expert in the field reviews the merits of the case and makes an assessment; this may then be used as a basis for further negotiations.

7. Multiple Choice

1.1 correct answer B

1.2 correct answer D

SUGGESTED ANSWERS TO COURSEWORK QUESTIONS 8–16, PAGES 174–7

THE LAW OF CONTRACT

8. An *offer* sets out the terms upon which an individual is willing to enter into a binding contractual relationship with another person. It is a promise to be bound on particular terms, which is capable of acceptance. The essential factor to emphasise about an offer is that it may, through acceptance by the offeree, result in a legally enforceable contract. The person who makes the offer is the offeror; the person who receives the offer is the offeree.

Offers, once accepted, may be legally enforced but not all statements will amount to an offer. It is important, therefore, to be able to distinguish what the law will treat as an offer from other statements which will not form the basis of an enforceable contract.

An offer must be capable of acceptance. It must therefore not be too vague (SCAMMEL V OUSTON (**1941**)). In CARLILL V CARBOLIC SMOKE BALL CO (**1893**) it was held that an offer could be made to the whole world and could be accepted and made binding through the conduct of the offeree.

In addition an offer should be distinguished, from the following:

(i) *A mere statement of intention.* Such a statement cannot form the basis of a contract even though the party to whom it was made acts on it (RE FICKUS (**1900**)).

(ii) *A mere supply of information.* As in HARVEY V FACEY (**1893**) where it was held that the defendant's telegram, in which he stated a minimum price he would accept for property, was simply a statement of information, and was not an offer capable of being accepted by the plaintiff.

Invitation to treat

However most difficulties arise in relation to invitations to treat, and it is most important, therefore, to distinguish offers from invitations to treat. These latter are distinct from offers in that rather than being offers to others, they are in fact invitations to others to make offers. The person to whom the invitation to treat is made becomes the actual offeror, and the maker of the invitation becomes the offeree. An essential consequence of this distinction is that, in line with the ordinary rules of offer and acceptance, the person extending the invitation to treat is not bound to accept any offers subsequently made to them.

The following are examples of common situations involving invitations to treat:

(i) *The display of goods in a shop window.* The classic case in this area is FISHER V BELL (**1961**) in which a shopkeeper was prosecuted for offering offensive weapons for sale, by having flick-knives on display in his window. It was held that the shopkeeper was not guilty as the display in the shop window was not an offer for sale but only an invitation to treat.

(ii) *The display of goods on the shelf of a self-service shop*. In this instance the exemplary case is PHARMACEUTICAL SOCIETY OF GREAT BRITAIN V BOOTS CASH CHEMISTS (**1953**). The defendants were charged with breaking a law which provided that certain drugs could only be sold under the supervision of a qualified pharmacist. They had placed the drugs on open display in their self-service store and, although a qualified person was stationed at the cash desk, it was alleged that the contract of sale had been formed when the customer removed the goods from the shelf. It was held that Boots were not guilty. The display of goods on the shelf was only an invitation to treat. In law, the customer offered to buy the goods at the cash desk where the pharmacist was stationed.

(iii) *A public advertisement*. Once again this does not amount to an offer. This can be seen from PARTRIDGE V CRITTENDEN (**1968**) in which a person was charged with 'offering' a wild bird for sale contrary to the *PROTECTION OF BIRDS ACT 1954*, after he had placed an advert relating to the sale of such birds in a magazine. It was held that he could not be guilty of offering the bird for sale as the advert amounted to no more than an invitation to treat. However, this should be contrasted with decisions such as that in CARLILL V CARBOLIC SMOKE BALL CO (**1893**), where the relevant newspaper advertisement in that case was held to be an offer. The differences between the groups of cases of which the above examples are representative illustrations rest in the intention of the advertiser (this was a particularly strong point in Carlill) and in the fact that the contract envisaged in such cases as Carlill is a unilateral contract and not a bilateral contract.

In other situations where a unilateral contract is envisaged (the 'reward' cases) newspaper and other advertisements are treated as offers. With regard to the contractual status of invitations to traders to submit tenders, the position is that a tender will be regarded as the offer which the person or body seeking the goods or services is free to accept or not.

(iv) *A share prospectus*. Contrary to common understanding such a document is not an offer. It is merely an invitation to treat, inviting people to make offers to subscribe for shares in a company.

9. This question asks candidates to consider the rules relating to the award of damages for breach of contract.

Damages is the common law remedy for breach of contract and, unlike discretionary equitable awards, is available as a right where a pecuniary loss has been sustained by the innocent party. In deciding what damages are to be paid, the courts deploy a number of rules and principles to guide their action. These various rules may be considered under two headings: the rules relating to remoteness of damage and rules relating to the measure of damages.

(a) *Remoteness of damage*

It would be unfair if the party in breach of contract were held to be liable for every consequence of their action no matter how far down the chain of causation it appeared. In order to limit potential liabilities, the courts have established clear rules about consequential liability in such a way as to deny the award of damages for consequences that are deemed to be too remote from the original breach. The rule relating to remoteness of damages was clearly stated for the first time in HADLEY v BAXENDALE (1854) to the effect that damages will only be awarded in respect of losses which:

(i) arise naturally, ie in the usual course of events; or

(ii) both parties may reasonably be supposed to have contemplated as a probable result of its breach when the contract was made.

As a consequence of the first part of the rule in HADLEY v BAXENDALE, the party in breach is deemed to expect the normal consequences of the breach, whether they actually expected them or not. It does not matter that they did not actually think of the consequences if those consequences were the natural outcome of their breach. Under the second part of the rule, however, the party in breach can only be held liable for abnormal consequences where they have actual knowledge that the abnormal consequences might follow. In VICTORIA LAUNDRY LTD v NEWMAN INDUSTRIES LTD (1949) it was decided that the plaintiff could claim damages in relation to the loss of normal profits due to the defendant's delay, as that loss was a natural consequence of the delay. A second claim for damages in relation to an especially lucrative contract failed, however, on the grounds that the loss was not a normal one, but was a consequence of an abnormal contract, about which the defendant knew nothing. The decision in the *Victoria Laundry* case was confirmed by the House of Lords in THE HERON II (1969), although the actual test for remoteness was reformulated in terms of whether the consequence should have been 'within the reasonable contemplation of the parties' at the time of the contract.

(b) *The measure of damages*

The courts use a number of rules and principles to determine the actual extent of monetary damages owed. The general rule is that damages in contract are intended to be compensatory rather than punitive. The aim is to put the injured party in the same position they would have been in had the contract been properly performed. As the object is not to punish the party in breach but to compensate the injured party for any financial loss sustained as a consequence of the other party's breach, so the amount of damages awarded can never be greater than the actual loss suffered. It should be noted that the exact amount of the loss may differ depending on whether the innocent party's reliance interest or expectation interest is used as the criterion against which damages are measured. In practice it is usually the expectation loss that is compensated except where this permits the innocent party to escape responsibility for any loss they would have made in the contract in the absence of breach (see CCC FILMS (LONDON) LTD v IMPERIAL QUADRANT FILMS LTD (1985)).

Where the breach relates to a contract for the sale of goods, damages are usually assessed in line with the market rule. This means that if goods are not delivered under a contract, the buyer is entitled to go into the market and buy similar goods, and pay the market price prevailing at the time. They can then claim the difference in price between what they paid and the original contract price as damages. Conversely, if a buyer refuses to accept goods under a contract, the seller can sell the goods in the market, and accept the prevailing market price. Any difference between the price they receive and the contract price can be claimed in damages.

The injured party is under a duty to take all reasonable steps to mitigate their loss. So in the above examples, the buyer of goods which are not delivered has to buy the replacements as cheaply as possible; and the seller of goods which are not accepted has to try to get as good a price as they can when they sell them. In such a way they are expected to minimise the actual loss they sustain, as may be seen in PAYZU v SAUNDERS (**1919**).

The foregoing has dealt with losses that are relatively easily quantified in monetary terms but matters are more complicated when it comes to assessing damages for non-pecuniary loss.

At one time, damages could not be recovered where the loss sustained through breach of contract was of a non-financial nature. The modern position is that such non-pecuniary damages can be recovered. Thus in JARVIS v SWAN TOURS LTD (**1973**) it was held that the plaintiff was entitled to recover, not just the substantial financial loss he suffered, but also for loss of entertainment and enjoyment which amounted to an even greater sum. The job of estimating damages may be made much simpler where the parties to an agreement make provisions for possible breach by stating in advance the amount of damages that will have to paid in the event of any breach occurring. Damages under such a provision are known as liquidated damages. They will be recognised by the court as long as they represent a genuine pre-estimate of loss, and are not intended to operate as a penalty against the party in breach. If the court considers the provision to be a penalty, it will not give it effect, but will award damages in the normal way (DUNLOP v NEW GARAGE & MOTOR CO (**1915**)).

10. The question is designed to test candidates' knowledge of the elements of agreement in the form of valid offers and acceptances.

Suggested Approach

– Identify offer and acceptance as the main elements of agreement.

– Proceed to explain what amounts to valid offers and acceptances in the various types of business communication.

Examiner's Comments

This was a question on one of the fundamental aspects of contract law.

Common Error

– The question only required an explanation of *agreement*. Far too many candidates wasted time by explaining all the elements of a *contract*.

11. Some contracts become impossible to perform though performance was possible at the time they were made; eg where countries go to war, as in AVERY v BOWDEN.

In the English law of contract the doctrine of 'frustration' has produced a rule which, in certain limited circumstances, the courts will apply to initially enforceable contracts rendering those contracts unenforceable against the parties involved. In other words, the contracts are frustrated in law. See eg DAVIES CONTRACTORS V FAREHAM UDC.

In the following, exceptional, situations frustration may take place:

a) Where a contract depends on the continued existence of some 'thing' and that 'thing' is destroyed: eg TAYLOR V CALDWELL.

b) Where a contract depends on some event taking place and that does not happen: eg KRELL V HENRY; HERNE BAY STEAMBOAT CO V HUTTON.

c) The death or illness of a party to a contract for personal services: eg CONDOR V BARRON KNIGHTS.

d) Where there is a Government prohibition or performance: eg METROPOLITAN WATER BOARD V DICK, KEER AND CO.

e) Where there is a change in the law, making performance illegal: eg AVERY V BOWDEN.

f) Where the method of performance becomes impossible, not where there is self-induced frustration and in some cases involving leases of land: eg NATIONAL CARRIERS LTD V PANALPONA LTD.

A frustrated contract is regarded as discharged, but it is not void 'ab initio'. Thus it is crucial that the parties should know who is to bear losses and who should pay for services already tendered.

The *LAW REFORM (FRUSTRATED CONTRACTS) ACT 1943* provides that

a) Money paid before frustration took place ceases to be payable;
b) Money payable before frustration took place ceases to be payable;
c) Any benefits conferred before frustration took place have to be paid for, and a party who had incurred expenses can claim compensation; eg BP V HUNT.

The Act can be excluded by agreement and does not apply to charter-parties, carriage of goods by sea, sales of specific goods and insurance contracts.

At common law, distribution of loss is only allowed where there has been a total failure of consideration: see the FIBROSA case.

In European contract law two articles in the principles provide for the situation where a contract is affected by a change of circumstances.

Article 6.111 provides that in general a change of circumstances, which makes the performance of a contract more onerous, does not allow a party to the contract to escape liability. However, where performance becomes 'excessively onerous' the parties have to 'enter into negotiations with a view to adapting the contract or ending it.'

Article 8.108 provides that a party may escape liability for non-performance due to an impediment' beyond the party's control.

Examiner's comments

Quite a popular question. Although there were some competent answers, many candidates merely listed all the forms of discharge.

This was a routine question on discharge of contract by *frustration* (in the *legal* sense) and the legal effects of a frustrated contract.

Arguments should always be supported by reference to decided authority, where available, and reason should always be given for those arguments.

12. Multiple Choice

    (a) correct answer B

    (b) correct answer B

    (c) correct answer C

    (d) correct answer B

    (e) correct answer A

    (f) correct answer D

    (g) correct answer C

13. a. A person who alleges that he has been the victim of a misrepresentation will have a remedy if either a fraudulent, negligent or innocent misrepresentation has been committed and neither a defence nor a 'bar' prevents him claiming his remedy.

    A misrepresentation is an untrue statement of fact which is one of the causes which induces the contract. A fraudulent misrepresentation is a statement which is known to be false, or made without belief in its truth, or recklessly, not caring whether it is true or false (DERRY v PEEK (1889)). A misrepresentation is innocent if the maker of the statement honestly and reasonably believes it to be true.

    A misrepresentation will be negligent if the maker believes it to be true, but has no reasonable grounds for that belief. A fraudulent misrepresentation makes a contract voidable, and whether or not it is avoided, it gives the innocent party a right to damages in tort for deceit.

    A statutory remedy for misrepresentation is provided by *S.2(1) MISREPRESENTATION ACT 1967* whereby the innocent party has a right to damages if he has suffered loss. However, if the maker of the statement proves that he had reasonable grounds for believing, and in fact did believe, up to the time the contract was made, that the facts represented were true, then he has a defence. If he is successful in this defence the misrepresentation will be innocent, if he is unsuccessful then it will be negligent.

    The equitable remedy of rescission is also available where there has been an innocent misrepresentation. Since the 1967 Act this remedy is no longer lost if the representation is incorporated into the contract *(S.1)*. In addition *S.2(2)* gives the court a discretion to award damages in lieu of rescission if it thinks it equitable to do so. These damages may be awarded even if the *S.2(1)* defence of reasonable belief is available.

    The remedy of rescission, or damages in lieu, may not be awarded if any of the bars apply. The bars are

i. *Impossibility of restoration to the pre-contract situation*, for example if the subject matter of the contract has deteriorated.

ii. *Affirmation.* If the innocent party, with knowledge of his right to rescind, affirms the contract.

iii. *The intervention of third party rights.* For example, a person cannot rescind an allotment of shares in a company if the company has gone into liquidation. The third party rights in question are the rights of creditors (and others) who are entitled to the company's assets.

iv. *Lapse of time.* Where the misrepresentation is fraudulent lapse of time does not itself bar rescission because time only begins to run from discovery of the truth. An example concerning innocent misrepresentation is LEAF v INTERNATIONAL GALLERIES (1950), where the plaintiff was induced to buy a painting by an innocent misrepresentation that it was by John Constable. Five years later he discovered the truth and immediately claimed rescission. He could not therefore have affirmed the contract but his claim was held to be barred by lapse of time.

b. The general rule is that a party is under no duty to disclose material facts known to him but not to the other party. Thus in FLETCHER v KRELL (1872) it was held that a person who applied for the post of governess did not need to disclose the fact that she was a divorcee. A person must, however, disclose facts that falsify an earlier statement made by him. In WITH v O'FLANAGAN (1936) a doctor who wished to sell his practice stated in January, at the start of negotiations, that it was worth £2,000 per year. He then fell ill and by May, when the contract was signed, the practice was almost worthless. The contract was set aside on the ground that the doctor should have communicated this change of circumstances to the purchaser.

Ivan cannot, however, base any claim on WITH v O'FLANAGAN since the case is only relevant if a later event falsifies an earlier representation. Since there is no 'later event' Ivan is restricted to arguing that the statement, although literally true, was misleading. It is difficult to succeed in such a claim. In NOTTS PATENT BRICK AND TILE COMPANY v BUTLER (1886) a solicitor stated that he was not aware of any restrictive covenants affecting some land. He did not say that this was because he had failed to read the relevant documents. The plaintiff was successful. However, in Ivan's case there is no authority to suggest that he would succeed. It is not a contract *uberrimae fidei*, there is no special relationship between Ivan and Henry and the facts are not especially unusual. If Ivan had asked for more detailed information presumably it would have been given. It is therefore suggested that the general rule of *caveat emptor* (let the buyer beware) applies, leaving Ivan without a remedy.

14.a. The general rule is that mistake does not affect the validity of a contract. For example if X purchases an imitation leather briefcase in the mistaken belief that it is real leather he cannot return it to the shop and claim his money back. There are several common law and equitable exceptions to this general rule.

If a common law exception applies the mistake is said to be 'operative' and the contract is void. This will occur

i.   When the parties make a mistake as to the existence of the subject matter. For example in GALLOWAY v GALLOWAY (1914) a separation deed between a man and woman who mistakenly thought they were married to each other was held to be void because it purported to deal with a marriage which did not exist.

ii. When there is a mistake as to the possibility of performing the contract. For example in COOPER v PHIBBS (1867) a person took a lease of land which, unknown to either party, already belonged to him. The lease was set aside since it was impossible to perform.

iii. When there is a mistake as to the identity (not the quality) of the subject matter. ie Where A intends to sell 'Product X', but B intends to buy 'Product Y'.

iv. When there is a mistake as to the identity of the other party. Such a mistake cannot be made if the parties deal face to face. Furthermore the innocent party must be led to believe that he is dealing with another existing person. The contract will not be void if he believes that he has made a contract with a person who in fact does not exist.

v.   When a person makes a mistake as to the terms of the contract of which the other party is aware. In HARTOG v COLIN AND SHIELDS (1939) a seller of skins mistakenly offered them at a price per pound instead of per piece. The buyer, knowing of the mistake, accepted the offer, but later failed in his attempt to sue for non-delivery.

The equitable remedies for mistake are rescission and rectification. Both are confined to fairly narrow limits. Rescission will only be granted if the party seeking to rescind was not at fault and provided justice can be done to the other party by imposing conditions.

In SOLLE v BUTCHER (1950) a flat was let for £250 per annum. The parties thought the flat was free from rent control, but this was not the case and it was subject to standard rent of £140 per annum. If the lessor had known this he could, before granting the lease, have increased the rent to about £250 per annum because of work done by him to the flat. The tenant claimed that the standard rent should apply and he sought repayment of the excess he had paid. The lessor claimed rescission of the lease. Rescission was granted, but since it was unjust to turn the tenant out of the flat the court gave him the option of staying on if he paid the standard rent plus the amount by which the landlord could have increased it, had he been aware of the position when he granted the lease. Rectification may be granted where a clear agreement between the parties has been incorrectly reduced into writing. The court will rectify the written document so that it reflects the true agreement of the parties.

Thus it can be seen that the effect of a mistake on the validity of a contract depends on the type of mistake that has been made.

b.   The situation with John is very similar to LEWIS v AVERAY (1971) where it was held that a person cannot make an operative mistake as to the identity of the other party if they deal face to face. Victoria is, however, the victim of a fraudulent misrepresentation.

With regard to Mary the basic rule is that a person who signs a document is bound even if they have not read the document. A plea of *non est factum* can occasionally assist where a document has been mistakenly signed, but Victoria would have to prove that she was not negligent. She could not do this since a normally sighted and literate person would undoubtedly be negligent if they sign a document without even finding out its basic purpose. Victoria is again the victim of a fraudulent misrepresentation.

Fraudulent misrepresentation renders a contract voidable. Therefore provided Victoria avoids the contract before the cars have been sold to an innocent third parties, she can recover them. However, since 'voidable' means valid until avoided, John and Mary will be able to pass title if they sell before avoidance, in which case Victoria would not be able to recover the cars. She would be limited to damages in tort for deceit. Since John and Mary may have disappeared or may be unable to pay damages, Victoria should avoid the contract as soon as possible by informing John and Mary (if they can be found), or by informing the police.

15. a. Consideration need not be adequate but it must be sufficient. ie It must be something of value in the eyes of the law, although not necessarily of proportionate value to the 'thing' given in return. Some 'things' although arguably of some value are not regarded as valuable consideration.

Thus in PINNEL'S CASE (1602) it was stated that payment on the day that a debt is due of less than the full amount of the debt is not consideration for a promise to release the balance. This rule was approved by the House of Lords in FOAKES v BEER (1884). F owed B a judgement debt of about £2,100. F asked for time to pay and a written agreement was entered into whereby F would make an immediate payment of £500 and the rest by stated instalments. In return B agreed not to take 'any proceedings whatsoever' on the judgement. After the full sum had been paid B claimed £360 for interest and the court upheld the claim.

The scope of the rule is, however, limited by the following factors:

i. Consideration for the creditor's promise to accept part payment can be provided if the debtor does an act which he was not bound by the contract to do. For example early payment of a smaller sum at the creditor's request is consideration for a promise to release the balance. This is an example of accord and satisfaction. The accord is the agreement by which the creditor agrees to waive his rights to the larger sum. Satisfaction is the consideration that the debtor gives for the creditor's promise.

ii. If payment is made by a third party and accepted by the creditor the debtor will have a good defence if sued for the balance. In HIRACHAND PUNAMCHAND v TEMPLE (1911) the father of a young man who was indebted to money lenders sent them a smaller sum of money 'in full settlement' of his son's debt. The money lenders accepted this payment and then sued the son for the balance. Their claim failed.

iii. Where the debtor makes a composition agreement with all his creditors (ie he agrees to pay each creditor an equal proportion of what is owed to them) a creditor who accepts a payment cannot sue for the balance of his debt.

iv. Finally equity has mitigated the hardship that could be caused to a person who relies on a promise that a debt will not be enforced in full. The principle is known as equitable estoppel. It may be expressed as follows:

If X, a party to a legal relationship, promises Y, the other party, that he (X) will not insist on his full rights under that relationship, and this promise is intended to be acted upon by Y, and is in fact acted upon, then X is estopped (stopped because of his own previous conduct) from bringing an action against Y which is inconsistent with his promise, even if Y gives no consideration. ie Y can use the principle of equitable estoppel as a defence against X should X attempt to enforce his original rights. In CENTRAL LONDON PROPERTY TRUST v HIGH TREES HOUSE (**1947**) the plaintiff leased a block flats from the defendant. Due to the war he was unable to sub-let the flats, and so the plaintiff agreed to accept half rent. Six months after the war the plaintiff claimed the full rent for the post-war period. This claim succeeded. However, the court also considered whether the plaintiff would have succeeded if he had claimed the full rent back to the start of the war. Denning, J. (as he then was) said that he would not have been successful because he would have been estopped in equity from going back on his promise.

The importance of equitable estoppel has been reduced by the decision in WILLIAMS v ROFFEY (**1990**) where it was held that a promise to pay an additional sum to secure the performance of an existing and unchanged duty is enforceable unless it was obtained by duress (including economic duress) or the promisor receives no benefit. A promise to perform on time is regarded as conferring a benefit.

b. i. This situation is quite straightforward, a variation of the contract has been agreed and there is consideration for that variation, ie extra remuneration in return for extra distance. D would be successful in his action to recover the agreed extra remuneration.

ii. There is some authority for the view that where D is bound to do something for F, D may rely on his performance of that act as consideration for a new promise made by G to D. For example in SCOTSON v PEGG (**1861**) A agreed to deliver coal to B, or to B's order. B ordered A to deliver it to C. C promised A that he would unload the coal. It was held that A could enforce C's promise because A's delivery of the coal was consideration for C's promise, despite the fact that A was already bound by his contract with B to deliver to C.

The facts of the problem resemble Scotson v Pegg and although a promise to 'assist with unloading' is more vague than a promise to unload, it is likely that Scotson's case would be followed.

16. It is a basic principle of the law of contract that parties should have freedom to contract on whatever terms they wish. However, it has become increasingly necessary to impose limits on the extent to which parties can use exclusion (or exemption) clauses to exclude or limit their liability if certain events occur, such as breach of warranty or negligence. Exclusion clauses are not necessarily undesirable. Between parties of equal bargaining power they are a quite proper means of allocating contractual risk and determining in advance who should insure against that risk. Problems have, however, occurred when large organisations or monopoly suppliers have imposed standard form contracts containing exclusion clauses on a 'take it or leave it' basis on consumers.

The courts firstly seek to control exclusion clauses by insisting that they are properly incorporated into the contract before it is made by signature or by reasonable notice. For example in OLLEY v MARLBOROUGH COURT (**1949**) an exclusion clause in a hotel bedroom was held to be ineffective because the contract had already been made when the guest signed the register at reception.

The exclusion clause must be a integral part of the contract. If it is contained in a document that a reasonable person would not assume contained any contractual terms then the clause will be ineffective. For example in CHAPELTON v BARRY UDC (**1940**) an exclusion clause in a receipt for the hire of a deckchair was not part of the contract, since the receipt was regarded as something which proved payment, rather than something in which one would expect to find contract terms.

If the parties have had long and consistent dealings on terms incorporating an exclusion clause, then the clause may be taken to apply to a particular transaction, even if the usual steps to incorporate it were not taken. Even if the clause has been properly incorporated into the contract by signature, notice or a course of dealings, it will still be ineffective if on interpretation the court does not consider that it has covered the breach that has occurred. The court will tend to interpret J's exclusion clause narrowly and where there is any doubt they will be interpreted against the person seeking to rely on it. Where the clause merely seeks to limit liability rather than exclude liability, the interpretation may not be so strict.

The main statute to impose limitations on the use of exclusion clauses is the *UNFAIR CONTRACT TERMS ACT 1977*. Its main provisions are:

a. A business cannot exclude or restrict its liability for death or personal injury resulting from negligence. Where the negligence causes other loss or damage the exclusion clause will only be effective if it is reasonable.

b. A business cannot exclude or restrict liability for breaches of consumer contracts or standard form contracts unless the exclusion clause is reasonable.

c. In a consumer sale it is not possible to exclude liability for breach of the implied conditions in the *SALE OF GOODS ACT* with regard to title, description, satisfactory quality, fitness for purpose and sale by sample. In a non-consumer sale the implied condition as to title cannot be excluded, but the others may be, provided the exclusion clause is reasonable. A consumer sale is where one party contracts in the course of a business and the other party does not, and the goods are of a type normally supplied for private use or consumption.

Reasonableness is assessed with regard to all of the circumstances which were, or ought reasonably to have been known to the parties when the contract was made. Relevant factors include:

i.   The relative bargaining strength of the parties

ii.   Whether the customer received an inducement (such as a lower price) to agree to the term.

iii. Whether the customer knew or ought to have known of the existence of the exclusion clause.

SUGGESTED ANSWERS TO COURSEWORK QUESTIONS 17– 29, PAGES 244–6

THE LAW OF TORTS

17. In the tort of negligence, even where a *factual* causal link between the commission of the tort and the damage suffered by the claimant is established, it is possible for a defendant to raise the issue of remoteness of damage in *law*. To put it another way, the breach of duty must be a cause of the damage in *law* as well as in *fact*.

Before 1961 the test of remoteness in *law* was based on the rule in RE POLEMIS. According to this rule once *some* reasonably foreseeable was established the defendant was responsible for all the *direct* consequences flowing from the damage.

However, in THE WAGON MOUND (1961), in fairness to defendants, it was held that a defendant would in future only be liable for damage of the *kind* or *type* reasonably foreseeable in the circumstances. Thus, eg if only property damage was reasonably foreseeable in a particular set of circumstances there would be no liability for personal injury suffered in that situation. See, eg, TREMAIN V PIKE; BRADFORD V ROBINSON RENTALS; STEWART V WEST AFRICAN AIR TERMINALS LTD.

There is no requirement under this rule that the damage must be sustained in a precisely foreseeable manner. See, eg, HUGHES V LORD ADVOCATE, but see DOUGHTY V TURNER MANUFACTURING; JOLLEY V SUTTON LBC. Neither is it necessary that the precise extent of the damage be reasonably foreseeable, eg VACWELL ENGINEERING V BDH CHEMICALS. Furthermore, the so-called 'egg-shell skull' rule (or the 'thin skull' rule) constitutes an exception to the WAGON MOUND rule.

This means that a defendant can be held responsible for damage aggravated by the physical or mental peculiarities of the claimant. For example, SMITH V LEECH BRAIN; DULIEU V WHITE; BRICE V BROWN; ROBINSON V THE POST OFFICE; PAGE SMITH.

Examiner's comments

This was not a popular question. A lot of candidates were 'lost' here, with many of them showing only the flimsiest of knowledge, in some cases confusing remoteness in contract with that in tort.

This was a routine question requiring an explanation of the 'reasonable foresight' test of 'kind' or 'type' of damage, as laid down in 'The Wagon Mound' and later cases.

18. (a) This Act imposes liability upon occupiers for the safety of lawful visitors on the premises. An 'occupier' is a person in 'control' of the premises ('occupier' is *not* synomous with 'owner'). See, eg, WHEAT V E LACON & CO LTD. Occupation may be shared.

    'Premises' includes land, buildings and 'any fixed or movable structure'.

    'Lawful visitors' is a term which encompasses invitees, licensees, contractual entrants, and those persons who enter premises under authority of law (eg, under special statutory powers, say the police). Those who enter under public or private rights of way must seek protection under the 1984 Act (or common law).

    The Act imposes the 'common duty of care' on occupiers (S2). This says that an occupier must take reasonable care for the reasonable safety of the visitor whilst that person is using the premises for the purpose (s) for which they are permitted to be there.

    Special care must be taken for the safety of children, and 'professional' visitors may expect a lower degree of care with regard to hazards, which are incidental to their calling, eg ROLES V NATHAN. A mere warning of danger is not sufficient, volenti and contributory negligence are defences and the *UNFAIR CONTRACT TERMS ACT 1977* applies to exclusions/modification of duty.

    (b) This Act is concerned with the duty owed by occupiers to 'non-lawful visitors'. Trespassers are included here.

    The 1984 Act imposes a considerably more limited duty upon occupiers than does the 1957 Act. Under the 1984 Act an occupier must only take reasonable care for the safety of the entrant in relation to specific dangers on the premises viz.

    - The occupier must be aware of the danger or have reasonable grounds to believe it exists.

    - The occupier must know or have reasonable grounds to believe that the entrant is in the vicinity of the danger or is likely to come into the vicinity.

    - The danger must be one against which, in all the circumstances of the case, it is reasonable to expect the occupier to offer some protection. Damage to the entrant's property is not covered under the 1984 Act (unlike the 1957 Act). A warning may have a stronger effect under this Act than under the 1957 Act, and the *UNFAIR CONTRACT TERMS ACT 1977* does not apply to the 1984 Act.

'Premises', etc, have the same meaning as under the 1957 Act, and the same general defences apply as under that Act.

In some situations trespassers may acquire implied licences and so gain the protection of the 1957 Act, eg, EDWARDS v RAILWAY EXECUTIVE.

Examiner's comments

This was not a popular question. A small number of reasonable marks were awarded here but on the whole answers were below the required standard. A fair number of candidates confused the two forms of statutory liability with common law liability even, in some cases, equating it with liability in nuisance and RYLANDS v FLETCHER.

This was an uncomplicated question, requiring only basic definition/explanations of liability of occupiers to lawful visitors under the 1957 Act (part (a) of the question) and liability of occupiers to other entrants under the 1984 Act (part (b) of the question). Case law is of considerable importance in this area of the law, a fact overlooked by too many candidates on this occasion.

19. Multiple Choice;

correct answer D

20. a. The general rule is that if the plaintiff is to succeed in a negligence action he must prove that the defendant has broken his duty of care. An exception occurs when the maxim *res ipsa loquitur* (the thing speaks for itself) applies. In SCOTT v LONDON AND ST CATHERINE DOCKS (**1865**) it was stated that the maxim applies where

> 'the thing is shown to be under the management of the defendant, and the accident is such as in the ordinary course of things does not happen if those who have the management use proper care'.

In such cases there is prima facie evidence of a breach of duty. The burden of proof is then shifted to the defendant who must prove that he did show reasonable care. The existence of *res ipsa loquitur* does not therefore guarantee success for the plaintiff, it is merely a rule of evidence.

For example in WARD v TESCO STORES (**1976**) an accident occurred due to a spillage of yoghurt on a shop floor. It was held that the facts placed a burden of proof upon the shopowners to show that it did not occur because of lack of care on their part. They were unable to do this and the plaintiff therefore succeeded.

b. Harry should consider the possibility of a negligence claim brought against him by Susan. Susan would have to show that Harry owed her a duty of care. She would be able to do this since a road user owes a duty to fellow road users. Susan would also be able to show that she had suffered damage. Susan's difficulty would be in proving that Harry has broken the duty of care since she is in no position to know why the car crashed.

The facts, however, infer negligence. It can be seen that the passage quoted in a. above will apply. '*Res ipsa loquitur*' will therefore shift the burden of proof from Susan to Harry. Thus if he is to avoid liability Harry must show that he has not broken his duty of care. He will be able to do this if he can show that he exercised the care and skill that a reasonable car driver would have exercised. This is an objective test. It therefore may not be sufficient if Harry merely proves that he has done his best.

It is clearly not possible to give any conclusion on the facts given. There are many possible explanations for the brakes failure, for example a negligent service at a local garage. Harry will, however, be presumed by the court to be negligent unless he can provide an alternative explanation indicating that he was not at fault.

21. a. A public nuisance is an unlawful act which endangers the health, safety, or comfort of the public (or some section of it), or obstructs the exercise of a common right. Examples are the sale of contaminated food, or obstruction of the highway. Principles of 'give and take' are relevant to the definition of nuisance. Thus, for example, a temporary highway obstruction of moderate size may be permissible. A private nuisance is an unlawful interference with the use or enjoyment of another person's land. It may consist of actual injury to property as where fumes kill shrubs, or it may be an interference with health or comfort, for example noise, smoke, or smells.

Public nuisance differs from private nuisance in that

(i) it is a crime as well as a civil wrong;

(ii) an isolated act may be a public nuisance;

(iii) it need not involve interference with the use or enjoyment of land;

(iv) several people must be affected;

(v) a right to commit a public nuisance cannot be acquired by long use; and

(vi) it is an unlawful activity, whereas private nuisance is only an unlawful interference, the activity itself normally being lawful.

b. Both noise and vibrations potentially fall within the definition of private nuisance stated above. However, it does not follow that such harm always constitutes a nuisance, regard must be had to the principle of 'give and take' between neighbours. It may be relevant to consider for example how far the act complained of is excessive, its duration and whether the defendant has shown only lack of care.

For example in ANDRAE v SELFRIDGE (1938) a hotel owner recovered damages from the defendant who was demolishing the adjoining premises. Although building and demolition do not usually constitute a nuisance, since they are socially desirable, if the amount of noise and dust created is unnecessarily great, a nuisance will be committed.

It thus appears that the residents will have a good chance of success if they sue Acme Plastics Ltd for private nuisance. They should claim an injunction to prevent the factory from operating until the noise and vibrations have been prevented, and damages for any loss suffered.

In respect of the damage to his house Mr Evans cannot sue for private nuisance since it was an isolated act which caused the damage. He should sue Acme Plastics Ltd for negligence. He would be able to show that he is owed a duty of care, and that he has suffered damage. He would not need to show that the company had broken their duty of care since *res ipsa loquitur* would apply and shift the burden of proof to Acme Plastics Ltd who would have to show that the accident did not occur due to their lack of care. It seems probable that they would not be able to show this. Mr Evans is also therefore likely to succeed.

22. a. CAPARO INDUSTRIES v DICKMAN (1990) is the most recent leading case concerning negligent statements by accountants causing economic loss. The House of Lords stated that the criteria for the imposition of a duty of care were foreseeability of damage, proximity of relationship, and the reasonableness or otherwise of imposing a duty. To establish proximity all of the following factors will typically need to be present.

    i.   The advice was required for a purpose made known to the adviser when the advice was given.

    ii.   The adviser knew that his advice would be communicated to the recipient in order that it should be used for this purpose.

    iii. It was known that the advice was likely to be acted on without independent inquiry.

    iv. It was acted on to the recipient's detriment.

To prove that the loss was foreseeable Thomas would need to show that Albert's advice was typical of the advice given by a practising accountant. He would have some difficulty doing this, since it is not normally within the province of an accountant to give investment advice, particularly since such advisers need to be authorised under the FINANCIAL SERVICES ACT 1986. With regard to proximity Thomas would need to show i. to iv. above. Clearly he would not be able to do this if Albert had made the statements generally or to other persons or for other purposes.

Even if it could be established that a duty was owed, the duty would only be broken if Albert fell below the standard that could be expected of a reasonably competent member of the accountancy profession.

On the facts given it is not possible to come to a firm conclusion, although it seems unlikely that Thomas could succeed.

b. In RONDEL v WORSLEY (1969) the plaintiff, who had been convicted of causing grievous bodily harm sued his barrister, claiming that he would not have been convicted if his case had been conducted properly. It was held that no action could be brought against the barrister. The main reason for the decision is that an action against the barrister would amount to a retrial of the original case, and this would not be in the public interest. However in HALL v SIMONS (2000) the House of Lords ruled that a barrister should no longer have immunity. It was suggested that someone convicted of a criminal offence would first have to exhaust normal judicial process before considering a negligence action against his barrister. Therefore Thomas should lodge an appeal with the Court of Appeal (Criminal Division).

   c.   Charles will be liable to Thomas if he

      i.   Owed him a duty of care,

      ii.   Broke the duty of care, and

      iii.   Thomas suffered damage, which was not too remote, as a result of the breach of duty.

i. and iii. above are present. The problem will be to establish a breach of duty by Charles. If he is to do this Thomas will have to show that Charles did not act as a reasonable car driver. It seems likely that he will be aided by the rule of evidence known as '*res ipsa loquitur*' (the thing speaks for itself). This applies where the 'thing' is under the control of the defendant and the accident is such as in the ordinary course of events does not occur if proper care is taken. If the maxim applies the burden of proof is shifted to the defendant who must show that he did exercise proper care. For example in RICHLEY V FAULL (**1965**) where the facts were similar to those stated in the question *res ipsa loquitur* was held to apply, and since the defendant could not give a satisfactory explanation he was held to be liable. This does not necessarily mean that Charles will be liable, there may be many satisfactory explanations for the skid which are consistent with Charles acting as a reasonable driver, for example the car may have been serviced incorrectly, or Charles may have swerved and skidded to avoid a pedestrian.

   d.   Generally a plaintiff will be entitled to compensation for damage suffered if the damage is the reasonably foreseeable result of the negligent act. However, even though nervous shock is often reasonably foreseeable, the courts are reluctant to apply the general principle of forseeability to such cases. There are two reasons for this, firstly, such injury would be far more easy to fake than physical injury, secondly, it would vastly increase the potential claimants in a particular case, putting pressure on the legal system and causing substantial increases in insurance premiums. Damages for nervous shock are therefore usually limited to situations where the plaintiff actually witnesses the death or serious injury of a close relative (ALCOCK V CHIEF CONSTABLE OF WEST YORKSHIRE (**1991**)). Furthermore the shock must be in the nature of a psychiatric illness, mere grief and sorrow do not entitle the plaintiff to damages. It is therefore clear that Thomas will not be able to sue David.

23. a.   Libel and slander are the two torts that comprise defamation. A defamatory statement is a false statement that tends to injure the plaintiff's reputation or causes him to be shunned by ordinary members of society.

Libel is defamation in a permanent form or a statement made for general reception. It includes writing, pictures and waxworks. Radio, television and theatrical performances are libel by virtue of statute (*DEFAMATION ACT 1952* and *THEATRES ACT 1968*). Slander is a defamatory statement that lacks permanence, for example words or gestures.

The distinction is important for two reasons. Firstly, libel is a crime where as slander is not. Secondly, libel is actionable per se (ie without the need to prove loss). Slander is only actionable per se in the following cases:

i.   If it imputes a crime punishable by imprisonment.

ii.   If it imputes certain diseases eg AIDS.

iii. If it imputes unchastity or adultery in a woman (but not a man).

iv.   If it calculated to damage the plaintiff in any trade, office or profession held or carried on by him.

b. If Quip is to succeed in a defamation action he must prove:

i.   That the statement is defamatory, ie it is false and would tend to lower the plaintiff in the estimation of right thinking members of society or make them shun or avoid that person.

ii.   That the statement refers to him.

iii. That the statement was published, ie communicated to at least one person other than him.

In this case the words (if taken literally) are clearly defamatory unless Red has actually sold secrets to the Russians. Quip's defence would be that such language is commonplace in political debate and that 'sold out' refers to a state of mind rather than acceptance of money, consequently Red's reputation would not suffer. However, it is suggested that this defence would not succeed. Concerning classification as libel or slander, tape recordings present a problem since there is no case on them, however, it is more likely to be libel and this would certainly be the case if the tape were broadcast.

24. a. Vicarious liability means liability for the torts of others, and it arises because of a relationship between the parties. The relationship may be either employer/independent contractor, or employer/employee (master/servant). A parent is not vicariously liable for his child's torts.

The general rule is that the employer is liable for the torts of his servant. A person is a servant if the employer retains the right to control not only the work he does, but also the way in which he does it. This classic test is often unsuitable for professional servants such as doctors. Here it may be necessary to consider such criteria as payment of salaries and the power of dismissal.

If the master is to be vicariously liable, the servant's tort must be committed within the course of his employment. The tortious act must be a wrongful way of going what the employee is employed to do. It may be negligent, fraudulent, or even forbidden provided it is within the scope of his employment.

In ROSE V PLENTY (1976), a notice at a milk depot, addressed to the milkmen stated,

'Children must not in any circumstances be employed by you in the performance of your duties'.

Contrary to this instruction the defendant employed a small boy who was later injured due to the defendant's negligent driving. Since the boy was the means by which the defendant did his job the employers were held liable despite their clear instruction that boys should not be employed by milkmen.

In contrast in BEARD v LONDON GENERAL OMNIBUS CO (1900), a bus conductor attempted to turn a bus around at the end of its route and in doing so caused an accident. His employers were not liable since he was employed only to collect fares, and not to drive buses.

Where the master is vicariously liable, the servant is generally also liable, but if a blameless master is held vicariously liable a term is implied in the servant's contract that he will indemnify the master – LISTER v ROMFORD ICE (1957).

b.   If the client is to be successful against Eric's employer he must show

    i.   That Eric was negligent; and

    ii.   That Eric was acting within the scope of his employment

To show negligence the client must prove

(a)   That Eric owes him a duty of care;

(b)   That Eric has broken the duty by failing to exercise reasonable care; and,

(c)   That the client has suffered reasonably foreseeable loss as a result of Eric's breach of duty.

(b)   and (c) above are clearly satisfied. However, in CAPARO INDUSTRIES v DICKMAN (1990) it was held that if a duty is to be owed it must be

    i.   Reasonably foreseeable that the statement will be relied on;

    ii.   That there is close proximity of relationship between the client and the adviser; and

    iii.   Reasonable to impose a duty.

In Eric's case it is arguable that it is not reasonably foreseeable that the client would rely on Eric's advice without independent enquiry, since Eric is an auditor, not somebody who would normally be expected to give investment advice.

It is therefore probable that Eric was not negligent. However, even if he was negligent, he may not be within the scope of his employment. An employee will be within the scope of their employment if the tortious act is a wrongful way of doing what they are employed to do.

For example in ROSE v PLENTY (1976) a milkman, contrary to clear instructions, allowed a young boy to help him deliver the milk. The boy was injured when his leg was caught between the van and the kerb. It was held that the employer was vicariously liable because the milkman was using the boy as a means of doing his job.

Even a fraudulent act will not necessarily be outside the scope of a person's employment. In Eric's case he is not auditing in an unauthorised manner, he is doing something quite different, ie giving investment advice. It is therefore likely that he is outside the scope of his employment and the employer would not be liable.

25. a. A nuisance is an unlawful interference with the use or enjoyment of another person's land. In contrast to trespass the interference is indirect rather than direct. At one time the courts held that a person could not be liable in nuisance for failure to act in connection with a condition naturally arising on his land for example in PONTARDAWE RDC v MOORE-GWYN (1929) the defendant was held not liable when there was a natural fall of rocks from his land onto the plaintiff's land. However, in DAVEY v HARROW CORPORATION (1958), a case which involved encroaching tree roots, the defendant was held liable.

It therefore seems clear that Mr A will be liable in nuisance (even if he did not plant the tree). It is also possible that he would be liable if sued for negligence.

   b. Trespass to land is the direct interference with a possession of another person's land without lawful authority. It includes entering on land, remaining on land after permission to stay has been withdrawn or placing objects on land. Moving the boundary fence onto Mrs Barker's land is a clear trespass to land. Mrs Barker would be able to obtain a court order that the fence be restored to its correct position. In addition the court would make an award of damages. If the fence actually belongs to Mrs Barker rather than Mr Adams there would also be a trespass to goods.

   c. Entry onto Mrs Barker's land to dig the hole is clearly trespass. Once the soil has been detached it ceases to be land and becomes goods. By removing the soil Mr Adams commits a trespass to goods as well as the tort of conversion. Conversion is a dealing with the plaintiff's goods which is a denial of the plaintiff's right to use and possess those goods. Any measure of damages related to the market value of the soil would probably be inappropriate. Mrs Barker should seek an injunction prohibiting any further trespass and sufficient damages to enable the land to be restored to its original state.

26. a. One of the general defences to a tort action is remoteness of damage. ie That the loss suffered by the plaintiff is not sufficiently closely linked to the defendant's tort because the loss is not reasonably foreseeable (THE WAGON MOUND (1961)). A *novus actus interveniens* is one factor which may break this link. It is an unforeseeable incident which changes the course of events. It could either be an act of the plaintiff himself, or of a third party over whom the defendant had no control. For example in HOGAN v BENTINCK COLLIERIES (1949) an employee sustained a broken thumb due to his employer's negligence. Acting on bad advice he had it amputated. It was held that the unreasonable amputation was a *novus actus interveniens* and therefore the plaintiff could only recover damages for a broken thumb.

There are, however, situations when an action which is arguably a *novus actus interveniens* will not break the link between the plaintiff and the defendant. For example in SCOTT v SHEPHERD (1773) a lighted squib was thrown onto a stall in a market place, and from there to another stall, and from there to Shepherd, whom it injured. It was held that the onward throwing was not a *novus actus interveniens* since it was an instinctive and foreseeable act done in the 'agony' of the emergency created by the defendant's tort. The same is true when the intervening act is a rescue. For example in HAYNES v HARWOOD (1935) a boy caused a horse to bolt into a crowded street. A policeman was injured whilst trying to bring the horse to a halt. His negligence action succeeded, since the defence of volenti cannot be invoked against a rescuer, nor could it be claimed that his act was a *novus actus interveniens* since the act of rescue was foreseeable.

If a *novus actus interveniens* is proved by the defendant it will enable the defence of remoteness to be invoked. This will not enable the defendant to avoid primary liability but it will enable him to avoid payment of some or all of the damages claimed by the plaintiff.

b. i. In an attempt to limit the award of damages AB Ltd should plead that the error by the surgeon was a *novus actus interveniens*. Although mistakes are occasionally made in hospitals such serious errors are rare. In addition, the actions of the surgeon are entirely out of AB Ltd's control.

The situation is very similar to HOGAN v BENTINCK COLLIERIES. The defence will succeed, and AB Ltd's liability will be confined to compensation for Arthur's broken leg.

ii. AB Ltd will again plead *novus actus interveniens*. In this case, however, success is in more doubt. It is reasonably well known that if a person is injured, and a fracture is suspected, it is best to leave him until medical help arrives. Many people, however, either do not realise this, or forget it in the 'heat' of the moment, and inflict greater injury on a person by trying to help him to his feet, or by pulling him out of wreckage. It is suggested that such action, although unwise, is reasonably foreseeable, and would not therefore amount to a *novus actus interveniens*.

If this suggestion were not accepted by the court Arthur would have two further chances of success. Firstly, he could claim that AB Ltd was negligent (for a second time) in failing to provide a system of supervision which prevented such unwise action by employees. Secondly, if Arthur could prove that the employees were themselves negligent, AB Ltd as their employer may be held vicariously liable for their tort.

On balance it seems that AB Ltd will be unable to avoid full liability for Arthur's injuries.

27. To succeed in a negligence action a consumer will need to prove, on the balance of probabilities, the following three elements.

That the defendant owed him a duty of care. To determine whether a duty is owed the courts will apply the 'neighbour test' laid down in DONOGHUE v STEVENSON (1932). In this case the plaintiff's friend purchased a bottle of ginger beer manufactured by the defendant and gave it to the plaintiff. She drank most of the bottle before discovering the decomposed remains of a snail. She became ill and sued for negligence. It was held that a person owes a duty to anyone who he can reasonably foresee would be injured by his acts or omissions. Such persons were described as 'neighbours'. Clearly therefore a manufacturer of goods owes a duty, not only to the purchaser of those goods, but to anyone who is likely to consume, use, or be affected by those goods.

That the defendant broke the duty of care. The duty will be broken if the defendant fails to act as a reasonable person in the defendant's position and with the defendant's knowledge, ie it is an objective test, it is not 'Did he do his best'?

Finally the plaintiff must show that he has suffered damage.

a.   This damage must be caused to a substantial extent by the defendant's conduct.

b.   The damage must be sufficiently closely related to the negligent act, ie it must not be too remote. Loss is not too remote if a reasonable man would have foreseen the type.

For example in LAMB V CAMDEN BOROUGH COUNCIL (**1981**) negligent council workers broke a water main and P's house was flooded. He recovered damages for loss due to flooding, but not for further damage caused by squatters who moved in while his house was unoccupied as a result of the flooding. This was not considered to be a reasonably foreseeable result of the negligence.

c.   In most cases the damage must be either physical injury to the plaintiff's person or property or economic loss consequential upon physical injury, eg lost wages as a result of a broken leg.

The *CONSUMER PROTECTION ACT 1987* provides an additional remedy to those already available in tort against suppliers of defective goods. Compensation may be recovered for death, personal injury or damage to private property but not for pure economic (financial) loss. As with negligence, persons other than the buyer may claim. Liability is strict.

The basic rule is that where damage is caused wholly or partly be a defect in a product the producer or supplier shall be liable for the damage. The injured person must still prove the product was defective and that the defect caused the injury. A 'product' must be movable and industrially produced, for example cars are products, but buildings are not. Farm produce is not a product unless subjected to a manufacturing process, thus potatoes are not products, but potato crisps are.

S.3 lays down the criteria for judging defectiveness. There is a defect in a product if the safety of the product is not such as persons generally are entitled to expect, taking all circumstances into account, including:

a.   The presentation of the product, including instructions and warnings.

b.   The use to which it could reasonably be expected to be put.

c. The time when the product was supplied. The omission of 'reasonably' from the phrase 'entitled to expect' suggests a stricter standard than that normally applied in tort. However, reasonableness is retained in the factors that the court must take into account.

S.4 provides a defence in the following situations:

a. That the defect is attributable to compliance with any enactment.

b. That he did not at any time supply the product.

c. That the supply was otherwise than in the course of a business.

d. That the defect did not exist in the product at the time of supply.

e. That the state of scientific and technical knowledge at the relevant time was not such that the producer might be expected to have discovered the defect.

f. That the defect constituted a defect in a product in which the product in question had been comprised and was wholly attributable to the design of the subsequent product.

g. More than 10 years has elapsed since the product was first supplied.

28. a. i. The defence of consent (also known as *volenti non fit injuria*) means that the defendant claims that the plaintiff was aware of the risk of harm and consented to that risk. The consent must be freely given, in full appreciation of the nature of the risk of injury. A consent given under protest, or in fear of dismissal from employment is no consent (BOWATER V ROWLEY REGIS CORPORATION (1944)). Similarly if a person is injured carrying out a rescue the defence will not apply since the moral duty to effect a rescue will negate the possibility of a freely given consent (HAYNES V HARWOOD (1935)).

The consent may be express (for example it may be an agreed contract term) or implied where, for example, the parties participate in a hazardous sport. Some statutes, for example the *ROAD TRAFFIC ACT 1972*, exclude the defence of consent. Under this Act a negligent driver cannot plead consent against a passenger who has been injured.

ii. To succeed in the defence of contributory negligence the defendant must show that the plaintiff failed to take reasonable care for his own safety. The failure may either contribute to causing the accident itself, or contribute only to the nature and extent of the plaintiff's injuries, for example by failing to wear a seatbelt. If the defence is successful the plaintiff's damages for the actual injuries suffered are reduced according to his share of responsibility. The court does not speculate on what injury the plaintiff would have suffered if there had been no contributory negligence.

iii. A Statute (or delegated legislation) as the supreme source of law can authorise acts that would in other circumstances constitute a tort. Absolute statutory authority imposes a duty on the public body to act. The body will not be liable for damage resulting from the exercise of that authority, provided it acted reasonably and there was no alternative way of performing the act. Where statutory authority is conditional the public body has the power to act but is not bound to do so. A defence will exist only if the relevant act is carried on without interference with the rights of others. Some statutes provide for compensation. In such cases the plaintiff can receive no more than the maximum allowed by the Act even if this is less than the actual loss. If the statute does not provide for compensation the presumption is that the plaintiff's private rights remain and an action may be brought for the full loss.

b.   The main remedy is an award of damages. They are intended to compensate the plaintiff by putting him in the position he would have been in if the tort had not taken place. They are not intended to punish the defendant. An award of damages may include compensation for personal injury, loss of goods or property or (in the case of negligent statements) pure economic loss.

In personal injury cases damages will be awarded under itemised headings, for example loss of amenity, pain and suffering, loss of expectation of life and so on. *Ordinary* damages are assessed by the court as compensation for losses which cannot be positively proved or ascertained, for example pain and suffering. They will depend upon the court's opinion as to the nature and extent of the plaintiff's injuries. *Special* damages are those which can be positively proved, for example damage to clothing or the cost of repairing a damaged car.

Where a plaintiff has won a case, but suffered no real loss the court may award *nominal* damages, for example £1, in recognition of the fact that a wrong has been suffered. *Exemplary* damages will be granted when the court intends to punish the defendant for his act and to deter others from similar action in future. Such awards are comparatively rare.

In some cases, for example where the plaintiff complains of nuisance, damages may not be an appropriate remedy. The court may therefore award an injunction. A *prohibitory injunction* forbids the defendant from doing something and a *mandatory injunction* orders something to be done. An injunction is an equitable remedy awarded at the discretion of the court.

Thus in MILLER v JACKSON (1977) although the plaintiff was able to establish that a cricket club were guilty of negligence and nuisance in allowing cricket balls to be struck out of their ground onto the plaintiff's premises, the plaintiff was not awarded an injunction, since the court felt that a greater public interest was served by allowing cricket to be played on a ground where it had been played for over 70 years. The plaintiff was, however, awarded damages for both past and potential future injury.

29. a.   The duty of occupiers of premises towards lawful visitors is governed by the OCCUPIERS' LIABILITY ACT 1957.

i.   An 'occupier' is a person who has some degree of control over the premises. He need not necessarily be the owner. It is also possible for there to be more than one occupier.

ii.   'Premises' includes land, buildings, fixed or moveable structures such as pylons and scaffoldings; and vehicles, including ships and aeroplanes.

iii.   'Visitors' are persons lawfully on the premises, such as customers in shops and factory inspectors.

The extent of the duty is laid down in *S2(2)* of the Act: 'A duty to take such care as in all the circumstances of the case is reasonable to see that the visitor will be reasonably safe in using the premises for the purpose for which he is permitted by the occupier to be there'.

This duty is merely an enactment of the common law duty to act as a reasonable man. The Act states that all circumstances of the case are relevant in determining the duty owed. Therefore the occupier:

(a) Must be prepared for children to be less careful than adults. In the case of very young children the occupier is entitled to assume that they will be accompanied by an adult.

(b) May expect a person who is doing his job to guard against the ordinary risks of his job. For example in ROLES v NATHAN (**1963**) the plaintiffs, who were chimney sweeps, were employed by D to block up holes in the flues of a coke fired heating system. Despite a warning from D they attempted to do this while the coke fire was lit, and they were both killed by carbon monoxide gas. Their executor's action failed since it was a risk incidental to their job which they should have foreseen and guarded against.

An occupier will not be liable if the injury results from the faulty work of an independent contractor, provided the occupier took reasonable steps to ensure that the contractor was competent. The occupier may also be able to escape liability by giving an adequate warning of the danger, although the *UNFAIR CONTRACT TERMS ACT 1977* prevents the exclusion of liability for causing death or personal injury by negligence. The occupier may also plead consent or contributory negligence as a defence.

b. As Simon is one of Walters' employees, he is a lawful visitor and he is owed the common duty of care described in *S2(2)* above. By placing a dangerous item such as poisoned bread in the workplace the premises are not reasonably safe, particularly if it is not obvious to employees that the bread is poisoned. As to whether Walter exercised reasonable care – if he knew that Simon had learning difficulties the standard of care is high, on the principle that Simon is a vulnerable person – PARIS v STEPNEY BOROUGH COUNCIL (**1951**).

It would appear that Walter is liable to Simon under the OLA *1957*. However, employees also have a responsibility for their own safety. Simon has clearly not had sufficient regard for his own safety by taking and eating the bread. He is therefore likely to be regarded as having contributed to the extent of his injury. His damages would be reduced under provisions in the *LAW REFORM (CONTRIBUTORY NEGLIGENCE) ACT 1945* by an amount reflecting the blame attributable to him.

Young is a trespasser. The *OCCUPIERS LIABILITY ACT 1984* governs the liability of occupiers of premises towards trespassers. Under the Act the occupier owes a duty if:

i. He is aware of the danger or had reasonable grounds to believe that it exists; and

ii. He knows, or had reasonable grounds to believe, that someone is in (or may come into) the vicinity of the danger; and

iii. The risk is one against which in all the circumstances of the case he may reasonably be expected to offer that person some protection.

Walter knows of the existence of the danger and that serious illness is a risk against which some protection ought to be offered. The matter on which the question gives no information is Walter's state of knowledge as to the likelihood of persons such as Young being within the vicinity of the poisoned bread. Assuming Walter is aware of some likelihood that young trespassers may enter, Young will be owed a duty of care under the OLA *1984*. The duty is to take such care as is reasonable in all the circumstances to see that the person to whom the duty is owed does not suffer injury on the premises by reason of the danger concerned. Circumstances which will be taken into account in deciding whether or not Walter has broken his duty include the seriousness of the danger, the type of trespasser likely to enter and, possibly the financial ability of Walter to guard against the danger.

It is unlikely that Walter could successfully raise a plea of contributory negligence against Young, because it is not reasonable to expect children to guard against their own safety.

Walter therefore owes a duty to Young and he has broken this by failing to prevent children entering the premises and coming into contact with dangerous substances. If a warning notice does exist it may prevent liability to an adult, but is unlikely to affect liaibility towards young children, who are known to take little or no notice of such warnings. Walter would therefore be liable to Young.

SUGGESTED ANSWERS TO COURSEWORK QUESTIONS 30–35, PAGES 339–40

COMMERCIAL LAW

30. This question required candidates to explain whether there was a binding contract between Graham and Peter. It follows therefore that the prerequisites to a valid contract have to be identified, explained and applied to resolve the case study. If there is a binding contract that has been breached, candidates were required to advise how the breach would be remedied.

There is the presence of an offer (a willingness to be bound on specific terms), acceptance of the offer stated without any qualification, consideration (something of economic value) and intention to be legally bound. Given that Graham is a book dealer there is a presumption of legal intention as it is a commercial or business agreement. The pre-requisites to a valid contract are in place and it is evident that Peter has breached the contract. In reliance on the contract Graham has agreed to sell one book to Eric and another to Helen by way of a part-exchange. In both situations Graham would be looking to seek a remedy for breach because he in turn is now in breach to both Eric and Helen. The measure of damages Graham would be able to claim may be subject to the 'remoteness of damage' test expounded in HADLEY V BAXENDALE and confirmed in VICTORIA LAUNDRY V NEWMAN INDUSTRIES.

The application of the 'remoteness' concept may mean that Peter could argue that he did not know Graham had agreed to sell the books on. However it is more likely that the assumption could be made that as a dealer he would be selling them on at a profit in the ordinary course of business. Applying the test of reasonable foreseeability Peter may be liable for the loss of £300 on the transaction with Eric and also the net loss of £300 on the transaction with Helen.

The remaining book is the only surviving copy and damages would not be an appropriate remedy, as the book cannot be obtained elsewhere no matter what amount of money is awarded in damages. An equitable and discretionary remedy is that of specific performance. This requires the person in breach to complete the contract as agreed and it is awarded in cases where rare or unique items, as in this situation, are involved.

The problem is more complicated however, as Peter now has a valid contract with Bertram to sell the three books for £2,000. If Bertram buys in good faith, which is presumed unless otherwise shown, then Bertram acquires a good title. This would of course give Peter the sale proceeds, which amount to £500 more than would have been received from Graham, to pay damages to Graham who would, in his role as a dealer, be able to claim the £500. This complicates the issue even further in that Graham may have difficulty in obtaining an appropriate remedy for the 'only surviving copy' if Bertram has good title.

Examiner's comments

Although many candidates were able to successfully identify the general areas of remedies for breach of contract within the question, a number did not recognise that there was a contract in the first place because it was verbal only. A number also thought that the three books sold to Bertram could be recovered from him, which is not the legal position as he bought in good faith.

31 (a) This question required candidates to explain the difference between the applicability of two consumer pieces of legislation in part (a) and in part (b) an explanation of the implied terms under the SUPPLY OF GOODS AND SERVICES ACT 1982. The determining feature in deciding whether to maintain an action under either of the statutes mentioned in the question is whether the contract involves a sale of goods or the supply of goods or services.

The SALE OF GOODS ACT 1979, as amended, provides under S.2 that a sale of goods is defined as being 'a contract by which the seller transfers, or agrees to transfer the property in goods to a buyer for a money consideration, called the price'. It is essential therefore that the contract involves 'goods' which are defined as being 'all personal chattels other than things in action and money'.

The SUPPLY OF GOODS AND SERVICES ACT 1982 applies to certain contracts that do not fall within the definition of a sale of goods, even though there might be a transfer of ownership. If the main purpose is one of skilled labour with an ancillary one of ownership being transferred, the 1982 Act applies. In ROBINSON v GRAVES a contract to paint a portrait would now be covered as the contract was essentially for work and materials. However in MARCEL (FURRIERS) LD v TAPPER the supply of a mink jacket, made to the customers specification, was held to be a contract of sale as the materials were not considered ancillary to the work performed because of their high value.

(b) The SUPPLY OF GOODS AND SERVICES ACT 1982 broadly reiterates the terms implied in the SALE OF GOODS ACT 1979. Where goods are supplied the implied terms of title, description, satisfactory quality and fitness for purpose (S.2–5) cannot be excluded where the supply is in the course of a business to a consumer.

Where the contract is wholly or substantially for the provision of services, there are implied terms that the supplier will carry out the service with reasonable care and skill, within a reasonable time and, in the absence of any contrary agreement, at a reasonable cost (S.13–15) but may be excluded if satisfying the test of reasonableness provided under UNFAIR CONTRACT TERMS ACT 1977.

Examiner's comments

This question was poorly answered mainly because candidates did not either read the question properly or were unable to include the appropriate responses in their answer. The first part of the question did not ask for the implied conditions in a sale of goods contract. The question asked candidates to determine whether a party affected by a breach of contract would sue for breach of the SALE OF GOODS ACT 1979 or breach of the SUPPLY OF GOODS AND SERVICES ACT 1982. Candidates should have explained the types of contracts that are covered by each Act. Part (b) on the other hand was competently answered.

32. (a) This two-part sale of goods question required candidates to explain the rights an unpaid seller has against the goods in part (a) and an explanation of three exceptions to the *nemo dat quod non habet* rule in part (b).

A seller will be deemed unpaid where the goods are sold without a stipulation as to credit, or if sold on credit and the credit period has expired, or the buyer becomes insolvent or payment has been made by cheque which has subsequently been dishonoured.

The unpaid seller can exercise the right of a lien (a hold or retention of the goods) until payment is tendered. The right, however, is forfeited where the buyer or his agent lawfully takes possession, or the whole of the price is tendered, or the seller waives the right to a lien, or the goods are in the possession of a carrier.

Stoppage in transit is similar to a lien except that the buyer must be insolvent and the goods are stopped en route whilst in the possession of an independent carrier. The right to stoppage in transit terminates where the buyer or his agent obtains lawful possession, or the carrier acknowledges to the buyer that the goods are now held on his behalf, or if the carrier wrongfully refuses to deliver the goods to the buyer.

The right of resale may apply automatically if the contract so provides. Where not applicable automatically, the right will apply where the unpaid seller gives notice of the intention to sell if payment is not made within a reasonable time, or if the goods are perishable.

32. (b) *(i) Estoppel*

If the true owner, by their conduct (ie through words or actions), leads the buyer to believe that the person who makes the sale owns the goods, the true owner is estopped from denying the seller's right to sell HENDERSON V WILLIAMS.

(ii) Common law or statutory power of sale

By court order where goods are perishable, or there is a falling market and at common law the power of sale of a pledge exists. Statutory powers of sale exist in favour of a pawnbroker, Baillie, an innkeeper or a sheriff.

(iii) Sale of a motor vehicle subject to hire purchase

An innocent private purchaser who buys a motor vehicle which is subject to a hire purchase agreement, or a conditional sale agreement, obtains a better title than the seller, leaving the true owner to sue the unauthorised seller for breach of contract or conversion.

Examiner's comments

Part (a) of the question was handled extremely well by the majority of candidates who attempted this question. However part (b) was poorly answered in the main, as many candidates clearly did not understand the concept of the three exceptions referred to in the question.

33. (a) This question required candidates to explain the ways in which an agency agreement can be formed in part (a) and the restrictions that may or may not apply on termination of such an agreement.

An agency agreement is generally just like any contract and can be formed:

- verbally, or in writing (eg the appointment of an auctioneer);

- it can also be formally established by deed (eg power of attorney vested in the hands of a solicitor or relative where a person lives abroad);

- it can also be implied and inferred through the relationship between the principal and his agent (eg the bank is the agent of its customer for collecting cheques).

The equitable doctrine of estoppel may also indicate the presence of an agency agreement where the conduct of the principal suggests to a third party that another person (the agent) has the authority to act for them. This may arise where words or conduct stop the principal denying the existence of the agent to the third party. Ratification may also validate the authority of an agent to bind a principal in contract. This has a retrospective effect providing that the principal existed and the agent must have indicated he was acting on behalf of the principal. The agent must however have had some authority to act even though it may have been exceeded and the actions must have been ratified within a reasonable period of time.

(b) The agency agreement, not regulated by the Commercial Agents Regulations 1993, can be terminated by completion of the agreement or through expiration of the agreed time. It can also be terminated by agreement between the parties, by revocation of the agreement by the principal who should notify the third party of revocation, or repudiation by the agent. In either of the latter two cases damages may arise for breach.

Furthermore, the agreement may be terminated through operation of the law because of:

- death of the principal or the agent

- mental incapacity of the parties

- bankruptcy of the principal and of the agent if in the latter case the agent has to use their own money

- the agreement being frustrated (eg destruction of the agency property or the agency becomes illegal).

Examiner's comments

Very popular question and generally candidates scored high marks on this question. There were however, a few candidates who answered part (b) with references to the Commercial Agents Regulations 1993 that the question specifically excluded.

34. (a) This question required candidates to explain copyright, the remedies available where copyright is infringed and any possible defences to any claim for infringement. Copyright involves the exclusive right to use one's own work and by implication the right to stop another from exploiting the skill and labour expended in the production of that work.

The COPYRIGHT, DESIGNS AND PATENTS ACT 1988 provides that the duration of copyright exists until the expiration of a certain period, depending upon the nature of the material. The introduction of the DURATION OF COPYRIGHT AND RIGHTS IN PERFORMANCE REGULATIONS 1995 made the following changes; in respect of literary, dramatic, musical or artistic works the period is seventy years from the end of the calendar year the author died, or if computer-generated, when created. In respect of film the period is seventy years from the end of the last to die of the principal director, the authors of the screenplay and dialogue, and the composer of the music created specifically for the film and similarly for broadcast or cable programmes, or sound recording, but fifty years from the end of the year of broadcast or publication. For typographical arrangements of a published edition the period is twenty-five years.

(b) (i) The remedies available for infringement include damages, being the amount required to compensate for actual harm suffered (eg loss of reputation). Alternatively an account of profits can be ordered in lieu of damages that are assessed on the sum of the profit made from the infringement of the copyright material. Further remedies include an injunction which amounts to an interim (temporary) order until such time as a permanent order can be obtained to prevent further infringement. A delivery-up order can also be obtained where the offending goods can be seized and destroyed following the issue of a search order (replacing an Anton Piller order).

(ii) There are a number of defences that can be raised such as:

- fair dealing, which would entail research or private study

- for the purpose of criticism or review

- reporting of current events

- use by licence or short extracts

- use by educational establishments and librarians

- use for the purpose of judicial or parliamentary proceedings.

Examiner's comments

A reasonably popular question that most of the candidates who attempted it completed successfully. Any mistakes made were in relation to the period of time that copyright existed in relation to the material covered.

35.(a) This question required candidates to consider the provisions of the CONSUMER CREDIT ACT *1974* as to 'extortionate credit bargains' in part (a) and 'protected goods' in part (b).

The standard limit of £25,000 for transactions covered under legislation does not apply where either the interest rate is prohibitive or the period for repayment of capital and interest is relatively short.

If the court is satisfied that the agreement is 'extortionate,' they can order the agreement be re-opened and make an appropriate order governing its terms. This may arise following an application by the debtor or in response as a defence to a claim made by the creditor. Consideration would however be given to the prevailing interest rates at the time, the age and experience of the debtor, the risk involved and the degree of pressure brought upon the debtor KETLEY v SCOTT

The above principles were highlighted in the recent case of LONDON NORTH SECURITIES v MEADOWS where a £5,750 loan had spiralled to a debt of £384,000, the interest rate being 34.9%. The sum was a significant amount because interest was compounded on arrears and there was a sum of £40,000 for legal costs.

(b) 'Protected goods' are defined as being where one-third of the total price for the goods has been paid, then the goods can only be re-possessed by way of a court order. In addition the creditor should have previously served a default notice upon the debtor, specifying the default alleged and the action to be taken to remedy the fault.

Where 'protected goods' are wrongly re-possessed, the effect is that the agreement is terminated and the debtor receives back any payments made Capital Finance v Bray. Whether 'protected' or not the creditor can only enter premises with a court order.

Examiner's comments

Candidates who attempted this question were able to demonstrate a sound understanding of the principles involved in both parts and there were no major issues that need to be highlighted.

SUGGESTED ANSWERS TO COURSEWORK QUESTIONS 36–42, PAGES 494–7

COMMERCIAL LAW

36. At common law a limited company which enters into a transaction that is not included in that company's objects clause in its Memorandum of Association, will be found to have entered into *ultra vires* contract. In other words, the contract will be beyond the legal powers of the company and thus a legal nullity ie, the contract is void. See ASHBURY RAILWAY CARRIAGE AND IRON CO V ROCHE.

This common law rule was developed to protect a company's shareholders. More recently, however, the view has gained ground that shareholders are really only mainly interested in the company being profitable (so swelling the dividends and raising the value of the shares) and not too worried about the exact nature of the business that the company's directors engage in on behalf of the company.

Outside parties, ie persons trading/dealing with the company (viz actual/potential creditors) are, on this view, more likely to be concerned by ultra vires transactions. Thus it has become customary over the years to put into the objects clauses of commercial companies a large number of objectives/powers to enable those companies to engage in a wide variety of transactions apart from their main business objectives. Furthermore, the practice has grown up of inserting a paragraph in the objects clause, which states that each clause contains a *separate* and *independent* main object, which can be carried on separately from the others. See COTMAN V BROUGHAM and BELL HOUSES V CITY WALL PROPERTIES. (It can be pointed out that an objects clause may make a decision depend on a resolution of the members of the company in order to place some control over the activities of directors.) These devices have much reduced the ambit of the ultra vires rules. In more recent times Parliament has legislated to *further* weaken the rule. The COMPANIES ACT 1985, S.35 inserted by the COMPANIES ACT 1989, gives further protection from the effects of the rule to outsiders dealing with a company in good faith. (It is the result of EU legislation.) The ultra vires rule, however, still fully operates *internally,* ie it defines the directors' duties to a company's *members*. A member may seek a court injunction to stop directors entering into ultra vires contract, and the directors are liable to the company for any loss, which may result from entering into such a contract. Of course, an injunction is useless *after* a contract has been formed. In such a case the members will have to rely on seeking recompense from the directors themselves. Members may *ratify* an ultra vires contract by means of a *special resolution*.

Examiner's comments

This was a fairly popular question. There was some very good answers and somewhat surprisingly for a routine question, there were also some very poor and bad answers. Some candidates merely explained the nature of a company, in a number of cases going to great lengths to explain the difference between public and private companies. The question required a straightforward explanation of the legal position where a company is found to have acted outside the powers given to it by its constitution.

37. Multiple Choice:

The correct answer are: D

A

A

B

C

C

D

D

C

A

C

B

C

CIMA November 2001

38. The question is designed to test candidates' knowledge of the distinction between fixed and floating charges.

Suggested Approach

Proceed by writing an essay which sets out the characteristics of fixed and floating charges.

Marking Guide Marks

Fixed charge is a charge over definite property which the company cannot deal with freely in the normal course of business. The charge has priority over a floating charge. Floating charges are peculiar to limited companies and are a charge over a class of assets which the company can deal freely with. The proceeds are first applied in paying any preferential creditors.

Examiner's Comments

Generally a well-answered question.

Common Errors

A number of candidates seem to mistakenly believe that a fixed charge means that the value of the asset cannot change and that a floating charge means that the value of the asset is constantly changing.

Others thought 'fixed' referred to the amount of interest charged and that if the asset is sold, the charge is transferred to the new owner.

39. This question requires candidates to explain the meaning and procedures involved in the course of 'winding-up' in company law.

   (a) One of the many consequences of incorporation is that a registered company becomes a legal entity in its own right having existence apart from its member shareholders. One of the attributes of this legal personality is that the company has not only separate, but perpetual existence, in that it continues irrespective of changes in its membership. Indeed the company can continue to exist where it has no members at all. Winding-up, or liquidation, is the process whereby the life of the company is brought to an end and its assets realised and distributed to its members and/or creditors. The rules governing winding-up are detailed in the provisions of the INSOLVENCY ACT 1986 (IA) and the exact nature of procedure depends on the type of winding-up involved and depends upon the solvency of the company at the time when liquidation commences. Winding-up can be conducted on a voluntary basis, in which case the members of the company themselves determine that the time has come for it to come to an end. Alternatively the court may make an order that the company's life should come to an end. This question refers to the first of these alternatives, voluntary winding-up.

   (b) *Section 84 IA* states that a company may be wound-up voluntarily:

      (i) When any period fixed for the duration of the company by the articles expires or any event occurs which shall, according to the articles, lead to its dissolution. Under such circumstances the winding-up has to be approved by an *ordinary resolution*.

(ii) For any other reason whatsoever. Under these circumstances a *special resolution* is required to approve the winding-up.

(iii) Where its liabilities make it advisable for it to be wound up. In this last case an *extraordinary resolution* is required to approve the winding-up. In any case the winding-up is deemed to have started on the date that the appropriate resolution was passed.

There are two distinct forms of voluntary liquidation:

(i) *Members' voluntary winding-up*

This takes place when the directors of the company are of the opinion that the company is solvent and is capable of paying off its creditors. The directors are required to make a formal declaration to the effect that they have investigated the affairs of the company and that in their opinion it will be able to pay its debts within 12 months of the start of liquidation. It is a criminal offence for directors to make a false declaration without reasonable grounds. On appointment, by an ordinary resolution of the company, the job of the liquidator is to wind up the affairs of the company, to realise the assets and distribute the proceeds to its creditors. On completion of this task the liquidator must present a report of the process to a final meeting of the shareholders. The liquidator then informs the Registrar of the holding of the final meeting and submits a copy of his report to it. The Registrar formally registers these reports and the company is deemed to be dissolved three months after that registration.

(ii) *Creditors' voluntary winding-up*

This takes place when the company is insolvent when it is decided to wind it up. The essential difference between this and the former type of winding-up is that, as the name implies, the creditors have an active role to play in overseeing the liquidation of the company. Firstly a meeting of the creditors must be called within 14 days of the resolution to liquidate the company at which the directors must submit a statement of the company's affairs. The creditors have the final say in who should be appointed as liquidator and may, if they elect, appoint a liquidation committee to work with the liquidator. On completion of the winding-up the liquidator calls and submits his report to meetings of the members and creditors. The liquidator then informs the Companies' Registry of the holding of these final meetings and submits a copy of his report to it. The Registrar formally registers these reports and the company is deemed to be dissolved three months after that registration.

40. This question asks candidates to provide some of the likely content of articles of association, to explain the effect of the articles and to detail the procedure for altering them. The constitution of a company is established by two documents: the memorandum of association, and the articles of association. Whereas the memorandum mainly governs the company's external affairs, the articles deal with the internal regulation of the company. If there is any conflict between the two documents, the contents of the memorandum prevail over anything to the contrary contained in the articles, although provisions in the articles may be used to clarify particular uncertainties in the memorandum.

(a) Model memorandums and articles of association are set out in the Companies (Tables A to F) Regulations 1985, although companies may alter the models to suit their particular circumstances and requirements. It is usual for companies to draw up their own particular articles but if they elect not to draw up their own, then Table A model articles apply automatically.

Table A also applies to the extent that the company's articles have not expressly excluded its provisions. The model articles cover such matters as the issue and transfer of shares, the rights attaching to particular shares, the rules relating to the holding of meetings, the powers of directors, and the payment of dividends.

(b) *Section 14* of the COMPANIES ACT provides that 'the memorandum and articles, when registered, bind the company and its members to the same extent as if they respectively had been signed and sealed by each member, and contained covenants on the part of each member to observe all the provisions of the memorandum and of the articles.' This section has three effects.

(i) The documents establish a contract which binds each member to the company. Thus in HICKMAN v KENT OR ROMNEY MARSH SHEEP-BREEDERS' ASSOCIATION (1915), the company was able to enforce an article against a member that provided that disputes involving the member and the company should go to arbitration.

(ii) The company is contractually bound to each of its members. On this basis in PENDER v LUSHINGTON (1877) a member was able to sue in respect of the wrongful denial of his right to vote at a company meeting.

(iii) The articles constitute a contract between the members. In RAYFIELD v HANDS (1960), the articles of the company provided that, where shareholders wished to transfer their shares, they should inform the directors of the company, who were obliged to take the shares equally between them at fair value. When the directors refused to purchase the plaintiff's shares, the court held that the directors were bound as members by the articles and therefore had to comply with the procedure set out there. Articles only operate as a contract in respect of membership rights and obligations. Consequently it has been held that, although members can enforce them, non-members, or members suing in some other capacity than that of a member, will not be able to enforce promises established in the company's articles.

In ELEY v POSITIVE GOVERNMENT SECURITY LIFE ASSURANCE CO (1876) the articles of a company stated that the plaintiff was to be appointed as the company's solicitor. It was held that Eley could not use the articles to establish a contract between himself and the company as those articles only created a contract between the company and its members. Although Eley was in fact a member, he was not suing in that capacity but in the capacity of solicitor, which was not a membership right.

(c) *Section 9* of the Companies Act 1985 allows companies to alter their articles by passing a special resolution. Any attempt in the articles to provide that a particular provision is unalterable is ineffective. The articles cannot be altered however, in such a way as to conflict with the memorandum or any provision of the Companies Act. In particular no member can be bound by any alteration to subscribe for more shares or increase their liability in any way (S.16). Any alteration must be made 'bona fide in the interest of the company as a whole', although the exact meaning of this phrase is not altogether clear. It is evident that it involves a subjective element in that those deciding the alteration must actually believe they are acting in the interest of the company. There is additionally, however, an objective element. In GREENHALGH v ARDERNE CINEMAS LTD (1951) it was stated that any alteration had to be in the interest of the 'individual hypothetical member'. In BROWN v BRITISH ABRASIVE WHEEL CO (1919) an alteration to the articles of the company was proposed to give the majority shareholders the right to buy shares of the minority. It was held that the alteration was invalid as it would benefit the majority shareholders rather than the company as a whole. However, in SIDEBOTTOM v KERSHAW LEESE & CO (1920), an alteration to the articles gave the directors the power to require any shareholder, who entered into competition with the company, to transfer their shares to nominees of the directors at a fair price. It was held that under those circumstances the alteration was valid as it would benefit the company as a whole.

41. This question invites candidates to consider the way in which companies acquire loan capital and specifically the mechanisms available for providing security against such loans. Companies ordinarily raise the money they need to finance their operations through the issue of share capital, but it is equally common for companies to raise additional capital through borrowing. The essential difference between share capital and loan capital is that whereas the share represents a proportionate interest in the business and constitutes the shareholder a member of the company, the lender, even where they hold loan-stock, remains a creditor of the company rather than a member. Such borrowing on the part of the company does not give the lender any interest in the company but represents a claim against the company. The relationship between company and the provider of loan capital is the ordinary relationship of debtor/creditor, although specific mechanisms exist to facilitate the borrowing of companies and secure the interests of their creditors.

(a) *Debentures*

A debenture is a document which acknowledges the fact that a company has borrowed money. The use of the term debenture, however, has been extended to cover the loan itself. A debenture may be issued to a single creditor or to a large number of people, in which case each of the creditors has a proportionate claim against the total 'debenture stock'. As creditors of the company, debenture holders receive interest on their loans and are entitled to receive payment whether the company is profitable or not. As regards repayment, debts rank in order of creation, so earlier debentures have to be paid before those created later. Where debentures are issued as part of a series, it is usual for a *pari passu* clause to be included in the document creating the debt, with the effect that all of the loans made within the series rank equally with regard to repayment.

Debentures which have no security are referred to as 'unsecured loan stock'. It is usual, however, for debentures to provide security for the amount loaned. Security means that if the company is wound up, the secured creditor will have priority in terms of repayment over any unsecured creditor. There are two types of security for company loans:

(b) *Fixed charge*

In this situation a specific asset of the company is made subject to a charge in order to secure a debt. Once the asset is subject to the fixed charge the company cannot dispose of it without the consent of the debentureholders. The asset most commonly subject to fixed charges is land, although any other long-term capital asset may also be charged, as may such intangible assets as book debts. It would not be appropriate, however, to give a fixed charge against stock in trade as the company would be prevented from freely dealing with it without the prior approval of the debentureholders. Such a situation would obviously prevent the company from carrying on its day to day business. If the company fails to honour the commitments set out in the document creating the debenture, such as meeting its interest payments, the debentureholders can appoint a receiver who will if necessary sell the asset charged to recover the money owed. If the value of the asset that is subject to the charge is greater than the debt against which it is charged then the excess goes to pay off the rest of the company's debts. If it is less than the value of the debt secured then the debenture holders will become unsecured creditors for the amount remaining outstanding.

(c) *Floating charge*

This category of charge is peculiar to companies and represents one of the advantages of the company over other business forms. The floating charge is most commonly made in relation to the 'undertaking and assets' of a company and does not attach to any specific property whilst the company is meeting its requirements as stated in the debenture document. The security is provided by all the property owned by the company, some of which may be continuously changing, such as stock in trade. Thus, in contrast to the fixed charge, the use of the floating charge permits the company to deal with its property without the need to seek the approval of the debentureholders. However, if the company commits some act of default, such as not meeting its interest payments, or going into liquidation, the floating charge is said to crystallise. This means that the floating charge becomes a fixed equitable charge over the assets detailed, and their value may be realised in order to pay the debt owed to the floating charge holder. All charges, including both fixed and floating, have to be registered with the Companies' Registry within 21 days of their creation. Failure to register the charge as required has the effect of making the charge void, ie ineffective, against any other creditor, or the liquidator of the company. The charge, however, remains valid against the company, which means in effect that the holder of the charge loses their priority as against other company creditors. In addition to registration at the Companies' Registry, companies are required to maintain a register of all charges on their property. Although a failure to comply with this requirement constitutes an offence, it does not invalidate the charge.

It is possible to obtain court permission for later registration of a charge, eg where failure to register was by mistake or due to inadvertence. However, the court cannot allow the rights of subsequent charge holders to be prejudiced. Thus, any charge that is now registered late is registered subject to those charges already registered. In relation to properly registered charges of the same type, they take priority according to their date of creation. However, as regards charges of different types, a fixed charge takes priority over a floating charge even though it was created after it. Generally there is nothing to prevent the creation of a fixed charge after the issuing of a floating charge, and, as a legal charge against specific property, that fixed charge will still take priority over the earlier floating charge. It is possible, however, for the debenture creating the original floating charge to include a provision preventing the creation of a later fixed charge taking priority over that floating charge. Such a negative pledge clause is effective if the subsequent fixed charge holder has actual notice of it.

42. This question requires candidates to consider the circumstances under which *private* companies are permitted to purchase their own shares and in particular it requires an explanation of the rules under which such companies can make use of their capital to finance such purchases.

(a) *Purchase of own shares*

It was once an extremely strict rule of company law that companies were not allowed to buy their own shares. Any such purchase was treated as a major contravention of the capital maintenance rules (TREVOR v WHITWORTH (1887). Subsequently, companies were granted the power to issue specifically redeemable shares and such a power still exists in *S.159* of the COMPANIES ACT (CA) 1985, although there are strict controls over how any such redemption has to be financed (*S.160*). However the right of companies to buy back their own shares has been extended to cover all, rather than just redeemable, shares as provided in *S.162–181* of the COMPANIES ACT *1985*.

The rules for financing the purchase by a company of its own shares are the same as those that apply to the redemption of redeemable shares as stated in *S.160 CA*. The most essential rule is that no purchase or redemption is to be financed from the company's capital, and can only be paid from profits properly available for distribution to the company's members (*S.162* applying *S.160 CA*).

(b) *Capital redemption reserve*

This concept reflects the controls that apply where companies buy their own shares. Thus even where the company uses distributable profits to pay for the purchase of its own shares, it is required under *S.170 CA* to establish a capital redemption reserve, equivalent to the value of the profits so used, which must be maintained in the same way as other capital. Any amount allocated to the capital redemption reserve may be reduced by transfer to a share capital account through the issue of bonus shares but otherwise cannot be reduced without the company going through the formal capital reduction process, requiring the approval of the court.

(c) *Permissible capital payment*

However, as in most areas of company law, there are relaxations of the strict rules in relation to private limited companies.

Thus in *S.171–175*, private companies are permitted to use the companies' capital to finance the purchase of their own shares, although even here the controls established are extremely rigorous. *Section 171* expressly allows the capital of a private company to be used to pay for the purchase of its own shares where its distributable profits are insufficient. However, *S.173* sets out strict conditions for such payments, requiring:

(i) the approval of the payment by a special resolution;

(ii) a statutory declaration by the directors to the effect that the company will be able to pay its debts within the coming year;

(iii) a statement from the company's auditors supporting the directors' declaration.

Section 175 requires the company to advertise the fact that it intends to use its capital to buy back its shares in the *Gazette* and an appropriate national newspaper, and *S.176* allows either members or creditors of the company to apply to the court to have any such resolution to be overturned.

SUGGESTED ANSWERS TO COURSEWORK QUESTIONS 43–46, PAGES 639–40

43. (a) Candidates were required to consider whether the employer and/or the employee were in breach of contract in part (a) and to explain the process of redundancy in part (b).

Mac will argue that Ronald has failed to give the appropriate period of notice to terminate his contract of employment, the requirement in this situation being one week. Mac may further argue that Ronald's claim must fail because he does not satisfy the requirement of one year's continuous service and is not therefore a qualifying employee.

Ronald will be stating his cause of action as being for unfair constructive dismissal in his Tribunal application. He will not be barred by the service requirement of one year, as his period of holiday entitlement will take his service over the minimum one year requirement.

His application will be on the basis of breach of contract, in that Mac did not provide him with a safe working environment, which is an implied term in his contract of employment. Despite several complaints no action was taken to remedy the situation, leaving Ronald with no alternative but to leave. In addition he suffered harassment, which was not prevented by his employer.

There is a range of remedies that may be awarded for unfair dismissal: re-instatement, involving a return to the old job, re-engagement, a return to a different job, and in the above case the most likely outcome would be that of compensatory damages.

43. (b) The answer should appear in report format, detailing who it is to, the date, subject matter and author.

The first thing that the board need to be aware of is the consultation procedure, and the length of time required is determined by the numbers of employees to be made redundant, ie below one hundred is thirty days and one hundred and above is ninety days. Even where there is only one redundancy, consultation still needs to take place to enquire as to whether there is any suitable alternative work.

The selection criteria should not be exclusively on the basis of last in first out. Consideration should be given to the following issues: attendance/absence records, annual appraisals, requirements of the employer, length of service. Different weightings may be attached to the above issues and they should be fairly applied.

Entitlement to redundancy is based on age and length of service and whether payment is to be calculated on salary or statutory awards. Eligibility is restricted to persons with a minimum of two years' continuous service and the following formula is applied:

Eighteen to twenty-one – half a week's pay for each completed year of service

Twenty-two to forty – one week's pay for each completed year of service

Forty-one to normal retirement age – one and a half weeks' pay for each completed year of service.

The maximum period of reckonable service is twenty years and calculation is based on the years of service in each band.

Redeployment should be considered, where possible. If a reasonable and effective mobility clause has been offered and the employee has rejected it, then the employee loses the right to a redundancy payment.

Examiner's comments

The standard achieved on this very popular question varied substantially between those candidates who recognised the 'constructive dismissal' issue and those who felt that the employee was in breach of contract for failing to give the appropriate notice. Part (b) was completed to varying degrees of competence, with some answers lacking sufficient detail as to the procedures to be adopted for a redundancy programme.

44. Candidates were required to explain in detail the main duties owed by employers to employees in the context of health and safety in the workplace.

The main duties owed by an employer under the *HEALTH & SAFETY AT WORK ACT 1974* are as follows: To provide and maintain plant and systems of work that are safe, and without risk. The employer has to make arrangements to ensure health and safety in relation to the use, handling, storage and transport of articles and substances. In addition, the employer has to provide adequate information, instruction, training and supervision, to maintain a safe place of work and ensure there is adequate access and egress and to provide a safe and healthy working environment.

Issues which have come to the fore in recent years include increased awareness of employees not to be subject to intolerable levels of stress WALKER V NORTHUMBERLAND COUNTY COUNCIL and also being subject to an environment free from tobacco smoke WALTONS & MORSE V DORRINGTON.

There are also other regulations that have been introduced that are specialist in nature in that they cover specific areas of the working environment. Whilst it may not be possible to identify and explain all of them the following are some of the more popular for application purposes: The MANAGEMENT OF HEALTH & SAFETY AT WORK REGULATIONS 1999 deals with risk assessment, implementation of measures to deal with risks, competent safety advisers to be appointed, procedures in place for emergencies, notification for employees and their training and also employee co-operation in this process.

The WORKPLACE (HEALTH, SAFETY AND WELFARE) REGULATIONS 1992 reformed parts of the FACTORIES ACT 1961, OFFICES, SHOPS AND RAILWAY PREMISES ACT 1963. The main issues centred round the working environment, safety, facilities and maintenance. Other specific regulations provide for Health & Safety (Display Screen equipment), Provision and use of work equipment, Manual Handling, Personal Protective Equipment at work.

Examiner's comments

Candidates who answered this popular question were able to demonstrate a sound understanding of the main HEALTH & SAFETY AT WORK ACT 1974 but were less competent in relation to other pieces of legislation that protect workers.

45. Multiple Choice

   The correct answer is **C**

46. Multiple Choice

   The correct answer is **B**

Variants in the Scottish Legal System

1. *Introduction*

Within the British political system there exist various forms of devolution and decentralisation above the level of Local Government.

a. Northern Ireland has a separately elected Parliament at Stormont, a local government structure and a system of courts. Apart from periods of 'direct rule' in the 1970s Northern Ireland has been governed mainly from Stormont and partly from Westminster, the division of power being laid down in the *GOVERNMENT OF IRELAND ACT 1920* and subsequent legislation.

b. Wales is also treated as a distinct area by British central government. There is a Welsh Office and the Secretary of State for Wales is a member of the Cabinet. However, there is no Welsh legal system and the identity of Wales is therefore based on language, religion and education rather than on political institutions.

c. Scotland falls between Northern Ireland and Wales. It has its own Parliament and a number of political and social institutions and a strong constitutional identity. Probably the most important factor contributing to this is the existence of a separate Scottish legal system.

2. *The Scottish Legal System*

The main features are described below:

a. *Law making*

Clearly most Acts of Parliament apply throughout the UK, but between five and ten Acts are passed each parliamentary session which apply exclusively to Scotland. Some of these are the result of recommendations by the Scottish Law Commission. The passage of these Acts through Parliament is scrutinised by several Scottish Committees in the House of Commons. In addition clauses which apply only to Scotland may be tacked on to British legislation.

b. *The Court Structure*

With one exception the court structure is different from and independent of the courts in the rest of Britain. The exception is that the final civil court of appeal is the House of Lords. All other cases must be tried in Scottish courts. Procedure in these courts differs from procedure in England. For example public prosecutions proceed under the direction of procurators-fiscal, rather than the police and the courts may return a verdict of 'not proven' rather than just 'guilty' or 'not guilty'. The court structure is as follows:

Civil Courts	Criminal Courts
House of Lords	Court of Criminal Appeal
Court of Session	High Court of Justiciary
Sheriff Court	Sheriff Court
	District Court

The same judges sit in the Court of Session and the High Court of Justiciary and at present they number about 20. The main local courts are the Sheriff Courts which have a wide jurisdiction in both civil and criminal cases.

c. *Law Officers*

The Scottish legal system is represented in the House of Commons by the Lord Advocate and the Solicitor General for Scotland. The Lord Advocate has a function similar to the Lord Chancellor in England and Wales, however, the Lord Advocate is not the head of the Scottish Judiciary, that position is held by the Lord President of the Court of Session.

d. *The Judiciary*

The senior judges sit in the Court of Session and the High Court of Justiciary. Below them are the Sheriffs-principal and the Sheriffs. In Scotland there is a much greater link between law and politics than in England. Often judges are appointed from principal government law officers as political reward. Scottish judges, in court and elsewhere see themselves as public figures. They often sit on important government committees and voice opinions on current affairs. Politics also pays a part in the lower courts where District Courts can have elected councillors as magistrates.

e. *The Legal Profession*

The Scottish Legal profession is different from that in England. It is recruited separately under the control of the Law Society of Scotland and the Faculty of Advocates (the equivalent of barristers) and judges are nearly always Scots. They receive their legal education in Scotland and they are generally not qualified to practise in England.

3. *Scottish Law and English Law*

All law in Scotland is technically 'Scottish' law since it is interpreted in Scottish courts, but in substance most law is 'British' since it lays down the same rights and duties for persons throughout the UK. For example civil liberties, ie the freedom of speech and assembly are the same as in England. Also the growth of the welfare state and of government regulation of the UK economy has resulted in more 'British' legislation. The main substantive differences concern private and property law rather than public and commercial law. The exclusively Scottish Acts of Parliament generally concern private matters such as local government and education. There is a different procedure for the sale of land and Scottish 'permissive' legislation concerning, for example divorce, homosexuality and licensing is more strict than in England.

4. *Conclusion*

In 1603 the monarchy of England and Scotland was united. In 1707 the ACT OF UNION passed by the parliaments of England and Scotland abolished separate parliaments and replaced them with a single parliament of the United Kingdom (a reform in which bribery and secret diplomacy played a significant part). Nevertheless the present system was not imposed on the Scots as it was on the Welsh. The Act of 1707 guaranteed certain rights, for example free trade with England, and certain institutions, in particular an independent church, legal system and universities. Lawyers, churchmen and educationalists may each claim that their institution is the foundation of Scottish nationality, but it is the legal system which must take priority because it lays down the rights and duties of the others.

GENERAL INDEX